Universal Precautions

Policies, Procedures, and Resources

Edited by Gina Pugliese, R.N., M.S., C.I.C.
Division of Quality Control Management
American Hospital Association

Contributing Editors
Patricia Lynch, R.N., M.B.A., C.I.C.,
and Marguerite M. Jackson, R.N., M.S., C.I.C.

AHA

AHA books are published by American Hospital Publishing, Inc.,
an American Hospital Association Company

The views expressed in this publication are strictly those of the contributing institutions and editors and do not necessarily represent official positions of the American Hospital Association.

Library of Congress Cataloging-in-Publication Data

Universal precautions : policies, procedures, and resources / edited by Gina Pugliese ; contributing editors, Patricia Lynch and Marguerite Jackson.
p. cm.
Includes bibliographical references.
Includes index.
ISBN 1-55648-055-5 (paper)
1. Bloodborne infections—Prevention. 2. Nosocomial infections—Prevention. 3. Hospitals—Sanitation. I. Pugliese, Gina. II. Lynch, Patricia, 1941- . III. Jackson, Marguerite.
[DNLM: 1. Communicable Diseases—transmission. 2. Cross Infection—prevention & control—United States. 3. Health Occupations—education—United States. 4. Occupational Diseases—prevention & control—United States. 5. Patient Isolation. WX 167 U58]
RA642.B56U55 1990
614.4'4—dc20
DNLM/DLC 90-1111
for Library of Congress CIP

Catalog no. 094119

Printed in the USA

AHA is a service mark of the American Hospital Association used under license by American Hospital Publishing, Inc.

Text set in Palatino
5M–10/90–0274

Audrey Kaufman, Product Line Manager
Sophie Yarborough, Editorial Assistant
Marcia Bottoms, Managing Editor
Peggy DuMais, Production Coordinator
Marcia Vecchione and Cheryl Clark, Designers
Brian Schenk, Books Division Director

Contents

About the Editors

Gina Pugliese, R.N., M.S., C.I.C., is the director of infection control and environmental safety for the Division of Quality Control Management of the American Hospital Association in Chicago.

Patricia Lynch, R.N., M.B.A., C.I.C., is the coordinator of the Epidemiology Department at Harborview Medical Center in Seattle.

Marguerite M. Jackson, R.N., M.S., C.I.C., is the director of the Medical Center Epidemiology Unit at the University of California Medical Center in San Diego.

Preface

The purpose of this manual is to provide health care facilities in the process of developing comprehensive infection control programs sample policies and procedures related to the prevention and management of bloodborne infections. The sample policies and procedures address many aspects of patient care and workplace practices, the use of protective barriers, and personnel management and training. Collectively, these strategies have become known as *Universal Precautions* and are recommended by the Centers for Disease Control (CDC) and mandated by the Occupational Safety and Health Administration (OSHA). The American Hospital Association has endorsed the adoption of Universal Precautions as recommended by the CDC as the most effective means of reducing the risk of transmission of bloodborne infections in health care settings.

The activities related to the development and implementation of Universal Precautions have assumed a major role in health care facilities. A variety of approaches have been taken, each of which requires significant resources, expertise, and cooperative effort among many individuals.

This manual reproduces sample policies and procedures from a number of hospitals and one long-term care facility. In 1989, the editor collected policies from facilities across the country. It was difficult to choose from among the many materials that were submitted. In general, those that were selected for reproduction in this manual are applicable in a variety of settings.

The material in this manual is organized into chapters that address the specific components of a comprehensive infection control program. The manual can be used as a general reference for developing an institutional strategy or revising specific components of an institutional strategy.

I hope that this manual will be a valuable resource as you develop or revise your policies and procedures and that it will reduce the need for you to "reinvent the wheel."

Gina Pugliese, R.N., M.S., C.I.C. June 1990

Acknowledgments

This manual represents the collective talents of many health care professionals committed to reducing the risk of transmitting infections in health care settings. Among the many colleagues whose contributions were essential to the completion of this book were Patricia Lynch, R.N., M.B.A., C.I.C., and Marguerite M. Jackson, R.N., M.S., C.I.C., who acted as contributing editors during the compilation and development of the manuscript for this manual. I also want to thank Deborah Bohr, director of the Division of Quality Control Management of the American Hospital Association, for her support and encouragement throughout the two years it took to develop this manual. She also reviewed the manuscript and offered valuable comments. I would also like to thank Sally Krause, R.N., B.S., C.I.C., for her assistance in the review and selection of sample materials. The advice and guidance of Barbara Soule, R.N., B.S., C.I.C., and Elizabeth Pantelick, R.N., M.P.H., C.I.C., in the early planning stages are also gratefully acknowledged. Finally, I want to extend my appreciation to Audrey Kaufman and the rest of the editorial staff at American Hospital Publishing, Inc.

This manual would not have been possible without the contributions of the facilities that generously shared their policies, procedures, and other materials for implementing Universal Precautions. It was very difficult to choose from among the many useful materials that were submitted. I would like to thank all those practitioners and facilities that submitted materials that could not be included because of practical constraints on the publication's length and cost.

Finally, I wish to acknowledge the following associations and health care facilities, as well as the practitioners affiliated with these organizations, for generously sharing the policies, procedures, and other materials that form the basis for this manual:

- Berks County Home/Berks Heim, Reading, Pennsylvania
- Charlotte Hungerford Hospital, Torrington, Connecticut
- Children's Hospital National Medical Center, Washington, D.C.
- Cleveland Clinic Foundation, Cleveland, Ohio
- Harborview Medical Center, Seattle, Washington
- Harper Hospital, Detroit, Michigan
- Johns Hopkins Health Care System, Baltimore, Maryland
- Kaiser Permanente Medical Center, San Francisco, California
- Lutheran General Hospital-Lincoln Park, Chicago, Illinois (closed since late 1989)
- Massachusetts General Hospital, Boston, Massachusetts
- North Carolina Memorial Hospital, Chapel Hill, North Carolina
- San Francisco General Hospital, San Francisco, California
- Tucson Medical Center, Tucson, Arizona
- University of California Medical Center, San Diego, California

- University of California at Irvine Medical Center, Orange, California
- University of Minnesota Hospital and Clinic, Minneapolis, Minnesota
- Veterans Administration Medical Center, Seattle, Washington
- Yale-New Haven Hospital, New Haven, Connecticut
- American Hospital Association, Chicago, Illinois
- Association for Practitioners in Infection Control, Dallas-Ft. Worth, Texas
- Marvick Educational Services, Inc., San Diego, California
- New Jersey Hospital Association, Princeton, New Jersey
- Society of Hospital Epidemiologists of America, Mundelein, Illinois
- Tennessee Hospital Association, Nashville, Tennessee

How to Use This Manual

This manual was created to serve as a guide for the development of institution-specific strategies for implementing Universal Precautions as recommended by the CDC and currently mandated by OSHA pending publication of the official OSHA standard in 1991. The sample materials provided by health care facilities represent both traditional and unique approaches to implementing Universal Precautions. The approaches reflect differences in the type and complexity of the health care organizations, as well as various philosophies of infection control, different patient populations and case mixes, various services and types of personnel, different levels of available resources, and various local and state regulatory environments.

The manual is divided into ten chapters: an introductory chapter, seven content chapters that address the main components of a Universal Precautions program (Universal Precautions and isolation systems, medical waste management, implementation plans, compliance monitoring, training and education, employee health, and OSHA's current requirements and proposed rule on occupational exposure to bloodborne pathogens), a discussion chapter, and a resource chapter. Each content chapter includes an introduction (which may be useful in developing a particular component of a Universal Precautions program) and sample policies and procedures. Within each content chapter, the material has been arranged by facility rather than by subject, and each example carries the title given to it by the facility that developed it. Some of the sample materials contain information that may also be useful in developing more than one component of the program. A detailed contents page at the beginning of the manual as well as an index at the end provide the reader with tools for locating examples from specific facilities and examples of policies and procedures covering key program components.

The sample policies in this manual are reproduced without significant editing. Some ideas and terms may not be entirely clear, and viewpoints are diverse and sometimes conflicting. Therefore, the policies and procedures, in some cases, may disagree with each other. However, each policy and procedure presented here represents a program that works for a specific facility. Chapter 9 provides commentary on a number of concepts, terms, and viewpoints. Throughout the sample materials, cross-references to chapter 9 indicate subjects that are included in the discussion chapter.

Chapter 10 reproduces key resources such as Universal Precautions guidelines from the CDC, relevant journal articles, references, an annotated bibliography on audiovisual teaching aids, and other materials useful for implementing Universal Precautions.

This manual should be useful to readers who are looking for new ideas about specific aspects of Universal Precautions programs or are planning minor revisions in existing policies. It should also be very useful for those who are considering making major revisions in their facilities' infection control policies. Chapter 2 would be especially valuable to readers planning such revisions. However, because the sample policies and procedures in this manual come from a variety of facilities, each of which has its own unique characteristics and circumstances, not every example provided is applicable to every health care organization. For example, some of the examples are very brief, even terse, while others are quite long and detailed. Hospitals that rely extensively on part-time or agency personnel but do not currently provide comprehensive training for such employees should develop sample policies that are detailed and clear.

In addition, the complex policies and implementation plans that large teaching facilities often use may not be needed by small hospitals. Conversely, large teaching facilities may find the policies and implementation plans written for small hospitals inadequate.

The philosophy of the institution should also be considered and so should the degree of commitment and support for the infection control program. Because making major revisions requires considerable planning and support from administrators, physicians, and department heads, major revisions should usually be avoided unless there is adequate support for the project. Exceptions to this suggestion include revisions to ensure consistency with applicable laws and regulations or consistency with infection control practices proved to be effective.

Chapter 1

Introduction

Isolation practices in health care facilities have been modified in response to changes in patient populations and technology and improvements in our knowledge about infectious diseases. The most recent revisions are the result of concern over the risk of transmitting hepatitis B virus (HBV) and human immunodeficiency virus (HIV) infection from patients to health care workers.

Recent History of Isolation Practices

During outbreak investigations conducted by the Centers for Disease Control (CDC) in the 1960s, investigators noted that few of the hospitals had consistent policies and procedures for isolating patients with infections.[1] In 1970, the CDC published a manual entitled *Isolation Techniques for Use in Hospitals* that advocated the use of seven categories of isolation.[2] Diseases with similar modes of transmission were grouped together into categories, and color-coded instruction cards were provided for each category. By 1976, the system had been adopted widely with few modifications.[3]

By 1980, a number of developments in hospitals made it apparent that a revision of the original isolation guidelines was needed.[4] First, as a consequence of grouping many infections into a few categories, unnecessary precautions were often used for some patients. Second, the increased use of intensive care units, the proliferation of invasive and immunocompromising technology, and the emergence of hospital pathogens resistant to multiple antibiotics increased the need for precautions that were specifically directed at nosocomial infections. Finally, most hospitals had infection control practitioners and other staff members with the specific knowledge and skill required to manage isolation precautions more effectively, as well as an interest in adapting isolation practices to meet the needs of their own facilities.

In 1983, the CDC revised its recommendations and published the *Guideline for Isolation Precautions in Hospitals*.[5] The revised isolation guidelines offered three alternative systems:

1. A modified category-specific system to reflect new epidemiologic knowledge
2. A new disease-specific system that suggested the specific precautions for each disease
3. The option for facilities to design their own systems

Other recommendations from the CDC for infection control are contained in the CDC's *Guidelines for the Prevention and Control of Nosocomial Infections,* first published in

1981 and revised periodically.[6] These guidelines describe practices that reduce the risk of specific types of patient infections and also include recommendations for hand washing, environmental control, and prevention of infections in hospital personnel.

Body Substance Isolation

In 1984, Lynch and Jackson developed a different approach to isolation and called it Body Substance Isolation (BSI).[7,8] This approach was designed to have two benefits: a decrease in the nosocomial transmission of infectious agents to patients and a reduction in the exposure of health care workers to viral and bacterial pathogens from patients. Body Substance Isolation requires personnel to put on clean gloves immediately before contact with the mucous membranes or nonintact skin of all patients and to wear gloves when contact with any moist body substances is likely. In addition, personnel wear aprons and other barriers as necessary to keep their skin and clothing clean. Personnel should be immune to, or immunized against, diseases transmitted by the airborne route, such as rubella, measles, and chickenpox, where barriers, including masks, may not prevent transmission. For diseases for which immunity is not possible, such as pulmonary tuberculosis, personnel are to wear masks. Soiled trash and linen are to be bagged and managed in the same fashion for all patients. Used sharps from all patients are to be handled carefully, and needles are not to be recapped by hand and are to be discarded in rigid puncture-resistant containers. Only laboratory and pathology wastes, sharps, and fluid-filled containers are considered to be potentially infectious and are to be managed as "medical" or infectious waste.

These precautions are used for all patients, regardless of whether they are diagnosed as having infections. This system is quite different from the traditional approach that recommended precautions only for patients diagnosed as or suspected of being infected. Body Substance Isolation continued to be evaluated during the late 1980s and has been adopted in a number of facilities.

Universal Precautions

In 1987, the CDC responded to increasing concern on the part of health care workers and others relating to the need to minimize the risk of infection from occupationally transmitted bloodborne diseases, such as hepatitis B and acquired immunodeficiency syndrome (AIDS). Published recommendations emphasized the need for health care workers to consider the blood and body fluids of all patients as potential sources of bloodborne pathogens. They recommended that the precautions outlined in the isolation category "blood and body fluid precautions" be consistently used for all patients and entitled the new recommendations Universal Precautions (UP) or Universal Blood and Body Fluid Precautions.[9]

This new approach requires health care workers to wear gloves and other protective barriers to reduce the risk of parenteral, mucous membrane, and nonintact skin exposures to blood and other body fluids. Specific precautions are to be taken with soiled linen, trash, and used sharps. Comprehensive postexposure management is indicated for all personnel experiencing mucous membrane, parenteral, or nonintact skin exposures to blood or body fluids, with an emphasis on hepatitis B immunization. Guidelines are provided for the content and frequency of employee education and training, with recommendations for monitoring for compliance. The CDC recommended that these precautions be used in conjunction with an isolation system specifically designed for patients with other diagnosed or suspected infectious conditions.

To clarify the specific body fluids covered by Universal Precautions, in 1988 the CDC revised their recommendations to include only those body fluids that had been implicated in the transmission of bloodborne infections.[10] Additional clarification was provided for glove use during phlebotomy, selection of gloves, and waste management practices. At the time the revision was published, many hospitals had already developed policies and procedures for their Universal Precautions systems and had successfully trained their personnel, which accounts for the great variety of approaches in use today.

Proposed OSHA Standard on Occupational Exposure to Bloodborne Pathogens

On May 30, 1989, OSHA published for public comment a proposed standard entitled Occupational Exposure to Bloodborne Pathogens.[11] Although a final standard is not expected until 1991 at the earliest, OSHA currently has the authority to conduct inspections of health care establishments to ensure that employers are providing appropriate safeguards against occupational exposure to bloodborne pathogens for their employees. The Occupational Safety and Health Administration is relying on the CDC's guidelines for Universal Precautions as the accepted standard of protection to be followed by employers in carrying out their responsibility to provide a safe work environment that is free from recognized hazards. At a minimum, employers must implement Universal Precautions as recommended by the CDC.

The proposed standard contains many of the recommendations from the CDC for Universal Precautions. In addition, the proposed standard contains requirements for the following elements of an occupational safety and health program:

- Identification of tasks that present a risk of exposure and the employees performing those tasks
- Establishment of the method and schedule for implementing protective barriers, workplace practices, and engineering controls to reduce the risk of exposure
- Requirements for general housekeeping, cleaning and disinfection, handling and disposal of infectious waste and sharps, and management of soiled linen
- Provision of hepatitis B vaccinations to employees who are frequently exposed to blood and potentially infectious materials
- Postexposure evaluation and medical follow-up
- Communication of hazards with warning signs and labels
- Special requirements for research laboratories and production facilities
- Training of employees
- Record keeping

The CDC's guidelines for Universal Precautions, which are endorsed by the American Hospital Association and mandated by OSHA, have prompted health care facilities to revise their infection control and isolation practices. A variety of approaches have been used. Some health care facilities have simply added Universal Precautions, as recommended by the CDC, to their existing programs; others have incorporated Universal Precautions into a broad institutional strategy for infection prevention and control. Body Substance Isolation is one example of the latter approach.

The field of infection prevention and control is an evolving one, and over the past 20 years there have been many changes in practice. As more is learned about bloodborne infectious agents and the efficacy of currently recommended practices, there will undoubtedly be a need for additional changes. Refinements in Universal Precautions programs may also be necessary when OSHA publishes the final standard on occupational exposure to bloodborne pathogens.

Planning a Universal Precautions Program

Universal Precautions, as recommended by the CDC, are currently mandated by OSHA and require health care workers to consider blood and certain body fluids from all patients to be potentially infectious for HIV, HBV, and other bloodborne pathogens. Universal Precautions also require the use of protective barriers, specific workplace practices, employee health management, education and training, and monitoring for compliance. The implementation of Universal Precautions for all patients theoretically eliminates the need for the use of the isolation category blood and body fluid precautions, which was previously recommended by the CDC for patients known or suspected to be infected with bloodborne pathogens.

When a hospital is considering revisions of its infection control program, careful planning is essential to ensure successful implementation. Making even a minor change may be a complicated project. Universal Precautions and isolation techniques touch many basic fears about safety, in particular fears about AIDS and HIV infection. Changing isolation precaution techniques often creates anxiety. In addition, there are often conflicting opinions regarding the precise method for adoption of specific practices or techniques. These changes require the cooperative effort of a number of individuals within the facility for planning and implementing an effective program.

Eight steps should be followed in order to ensure the successful implementation of a Universal Precautions program:

1. Identify key elements.
2. Assess the facility and its regulatory environment.
3. Review existing policies and procedures.
4. Develop a written proposal.
5. Meet with key personnel.
6. Implement the plan.
7. Provide training and education.
8. Monitor for compliance.

Step 1: Identify Key Elements

The first step is to identify the key components of a Universal Precautions program. Universal Precautions programs must include at least the specific recommendations of the CDC. In addition, the program should take into consideration OSHA's proposed standard on occupational exposure to bloodborne pathogens, which contains many of the elements for Universal Precautions as recommended by the CDC as well as additional requirements for an occupational safety and health program. The proposed standard has not yet become a regulation, but it does indicate the direction in which OSHA is heading for the future. The CDC's guidelines for Universal Precautions are included in chapter 10 of this manual, and the current and proposed requirements from OSHA are contained in chapter 8.

Step 2: Assess the Facility and Its Regulatory Environment

Any assessment of the facility should include information on its philosophy of infection control and its degree of commitment and support for the program. Policies that call for great changes in the practices of personnel are complicated to implement and require support from administration and hospital committees. The lack of such support may preclude implementation of a complex change unless changes are necessary to comply with applicable laws and regulations or with practices that have proven efficacy.

An assessment of the complexity of the facility is also important because large facilities that deliver technologically sophisticated care to severely immunocompromised patients need policies that recognize that fact. The level of expertise among personnel is also an important consideration because knowledgeable personnel often resist simple categories for precautions and prefer to rely on their expertise to make judgments about appropriate precautions. In addition, training programs must be appropriate for the staff's level of expertise.

An assessment of the state and local regulations that mandate certain practices is necessary to ensure that appropriate policies are developed to meet these requirements. Although many local regulations may be excessive, adopting different practices may be very time-consuming and difficult. Some state associations of infection control practitioners have been successful in influencing changes in state and local regulations to reflect current knowledge and practice.

Step 3: Review Existing Policies and Procedures

A review and evaluation of existing policies and procedures determines the need for revisions in existing policies or development of additional ones. The components of existing policies and procedures should be compared with the key elements recommended by the CDC and required by OSHA. This review should also include the reasons for any proposed changes, such as consistency with regulatory or guideline-setting agencies or current infection control practice, as well as information on the benefits of the proposed changes.

Step 4: Develop a Written Proposal

The next step is to develop a written plan for designing the elements of the new program. The titles and key elements of desired policies, procedures, and program components should be included. Tentative deadlines should be set for accomplishing the tasks in the development or revision of each of the key elements, and the responsibility for each task should be assigned to appropriate personnel. A review of the sample policies and procedures throughout this manual will provide ideas for designing the elements of the program.

Step 5: Meet with Key Personnel

After the written plan is complete, meetings should be set up with administrators, department heads, committee chairs, and others who are key to building support for the plan and marketing it to their staff and who will need to approve or implement the plan. After input from these key personnel, the plan and deadlines should be adjusted to reflect the information and comments received.

Step 6: Implement the Plan

Implementation of the plan requires the development of written policies, procedures, and materials to document the necessary components of each of the elements of the Universal Precautions program. The structure and format of the policies and procedures vary. Some facilities may develop general hospitalwide policies that incorporate all the components into a single policy. Others may develop individual policies and procedures for each specific component. Department-specific policies and procedures may also need to be developed.

It may be helpful to form task forces to develop specific policies and implementation plans. Individual departments may assist with the development of department-specific policies. An action plan should be developed for each specific component, task, or activity that has been identified, including developing or revising policies and procedures and obtaining any supplies or materials needed to implement that specific component. The action plan should identify the individual who will coordinate that particular component of the plan and the deadline for completion. Samples are included in chapter 2 for both hospitalwide and department-specific policies and procedures, as well as implementation policies, plans, and time lines. An article entitled "Implementing and Evaluating a System of Generic Infection Precautions: Body Substance Isolation," written by Patricia Lynch and others (*American Journal of Infection Control,* 1990), is reprinted in chapter 10.

Step 7: Provide Training and Education

The training and education of personnel is an essential component of the process and must be provided to all staff, including physicians, house staff, students, and other personnel who will be involved in following the program. The content of the training and education programs should include information that will be relevant to the specific work practices of each group. Chapter 6 provides strategies for developing, presenting, and evaluating training and education programs. Sample materials are also included for "train-the-trainer" programs, self-learning programs, and pretests and posttests.

Step 8: Monitor for Compliance

When the Universal Precautions program is established, monitoring for compliance is essential to ensure that the recommended practices are being followed. Any problems identified during this monitoring should be documented and corrected as soon as possible. When monitoring reveals a failure to follow recommended practices, the CDC recommends that counseling, education, and/or retraining be provided to staff and, when necessary, that appropriate disciplinary action be considered. Chapter 5 provides strategies for monitoring compliance and sample tools for monitoring compliance with specific components of the Universal Precautions program.

□ References

1. Garner, J. S., and Hughes, H. M. Editorial: options for isolation precautions. *Annals of Internal Medicine* 2:248–50, 1987.
2. Centers for Disease Control. *Isolation Techniques for Use in Hospitals.* DHEW publication no. (PHS) 70-2054. Washington, DC: U.S. Government Printing Office, 1970.
3. Haley, R. W., and Shactman, R. H. The emergence of infection surveillance and control programs in U.S. hospitals: an assessment. *American Journal of Epidemiology* 111:574–91, 1980.
4. Haley, R. W., Garner, J. S., and Simmons, B. P. A new approach to the isolation of hospitalized patients with infectious diseases: alternative systems. *Journal of Hospital Infection* 6:128–39, 1985.
5. Garner, J. S., and Simmons, B. P. Guideline for isolation precautions in hospitals. *Infection Control* 4:245–325, 1983.
6. Centers for Disease Control. *Guidelines for the Prevention and Control of Nosocomial Infections.* Atlanta: U.S. Department of Health and Human Services, 1981.
7. Lynch, P., and Jackson, M. M. Rethinking the role of isolation precautions in the prevention of nosocomial infections. *Annals of Internal Medicine* 107:243–46, 1987.
8. Lynch, P., Cummings, M. J., Roberts, P. L., and others. Implementing and evaluating a system of generic infection precautions: Body Substance Isolation. *American Journal of Infection Control* 18:1–12, 1990.
9. Centers for Disease Control. Recommendations for prevention of HIV transmission in health care settings. *Morbidity and Mortality Weekly Report* 36(25, Suppl.):1S–16S, Aug. 21, 1987.
10. Centers for Disease Control. Update: Universal Precautions for prevention of transmission of human immunodeficiency virus, hepatitis B virus, and other bloodborne pathogens in health care settings. *Morbidity and Mortality Weekly Report* 37:377–88, June 24, 1988.
11. Department of Labor and Department of Health and Human Services. Occupational exposure to bloodborne pathogens: proposed rule and notice of hearings. *Federal Register* 54(102): 23042–139, May 30, 1989.

Chapter 2

Universal Precautions and Isolation Systems

Introduction

Universal Precautions, as recommended by the Centers for Disease Control (CDC), require health care workers to consider the blood and certain body fluids of all patients to be potentially infectious for bloodborne pathogens and to use protective barriers and workplace practices to reduce the risk of exposure. Theoretically, the adoption of Universal Precautions techniques for all patients eliminates the need for the specific isolation of patients known to be or suspected of being infected with bloodborne pathogens. Health care facilities have used a variety of approaches for designing programs to incorporate the Universal Precautions techniques as recommended by the CDC.

Some of the important variables in the design of a program include: (1) the specific body fluids to be considered under Universal Precautions, (2) the method for incorporating Universal Precautions into an existing isolation system, and (3) the number and types of specific isolation categories to be used for patients with known or suspected nonbloodborne infections, such as respiratory infections.

The specific body fluids to be considered under Universal Precautions were clarified by the CDC in June 1988. These body fluids include blood, semen, vaginal secretions, tissues, cerebrospinal fluid, synovial fluid, pleural fluid, pericardial fluid, amniotic fluid, bloody saliva in dental settings, breast milk in special settings such as breast milk collection and banking, and any other body fluid that contains visible blood. Universal Precautions, as defined by the CDC, do not apply to feces, saliva, nasal secretions, sputum, sweat, tears, or urine unless they are visibly contaminated with blood. Some health care facilities have adopted the CDC's list of body fluids to be considered under Universal Precautions, but others have found it easier to include all body fluids. Each facility must specify in its policy those body fluids to which Universal Precautions apply.

A variety of approaches have also been used for incorporating Universal Precautions into an existing isolation policy. Some facilities have simply added Universal Precautions to their existing category-specific or disease-specific isolation policy. Others have replaced their existing isolation policy with an approach similar to Body Substance Isolation. (See the discussions of Body Substance Isolation in chapter 1.) Still others have developed policies that are a combination of the two approaches.

The next step is to determine the number and types of specific isolation categories for patients with known or suspected infections transmitted by routes other than the bloodborne infection route, for example, patients with tuberculosis or infectious diarrhea. This determination depends on the strategy chosen for isolation techniques. Some facilities have chosen to retain their category-specific isolation model with no changes or with revisions in both the numbers of categories and the diseases to be included in each category. Other facilities have replaced their category-specific models with an approach similar to the Body Substance Isolation system and retained only one category of isolation for diseases transmitted by the respiratory route.

After the method for incorporating Universal Precautions into the infection control and isolation program and the body fluids to be considered potentially infectious have been determined, the structure and content of each policy and procedure must be established. There is no correct method for developing the components of each policy and procedure. One method is to develop a comprehensive hospitalwide policy that contains all the necessary elements of the program. Another method is to develop individual policies for specific elements of the program. Department-specific policies and procedures may also be useful for providing information on protective barriers and workplace practices that are unique for each department. Regardless of the approach chosen, policies and procedures must contain, at a minimum, the recommendations from the CDC that are currently mandated by OSHA. The CDC's recommendations are reproduced in chapter 10 and OSHA's current proposed requirements are included in chapter 8.

The sample materials contained in chapter 2 include hospitalwide and department-specific policies for Universal Precautions. Table 2-1 provides information on each of the facilities represented in this chapter, including bed size, the body fluids covered, the number and titles of specific isolation categories used, and the title given to each system of Universal Precautions.

A careful review of each of the policies and procedures in this chapter is necessary before any particular model can be chosen. The title given to the policy by a facility may not provide complete information on the strategy used for implementing Universal Precautions. Some hospitals have retained the title "Isolation Precautions" to describe their existing isolation systems and added a second title such as "Universal Precautions" or "Universal Blood and Body Fluid Precautions" to represent the addition of the CDC's specific recommendations. Facilities that have adopted the Body Substance Isolation approach have also used a variety of titles, including "Universal Precautions," "Body Substance Precautions," "Body Substance Isolation," and "Universal Body Substance Technique" as well as other titles.

Materials for implementing several of the facilities' policies reproduced in this chapter are provided in chapter 4. These include policies and procedures from Tucson Medical Center, San Francisco General Hospital, Yale-New Haven Hospital, Harborview Medical Center, and Marvik Educational Services.

Table 2-1. Characteristics and Systems for Infection Precautions of Facilities Represented by Policies and Procedures in Chapter 2

			Body Fluids/Substances Covered by Precautions		Isolation Categories in Addition to Universal Precautions						
Name of Institution	Number of Beds	Title Given to System of Precautions	All	1988 CDC*	Airborne/ Respiratory	Blood and Body Fluids	Strict	Contact	Enteric/ Secretion	Protective	"Special Isolation"
Berks County Home/Berks Heim	—	Universal Precautions	X		X		X		X		
Children's Hospital National Medical Center	279	Universal Precautions		X	X		X	X	X	X	
Tucson Medical Center	562	Body Substance Precautions	X		X						
University of Minnesota Hospital and Clinic	591	Universal Blood and Body Substance Technique	X		X	X		X			X
San Francisco General Hospital	444	Body Substance Precautions	X		X						
Yale-New Haven Hospital	829	Universal Precautions	X		X						
Kaiser Permanente Medical Center	264	Universal Precautions	X		X						
Harborview Medical Center	330	Body Substance Isolation	X		X						

*Body fluids as defined by the CDC in the June 24, 1988, issue of *Morbidity and Mortality Weekly Report* include blood, semen, vaginal secretions, tissues, cerebrospinal fluid, synovial fluid, pericardial fluid, amniotic fluid, bloody saliva in dental settings, breast milk in special settings such as breast milk collection and banking, and any other body fluid that contains visible blood.

Berks County Home/Berks Heim
Reading, Pennsylvania

Isolation/Precautions Program

Policy

It is the policy of Berks County Home/Berks Heim to use the following CDC-approved categories of Isolation/Precautions:

Isolation

An acutely sick resident who requires skilled nursing care and observation. Resident may need to change level of care; resident with a highly communicable disease spread by air and by contact with some diseases.

Isolation Categories: Strict Isolation
Respiratory Isolation

Precautions

The use of nursing care measures to prevent spread of infection by direct or indirect contact; use of "barrier techniques." Resident probably does not require a level of care change.

Precaution Categories: Enteric Precautions
Drainage/Secretion Precautions

Universal Precautions

Consists of the application of Blood and Body Fluid Precautions to the care for all residents. See Policy #2702-45 "Isolation Precautions Program: Universal Precautions" for specific policy of Universal Precautions care of the resident.

The Infection Disease Index is used to determine which category to use for an infection in addition to Universal Precautions.

Note: As long as employees follow the specified technique, they are not at risk to acquire the infection.

Any resident with a known or suspected communicable disease/infection is to be placed in the appropriate category of (or combination of) Isolation/Precautions.

The resident may remain on the unit unless a special room or level of care change is required.

Isolation/Precautions are not discontinued until a definite diagnosis is made or treatment received that renders the resident noninfectious.

The attending physician or the Director of Infection Control is responsible for initiating Isolation/Precautions for residents with known or suspected infection. In the absence of the above, the charge nurse on the unit is responsible for initiating the appropriate Isolation/Precautions after consultation with the Director of Infection Control and Nursing Supervisor.

If a difference of opinion arises concerning the advisability of Isolation/Precautions, the decision of Administration will be final.

Residents with infections needing strict or respiratory isolation require a physician's written order and must be moved to a designated private isolation room. See approved list of designated isolation rooms. Utilization review must be notified.

Residents with infections needing enteric precautions or drainage/secretion precautions do not require a physician's order if the resident does not require skilled nursing care:

- The precautions must be listed on the physician's progress note by the charge nurse as a notification to the attending physician, the charge nurse, or the Director of Infection Control.
- If the resident requires a change to skilled nursing care, a physician's order must be obtained.

If the resident is in a semiprivate room, the Isolation/Precautions sign should identify the resident's name and bed number (location in room).

The appropriate Isolation/Precautions are implemented for the resident until a definite diagnosis is made and treatment is received that will allow for the termination.

Isolation/Precautions are discontinued on 7-to-3 shift to facilitate proper cleaning procedures by the Housekeeping Department.

Procedure: Initiation of Isolation/Precautions

Charge Nurse, R.N., L.P.N.

- Discusses with the Director of Infection Control and Nursing Supervisor the need for isolation or precautions and determination made.
- Determines isolation or precautions based on the mode or transmission of the known or suspected infection using the Infection Disease Index (Policy #2702-05).
- Reports to attending physician and Infection Control when resident requires Isolation/Precautions.
- Posts Isolation/Precautions sign on the resident's door. *Note:* Sign should identify resident's name and bed number.
- Explains the necessity and procedure of the type of isolation or precautions to the resident, family members, and visitors.
- Records type of isolation or precautions category on Kardex® (under treatment section).
- Records on the individual care plan (ICP).
- Notifies unit coworkers of resident's isolation or precautions.
- Records the following information in the resident's chart under nursing notes:

  1. Clinical S/S of infection or disease
  2. Category of Isolation/Precautions
  3. Explanation to resident, family, and visitors
  4. Persons notified: Director of Infection Control, Nursing Supervisor
  5. Any specimens sent

- Records Isolation/Precautions category on physician's progress notes.
- Reports the above information to the Director of Infection Control as soon as possible.

Nursing Assistant

- Sets up Isolation/Precautions room under direction of nurse.

Charge Nurse, Ward Clerk, or Designee

- Sends referral to Social Services and Utilization Review with resident's name, room, and category of Isolation/Precautions.
- Notifies Dietary using Dietary Request form.
- Notifies Laundry.
- Labels resident's Line-o-vision® and front of chart with category of Isolation/Precautions.
- Notifies Housekeeping Supervisor of rooms used by Isolation/Precautions residents for proper daily cleaning and discharge.

Procedure: Termination of Isolation/Precautions

Physician

- Attending physician will order the discontinuation of isolation.

Charge Nurse, R.N., L.P.N.

- Consult the Director of Infection Control and attending physician to discontinue precautions.
- Nurse discontinues Isolation/Precautions.

  1. Explains to resident and staff.
  2. Documents on chart.
  3. Informs nursing assistant to discontinue room setup.
  4. Notifies Nursing Supervisor.

Nursing Assistant

- Removes sign from door.
- Removes Isolation/Precautions trash and laundry.
- Returns reusable equipment to Central Supply according to policy.

Charge Nurse, Ward Clerk, or Designee

- Notifies Housekeeping to clean room.
- Notifies Dietary with Dietary Request form.
- Notifies Laundry.
- Removes Line-o-vision®.
- Notifies Social Services department.
- Notifies Utilization Review if skilled nursing.
- Notifies departments that resident attends of discontinuation (for example, Physical Therapy, Activities, Clinics).
- Removes label from front of resident's chart.
- Deletes entry in Kardex®.
- Deletes entry in individual care plan (ICP).

☐ References

Centers for Disease Control Guideline for Isolation/Precautions in Hospitals, July/August 1983.

Universal Precautions Policy No. 2702-45.

Children's Hospital National Medical Center
Washington, D.C.

Universal Precautions for Exposure to Blood and Body Fluids

I. Statement of Policy

Universal Precautions are intended to prevent parenteral, mucous membrane, and nonintact skin exposures of health care workers to bloodborne pathogens. Universal Precautions should be used in the care of all patients. Body fluids to which Universal Precautions apply are: blood and other body fluids containing visible blood. Universal Precautions also apply to tissues and to the following fluids: cerebrospinal fluid (CSF), synovial fluid, pleural fluid, peritoneal fluid, pericardial fluid, amniotic fluid, semen, and vaginal secretions. Universal Precautions *do not apply* to feces, nasal secretions, sputum, sweat, tears, urine, and vomitus unless they contain visible blood.

Universal Precautions mandates that all health care workers shall routinely use appropriate barrier precautions when exposure to bloodborne pathogens is anticipated. Medical history and examination cannot reliably identify all patients infected with HIV, HBV, or other bloodborne pathogens; hence the institution of these Universal Precautions.

II. Purpose

To protect health care providers and patients from contamination by potentially infective body fluids/substances. Health care providers are defined as persons, including students and trainees, whose activities involve contact with patients or with blood or other body fluids/substances from patients in a health care setting.

Materials: Gloves, gowns, goggles, masks

III. Implementation

1. Gloves should be worn for touching blood and body fluids, mucous membranes, or nonintact skin of all patients, for handling items or surfaces soiled with blood or body fluids/substances, and for performing venipuncture and other vascular access procedures. Gloves should be changed after contact with each patient and hands should be washed. Masks and protective eyewear or face shields should be worn during procedures that are likely to generate droplets of blood or other body fluids to prevent exposure of mucous membranes of the mouth, nose, and eyes. Gowns or aprons should be worn during procedures that are likely to generate splashes of blood or other body fluids.
2. Hands and other skin surfaces should be washed immediately and thoroughly following contact with blood or other body fluids/substances. Hands should be washed immediately after gloves are removed.
3. All health care workers should take precautions to prevent injuries caused by needles, scalpels, and other sharp instruments or devices during procedures; when cleaning used instruments; during disposal of used needles; and when handling sharp instruments after procedures. To prevent needlestick injuries, needles should not be recapped, purposely bent or broken by hand, or removed from disposable syringes. Needles, scalpel blades, and other sharp items should be placed in puncture-resistant containers for disposal; the puncture-resistant containers will be located in all areas where patient care is provided. The method of disposal for these containers will be incineration. See Disposal of Waste Policy II:I:9. [See the discussion of needle recapping in chapter 9.]
4. To minimize the need for emergency mouth-to-mouth resuscitation, mouthpieces, resuscitation bags, or other ventilation devices should be available for use in areas in which the need for resuscitation is predictable.

5. Health care workers who have exudative lesions or weeping dermatitis should refrain from all direct patient care and from handling patient-care equipment until the condition resolves.
6. Pregnant health care workers are not known to be at greater risk of contracting HIV or HBV infection than health care workers who are not pregnant; however, if a health care worker develops HIV or HBV infection during pregnancy, the infant is at risk of infection resulting from perinatal transmission. Because of this risk, pregnant health care workers should be especially familiar with and strictly adhere to precautions to minimize the risk of HIV, HBV transmission.
7. Implementation of Universal Blood and Body Fluid Precautions for all patients eliminates the need for use of the isolation category of "Blood and Body Fluid Precautions" previously recommended by the CDC for patients known or suspected to be infected with bloodborne pathogens. Modified category-specific isolation precautions (e.g., Strict, Respiratory, Enteric/Skin) should be used as necessary if associated conditions, such as infectious diarrhea, are diagnosed or suspected. See Isolation Precautions Policy II:I:1.
8. Each department–including those where invasive procedures are performed, Dialysis, Laundry, Dentistry, Housekeeping, and those responsible for handling and transporting infective waste–will develop policies that support its compliance with Universal Precautions.
9. Staff education will be presented at the New Employees Orientation and updates will be given in the annual Infection Control Briefing. Attendance at these meetings is mandatory. Each department will be responsible for ensuring that newly assigned personnel receive orientation to department-specific Universal Precautions policies and procedures.

Children's Hospital National Medical Center
Washington, D.C.

Isolation Precautions: Universal and Specific [Excerpt]

I. Statement of Policy
Universal Precautions for Blood and Body Fluids will be used in the care of all patients. Specific isolation precautions (e.g., Strict, Respiratory, Enteric/Skin) must be used for a patient with a suspected or diagnosed communicable infection whether community acquired or nosocomial.

II. Purpose
To reduce the risk of transmission of pathogens within the hospital.

III. Implementation

1. *Universal Precautions* are intended to prevent parenteral, mucous membrane, and nonintact skin exposures of health care workers to bloodborne pathogens. Body fluids to which Universal Precautions apply are: blood and other body fluids containing visible blood. Universal Precautions also apply to tissues and to the following fluids: cerebrospinal fluid (CSF), synovial fluid, pleural fluid, peritoneal fluid, pericardial fluid, amniotic fluid, semen, and vaginal secretions. The risk of transmission of HIV and HBV from these fluids is unknown. However, HIV has been isolated from CSF, synovial, and amniotic fluid, and HBsAG has been detected in synovial fluid, amniotic fluid, and peritoneal fluid.

   Body fluids to which Universal Precautions *do not apply* are: feces, nasal secretions, sputum, sweat, tears, urine, and vomitus unless they contain visible blood. Additionally, some of the above body fluids present a potential source for infections with other pathogens and specific barriers and/or isolation precautions are required for prevention of transmission of nonbloodborne pathogens.

   Protective barriers reduce the risk of exposure to blood and body fluids. Examples of protective barriers include gloves, gowns, masks, and protective eyewear.

   Universal Precautions are intended to supplement rather than replace recommendations for routine infection control, such as hand washing and using gloves to prevent gross microbial contamination of hands. Because specifying the types of barriers needed for every possible clinical situation is impractical, some judgment must be exercised.
2. *Specific Isolation Precautions* are required for prevention of the transmission of nonbloodborne pathogens. Modified category-specific isolation techniques will be used.

   Three categories apply to Specific Isolation Precautions.
   a. *Strict Isolation*
   b. *Respiratory Isolation*
   c. *Enteric/Skin Precautions*
3. The precautions for specific diseases are listed in the Isolation Precaution Manual in alphabetical order according to disease.
   a. In addition to showing the category of isolation for each disease, Category-Specific Isolation Precautions identify which protective barrier precautions are used; which secretions, excretions, discharges, body fluids, and tissues are infective or might be infective; and duration required for precautions. Additional information regarding employees, cohorting, and public health responsibilities is noted in the manual.

b. In other special circumstances, notation on the precautions sign must be approved by Epidemiology/Infection Control. For example, Neutropenic Precautions category is determined by the attending physician for the individual patient. Reverse isolation is used only for bone marrow transplant patients.
c. *Specific Isolation Precautions* must be ordered and discontinued by the physician. In the event this is not done, nursing will initiate specific isolation precautions and notify the physician. Additionally, the hospital infection control officer and nurse epidemiologist have authority to institute appropriate control measures.
d. The Category-Specific Isolation Manual will be kept on each unit and in each admitting office.
e. *Signage* for Universal and Specific Precautions will be posted at the entrance of the patient's room.
   (1) **Wash Hands before and after Patient Contact.**
   (2) Gloves usage should reduce the incidence of contamination of hands, but gloves cannot prevent penetrating injuries due to needles or other sharp instruments.
   - Gloves will be worn for performing phlebotomy when the health care worker has cuts, scratches, or other breaks in his/her skin.
   - Gloves will be worn in situations where the health care worker judges that hand contamination with blood may occur, for example, when performing phlebotomy on an uncooperative patient.
   - Gloves will be worn when performing finger and/or heel sticks on infants and children.
   - Gloves will be worn when persons are receiving training in phlebotomy.
   - Gloves should be worn for digital examination of mucous membranes and endotracheal suctioning.
   - Gloves need not be worn when feeding patients and when wiping saliva from skin.
   - Gloves will be worn when specified for contact with patients on Specific Isolation Precautions. (See manual.)
   - Gloves will be worn once and discarded.

   (3) Gowns will be worn if soiling of clothing is likely with blood or body fluids/substances and when specified for contact with patients on Specific Isolation Precautions. (See manual.) Gowns must be full length with long sleeves and tight-fitting cuffs, with ties at neckline and waist. The gown is to be discarded after use. Gowns should not be worn outside of the patient's room or treatment room, unless transporting an isolated patient.
   (4) Masks and protective eyewear or face shields may reduce the incidence of contamination of mucous membranes of the mouth, nose, and eyes.
   - Masks and protective eyewear will be worn anytime when aerosolization or splashing is likely and for patients on specific isolation when specified. (See manual.)
   - Masks should cover nose and mouth and should be used once and discarded.
   - Masks become ineffective when moist and should be changed every 30 minutes. [See the discussion of masks in chapter 9.]
   - Masks should never be lowered around neck and then reused.
   - Masks should never be lowered around neck and then reused.

   (5) Equipment and other articles necessary to protect personnel and visitors are kept available in the nurse server or near the patient's bedside (in the NICU, ICU).
   - Sharps and all used needles and syringes are placed in an impervious container. For patients in strict isolation, the container will be wiped with 0.5% staphene and picked up by ESD for incineration.

Tucson Medical Center
Tucson, Arizona

Body Substance Precaution System

Introduction

The Body Substance Precaution (BSP) System focuses on isolating body substances (blood, feces, urine, wound drainage, oral secretions, lesion secretions, etc.) from the hands of personnel, primarily by increased glove use and hand washing. The system eliminates many of the ritualistic practices associated with traditional isolation systems while increasing the use of barriers for all contacts with body substances. In actual hospital practice, it is more reliable to provide the same high level of infection precautions for all patients, rather than only performing special practices for those with diagnosed infections as in the past. All patients' blood and body fluids are to be considered infectious. Any task that includes exposure to blood or body fluid requires the use of precautions.

The BSP System is consistent with recommendations from the Centers for Disease Control and the TMC Task Force on AIDS that point out the need to consider *all* blood and body fluids as potentially infectious, regardless of the patient's diagnosis. In order to follow these recommendations, the need to use barriers must focus on the care provider's interaction with the patient at the time, rather than on the diagnosis of the patient.

Another reason for the BSP System is that for virtually all infectious diseases the diagnosed cases represent only the tip of the iceberg. This is certainly true for human immunodeficiency virus (HIV) infection and for hepatitis B virus (HBV) infection. Focusing isolation precautions only on diagnosed cases of AIDS and hepatitis B misses the vast majority of persons who have the infectious agents in their blood. Because the status of all patients' blood cannot be known for these or other infectious diseases, it makes far more sense to treat all blood and body substances as potentially infectious rather than to focus on precautions only for the patients diagnosed with infectious diseases.

In addition, colonized body substances (a site where there is no infection though the microorganism is present) are a major reservoir for multiple-drug-resistant organisms that can be easily transmitted from patient to patient on the hands of personnel. The BSP System also reduces the risks of such transmission by the consistent use of barriers whenever any body substances are likely to be in contact with the care giver's hands.

Body Substance Precautions provide a consistent approach to managing body substances from all patients and are essential to prevent transmission of potentially infectious agents.

Implementing the Body Substance Precaution (BSP) System

Implementing the BSP System includes the following elements and should be followed by all personnel at all times, regardless of the patient's diagnosis:

1. Wear gloves when it is likely that hands will be in contact with body substances (blood, urine, feces, wound drainage, oral secretions, sputum, vomitus, and any other fluid or tissue).
2. Protect clothing with a plastic apron or gown when it is likely that clothing will be soiled with body substances.
3. Wear masks and/or eye protection when it is likely that eyes and/or mucous membranes will be splashed with body substances (for example, when suctioning a patient).
4. Wash hands often and well (10-second hand washing).
5. Discard uncapped needle(s) and sharps in puncture-resistant containers for sharps. Containers are in all patient rooms.
6. Discard trash and linen in impervious (leak-proof) plastic bags. [See the discussion of the term *impervious* in chapter 9.]

Use individual judgment in determining when barriers (protective wear) are needed based on your skills and interactions with the patient's body substances, nonintact skin, and mucous membranes.

Certain department policies/procedures may mandate the use of appropriate protective wear and must be followed per written policy.

Role of Direct Care Providers in the Body Substance Precaution System

1. Each direct care provider (for example, nurse, respiratory therapist) needs to evaluate his/her own interactions with the patient and use barriers as appropriate, based on anticipated contact with body substances, not on the patient's diagnosis of infection. Use the information on p. 23 as guidelines in making these judgments.
2. Each direct care provider needs to know his/her own chickenpox status so as not to put themselves at risk of exposure. All new employees will be immunized for measles and rubella unless evidence of immunity can be provided.
3. All direct care providers who have frequent contact with blood or body fluids should be immunized against hepatitis B. Hepatitis B vaccine is a benefit of employment at Tucson Medical Center.

The When's, What's, and Why's of Judgment for the BSP System

The BSP System is a judgment-based system. This indicates that unless protective measures (for example, hand washing, gloves) are already required for the procedure, it is the direct care giver's (DCG's) responsibility to anticipate the need for protective measures. When deciding what protective measures are appropriate for any given task or procedure, ask yourself these questions:

1. Will I come in contact with blood or body fluids?
2. What kind (blood, sputum, etc.) and in what quantity? (Large quantities of body fluids should always be handled with gloves.)
3. What condition are my hands in (intact, cuts, or sores)?
   a. If any broken skin, always wear gloves for any contact with blood or body fluids.
   b. If skin is intact, it may be appropriate not to wear gloves. If skin is exposed, hand washing is an appropriate protective measure.
4. What is the patient like? Is the patient alert, cooperative, confused, disoriented, or combative?
5. What is your skill level for this procedure or task? You generally know your individual skill level for procedures. Judgment is frequently based on what your individual practice is (for example, standing to one side of the bed while suctioning).

Examples

1. Starting an I.V. or lab draw—If a policy or procedure requires the use of protective care barriers, it is the health care worker's responsibility to wear the appropriate protective barrier(s) listed in the procedure.
2. Suctioning a patient—Patient is combative. She has a history of coughing while being suctioned and produces large amounts of sputum. In this situation, the use of a mask and eyewear is indicated. The patient could turn her head and the likelihood of droplets is high. Even if you stand at the side of the bed, the situation is not well controlled.

   If the patient was cooperative, had been suctioned previously and was dry, or doesn't cough with suctioning, a mask and eyewear may not be indicated.
3. You enter a patient's room to see if the patient wants a book or help with menu selection. The patient is in the bathroom. The phone rings and you answer it. The

patient returns to bed and shakes your hand upon introducing himself. What kind of protective measures should be taken?

In this situation, all of the above contacts are considered casual contacts. No protective wear is indicated. Hand washing following patient contact is always good practice.

As you can see, it is important to consider:

- The task itself
- The patient's condition
- Your practice for the procedure or task
- Whether the procedure requires protective barriers

Body Substance Precaution System Reminders

Labeling of Specimens

There is no need to place "blood precautions" or other labels on specimens from patients with identified infections (with the exception of a patient admitted or diagnosed with Creutzfeldt–Jakob disease). This is consistent with the need to treat all blood and body substances as if they are potentially infectious. Using special precautions and labels on specimen tubes and containers encourages a false sense of security. It also potentially increases risk to personnel who may handle unlabeled specimens less carefully than they should. However, it is always important to note the patient's diagnosis on laboratory requests, X-ray requests, pathology requests, and so on because the diagnosis has clinical relevance.

Soiled Linen from Patient Rooms

All soiled linen is to be put into regular plastic laundry bags. When a bag is no more than two-thirds full it is to be tied securely closed and put in the dirty linen room.

Waste from Patient Rooms

All trash generated from individual patient rooms, with the exception of fluid-filled containers, can be disposed of in regular trash bags as per usual practice.

Large spills of blood or body fluids (greater than 10 ml) should be cleaned immediately with a 1:10 dilution of bleach or a high-level disinfectant. [See the discussion of disinfectants in chapter 9.]

Fluid-Filled Containers

Fluid-filled containers (for example, Pleur-evacs®, suction canisters with liners) are not to be emptied by nursing or other personnel but are to be disposed of as follows (special instructions for emptying fluid-filled containers have been provided for personnel in the Operating Room):

1. Obtain a red "infectious waste" plastic bag from clean utility room.
2. Place the container into the bag and tie it securely closed. Place the container into a second bag if needed for strength.
3. Carry the red bag to the trash room and place it into the "infectious waste" container.

Fluid-filled containers that must be emptied (for example, Hemovacs® for reactivation) should be emptied with care. The health care worker should wear protective barriers to prevent exposure from splashing.

Wound Dressings

All wound dressings are to be disposed of in a manner so as to "confine and contain" any blood/body fluids that may be present:

1. Small dressings can be enclosed in the disposable glove used to remove the dressing. Pull the glove off inside out containing the dressing inside the glove. This dressing and glove can then be discarded into the regular trash container in the patient's room.
2. Larger dressings should be removed using gloved hands and placed into an impervious bag. This bag can be used for the old dressing, gloves, and other trash from the dressing change procedures. This bag can then be deposited into the regular trash container in the patient's room. [See the discussion of the term *impervious* in chapter 9.]

Tucson Medical Center
Tucson, Arizona

Barrier Usage Guidelines

Procedure	Wash Hands	Gloves	Gown	Mask	Eyewear
Talking with patient					
Adjusting I.V. rate or noninvasive equipment					
Examining patient without touching blood, body fluids, mucous membranes	*				
Examining patient with contact with blood, body fluids, mucous membranes	*	*			
Drawing blood	*	*			
Inserting venous access devices	*	*	Use gown, mask, eyewear if bloody fluid splattering is likely		
Handling soiled waste, linen, other materials	*	*	Use gown, mask, eyewear if bloody fluid splattering is likely		
Operative and other procedures that produce extensive splattering of blood or body fluids	*	*	*	*	*
Handling lab specimen	*	*	Use gown, mask, eyewear if bloody fluid splattering is likely		
Inserting arterial access devices	*	*	*	*	*

University of Minnesota Hospital and Clinic
Minneapolis, Minnesota

Universal Blood and Body Substance Technique and Isolation

Policy

This policy describes techniques designed to prevent cross-transmission and protect personnel. All patient specimens and body substances encountered during patient care must be regarded as infectious and will be managed using the Universal Blood and Body Substance Technique (UBBST). Patients suspected of having or diagnosed with certain specified infections will be cared for in Isolation. Contact Precautions will be used for patients whose body substances are not controlled or contained using standard nursing measures. Blood Precautions will be used for patients known to have a blood-transmissible agent.

It is the responsibility of individual departments to apply, in consultation with the Infection Control Department, the following general guidelines. The individual hospital department has the responsibility for education and monitoring of employee compliance.

The delivery and quality of patient care will not be compromised for any patient whose condition requires Isolation, Contact Precautions, or Blood Precautions.

Procedures

1. Universal Blood and Body Substance Technique (UBBST)
   A. Description. The essence of UBBST is the recognition that all blood and body substances, regardless of what is known about the source, must be regarded as hazardous. Body substances, for the purpose of policy, include all body fluids, excretions, secretions, sputum, and any drainage, but not perspiration. Avoiding contact with body substances requires avoidance of contact with nonintact skin and mucous membranes.

      When it is anticipated that there will be contact with any blood or body substance, health care workers should use the appropriate barrier precautions to prevent cross-transmission and exposure of their own skin and mucous membranes.
      (1) Barriers. [See the discussion of protective apparel in chapter 9.]
         (a) Gloves should be worn when it is anticipated that there will be touching of blood, body substances, mucous membranes, or nonintact skin of all patients, for handling items or surfaces soiled with blood or body fluids, for performing venipuncture and other vascular access procedures, and for most contact with hospitalized infants (less than 12 months old). Gloves should be changed (not washed) between patients. Hands should be washed immediately after gloves are removed.
         (b) Cloth gowns or laboratory coats should be worn when it is anticipated that there will be (1) body contact with surfaces, items, or patients soiled with blood or body substances or (2) minor splashes of blood or body substances, that is, of insufficient volume to soak through to the next layer of clothing or skin. When caring for children under the age of 12 months, a cover gown should be worn by personnel whose uniform could otherwise come into contact with the child's body (holding, feeding, etc.).
         (c) A moisture-resistant gown should be worn when it is anticipated that there will be a splash of blood or body substances of sufficient volume to soak through ordinary fabric. [See the discussion of the term *impervious* in chapter 9.]
         (d) Masks and protective eyewear should be worn when it is anticipated that there will be splatter or spray of droplets of blood or body substances to the mouth, nose, or eyes. Eyeglasses will suffice for most situations, but

goggles or safety glasses with side protection may be needed, depending on the procedure and the direction of the anticipated splash.

(e) In the event of unprotected contact with blood or other body substance, hands and/or other skin surfaces should be washed immediately and thoroughly.

(2) Handling and Disposal of Needles and Sharps. All health care workers should take precautions to prevent injuries caused by needles, scalpels, and other sharp instruments or devices during procedures; when cleaning used instruments; during disposal of needles; and when handling sharp instruments after procedures. To prevent needlestick injuries, needles should not be recapped, purposely bent or broken by hand, removed from disposable syringes, or otherwise manipulated by hand. After they are used, disposable syringes and needles, scalpel blades, and other sharp items should be placed in puncture-resistant containers for disposal; the puncture-resistant containers should be located as close as practical to the use area (in patient rooms when patient safety is not compromised). Before transport to the reprocessing area, reusable needles or sharps should be taped to a solid surface or otherwise secured.

(3) Resuscitation. To minimize the reliance on emergency mouth-to-mouth resuscitation, a safety ventilation device (bag/mask) will be placed at the bedside of all patients. When a patient (inpatient or outpatient) is transported from his "home base" (that is, clinic, ward), his ventilation device should be brought along whenever, in the opinion of his primary care givers, he is at increased risk for cardiopulmonary difficulties. Ventilation devices will also be available in all clinics, in diagnostic and therapeutic areas, and in highly frequented areas of the hospital complex isolated from resuscitation equipment.

(4) Pediatric Considerations. Interactions between children in the hospital will be closely supervised by a reasonable adult to prevent sequential mouthing of toys, biting, and any other activity that might result in transfer of body substances or fluids.

B. Conditions Requiring UBBST. Universal technique should be applied to all patients and procedures.

C. Institution of UBBST. A physician's order is not required. A UBBST card will be placed at the door of all inpatients.

D. Transportation

(1) Patient. In the event that the patient may require care during transport, personnel should have appropriate barriers available.

(2) Specimens. All specimen containers will be visibly clean and placed in sealed plastic bags for transportation to the laboratory. The request form will be attached to the outside of the bag. [See the discussion of bagging specimens in chapter 9.]

E. Visitors

(1) Visitors, including children, who have only casual contact with patients may require instruction in standard hygienic measures.

(2) Visitors who are also care givers should be instructed in the practice of UBBST and the use of barriers.

2. Isolation

A. Description. Inpatients requiring Isolation will be assigned to a private room with an isolation card at the door. For certain diseases (see below) the room should have an anteroom and a ventilation design producing corridor-to-room airflow. Patients requiring Isolation will be cared for using UBBST. In addition, all personnel will wear a mask to enter the room. Gown and gloves will be worn by all personnel for direct contact with the patient, linens, or anything likely to be contaminated with secretions. Outpatients requiring Isolation should be placed in the clinic room immediately. Time spent in the hospital complex should be minimized.

B. Conditions or diseases (suspected or confirmed) requiring Isolation:

Adenovirus–interstitial pneumonia in immunosuppressed patients
Diphtheria
Herpes simplex virus in postpartum, newborn, and obstetrical areas (see Policy 33.12)
Herpes zoster, disseminated[1]
Herpes zoster, localized
Influenza[1]
Lassa fever[1,2]
Marburg virus disease[1,2]
Measles[1]
Meningitis, bacterial or viral
Meningococcal pneumonia or tracheitis[1]
Meningococcemia
Mumps[1]
Pertussis
Plague
Rabies
Respiratory syncytial virus (eye protection recommended)
Rubella[1]
Staphylococcus aureus or group A *Streptococcus* causing: pneumonia, puerperal sepsis, endometritis, or vaginitis
Tuberculosis, pulmonary or laryngeal (mask only plus UBBST)[1]
Varicella (chickenpox)[1]

Notes: (1) Anteroom-to-room and corridor-to-room airflow required. (2) Call Infection Control Department.

C. Institution of Isolation. Doctor's orders for institution or discontinuation of Isolation should be written by the responsible physician, either as part of the admission orders or during the hospitalization. The order should specify Isolation. The charge nurse, with the assistance of the physician, should consult the above list of conditions and diseases to determine if a corridor-to-room airflow room is needed. Isolation should be instituted by the charge nurse on the patient care unit when the responsible physician is not immediately available. The physician's order should be written as soon thereafter as practical. The institution, observation, and discontinuation of Isolation should be documented in the treatment record or acute care record.

D. Transportation

(1) Patients. Patients in Isolation may leave their rooms for essential procedures when appropriate barriers are used. Patients in Isolation must wear mask, gown, and gloves during transportation. In the event that the patient requires care during transport, the transportation employee should have mask, gown, and gloves available. Arrangements should be made in advance with the receiving department. The patient should be placed directly into the diagnostic exam room to avoid contact with susceptible patients.

Patients with the diagnosis of varicella or disseminated herpes zoster should arrive in the receiving department at a time that would avoid contact with susceptible patients. Personnel involved in the exam should wear mask, gown, and gloves.

(2) Specimens. See I.D.(2) above.

E. Visitors. Visitors should be instructed to wear mask, gown, and gloves during the visit to the patient. Visitors who also provide care and long-term support and are not susceptible to the disease for which the patient is being isolated may abridge full technique in coordination with the Infection Control Department.

3. Contact Precautions
   A. Description. Inpatients requiring Contact Precautions will be placed in a private room with a Contact Precautions sign at the door. Patients requiring Contact Precautions will be cared for using UBBST. In addition to the protective measures outlined under UBBST, personnel will wear gown and gloves for all direct contact with the patient, linens, or anything likely to be contaminated. Patients may leave their rooms when, in the judgment of their care givers, it is unlikely that they will soil the environment and when precautions are taken to prevent cross-transmission.
   B. Conditions Requiring Contact Precautions:
      - Patients with unconfinable sources of blood or body substances (for example, wounds producing large volumes of drainage)
      - Patients with greater than or equal to three diarrheic stools in a 24-hour period
      - Patients who uncontrollably soil their environment with blood or body substances
      - Patients infected with oxacillin-resistant (equals methicillin-resistant) *Staphylococcus aureus* [as identified and directed by the Infection Control Department]
      - Patients infected with aminoglycoside-resistant gram-negative rod [as identified and directed by the Infection Control Department]
      - Patients with wound or skin infections with *Staphylococcus aureus* or a group A *Streptococcus*
      - Patients with major burns and skin infections
      - Patients infected with:
        - *Campylobacter* species
        - *Clostridium difficile*
        - *Cryptosporidium* species
        - *Escherichia coli,* enteropathogenic
        - Norwalk agent
        - Rotavirus
        - *Salmonella* species
        - *Shigella* species
        - *Vibrio cholerae*
        - *Yersinia enterocolitica*
      - Patients infected with cytomegalovirus (CMV):
        - Infants and toddlers shedding CMV (less than or equal to 4 years old)
        - Neonates with CMV disease
        - Recipients of solid organ transplants shedding CMV
      - Postpartum patients with:
        - Wound infections
        - Nonviral genital infections
        - Puerperal sepsis with vaginal discharge (caused by other than *Staphylococcus aureus* or group A *Streptococcus*)
        - Purulent vaginal discharge
      - Patients with herpes simplex virus in postpartum, newborn, and obstetrical area (see Policy 33.12)
      - Patients with untreated lice and scabies
   C. Institution of Contact Precautions. Contact Precautions may be instituted or discontinued by physician's order or by the charge nurse on the station. If instituted or discontinued by the charge nurse, the action must ultimately be supported by a physician's order. The institution, observation, and discontinuation of Contact Precautions should be documented in the treatment record or acute care record.
   D. Transportation
      (1) Patient. See 1.D.(1) above.
      (2) Specimens. See 1.D.(2) above.

E. Visitors. See 1.E above.

4. Blood Precautions

A. Description. Inpatients requiring Blood Precautions will be placed in a private room with a Blood Precautions sign at the door. Patients requiring Blood Precautions will be cared for using UBBST. Patients known to be infected with hepatitis B virus (HBV) and/or human immunodeficiency virus (HIV) will have the letter "B" embossed on their addressograph plates and the words "Blood Isolation" will appear on certain hospital computer screens. Blood Precautions may be superimposed on UBBST, Isolation, or Contact Precautions. Patients may leave their rooms when, in the judgment of their care givers, it is unlikely that they will soil the environment and when precautions are taken to prevent cross-transmission.

HIV- or HBV-infected (see 4.B.) children who are not toilet trained, who are neurologically handicapped and lacking control of their body secretions, who may spontaneously bite other children, or who have uncoverable, oozing lesions should not be permitted to engage in unsupervised interaction with other children. Such supervision, which may be delegated to a responsible adult, should prevent sequential mouthing of toys and any other activity that may result in contact with body fluids.

B. Conditions Requiring Blood Precautions

- Hepatitis B, acute hepatitis B. HBsAg positive (regardless of HBeAg result) and those patients who in the physician's judgment require Blood Precautions.
- Human immunodeficiency virus (HIV), all types. Anti-HIV seropositive (Western blot positive or EIA positive, Western blot not done), HIV culture positive, or HIV antigen positive. Untested patients with AIDS, AIDS-related complex, and those patients who in the physician's judgment require Blood Precautions.
- Malaria.
- Arthropod-borne viral infections.
- Human T-cell leukemia virus types I and II (HTLV-I, HTLV-II).
- Human herpesvirus type 6.

C. Institution of Blood Precautions. Blood Precautions may be instituted or discontinued by physician's order or, if the patient has a B code, the charge nurse on the station. If instituted or discontinued by the charge nurse, a physician's order must ultimately be written. If a patient who does not have a B code is placed in Blood Precautions, the Infection Control Department should be notified. Institution, observation, and discontinuation of Blood Precautions should be documented in the treatment record or acute care record.

D. Transportation

(1) Patient. See 1.D.(1) above.

(2) Specimens. All specimen containers and request forms will be labeled "Blood Precautions."

E. Visitors. See 1.E above.

5. In unusual circumstances, the Hospital Epidemiologist or his/her designee has the authority to institute additional control measures to minimize transmission of infection.

6. Admissions. Physicians arranging the admission of a patient requiring Isolation, Contact Precautions, or Blood Precautions are responsible for notifying the Admissions Department. Patients admitted from outside UMHC who require Isolation should be admitted through the Emergency Department. Patients requiring Isolation who are admitted from a clinic should not go to Admissions. If an inpatient room will be available in a short period of time, the patient should wait in a clinic room and be transported directly to the inpatient room. Otherwise, the patient should go through the Emergency Department.

7. Exposures. All actual or potential unprotected exposures of personnel to patients shall be reported to Employee Health Service/Emergency Department (see Policy 33.18,

Needlestick or Other Significant Exposure to Blood and Body Fluids). Exposures include parenteral (for example, needlestick or cut) or mucous membrane (for example, splash to the eye or mouth) exposure to blood or other body fluids or cutaneous exposure involving large amounts of blood or prolonged contact with blood—especially when the exposed skin is chapped, abraded, or afflicted with dermatitis. Hands and other skin surfaces should be washed immediately and thoroughly if there has been contact with blood or other body substances. Consult the Infection Control Department if the exposure is other than described above.

8. Care of the Body after Death
   A. Patients who were in Blood Precautions at the time of death shall have the words "Blood Precautions" written on the Report of Death and the morgue tags, one of which is affixed to the ankle, the second at chest level on the outside of the shroud.
   B. Patients who were in Isolation at the time of death should have the specific disease for which they were isolated written on the Report of Death (Form 153) and the morgue tags.
   C. Information as in 8.A and 8.B above will accompany the body when it leaves the hospital.

San Francisco General Hospital
San Francisco, California

Body Substance Precautions Handbook for Clinical Staff [Excerpt]

Rationale for Body Substance Precautions (BSP)

Infection control systems are designed to prevent health care workers from transferring infections to patients and to prevent health care workers from acquiring infections themselves.

Traditionally, hospitals and health care facilities have used isolation for patients with diagnosed or suspected infections only.

Body Substance Precautions improve on the traditional systems because they protect workers during the period before a patient's diagnosis is known. It is not possible to tell by looking which patients are infected. It is not practical to test all patients for all possible infections and not timely, as exposure would occur prior to obtaining the results.

Body Substance Precautions are designed to be used with all patients, not just the identified infected patient.

Body Substance Precautions are based on the knowledge of disease transmission and the prevention of disease transmission.

In hospitals, diseases are transmitted:

- Through an opening in the body by contaminated hands or materials
- By blood to blood, broken skin, or mucous membrane contact
- By breathing airborne organisms

Body Substance Precautions are based on degree of risk of exposure to blood and other body substances, not on diagnosis. Staff should determine precautions based on degree of risk.

Precautions with all patients should include routine use of appropriate barrier precautions to prevent skin and mucous membrane exposure when contact with blood or other body substances of any patient is anticipated.

Since the BSP method considers all patients and laboratory specimens as potentially infected, it provides protection from not only the known infected cases but the unrecognized cases as well, and therefore protects patients and health care workers alike.

Hand Washing

Body substances that may contain disease organisms easily contaminate your hands. Should these organisms enter an opening in the body, the mouth, for example, infection may occur. Hand washing is one of the most effective means of infection control.

Most routine brief patient care activities (such as taking blood pressures) do not require hand washing between contacts.

According to San Francisco General Hospital policy, you should wash your hands:

- *Before* eating or preparing food
- *Before* performing clean or sterile invasive procedures
- *Before and after* touching wounds or other drainage
- *After* contact with blood or body fluids, mucous membranes, secretions, or excretions, such as:
  - Saliva
  - Urine
  - Blood
  - Feces
- *After* handling soiled linen or waste
- *After* handling devices or equipment soiled with body substances (urine collection containers, bedpans, bloody linen, etc.)
- *After* removing gloves if gloves or hands have been soiled

Hands and other skin surfaces exposed to blood or body fluids should be washed as soon as patient safety permits.

How to Wash Your Hands

1. Use either bar or liquid soap and running water at a comfortable temperature. Work up a lather and use friction. Wash between your fingers. You need only scrub for a few seconds unless you are in an area with a special protocol or you are performing a surgical scrub.
2. Use plenty of running water so that no soap remains on your hands. Residual soap may cause skin irritation, dermatitis, and chapping.
3. Dry your hands well with paper towel to remove water. Air drying may cause chapping. Use your towel to turn off the faucet.
4. If your hands are chapped or you have dermatitis, evaluate your hand washing technique.

Soap

The most important function of hand washing is to remove infectious organisms. No hand washing product on the market kills all disease-causing organisms. Physical removal—washing soil and organisms down the drain—is the most effective practice. If properly used, any hand washing product approved by this hospital, whether antibacterial or not, will achieve this goal.

Soap-impregnated towelettes should be used only out in the field where hand washing facilities are not available. They should not be substituted for soap and running water in the hospital except during an internal disaster.

Do not use other chemicals such as alcohol or bleach to wash your hands. They may damage your skin and cause open or chapped areas that are more easily infected.

Lotion

Your skin may become dry and chapped with frequent hand washing. Use lotion to replace the oils removed by hand washing.

Always wash your hands before using lotion. If you use a lotion bottle while your hands are dirty, you are likely to contaminate the lotion container and, thereafter, contaminate your hands each time you touch it. Medicated lotion claims to control this problem have less-than-satisfactory test data.

Use your own bottle of lotion. Leave it in a locker or other location where you will be the sole user. In this way you will be aware if the lotion becomes contaminated.

Do not leave "community" lotion bottles in staff bathrooms.

Do not use lotion for patients as your post-hand-washing lotion.

Gloves

Gloves provide additional safety and should be worn whenever contact with blood or other body fluids or tissue is expected. Both vinyl and latex gloves are suitable for patient care activities. Each has a 95 percent effectiveness rate. [See the discussion of gloves in chapter 9.]

Wear gloves when touching:

- Body substances, mucous membranes, and nonintact skin
- Surfaces and articles moist with blood or body substances

Wear gloves for performing venipuncture or other vascular access procedures.

Wear sterile gloves for all sterile procedures to protect both the patient and yourself.

Wear nonsterile gloves for nonsterile patient care procedures where worker protection is needed.

Wear finger cots or gloves to cover cuts, abrasions, rashes, or minor infections on your hands while working.

Wear gloves when cleaning up blood spills and other contaminated areas. Wipe up small spills with disposable absorbent towels. If there is broken glass, scoop it up with several paper towels and dispose of it in the red sharps container. Then mop the area with a hospital disinfectant. Large blood spills should also be mopped up with hospital disinfectant. Wash your hands after you remove your gloves.

If your glove is torn or punctured by a needlestick or other accident, remove the damaged glove, wash your hands, and put on a new glove as promptly as patient safety permits.

If your gloves are contaminated, don't touch telephone receivers, other uncontaminated surfaces, or other areas of the same patient's body that may be uncontaminated.

Phlebotomy station staff may either wash or change gloves between patients. However, if your gloves are soiled or torn, you should change them and wash your hands. [See the discussion of gloves in chapter 9.]

Aprons and Gowns

Wear an apron or gown during all procedures that are likely to generate splashes or soiling from blood or body fluids.

Most ordinary patient care activities at the bedside do not require a gown. Activities such as changing the bed of an incontinent patient, lifting and moving a dependent patient with draining wounds, and certain diagnostic and therapeutic procedures that cause splattering might require the use of a gown.

Masks

When to Wear a Mask

Wear a mask to prevent exposure of the mucous membranes of your mouth and nose during procedures that are likely to generate aerosol droplets or splashes of blood or other body fluids.

Anyone who enters the room of a patient on Respiratory Precautions should wear a mask unless they know they are immune to that disease. [See the discussion of masks in chapter 9.]

Since protective garb should be worn only when needed, hospital personnel should not wear masks in the hallway. It is appropriate for patients on Respiratory Precautions to wear masks outside of their rooms for the safety of others in hallways, elevators, and waiting rooms. [See the discussion of masks in chapter 9.]

How to Wear and Dispose of a Mask

Masks should cover both the nose and mouth. Masks should fit close to the face so that air can be breathed only through the mask.

Do not loosen your mask. Over time, your mask will become impregnated with moisture from your breath and it will become harder to breathe. When this occurs, change the mask—do not loosen it.

Discard masks after each use or when they become damp. Dispose of masks as regular, not infectious, waste.

Protective Eyewear

Wear protective eyewear—glasses or face shields—for protection from splashes to your face. Situations in which eyewear might be needed include certain diagnostic procedures such as endoscopies, invasive surgical procedures, and certain dental and obstetrical procedures.

Protective eyewear is available through CPD.

Eyewear that has been soiled but not damaged is reusable. Eyewear should be washed with soap and water and dried. Eyewear does not require decontamination by CPD.

Respiratory Precautions

Respiratory Precautions will continue to be used for diseases known to be spread by droplet. Airborne diseases infect by entering the body through the nose or mouth.

When a patient is suspected or known to have an airborne disease, the following measures should be taken:

1. Private Room. The physician must request a private room. Bed control will work with nursing on private room assignments.
2. Stop Sign Alert on door. The nurse will place this sign on the patient's door. This sign instructs anyone about to enter to "Check with the nurse before entering." The nurse is responsible for providing instructions regarding masks and for screening for immune status when appropriate. Visitors and care providers who do not have immunity to chickenpox or herpes zoster, measles, rubella, and mumps should not enter the room even with a mask on.
3. The door should remain closed.
4. Anyone who enters the room of a patient on Respiratory Precautions should wear a mask unless they know they are immune to that disease.
5. If a patient leaves their room, they should wear a mask.
6. Continue using Body Substance Precautions.

The following diseases are transmitted in whole or in part by the airborne route. For diseases marked with an asterisk, all care providers who are not immune to these diseases should not enter the room of these patients.

Disease	Apply Airborne Precautions for How Long
Anthrax, inhalation	Duration of illness
Chickenpox (varicella)*	Until all lesions are crusted
Diphtheria	Until two cultures from both nose and throat taken at least 24 hours after cessation of antimicrobial therapy are negative for *Corynebacterium diphtheriae*
Erythema infectiosum	For 7 days after onset
Hemorrhagic fevers	Duration of illness
Herpes zoster/varicella* localized in immunocompromised patient or disseminated	Duration of illness
Lassa fever	Duration of illness
Marburg virus disease	Duration of illness
Measles (rubeola)*	For 5 days after start of rash, except in immunocompromised patients, with whom precautions should be maintained for the duration of the illness
Mumps (infectious parotitis)*	For 9 days after onset of swelling
Pertussis (whooping cough)	For 7 days after the start of effective therapy
Plague, pneumonic	For 3 days after the start of effective therapy
Rubella (German measles)*	For 7 days
Tuberculosis, pulmonary, confirmed or suspect	In most instances, duration can be guided by clinical response and a reduction in numbers of TB organisms on sputum smear. Precautions can usually be discontinued after two weeks of appropriate antituberculosis chemotherapy. When the patient is known to be infected with INH-resistant organisms, it is the responsibility of the physician to order precautions until the patient is improving and the sputum smear is negative for TB organisms.

Needles and Sharps

Handle needles and other sharp instruments with extreme care to prevent infection with HIV and hepatitis. Most needlesticks occur when used needles are not handled properly. Broken skin or mucous membrane contact and a needlestick or other blood-to-blood accident may transmit infection.

Recapping Needles

Clinical staff should never bend, break, or recap a used needle except in special circumstances approved by the Infection Control Committee.

Drawing blood gases is an example of a special circumstance in which the needle should be recapped.

If recapping is necessary, you should use:

- One-handed method, for example, using the plastic outer cover of the Monojet® as a cap stand for the needle or
- Two-handed method, for example, employing a shielding device to prevent sticks

Red Sharps Containers

Dispose of used needles and sharps into puncture-resistant red containers immediately.

Never put needles or sharps in the trash or linen. This is dangerous to other hospital employees.

Porters should regularly check and empty the red sharps containers. However, if you discover that a red sharps container is full, notify the porter to replace it.

Pick up improperly discarded needles with extreme caution and dispose of them in the nearest red sharps container. Do not attempt to cap the needle. Wash your hands after you dispose of it. Use tongs or forceps to pick up sharps.

Preventing Needlesticks

Needlesticks are a problem for all hospital employees. Following these recommendations should help prevent them:

1. Slow down when you handle needles.
2. Dispose of needles properly in the red plastic needle disposal boxes in patient bathrooms and at nursing stations. Needles left where they do not belong can injure workers, patients, and visitors.
3. Do not recap unless absolutely necessary. Recapping needles is a major source of injury to nurses. To recap Vacutainer® needles, put the cap on the table and slide the needle into it without holding the cap. Then tighten the cap at the needle hub.
4. Never put a used needle in your pocket.
5. As soon as you use a disposable needle, put it into the nearest red needle box.
6. Never try to take anything out of a needle box. If a needle will not go in easily, and the box is not full, use a large syringe to dislodge it. If the box is full, arrange to have it replaced.

Note: If you are stuck with a needle, go to CMOSH, Building 9, Second Floor, immediately. If CMOSH is not open, go to the Emergency Room and then report to CMOSH as soon as possible.

Ventilation Devices

Use mouthpieces, resuscitation bags, or other ventilation devices on all patients instead of mouth-to-mouth resuscitation.

Resuscitation bags are located on the emergency cart in every patient care area.

Ventilation devices are obtained from Respiratory Therapy.

Laboratory Specimens

All patient specimen containers, when transported to the laboratory by the Messenger Service, should be placed into a Ziploc® or other hand-sealed plastic bag and sealed shut. [See the discussion of bagging specimens in chapter 9.]

If the specimen container is too large to fit in a Ziploc®, use tape to secure the cap and enclose the entire item in a plastic bag with a twist tie.

The lab slip should be attached by rubber band or tape to the outside of the bag.

If the specimen container is not bagged or the bag is not visibly clean, the messenger will ask the charge nurse to bag the specimen correctly.

If an accidental specimen spill occurs, the messenger should place paper towels over the spill and notify Housekeeping immediately for cleanup.

Specimens collected and transported by personnel themselves (that is, phlebotomists) or specimens transported within the laboratory need not be bagged.

Laboratory workers should use gloves for handling specimens when contamination of hands is anticipated.

Linen

All soiled linen will be placed in leak-proof blue bags mounted on covered hampers in all patient care areas. In the OR, the linen bags will be mint green. [See the discussion of the term *impervious* in chapter 9.]

Postmortem

During the postmortem handling of bodies, it is important to continue BSP while preparing the body for transport and performing autopsies.

Reusable Patient Care Equipment

Patient care items not classified as sharps and not required by CPD to be soaked should be returned by placing them on the CPD cart in the soiled utility room.

OR instruments requiring soaking should be placed in an approved detergent (contact CPD) and transported to CPD in a covered cart.

Reusable sharps should be transported to CPD in a closed container.

San Francisco General Hospital
San Francisco, California

Memo from Infection Control Committee Co-Chair

Important Points to Understand about Proposed Infection Control Procedure

1. Universal Blood and Body Fluid (Substance) Precautions, recommended by the CDC, are recommended unanimously by the SFGH Infection Control Committee (ICC) for adoption by SFGH.
2. Precautions are defined by what you are doing with *any* patient or material (for example, wear gloves when touching blood; dispose of needles and syringes in rigid-walled red containers; wash hands before going to next patient). Precautions are not directed by diagnosis of patient's disease process except for a few respiratory diseases, including tuberculosis. In most cases, there will not be precaution signs on patients' doors, just as we no longer put H/A stickers on patients' specimens.
3. There will be a change in definition of infectious waste to conform to the CDC point that hospital/clinic unit waste is not any more infectious than household waste. Pleur-evacs® with large volume exudates or large quantities of blood will be infectious–tissues with small quantities of blood, dressings with small quantities of blood or exudate, Chux® with stool will be regular waste. Regular waste handling will be upgraded with covered containers in each patient room. The hospital will use a sterilizer compactor for infectious waste rather than the expensive ($400,000/year) Scavenger pickup incineration system.
4. *No* laundry will be sorted into contaminated or regular soiled linen on the hospital/clinic unit. All linen will be put into an upgraded, nonleaking nylon bag.
5. Each service and department will have to rewrite its infection control policy and procedure. Infection Control Committee staff and members will support you in doing this.
6. A training unit has been set up for health and safety training. Training must be documented and available to any inspector.
7. Supervisors must assume responsibility for enforcement of precautions that they have decided are important in consultation with Infection Control. Quality assurance system must document that procedures are being followed.
8. We can expect more enforcement action, which will review our performance. State, federal, and JCAHO representatives will examine us. OSHA has visited SFGH to develop enforcement guidelines. State–HCFA inspection of Infection Control was completed today. We can expect more environmental law action.
9. State Title 22 regulation is out-of-date. It emphasizes large-scale surveillance of hospital-associated infections, rather than problem-related surveillance and disease-related precautions. Nevertheless, we must show evidence of review and analysis of infections by services along with external review of services to inspectors.

Projects Being Studied

1. HIV antibody testing and counseling of employees who have work-related exposures
2. System of counseling patients who are being asked to have HIV antibody test done
3. Worker's compensation
4. Technological innovation for health worker safety

Yale-New Haven Hospital
New Haven, Connecticut

Universal Precautions Policy—Department of Nursing

I. Purpose

The purpose of this policy is to establish individual responsibilities to minimize transmission of contagious microorganisms to, from, and between patients and all other persons at Yale-New Haven Hospital.

II. Definitions

A. *Persons:* All hospital employees, students, volunteers, visitors, and/or any other individuals who enter the hospital.

B. *Universal Precautions:* The routine and consistent use of appropriate barrier protection to prevent skin and mucous membrane transmission of microorganisms resulting from contact with blood and body fluids, and as part of the practice of general hygiene. Patients with a documented or potentially contagious respiratory infection will be hospitalized in Respiratory Isolation, as defined in the Infection Control Manual.

C. *Blood and Body Fluids:* This includes all body tissues and body fluids that may potentially harbor contagious microorganisms. Blood and Body Fluids include but are not limited to the following:

amniotic fluid
blood
body tissues
breast milk
cerebrospinal fluid
feces
nasal secretions
nonintact skin
pericardial fluid
peritoneal fluid
pleural fluid
saliva
semen
sputum
synovial fluid
urine
vaginal secretions
vomitus
wound drainage

Blood and body fluids do not include tears or perspiration unless they contain visible evidence of blood.

D. *Exposure:* Actual or potential skin, mucous membrane, or parenteral contact with blood or body fluids.

E. *Hand Washing/Barrier Protection:* The appropriate use of hand washing, gloves, gowns, masks, goggles, and face shields to minimize exposure to blood and body fluids.

F. *Occupational Safety and Health Administration Exposure Categories:*

1. Category I—jobs with tasks that routinely involve exposure or potential exposure to blood, body fluids, or tissues
2. Category II—jobs with tasks that do not routinely involve exposure to blood, body fluids, or tissues, but exposure or potential exposure may be required as a condition of employment
3. Category III—jobs with tasks that do not routinely involve exposure to blood, body fluids, or tissues (persons in this category are not called upon to perform or assist in emergency medical care or first aid or to be potentially exposed in any other way as a condition of employment)

III. Scope

This policy applies to all persons who are or may be administratively responsible to the Department of Nursing.

IV. Responsibilities

A. The Nursing Department shall:

1. Provide appropriate types and supplies of protective equipment (that is, gloves, goggles, masks, gowns, etc.).
2. Assure that employees, students, and volunteers affiliated with department receive education and training in hospital Universal Precautions and Infection Control policies and procedures that are specific to their responsibilities prior to assuming these responsibilities.
3. Monitor and document individual compliance with the practice of hospital Universal Precautions and Infection Control policies and procedures in a fair and equitable manner.
4. Include compliance with hospital Universal Precautions and Infection Control policies and procedures as part of each employee's performance review.
5. Provide appropriate retraining and progressively discipline, if necessary, individuals who fail to comply with department procedures for Universal Precautions and Infection Control.
6. Inform visitors that they are not allowed in areas where contagion is likely unless there is specific need and the visitor receives instruction in hospital Universal Precautions and Infection Control policies and procedures specific to the area/tasks involved.
7. Submit a Supervisor's Report of Employee Accident/Injury (F.1797) following all incidents of actual exposure to blood or body fluids.
8. Submit an incident report for all instances where an individual's technique is not consistent with hospital Universal Precautions and Infection Control policies and procedures.

B. Each individual shall:

1. Comply with the guidelines of the Personnel Health Service. They are required to have a preemployment examination, not to work when they have communicable diseases, and to be cleared by the Personnel Health Service after a three-day or longer absence due to illness. Affiliating students shall have fulfilled any contractual health examinations and/or obligations negotiated between their parent school and Yale-New Haven Hospital.
2. Understand the principles of hospital Universal Precautions and Infection Control policies and procedures, with specific knowledge of the tasks that they may assume.
3. Routinely apply the practices of hospital Universal Precautions and Infection Control policies and procedures to each task they perform.
4. Report incidents to their supervisor of actual exposure to blood or body fluids.
5. Report incidents to their supervisor when other individuals are noncompliant with Universal Precautions and Infection Control practices.

V. Guidelines

A. Implementation of Hand Washing and Barrier Precautions

1. *Hand washing:* Hands shall be washed using warm water and soap before and after contact with all patients or following contamination with blood or body fluids. Particular attention shall be given to areas around and under fingernails and between fingers.
2. *Gloves:* Gloves shall be worn for anticipated or potential exposure of the hands to blood and body fluids or surfaces soiled with blood and body fluids. Gloves shall be discarded when torn, following contact with each patient (before leaving the patient's room), or following contact with contaminated items.
3. *Gowns/plastic aprons:* Fluid-repellant gowns/plastic aprons shall be worn when splattering of blood or body fluids is likely (gloves shall be worn in addition to gowns). Gowns shall be discarded when torn, following contact with each

patient (before leaving the patient's room), or following contact with contaminated items. Cloth lab coats are not acceptable substitutes for gowns.

4. *Masks:* Masks shall be worn if the patient has a documented or potential contagious respiratory infection. Masks shall be discarded following contact with each patient.
5. *Glasses/goggles plus masks or face shields:* Glasses/goggles plus masks or face shields shall be worn if splattering or aerosolization is likely to occur. Glasses, goggles, and face shields shall be cleansed with phenolic solution following contamination with blood or body fluids. Masks shall be discarded following contact with each patient.

B. Standard Operating Procedures

1. All patients who are on respiratory isolation shall be handled according to the recommendations of the Infection Control Manual.
2. Protective pads shall be placed on all chairs, wheelchairs, and stools on which patients sit if their skin is likely to come in contact with the seat.
3. Examining/treatment tables shall be covered with a clean sheet before each patient use. They shall be wiped with a phenolic solution and dried at the end of each day or following contamination with blood or body fluids.
4. Portable equipment (that is, cardiac chair, shower chair, intravenous poles/pumps) shall be cleaned and decontaminated with a phenolic solution after each patient's use.
5. Blood pressure cuffs shall be cleaned with a phenolic solution when visibly soiled.
6. Multiple-use stock containers of topical medications shall not be brought into the patient's bedside unit; the medications shall be transferred to individual containers, labeled, and dated for patient use at the bedside.
7. Contaminated instruments shall be bagged in specially marked plastic bags before being returned to Central Supply.
8. All patient specimens being transported to clinical laboratories shall be placed in plastic bags; laboratory requisitions shall be attached to the outside of the plastic bag.
9. All disposable sharps shall be disposed of in the yellow Eagleguard® containers. Scalpel blades shall not be removed from their handles.
10. Bandage scissors shall be washed with soap and water, wiped with a phenolic solution, and rinsed with clear water after each use.
11. Soiled linen shall be placed in the designated laundry bag.
12. Trash shall be placed in the designated trash receptacle.
13. Counters and other horizontal surfaces shall be wiped down with a phenolic/diluted bleach (1:10) solution following contamination with blood or body fluids.
14. A clean barrier shall be placed on horizontal surfaces in the patient's unit before placing portable equipment on these surfaces to avoid contamination of the equipment.

VI. Applications

Universal Precautions shall be applied at all times and for all patients regardless of diagnosis. Examples of applications are provided for illustrative purposes but should not be considered all-inclusive. Good judgment shall be exercised.

Yale-New Haven Hospital
New Haven, Connecticut

Barrier Requirements for Patient Care Activities—Department of Nursing

Listed below are the minimum requirements (recommended during controlled situations to protect the health care worker from potentially infectious agents). This list is not all-inclusive, and so judgment is required on the part of the health care worker to assess the need for additional barrier protection in less-controlled situations.

Other barriers may be required to protect the patient/employee during certain procedures. Refer to your department policy and procedure manual.

If an employee has an open cut or abrasion on their hands, they are responsible for protecting it through the use of gloves.

Sterile technique is to be used during sterile procedures.

Procedure	Hand Washing	Gloves	Gown/ Plastic Apron	Mask	Eye Protection
Bath (open lesions)	X	X			
Bath, routine (skin intact)	X				
Bleeding, pressure application to control	X	X	S	*	*
Blood glucose (capillary), testing	X	X			
Breathing treatment, routine	X	S			
Changing visibly soiled beds	X	X	S		
Cleansing, anal	X	X			
Cleanup of:					
Incontinent patient (feces)	X	X	S		
Incontinent patient (urine)	X	X			
Spills of blood/body substances	X	X	S		
Surfaces contaminated by blood/body substances	X	X	S		
CPR	X	X			
CVP measurement	X	X			
Decubitus care	X	X			
Direct contact with patients with frequent, forceful coughing	X			X	X
Dialysis, peritoneal:					
Initiation of acute treatment	X	X	X	*	*
Performing an exchange	X	X	X	*	*
Termination of acute treatment	X	X	X	*	*
Setting up tubing to cycler	X				
Dismantling tubing from cycler	X	X	X	*	*
Addition of medications to dialysate solution	X				
Discarding peritoneal drainage	X	X	X	*	*
Irrigation of peritoneal catheter	X	X	X	*	*
Specimen collection	X	X			
Tubing change	X	X	X	*	*
Skin care (catheter site)	X	X		X	X

Procedure	Hand Washing	Gloves	Gown/ Plastic Apron	Mask	Eye Protection
Dialysis, peritoneal: *(continued)*					
Assisting with insertion of acute peritoneal catheter (outside sterile field)	X	X	X	*	*
Accidental disconnection from cycler (wash hands immediately after exposure)	X				
Dressing change, burn	X	X	X		
Dressing removal/change for wounds with little or no drainage	X	X			
Dressing removal/change for wounds with large amount of drainage	X	X	S		
Emptying drainage receptacles, including suction containers, urine receptacles, bed pans, emesis basins	X	X	S	*	*
Emptying wastebaskets	X	X			
Enema	X	X	S		
Fecal impaction, removal of	X	X			
Fecal incontinence, placement of Foley catheter for and emptying bag	X	X	*		
Feeding patient	X				
Gastric lavage	X	X	S		
Intravenous/intraarterial:					
Initiation	X	X			
Termination	X	X			
Tubing change at hub of catheter	X	X			
Irrigation:					
Foley	X	X			
Vaginal	X	X	S		
Wound	X	X	S	*	*
Medication administration:					
Eye, ear, and nose drops	X	X			
Intramuscular/subcutaneous	X	X			
Intravenous:					
Direct or into hub of catheter/Heplock®	X	X			
Piggyback	X				
Oral, nurse administered:					
Handed to patient	X				
Placed in patient's mouth by nurse	X	X			
Rectal/vaginal suppository	X	X			
Topical medication to intact skin	X				
Topical medication to lesion	X	X			
Nasogastric tube, insertion/irrigation	X	X	S	*	*
Oral/nasal care	X	X			
Ostomy care, irrigation and teaching	X	X	S		

(Table continues.)

Procedure	Hand Washing	Gloves	Gown/ Plastic Apron	Mask	Eye Protection
Oxygen:					
Draining of tube condensate	X	X			
Placing of cannula or mask	X				
Perineal cleansing	X	X			
Physical assessment	X				
Pleur-evac® change	X	X	*		
Postmortem:					
Care	X	X	S		
Transportation of body in shroud	X				
Pulse oximetry	X				
Shaving	X	X			
Sitz bath	X				
Specimen collection (blood, stool, urine, sputum, wound)	X	X			
Suctioning:					
Nasotracheal or endotracheal	X	X	S	*	*
Oral/nasal	X	X			
Temperature, rectal	X	X			
Trach care (suctioning and cleansing of cannula)	X	X	S	*	*
Traction	X				
Tube feeding	X				
Urine/stool testing	X	X			
Vital signs (oral temperature, pulse, respiration, blood pressure)	X				
Washing hair	X				
Wound packing	X	X	S		
Assisting with:					
Central line insertion/venesectomy (cut down)	X	X			
Cervical cauterization	X	X			
Chest tube insertion	X	X	S	*	*
Chest tube removal	X	X	S	*	*
Colonoscopy, flexible sigmoidoscope	X	X			
Incision and drainage of abscess	X	X	*		
Intubation/extubation	X	X	*	*	*
Invasive procedures (lumbar puncture, bone marrow aspiration, paracentesis, liver biopsy) outside sterile field	X	X			
Joint/nerve injection	X	X			
Lesion biopsy/removal	X	X			
Pelvic exam and Pap smear	X	X			
Tracheostomy tube change	X	X		*	*

LEGEND: X = Routinely S = If soiling is likely * = If splattering is likely

Yale-New Haven Hospital
New Haven, Connecticut

Universal Precautions—Questions and Answers

Universal Precautions/Respiratory Isolation System

The Universal Precautions/Respiratory Isolation system is a method to prevent the transmission of infectious agents. It requires the use of barriers for all contact with blood and body fluids, but continues to use Respiratory Isolation for patients with diseases known to be transmitted by the airborne route. Universal Precautions will replace the old category-specific system of isolation (Strict Isolation, Contact Isolation, and Enteric, Drainage/Secretion, Blood/Body Fluids, and Multiple-Drug-Resistant Organism Precautions). Therefore, isolation signs will no longer be placed on patients' rooms, with the exception of patients on Respiratory Isolation. This system is designed to protect health care workers and patients from exposure to infectious agents and to prevent the nosocomial transmission of infections from patient to patient.

1. What is the main focus of Universal Precautions?

   Universal Precautions focus on isolating blood and body fluids from the hands, skin, and mucous membranes of health care providers. This is accomplished by frequent hand washing and the use of barrier techniques (gloves, gowns, masks, and goggles) whenever exposure to blood and body fluids is anticipated. Barrier protection is worn for designated procedures regardless of the patient's specific diagnosis.

   Universal Precautions are intended to supplement other infection control measures, such as hand washing. Gloves should be worn for contact with blood or body fluids, mucous membranes, and nonintact skin of all patients. They should also be worn when touching contaminated items or surfaces. Gloves must be changed after contact with each patient, when torn or punctured, and as needed during the care of an individual patient. They should not be washed or disinfected. General-purpose utility gloves, such as household rubber gloves used for housekeeping and equipment cleaning, may be washed and disinfected, but they must be discarded if there is any evidence of peeling, cracking, punctures, tearing, or any other form of deterioration. Workers must wash their hands each time the gloves are removed. Masks and goggles should be worn during procedures where blood or body fluids may be aerosolized or splashed. Gowns are used for procedures that are likely to soil clothing.

2. What are some considerations in patient placement, bed assignment, and roommate selection?

   If Universal Precautions are appropriately applied, placing the patient in a private room is not necessary. However, a private room may be necessary for infection control purposes if a patient:
   (a) Has poor personal hygiene (such patients may include infants, children, or patients with altered mental functioning, who are unable/unwilling to wash their hands appropriately, contaminate the environment with infective materials, share contaminated articles with other patients, etc. If a patient's personal hygiene is questionable or cannot be accurately assessed, a private room is indicated)
   (b) Has an infection that is transmissible by the *respiratory/airborne* route that requires a private and/or negative-pressure room
   (c) Produces infectious/bloody materials that are large in quantity and/or cannot be properly contained by the patient or by personnel (for example, patients who have frank gastrointestinal bleeding)
   (d) Has an infection involving organisms that are highly resistant to multiple antibiotics

(e) Or if other conditions exist that may enhance the possibility of hazardous consequences to other patients

Note: A private room is not necessary for patients with AIDS or HIV infection. However, a private room may be indicated if other circumstances are present, such as if the HIV-infected patient has other infections that are transmitted by the airborne route, poor personal hygiene, etc.

3. When is Respiratory Isolation necessary?

Patients who have, or may have, a disease that is transmissible by the respiratory/airborne route (which includes diseases formerly requiring Strict Isolation and AFB Isolation) are to be placed on Respiratory Isolation in addition to Universal Precautions.

(a) Place these patients in a private room with the door closed at all times, except for entering and exiting the room.
(b) Certain diseases, such as active pulmonary tuberculosis, measles, disseminated herpes zoster, and chickenpox, require a private, negative-pressure room. Refer to appendix A [reproduced as p. 48 of this manual] for examples of infectious diseases that require Respiratory Isolation.
(c) Display the blue Respiratory Isolation sign on the door to the patient's room, which will instruct persons who enter to follow the directions outlined. The patient's nurse will inform visitors and other persons to wear a mask at all times.
(d) Place a Respiratory Isolation card on the cover of the patient's medical record. (All patients will have blue medical record binders since the yellow binders will no longer be used.)
(e) Waste removal from the rooms of patients on Respiratory Isolation is managed in a manner that is identical to patients on Universal Precautions, in accordance with the hospital's Regulated and Nonregulated Waste policies. (See question 9 below for exceptions to this general rule.)
(f) Patients on Respiratory Isolation may share a room only if they have identical infections and there are no other transmissible factors.
(g) Refer to appendix A [p. 48 of this manual] for examples of infectious diseases that require respiratory isolation.

4. Are there any extraordinary procedures for cleaning the equipment, rooms, and linen used by AIDS patients or handling their waste materials, beyond routine measures?

No. The AIDS virus is not stable in the external environment outside of the body. It is rapidly inactivated after drying and exposure to commonly used chemical germicides. Therefore, no extraordinary procedures are required in sterilization or decontamination of equipment, environmental surfaces, or materials exposed to the AIDS virus. All patient rooms will be cleaned thoroughly and consistently according to the hospital's environmental standards.

5. What is the procedure for cleaning spills involving blood and body fluids on environmental surfaces?

All spills of blood and body fluids should be cleaned as soon as possible. Personnel must wear gloves during this procedure and a gown if the spill might be expected to contaminate clothing. Use an absorbent cloth to wipe excess liquid that may accidentally splash. Clean the spill area with a solution of SaniMaster® III diluted according to the manufacturer's directions (one ounce per gallon of water) or a solution of sodium hypochlorite (household chlorine bleach) in a concentration of 5,000 parts per million (1:10 dilution). Please note that these germicides are highly caustic unless properly diluted and are intended for use on environmental surfaces only since they can damage instruments and equipment.

6. What is the procedure for handling reusable instruments and equipment prior to decontamination in Central Sterile Supply?

   When reusable instruments and equipment are contaminated, the items should be rinsed with water to eliminate visible soiling and placed in a clear orange plastic "decontamination" bag before being removed from the patient's room. The bag, which is labeled "Infectious Matter to Be Autoclaved," must be closed tightly, secured with a tie, and tagged with an "F-9 Requisition" form. The bag should then be sent to the Central Sterile Supply Department for decontamination or sterilization. Questions regarding equipment decontamination can be directed to Central Sterile Supply. The responsibility for cleaning equipment is multidisciplinary and must be clearly delineated by nursing and unit management on each patient care unit.

   (a) Autoclavable Instruments and Equipment—Items that can withstand heat, high temperature, and moisture should be sent to Central Sterile Supply for reprocessing and sterilization by steam. Reusable glass syringes, rubber articles, glass bottles, and metal instruments are examples of items that should be steam-autoclaved.
      (1) Always wear gloves when handling contaminated equipment.
      (2) Rinse items under running water to remove gross soiling. Dry nonsharp items with a paper towel.
      (3) Place nondisposable needles, syringes, and other delicate instruments on the tray that was included in the original package. Always hold the tray in an upright position so that sharp implements do not puncture the bag.
      (4) Separate linen, such as towels and drapes, from reusable equipment. Dispose of linen according to the procedure outlined in question 7. Do not return linen to CSS.
      (5) Place the items in a clear orange plastic "decontamination" bag and return to CSS.

   (b) Equipment Requiring Reprocessing by Ethylene Oxide—Some items, such as plastics, synthetic materials, delicate instruments, electrical equipment, gauges, otoscopes, flashlights, etc., cannot withstand heat or moisture. These items should be terminally sterilized by ethylene oxide gas.
      (1) Always wear gloves when handling contaminated equipment.
      (2) Remove all gross soiling from equipment. Do not place gauges and electrical equipment under running water. Dry the item with a paper towel.
      (3) Place the item into a clear orange plastic "decontamination" bag and return to CSS.

   (c) Portable Equipment Requiring Terminal Disinfection
      (1) Always wear gloves when handling contaminated equipment.
      (2) Clean gross soiling on equipment and wipe all surfaces thoroughly using a cloth moistened with an EPA-approved germicide or detergent disinfectant solution.
      (3) Return equipment to the department of origin or to the proper storage area on the patient care unit.

7. What is the procedure for linen handling?

   All soiled linen is handled in the same manner regardless of the patient's specific diagnosis. Place linen into a yellow leak-proof laundry bag with a biohazard label. If a supply of these bags is not available, insert a plastic liner into an ordinary white laundry bag to prevent strike through of moist linen to the outside. [See the discussion of biohazard labeling in chapter 9.]

8. What is the procedure for handling laboratory specimens on the divisions?

   (a) Place each lab specimen in an appropriate leak-proof container.
   (b) Secure lids tightly to prevent leakage.

(c) Place the specimens into a plastic bag with a biohazard label. [See the discussion of biohazard labeling in chapter 9.]
(d) Seal the bag before transporting it to the lab by the pneumatic tube system or by hand.
(e) Insert the requisition slips into the outside pocket of this bag.

9. What is "regulated waste," and how is it handled?

Refer to the Biomedical Waste Segregation Procedures memo for specific information regarding the definition and disposal of regulated waste. A summary of this memo is given in appendix B [reproduced as pp. 92–93 of this manual].

Waste produced from the care of all patients on Universal Precautions and most patients on Respiratory Isolation is handled in the same manner. However, all waste generated from the rooms of patients on Respiratory Isolation who have certain rare diseases that are classified as Biosafety Level 4 by the federal Centers for Disease Control is regulated waste. These infections are rarely, if ever, seen at Yale-New Haven Hospital and include diseases such as Lassa, Ebola, Marburg, and several others. A complete list of infections in this classification can be found in appendix C [reproduced as p. 94 of this manual].

10. Where should patients place their own waste materials?

All patients need to be informed not to use the regulated trash receptacles in their rooms when disposing of their waste materials. Patients should be instructed to discard personal items into the general/routine trash containers. However, patients who might be expected to generate regulated waste products, such as OB pads, should be informed of the location of the regulated waste receptacle and directed to dispose of these items in the correct container. This requirement may pose some confusion for patients, but it is important to anticipate this with proper instruction in order to minimize the cost of waste removal.

11. Will the procedure for cleaning patients' rooms change under Universal Precautions?

No. Environmental surfaces, such as walls, floors, and other surfaces, have not been associated with the transmission of infectious diseases to patients or health care workers. Common housekeeping procedures, using EPA-approved germicides according to the manufacturer's directions, are adequate for cleaning environmental surfaces. In patient care areas, horizontal surfaces, such as bedside tables and floors, should be cleaned on a regular basis, when soiling or spills occur, and when a patient is discharged. Cleaning of other surfaces, such as walls and curtains, is needed periodically or when soiling is visible.

12. Will the handling of used needles and sharp implements change under the Universal Precaution system?

The management of needles and sharps will remain the same.
(a) All needles and sharps are discarded in Eagleguard® containers. It is imperative that these items not be left in patient care areas or inadvertently deposited in trash containers.
(b) Used needles should not be recapped by hand, removed from disposable syringes by hand, or purposely bent, broken, or otherwise manipulated by hand.

13. Where will supplies of gloves, gowns, masks, and goggles be stored?

Supplies of barrier equipment will be stored on Universal Precautions stations, which will be placed in several areas on each patient care unit. Each station will house a supply of gowns, masks, goggles, bags for lab specimens, bags for equipment to be returned to CSS, and two boxes of large-, medium-, and small-size gloves. Generally,

Kaiser Permanente Medical Center
San Francisco, California

Barrier Techniques to Reduce Infection Risk for Specific Clinical Situations

Most infection control situations are addressed in these general guidelines. These techniques should be applied to all body substances from all patients, not only those patients with diagnosed infections, since the presence of infectious organisms *always* precedes diagnosis. In general, contact with blood or body fluids/substances from patients, infected or uninfected, should be avoided. Gloves should be worn for all contacts with blood or body fluids/substances. Gowns should be worn when the amount or location of the blood or body fluid/substance makes it difficult to keep clothing clean.

Clinical Situations by Body System	Barrier and Containment Techniques
	Gastrointestinal
• Diagnostic equipment entering the gastrointestinal tract • Diarrhea due to any cause • Feces • Gallbladder drainage • Ostomy drainage • Saliva	• Wash hands after contact with fecal or gastrointestinal fluid or saliva • Wear gloves when handling fecal or gastrointestinal fluid or giving oral hygiene • Wear gown when soilage of clothing is likely • Place linen and trash soiled with feces into their appropriate impervious bags • Rinse contaminated reusable equipment/instruments under running water or wipe with appropriate disinfectant before returning them to CSR for decontamination or sterilization • Instruct patient in care of feces, gastrointestinal drainage, and saliva and in hand washing
	Genitourinary
• Urine –Urinary catheter drainage –Urine specimens: Outpatient measurement Fractionals Specific gravity • Urinary incontinence	• Wash hands after contact with urine • Wear gloves when handling urine • Wear a gown when soilage of clothing is likely • Contain specimens so that urine/fluids do not leak or contaminate environment • Dispose of urine into sanitary sewer • Place linen and trash soiled with urine into their appropriate bags • Use individual urine measurement devices • Maintain sterile closed drainage system • Instruct patient in care of urine/catheter and hand washing
• Vaginal drainage/discharge –Amniotic fluid –Blood from menses and postpartum lochia • Placental tissue	• Wear gloves for contact with drainage and soiled perineal pads • Wash hands after contact with drainage and soiled perineal pads • Contain perineal pads in a bag prior to disposal • Rinse contaminated reusable equipment/instruments under running water or wipe with appropriate disinfectant before returning them to CSR for decontamination and sterilization • Dispose of placentas into two red bags • Instruct patient in hand washing and disposal of perineal pads

one station will be located in a position to service four patient rooms. The exact location of the stations will be determined by nursing personnel in conjunction with unit managers and the Engineering Department. Each unit will determine its minimum stock needs for barrier equipment, and supplies can also be placed in other convenient locations. Station supplies will be restocked by the unit assistants during the day shift. New supplies can be reordered from the storeroom at other times.

Until the Universal Precautions stations are constructed and installed, isolation carts containing this equipment will be used on all divisions in the Memorial unit and designated areas in the new facility. Barrier equipment will also be stored in the drawers and cabinets adjacent to the hallway sinks in the new facility.

14. What is the procedure for handling and reporting occupational exposures to blood and body fluids?

    An employee who experiences a significant exposure to the blood or body fluids of any patient should clean the skin wound thoroughly with a betadine solution and/or rinse mucous membranes that were exposed. Use a sterile saline solution to flush the eyes, water to rinse the mouth, etc. The exposed employee should immediately report the incident to his or her supervisor, have a Supervisor's Report of Employee Incident (AR) completed, and report to the Personnel Health Service (PHS) at the first opportunity. A significant exposure is defined as contact between the blood or body fluids of any patient and the blood (from needlesticks, cuts, bites), mucous membranes, or broken skin of an employee.

    While an exposure such as this is distressing, emergency medical attention is not necessary for the exposure itself. The exposed employee should not go to the Emergency Room unless the exposure site requires direct medical treatment (for example, stitches). The employee should report to PHS on the first day that it is open after the exposure. Reporting must be done within one week of the injury. Only in PHS can HIV testing and counseling be done in accordance with the YNHH AIDS in the Workplace Guidelines.

15. What else can I do to protect myself?

    The hepatitis B vaccine is available free of charge to all category I and II employees. This is a very safe and effective vaccine that is highly recommended for persons who are exposed to blood or body fluids. The vaccine is available through Personnel Health Service. For additional questions and information regarding Universal Precautions, please contact the Department of Epidemiology and Infection Control.

Yale-New Haven Hospital
New Haven, Connecticut

Examples of Infectious Diseases Requiring Respiratory Isolation for Specific Periods of Time

1. Anthrax–duration of illness
2. B19 (human parvovirus) transient aplastic crisis, B19 infection in immunodeficient patients, and chronic B19 infection–duration of illness or until the infection has been cleared
3. Chickenpox*–until all lesions are crusted
4. Diphtheria–24 hours after antimicrobial therapy and two negative throat cultures
5. Epiglottitis due to *Haemophilus influenzae*–24 hours after start of effective antibiotic therapy
6. Hemorrhagic fevers–duration of illness
7. Herpes zoster/varicella*–duration of illness (localized in immunocompromised patients)
8. Lassa fever–duration of illness
9. Measles (rubeola)*–for four days after start of rash (except in immunocompromised patients–duration of illness)
10. Meningitis (*Haemophilus influenzae,* known or suspected)–24 hours after start of effective antibiotic therapy
11. Meningococcal meningitis (*Neisseria meningitidis*)–24 hours after start of effective antibiotic therapy
12. Meningococcal pneumonia (*Neisseria meningitidis*)–24 hours after start of effective antibiotic therapy
13. Mumps (infectious parotitis)–nine days after onset of swelling
14. Pertussis (whooping cough)–seven days after start of effective therapy
15. Plague pneumonia–three days after start of effective therapy
16. Pneumonia, *Haemophilus,* in infants and children–24 hours after start of effective antibiotic therapy
17. Rubella (German measles)–seven days after onset of rash
18. Tuberculosis, pulmonary* (confirmed or suspected)–In most instances, duration can be guided by clinical response and a reduction in numbers of TB organisms on sputum smears. Usually, this occurs within two to three weeks after chemotherapy is begun. When the patient is likely to be infected with INH-resistant organisms, continue isolation until the patient is improving and sputum smear is negative for TB organisms.

Note: An asterisk indicates an infectious condition that requires a negative-pressure room in addition to a private room. Negative-pressure rooms are specially designed to limit the flow of contaminated air into the hallway. This is accomplished through fans and vents that direct the airflow outside of the building and/or through special air filters.

Kaiser Permanente Medical Center
San Francisco, California

Rationale for Universal Precautions [Excerpt from Infection Control Manual]

I. Introduction

The Kaiser Permanente Medical Care Program – San Francisco, the American Hospital Association, and the Centers for Disease Control have endorsed adoption of Universal Precautions. They are believed to be the most effective means of reducing the risk of infection in health care settings. Universal Precautions minimize transmission of bloodborne diseases including hepatitis B virus (HBV) and human immunodeficiency virus (HIV or AIDS virus) by reducing the chances of exposure to patients' blood or body fluids/substances.

For many years, isolation has been viewed as the cornerstone of a medical center's program of infection prevention and control. This concept is an outgrowth of the earlier practice of placing patients with selected diagnosed diseases in quarantine. Universal Precautions provides the same high level of precautions for all patients, rather than singling out only those with diagnosed infections and then performing special practices only for them.

The new system is called Universal Precautions because it focuses on isolating body substances (blood, feces, urine, wound drainage, oral secretions, etc.) from the hands of health care workers, primarily by increased glove use and hand washing. This system eliminates many of the ritualistic practices associated with traditional isolation systems, while increasing the use of barriers for all contacts with blood or body fluids/substances.

The Universal Precautions system is consistent with recommendations from the Centers for Disease Control and the University of California – San Francisco Task Force on AIDS that point out the need to consider all blood or body fluids/substances as potentially infectious, regardless of the patient's diagnosis. In order to follow these recommendations, the need to use barriers must focus on the care provider's interaction with the patient at the time, rather than on the diagnosis of the patient, which has been the cornerstone of traditional isolation systems.

Another reason for this change from a traditional "diagnosis-driven" isolation system to the new "interaction-driven" Universal Precautions system is that for many infectious diseases, the diagnosed cases represent only the tip of the iceberg. This is certainly true for HIV infection and for hepatitis B virus (HBV) infection. Focusing isolation precautions only on diagnosed cases of AIDS and HBV infections often misses the vast majority of persons who have the infectious agents in their blood or body fluids/substances. Because the status of all patients' blood cannot be known for these or other infectious diseases, it is imperative to treat all blood or body fluids/substances as potentially infectious, rather than to focus precautions only on the patients diagnosed with infectious diseases.

In addition, colonized body substances are a major reservoir for multiple-drug-resistant organisms that can be easily transmitted from patient to patient on the hands of health care workers. The Universal Precautions system also reduces the risks of such transmission by the consistent use of barriers whenever any body substances are likely to be in contact with the care giver's hands.

Universal Precautions provide a consistent approach to managing blood or body fluids/substances from all patients and are essential to prevent transmission of potentially infectious agents.

II. Elements of Transmission of Infection

Spread of infection within a medical center requires three elements: a source of infecting organisms, a susceptible host, and a means of transmission for the organism.

A. *Source.* The source of the infecting agent may be patients, health care workers, or, on occasion, visitors and may include persons with acute diseases, persons in the incubation period of the disease, or persons who are colonized by the infectious agent but have no apparent disease. Another source of infection can be the person's endogenous flora (autogenous infection). Other potential sources are inanimate objects in the environment that have become contaminated, including equipment and medications.

B. *Host.* Patients' resistance to pathogenic microorganisms varies greatly. Some persons may be immune to or able to resist colonization by an infectious agent; others exposed to the same agent may establish a commensal relationship with the infecting organism and become asymptomatic carriers; still others may develop clinical disease. Persons with diabetes mellitus, lymphoma, leukemia, neoplasia, granulocytopenia, or uremia and those treated with antimicrobials, corticosteroids, irradiation, or immunosuppressive agents may be particularly prone to infection. Age, chronic debilitating disease, shock, coma, traumatic injury, or surgical procedures also make a person more susceptible.

C. *Transmission.* Microorganisms are transmitted by various routes, and the same microorganism may be transmitted by more than one route. For example, varicella-zoster virus can spread either by the airborne route (droplet nuclei) or by direct contact.

There are four main routes of transmission—contact, vehicle, airborne, and vectorborne.

1. Contact transmission, the most important and frequent means of transmission of nosocomial infections, can be divided into three groups: direct contact, indirect contact, and droplet contact.
   a. Direct contact involves direct physical transfer between a susceptible host and an infected or colonized person, such as occurs when medical center personnel turn patients, give baths, change dressings, or perform other procedures requiring direct personal contact. Direct contact can also occur between two patients, one serving as the source of infection and the other as a susceptible host.
   b. Indirect contact involves personal contact of the susceptible host with a contaminated intermediate object, usually inanimate, such as visibly soiled bed linens, clothing, instruments, and dressings.
   c. In droplet contact, infectious agents may come in contact with the conjunctivae, nose, or mouth of a susceptible person as a result of coughing, sneezing or talking by an infected person who has clinical disease or is a carrier of the organism. This is considered "contact" transmission rather than "airborne" since droplets usually travel no more than about three feet.
2. The vehicle route applies in diseases transmitted through these contaminated items:
   - Food, such as in salmonellosis
   - Water, such as in legionellosis
   - Drugs, such as in bacteremia resulting from infusion of a contaminated infusion product
   - Blood, such as in hepatitis B or in non-A, non-B hepatitis
3. Airborne transmission occurs by dissemination of either droplet nuclei (residue or evaporated droplets that may remain suspended in the air for long periods of time) or dust particles in the air containing the infectious agent. Organisms carried in this manner can be widely dispersed by air currents before being inhaled by or deposited on the susceptible host.
4. Vectorborne transmission is of greater concern in tropical countries, for example, with mosquito-transmitted malaria. It is of little significance in medical centers in the United States.

Kaiser Permanente Medical Center
San Francisco, California

Implementing Universal Precautions

The Kaiser Permanente Medical Care Program mandates the application of Universal Blood or Body Fluids/Substances Precautions for all patients as recommended by the American Hospital Association and the Centers for Disease Control. These guidelines are implemented in order to protect employees, physicians, and patients from the transmission of infections and are inclusive of protection against the transmission of human immunodeficiency virus (HIV) in health care settings. Precautions must be strictly followed whenever there is a possibility of exposure to blood or other body fluids/substances. Health care workers need to exercise judgment in making decisions about anticipating exposure and when to use appropriate barrier precautions.

Guidelines for Infection Control Precautions

1. Handle the blood or body fluids/substances of *all* patients as potentially infectious.
2. Wash hands before and after *all* patient or specimen contact.
3. Wear gloves when contact with blood or body fluids/substances is anticipated; remove gloves after each individual task.
4. Wear a gown or disposable plastic apron when splashing with blood or body fluids/substances is anticipated.
5. Wear a mask for protection against airborne transmitted diseases (HIV is not airborne).
6. Wear protective eyewear and mask if facial splatter with blood or body fluids/substances is anticipated.
7. Immediately place used needles/syringes in a nearby puncture-resistant container. Generally, needles should not be recapped or manipulated in any way.
8. Process *all* laboratory specimens as potentially infectious.
9. Place equipment needed for emergency resuscitation, for example, Ambu bags and/or mouthpieces, in areas in which the need for resuscitation is predictable.

Employee Health Issues

1. Wash your hands, arms, face, etc., immediately and thoroughly if you have had unprotected contact with blood or body fluids/substances.
2. Protect your nonintact skin (for example, skin that is chapped, abraded, or afflicted with dermatitis) from contact with blood or body fluids/substances.
3. Contact your supervisor when you have had an exposure to blood or body fluids/substances such as a needlestick or a splash of blood onto nonintact skin or mucous membranes.

The Role of Direct Care Givers in Implementing Universal Precautions

I. All Direct Care Givers' Responsibility
   A. Each care giver should evaluate his/her own interactions with the patient and use barriers as appropriate based on judgments of anticipated contact with blood or body fluids/substances, not on the patient's diagnosis of infection. See Barrier Techniques to Reduce Infection Risk for Specific Clinical Situations [pp. 56–57 of this manual].
   B. All direct care givers should know their own varicella (chickenpox) and rubella status and participate in the annual TB screening program.
   C. All care givers who have contact with blood or body fluids/substances should be immunized against hepatitis B. The new hepatitis B vaccine, Recombivax HB® (Merck), is free of association with human blood or blood products. It is available without charge to all Kaiser Health Plan members or may be obtained from the employee's direct care provider.

II. Physician's Responsibility
   A. The physician no longer needs to write an order for isolation of diseases that are not transmitted by the airborne route.
   B. The physician shall be responsible for documenting on the physician's order sheet if the patient has, or is suspected of having, a disease that is transmitted in whole or in part by the airborne route. The physician shall write "Respiratory Precautions" and state the disease or suspected disease.

III. Nurse's Responsibility
   A. The nurse shall be responsible for placing a Stop Sign Alert on door of a patient with a disease requiring Respiratory Precautions.
   B. This sign signifies that anyone who desires to enter the room must report first to the nurse to be instructed in special precautions that must be taken. (See Guidelines for Patients with an Airborne Disease Requiring Respiratory Precautions [pp. 61–65 of this manual] and Airborne Diseases for Which Exclusion of Susceptible Individuals May Be Indicated [p. 66 of this manual].)

Techniques and Recommendations for Universal Precautions

This section contains information essential to understanding and properly applying Universal Precautions to interrupt the transmission of infection.

Hand Washing

I. Hands should be washed before and after *all* patient and specimen contact. Hand washing is the single most important means of preventing the spread of infection.

II. Hands should be washed for at least 10 seconds with soap and lukewarm running water.

III. Hands should be washed when gloves are removed after performing each task that involves contact with blood or body fluids/substances, mucous membranes, or nonintact skin.

IV. Hands should be washed before performing invasive procedures and before touching immunocompromised patients.

V. Soap without antibacterial ingredients may be used for hand washing when caring for patients who are not on a special area unit (for example, patients on medical, surgical, pediatric units). If bar soap is used, it should be kept on a rack that allows drainage of water. If liquid soap is used, the dispenser should be replaced or cleaned and filled with fresh product when empty; liquids should not be added to a partially full dispenser.

VI. Antiseptic soaps should be used for hand washing when caring for patients in special high-risk units (for example, intensive care units, the pediatric special care unit, and the intensive care nursery). Antiseptic soaps will inhibit or kill many microorganisms that may not be completely removed by normal hand washing. Some antiseptics also have residual effects that will continue to suppress microbial growth several hours after hand washing. Such antiseptics should not be used as a substitute for adequate hand washing with soap and water.

VII. When an inadvertent, unprotected exposure to blood or body fluids/substances occurs, the contaminated area should be washed immediately and thoroughly with soap and water.

Protective Apparel

Protective apparel supplies will be placed in convenient locations in all patient care areas throughout the medical center.

I. Gloves: Gloves should be worn when contact with blood or body fluids/substances is anticipated. Remove gloves after each individual task.
   A. There are three distinct reasons for wearing gloves.
      1. Gloves will reduce the possibility that health care workers will become infected with microorganisms that are infecting patients. For example, gloves should prevent transmission of bloodborne diseases during exposure to blood or body fluids/substances.
      2. Gloves reduce the likelihood that health care workers will transmit their own endogenous microbial flora to patients. For example, sterile gloves are used for this reason when health care workers perform surgery or touch surgical wounds.
      3. Gloves reduce the possibility that health care workers will become transiently colonized with microorganisms that can be transmitted to other patients.
   B. Gloves should be worn for contact with blood or body fluids/substances, mucous membranes, or nonintact skin of all patients and for handling items or surfaces contaminated with body fluids. Pathologic agents may be present in body substances whether or not they are recognized to be present.
      1. These agents may be transmitted from clinically healthy individuals.
      2. Use of gloves in a nonpatient care area such as the hall or nursing stations is only indicated when performing a task that may involve contact with blood or body fluids/substances, that is, emptying trash or cleaning surfaces visibly contaminated with blood or body fluids/substances.
      3. Pathologic agents are carried on gloves as easily as they are carried on unwashed hands. Gloves should be removed immediately and hands washed after each task is completed. If gloves are not removed, contamination of the environment, other patients, or other body sites on the same patient can occur.
      4. Gloves do not provide protection against needlesticks.
   C. Selection of Gloves
      When gloves are indicated, disposable single-use gloves should be worn.
      1. Sterile gloves should be worn only for procedures involving contact with sterile areas of the body.
      2. Nonsterile gloves should be worn when asepsis is not required.
      3. Vinyl and latex gloves provide equal protection against all microorganisms found in blood or body fluids/substances, mucous membranes, or nonintact skin.
         a. Vinyl gloves should be used for most patient care procedures involving contact with body substances. Choosing a size that fits best will increase manual dexterity and tactile sense when performing a task.
         b. Latex gloves should be used for handling chemotherapeutic agents and blood or body fluids/substances of patients receiving chemotherapy.
      4. General-purpose utility gloves (for example, rubber household gloves) should be used for housekeeping chores involving potential blood or body fluids/substances contact and instrument cleaning and decontamination procedures. Utility gloves may be decontaminated and reused but should be

discarded when they show evidence of deterioration such as peeling, cracks, discoloration, punctures, or tears.

II. Gowns

A. Wear a gown or disposable plastic apron when splashing of blood or body fluids/substance is anticipated.

1. Gowns or disposable plastic aprons are recommended to prevent soiling of clothing when caring for patients. Such soilage may occur when clothing comes into direct contact with blood or body fluids/substances.
2. Gowns or disposable aprons should prevent organisms from being carried on the clothing of health care workers.
3. When gowns or plastic aprons are indicated, they should be worn only once and discarded in an appropriate receptacle.
4. Clean, freshly laundered gowns or nonsterile plastic aprons may be worn in most circumstances.

B. Gowns are not indicated in patient care situations when soiling is not likely.

C. Sterile gowns should only be used in procedures that require asepsis, such as performing surgical procedures.

III. Masks/Protective Eyewear: Wear a mask for protection against airborne diseases (HIV is not airborne). Wear protective eyewear and a mask if facial splatter with blood or body fluids/substances is anticipated. [See the discussion of masks in chapter 9.]

A. A mask may be required when health care workers enter the rooms of patients on Respiratory Precautions. (See the list of airborne diseases [pp. 62–65 of this manual] and the list of airborne diseases for which exclusion of susceptible individuals may be indicated [p. 66 of this manual].)

1. A mask should be placed on patients with airborne diseases while they are being transported in the halls or elevators and while they are in open areas, such as Radiology.
2. A Stop Sign Alert will be placed on the door of each patient with an airborne disease to alert health care workers to the need for Respiratory Precautions and the possible need for a mask.
3. Nursing personnel are responsible for instructing any person who wishes to enter the room as to whether or not a mask is indicated. Exclusion of susceptibles is indicated in some situations. (For more details see Guidelines for Persons with an Airborne Disease Requiring Respiratory Precautions [p. 61 in this manual] and Airborne Diseases for Which Exclusion of Susceptible Individuals May be Indicated [p. 66 in this manual].)
4. Masks should only be used once and discarded after use because moist masks are not effective filters for microorganisms.
5. Masks should cover both the nose and mouth with no gaping on the sides.
6. Eye protection is not necessary unless a splash or splatter of blood or body fluids/substances is anticipated.

B. A mask plus eye protection (glasses, goggles, or face shields) should be worn to prevent exposure of the care giver's eyes and nasal/oral mucosa when a splash, splatter, or generation of droplets of any blood or body fluids/substances from any patient is anticipated.

1. Masks and goggles may be carried with health care workers when facial exposure to blood or body fluids/substances is anticipated.
2. Masks should be discarded when soiled with blood or body fluids/substances.
3. Reusable goggles should be cleaned when visibly soiled with blood or body fluids/substances.

C. A mask is indicated during procedures that require surgical asepsis.

1. Protective eyewear should be worn if generation of droplets or splatter of blood or body fluids/substances is anticipated.
2. Refer to procedure manual in your department for the specific procedures where masks are indicated.

General Guidelines for Procedures (Casual, Routine, Invasive, Perinatal)

Handle the blood or body fluids/substances from *all* patients as potentially infectious.

I. Casual Contact: Protective apparel is not needed for casual contact with intact skin during routine patient care or for walking into the room of any patient, with the exception of masks for patients on Respiratory Precautions. Protective apparel is also not necessary for performing nonpatient tasks that do not involve potential contact with blood or body fluids/substances, such as routine mopping of floors, delivering dietary trays, taking vital signs, etc.

II. Routine Procedures: All health care workers should routinely use appropriate barrier precautions to prevent skin and mucous membrane exposure when contact with blood or body fluids/substances is anticipated. Gloves should be worn for touching blood or body fluids/substances, mucous membranes, and nonintact skin of all patients and for handling surfaces soiled with blood or body fluids/substances. Masks and protective eyewear/face shields should be worn during procedures that are likely to generate droplets of blood or body fluids/substances to prevent exposure of the mucous membranes of the mouth, nose, and eyes. Gowns or aprons should be worn during procedures that are likely to generate splashes/soilage from blood or body fluids/substances.

III. Invasive Procedures: All health care workers who participate in invasive procedures must routinely use appropriate barrier precautions to prevent skin and mucous membrane contact with blood or body fluids/substances. Barrier precautions also prevent transmission of microorganisms from health care workers to the patient during invasive procedures. Invasive procedures include any surgical entry into tissues or repair of traumatic injury in any health care setting.

IV. Perinatal Procedures: All health care workers should wear gloves when handling newborns until visible blood and amniotic fluids have been removed by dry wiping or washing from the infant's skin.

Reminder Sign/Stop Sign Alert

I. Reminder signs indicating precautions for patient care activities when contact with blood or body fluids/substances is anticipated will be placed in visible locations throughout patient care areas in the medical center.

II. A Stop Sign Alert will be placed on the door of each patient with an airborne disease to alert health care workers that Respiratory Precautions are indicated.

Clinical Situations by Body System	Barrier and Containment Techniques
Respiratory	
• Sputum production –Bronchitis –Pneumonia –Productive cough	• Wash hands after contact with sputum • Wear gloves for contact with sputum • Position self to avoid being in direct line with respiratory secretions
• Suctioning	• Wear protective eyewear and mask if splatter with respiratory secretions likely • Rinse contaminated reusable equipment/instruments under running water or wipe with appropriate disinfectant before returning them to CSR for decontamination and sterilization • Follow Respiratory Precautions if airborne disease is suspected • Instruct patient as to the importance of handling secretions/sputum
• CPR exposure to airway secretions	• Use a mouthpiece or use Ambu® bags during resuscitation
Other	
• CSF • Joint fluid • Peritoneal fluid	• Wash hands after contact with body substances • Wear gloves for contact with body fluids/substances • Instruct patient in care of body substances and hand washing
Skin	
• Lesion drainage –Boils –Exanthems –Open skin ulcers –Pustular lesions –Wound infections –Wounds	• Wash hands after patient contact • Wear gloves for contact with drainage/open wound • Wear gown/apron if soiling of clothing is likely • Dispose of dressing by confining and containing into an inverted glove or bag and by placing into impervious bag • Place soiled linen in an impervious bag • Follow Respiratory Precautions for airborne diseases that have exanthems (for example, chickenpox) • Instruct patient in care of drainage and hand washing
Blood	
• Frank bleeding • G.I. bleeding • Hemoptysis • Serosanguinous wound/lesion drainage • Starting I.V. therapy or drawing blood (if the practice usually results in getting blood on care giver's hands) • Manipulating stopcocks	• Wash hands after contact with blood • Wear gloves when contact with blood is anticipated • Wear masks and protective eyewear when aerosolization of blood may occur • Wear gown/apron when soiling of clothing is likely • Place soiled linen/trash into its appropriate impervious bags • Discard large volumes of blood from containers that can be emptied into the sanitary sewer • Place large volumes of blood in containers that cannot be emptied into the sanitary sewer into two red bags and discard as infectious waste • Instruct patient in care of bloody discharge and in hand washing

Kaiser Permanente Medical Center
San Francisco, California

Guidelines for Patient Room Placement

Definition	Examples	Room Placement
1. Patients with communicable diseases spread through the airborne route	Anthrax (inhalation) Chickenpox Diphtheria (pharyngeal) Erythema infectiosum *Haemophilus* influenza • Epiglottitis • Meningitis • Pneumonia Herpes zoster (shingles) • Localized, immunocompromised host • Disseminated, immunocompetent host Lassa fever Marburg virus disease Measles (rubeola) Meningococcal infection Mumps Pertussis (whooping cough) Plague (pneumonic) Rabies Rubella Tuberculosis (pulmonary)	See Guidelines for Patients with an Airborne Disease Requiring Respiratory Precautions for duration of precautions. Private room with door closed. Stop Sign Alert on door. Patients may share a room if they have the same organism. Children with chickenpox will be housed on an adult medical or surgical ward if possible or transferred to another facility.
2. Susceptible patients recently exposed to airborne communicable disease who are in their potentially infectious period	Chickenpox Diphtheria (pharyngeal) Measles Mumps Pertussis Rubella	Consider postponing elective admission. If not possible, private room or share room with immune roommate. Respiratory precautions should be initiated as indicated. (See list of airborne diseases [pp. 62–65 of this manual] and list of airborne diseases for which exclusion of susceptible individuals may be indicated [p. 66 of this manual].)
3. Patients with *Staphylococcus aureus* pneumonia		Private room until 48 hours after the start of effective antibiotic therapy
4. Patients with localized herpes zoster who are immunocompetent (shingles)		Roommate must have had chickenpox. Direct care givers must have had chickenpox. Place a Stop Sign Alert on door or bed. Room assignment applies until all lesions are crusted over.

Definition	Examples	Room Placement
5. Patients who consistently soil environment with body substances. Patient's or health care workers' efforts cannot contain blood, urine, feces, sputum, etc.	Incontinent patients who soil the environment Upper gastrointestinal bleeding with projectile emesis	Private room until blood or body fluids/substances can be contained by patient or health care workers.
6. Patients with large major draining wounds that cannot be covered or adequately contained by dressings	Cellulitis Infected pressure sores Wound infections	Can share rooms with patients with medical conditions who have no open skin sites or no mechanical respiratory assistance (for example, patients with back pain, diabetes, ulcer disease, etc.) and patients with wounds infected with the same organism.
7. Patients with infected wounds that can be adequately contained by dressings	Cellulitis Infected pressure sores Wound infections	Can share rooms with patients with medical or surgical conditions who have wounds contained by dressings or closed drainage systems and patients with uncontained wound infections with the same organism.
8. Patients with group A beta-hemolytic *Streptococcus* infections	Cellulitis Endometritis Pharyngitis Pneumonia Scarlet fever Wound infections	Private room until 24 hours after start of effective antibiotic therapy. See exposure guidelines for procedure to be followed for surgical or obstetrical team members who have operated on or delivered a patient who developed a nosocomial or community-acquired streptococcal infection [not reproduced in this manual].
9. Patients with neutropenia (<1000 neutrophils)		A private room is preferred; but if there is none available, can share room with patients making an uneventful recovery from medical conditions who have no open skin sites, no urinary catheters, no drains or no mechanical respiratory assistance. Roommate must be free of airborne communicable disease. See Care of Severely Compromised Patients [p. 67 of this manual].

(Table continues.)

Definition	Examples	Room Placement
10. Patients with extrapulmonary tuberculosis with draining lesions (including scrofula)		Private room for children until drainage ceases.
11. Patients infected or colonized with multiply resistant bacteria whose infected or colonized site is open to the environment	Wounds, indwelling urinary catheters, sputum, etc., infected with: • Gram-negative rods, resistant to multiple antibiotics • *Haemophilus* influenza resistant to ampicillin • *Staphylococcus aureus* resistant to nafcillin and methicillin • *Pneumococcus* resistant to penicillin • Other resistant bacteria judged to be significant by Infection Control Department	Private room or can share room with roommate infected or colonized with the same organism for the duration of hospitalization. Patients with an indwelling urinary catheter may have to be spatially separated from other patients with an indwelling urinary catheter. Room assignment applies until patient is discharged from the medical center.
12. Patients infected or colonized with the same organism during outbreak situations	Adenovirus infection Chickenpox Gram-negative enteric meningitis in neonates Group B *Streptococcus* in neonates Influenza virus Multiply resistant organisms Necrotizing enterocolitis in neonates Parainfluenza virus Respiratory syncytial virus Staphylococcal infections in neonates	Can share room with roommate infected or colonized with the same organism (cohorting).

Kaiser Permanente Medical Center
San Francisco, California

Guidelines for Patients with an Airborne Disease Requiring Respiratory Precautions

The following are the general guidelines to follow when patients are put on Respiratory Precautions because they have a known or suspected airborne disease. (See the list of airborne diseases requiring respiratory precautions [pp. 62–65 in this manual].)

I. A chart order will be written by the physician on the physician's order sheet stating the name of the known or suspected disease and "Respiratory Precautions."

II. A private room is indicated and the door should remain closed. Patients known to be infected with the same organism may share a room.

III. The nurse will place a Stop Sign Alert on the door of the patient's room.

IV. Nursing personnel are responsible for instructing persons who wish to enter the room whether or not a mask is indicated (for example, for a patient with active tuberculosis) or for determining the immune status of the person wishing to enter the room (for example, for a patient with chickenpox).

   A. Exclusion of susceptibles may be indicated with some airborne diseases. (See Airborne Diseases for Which Exclusion of Susceptibles May Be Indicated [p. 66 of this manual].)

   B. If the person wishing to enter the room is immune, s/he may enter the room without a mask. (See the list of airborne diseases [pp. 62–65 of this manual] and the list of airborne diseases for which exclusion of susceptible individuals may be indicated [p. 66 of this manual].)

   C. If the person is susceptible to the disease and must enter the room of a patient with an airborne disease, a mask should be worn. [See the discussion of masks in chapter 9.]

V. Masks should cover both the nose and mouth with no gaping on the sides.

VI. Universal Precautions should also be practiced as indicated for exposure to blood or body fluids/substances. (See the list of airborne diseases [pp. 62–65 of this manual].)

VII. Elective admissions should be postponed for susceptible patients who have recently been exposed to or who currently have a disease spread through the airborne route (for example, chickenpox). If the patient must be admitted, the physician must contact the receiving nursing unit and write in the chart an order indicating that the exposed susceptible patient is on Respiratory Precautions for the length of time that the patient might be susceptible (for example, day 10 until day 21 postexposure to chickenpox).

VIII. Susceptible patients who have been recently exposed to or currently have an airborne disease should be discharged as soon as possible. If not possible, place patient in private room or with an immune roommate.

IX. Patients on Respiratory Precautions should wear a mask when they leave the room. Transport personnel should wear a mask and protective apparel as indicated. The receiving department should be notified in advance by nursing personnel because it may be appropriate to select immune persons to do the procedure. (See the list of airborne diseases for which exclusion of susceptible individuals may be indicated [p. 66 of this manual].)

X. Patients may be taken off Respiratory Precautions when they are no longer infectious. For duration of Respiratory Precautions for each disease, see list of airborne diseases [pp. 62–65 of this manual].

Airborne Diseases Requiring Respiratory Precautions

Disease	Apply Respiratory Precautions for How Long	Comments
Anthrax (inhalation)	Duration of illness	Please report by telephone to San Francisco Health Department and Infection Control Department.
Chickenpox (varicella)	Until all lesions are crusted	Persons who have had chickenpox do not require a mask. Susceptible persons should, if possible, stay out of room. Exposed susceptible patients should be placed on Respiratory Precautions days 10 through 21 after exposure. Children should be housed on an adult medical/surgical floor in a private room or with an immune roommate. OB patients should labor, deliver, and recover in the same private room and remain there until discharge. Neonates born to mothers with active varicella should be placed on Respiratory Precautions at birth. Please report to Infection Control Department. For workup of exposed susceptible health care workers, see Exposure to Chickenpox [not reproduced in this manual].
Diphtheria (pharyngeal)	Until cultures from both the nose and throat taken at least 24 hours after cessation of effective antimicrobial therapy are negative for *Corynebacterium diphtheriae*	Please report by telephone to the San Francisco Health Department and Infection Control Department. Susceptible persons should, if possible, stay out of the room. See Airborne Diseases for Which Exclusion of Susceptible Individuals May Be Indicated [p. 66 of this manual].
Epiglottitis, due to *Haemophilus influenzae*	For 4 hours after start of effective antibiotic therapy	Please report to Infection Control Department.
Erythema infectiosum	For 7 days after onset	
Haemophilus influenzae: epiglottitis meningitis pneumonia	For 4 hours after start of effective antibiotic therapy	Please report to Infection Control Department.
Hemorrhagic fevers (for example: Lassa fever, Marburg virus disease)	Duration of illness	Please report by telephone to State Health Department, Centers for Disease Control, and Infection Control Department for advice about management of a suspected case.

Disease	Apply Respiratory Precautions for How Long	Comments
Herpes zoster (shingles) localized in an immunocompromised host or disseminated in an immunocompetent host	Duration of illness	Disseminated herpes zoster occasionally manifests itself as pneumonia and can be spread via the airborne route. Localized lesions in immunocompromised patients occasionally become disseminated. Because such dissemination is unpredictable, use the same precautions as for disseminated disease. Persons who have not had chickenpox should stay out of the room if possible. Persons who have had chickenpox do not require a mask. See Airborne Diseases for Which Exclusion of Susceptible Individuals May Be Indicated [p. 66 of this manual].
Lassa fever and Marburg virus disease	Duration of illness	Please report by telephone to State Health Department, Centers for Disease Control, and Infection Control Department for advice about management of a suspected case.
Measles (rubeola)	For 4 days after start of rash, except in immunocompromised patients, for whom precautions should be maintained for duration of illness	Please report by telephone to San Francisco Health Department and the Infection Control Department. Persons who are immune do not require a mask. Susceptible persons should, if possible, stay out of room. See Airborne Diseases for Which Exclusion of Susceptible Individuals May Be Indicated [p. 66 of this manual].
Meningitis a. *Haemophilus influenzae* known or suspected	For 4 hours after start of effective therapy	Please report to San Francisco Health Department and Infection Control Department.
b. Meningococcal *(Neisseria meningitidis)* known or suspected	For 4 hours after start of effective therapy	Please report to San Francisco Health Department and Infection Control Department. See recommendations for postexposure prophylaxis [not reproduced in this manual].
Meningococcal disease *(Neisseria meningitidis)*: meningitis, meningococcal sepsis, pneumonia	For 4 hours after start of effective therapy	Please report to San Francisco Health Department and Infection Control Department. See recommendations for postexposure prophylaxis [not reproduced in this manual].
Mumps	For 9 days after onset of swelling	Persons who are immune do not require a mask. Susceptible persons should stay out of the room. See Airborne Diseases for Which Exclusion of Susceptible Individuals May Be Indicated [p. 66 of this manual].

(Table continues.)

Disease	Apply Respiratory Precautions for How Long	Comments
Pertussis (whooping cough)	For 7 days after start of effective therapy	Please report to Infection Control Department. For recommendations for post-exposure prophylaxis and outbreak measures [not reproduced in this manual].
Plague (pneumonic)	For 3 days after start of effective therapy	Please report by telephone to San Francisco Health Department and Infection Control Department.
Pneumonia		
a. *Haemophilus influenzae*	For 4 hours after start of effective therapy	Please report to San Francisco Health Department and Infection Control Department.
b. Meningococcal	For 4 hours after start of effective therapy	Please report to San Francisco Health Department and Infection Control Department.
Rabies	Duration of illness	Please report by telephone to San Francisco Health Department and Infection Control Department.
Rubella (German measles)	For 7 days after onset of rash	Persons who are immune do not need to wear a mask. Susceptible persons should, if possible, stay out of room. See Airborne Diseases for Which Exclusion of Susceptible Individuals May Be Indicated [p. 66 of this manual].
Rubella, congenital	For the first year of life unless nasopharyngeal cultures are negative for the rubella virus after 3 months of age	Persons who are immune do not need to wear a mask. Susceptible persons should, if possible, stay out of room. See Airborne Diseases for Which Exclusion of Susceptible Individuals May Be Indicated [p. 66 of this manual].
Shingles (see herpes zoster)		
Smallpox (variola)	Duration of illness	As long as smallpox is kept stocked in laboratories, the potential exists for cases to occur. Please report by telephone to state Health Department, Centers for Disease Control, and Infection Control Department for management of suspected case.

Disease	Apply Respiratory Precautions for How Long	Comments
Tuberculosis, pulmonary, confirmed or suspected	Duration of precautions can be guided by clinical response and reduction in numbers of TB organisms in the sputum smear. Usually this occurs 10-21 days after the start of effective therapy. When the patient is likely to be infected with isoniazid-resistant organisms, apply precautions until the patient is improving and the sputum smear is negative for TB organisms.	Please report to San Francisco Health Department and Infection Control Department. Infants do not usually require isolation precautions because they rarely cough and their bronchial secretions contain few TB organisms compared to adults with pulmonary TB. For workup of exposed health care workers, see exposure guidelines for AFB [not reproduced in this manual].
Varicella (see chickenpox)		

Kaiser Permanente Medical Center
San Francisco, California

Airborne Diseases for Which Exclusion of Susceptible Individuals May Be Indicated

Individuals are susceptible to:	If they have never had:
Chickenpox, herpes zoster, varicella	Chickenpox, herpes zoster (shingles), or positive varicella titer
Diphtheria, pharyngeal	Diphtheria vaccination (DPT in childhood and boosters of DT every 10 years)
Measles (rubeola)	Measles, measles vaccination (MMR in childhood), or positive serology for measles (rubeola)
Mumps	Mumps, mumps vaccination (MMR in childhood), or positive serology for mumps
Pertussis (whooping cough)	Pertussis (whooping cough) or pertussis vaccination (DPT in childhood)
Rubella (German measles)	Rubella, rubella vaccination (MMR in childhood/adult), or positive serology for rubella

Kaiser Permanente Medical Center
San Francisco, California

Modification of Universal Precautions for Immunocompromised Patients and Newborns

I. **Care of Severely Compromised Patients**

A. Patients with certain diseases (for example, leukemia, cancer, and extensive skin conditions, such as severe burns or dermatitis) and patients who are receiving certain therapeutic regimens (for example, total body irradiation, steroid or antimetabolite therapy) are highly susceptible to infection. These compromised patients are often on special "protective" patient care regimens intended to reduce the risk of infection. One such regimen, Protective Isolation (as outlined in the previous editions of *Isolation Techniques for Use in Hospitals*), does not appear to reduce this risk any more than strong emphasis on appropriate hand washing during patient care.

B. Protective Isolation, as previously outlined, may fail to reduce the risk of infection because compromised patients are often infected by their own (endogenous) microorganisms or are colonized and infected by microorganisms transmitted by the inadequately washed hands of health care workers or by nonsterile items used in routine Protective Isolation. Such items may include patient care equipment, food, water and air. Some studies suggest that vigorous efforts to exclude all microorganisms by using patient-isolator units, eradicating endogenous flora, and sterilizing food, water, and fomites may prevent or delay onset of some infections; thus, these procedures have been recommended by some for use with very high risk patients who have a predictable temporary period of high susceptibility. However, these extraordinary and expensive precautions do not appear warranted for most compromised patients.

C. In general, compromised patients should be taken care of by using precautions that are no different from routine good patient care techniques, but for these patients, routine techniques must be emphasized and enforced. All health care workers must frequently and appropriately wash their hands before, during, and after patient care. Compromised patients should be kept separate from patients who are infected or have conditions that make infection transmission likely. They should be put in private rooms whenever possible. (See Guidelines for Patient Room Placement [pp. 58–60 of this manual].)

II. **Modifications of Universal Precautions for Newborns and Mothers**

Universal Precautions and Respiratory Precautions for newborns and infants are modified from those recommended for adults for several reasons: (1) Usually only a small number of private rooms are available for newborns and infants, (2) during outbreaks, it is frequently necessary to establish cohorts of newborns and infants, and (3) a newborn may require special precautions at delivery because its mother has an infection (for example, herpes simplex, chickenpox, etc.).

A. Appropriate Use of Universal Precautions

1. See Guidelines for Infection Control Precautions [p. 51 of this manual].
2. If the infant is infected, the mother should demonstrate an understanding that anticipated exposure to blood or body fluids/substances requires a protective barrier, that is, gloves, gowns, etc., to minimize the risk of transmission to herself.
3. If the mother is infected, the mother should demonstrate an understanding that anticipated exposure of her baby to blood or body fluids/substances requires a protective barrier, that is, gloves, gowns, etc., to minimize the risk of transmission to her baby.

B. Private Rooms

1. If the guidelines state that a private room is indicated and mother–infant contact is permitted, the mother and the newborn infant may share the private room.
2. In the past, private rooms were recommended so that infected newborns or those suspected of being infected (regardless of the pathogen and clinical manifestations) could be put into a separate private room. This recommendation was based on the assumption that a geographically isolated room was necessary to protect uninfected newborns and that infected newborns would receive closer scrutiny and better care in such a room. Neither of these assumptions is completely correct.
3. Private rooms are seldom indicated for newborns with many kinds of infection if the following conditions are met: (a) An adequate number of nursing and medical personnel are on duty and have sufficient time for appropriate hand washing, (b) sufficient space is available for a 4- to 6-foot aisle or area between newborn stations, (c) an adequate number of sinks for hand washing are available in each nursery room or area, and (d) continuing instruction is given to health care workers about the mode of transmission of infections. When these criteria are not met, a separate room with hand washing facilities may be indicated.

C. Forced-Air Incubators

Another incorrect assumption regarding special precautions for newborns and infants is that forced-air incubators can be substituted for private rooms. These incubators may filter the incoming air but not the air discharged into the nursery. Moreover, the surfaces of incubators housing newborns or infants can easily become contaminated with organisms infecting or colonizing the patient, and so health care workers working with the patient in the Isolette® may have their hands and forearms colonized. Forced-air incubators, therefore, are satisfactory for limited "Protective" Isolation of newborns and infants but should not be relied on as a major means of preventing transmission from infected patients to others.

D. Criteria for Special Precautions

Precautions for an infected or colonized newborn or infant, or for a newborn of a mother suspected of having an infectious disease, can be determined by the specific viral or bacterial pathogen, the clinical manifestations, the source and possible modes of transmission, and the number of colonized or infected newborns or infants.

Kaiser Permanente Medical Center
San Francisco, California

Guidelines for Handling and Disposal of Used Hospital Items

I. Handling and Disposal of Patient Care Equipment

A. Disposable Patient Care Equipment

A variety of disposable patient care equipment is available and should be considered for patients. Use of these disposable articles reduces the possibility that equipment will serve as a fomite; however, disposables must be disposed of safely. No special precautions are indicated for disposable equipment other than large-volume fluid-filled containers. (See subsequent section I.C and the section on Disposal of Waste [pp. 98–99 of this manual].)

B. Reusable Patient Care Equipment

1. As defined by patient care procedure, such equipment should be returned to Central Supply Reprocessing (CSR) for decontamination and reprocessing by trained personnel.
2. All equipment that is not sent to CSR or discarded should be cleaned with a disinfectant–detergent solution.
3. Reusable contaminated instruments that can be immersed in water, such as syringes and metal hardware, should be rinsed under running water and delivered to CSR or placed in a designated container to be picked up by CSR.
4. Reusable contaminated equipment that cannot be immersed in water should be wiped with an appropriate hospital disinfectant approved for hospital use by the Environmental Protection Agency (EPA) to remove gross contaminants before being labeled for return to CSR for decontamination and sterilization. [See the discussion of disinfectants in chapter 9.]

C. Large-Volume Fluid-Filled Containers

1. The contents of collecting devices containing large volumes of blood or drainage that can be emptied, such as suction canisters, etc., should be flushed down the sanitary sewer.
   a. The emptied canisters may be discarded in the regular trash.
   b. Appropriate precautions should be taken to guard against spillage.
   c. Protective apparel should be worn if exposure to blood or body fluids/substances is anticipated.
2. Collecting devices containing large volumes of blood or drainage that cannot be emptied should be sealed to prevent leakage of body fluids, then confined and contained in two red bags and discarded as infectious waste (see section on Infectious Waste [pp. 98–99 of this manual]).

D. Needles, Syringes, Sharps

Health care workers should use caution when handling all used needles and syringes because it is not usually known which patients' blood is contaminated with HIV, HBV, or other bloodborne pathogens. There are several things that health care workers can do to reduce the risk of needlestick injuries.

1. Place used needles/syringes immediately in a nearby puncture-resistant container.
2. Generally, needles should not be recapped or manipulated in any way. Recapping needles is a major cause of needlestick injuries.
3. Recapping may be necessary in some situations such as transportation of blood gas syringes. Recapping may be safely accomplished by placing the needle cap horizontally on a flat surface and inserting the needle into the cap with one hand. Once the needle is covered by the cap, two hands may be used to tighten the cap to the needle hub.

4. Assistance should be obtained when injections are administered or infusion therapy is given to uncooperative patients.
5. Adequate lighting should be used when performing procedures that involve needles or sharps.
6. Needles should never be left on beds, gurneys, bedside tables, etc., because they may injure unsuspecting patients, visitors, or other health care workers.
7. Needles or other sharp instruments should be removed from I.V. tubing or disposable trays, etc., prior to discarding because persons emptying trash cans may be injured by a needle or sharp protruding through the plastic bag.
8. Needles and other sharp objects should also be removed from reusable instrument trays prior to removal from the unit to prevent injury to personnel reprocessing those trays.
9. Hands of health care workers should never go inside the opening of the puncture-resistant container.
   a. Needles or other sharp objects should not be forced into full containers.
   b. If the container is more than three-fourths full, the opening should be securely closed. Notify the Environmental Services Department to change the container.
10. If an inadvertent needlestick or injury from a sharp object does occur, health care workers should notify their supervisor immediately so that corrective action may be taken. (See Exposure to Blood and Body Fluids/Substances [pp. 218–21 of this manual] and the algorithm for hepatitis B postexposure prophylaxis protocols [figure 7-18 of this manual].)

E. Resuscitation Devices

Mouthpieces, resuscitation bags, or other ventilation devices shall be available for use in areas in which the need for resuscitation is predictable.

F. Sphygmomanometer and Stethoscope

1. No special precautions are indicated unless this equipment is contaminated with blood or body fluids/substances.
2. If visibly contaminated, the equipment should be wiped with a hospital disinfectant approved for hospital use by the EPA. (See CDC's *Guideline for Hospital Infection Control: Cleaning, Disinfection, and Sterilization of Hospital Equipment.*)

G. Thermometers

1. On admission, each patient will be issued a thermometer and suitable holder.
2. Thermometers are used with a disposable plastic sheath according to the procedure in the Inpatient Nursing Manual.
3. On discharge, thermometer should be given to patient to take home or disposed of in a puncture-resistant container.

II. Guidelines for Handling and Disposing of Linen

A. Introduction

"Although soiled linen has been identified as a source of large numbers of certain pathogenic microorganisms, the risk of actual disease transmission is negligible. Rather than rigid procedures and specifications, hygienic and commonsense storage and processing of clean and soiled linen are recommended. Soiled linen should be handled as little as possible and with minimum agitation to prevent gross microbial contamination of the air and of persons handling the linens. All soiled linen should be bagged at the location where it was used; it should not be sorted or rinsed in patient care areas. Linen soiled with blood or body fluids/substances should be placed and transported in bags that prevent leakage" (Centers for Disease Control, *Morbidity and Mortality Weekly Report* 36(2S):11S, August 21, 1987).

B. Soiled linen for all patients should be handled in the following manner.

1. Bed linen shall be removed by gently rolling it toward the center of the bed in such a way as to contain blood or body fluids/substances if present. Linen should never be shaken or agitated in any way.
2. Soiled linens should be held away from the body at all times.
3. Soiled linen should be placed in a single impervious bag at the location where the linen was used. [See the discussion of the term *impervious* in chapter 9.]
4. Bags shall be such that they can be securely closed and will withstand transportation to the laundry facility without rupture.
5. When bag is no more than two-thirds full, it is to be securely closed.
6. A second bag is indicated if there is visible outside contamination or if puncture is likely.
7. Gloves should be worn when handling linen that may be soiled with blood or body fluids/substances.
8. Linen transport carts should be cleaned with appropriate detergent when visibly soiled and as scheduled.
9. Health care workers should wash their hands after handling linen, the hamper stand or transport carts.

III. Dietary Precautions

A. No special precautions are necessary for dishes/trays unless they are visibly contaminated with blood or body fluids/substances.
   1. Disposable dishes contaminated with blood or body fluids/substances can be handled as disposable patient care equipment.
   2. Tray mats contaminated with blood or body fluids/substances should be removed from the tray and disposed of in regular trash by the nursing staff prior to return of trays to the Dietary Services Department.
   3. Reusable dishes, utensils, and trays contaminated with blood or body fluids/substances should be rinsed under running water to remove gross soilage before being returned to the Dietary Services Department.
   4. Families should be instructed to wash personal dishes, etc., in dishwasher or with soap and hot water.
   5. Food service personnel who handle dishes should wear gloves, and they should wash their hands before handling clean dishes or food.

B. No special precautions are indicated for drinking water. Water containers and water glasses for patients should be handled the same way dishes are (see above).

IV. Handling and Disposal of Soiled Dressings

All wound dressings are to be disposed of in such a manner as to "confine and contain" any blood or body fluids/substances that may be present.

A. Small dressings can be enclosed in the disposable glove used to remove the dressing. Pull the glove off inside out containing the dressing inside of it. This dressing and gloves can then be discarded into the regular trash container in the patient's room.

B. Larger dressings should be removed using gloved hands and placed into a bag. This bag can be used for the old dressing, gloves, and other trash from the dressing change procedure. This bag can then be deposited into the regular trash container in the patient's room.

V. Handling and Disposal of Urine and Feces

A. Urine and feces from all patients should be flushed down the toilet.

B. All reusable urinals or bedpans from a patient should be cleaned and disinfected or sterilized before being used by another patient.

C. Disposable urinals or bedpans can be placed into the regular trash.

D. Discontinued Foley bags or rectal tube collection containers should be emptied prior to disposal.

VI. Laboratory Specimens

A. Process *all* laboratory specimens as potentially infectious.

B. Laboratory specimens will be prepared for transport in the following manner.

1. Specimens should be put in a well-constructed container with a secure lid (preferably screw-top) to prevent leakage.
2. Care should be taken when collecting specimens to avoid contamination of the outside of the container and the laboratory form accompanying the specimen.
   a. If the outside of the container becomes contaminated, clean the container appropriately before sending to the laboratory.
   b. If the laboratory form becomes contaminated, discard it and fill out a new form. The laboratory will not accept soiled requisitions.
3. Specimens should be transported in a manner such that blood or body fluids/substances will not be accidentally spilled.
   a. Use a secondary leak-proof bag or container in order to protect against a possible spill.
   b. Tubes of blood can also be placed on a rack inside of a leak-proof container for transport.
   c. Keep laboratory requisitions separate from the specimens.
   d. Intralaboratory handling does not necessitate the secondary container as long as breakage and spillage can be avoided.

C. Laboratory request slips should not be labeled to identify patients with blood-borne diseases because all laboratory specimens will be processed with equal caution.

1. Using special precaution labels on specimen tubes, containers, and request slips encourages a false sense of security and potentially increases risk to health care workers who may handle unlabeled specimens less carefully than they should.
2. It is important to note relevant patient information on all requisitions, such as radiology, pathology, laboratory, etc.
3. Laboratory request slips from patients whose cultures are likely to yield *Coccidioides immitus* must be clearly marked to alert laboratory personnel to the potential hazard associated with the handling and processing of such specimens.

VII. Patient's Property

A. Patient's Clothing

Patient's clothing soiled with blood or body fluids/substances should be bagged before being sent home. The patient/family should wash the clothing with a detergent and, if possible, hot water and bleach.

B. Books, Magazines, and Toys

In general, any of these articles visibly soiled with blood or body fluids/substances should be disinfected or destroyed. A child should not share toys with other children.

Kaiser Permanente Medical Center
San Francisco, California

Miscellaneous Procedures for Hospital Infection Control

I. Visitors

A. Visitors should be instructed to follow Universal Precautions when handling blood or body fluids/substances. (See Guidelines for Infection Control Precautions [p. 51 of this manual].)

B. A Stop Sign Alert will be placed on the door of the patient's room to notify visitors and health care workers that the patient has a disease spread by the airborne route.

C. Nursing personnel should instruct each visitor on the appropriate use of a mask and/or exclude persons who are susceptible when indicated. (See Guidelines for Patients with an Airborne Disease Requiring Respiratory Precautions [pp. 61–65 of this manual] and Airborne Diseases for Which Exclusion of Susceptible Individuals May Be Indicated [p. 66 of this manual].)

II. Transporting Patients

A. Appropriate barriers (that is, masks, impervious dressings, etc.) should be used by the patient and transport personnel.

B. Patients with diseases transmitted by the airborne route should not be transported unnecessarily to other departments. (See Airborne Diseases for Which Exclusion of Susceptible Individuals May Be Indicated [p. 66 of this manual].)

1. If such patients are transported, the patient should wear a mask and the transporter should be immune to the disease, if possible.
2. The receiving department is notified in advance by nursing so that immune health care workers may be selected for performing the procedure, if possible.

C. Patients should be alerted to the potential spread of their disease and informed how they may assist in maintaining a barrier against transmission of their infection to others.

III. Room Cleaning

A. Although microorganisms may be present on environmental surfaces such as walls, floors, and other surfaces, these surfaces, unless visibly contaminated, are not associated with transmission of infections to patients or health care workers. Therefore, extraordinary attempts to disinfect or sterilize these environmental surfaces are not necessary. However, cleaning and removal of visible soil should be done routinely.

B. Disinfectant–detergent formulations registered by the EPA and approved by the Medical Center Infection Control Committee can be used for cleaning environmental surfaces, but the actual physical removal of microorganisms by scrubbing is probably at least as important as any antimicrobial effect of the cleaning agent used. The manufacturer's instructions for appropriate use should be followed.

C. Health care workers should wear appropriate protective apparel when they anticipate exposure to blood or body fluids/substances while cleaning rooms. Gloves may also protect hands from possible irritating effects of disinfectants.

D. The same routine daily cleaning procedures should be used to clean all medical center rooms. Cleaning schedules and methods vary according to the area of the medical center, the type of surface to be cleaned, and the amount and type of soilage present.

1. Horizontal surfaces, such as bedside furniture and hard-surfaced floors, sinks, bathroom fixtures, etc., in patient care areas should be cleaned on a regular basis and when soilings or spills occur.
2. Cleaning of walls, blinds, and/or curtains is recommended only when they are visibly soiled.
3. Disinfectant fogging is an unsatisfactory method of decontaminating surfaces; therefore, it is not recommended.

E. In addition to the routine daily cleaning procedures, the following procedures should be used to clean all medical center rooms of discharged patients.
1. All reusable equipment (drainage bottles, flowmeter jars, etc.) should be returned to CSR for decontamination and reprocessing (see procedure for handling reusable patient care equipment [p. 69 of this manual]).
2. All disposable items should be discarded (see procedure for discarding disposable patient care equipment [pp. 69–72 of this manual]).
3. All equipment that is not sent to CSR or discarded should be cleaned with a disinfectant–detergent solution.
4. All floors should be wet vacuumed or mopped with a disinfectant–detergent solution.
5. Airing a room from which a patient has been discharged is not effective or necessary.
6. The State Department of Health, the Centers for Disease Control, and the Infection Control Department should be consulted about cleaning the room of a patient who has or is suspected to have smallpox, Lassa fever, Ebola fever, or other hemorrhagic fevers such as Marburg virus disease.

IV. Cleaning and Decontaminating Spills of Blood or Other Body Fluids

A. Chemical germicides that are approved for use as "hospital disinfectants" and are tuberculocidal when used at recommended dilutions can be used to decontaminate spills of blood and other body fluids.

B. Strategies for decontaminating spills of blood and other body fluids in patient care settings are different than for spills of culture or other materials in the clinical laboratory.
1. In patient care areas, visible material should be first removed and then the area should be decontaminated with a chemical germicide.
2. With large spills of cultured or concentrated infectious agents in the laboratory, the contaminated area should be flooded with a liquid germicide before cleaning and then decontaminated with a fresh germicidal chemical.
3. In both settings, gloves should be worn during the cleaning and decontaminating procedures.

V. Postmortem Handling of Bodies

A. Health care workers should use the same precautions to protect themselves during postmortem handling of bodies that they would use if the patient were still alive.

B. Autopsy personnel who perform or assist in postmortem procedures should wear gloves, masks, protective eyewear, and gowns.

C. Instruments and surfaces contaminated during postmortem procedures should be decontaminated with an appropriate chemical germicide.

D. Morgue attendants and morticians should handle all bodies as potentially infectious.

VI. Eating or Drinking in Patient Rooms

Employees should not eat or drink in patient care areas. Such activities should be confined to designated areas such as the cafeteria or lounge area.

Harborview Medical Center
Seattle, Washington

Body Substance Isolation

Introduction

For many years, isolation has been viewed as the cornerstone to a program of infection prevention and control. This concept is an outgrowth of the earlier practice of placing patients with selected diagnosed diseases in quarantine. In hospital practice, it is more reliable to provide a high level of infection precautions for all patients, regardless of whether an infection has been diagnosed.

Why is this? First of all, a system like the isolation used in most hospitals is not initiated until the diagnosis of an infectious disease is suspected or proven. The causative agent is always present in the affected body site or substance before the diagnosis is established. Thus, transmission may often occur before isolation is begun.

Second, infectious diseases occur in a variety of forms, ranging from inapparent, unrecognized infection to moderate or severe illness. Inapparent infection may be clinically unrecognized and yet still be communicable. The higher incidence of serological markers for hepatitis B in health care workers with frequent blood contact illustrates this point.

Third, isolation focuses on special techniques for only those body substances identified as containing the infective agent. However, other substances are often handled without the awareness that they also may be colonized with the same microorganism. For instance, a patient with a wound infected with *Staphylococcus aureus* might also have the same organism in sputum or saliva.

Fourth, the majority of hospitalized patients with infection don't really require isolation based on CDC or other guidelines. Yet, these infected or colonized patients frequently serve as a source of spread to other patients or personnel. The distinction between isolated and nonisolated patients may give personnel a false sense of security with such patients and promote a lesser standard of care.

A consistent approach to managing body substances from all patients is essential to prevent transmission of infectious agents. The following strategy is recommended for use with all patients at all times to prevent transmission of hospital infections.

1. When direct contact with moist body substances (pus, sputum, urine, feces, blood, saliva, etc.) from any patient is anticipated, gloves are worn.
2. When soilage of clothing by these body substances is anticipated, a gown is worn.
3. When splattering of these body substances into the mouth, nose, or eyes is anticipated, masks and/or goggles or glasses are worn.
4. If unanticipated contact with these body substances occurs, washing is done as soon as possible (hand washing, face washing, etc., as appropriate).

Most infection control situations are addressed in these general guidelines. These techniques should be applied to all body substances from *all* patients, not only those of patients with diagnosed infections, since the presence of infectious organisms *always* precedes diagnosis. In general, contact with body substances from patients, infected or uninfected, should be avoided. Gloves should be worn for all contacts with body substances, and when the amount or location of the substance makes it difficult to keep clothing clean, personnel should wear gowns.

Harborview Medical Center
Seattle, Washington

Barrier Techniques to Reduce Infection Risk

Patient's Condition	Always Requires	Sometimes Requires
Sputum production: suctioning coughing patients pneumonia bronchitis	• Wash hands after contact • Glove for sputum contact • Contain sputum in tissues • Instruct patient in hand washing and care of sputum • Gown when soilage of clothing is likely	• Roommate restriction when either roommate has poor personal hygiene[a] • Mask if patient is likely to cough or spit in your face • Special TB precautions if this diagnosis is suspected
Lesion drainage: open skin ulcers pustular lesions boils wounds wound infections	• Wash hands after drainage contact • Glove for contact with drainage or open wound • Use "no-touch" dressing technique • Gown for activities where soilage of uniform is likely • Bag soiled linen, dressings • Instruct patient in hand washing • Cover draining wounds with dressings	• Roommate restriction when drainage is excessive or if patient or roommates have poor personal hygiene • Special precautions for selected patients with skin lesions that are manifestations of systemic infection, such as chickenpox or measles
Urine drainage: urine incontinence urinary fistula catheter drainage specimen handling fractionals specific gravity output measure	• Wash hands after urine contact • Glove for urine contact • Use individual urine measurement devices • Maintain sterile closed drainage system • Bag urine-soaked linen and trash • Instruct patient in care of urine and in hand washing	• If possible, do not assign roommates with urinary catheters
Fecal drainage: fecal incontinence ostomy drainage gallbladder drainage diarrhea due to any cause	• Wash hands after contact with feces • Glove for fecal contact • Gown when soilage of clothing is likely • Bag heavily soiled linen and trash • Instruct patient in care of feces and in hand washing	• Roommate restriction when fecal soilage is excessive or if either patient or roommate has poor personal hygiene
Blood: G.I. bleeding serosanguinous wound or lesion drainage hemoptysis post-TURP CPR	• Wash hands after contact with blood • Glove for blood contact • Gown when soilage of clothing is likely • Bag bloody linen or trash • Instruct patient in care of bloody discharge and in hand washing	• Roommate restriction when soilage is excessive or if patient or roommate has poor personal hygiene

Patient's Condition	Always Requires	Sometimes Requires
Other body substances: peritoneal fluid, vaginal discharge, joint fluid, CSF	• Wash hands after contact • Glove for body substance contact • Gown when soilage of clothing is likely • Bag soaked or heavily soiled linen or trash • Instruct patient in care of body substances and hand washing	• Roommate restriction when soilage is excessive or if patient or roommate has poor personal hygiene[a]
Diseases transmitted by airborne route: measles, mumps, chickenpox (varicella), disseminated zoster (shingles), rubella, tuberculosis, meningitis[b], diphtheria, pharyngeal or cutaneous, whooping cough (pertussis), plague	• Infection control notification • Private room (immune roommate sometimes acceptable) • Personnel who are immune to the disease always desirable • Hand washing after body substance contact • Glove for contact with body substance • Gown if soilage of clothing is likely • Instruct patient regarding spread of disease and hand washing	• Direct exhaust of air from room to outdoors • Use of ultraviolet light • Cohorting of patients with the same disease • Discharging patients
(Refer to pp. 83–84 [of this manual] for special instructions and comments about infectious diseases and duration of infectivity.)	(Masks to protect personnel from airborne agents have not proven effective in protecting susceptible personnel, but are recommended.)	

[a]Personal hygiene is considered good if the patient does not soil the environment with body substances, covers the mouth and nose when coughing, and washes hands after soiling them. In seriously ill patients, the management of body substances is performed by personnel; if body substances cannot be contained by the patient or personnel, consider the patient to have poor personal hygiene and restrict roommates when indicated.

[b]Until meningococcal meningitis is ruled out or treated for 24 hours.

Harborview Medical Center
Seattle, Washington

Roommate Selection for Infection Prevention

In an ideal world, every hospitalized patient would have a private room. However, in practice this does not always occur. These guidelines are provided as a model for determining safe roommate combinations that reduce the risk of transmission of organisms between patients and are most effective when practiced with recommended body substance barrier techniques. Personal hygiene, the ability to control body substances, is the most important element to consider in roommate assignments.

A patient may fit into more than one level. When placing a patient with a roommate, select the single highest level that describes the patient.

Level	Definition	Examples	Combinations
1	Patients making uneventful recovery from medical conditions, who have no open skin sites, catheters, or incontinence, and who do not fit into levels 2, 3, or 4	M.I., diabetes, G.I. bleed, hypertension, ulcer disease, back pain	YES–1, 2, 3 NO–4
2	Oncology patients, preoperative patients, and patients who are making uneventful recoveries from surgical procedures that entail no open drains, catheters, or mechanical respiratory assistance and who do not fit into levels 3 or 4[a]	Cholecystectomy, appendectomy, orthopedic surgery, hysterectomy, vaginal delivery, C-section, chemotherapy or radiation therapy, minor burns, leukemia, AIDS[b]	YES–1, 2 NO–3, 4
3	Patients likely to be sources of large numbers of microorganisms, either infected or colonized, and who do not fit into level 4	Fecal/urinary incontinence, open drains, major decubitus, extensive dermatitis, ventilator assistance	YES–1 NO–2, 3, 4
4	(A) Patients with communicable diseases spread through the airborne route *or* (B) Patients who consistently soil the environment with body substances	(A) Measles, mumps, chickenpox, rubella, tuberculosis, major burns, disseminated zoster, meningococcal meningitis *or* (B) containment of pus, blood, urine, feces, sputum unable to be accomplished by patient or personnel	(A) YES–4[c] (B) NO–1, 2, 3, 4

[a]Patients very susceptible to infections due to diminished immune responses such as post bone marrow transplant or severe leukopenia may benefit from a private room. "Protective Isolation," the use of gown, gloves, and masks, does not reduce the incidence of infection in compromised patients and is not recommended.

[b]Patients with AIDS usually have infections, but may also be more susceptible to exogenous infections.

[c]Patients with the same airborne communicable disease may room together. For example, a patient with chickenpox may room with any other patient who has a history of chickenpox, herpes zoster, or has active varicella infection.

Harborview Medical Center
Seattle, Washington

Susceptibility and Communicable Diseases

Certain diseases are transmitted either in part or entirely by the airborne route. Some of these are the usual childhood diseases such as measles, mumps, rubella, whooping cough, and chickenpox. The remainder are infectious diseases more often seen in adults that are known to be spread by contact but that may also have an airborne component. These include pharyngeal diphtheria, herpes zoster (shingles), and tuberculosis.

A person who is susceptible has little or no resistance to the disease and should avoid contact with body substances and sharing of enclosed air space with individuals known to have that disease. A nonsusceptible person is immune. Some people may lose their immune response through age or disease.

The following table is designed to assist you in determining an individual's susceptibility to specific airborne diseases.

You may be susceptible to:	If you have never had:
Chickenpox	Chickenpox Herpes zoster (shingles)
Diphtheria, pharyngeal	Diphtheria vaccination (DPT in childhood and boosters of DT every 10 years)
Measles (rubeola)	Measles Measles vaccination (MMR in childhood) Positive serology for measles
Mumps	Mumps Mumps vaccination (MMR in childhood) Positive serology for mumps
Pertussis (whooping cough)	Pertussis (whooping cough) Pertussis vaccination (DPT in childhood)
Rubella	Rubella Rubella vaccination (MMR in childhood/adult) Positive serology for rubella
Tuberculosis	Positive PPD Active tuberculosis

Harborview Medical Center
Seattle, Washington

Summary of Body Substance Isolation

Infection Precautions

Infection precautions place a barrier of plastic (gloves), fabric (gowns), or paper (masks) between potentially infectious body substances and the care giver. All humans have potentially infectious agents in pus, feces, and sputum. Many persons also have potentially infectious agents in blood, urine, and other body fluids. Precautions to prevent transmission of these potentially infectious agents should be practiced for all patients, not only those who have diagnosed infectious diseases. Body Substance Isolation is used at HMC instead of the usual card-category isolation. A brief description of the procedures follows.

Articles Used for Infection Precautions

Gloves
Gloves are worn for anticipated contact with any patient's blood, pus, feces, urine, or oral secretions. Gloves are not necessary for contact with unsoiled articles or intact skin. Put on clean gloves just before contact with mucous membranes or nonintact skin.

Gowns
Gowns are worn when it is likely that personal clothing will be soiled with any patient's blood, pus, feces, urine, or oral secretions. Gowns are not necessary for other contact.

Masks
Masks are worn for anticipated contact with respiratory droplet secretions, for example, a coughing patient who does not cover mouth or nose, suctioning patient, splatter into mouth or nose while cleaning or performing procedures. A coughing patient may need to be masked for transport outside the room.

Protective Eyewear
Protective eyewear may be useful in situations in which splatter with blood or other body substances such as sputum is anticipated.

Isolation Cards
Cards to remind staff of infection precautions are located in all patient rooms. In addition, Stop Sign cards are used to identify the rooms of patients with airborne communicable diseases.

Physician's Orders
Record diagnosis of suspected infections on the order sheet. It is unnecessary to write special orders, for example, wound isolation, etc.

Disposable Dishes
Not necessary.

Care of Articles from Patient Rooms

Laboratory Specimens
Laboratory specimens from all patients are handled with equal care. After specimens are taken to the laboratory, transporting personnel wash their hands. The outside of

specimen containers should be clean; visibly soiled containers may be rejected by the laboratory. See Biohazard Policy.

Reusable Articles

The purpose of bagging reusable soiled articles is to prevent leakage and to identify the contents as soiled so that Central Supply personnel will glove to handle them. Soiled instruments are placed in marked containers located in the dirty utility rooms.

Syringes, Needles, and Disposable Sharps

Syringes, needles, and other sharp objects are placed in a heavy plastic needle container. Used needles should not be broken off or recapped by hand before disposal. If it is necessary to recap, a recapping device or technique is used.

Harborview Medical Center
Seattle, Washington

Body Substance Isolation Guidelines for Physicians and Medical Students

Harborview Medical Center has instituted a system of infection prevention practices that is different from the isolation systems used in other hospitals. The reason for the change is that traditional isolation systems fail to identify the major reservoir for nosocomial organisms: the colonized body substances of persons who are not diagnosed as infected. The result is a two-tiered system that focuses too many precautions on diagnosed cases and not enough on undiagnosed cases. The Infection Control Committee wished to correct these deficiencies, reduce the colonizaton and infection rates, and also reduce costs associated with the infection prevention program. The system has been successful, but is dependent on cooperation from all personnel, including physicians and students. The following information is provided to make it simple and easy to cooperate with the infection prevention program at HMC.

Do	Don't
• Glove for contact with mucous membranes, nonintact skin, and moist body substances from all patients, all the time. • Wear a cover gown, mask, or eye protection as necessary for procedures in which you are likely to be splashed with moist body substances from any patient. • Wash your hands for at least 10 seconds before touching any patient. • When infectious or communicable diseases are suspected, particularly if immunity of personnel or patient roommates is a consideration, record the information on the order sheet as well as the progress note. • If a patient has poor personal hygiene and soils articles in the room or if the patient has a disease transmitted by the airborne route, the patient may need to be in a private room. Consult the nurses. A manual of information about Body Substance Isolation is available on each nursing unit and in each clinical department. • Report cases of reportable communicable diseases to the Seattle-King County Health Department or to the HMC Epidemiology Department.	• Order category isolation. Terms such as "Wound Isolation" are confusing to personnel and do not provide clear direction. Instead, identify the suspected infection and discuss the potential impact on care, remembering that the standard of care at HMC includes gloves for contact with mucous membranes, nonintact skin, and moist body substances for all patients, all the time. Gowning, trash and linen management, and wearing protective garb are also uniform for all patients. • If you are susceptible to an airborne communicable disease, e.g., chickenpox or rubella, do not have contact with known cases. Wearing a mask is not an effective prevention strategy. If you have an exposure, contact the Employee Health Service for instructions before the end of the incubation period.

Harborview Medical Center
Seattle, Washington

Precautions for Patients with Diseases Transmitted by the Airborne Route (Stop Sign Isolation)

Whenever patients are believed to have diseases transmitted in whole or in part by the airborne route, they should be placed in "Stop Sign Isolation." A Stop Sign Alert card is placed on the patient's door, the patient is placed in a private room or with an immune roommate, and all personnel or visitors must check with the nurse before entering. The nurses are responsible for determining the immune status of persons wishing to enter the room when patients have certain diseases on the following list, for example, chickenpox. If persons wishing to enter the room have not had the disease or immunization for it, they should not enter, with or without a mask. The nurses are also responsible for instructing persons to wear masks when necessary, for example, for tuberculosis patients.

The following diseases are transmitted in whole or in part by the airborne route. Patients with these diseases need to be assigned to private rooms and have a Stop Sign Alert posted on the door. The door should remain closed.

For diseases marked with an asterisk (*), all care providers who are not immune to these diseases should not enter the room of these patients.

Disease	Apply Airborne Precautions for How Long	Comments
Anthrax, inhalation	Duration of illness	Report promptly to Health Department. Call the Epidemiology Department.
*Chickenpox (Varicella)	Until all lesions are crusted	Persons who are not susceptible do not need to wear a mask. Exposed susceptible patients should be isolated beginning 10 days after exposure until 21 days after last exposure.
Diphtheria, pharyngeal	Until two cultures from both nose and throat taken at least 24 hours after cessation of antimicrobial therapy are negative for *Corynebacterium diphtheriae*	Report promptly to Health Department. Call the Epidemiology Department.
Hemorrhagic fevers	Duration of illness	Call the Epidemiology Department immediately. Physicians can call the State Health Department and the Centers for Disease Control for advice about management of a suspected case.
*Herpes zoster/varicella localized in immunocompromised patient or disseminated	Duration of illness	Localized lesions in immunocompromised patients frequently become disseminated. Because such dissemination is unpredictable, use the same precautions as for disseminated disease.

(Table continues.)

Disease	Apply Airborne Precautions for How Long	Comments
Lassa fever Marburg virus disease	Duration of illness	Call the Epidemiology Department immediately. Physicians can call the State Health Department and the Centers for Disease Control for advice about the management of a suspected case.
*Measles (rubeola)	For 4 days after start of rash, except in immunocompromised patients, with whom precautions should be maintained for duration of illness	Persons who are not susceptible do not need to wear a mask. Report promptly to Health Department. Call Epidemiology Department.
Neisseria meningitidis (meningococcal), known or suspected	For 24 hours after start of effective antibiotic therapy	Report promptly to Health Department.
Meningococcal pneumonia	For 24 hours after start of effective antibiotic therapy	Report promptly to Health Department
*Mumps (infectious parotitis)	For 9 days after onset of swelling	Persons who are not susceptible do not need to wear a mask. Call Epidemiology Department.
Pertussis (whooping cough)	For 7 days after start of effective therapy	Persons who are not susceptible do not need to wear a mask. Call Epidemiology Department.
Plague, pneumonic	For 3 days after start of effective therapy	Report promptly to Health Department. Call Epidemiology Department.
Rubella (German measles)	For 7 days after rash appears	Persons who are not susceptible do not need to wear a mask. Call Epidemiology Department.
Tuberculosis, pulmonary, confirmed or suspected	In most instances, duration can be guided by clinical response and a reduction in numbers of TB organisms on sputum smear. Usually this occurs within 2 to 3 weeks after therapy is begun. When the patient is likely to be infected with INH-resistant organisms, apply precautions until patient is improving and sputum smear is negative for TB organisms.	

Harborview Medical Center
Seattle, Washington

Management of Contaminated Needles and Sharps

Purpose
To provide a safe and efficient means for handling and disposal of needles, syringes, and sharp objects.

Policy
Needles and sharp objects are to be cautiously handled to minimize risk of inadvertent puncture or other such injuries. Recapping of needles is to be avoided whenever possible. Needles and other sharp objects such as trochars, glass, scalpels, etc., must not be bent, broken, or otherwise manipulated by hand and are to be disposed of into puncture-resistant containers.

Inclusion
Staff, faculty, and students who handle needles and sharp objects.

Implementation
1. All sharp objects are kept separated from general waste by placing them in puncture-resistant containers that are clearly labeled for such disposal.
2. Disposal containers are located at the point of use whenever feasible and safe. Disposal containers are to be sealed and discarded when they have been filled to the designated fill line on the container (usually about two-thirds full).
3. All used sharps are considered contaminated. Contamination occurs as a result of contact with blood or other body fluids, chemicals, drugs, etc.
4. Do not recap contaminated needles unless recapping is unavoidable such as:
   (a) When giving serial injections of a solution for the same patient over a short period of time.
   (b) When disposal container is not available due to the unpredictable nature of the patient population (for example, psychiatric unit patient rooms).
   (c) When removal of a contaminated needle is essential in order to replace it with a new sterile needle or cap, for example, collecting anaerobic specimen or blood gases.
   (d) When repeated trips to the sharps container are impractical (for example, during sterile procedures, managing a critical care patient).
5. Acceptable methods of recapping include:
   (a) Use of a device that holds the cap vertically while the needle is inserted. (See Recapping Guidelines [p. 86 of this manual].)
6. Evaluate products and techniques for the feasibility of eliminating or minimizing the use of needles in procedures.

Harborview Medical Center Seattle, Washington

Recapping Guidelines

Situation	Recommended Solution
1. Serial injections from the same syringe	1. Use a recapping device*
2. Puncture-resistant sharps container not available; transport of unsheathed needle dangerous to nurse/patient	2. Use a recapping device*
3. Removal of contaminated needle without sheath	3. Remove needle with forceps or 3. Deposit syringe with needle attached into sharps container
4. Aerobic/anaerobic culture collection/ transport (blood, pleural fluid, etc.)	4. Remove needle with recapping device* or forceps if necessary; affix syringe cap** (Luer-tip cap) for transport
5. Blood gas collection/transport	5. Remove needle with recapping device* or forceps if necessary; affix syringe cap** for transport

Product	Source	Order Number
*Recapping device	Medical Stores	23360 (each) Concord®
**Syringe cap (Luer-tip cap)	Medical Stores	23370 (10 each)

Harborview Medical Center
Seattle, Washington

Biohazard Labeling for Clinical Laboratory Specimens

Policy Statement
All patient specimens may potentially contain infectious agents and are handled consistently to prevent contact with the specimens by personnel. Since all specimens at HMC are handled as potentially infectious, special tags or labels to denote infectivity for specimens processed within HMC are not used.

Implementation
1. Gloves are worn during collection and processing of specimens when body substances are likely to contaminate hands of personnel.
2. Gloves are worn by personnel transporting specimens.
3. Labels are not used for specimens processed within HMC laboratories.

Chapter 3

Medical Waste Management

Introduction

The CDC has emphasized that Universal Precautions were not intended to change waste management programs in health care facilities. However, the medical waste that washed ashore on East Coast beaches in the late 1980s drew the nation's attention to medical waste management practices. This attention prompted the swift passage of local, state, and federal legislation on medical waste management, which made it difficult for health care facilities attempting to develop waste management policies and procedures consistent with current legal requirements. This chapter discusses issues related to medical waste management and contains sample materials that may be useful in developing institutional programs.

In 1990, approximately 44 states regulated the handling of medical waste to some degree. At the time of this publication, there are inconsistencies among the regulations of different states and between state and local regulations. In addition, a two-year demonstration project, mandated by the Medical Waste Tracking Act of 1988, requires the Environmental Protection Agency (EPA) to establish a two-year demonstration project. This demonstration project includes requirements for the packaging, labeling, and tracking of medical waste from its generator to its final disposition. Participation in this demonstration project is mandatory for New York, New Jersey, and Connecticut, and a few additional states voluntarily agreed to participate. The seven Great Lakes states were given the opportunity to participate; however, all have opted out. The greatest concern is that Congress will preempt the demonstration project by enacting a mandatory national waste tracking law before the demonstration project has yielded its final results.

For those states that are not participating in the demonstration project, there are no federal requirements for medical waste management at this time. However, OSHA has proposed some standards for defining, labeling, and packaging medical waste, and health care facilities have urged OSHA to develop regulations that are consistent with the regulations being developed by other federal agencies.

One of the most controversial aspects of discussions of medical waste management is the definition of just what infectious waste is. *Infectious waste* can be defined as waste capable of producing an infectious disease. This definition requires that factors in the chain of infection necessary for disease transmission are considered. The factors include dose, presence of pathogen, portal of entry, and a susceptible host. Therefore, to be considered infectious, waste must contain pathogens with sufficient virulence and quantity that exposure to waste by a susceptible host could result in an infectious disease.

In the absence of an objective test to define infectious waste, subjective and overly inclusive definitions have been adopted at the federal, state, and local levels. The implications of such broad definitions are significant. First, the options for on-site waste treatment are diminishing due to restrictions on incineration and bans on accepting even treated medical waste at some landfills. Second, medical waste management programs have become unnecessarily expensive with no added health or environmental benefits. As the CDC has consistently stated:

> There is no epidemiologic evidence to suggest that most hospital waste is any more infectious than residential waste. Moreover, there is no epidemiologic evidence to suggest that hospital waste disposal practices have caused disease in the community; therefore, identifying waste for which special precautions are indicated is largely a matter of judgment about the relative risk of disease transmission. Hospital waste for which special precautions appear prudent includes microbiology laboratory waste, blood and blood products, pathology waste, and sharp items (especially needles).[1]

The CDC has also emphasized this point in their Universal Precautions guidelines:

> While any item that has had contact with blood, exudate or secretions may be considered potentially infective, it is not usually considered practical or necessary to treat all such waste as infective.[2]

Defining a facility's medical waste may be the most challenging aspect of policy development. There are three possible different sets of federal definitions for medical waste, that is, the CDC's, the EPA's according to the Medical Waste Tracking Act, and OSHA's proposed standard on bloodborne pathogens, as well as various state and local definitions.

Prior to developing a medical waste management program, a thorough review of applicable local, state, and federal regulations is necessary. In addition to the CDC's guidelines for medical waste management (published in 1985, 1987, and 1988), the EPA has also published a *Guide for Infectious Waste Management.*[3-5] Those facilities in states participating in the two-year demonstration project as part of the Medical Waste Tracking Act must be in compliance with the specific requirements of the act. Many infection control practitioners have been influential in working with elected officials and governmental agencies at the local and state levels to modify outdated regulations and make them consistent with current knowledge, practice, and the intent of Universal Precautions. Further information is available in the literature on the subject.[6-10]

The sample policies and procedures in this chapter are from facilities in several states and reflect differences in definitions as well as influences from federal, state, and local regulations. A biomedical waste policy is included from a facility in one of the states participating in the Medical Waste Tracking Project: Yale-New Haven Hospital, New Haven, Connecticut. Also included is a policy from Harper Hospital in Detroit, Michigan, which is based on the State of Michigan's Emergency Rules for Infectious Medical Waste. Three medical waste policies are included from facilities in California—Kaiser Permanente Medical Center in San Francisco, the University of California Medical Center in San Diego, and San Francisco General Hospital. A policy on in-room needle disposal maintenance from Lutheran General Hospital-Lincoln Park in Chicago is also included.

☐ References

1. Centers for Disease Control. *Guideline for Handwashing and Environmental Control—Infective Waste.* Atlanta: CDC, 1985, p. 15.
2. CDC, p. 15.
3. Environmental Protection Agency. *Guide for Infectious Waste Management.* Washington, DC: EPA, 1986.

4. Centers for Disease Control. Recommendations for prevention of HIV transmission in health care settings. *Morbidity and Mortality Weekly Report* 36(25, Suppl.):1S–16S, Aug. 21, 1987.
5. Centers for Disease Control. Update: Universal Precautions for prevention of transmission of human immunodeficiency virus, hepatitis B virus, and other bloodborne pathogens in health care settings. *Morbidity and Mortality Weekly Report* 37:377–88, June 24, 1988.
6. American Medical Association. Council on Scientific Affairs: council report—infectious medical wastes. *Journal of the American Medical Association* 262(12):1669–71, 1989.
7. Environmental Protection Agency. Standards for the tracking and management of medical waste: 40 CFR Parts 22 and 259. *Federal Register* 54(56):12326–95, Mar. 24, 1989.
8. Hedrick, E. R. Editorial: infectious waste management—will science prevail? *Infection Control and Hospital Epidemiology* 9:488–90, 1988.
9. Medical Waste Policy Committee. Report, June 1989. Albany, NY: Nelson A. Rockefeller Institute of Government.
10. Rutala, W. A., Odette, R. L., and Samsa, G. P. Management of infectious waste by US hospitals. *Journal of the American Medical Association* 262:1635–40, 1989.

Yale-New Haven Hospital
New Haven, Connecticut

Summary of Information Given in the Biomedical Waste Segregation Procedures Memo

New federal regulations require that certain waste materials be segregated from the general/routine trash. These "regulated" waste items are disposed of using one of the following methods:

1. In designated "regulated waste" receptacles containing biohazard-labeled red polyliners,
2. In Eagleguard® sharps containers, and
3. In the sanitary sewer system (hopper or toilet)

Regulated waste includes the following types of items:

1. Sharp implements, such as needles, blades, safety pins, disposable scissors, Vacutainers®, small glass slides, and slip covers—Sharps are discarded directly into the Eagleguard® container system.
2. Containers contaminated with blood or bloody drainage.
   a. Sealed collection units, such as Pleur-evacs®, should not be emptied, but will be placed in a biohazard-labeled red polyliner, sealed, and deposited into a regulated waste receptacle.
   b. Open containers, such as bedpans, collection bottles, and specimen cups, should be emptied by pouring the accumulated liquids into the sanitary sewer system. If blood or bloody drainage is still visible, the container should be deposited into a regulated waste receptacle. If no blood is visible, the container may be discarded into the general/routine waste.
3. Any items that are saturated with blood or bloody drainage, such as dressing materials, sponges, Chux®, gloves, masks, diapers, OB pads, or padding—An item is considered saturated if it may contain more than 20 milliliters of fluid. Materials that have been contaminated with blood or bloody drainage in small amounts (not saturated) may be disposed of by using the general/routine wastebaskets.
4. All types of contaminated and uncontaminated tubing and tubing supplies, such as that used for intravenous and arterial lines, irrigations, suction, respiratory tubing, urinary and other catheters, airways, cannulas, stopcocks, or transducers—All tubing is discarded in regulated waste receptacles regardless of whether the item is new or used.
5. All intravenous fluid containers and glass vials—All remaining liquid from I.V. fluid bags or bottles should be discarded into the sanitary sewer system, and the containers should be deposited into the regulated trash receptacle.
6. Waste generated from the rooms of patients who are diagnosed with an infection specifically listed in the list of Infectious Diseases Classified as Biosafety 4 Level by the Centers for Disease Control [p. 94 of this manual]—All waste items that are used in the care of these patients are disposed of as regulated waste using the appropriate procedure; that is, for sharps, use the Eagleguard® container; for liquids, use the sanitary sewer system; and for other disposable items, use the designated regulated waste receptacle. Rooms of patients with these diagnoses should not have general/routine wastebaskets in them. Upon the discharge of these patients, the Eagleguard® sharps container will be replaced.
7. Waste generated as a result of dialysis treatments—All waste items that are used in the care of dialysis patients are disposed of as regulated waste by using the appropriate procedure; that is, for sharps, use the Eagleguard® container; for liquids, use the sanitary sewer system; and for other disposable items, use the designated regulated waste receptacle.

8. All waste generated from chemotherapy treatment, including items associated with medication administration, and the blood or body fluids of chemotherapy patients—Employ the appropriate procedure when removing the waste of chemotherapy patients; that is, for sharps, use the Eagleguard® container; for liquids, use the sanitary sewer system; and for other disposable items, use the designated regulated waste receptacle.

General/routine waste is disposed of in unmarked trash receptacles lined with a clear, brown, or buff polyliner. General/routine waste includes a variety of items, such as:

1. Patient care materials contaminated with small amounts of blood or bloody drainage, but not saturated—These items may be contained by pulling a glove over the object to enclose the waste before disposal into a general/routine trash receptacle.
2. General fluid containers, such as paper cartons, and metal or plastic containers—Empty all liquids into the sanitary sewer system before disposing of the container into the general/routine waste.
3. Other routine/general waste items, such as paper, packaging, foodstuffs, and items that are considered to be normal household waste.

Yale-New Haven Hospital
New Haven, Connecticut

Infectious Diseases Classified as Biosafety Level 4 by the Centers for Disease Control

1. All waste items that were used in the care of patients with infections caused by organisms classified as Biosafety Level 4 by the CDC will be considered regulated waste.
2. Infectious diseases classified as Biosafety Level 4 by the CDC include the following:

   Congo-Crimean hemorrhagic fever
   Ebola
   Hyper
   Junin
   Kumlinge
   Kyasanur Forest disease
   Lassa fever
   Marburg
   Machupo
   Omsk hemorrhagic fever
   Russian spring-summer encephalitis
   Tick-borne encephalitis virus complex

Note: Recognition of these diseases requires immediate notification of the hospital Epidemiology Office and the Connecticut Department of Public Health by the patient's physician.

Harper Hospital
Detroit, Michigan

Guidelines for Infectious Medical Waste Management

Introduction

These guidelines focus on infectious medical waste only. Management of waste considered hazardous primarily because of its toxicity, corrosiveness, ignitability, or radioactivity is described in the general Guidelines for Waste Management, is reviewed by the Safety Committee, and is documented in other manuals.

Some infectious medical waste has a hazardous component that must be considered in disposal, for example, contaminated needles. The U.S. Environmental Protection Agency (EPA) defines infectious waste as that waste which, in all probability, contains pathogenic agents that because of their type, concentration, and quantity may cause disease in persons exposed to the waste. Regulations governing management of infectious medical waste as defined by the Michigan legislature were enacted April 1989 by Governor Blanchard, and the following guidelines for infectious medical waste are effective June 10, 1989.

These guidelines stand as a policy statement of infectious waste disposal for Harper-Grace Hospitals and will be reviewed annually. Each department will apply the policy to its area and develop appropriate procedures.

Definitions and Classification of Infectious Medical Waste

1. Cultures and stocks of infectious agents and associated biologicals, including laboratory waste, biological production wastes, discarded live and attenuated vaccines, culture dishes and related devices.
2. Pathological waste: human tissues, organs, products of conception, body parts other than teeth, and body fluids removed by trauma or in surgery, autopsy, or other medical procedure and not fixed in formaldehyde.
3. Liquid human and animal waste, including blood and blood products and body fluids, but not including urine or materials stained with blood or body fluids.
4. Sharps: needles, syringes, scalpels, intravenous tubing with needles attached, and any other medical or laboratory instruments or glassware that might cause punctures or cuts.
5. Contaminated wastes from animals that have been exposed to agents infectious to humans, these being primarily research animals.

Infectious Waste Management

1. Harper Hospital shall package, contain, and locate infectious medical waste in a manner that prevents and protects the waste from release at the facility or at any time before ultimate disposal.
2. Harper Hospital shall separate the categories of waste at the point of origin into appropriate, properly labeled containers.
3. Harper Hospital shall clearly label containers used to collect, transport, or store infectious medical waste with a biohazard symbol or with the words "infectious medical waste" or "pathological waste" written in letters 1 inch high.
4. Harper Hospital shall not compact or mix infectious medical waste with other waste materials before decontamination or incineration and disposal. Decontaminated waste that is mixed with other solid waste that is not infectious waste shall be clearly labeled on the container used for transport, or Harper shall otherwise notify the handlers of the waste that decontaminated infectious medical waste is included.

5. Infectious medical waste is stored in such a manner that putrefaction will not occur and infectious agents will not come in contact with the air or individuals.
6. If Harper stores infectious medical waste outside, it shall be stored in a secure area or locked in rigid containers weighing more than 500 pounds and prevent access to container by vermin or unauthorized individuals.

Methods for Decontamination or Disposal

1. Cultures and stocks of infectious material shall be stored in closed, puncture-proof containers, decontaminated by autoclaving, and disposed of in approved sanitary landfill.
2. Human blood and blood products and body fluids shall be flushed down a sanitary sewer or autoclaved before incineration.
3. Pathological waste shall be disposed of by grinding and flushing down a sanitary sewer system. Small amounts are autoclaved or incinerated.
4. Sharps shall be disposed of by placement in rigid, puncture-proof containers that are appropriately labeled and transported to a sanitary landfill or incinerator in a manner that retains the integrity of the container.

Management of Infectious Medical Waste

Harper Hospital's primary infectious medical waste that requires packaging, handling, and transportation is Category 4, Sharps.

1. Sharps and containers: Needles and syringes shall be placed into rigid, puncture-proof disposable containers without cutting, bending, or recapping. Needles and syringes shall be discarded as a unit without recapping whenever possible. The rigid liners shall remain labeled and tightly sealed before safe transport by Environmental Services to the designated dock area.
2. Protective clothing and impervious gloves must be worn when handling, packaging, and transporting infectious medical waste. Environmental Services has protocols governing the use of protective clothing and personnel training for collection, internal transport to the dock, and appropriate loading of disposal units for external transport to approved sanitary landfill.
3. Collection: Filled sharps containers from all areas will be placed in designated areas of soiled utility rooms, separate from other waste for pickup by Environmental Services.
4. Loading: Environmental Services has protocols governing the transfer of separately collected sharps containers to the vehicle used for transport to incinerator. Facility Services provides training to the staff in the use of protective barriers during transport of containers to Hutzel Hospital for incineration.

Harper Hospital
Detroit, Michigan

Medical Waste Emergency Rules [State of Michigan]

Generators	Categories of Infectious Medical Waste	Suggested Methods of Infectious Medical Waste Management
• Ambulance operations • Advanced mobile emergency care services • Limited advanced mobile emergency care services • Laboratories (research, analytical, or clinical) • County medical care facility • Freestanding surgical OP clinics • Health maintenance organizations • Homes for the aged • Hospitals • Nursing homes • Hospices • Physicians • Dentists • Veterinary clinics • Podiatrists	• Cultures and stocks of infectious agents and associated biologicals, including laboratory waste, biological production wastes, discarded live and attenuated vaccines, culture dishes, and related devices	• Store in closed, labeled, puncture-proof containers, decontaminated by autoclaving or incineration
	• Liquid human and animal waste, including blood and blood products and body fluids, but not including urine or materials stained with blood or body fluids	• Flushing down sanitary sewer • Decontamination by autoclaving or incineration • Solidifying • Sanitary landfill
	• Pathological waste—human tissue, organs, products of conception, body parts other than teeth, and body fluids removed by trauma or in surgery, autopsy, or other medical procedure and not fixed in formaldehyde	• Incineration or cremation • Grinding and flushing into a sanitary sewer • Burial in a cemetery (must be transported in leak-proof containers) • Grinding to render unrecognizable, stored in closed, puncture-proof containers and disposed of in a sanitary landfill
	• Sharps—needles, syringes, scalpels, intravenous tubing with needles attached, and any other medical or laboratory instruments or glassware that might cause punctures or cuts, excluding needles used by an individual in his home as prescribed by his physician	• Stored at the facility in rigid, puncture-proof containers, labeled and disposed of in a sanitary landfill • Incineration or decontamination and grinding that renders the objects unrecognizable and placed in sealed, rupture-proof containers and disposed of in a sanitary landfill • Other process approved by the department
	• Contained wastes from animals that have been exposed to agents infectious to humans, these being primarily research animals	• Incineration or burial in sanitary landfill or burial in sanitary landfill in labeled, double containers that are leak-proof and puncture resistant and sealed to prevent escape of fluids or materials. Contaminated animal organs disposed of separately shall be rendered unrecognizable.

Adapted from Bureau of Health Facilities Administration, State of Michigan.

Kaiser Permanente Medical Center
San Francisco, California

Guidelines for Identification and Disposal of Medical Center Waste

I. Introduction

"There is no epidemiologic evidence to suggest that most hospital waste is any more infective than residential waste. Moreover, there is no epidemiologic evidence that hospital waste has caused disease in the community as a result of improper disposal. Therefore, identifying wastes for which special precautions are indicated is largely a matter of judgment about the relative risk of disease transmission. The most practical approach to the management of infective waste is to identify those wastes with the potential for causing infection during handling and disposal and for which some special precautions appear prudent. Hospital wastes for which special precautions appear prudent include microbiology laboratory waste, pathology waste, and blood specimens or blood products. While any item that has had contact with blood, exudates, or secretions may be potentially infective, it is not usually considered practical or necessary to treat all such waste as infective" (Centers for Disease Control, *Morbidity and Mortality Weekly Report* 36(2S):12S, August 21, 1987).

II. Infectious Waste

A. The following materials are classified as infectious waste:
   1. Microbiology laboratory waste, including cultures of etiologic agents, which significantly contribute to the cause of increased morbidity or mortality of humans
   2. Pathological specimens
   3. Surgical specimens
   4. Human dialysis waste
   5. Any large volume of blood or body fluids/substances
   6. Needles and sharps

B. Methods of disposal for infectious waste (other than needles and sharps):
   1. Infectious waste should be confined and contained in two red, 2-millimeter impervious bags that are clearly labeled as "infectious waste" or marked with the biohazard symbol. An additional bag may be used if there is visible outside contamination.
   2. The bags should be secured for disposal when no more than three-fourths full.
   3. Heavy utility gloves should be worn when handling waste bags.
   4. Infectious waste bags should be transported in a sturdy container and placed in a secured holding area for final processing.
   5. Bags should be held away from the body during transport to prevent inadvertent injury from sharp objects that may protrude through the bags.
   6. Collecting devices that contain large volumes of blood or drainage that can be emptied, such as suction canisters, etc., should be emptied down the sanitary sewer. The emptied canisters may be discarded in the regular trash. Appropriate precautions should be taken to guard against spillage.
   7. Collecting devices that contain large volumes of blood or body fluids/substances that cannot be emptied should be sealed to prevent leakage of body fluids, placed into two red bags, and disposed of as infectious waste.
   8. Urine, stool, or dialysate should also be flushed down the sanitary sewer. Appropriate precautions should be taken to guard against spillage.
   9. Health care workers who anticipate spraying or splashing of blood or body fluids/substances while emptying containers should wear protective apparel.

C. Method of disposal for needles and sharps
   1. Needles/syringes and other sharp objects should be placed intact (unclipped) into the opening of a rigid, puncture-resistant container.
   2. When the disposal container is three-fourths full, the opening of the container should be permanently secured.
   3. Environmental Services will remove and replace the puncture-resistant containers.

III. Noninfectious Waste

A. Noninfectious waste includes any trash that does not fit into the infectious waste category. Trash and soiled articles from the general medical center environment, including patient room waste, do not require handling as "infectious." Only materials containing large volumes of blood or body fluids/substances may require special precautions.

B. Method of disposal for noninfectious waste
   1. Noninfectious waste will be handled the same for all patients.
   2. Noninfectious waste should be confined and contained in an impervious bag.
   3. A second bag may be used over the first if there is visible outside contamination on the bag.
   4. All wound dressings are to be disposed of in a manner so as to "confine and contain" any blood or body fluids/substances that may be present.
      a. Small dressings can be enclosed in the disposable glove used to remove the dressing. Pull the glove off inside out to contain the dressing inside of it. This dressing and the gloves can then be discarded into the regular trash container in the patient's room.
      b. Larger dressings should be removed using gloved hands and placed into a bag. This bag can be used for the old dressing, gloves, and other trash from the dressing change procedure. This bag can then be deposited into the regular trash container in the patient's room.
   5. Large volumes of blood or drainage from suction canisters or collecting devices that can be emptied should be flushed down the sanitary sewer with appropriate precautions to guard against spillage. Emptied canisters are discarded in the regular trash.
   6. Large volumes of urine, stool, or dialysate should be flushed down the sanitary sewer with appropriate precautions to guard against spillage.
   7. Noninfectious waste bags should be secured for disposal when three-fourths full and then transported in a sturdy container to the waste storage and processing area.
   8. Health care workers should wear heavy utility gloves when handling waste bags.
   9. Only the visible tops of the bag should be touched when handling trash. The bag should be held away from the body during transport to prevent inadvertent injury from sharp objects protruding through the bags.

Lutheran General Hospital-Lincoln Park
Chicago, Illinois

In-Room Needle Disposal Maintenance

I. Policy

This policy outlines the procedures for emptying and refilling needle-disposal containers located in patient rooms.

II. Definitions

The in-room needle disposal system consists of disposal units strategically mounted in all patient rooms. This will facilitate needle disposal as close to the point of use as possible.

The in-room disposal system contains the following components:

A. A locking wire bracket or locking plastic cabinet to house the liner
B. A liner made of puncture-resistant plastic, available in three sizes
C. A plastic table stand for use in areas where wall mounting cannot be done

III. Procedure

A. The Maintenance Department will be responsible for mounting the appropriate wall mount in the designated areas.
B. The unit managers and Infection Control will designate the location of the disposal unit. The location will be standardized throughout the units, when possible.
C. Central Service will stock the disposal liners. A supply of three clean liners will be maintained on the clean utility cart for each area with the in-room system. If additional liners are needed, it is the responsibility of the unit to call Central Service and request the necessary item.
D. The Nursing staff is responsible for closing off full containers. (See the Procedure for Sealing and Changing Full Liners [p. 101 of this manual].)
E. During the day shift (7 a.m to 3 p.m.), Nursing is to notify the housekeeper assigned to that unit to remove and replace the full, sealed needle disposal container.

   Between 3 p.m. and 7 a.m., the Nursing staff is responsible for sealing, removing, and replacing the disposal lining.
F. New liners are to be placed in the wall mount immediately. They are found on the clean utility cart.
G. Full, sealed liners are to be placed in the soiled utility room awaiting disposal. They will be taken to the incinerator daily, around 3 p.m., by Housekeeping personnel.
H. Keys for wall mount units will be located with:
   1. Unit managers
   2. Housekeeping supervisors
   3. Unit key ring
   4. Housekeeping unit key ring
   5. Infection Control
   6. Patient care coordinator
I. All wall brackets and wall mounts will remain locked at all times.
J. No units are to be used without a liner in place. *No exceptions.*
K. Any needlesticks or puncture wounds sustained are to be reported and followed up according to set policy.

Lutheran General Hospital-Lincoln Park
Chicago, Illinois

Procedure for Sealing and Changing Full Liners

I. The following steps are to be taken when closing off a full needle disposal container.
   A. Identification of a full container
      The container/liner is full when the door meets resistance when someone tries to open it. The door operates like a swinging door on a mailbox. When any resistance is met, the liner should be changed.
   B. Sealing a full container/liner
      In order to secure the opening of the disposal container, simply press the lid *in toward the box and down* until you hear it snap past three sets of "teeth." Since this is a horizontal drop system, when the container is closed off at the proper time, the level of contaminants will be far below the level of the opening, posing no risk of puncture through the lid.
   C. The liner can now be removed safely and the unit relined or replaced.

II. Make sure you have the following available when emptying and refilling one of these units.
   A. A key is necessary to unlock the wall mount or wall bracket for removal.
   B. Replacement liners are found in the clean utility room.

III. Never leave a unit unlocked or unlined.

University of California Medical Center
San Diego, California

Waste Management Plan

All infectious waste (as defined by the state of California Health and Safety Code), except certain recognizable anatomical remains and/or pathological specimens, will be disposed of by the Environmental Services Department under the supervision of the Executive Housekeeper. Certain recognizable anatomical remains and/or pathological specimens will be disposed of by incineration in the medical center's incinerator located behind the Plant Services Department at UCSD Medical Center.

Procedure

1. As a minimum, all infectious waste will be collected within the area of origin in red plastic bags of at least 165-gram-dart-impact-resistant strength. Bagging is to be done in a manner that will reduce the hazard of injury or risk of transmission of potentially infectious agents.
2. All used needles and syringes are considered infectious waste and will be disposed of at the point of origin in an appropriate sharps collection container. These filled containers will be collected by Environmental Services personnel from designated holding locations in each area.
3. The Environmental Services personnel who have collected the infectious waste will then transport it to the basement and place it in the infectious waste bin for daily pickup by the contract service.
4. In the basement, the bags of infectious waste will be placed into a leak-proof, rodent-proof storage container with a tight-fitting lid provided and maintained by the contract waste hauler. The storage container will be identified with a numerical code designating the generating institution and labeled with the words "infectious waste" or the international biohazard symbol and the word "biohazard."
5. The storage containers will be maintained at UCSD Medical Center in a secured bin to prohibit access by unauthorized personnel. This area will display prominent warning signs in English: "Caution–Infectious Waste Storage Area–Unauthorized Persons Keep Out," and in Spanish, "Cuidado–Zona de Residuos–Prohibida la Entrada A Personas No Authorizadas." This area will be well ventilated and kept clean at all times.
6. The storage containers will be picked up by the contract waste hauler, intact as units, daily, except on Sundays.
7. The volume of infectious waste transported and incinerated or autoclaved is estimated at 7,300 pounds per week.
8. Each newly hired Environmental Services employee will receive an orientation to the procedure for the in-house collection, transportation, and storage of infectious waste at the medical center prior to his/her first day on the job. Continual on-the-job training will be provided by the individual in charge of this area.
9. The local Director of Health will be promptly notified if this Individual Plan for Off-Site Infectious Waste Disposal is either discontinued or altered.

☐ Reference

HU-531.2B: Hazardous Waste Management Policy and Procedure.

University of California Medical Center
San Diego, California

Guidelines for Disposal of Waste

Type of Waste	Red Bag	Regular Bag	Sharps Container
Blood, blood elements, vials of blood, specimens for microbiologic culture, used culture plates, and used culture tubes	X		
Containers of CSF, synovial, pleural, peritoneal, pericardial and amniotic fluid	X		
Fluid-filled containers from patients on nursing units, ER, RR, OPC (for example, Pleur-evacs®, Hemovacs®, suction canisters)*	X		
Surgical specimen	X		
Needle/syringe units, needles, scalpels, suture needles, etc.			X
Glass slides and pipettes			X
Empty urine cups, empty stool containers, and other empty specimen containers; empty urinary drainage bags, empty bedpans		X	
Dressings, bandages, cotton balls, peripads, Chux®, diapers, cotton swabs, etc.		X	
Used gloves, aprons, masks, and shoe and head covers		X	
Paper towels for hand washing		X	
Computer paper		X	
Packaging materials, paper		X	
Materials used to clean up spills		X	
Food waste (for example, soda cans, paper cups, plastic cutlery, etc.)	X		

*These containers can be emptied by Environmental Services personnel in the *operating room only.*

San Francisco General Hospital
San Francisco, California

Infectious Waste Handling

Definitions

Infectious waste consists of those items that are judged to have a relative risk of disease transmission and therefore special handling is indicated for their disposal. Infectious wastes are:

1. Needles/sharps and syringes used for injection or aspiration
2. Fluid-filled disposable suction devices/bags
3. Blood transfusion bags and administration sets
4. Blood-soaked waste from the Operating Room, Delivery Room, and Trauma Room in the Emergency Department
5. Dialyzers, peritoneal dialysis bags, blood or dialysis lines
6. Large-volume urine and stool collections
7. Lab specimens and their disposable containers
8. Cultures of patient specimens
9. Body parts, both human and animal

The following list identifies infectious waste by location.

Clinical Laboratories

1. Patient specimens, their containers, and disposable items used to work with them
2. Vacutainers® with blood and body fluids
3. Screw-cap tubes and cups used for fluids, sputum, urine, and stool
4. Disposable glass or plastic items to contain, measure, or transport specimens
5. Cultures made in microbiology laboratories from patient specimens.
6. Petri dishes, tubes, slides, and plastic modules that contain cultures

Anatomic Pathology

- Body parts removed at surgery and sent to surgical pathology, excess tissues from surgical pathology, and excess tissues from autopsies

Patient Care Areas

1. Needles/syringes for injection or aspiration/sharps (this does not include syringes for tube feeding or irrigations)
2. Unprocessed blood specimens
3. Fluid-filled disposable suction devices/bags
4. Blood transfusion bags and their administration sets

Operating Room, Delivery Room, and Trauma Rooms in Emergency Department

- Blood-soaked waste in addition to wastes mentioned under patient care areas

Dialysis Unit (Acute and Chronic)

- Dialyzers, peritoneal dialysis bags, and lines

Everything that is *not* listed above as infectious waste is regular waste. It may include food, office waste, and patient care waste including blood-spotted tissues and dressings not from the Operating Room, Delivery Room, or Trauma Rooms.

Containment, Transport, and Disposal: General Principles

Infectious Waste

While awaiting transport, infectious waste must be contained at the site of origin in covered or bagged leak-proof waste containers. Infectious waste must be collected in identifiable containers or bags and transported to a separate disposal site.

Regular Waste

For disposal, regular waste should be placed in waste cans with brown liners. Liners should be tied shut and used as bags for transport. Regular waste from patient care areas must be removed at least once a day or more often to prevent excessive accumulation and taken to the storage site for final disposal.

All Waste

Waste container liners must be removed as a single unit and tied shut without turning the container upside down to consolidate waste. Waste containers must be strong enough to resist tears and leaks under normal handling. Final disposal of waste is by approval of the County Health Officer and includes incineration, autoclaving, sewer system, or sanitary landfill.

Please refer to the Waste Collection Transport and Disposal Chart [pp. 106–7 of this manual] for specific waste handling.

San Francisco General Hospital
San Francisco, California

Waste Collection Transport and Disposal Chart

Waste	Containment and Transport	Responsibility	Final Disposal
	Infectious Waste		
1. Needles/sharps and syringes for injection and aspiration	1–2. Rigid-walled container located as near site of use as possible; place in "Infectious Waste" box located in chute room	1–6. Housekeeping	1–6. Off-site incineration
2. Unprocessed blood specimens for disposal			
3. Fluid-filled disposable suction devices/bags	3–6. Infectious waste-covered* containers lined with red bags		
4. Blood transfusion bags and administration sets			
5. Blood-soaked waste from Operating Room, Delivery Room, and Trauma Rooms	1–6. Transported by infectious waste cart		
6. Dialyzer peritoneal dialysis bags			
7. Large-volume urine and stool	7. Utility hoppers/sinks (not used for hand washing or food preparation)	7. Care providers	7. Sanitary sewer
8. Specimens and their disposable containers	8–9. Step-on pedal cans lined with tan/buff liners	8–9. Lab utility area	8–9. Autoclaved in utility area and disposed of by sanitary landfill
9. Cultures of patient specimens			
10. Body parts, animal and human	10. Transported by utility cart	10. Morgue attendant and animal lab attendant	10. Incineration on site

Waste	Containment and Transport	Responsibility	Final Disposal
	Regular Waste		
1. Moist patient care waste not defined above	1. Covered* trash cans lined with brown plastic and tied shut for transport	1–2. Housekeeping	1–3. Sanitary landfill
2. General office nonpatient care waste	2. Trash cans lined with brown plastic and tied shut for transport		
3. Kitchen wet garbage	3. Nonabsorbent cans with tight-fitting lids	3. Kitchen	

*If a can that does not have a working lid must be used, moist trash must be bagged before being placed in an open can.

Chapter 4

Implementation Plans

Introduction

Implementing Universal Precautions requires health care workers to assume that blood and certain body fluids from all patients are potentially infectious. This represents a significant change from previous practices, which were based on the facility's information about the infection status of each patient. Such complex changes in policies and procedures require skill, planning, and a significant commitment of time and resources. In many hospitals, the successful implementation of Universal Precautions programs has taken a year or more to complete.

Before the implementation process can begin, several preliminary steps must be accomplished: (1) identification of key elements of the desired program, (2) assessment of the facility and its regulatory environment, (3) review of existing policies and procedures, (4) development of a written plan, (5) meetings with key personnel, and (6) approval of implementation plan. These steps are discussed in the section on planning a Universal Precautions program in chapter 1, pp. 4–6.

Implementation requires the support and cooperation of many individuals. One person cannot do it alone. The support of key personnel must be enlisted, including committee chairmen, administrators, department heads, labor union representatives, and others. Before meeting with key personnel, the program planner should determine the specific outcomes to be accomplished. These may include developing additional policies, purchasing necessary supplies and equipment, and agreeing to assist with the implementation of specific components of the plan such as the training and education of staff and monitoring for compliance. During these meetings, an action plan is developed. It should include the activities for which each person will be responsible and the deadline for completion. The program planner may find it necessary to set up a task force to develop specific action plans for some of the activities that affect many departments, such as sharps disposal.

After the action plans have been developed, it is useful to develop a comprehensive time line for the completion of each step in the process. This time line, of course, may need to be revised periodically.

This chapter contains sample materials that may be useful in the implementation of a Universal Precautions program. Answers to frequently asked questions about Body Substance Isolation from Harborview Medical Center are included. Implementation models and plans from Tucson Medical Center and San Francisco General Hospital are also reproduced. A policy outlining staff responsibilities for developing, implementing, and enforcing Universal Precautions at Yale-New Haven Hospital may also be useful. Finally, an action plan for evaluating and implementing a sharps disposal system, developed by Marvick Educational Services, Inc., is provided.

Harborview Medical Center
Seattle, Washington

Implementing Body Substance Isolation

Several questions about Body Substance Isolation (BSI) are asked very frequently.

1. How long did it take to develop and implement BSI at Harborview?

   The ideas that resulted in BSI as an isolation system had been discussed by Marguerite Jackson and Patricia Lynch since 1982. "Infection Control: Too Much or Too Little?" was published in the *American Journal of Nursing* in February 1984 (volume 84, pp. 208–10). Concurrently, Jeanne Cummings and Patricia Lynch at Harborview began using BSI along with category-specific isolations. However, compliance with the two systems was inadequate: personnel continued to use gloves and other barriers for patients who were in category isolation and had isolation signs on their doors rather than using the precautions systematically for all patients.

   In 1985, after 15 months of promoting the use of the two systems together and noting that compliance was not increasing substantially, we decided to discontinue category isolation and only use BSI, thus removing the diagnosis-based signal system for using precautions. Full implementation of BSI alone took an additional 10 months from this time. In October 1985, BSI alone was formally adopted as Harborview Medical Center's isolation system.

2. What took you so long?

   Using a judgment-based system instead of a diagnosis-based system represented a major conceptual as well as behavioral change and entailed a great deal of preparation.

   The ICPs from the Epidemiology Department served as the central project coordinators, developing the training programs and plan for change.

   Several implementation committees were formed to manage the change. Inpatient nursing, medical staff, nonnursing clinical (RT, lab, etc.), and nonclinical employees (Dietary, Environmental Services, etc.) all had different concerns sufficient to warrant separate implementation committees; each committee discussed their education, supply, and procedure needs; presented the ideas to their own departments; gathered feedback and information; and then met again to discuss the final plan and to set the date for the formal change.

   Many other essential activities required several months:

   - Revising department policies and procedures; this was accomplished by individual managers who requested help from the Epidemiology Department when needed
   - Finding suitable supplies such as gloves, gowns, aprons, and eyewear and deciding where they should be located
   - Developing the Infection Control Manual including the signs, review of these materials by the Infection Control Committee, and revisions
   - Developing and testing the training materials; scheduling the programs for all personnel including house staff

3. What cost impact does implementing BSI have?

   The cost of the system will depend on various factors at each facility, and so no overall figure can be given. At one end of the cost spectrum are facilities that routinely used expensive, unnecessary tools such as tacky mats and water-soluble laundry bags; these hospitals may actually save money by simplifying procedures. At the other end of the spectrum are facilities where personnel routinely have bare-hand contact with mucous membranes, nonintact skin, and moist body substances of patients and have no point-of-use needle disposal devices; these hospitals will find implementing any system of Universal Precautions expensive. Most hospitals are somewhere between these two extremes.

Costs for some items are given below:

Gloves: Harborview has six critical care units, and glove use tripled in these units. We buy a variety of sizes of gloves in both latex and vinyl, powdered and unpowdered. Few people are sensitive to both latex and vinyl, and having a great variety makes selection convenient for the users. There is no apparent difference in quality, and each costs about $9 per box of 100. Gloves are located at each patient bedside. In the wards, glove use almost doubled; this included outpatient areas as well.

Gowns and aprons: Fabric gowns or plastic sleeved or unsleeved aprons are appropriate for various activities. The purpose is to keep personnel from soiling their clothing and skin, and personnel select the degree of protection necessary for the anticipated task. The plastic aprons cost about the same as laundering the gowns, and use was not an expense factor.

Masks and eyewear: Masks and glasses or goggles are available in utility rooms; these items are usually worn together to protect personnel during "splashy" jobs. Goggles create visual distortion and most personnel performing fine tasks prefer to buy good-quality plain-pane eyeglasses.

Sharps containers: Sharps containers are located in each patient room except on psychiatric units and in the Emergency Room. These represented an initial cost but not a continuing increase, since sharps had previously all been disposed of in centrally located containers, such as on medication carts. Point-of-use boxes make uncapped disposal more convenient.

Isolation carts: We do not use isolation carts except to store supplies on some units that have long halls and few utility rooms.

Hand washing: We have not changed our recommendations for hand-washing products or frequency and continue to use an antimicrobial product in critical care units.

Housecleaning: Housecleaning is now done to a high standard for all rooms regardless of the patient's diagnosis; degree of soilage is the indicator for special cleaning. Housekeepers wear heavy-duty utility gloves for all activities likely to result in contact with moist body substances.

4. What do you do with soiled linen?

   All soiled linen is placed in fabric laundry bags; heavily soiled linen that might leak is placed in a plastic bag first. At the laundry, the employees wear heavy-duty gloves and gowns to sort all linen; visibly soiled linen is run through a cold-water rinse-spin cycle first, and then a regular wash to prevent staining. There are no isolation laundry bags.

5. What do you do with soiled trash?

   All trash is collected in plastic trash bags, as many as are necessary to prevent leaking. All trash is compacted and taken to a landfill. Some items require special handling:

   - All sharps containers and waste from the clinical and research laboratories and the Pathology Department are autoclaved before compacting.
   - Fluid-filled containers such as chest drainage and wound suction devices are placed in plastic-lined metal cans in the soiled utility rooms on the nursing units; these are collected by Housekeeping and carried away by cart rather than being sent down the chute. They are also autoclaved before compacting.

   The county and state regulations require the Infection Control Committee in each facility to define and prescribe handling for infectious waste. In the absence of any evidence that waste from medical facilities is potentially more infectious than residential waste, Harborview has defined potentially infectious waste as sharps, laboratory and pathology waste, and fluid-filled containers. Review of local and state regulations regarding identification and handling of infectious wastes needs to be accomplished for compliance by hospitals planning to implement BSI.

6. What do you do with soiled equipment?

   Soiled equipment is placed in plastic bags in the utility rooms before being hand processed by gloved workers in Central Supply. All soiled equipment is managed in the same fashion for all patients, regardless of diagnosis. We do not have a washer sterilizer. All soiled equipment receives a level of disinfection appropriate for the type of patient contact rather than special handling for certain diagnoses.

7. Do you do anything different for people who are known to be HIV or HBV positive?

   No. They are assigned to rooms on the basis of their severity of illness, ability to control their body substances, and need for privacy. Use of protective barriers for personnel is based on the anticipated interactions. Personnel do not usually provide people assigned to the same room with information about each other's diagnosis, but we believe it is usual for roommates to be aware of each other's diagnosis, given the lack of privacy in multibed rooms.

8. How do you evaluate BSI?

   We believed it was important to evaluate several aspects of the implementation process.

   - We administered a written pre- and posttest to all personnel attending our training programs. The test identified changes in their attitudes, knowledge, and reported past practices. Eight months later, we gave the test again to a random sample of personnel to determine whether they had retained the knowledge. Significant changes in attitudes, knowledge, and practices did occur.
   - We determined attendance at the training programs by using personnel rosters. It is important to have at least 75 percent of employees and medical staff attend. Departments with poor attendance tended to have poor compliance with the new practices. Subsequent programs were scheduled for departments with poor initial attendance.
   - Compliance with the new practices was evaluated by a formal observation study. Patient–care giver interactions were recorded by site of contact, care giver discipline, and whether hand washing and/or gloving were performed correctly. Contacts with mucous membranes, nonintact skin, and indwelling device insertion sites were defined as recordable events. Information on compliance was reported to departments. Compliance gradually rose to more than 80 percent.
   - The effect of BSI on nosocomial transmission with certain organisms was evaluated by recording incidence of first positive isolates for *Serratia* and *Acinetobacter.* The incidence declined substantially as compliance increased.

9. Do any small hospitals use Body Substance Isolation?

   Yes. In fact, BSI was first implemented at a small community hospital.

San Francisco General Hospital
San Francisco, California

Implementing Body Substance Precautions in a Health Care Facility (A Model for Increasing Employee Safety and Decreasing Anxiety While Preserving Quality Health Care)

A major step in reducing AIDS anxiety has been taken when the employee increases his/her control over work conditions by being allowed an opportunity to have constructive input into the implementation of infection control practices.

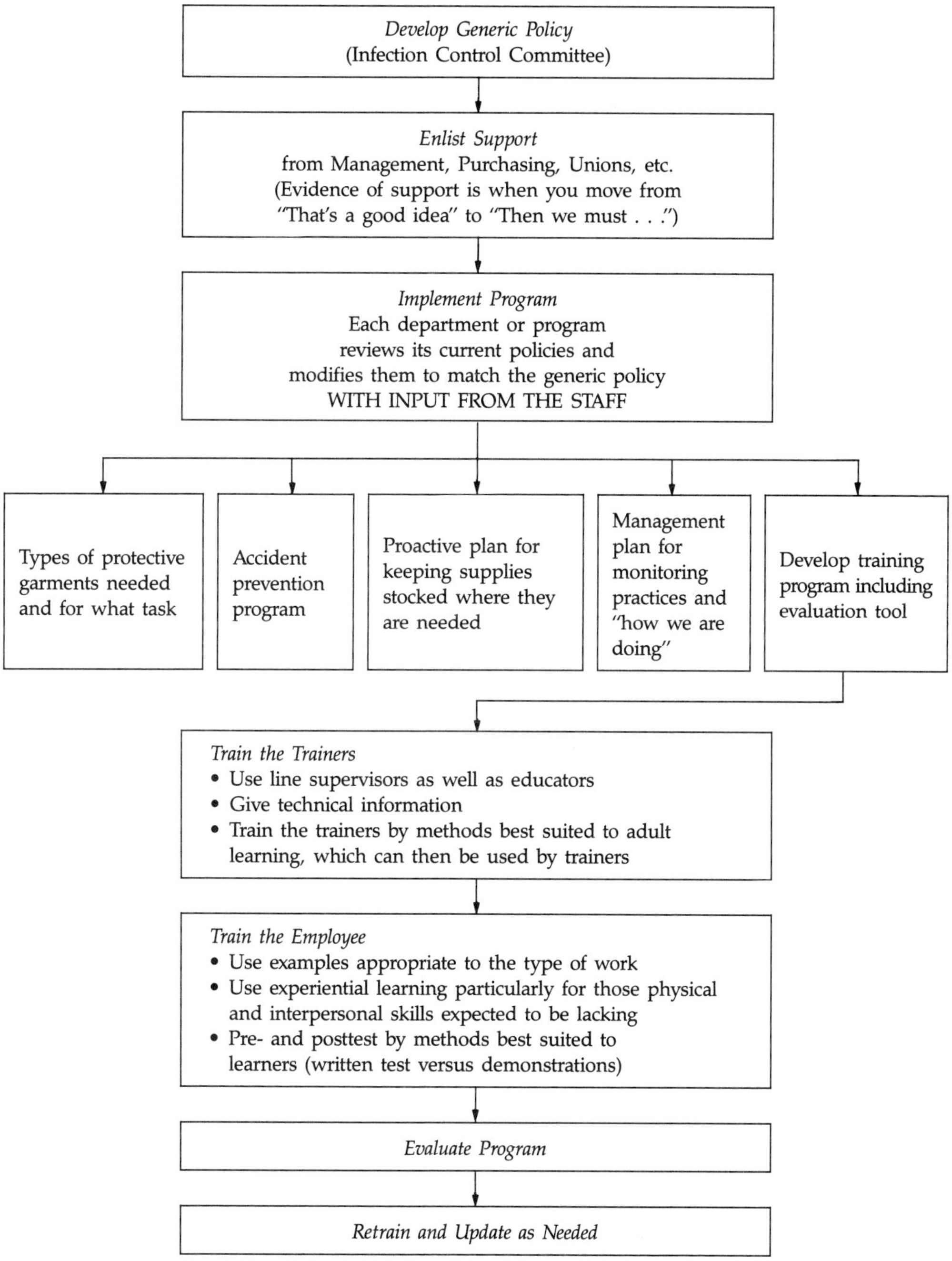

☐ References

American Hospital Association. AIDS: Protecting the Hospital Worker. Panel discussion by Patricia Lynch, Marguerite Jackson, Steven Trosty, and Carson Dye, Aug. 12, 1987. Chicago: AHA, Sept. 1987. [Videotape copies provided to all AHA member hospitals.]

Jackson, M. M., and Lynch, P. Education of the adult learner: a practical approach for the infection control practitioner. *American Journal of Infection Control* 14:257–71, 1986.

Jackson, M. M., Lynch, P., McPherson, D. C., Cummings, M. J., and Greenawalt, N. C. Clinical savvy: why not treat all body substances as infectious? *American Journal of Nursing* 87:1137–39, 1987.

Lynch, P., Cummings, M. J., Roberts, P. L., Herriott, M. J., Yates, B., and Stamm, W. E. Implementing and evaluating a system of generic infection precautions: Body Substance Isolation. *American Journal of Infection Control* 18:1–12, 1990.

Lynch, P., Jackson, M. M., Cummings, M. J., and Stamm, W. E. Rethinking the role of isolation practices in the prevention of nosocomial infections. *Annals of Internal Medicine* 107:243–46, 1987.

McPherson, D. C., and Jackson, M. M. Isolation precautions for a changing environment: a new approach. *Journal of Healthcare Materiel Management* 5(6):28–32, 1987.

Weiss, C. H. *Evaluation Research: Methods for Assessing Program Effectiveness.* Englewood Cliffs, NJ: Prentice-Hall, 1972.

Tucson Medical Center
Tucson, Arizona

Body Substance Precautions System Implementation Plan

I. Develop AIDS Task Force

A. Multidisciplinary
B. Elected to implement the CDC's Guidelines for Universal Precautions

II. Plan the Implementation of the System

A. Develop actual policies and procedures
- BSP–general
- Infectious waste
- Soiled linen
- Sharps disposal

B. Consents
- HIV testing of patients
- HIV testing of employees
- Transfusion of donor blood

C. Materials management
- Estimate increased glove usage
- Evaluation of protective gear
  - –Needle disposal systems
  - –Protective eyewear
  - –Protective care carts (unit use)

D. Employee health issues
- Exposure testing for HIV and hepatitis B
- Cost issues
- Policy on employees with AIDS

III. AIDS Task Force (Periodic Meetings)

- Take all revisions, proposals, and estimates to this body to document consensus during development process

IV. Set Up a BSP Core Group

Representatives from Nursing, Patient and Family Counseling, Forms Committee, Education, and Infection Control

A. Counseling (pre- and posttesting)
- Patient and Family Counseling to perform

B. Consent revisions
C. Education suggestions
D. Revision in policy and procedure (BSP)

V. Additional Groups to Interface with Core Group

A. Plant services
- Infectious waste issues (what, how, where, etc.)

B. Education
- Development of education for the following groups:

Supervisory	Residents
Staff–hospital	Paramedics
Physicians	Auxilians
Per diem staff	Affiliates
Agency	(off-campus facilities)
Students	Ongoing education
New physicians	(orientation)

C. Quality assurance
Development of housewide observational compliance audits to be used in all areas that have any patient or blood/body fluid contact
- Patient care audits
- Needlestick audits
- Exposure follow-up
- Infectious waste audits

D. Materials management
Set up the purchasing of supplies and distribution of protective gear and equipment and develop a rotation system to keep departments supplied.

VI. Committee Communication
- To AIDS Task Force for consensus
- To Medical Executive Committee for approval
- To TMC Board for approval

VII. Education
Provide mandatory education to all personnel in supervisory positions.
- Supervisory personnel provide education to all employees under their direct supervision.

VIII. Revision of All Housewide Policies and Procedures
- Revision of all job descriptions

IX. Compliance
- Supervisor responsibility
- Disciplinary action possible
- Include on performance evaluation as goal for next year

Tucson Medical Center
Tucson, Arizona

Estimate of Necessary Time and Sequence for Planning and Implementing Body Substance Precautions

	Oct.	Nov.	Dec.	Jan.	Feb.	Mar.	Apr.	May	June
Enlist support and committee action	—	—	—	—					
Plan implementation of system (consents, policies, supplies, etc.)	—	—	—	—					
Sharps disposal issue	—	—							
Infectious waste issues	—	—							
Soiled linen management	—	—							
Purchasing supplies in areas		—	—	—					
Placing supplies in areas				—	—	—			
Revise policies and procedures for all departments incorporating the BSP system (laundry, E.D., lab, etc.)	—	—	—	—					
Plan and present education program			—	—	—	—			
Implement changeover							—		
Evaluate process				—	—				
Audit program							—	—	—
Incorporate BSP into all orientation programs					—		—	—	—

Yale-New Haven Hospital
New Haven, Connecticut

Universal Precautions Policy Implementation

I. Introduction

The purpose of this document is to outline hospital, department, and individual responsibilities in the development, implementation, and enforcement of Universal Precautions throughout Yale-New Haven Hospital. The result should be consolidation of Universal Precautions with current infection control practices in an effort to provide a safe working environment within the hospital and to ensure compliance with Occupational Safety and Health Administration (OSHA) requirements.

Through the use of this document, department managers should be able to successfully develop and implement a Universal Precautions Policy that is specific to their department, but consistent with other departmental Universal Precautions policies throughout the hospital.

In order to ensure consistency of content among departmental policies and procedures throughout the hospital, the Policies and Procedures Subcommittee recommends that two (2) FTEs be allocated for a period of six (6) months to serve as working coordinators to supervise hospitalwide implementation. Hospital Epidemiology will have responsibility for supervising the coordinators.

II. Hospital Universal Precautions Policy

The hospital Universal Precautions Policy includes the following sections:

A. Purpose
B. Definitions
C. Scope
D. Implementation
E. Responsibilities
F. Applications

The policy addresses the procedures to be utilized for protection from contagious microorganisms as well as for the practice of general hygiene. Most important, this policy eliminates the need for the various categories of Isolation Precautions in the Infection Control Manual with the exception of Respiratory Isolation. The Infection Control Manual is currently being updated to bring these and other procedures into compliance with Universal Precautions.

Universal Precautions shall be utilized at all times and for all patients regardless of diagnosis.

A. Purpose

The purpose of this policy is to establish hospital, departmental, and individual responsibilities to minimize transmission of contagious microorganisms to, from, and between patients and all other persons at Yale-New Haven Hospital.

B. Definitions

1. Persons–All hospital employees, physicians, students, volunteers, visitors, and/or any other individuals who enter the hospital.
2. Universal Precautions–The routine and consistent use of appropriate barrier protection to prevent skin and mucous membrane transmission of microorganisms resulting from contact with blood and body fluids, and as part of the practice of general hygiene. Patients with a documented or potentially contagious respiratory infection will be hospitalized in Respiratory Isolation, as defined in the Infection Control Manual.

3. Blood and body fluids–This includes all body tissues and body fluids that may potentially harbor contagious microorganisms. Blood and body fluids include but are not limited to the following:

amniotic fluid	peritoneal fluid
blood	pleural fluid
body tissues	saliva
breast milk	semen
cerebrospinal fluid	sputum
feces	synovial fluid
nasal secretions	urine
nonintact skin	vaginal secretions
pericardial fluid	vomitus

   Blood and body fluids do not include tears or perspiration unless they contain visible evidence of blood.
4. Exposure–Actual or potential skin, mucous membrane, or parenteral contact with blood or body fluids.
5. Hand washing/barrier protection–The appropriate use of hand washing, gloves, gowns, masks, goggles, and face shields to minimize exposure to blood and body fluids.
6. Occupational Safety and Health Administration exposure categories:
   a. Category I–Jobs with tasks that routinely involve exposure or potential exposure to blood, body fluids, or tissues.
   b. Category II–Jobs with tasks that do not routinely involve exposure to blood, body fluids, or tissues, but exposure or potential exposure may be required as a condition of employment.
   c. Category III–Jobs with tasks that do not routinely involve exposure to blood, body fluids, or tissues. Persons in this category are not called on to perform or assist in emergency medical care or first aid or to be potentially exposed in any other way as a condition of employment.

C. Scope
This policy applies to all departments and all persons within Yale-New Haven Hospital.

D. Implementation of Hand Washing and Barrier Precautions
1. Hand washing–Hands shall be washed using warm water and soap before and after contact with all patients or following contamination with blood or body fluids. Particular attention should be given to areas around and under fingernails and between fingers.
2. Gloves–Gloves shall be worn for anticipated or potential exposure of the hands to blood and body fluids or surfaces soiled with blood and body fluids. Gloves shall be discarded when torn, following contact with each patient (before leaving the patient's room), or following contact with contaminated items.
3. Gowns–Fluid-repellant gowns shall be worn when splattering of blood or body fluids is likely (gloves shall be worn in addition to gowns). Gowns shall be discarded when torn, following contact with each patient (before leaving the patient's room), or following contact with contaminated items. Cloth lab coats are not acceptable substitutes for gowns.
4. Masks–Masks shall be worn if the patient has a documented or potentially contagious respiratory infection. Masks shall be discarded following contact with each patient.
5. Glasses/goggles plus masks, or face shields–Glasses/goggles plus masks, or face shields shall be worn if splattering or aerosolization is likely to occur. Glasses, goggles, and face shields shall be cleansed with germicidal solution following contamination with blood or body fluids. Masks shall be discarded following contact with each patient.

E. Responsibilities
1. Hospital responsibilities–The hospital shall:
   a. Require use of appropriate safeguards for persons to minimize direct contact with contagious microorganisms.
   b. Provide all employees, students, and volunteers with education and training in hospital Universal Precautions and Infection Control policies and procedures that are specific to their responsibilities prior to assuming responsibilities.
   c. Provide appropriate types and supplies of protective equipment (for example, gloves, goggles, masks, gowns, etc.).
   d. Categorize all job descriptions as including category I, II, or III tasks as defined by OSHA.
   e. Regularly review departmental compliance with hospital Universal Precautions.
   f. The Department of Epidemiology and Infection Control shall annually review departmental policies and procedures for completeness.
2. Departmental responsibilities–Each department shall:
   a. Categorize all job descriptions as including category I, II, or III tasks as defined by OSHA.
   b. Develop and implement a departmental Universal Precautions policy based on this hospital policy, which indicates the necessary types of hand washing/barrier precautions as part of the standard operating procedures for each task. The type of hand washing/barrier precautions required is based on the:
      - Type and volume of blood or body fluids with which there will or may be contact
      - Probability of an exposure taking place
      - Probable route of exposure

      All departmental policies shall be submitted to the Policies and Procedures Coordinator for approval prior to implementation. Once approved, departmental policies shall be submitted to the Department of Epidemiology and Infection Control for review annually.
   c. Ensure that all applicants are apprised of the risk for exposure to blood and body fluids at the time of the applicant's interview.
   d. Provide all employees, students, and volunteers with education and training in hospital Universal Precautions and infection control policies and procedures that are specific to their responsibilities prior to assuming responsibilities.
   e. Provide regular employee inservice training in hospital Universal Precautions and infection control policies and procedures as part of ongoing staff education.
   f. Design a system to monitor and document, in a fair and equitable manner, individual compliance with the practice of hospital Universal Precautions and infection control policies and procedures.
   g. Include compliance with hospital Universal Precautions procedures as part of each employee's performance review.
   h. Provide appropriate retraining and progressively discipline, if necessary, individuals who fail to comply with department policies and procedures for hospital Universal Precautions and infection control.
   i. Ensure that visitors are not allowed in areas where contagion is likely, unless there is specific need and the visitor receives instruction in the Universal Precautions and infection control policies and procedures specific to the area/tasks involved.
   j. Submit an incident report for all instances where an individual's technique is not consistent with hospital Universal Precautions and infection control policies and procedures.

k. Submit a Supervisor's Report of Employee Accident/Injury (F-1797) following all incidents of actual exposure to blood or body fluids.

3. Individual responsibilities—Each individual shall:
   a. Comply with the guidelines of the Personnel Health Service.
   b. Understand the principles of hospital Universal Precautions and infection control, with specific knowledge of the tasks that individual may assume.
   c. Routinely apply the practices of Universal Precautions and infection control to each task performed.
   d. Report incidents to their supervisor of actual exposure to blood or body fluids.
   e. Report incidents to their supervisor when other individuals are noncompliant with hospital Universal Precautions and infection control policies and procedures.

F. Applications

Universal Precautions shall be utilized at all times and for all patients, regardless of diagnosis.

III. Implementation of Universal Precautions into All Hospital Departmental and Interdepartmental Policies and Procedures

The implementation and enforcement of a Universal Precautions policy that applies to all patients is intended to protect health care workers and patients from nosocomial transmission of contagious microorganisms.

Departmental and interdepartmental policies and procedures currently in place need to be reviewed and revised to include guidelines for Universal Precautions specific to each employee's responsibilities and tasks.

Adequate protection of patients and hospital staff requires appropriate controls, adequate supplies, and informed workers who have a working knowledge of standard operating procedures. Therefore, it is imperative that departments establish policies that identify departmental and individual responsibilities and that contain detailed standard operating procedures for all tasks or work areas having the potential for exposure to blood, body fluids, or tissues. A worker education program is necessary to ensure familiarity with the standard operating procedures.

In order to ensure consistency of content among departmental policies and procedures throughout the hospital, two working coordinators should be allocated for a period of six (6) months to supervise hospitalwide implementation. Hospital Epidemiology will be responsible for supervising the coordinators.

Coordinator Responsibilities: The Universal Precautions Coordinators shall:

1. Provide managers with the necessary information and training to ensure the successful implementation of departmental Universal Precautions policies and procedures.
2. Assist managers in developing standard operating procedures for routine tasks. The standard operating procedures shall include the minimum level of protective barriers required to perform each task safely.
3. Assist managers, as required, in providing inservice education and training for all employee and nonemployee groups.
4. Review and revise departmental Universal Precautions policies and procedures to ensure consistency between departments.
5. Coordinate the review and approval of Universal Precautions policies and procedures with members of hospital Epidemiology and members of the Infection Control Committee.
6. Coordinate the changes in personnel policies and job descriptions with the Department of Human Resources.
7. Identify and develop policies for university and community activities that overlap with Yale-New Haven Hospital.

Yale-New Haven Hospital
New Haven, Connecticut

Universal Precautions Implementation Model

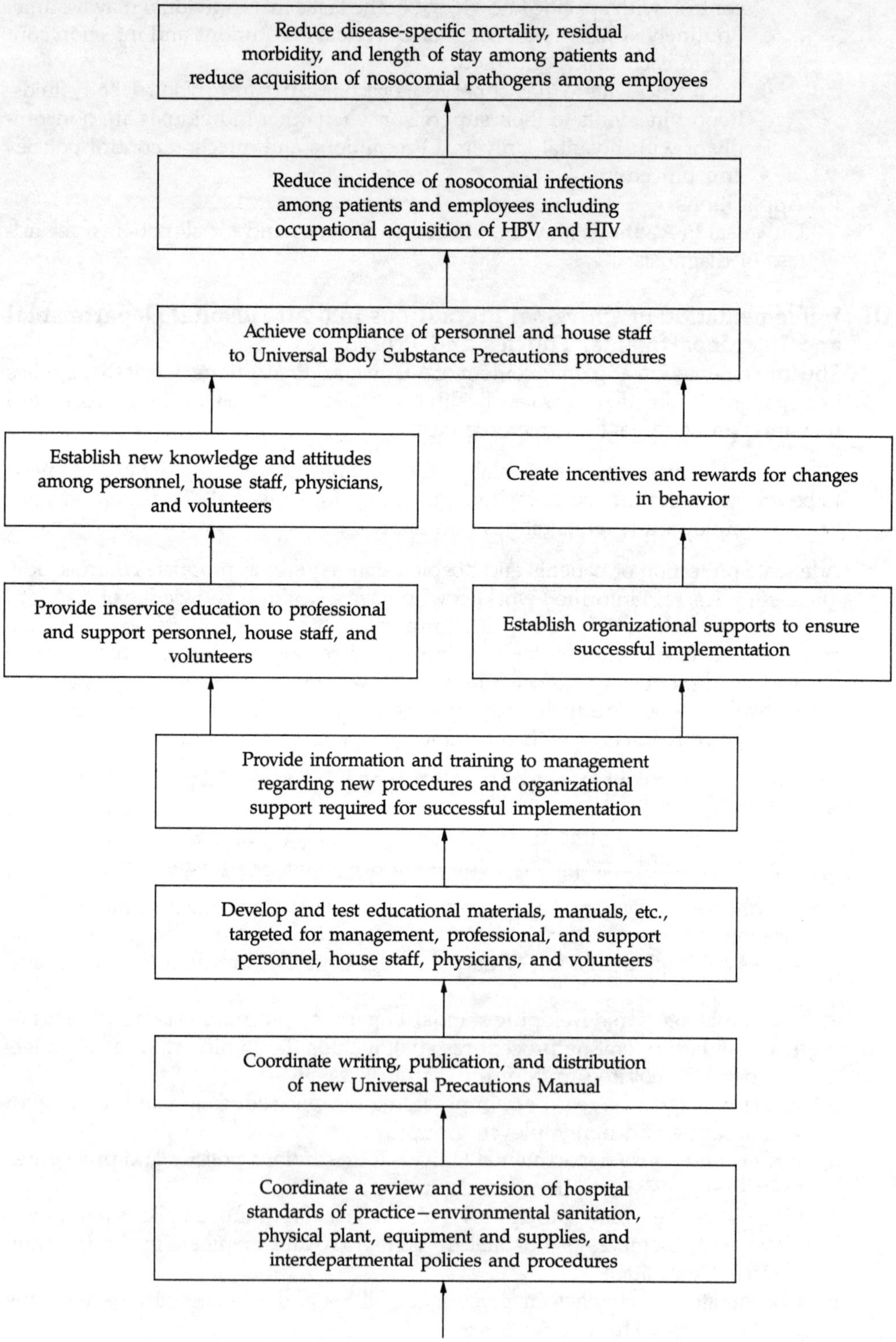

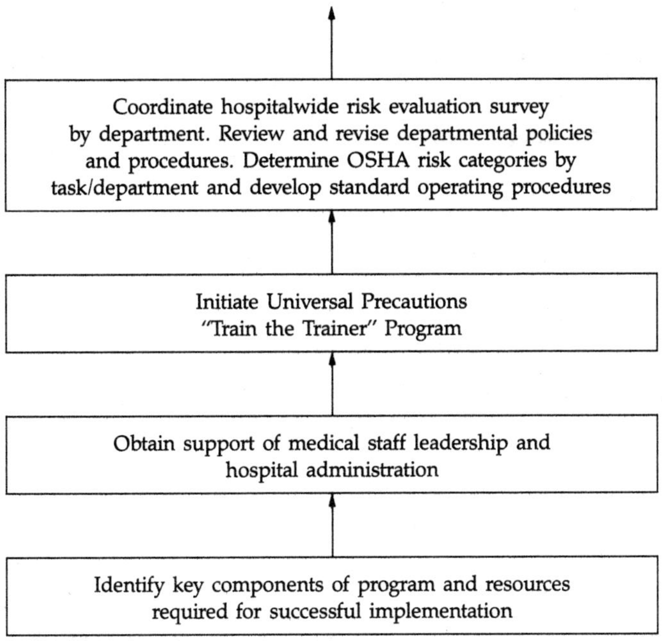

Adapted from Lynch, P., Cummings, M. J., Roberts, P. L., Herriott, M. J., Stamm, W. E., and Yates, B. Implementing and evaluating a system of generic infection precautions: Body Substance Isolation. *American Journal of Infection Control* 18:1-12, 1990 [implementation model modified by E. Pantelick].

Marvick Educational Services, Inc.
San Diego, California

Action Plan: Sharps Disposal

Project Coordinator: ____________________

Action	Responsibility	Deadline	Deadline Met?
A. Evaluate current system for convenience at point of use			
B. Evaluate needle boxes for percent recapped now—are they used correctly at present?			
C. If supply and location of sharps containers needs to be improved: 1. Get administrative agreement that point of use is needed; resources will be available for new system			
2. Determine additional locations and tabulate supply needs			
3. Determine type of system (for example, labor-intensive exchange system; price-intensive disposable system)			
4. Determine ultimate disposal (for example, autoclave, incinerate, outside vendor removal/disposal)			
5. Contact vendors, estimate cost, allocate cost to departments			
6. Let contracts for installations			
7. Write/update policies/procedures for sharps disposal to include new point-of-use system			
8. Train personnel to use new system			
9. Install point-of-use system			
10. Determine responsibility for maintenance on ongoing basis			
D. Evaluate correct use of system			
1. Repeat survey to determine proportion of recapped needles in disposal devices			
2. Determine whether system is satisfactory to personnel			
a. Are devices emptied/changed frequently enough?			
b. Are devices in convenient locations?			
c. Are more devices needed in certain areas?			

E. Estimate of time necessary: Depending on the facility, this project will take one to four months to complete.

Additional issues for your plan:

Reprinted with permission from Lynch, P., and Jackson, M. M. *The Body Substance Isolation System: A Workbook for Implementing Universal Infection Precautions.* San Diego: Marvick Educational Services, Inc., 1988.

Chapter 5

Compliance Monitoring

Introduction

Monitoring staff compliance is an essential component of a Universal Precautions program that ensures that recommended practices are being followed. However, few models for evaluating compliance with Universal Precautions have been published. This chapter discusses strategies for monitoring compliance with Universal Precautions. Sample tools for monitoring specific components of the program are also included.

Compliance monitoring is an ongoing process that is carried out during the planning, implementation, and evaluation stages of Universal Precautions programs. To ensure compliance, the responsibilities of all staff must be specified. Policies and procedures should indicate the responsibilities of department heads, managers, and staff for implementing each component, complying with the recommended practices, reporting noncompliance, and taking action in response to noncompliance. Some health care facilities have made compliance with recommended practices a requirement for satisfactory job performance and incorporated it into the employees' performance review criteria.

A mechanism needs to be established to identify and evaluate the reasons for noncompliance so that appropriate action can be taken. Compliance with Universal Precautions techniques often requires fundamental changes in infection control practices, and employees may resist such changes because they feel that the changes will affect them adversely. For example, employees may consider compliance with Universal Precautions to be an added burden in a work schedule that is already demanding. They may feel that compliance will necessitate cutting corners in their normal work load at the "expense" of the patient. In addition, employees who have been trained to exercise professional judgment are likely to resist changes that restrict their power to make judgments in practice.

Compliance monitoring may also identify a need to modify a procedure, allocate additional supplies or equipment, or provide additional education and training. Staff input during compliance monitoring should be encouraged in order to provide an incentive for commitment to the recommended practices. Providing positive incentives for staff or departments that achieve compliance has been found to be a very successful approach. Training and retraining programs also reinforce the facility's commitment to employee safety.

When monitoring reveals repeated failure to follow recommended practices after additional supplies, education and/or retraining, and counseling have been provided, disciplinary action may be necessary.

Many of the activities currently being used to monitor and evaluate the success of infection prevention and control programs are part of compliance monitoring, for example, following up on problems identified through sources such as informal reports or complaints from staff, reports or minutes from committees, employee questionnaires, staff logs, and comments received during evaluations of education and training programs. Accident/incident reports also provide information on staff compliance and identify specific problems in need of corrective action. Because education and training are necessary to ensure that staff members are both knowledgeable about Universal Precautions and capable of performing the recommended protective practices, a review of attendance records provides useful information.

Compliance monitoring can also be achieved by directly observing individual employees' performance, such as handling needles properly or wearing protective apparel during specific procedures. It can also be done indirectly. For example, needle disposal practices can be monitored by observing the location of needle disposal containers in each department or the identification of overfilled needle disposal containers. Compliance monitoring can also be done by evaluating outcomes, for example, a reduced incidence of needlestick injuries, as a result of the successful implementation of a sharps injury reduction program.

Observing employees' performance can be done in an informal manner, for example, on walking rounds that are either announced or unannounced. Recording of observations of staff compliance can be done using a simple tool that contains information on the person recording the observations, the specific unit or department being monitored, and the number of observations of compliance or noncompliance with the specific practices or activities. Information can also be collected on specific personnel observed to be in noncompliance with recommended practices.

Compliance monitoring can also be done by conducting a formal study that randomly samples the performance of personnel. An important consideration in a formal study is the sampling or observation of a significant number of behaviors or events to ensure that the events being observed are not occurring infrequently, by chance alone, or in response to the observer's presence. When the formal study design includes the recording of behavioral observations without the observed employee's knowledge, it is important to maintain this method throughout the study period. When the study is designed so that personnel know that they are being observed, it is assumed that their behavior may be consistently modified.

Regardless of the method used to monitor staff compliance, the mere presence of an observer may prompt modification of staff behavior and compliance with recommended practices. In addition, staff may be more motivated to change their behavior when the results are reported back to them as well as being used for their performance evaluations.

Compliance monitoring requires the cooperation of many individuals. Information that can be used for monitoring compliance may be collected by many different departments within a facility. Therefore, an organized plan is needed (1) to identify the information that is currently available for monitoring compliance, (2) to determine which additional data need to be collected, (3) to analyze the information in a regular and systematic manner, (4) to implement corrective action, and (5) to evaluate results.

Because monitoring every activity and every staff member is impossible, it is important to focus on those practices that are associated with the greatest risk of exposure and infection. Proper handling and disposal of needles and sharps is one example. A sample tool for monitoring compliance with sharps disposal, developed by the Tucson Medical Center, is included in this chapter. Also included from Tucson Medical Center is a policy establishing departmental responsibilities for compliance monitoring, as well as a sample tool for monitoring disposal of containers filled with body fluids and a sample tool for monitoring physicians' compliance.

Questionnaires have also been used to assess compliance. The University of California at Irvine Medical Center has incorporated compliance questions into an employee health questionnaire, which is included in this section. Additional compliance monitoring tools and policies delineating specific responsibilities are also included.

Harborview Medical Center
Seattle, Washington

Frequency and Indications for Glove Use and Hand Washing in Patient Care Areas: Observation of Personnel Practices

Definitions

Mucous membrane contact is defined as direct physical contact of the practitioner's hand(s) with oral, genital, rectal, nasal, or conjunctival mucosa. Specify site.

Surgical wound/burn/open lesion contact is defined as direct physical contact of the practitioner's hand(s) with a surgical incision, open skin, lesion, wound, or burn surface. Specify type and site.

Device contact is defined as direct physical contact of the practitioner's hand(s) with the exit/entrance wound or indwelling device within 1 inch of the exit/entrance wound. Specify device and site.

Moist body substance (MBS) contact is defined as direct physical contact of the practitioner's hand(s) with any body fluids or solid substances (for example, blood, feces, secretions, pus, etc.) that are not categorized in any of the other contacts.

Hand washing takes place when the practitioner/subject is at the sink with water running and elbows moving for 10 seconds. Indicate "yes" if all criteria are met.

Gloves refers to clean or sterile vinyl, latex, or plastic gloves. Indicate "yes" if the practitioner/subject put gloves on immediately before the contact; if gloves worn for another activity are worn for subsequent activities, record as "no" for the second and subsequent activities.

Compliance with hand washing procedure occurs when the observer sees hand washing and the hands having no potential contact with moist substances between the hand washing and the next patient care contact.

Compliance with glove use procedure occurs when the observer sees clean gloves put on just before patient contact.

Observation of Personnel Glove Use Practices: Methods

1. Locate the charge nurse and introduce yourself. Explain that you are the observer for the Infection Control Committee study and that you will be observing patient care practices relative to glove use.
2. Identify patients at high risk for mucous membrane, wound/open skin, or device contacts by reviewing the Kardex® with the charge nurse. Record the bed numbers of patients who are incontinent of urine or feces and dependent on personnel for oral hygiene. List the room numbers of these patients on the Patient Care Unit Summary.
3. Randomization: Using the table of random digits and the room numbers of high-contact patients, select three patients for observation. Since all patients in the ICUs are high-contact patients, observation sites, located on the maps for each unit, are randomly selected for observation order.
4. If the patient is alert, ask the charge nurse to explain the study to the patient and elicit cooperation. The explanation should be similar to the following: "The hospital is doing a study of the quality of care being provided to patients. A professional nurse will sit in your room for 20 minutes to observe the practitioners who care for you. She will not participate in your care or distract the personnel from what they are doing. She will leave if it bothers you to have someone else in the room." If the patient agrees, have the charge nurse introduce you to the patient. (Most patients who meet the study criteria will not be alert.)
5. Position yourself unobtrusively in the room or outside it if good visibility can be maintained.

6. Each time contact with a mucous membrane, skin lesion, or device occurs, enter the information on a new line. The same activity repeated is entered as a new activity each time. Enter every bit of information on the form.
7. Designate each practitioner's discipline as accurately as possible. Ask for clarification if necessary after the individual has completed the task being performed. Identify each different practitioner in the same discipline by a code such as RN 1, RN 2, ...
8. If personnel question your purpose, explain that you are collecting data for a quality assurance study of patient care practices. Answer questions accurately but as incompletely as possible since knowledge of the exact practices being monitored may influence personnel behavior. Use the following worksheets to record and summarize your observations [figures 5-1 through 5-3]. Refer persistent or difficult questions to appropriate Infection Control personnel.

Figure 5-1. Sampling Worksheet

Unit	Location (Station or Bed Number)		
______ 2N TICU	(1) ______	(2) ______	(3)______
______ 2N MICU	(1) ______	(2) ______	(3)______
______ 2N CCU	(1) ______	(2) ______	(3)______
______ 3N	(1) ______	(2) ______	(3)______
______ 4N	(1) ______	(2) ______	(3)______
______ 4C	(1) ______	(2) ______	(3)______
______ 5N	(1) ______	(2) ______	(3)______
______ 6N	(1) ______	(2) ______	(3)______
______ 6C	(1) ______	(2) ______	(3)______
______ 7N	(1) ______	(2) ______	(3)______
______ 9NC NICU	(1) ______	(2) ______	(3)______
______ 9NA BURN	(1) ______	(2) ______	(3)______
______ 9NB BURN	(1) ______	(2) ______	(3)______
______ 8N	(1) ______	(2) ______	(3)______

Sampling for ICUs:

1. Identify observation sites from the map of the specific unit.
2. Randomize order in which you observe the sites.
3. Select three observation sites. If a site is unsuitable, move on to the next site; cross off the unused site on the recording form.

Sampling for Medical/Surgical Units:

1. From charge or head nurse, obtain list of all patients who fit the criteria.
2. Draw chips equal to the number of observation sites of patients meeting the criteria and randomly choose three.

Figure 5-2. Patient Care Unit Summary Sheet

1. Unit designation:______________________________
2. Number of bed on unit:______________________________
3. Number of patients who meet study criteria (incontinent and require oral hygiene by personnel):______________
4. List of room numbers of patients who meet study criteria:

__________ __________ __________ __________ __________ __________

__________ __________ __________ __________ __________ __________

__________ __________ __________ __________ __________ __________

5. Circle room numbers of the patients randomly selected for monitoring from the list above.
6. For each patient monitored, record the following information:

Name:	______________	______________	______________
Number:	______________	______________	______________
Age/Sex:	______________	______________	______________
Diagnosis:	______________	______________	______________
Date/Time:	______________	______________	______________
Ending Time:	______________	______________	______________

Figure 5-3. Glove Use Evaluation: Infection Control Committee

Room/Bed Number	Event	Gloves		Hand Washing			Practitioner
	Mucosal (circle one only) (1) Oral (2) Nasal (3) Conjunctival (4) Rectal (5) Genital (6) Surgical wound (7) Burn (8) Open lesion (9) Devices (specify site) ____ (10) MBS Contact Yes No Site ____	Yes ____ 1	No ____ 2	Yes ____ 1	No ____ 2	? ____ 3	(1) R.N. (2) M.D. (3) R.T. (4) P.T. (5) L.P.N. (6) Undetermined (7) Other (specify) ____
	Mucosal (circle one only) (1) Oral (2) Nasal (3) Conjunctival (4) Rectal (5) Genital (6) Surgical wound (7) Burn (8) Open lesion (9) Devices (specify site) ____ (10) MBS Contact Yes No Site ____	Yes ____ 1	No ____ 2	Yes ____ 1	No ____ 2	? ____ 3	(1) R.N. (2) M.D. (3) R.T. (4) P.T. (5) L.P.N. (6) Undetermined (7) Other (specify) ____
	Mucosal (circle one only) (1) Oral (2) Nasal (3) Conjunctival (4) Rectal (5) Genital (6) Surgical wound (7) Burn (8) Open lesion (9) Devices (specify site) ____ (10) MBS Contact Yes No Site ____	Yes ____ 1	No ____ 2	Yes ____ 1	No ____ 2	? ____ 3	(1) R.N. (2) M.D. (3) R.T. (4) P.T. (5) L.P.N. (6) Undetermined (7) Other (specify) ____
	Mucosal (circle one only) (1) Oral (2) Nasal (3) Conjunctival (4) Rectal (5) Genital (6) Surgical wound (7) Burn (8) Open lesion (9) Devices (specify site) ____ (10) MBS Contact Yes No Site ____	Yes ____ 1	No ____ 2	Yes ____ 1	No ____ 2	? ____ 3	(1) R.N. (2) M.D. (3) R.T. (4) P.T. (5) L.P.N. (6) Undetermined (7) Other (specify) ____
	Mucosal (circle one only) (1) Oral (2) Nasal (3) Conjunctival (4) Rectal (5) Genital (6) Surgical wound (7) Burn (8) Open lesion (9) Devices (specify site) ____ (10) MBS Contact Yes No Site ____	Yes ____ 1	No ____ 2	Yes ____ 1	No ____ 2	? ____ 3	(1) R.N. (2) M.D. (3) R.T. (4) P.T. (5) L.P.N. (6) Undetermined (7) Other (specify) ____

University of California at Irvine Medical Center
Orange, California

Employee Health Questionnaire

UCIMC EMPLOYEE HEALTH QUESTIONNAIRE 1989

Name: ______________________ Home Phone: ( ) ________ Birth Date: ________

?? Previous name at UCIMC: ______________________

Job Title: ________________ Department: ____________ Shift: ______ Ext.: ______

		YES	NO
1.	Other than common colds, have you had a healthy year?	☐	☐
2.	Number of workdays lost due to illness/injury/surgery? ________ (Number of days)	☐	☐
3.	Do you take medicine on a daily basis? ________________ (Name of medication(s))	☐	☐
4.	Have you had a constant, productive cough, accompanied by drenching night sweats?	☐	☐
5.	Do you smoke?	☐	☐
6.	Have you ever had chickenpox?	☐	☐
7.	Are you aware of our Employee Assistance Counselor, available to any concerned/ troubled employee, absolutely free and totally confidential?	☐	☐
8.	Do you feel you work in a safe environment? .... If not, suggest improvements: ______________________	☐	☐
9.	Do you work with any toxic products, such as: chemicals, anesthetic gases, asbestos, ethylene oxide, chemotherapeutic drugs, formaldehyde, mercury, lasers, radiation, excessive noise or heat? Other? __________ (Please circle) Would you like additional information or training on any of the above?	☐	☐
10.	While working at UCIMC, are you exposed to blood, body fluids, tissue? ...... Please circle how often: Often (daily or weekly); Rarely (monthly); Never	☐	☐
11.	Do you know how to protect yourself while handling patient body fluids, tissue? This means using gloves, gowns/aprons, goggles, masks, and MOST IMPORTANTLY hand washing for at least 10 seconds after each patient contact.	☐	☐
12.	Do you know where these supplies are kept on the unit where you work?	☐	☐
13.	Each employee handling patient body fluids is at risk for hepatitis B. The hospital provides the hepatitis B vaccine free to employees working with these exposures. Have you had the vaccine? __________ (Year completed) Would you like this vaccine?	☐	☐
14.	**New Isolation Standards:** Body Substance Precautions mean that *all* patient body fluids (anything wet from the body) are considered potentially infectious and require whatever it takes to keep the substance off of you (gloves, mask, gown, goggles . . .) and hand washing at least 10 seconds. Do you need additional training or information on protecting yourself?	☐	☐
15.	Our AIDS Coordinator/Educator is available to discuss any questions or concerns about AIDS issues. This is a free and confidential service.		

Height: __________ Weight: __________ Last tetanus shot? __________

Blood Pressure: ________ PPD/TBC skin test __________ (Date) __________ (Result)

Last CXR __________ (Date) __________ (Result)

Date: ______________ ______________________ (UCIMC Employee Health)

Tucson Medical Center
Tucson, Arizona

Body Substance Precautions Staff Compliance Monitoring Policy

Purpose
To observe and document employee compliance with Body Substance Precautions (BSP) policies and procedures, as well as competency in technique, to prevent the transmission of infections in patients and personnel.

Policy
Monitoring of staff compliance to BSP policy and procedure will be performed at least annually by all departments that have employees who engage in health care activities involving potential exposure to blood and body fluids (category I or II procedures or employees).

Procedure

1. The Infection Control (IC) Department will determine criteria necessary for monitoring. Criteria include hand washing, protective gear, sharps disposal, and fluid-filled container disposal. Criteria will be based on OSHA guidelines and the Infection Control Manual (BSP policy and procedure).
2. The Infection Control Department will determine the quantity of monitoring tools that need to be completed by each department.
3. Monitoring tools will be distributed to the ancillary departments by the IC Department. Monitoring tools will be distributed to the nursing departments by the Nursing Quality Assurance (QA) Department. [Sample monitoring tools are reproduced as figures 5-4 through 5-7, pp. 133–35 in this manual.]
4. Supervisors will observe for adherence to the BSP system during designated health care activities on an ongoing incidental and scheduled basis. The monitoring tool is to provide feedback to the supervised health care worker. Feedback shall include reinforcing recognition for adherence to policies and or reinforcing corrective action for failure to adhere to policies.
5. Departments will return the completed monitoring tools within the allotted time to either the IC Department (ancillary) or the Nursing QA Department (nursing).
6. The Infection Control Department will review and summarize the ancillary data collected. Summarized quarterly reports will be sent to each participating department. Corrective or follow-up action must be documented by the department for any compliance percentage less than 90 percent. A summary of corrective or follow-up action must be sent to the Infection Control Department within the allotted time. A BSP audit of compliance summary will be submitted to the QA Department quarterly. Information will be made available to the pertinent departments.
7. The Nursing QA Department will review and summarize the nursing data collected. A summary will be sent to the nursing patient care managers quarterly. An annual BSP audit of compliance summary will be submitted to the QA Department.
8. The institution of changes and/or staff education will be based on the results of the quarterly summaries.

Tucson Medical Center
Tucson, Arizona

Infection Control/Quality Assurance Monitoring Tools

Figures 5-4 through 5-7 show examples of the monitoring tools used at the Tucson Medical Center to monitor compliance with Universal Precautions.

Figure 5-4. Monitoring Tool: Use of Protective Gear

Tucson Medical Center
Infection Control/
Quality Assurance
Monitoring Tool

Date ____________
Unit ____________
Monitor's Initials ______

Title: BSP Protective Gear

Instructions: Observation of competency and/or procedure compliance of the health care staff in the performance of direct patient care.

Criteria	Yes	No*	NA
1. Gloves are worn when touching blood, body fluids, mucous membranes, or nonintact skin.			
2. Gloves are worn for handling of items or surfaces soiled with blood or body fluids.			
3. Gloves are worn when contact with blood is possible (I.V. initiation, fingersticks, etc.).			
4. Gloves are worn when policy or procedure requires them.			
5. Hands are washed immediately after gloves are removed.			
6. Gowns or aprons are worn when there is potential for blood and/or body fluids to splash onto the care giver.			
7. Masks, eyewear, and/or face shields are worn when policy or procedures require them.			
8. Protective facewear is worn when care is likely to generate droplets or splashing that could expose mucous membranes of care giver.			
9. Protective gear is available for use.			

Title of person being observed ______________________________

*Document any follow-up action for noncompliance on Follow-up Action Form.

Figure 5-5. Follow-up Action Form Printed on Reverse Side of All Compliance Monitoring Tools

Tucson Medical Center
Infection Control/
Quality Assurance
Follow-up Action Form

Document noncompliant activity and follow-up action for each response in the "No" column on the audit. Follow-up action includes any action such as reeducation, obtaining necessary equipment, inclusion in staff meeting discussions, etc. Infection Control is available to assist with recommendations if needed. If you wish to keep your own documentation, please copy and send original to the Infection Control Department.

Activity ____________________

Figure 5-6. Monitoring Tool: Sharps Disposal

Tucson Medical Center
Infection Control/
Quality Assurance
Monitoring Tool

Date ________
Unit ________
Monitor's Initials ______

Title: BSP Sharps Disposal

Instructions: Observation of competency and/or procedure compliance of the health care staff in the performance of direct patient care.

Criteria	Yes	No*	NA
1. All used needles/syringes contaminated with blood/body fluids are placed uncapped in the sharps box immediately after using.			
2. Used needles/syringes that are recapped are done so with a recapping device or with a one-hand technique.			
3. Biohazardous sharps disposal boxes are present in all patient rooms, med. room, med. cart, and dirty utility room.			
4. All sharps from patient procedure trays are placed in the sharps box immediately after the procedure is completed.			
5. Sharps disposal boxes are not overfilled and are properly disposed of when full.			
6. Sharps disposal box key is available to all personnel for the exchanging of inner liners.			
7. Needles are left intact after use and no needle cutters are present in the unit or area.			
8. Appropriate equipment/resources are available for use for sharps disposal.			

Title of person being observed ____________________

*Document any follow-up action for noncompliance on Follow-up Action Form.

Figure 5-7. Monitoring Tool: Physicians

Tucson Medical Center
Infection Control/
Quality Assurance
Monitoring Tool

Date ______________
Unit ______________
Monitor's Initials ______

Title: BSP Compliance Monitor for Physicians

Instructions: Observation of competency and/or procedure compliance of the physician in the performance of direct patient care.

Criteria	Yes	No*	NA
1. Washes hands between patients.			
2. Washes hands after performing any procedures on the patient.			
3. All used needles/syringes contaminated with blood/body fluids are placed uncapped in the sharps disposal box after use.			
4. Needles that are recapped are done so with a recapping device or with a one-hand technique.			
5. Gloves are worn when touching blood or body fluids, mucous membranes, or nonintact skin of all patients.			
6. Gloves are worn for handling of items or surfaces soiled with blood or body fluids.			
7. Gloves are worn when performing any procedure that may expose the physician to blood or body fluids or when policy or procedure requires.			
8. Hands are washed immediately following removal of gloves.			
9. Masks, eyewear, face shields, or gowns are worn when policy or procedure requires or when care is likely to generate droplets or splashing.			

*Document any follow-up action for noncompliance on Follow-up Action Form.

Yale-New Haven Hospital
New Haven, Connecticut

Compliance Monitoring and Enforcement for Universal Precautions

Employees and nonemployees must be provided with education about Universal Precautions requirements and given notice that failure to comply with Universal Precautions (and other infection control requirements) will be considered as part of the performance evaluation process and as a potential disciplinary ground (to the extent that this is applicable).

The compliance section addresses the mechanisms for compliance monitoring and enforcement of the Universal Precautions Program for the following categories of personnel:

A. Medical staff
B. Employees
C. Other nonemployees (inclusive of students and volunteers)

Medical Staff

1. Education of the medical staff about YNHH infection control requirements should initially be continued via an informational column published in the Medical Staff Bulletin. We recommend that an update appear in that publication at least annually.
2. A resolution is to be proposed to the Medical Board that educational information be mailed to members of the medical staff. Education of the medical staff and their commitment to comply is reflected on a signature page to be signed by individual members of the medical staff and returned to the Chief of Staff's office for inclusion in their individual files.
3. Members of the medical staff who are particularly involved in resident supervision (at least chiefs and associate chiefs of service and chiefs of clinical sections in diagnostic imaging, for example) should receive copies of information that is provided the house staff during orientation. This will enable the chiefs to reinforce hospital requirements with the house staff and leave no doubt as to what information the house staff has received.
4. Rule #25 of the medical staff rules and regulations needs revision; this process has already begun.
5. The Chief of Staff should receive summary reports as described below (having to do with employee compliance with Universal Precautions) and should receive information on incident reports from Risk Management.

Employees

1. The Code of Employee Conduct must be revised to include the following language: Employees are expected to conform to appropriate infection control policies in their contacts with patients and with blood and body fluids. (Precise language to be discussed with Human Resources.)

   The new code should be distributed to all employees, including casual-status employees, in high-risk areas. The brochure is already being distributed to new orientees.
2. All job descriptions should be categorized as including category I, II, or III tasks as defined by OSHA.
3. All employees should be informed that compliance with appropriate infection control procedures is expected and will be addressed during performance appraisals. There seems to be no need to create a separate category on the appraisal form.
4. Notice of expected compliance and the consequence of noncompliance should be given to the collective bargaining unit representing the Food and Nutritional Service

Workers. The Director of Employee Relations believes that such notice can be delivered in writing at the time the code of employee conduct is revised or before if needed.

5. During orientation, the code of employee conduct should be distributed, and house staff members should be informed that discipline will follow for inadequate compliance with hospital Universal Precautions and infection control policies and procedures. The chief of each section (and subsection where appropriate) should receive copies of materials distributed during orientation. Attendance at these sessions should be documented.

   We suggest that the house staff be informed by letter from the Chief of Staff about Universal Precautions and infection control expectations.

Incident Reports

We suggest that the incident-reporting procedure be reviewed and updated to include failures of Universal Precautions and infection control technique (already being reported in the OR). Incident reports (or some modification of the form) should be used to report lack of compliance by any person, employee or nonemployee (including members of the medical staff). The data should be accumulated and collated by Risk Management and distributed at appropriate intervals to the Chief of Staff, Chiefs of Service, and Epidemiology and Infection Control. Incidents of particular concern should be followed up immediately with the appropriate individual.

Nonemployees (Others)

This category includes nursing and other students, volunteers, etc. Students and others should have received appropriate Universal Precautions and infection control training before arrival here (or we can make arrangements for training if we wish). Failure to comply with our policies should result in the removal of the student from hospital premises. Contracts with educational facilities that send students here should address this issue.

Guidelines for Universal Precautions Monitoring and Documentation

Each manager shall design a system to monitor and document, in a fair and equitable manner, individual compliance with the practice of hospital Universal Precautions and infection control policies and procedures.

Compliance monitoring and enforcement should include the direct observation of each employee at least one day every six months to ensure that the required work practices are observed and that the appropriate protective clothing and equipment are properly used.

Interdepartmental Reporting

1. An incident report shall be submitted to the Department of Risk Management and Medicolegal Affairs for all instances where an individual's technique is not consistent with hospital Universal Precautions and infection control policies and procedures. An incident report shall also be submitted for instances where protective barrier equipment or supplies fail to provide adequate protection against blood, body fluids, and tissues.
2. All defective protective barrier equipment/supplies shall also be reported to the Department of Purchasing by the responsible manager.
3. A Supervisor's First Report of Accident/Injury (F-1797) shall be submitted to Personnel Health Service following all incidents of actual exposure to blood, body fluids, or tissues.

Departmental Records

Following compliance monitoring, records shall be maintained for all instances that an employee is observed to be either compliant or noncompliant with the practice of Universal Precautions and infection control.

Departments shall maintain the following documentation:

1. Individual compliance and noncompliance as observed during the routine and incidental observation of individual work practices shall be documented. Routine monitoring should occur at least once every six months.
2. Educational sessions provided to employees and nonemployees shall be documented, including:
   a. Outline of content
   b. Date of session
   c. Length of session
   d. Signatures of those in attendance

   Initial education and training sessions should occur before individuals assume their responsibilities.
3. Actions taken in the event that instances of noncompliance or patterns of noncompliance are noted shall be documented. Educational sessions should occur for initial instances of noncompliance. If noncompliance continues, disciplinary action may be necessary.
4. Patterns of compliance and noncompliance shall be reflected in each employee's performance review.

Chapter 6

Training and Education

Introduction

Employee training and education have always been major components of infection prevention and control programs in health care facilities.[1] Employees must have the necessary knowledge and skills to perform the required protective practices to reduce their risk of occupational exposure to bloodborne pathogens. This chapter discusses strategies for developing a comprehensive education and training program, including methods for planning, presenting, and evaluating programs.

Successful training and education programs are the result of a cooperative effort of a number of individuals, including members of the infection control and employee health staff, education department, and management and staff in clinical and support departments. However, the coordination of all planning and implementation activities for the program will need to be assigned to a specific individual or a small group of individuals, with input from key staff members. The key components of the training and education program that must be addressed in the planning stages include the following:

- The target audience
- Individual(s) to conduct training programs
- Objectives and learning outcomes
- Content and duration of each training session
- Time period for the completion of each component of the training program
- Presentation methods and style
- Evaluation methods

Each target audience identified will require programs that are tailored to its specific job, educational background, level of expertise, and language. This can be achieved by involving employee representatives from each of the identified target audiences. Specific information on different job functions can also be obtained by the trainer at the beginning of an educational session by asking the participants to identify those activities that are unique to their jobs. This information can be used to train the audience on protective practices that are applicable to its specific jobs or tasks.

The primary trainers will also need to be identified. Because it is often impossible for one individual to conduct training sessions for all employees, many facilities have enlisted the help of additional trainers through a "train the trainer" program. This strategy involves the training of specific individuals who will be responsible for the training of staff assigned to them or in their department.

Most facilities have an organized method to train newly hired personnel, but some may be less systematic in training personnel who are already employed. Some facilities have an "annual infection control update" program; others target specific departments on a rotating basis throughout the year. The most difficult groups to reach in these training programs are usually the medical staff and contract personnel.

The development of clear instructional objectives and specific learning outcomes will be useful for establishing the presentation and evaluation methods. These objectives and outcomes become essential when a number of different trainers are used, such as in train-the-trainer programs.

The specific content of the program will need to be related to the established objectives and learning outcomes and the identified needs of the target audience. The Occupational Safety and Health Administration (OSHA) has specific requirements for the content of education and training programs, which incorporate recommendations on Universal Precautions from the Centers for Disease Control (CDC). The requirements include initial and periodic training with the following content:

- Modes of transmission of bloodborne pathogens
- Methods for identification of tasks and activities that involve potential exposure
- Engineering controls and workplace practices to reduce the risk of exposure, including proper handling of sharps, cleaning of blood and body fluid spills, and handling and disposal of contaminated/infectious waste
- Type, selection, location, indications, proper use, removal, handling, and disposal or reprocessing of personal protective equipment
- Explanation of warning signs, warning labels, and/or color coding identifying potentially infectious material
- Explanation of the procedure to be followed when an exposure incident occurs, including the reporting method and availability of medical follow-up
- Information on the availability and benefits of hepatitis B vaccination

In addition, OSHA's proposed standard on Occupational Exposure to Bloodborne Pathogens requires that a copy of the actual standard and an explanation of its content be provided to all employees. This requirement is consistent with other OSHA standards. (Information on OSHA's current and proposed training requirements is included in chapter 8.)

Ideally, training and education should begin before the employee is expected to perform a specific task or procedure and periodically in refresher sessions to ensure that the knowledge and skills have been retained. After initial training is provided, additional training may need to be targeted to problems identified with specific employees or noncompliance with procedures. The amount of time needed for initial and repeated education and training sessions is a function of several factors, including the following:

- The number of personnel to be trained
- The size of the audience at each training session
- The duration of each training session
- The time period for completion of training of all personnel
- The number of personnel successfully trained at the end of the initial training period
- The number of annual sessions needed to accommodate staff turnover

Each of these factors will need to be assessed. For example, if a facility had 1,000 employees (including members of the medical staff) and the maximum number of employees per session were about 30, 30 to 35 individual training sessions would need to be conducted. If the training was to be conducted during a period of six weeks, 5 or 6 sessions would need to be arranged each week. Staffing also needs to be considered for all shifts. Training sessions may need to be provided to staff during their regularly scheduled hours or after a shift is completed when attendance is mandatory and employees are paid for their time.

The presentation method and style may vary depending on the established objectives, target audience, available resources, amount of time available, and location of the presentation. Successful presentations combine lectures, written materials, audiovisual aids, and audience participation. Combining two or three approaches to present information maximizes the learners' opportunity to master the material in a short time.

Many different types of audiovisual aids can be used in presenting educational sessions. In addition to using commercially available products, many facilities have developed their own materials. For example, written handouts can be provided that outline or summarize important points and provide a space for note taking. If more than one person will be conducting the training sessions, guidelines outlining each step in the training program must be developed for each trainer to follow.

Evaluation methods can range from informal interactions among participants to formal evaluation techniques. Informal evaluations of the knowledge gained during the training session can consist of asking the learners whether they understood the information provided or asking them to explain what they have learned. Using an informal question-and-answer evaluation method at the end of a program is a quick way to assess whether learners have understood the content of the presentation. Another method is to prepare a short quiz to be given at the end of the session. The trainer can review the correct responses to the quiz verbally with each learner, who scores his or her own answers. This will reinforce what was presented and prompt questions on specific topics that may still be unclear. More formal methods of assessing the outcomes of training programs include the use of pretests and posttests to compare the learners' knowledge before and after the session. Posttests can also be given several weeks or months after the initial training session to determine whether the information has been retained over time.

It is more difficult to evaluate changes in behavior. Formal observational studies are needed to evaluate behavioral changes and require significant resources and trained observers not available in many facilities. Considerations for formal observational studies to evaluate behavior and monitor compliance with recommended practices were discussed in chapter 5.

Employees should be provided with the results of any program evaluations. These evaluations may also provide information that will be useful for modification of both future training programs and specific components of the overall Universal Precautions program.

Records must be kept on all training and education. The records should include the dates and content of all programs, the names of the individuals conducting the programs, and the names of all persons in attendance. Because these training sessions are *required* by OSHA, methods need to be established to ensure that *all* employees whose jobs put them at risk of occupational exposure to bloodborne pathogens attend the training sessions. The responsibility for verifying attendance and keeping records may be assigned to individual department managers or managed through a centralized system.

Training and education programs provide the basic knowledge and skills necessary to comply with Universal Precautions. However, when performance problems are identified, the nature of the problem should be assessed before the education and training session is repeated. Not all performance problems are caused by knowledge and skill deficits and not all will respond to education as the corrective strategy. Reasons for poor performance can be grouped into three major categories[2]:

- *Lack of knowledge or skill.* When staff members are unable to perform a task properly either because of a lack of skill or because of a lack of critical information, then providing additional training and education will often solve the problem.
- *Lack of equipment or supplies.* When equipment or supplies are inadequate for the job, are maintained poorly, or are not placed in convenient locations, performance may be unacceptable, but it will *not* improve with education alone.

- *Management problems.* When personnel fail to perform even though they know what to do and have adequate resources, it is often a management problem that can only be solved through appropriate management strategies. It will not be corrected by further training and education.

Learning to assign a performance problem to the correct category will help define the type of strategy to be followed to correct it. Future education and retraining programs can then be targeted as needed.

This chapter contains a number of materials that will be useful in developing training and education programs. A unique self-learning module was developed by the Children's Hospital National Medical Center, Washington, D.C. This self-learning module and the accompanying posttest and evaluation are reproduced in this chapter.

Sample materials for developing specific components of train-the-trainer programs have been included from two facilities, Tucson Medical Center and Yale-New Haven Hospital. A worksheet to assist managers in developing department-specific guidelines for the use of protective barriers is included in the materials from Yale-New Haven Hospital.

☐ References

1. Soule, B. M., editor. *The APIC Curriculum for Infection Control Practice.* Dubuque, IA: Kendall/Hunt Publishing Co., 1983.
2. Jackson, M. M., and Lynch, P. Education of the adult learner: a practical approach for the infection control practitioner. *American Journal of Infection Control* 14:257–71, 1986.

Children's Hospital National Medical Center
Washington, D.C.

Universal Precautions Self-Learning Module

This self-learning module is used to educate staff initially about Universal Precautions and is also used to orient new employees in a decentralized fashion at the departmental level. It is also used as an adjunct to the annual infection control educational review. It is used after viewing the American Hospital Association (AHA) videotape "Is It Worth the Risk" and our own institution-specific film, for a total of one hour of viewing time. The first part of the self-learning module (part I) is for all hospital workers. Part II is used in addition to part I for all physicians and nurses. A self-test and learning module evaluation form are also included.

Part I Directions: All Employees

Preparation

1. Complete the Attitude Response Survey (completed in U.P. General Inservice).
2. View the film (completed in U.P. General Inservice).
3. Review the following policies and/or associated fact sheets:
   - Universal Precautions for Exposure to Blood and Body Fluids
   - Disposal of Waste: General, Potentially Infectious, and Cytotoxic

Guidelines

1. Study the learning module objectives.
2. Review the learning module. This may be done in one of two ways:
   - A group leader may use the questions to structure discussion/learning or
   - As a self-instructional module
3. Complete the self-test through:
   - Group discussion
   - The self-instructional module
4. Complete the learning module evaluation form.
5. Submit the attitude response survey, self-test, and module evaluation form to your supervisor or designee.

Part II Directions: The Clinical Staff/Direct Care Givers, Including Nursing and Medical Staff

1. Study the learning module objectives.
2. Review the following policies and/or associated fact sheets:
   - Employee Infection Control
   - Department Infection Control/Universal Precautions
3. Review the learning module. This may be done in one of two ways:
   - A group leader may use the questions to structure discussion/learning or
   - As a self-instructional module
4. Complete the self-test through:
   - Group discussion
   - The self-instructional module
5. Discuss specific examples for your work area with the supervisor or designee.
6. Complete the learning module evaluation form.
7. Submit the self-test and module evaluation form to your supervisor or designee.

Part I Objectives

At the completion of the program Universal Precautions Learning Module, Part I, the participant will be able to:

1. State why health care workers and patients are at risk for acquiring communicable bloodborne diseases in the hospital.
2. Describe what is being done to provide protection in the workplace against communicable bloodborne diseases.
3. Identify the major communicable bloodborne disease in the health care industry today.
4. Recognize those areas at CHNMC considered to be at high risk for exposure to bloodborne diseases.
5. Recognize what to do if an employee is stuck by a contaminated needle.
6. Describe the risks of acquiring HIV as a health care worker.
7. Describe the modes of transmission for HIV and HBV.
8. Recognize which body fluids/substances Universal Precautions apply to.
9. Describe how exposure to blood and/or body fluids/substances may occur.
10. Delineate why routine testing for HIV is not recommended for all patients admitted to the hospital.
11. Recognize what patients and health care workers should be tested for HIV.
12. Recognize steps to take if a worker is exposed to HIV at CHNMC.
13. Describe how health care workers can be adequately protected against communicable bloodborne diseases.
14. Specify what is included in Universal Precautions.
15. Recognize what protective barriers are available to health care workers.
16. Differentiate between general versus low and high potentially infectious waste.
17. Recognize how to dispose of all waste.

Part I

Introduction

- In 1983, the Centers for Disease Control (CDC) published the document *Guidelines for Isolation Precautions in Hospitals,* which contained a section entitled "Blood and Body Fluid Precautions." This called for blood and body fluid precautions when a patient was known or suspected to be infected with a bloodborne pathogen.
- In 1987, the CDC published the document *Recommendations for Prevention of HIV Transmission in Care Settings.* This recommends that blood and body fluid precautions be consistently used for all patients regardless of their bloodborne infection status.
- This extension to all patients is referred to as Universal Blood and Body Fluid Precautions or Universal Precautions.

Why Are Health Care Workers and Patients at Risk for Acquiring Communicable Bloodborne Diseases in the Hospital? (1)

- Health care workers perform numerous tasks involving direct and indirect patient contact every day.
- In many hospitals, isolation is not initiated until the diagnosis of an infectious disease is suspected or proven.
- The causative agent is always present in the affected body site or substance before the diagnosis is established.

Transmission before Isolation

- Therefore, transmission of communicable bloodborne diseases before isolation may occur from:
  - Patient to patient
  - Patient to health care worker
  - Health care worker to health care worker
  - Health care worker to patient

Carriers' Inapparent Infection	• In addition, patients and/or health care workers may be carriers of infection; inapparent infection may be clinically unrecognized, yet still communicable.
Infectious Pathogens	• Finally, without their being aware, health care workers may handle blood and body fluids/substances that are infectious with bloodborne pathogens.
Critical Points	• Health care workers want to be assured that both the risk of becoming infected and infecting others while caring for patients is minimized. • And patients want assurance that treatments in hospitals do not put them at risk. • Recently, for health care workers and patients, one of the most difficult issues raised by HIV concerns actions that are needed to ensure a safe hospital environment.

What Is Being Done to Ensure a Safe Hospital Environment and Protection in the Workplace against Communicable Bloodborne Diseases Like HIV? (2)

Critical Point	• It is the responsibility of employers to provide appropriate safeguards for health care workers who may be exposed to blood and body fluids/substances.
CDC	• The CDC has prepared a new category of isolation called Universal Precautions, developed to protect health care workers from exposure to bloodborne pathogens.
OSHA	• For this reason, OSHA of the Department of Labor has issued an advisory notice calling for the timely implementation of Universal Precautions. • This report emphasized that hospitals have the responsibility to: –Provide appropriate barriers –Educate health care workers –Monitor compliance with Universal Precautions and develop a procedure for handling noncompliance among employees
CHNMC	• At Children's Hospital, the Hospital Operations Committee has agreed to implement Universal Precautions for blood and body fluids/substances during 1988–1989. • A task force representative of all key departments has been appointed to oversee the development and implementation of several policies.
Universal Precautions Policy	• Universal Precautions for Exposure to Blood and Body Fluids: –All health care workers should routinely use appropriate barrier precautions when exposure to bloodborne pathogens is anticipated. –Universal Precautions are intended to prevent parenteral, mucous membrane, and nonintact skin exposures of health care workers to bloodborne pathogens.
Waste Policy	• Disposal of waste–general, potentially infectious, and cytotoxic: Disposal of hospital waste shall be

performed in such a manner as to prevent the exposure of hospital employees to potentially hazardous waste and in doing so to help provide a safe working environment.

- The Infection Control Committee has revised the Isolation Policy.

Isolation Precautions

- Isolation precautions—universal and specific:
  - –Universal Precautions for Blood and Body Fluids/Substances will be used in care of all patients.
  - –Specific isolation precautions (for example, strict, respiratory, enteric/skin) must be used with a suspected or diagnosed communicable infection whether community acquired or nosocomial.
  - –Specific isolation precautions are required for prevention of the transmission of nonbloodborne pathogens. Modified category-specific isolation (based on disease) will be used beginning December 1988.

Employee Infection Control Policy

- Employee Health continues to strongly recommend through the Employee Control Policy
  - –Immunization with an approved HBV vaccine as an important adjunct to Universal Precautions for any health care worker exposed to blood and body fluids.
  - –Prompt reporting of any percutaneous or mucous membrane exposure.

Critical Point

- Remember, it is the responsibility of each health care worker to comply with hospital policy and recommended guidelines to protect themselves from communicable bloodborne diseases like HIV.

Is HIV the Major Communicable Bloodborne Disease in the Health Care Industry Today? (3)

Hepatitis B

- No, hepatitis B is considered the major communicable bloodborne disease in the health care industry.
- Hepatitis B is a viral illness that can cause serious damage to the liver.
- Over 300,000 new cases of HBV are diagnosed each year, with 18,000 cases in health care workers.
- Of the 18,000 cases in health care workers, two-thirds are a result of an occupational exposure.
- Of the 18,000 cases diagnosed, 10 percent will be long-term carriers, and such health care workers will have to give up their work.
- In addition, 500 to 600 health care workers whose jobs entail exposure to blood are hospitalized annually with the infection.
- Finally, over 200 deaths per year among health care workers result from hepatitis B infection.
- The risk of infection with the hepatitis B virus following a needlestick from a patient with hepatitis B is estimated to be between 90 and 370 infections per 1,000 adverse exposures.

Critical Point

- The high incidence of infection in some clinical settings is unfortunate because the mode of transmission is well known and infection is readily avoided by attention to work practices and protective barriers as described in Universal Precautions.

What Areas at CHNMC Are Considered High Risk for Exposure to Bloodborne Disease? (4)

- At CHNMC persons at high risk for exposure to hepatitis B infection include:
  - Emergency Room attending physicians
  - Pediatric house staff (including fellows)
  - Surgical chief residents
  - Attending dentists, dental residents, fellows, technicians, and hygienists
  - Nephrology attending physicians
  - All dialysis personnel (nurses, technicians)
  - Pathologists, pathology technicians
  - Clinical Hematology personnel
  - Clinical Chemistry personnel
  - Phlebotomists
  - All attending surgeons and subspecialty surgical fellows
  - Anesthesiologists
  - Respiratory Therapy personnel
  - Burn nurses 3 Green
  - ICU attending physicians
  - ICU nurses
  - Intermediate care nurses 3 Green
  - Operating room personnel having intimate contact with patients
  - Renal nurses
  - Hematology–oncology nurses
  - Cardiac catheterization personnel
  - Decontamination personnel from Environmental Services and Sterile Processing
  - Comp Care phlebotomists
  - Float nurses who work more than 20 hours per week in one of the high-risk areas

Critical Point

- Fortunately, there is a vaccine available, free of charge, to *all* employees who are at risk for exposure to blood and body fluids regardless of where they work.

How Do CHNMC Employees Go about Getting Vaccinated?

- The best way to prevent hepatitis B infection is to receive one of the two vaccines from Employee Health.

Heptavax-B®

- Heptavax-B®, produced from pooled plasma, has been available for several years and is safe.

Recombivax-HB®

- A new vaccine, Recombivax-HB®, produced in yeast using recombinant DNA technology appears to be equally safe and effective.

- Hepatitis B high-risk personnel will have HBsAG and anti-HBs serology screening obtained at the time of employment. If the tests are negative, a currently approved hepatitis B vaccine will be offered.
- The immunization regimen consists of three doses of vaccine.
- The first dose is provided initially, followed at one month and six months.
- Supervisors of employees who do not comply with recommendations will be contacted.
- During the implementation of Universal Precautions, all direct care givers will be asked to review and sign the Hepatitis B Vaccination Consent Form to indicate agreement to be or not be immunized. Those employees who choose to be immunized should contact Employee Health Services for an appointment and bring their consent form with them to their appointment.

What Happens if an Employee Is Stuck by a Needle That Has Penetrated Another Person's Skin? (5)

Needlestick

- The following steps will be taken in all types of needlesticks, regardless of the needle source:
  - Milk the puncture site to expel blood.
  - Clean the wound vigorously with one-half teaspoon of soap and water for 10 to 15 seconds, using friction.
  - Complete and forward to Employee Health a nonpatient incident report and notify your (the employee's) supervisor (report to Employee Health for treatment/policy).
  - Determine the hepatitis B status of the patient.
  - Determine the vaccine status of the employee.
  - Initiate an HB vaccine if the employee was not previously vaccinated.
  - Or give HBIG immediately to an employee not previously vaccinated if the patient is HBsAG positive or if a previously vaccinated employee has inadequate antibodies or is a vaccine nonresponder.
  - Initiate the HB vaccine booster to a previously vaccinated employee if the employee has inadequate antibodies or is a vaccine nonresponder.
  - Draw liver enzymes if the employee develops symptoms suggestive of hepatitis.
  - The HIV status of the patient must be determined.

Given That Hepatitis B Is the Number-One Occupational Hazard in the Health Care Industry, What Exactly Is the Risk of Acquiring HIV? (6)

Small but Recognizable Risk

- There is a small but recognizable risk associated with HIV.
  - Prospective studies suggest that the risk of HIV acquisition (by accidental needlestick) with contaminated needles is under 1 percent, and from

other types of nonsexual contact it is considerably smaller.

- The HIV virus can lead to AIDS.
  - Most people infected with the virus will develop AIDS. This is a serious condition affecting the body's ability to fight infection.
- As of September 1988, there have been 72,648 known persons with AIDS reported to the CDC in the United States.

Pediatric Patients

  - 1,154 are pediatric patients (0 to 13 years old, 78 percent infected in utero or perinatally secondary to maternal infection).
  - 291 are adolescents (13 to 19 years old).
  - 100 children/adolescents infected with HIV are presently followed at CHNMC.

Critical Point

- Recent data on HIV transmission indicate that infection is not more likely to occur in the hospital or health care setting. The rate of infection appears to be no greater among health care workers than in the general population.
- HIV is not highly contagious, and transmission ordinarily requires repeated sexual contact or intravenous inoculation.

How Are HIV and HBV Transmitted? (7)

- Both HIV and HBV are transmitted in the same way, that is, through:

Sexual Contact/Blood and Body Substances

  - Sexual contact
  - Mucous membrane or parenteral exposure to infected blood and body fluids/substances

Mother/Infant

  - Mother/infant (in utero/perinatally)

Critical Points

- All health care workers are concerned about contracting AIDS because of its fatal outcome.
- Pregnant health care workers are not known to be at greater risk of contracting HIV or HBV infection than health care workers who are not pregnant; however, if a health care worker develops an HIV infection during pregnancy, the infant has a 50 percent risk of infection resulting from perinatal transmission.
- If a health care worker develops HBV during pregnancy, the infant has a 70 to 90 percent risk of infection resulting from perinatal transmission.
  - The baby may then become a carrier and has a 25 percent chance of developing chronic liver disease.
- The primary potential risk for health care workers is a percutaneous or mucous membrane exposure to infected blood and body fluids/substances.

What Body Fluids/Substances Do Universal Precautions Apply To? (8)

Body Fluids/Substances

- Body fluids/substances to which Universal Precautions apply are:
  - Blood
  - Body fluids containing visible blood

- –Human tissues
- –and the following fluids:
  Cerebrospinal fluid
  Synovial fluid
  Pleural fluid
  Peritoneal fluid
  Pericardial fluid
  Amniotic fluid
  Semen
  Vaginal secretions

Critical Point

- Universal Precautions do not apply to the following unless they contain visible blood:
  - –Feces
  - –Nasal secretions
  - –Sputum
  - –Sweat
  - –Tears
  - –Urine
  - –Vomitus

How Might Exposure to Blood and/or Body Fluids/Substances Occur? (9)

- An exposure to blood and/or body fluids/substances requires very specific conditions.
- The infectious agent must be directly introduced into the person's body. This means blood and/or body fluids/substances must be introduced through the skin (percutaneous) or by contact with mucous membranes such as the eye, mouth, or nose.

Percutaneous Exposure

- A percutaneous event occurs when body fluids/substances are introduced through the skin.
  - –This can occur by being injured by a needlestick, sustaining a cut by a sharp object, or having blood and/or fluids/substances contaminate nonintact skin, that is, an existing wound, sore, broken cuticle, or chapped skin.

Mucous Membrane Exposure

- A mucous membrane exposure occurs when blood and/or body fluids/substances are splashed into the eye, mouth, or nose.

Critical Points

- There are no known cases of HIV developing after mouth-to-mouth resuscitation.
- HIV (and HBV) are not transmitted by casual contact or through intact skin.
- Limiting means of exposure means instituting Universal Precautions to ensure that health care workers will be adequately protected.

Why Universal Precautions? Why Not Test All Patients at the Time of Admission to the Hospital (Particularly for HIV and HBV)? (10)

- Routine testing has not been recommended for several reasons.

Prompt Treatment in ER

- –Emergency room patients must be treated promptly; results from HIV and HBV screening, however, would not be returned promptly.

Window Period

– For HIV there is a window period wherein it usually takes from 6 to 12 weeks to develop antibodies; this window may extend to 14 months. Transmission may occur during this time.
– For HBV, there is a window period of 90 days.

False Negatives

– Falsely negative serology can occur with improperly performed tests or laboratory errors.

Critical Points

- If work practices are upgraded only following a return of a positive HIV or HBV, then workers would be inadequately protected before diagnosis is made.
- Therefore, blood and body fluids/substances must always be considered potentially infectious for bloodborne pathogens.
- In certain situations, however, patients and health care workers should be tested for HIV.

Which Patients and Health Care Workers Should Be Tested for HIV? (11)

Diagnosis/Screening/ Exposure/Request

- Testing should occur:
  – To determine a diagnosis
  – To screen donor blood and organs
  – To track an occupational exposure
  – When an employee requests testing
- When testing is felt to be a part of a diagnostic workup.
  – General implied consent or written consent at the time of admission is sufficient.
  – However, a health care worker must inform the parents of children tested about the testing and the results.

Critical Point

- It is important to recognize the extreme sensitivities associated with HIV for both patients and health care workers and their right to privacy and confidentiality.

What Steps Should Health Care Workers Take if an Occupational Exposure to HIV Should Occur? (12)

Steps to Take after Occupational Exposure

- If a percutaneous or mucous membrane exposure to the blood or body fluids/substances of a patient infected with HIV should occur, you must:
  – Milk the puncture to express blood.
  – Clean the wound vigorously with one-half teaspoon of soap and water, using friction for 10 to 15 seconds.
  – Complete and forward to Employee Health a non-patient-related incident report and notify your supervisor (report to Employee Health for treatment/policy) for any exposure.
  – Be tested at the time of exposure and at 6 weeks, 12 weeks, 6 months, and 1 year after exposure.

If Routine Testing Is Not Recommended, Then What Can Be Done to Adequately Protect Health Care Workers from Communicable Bloodborne Disease? (13)

Minimize Direct Contact with Blood and Body Fluids/Substances

- Because it is not possible to know when an individual may be infected, consistent use of Universal Precautions reduces the chances of direct contact with blood and body fluids/substances.

- Universal Precautions may provide the additional benefit of protecting employees and patients from a wide variety of other infections.

What Exactly Are Universal Precautions? (14, 15)

Critical Point
- Fundamental to the concept of Universal Precautions is treating blood and body fluids/substances as if they were infected with bloodborne pathogens and taking appropriate protective measures, including the following.

Good Hand Washing
- Hands and skin surfaces should be washed after contact with blood and body fluids/substances and after removing gloves.

Gloves
- Gloves should be worn for touching:
  - –Blood and body fluids/substances
  - –Mucous membranes
  - –Nonintact skin
  - –Items or surfaces soiled with blood or body fluids/substances
- Gloves should be worn for performing venipuncture or vascular access procedures.

Critical Points
- Gloves should be changed after contact with each patient.
- Though gloves reduce the incidence of contamination, they cannot prevent penetrating injuries from needles and other sharp instruments.

Gowns and Aprons
- Gowns and/or aprons should be worn during procedures that are likely to soil clothing or generate splashes of blood and body fluids/substances, for example, exchange transfusions.

Masks and Protective Eyewear
- Masks and protective eyewear should be worn during procedures that are likely to generate splashes or droplets of blood and body fluids/substances, for example, suctioning.

Handling Sharps
- Needles and sharp objects should be correctly handled and disposed of.

Resuscitative Devices
- Resuscitative devices should be used in an emergency.

Work Restrictions
- Health care workers with rashes, exudative lesions, or weeping dermatitis should not perform direct patient care.

Spills
- Spills should be correctly cleaned up.

Waste
- General and potentially infectious waste should be separated.

Critical Point
- Universal Blood/Body Fluid Precautions signage will be posted in all areas where patient care occurs.
- All protective barriers are located in patient care areas.
- A Laerdal pocket resuscitative mask will be available to all direct care givers through their departments.

What Is General versus Potentially Infectious Waste? (16)

General Waste
- General waste is garbage or rubbish that is not contaminated with potentially infectious or cytotoxic substances.

Potentially Infectious Waste

- Potentially infectious waste is that which is visibly contaminated by any of the following:
  - Blood
  - Body fluids containing visible blood
  - Human tissues
  - The following fluids:
    Cerebrospinal fluid
    Synovial fluid
    Pleural fluid
    Peritoneal fluid
    Pericardial fluid
    Amniotic fluid
    Semen
    Vaginal secretions

Critical Point

- Potentially infectious waste is further classified into two categories for the purpose of waste disposal.

What Two Categories Is Potentially Infectious Waste Classified into for the Purpose of Waste Disposal? (16)

- Potentially infectious waste falls into two categories.
- High-risk potentially infectious waste includes:
  - Microbiologic laboratory waste and specimens
  - Other laboratory waste and specimens
  - Pathology waste and specimens
  - Operating room waste
  - Sharps and needles
  - Containers filled with blood or potentially infectious body fluids
  - Disposable items visibly contaminated with potentially infectious substances
- Low-risk potentially infectious waste includes:
  - Partially eaten patient food
  - I.V. tubing
  - Anesthesia and respiratory care equipment
  - Disposable items not visibly contaminated with potentially infectious substances
- Note: See the Waste Policy for the definition and disposal of microbiologic waste, laboratory waste, pathology waste, and operating room waste.

Critical Point

- Low-risk potentially infectious waste and high-risk potentially infectious waste are disposed of differently.

How Are High-Risk Waste, Low-Risk Waste, and General Waste Disposed Of? (17)

Low-Risk and General Waste

- Low-risk waste and general waste are disposed of in single brown plastic bags.

High-Risk Waste

- High-risk waste is placed in clear plastic bags within covered waste receptacles.

Needle/Sharps Containers

- Needle/sharps containers will be located in all rooms where they are used. When full, the containers will be picked up by ESD and placed in red bags for incineration.

Cytotoxic Waste

- Cytotoxic waste (contaminated with drugs that have a toxic effect on cancerous and normal cells) shall be placed in red plastic bags that will be picked up by ESD and sent to the incinerator.

Linen
- All linen will be placed in hampers within the nurse server lined with a clear plastic bag.
  - Linen is not separated.
  - Linen is not double bagged.

Summary
- Blood is the single most important source of HIV, HBV, and other bloodborne pathogens in the occupational setting.
- Infection control efforts for HIV and HBV and other bloodborne pathogens must focus on preventing exposures to blood, body fluids/substances containing blood, and other body fluids to which Universal Precautions apply, as well as the delivery of the HBV immunization.

Part I Self-Test

The self-test for part I is shown in figure 6-1.

Part II Objectives

At the completion of the program Universal Precautions Learning Module, Part II, the participant will be able to:

1. Describe how Universal Precautions will interface with our infection control practices.
2. Recognize the difference between Universal and Specific Precautions.
3. State when and how hands are to be washed.
4. Describe how the health care worker will determine what protective barriers are appropriate.
5. Recognize what factors influence the likelihood of infection with bloodborne pathogens.
6. Apply all principles of Universal Precautions in order to determine what protective barriers should be used.
7. State where protective barriers are located on the inpatient units.
8. Describe how to handle sharp objects, for example, needles and scalpels.
9. Describe what to do if a personal exposure or spill should occur.
10. Describe how to protect self from personal exposure while administering CPR.
11. Describe what should be told to children and families about Universal Precautions.

Part II

Introduction

- All children who are in hospitals should be treated as if they were carrying bloodborne infections.
- The risk of transmission from exposure to infected blood during patient care either by splashing on skin or mucous membranes or by needlestick is certainly low, even when the child is known to be infected.
- Reducing the risk of infection for hospital staff to zero is not possible; however, it is the responsibility of health care workers to learn where barriers are stored in their work area and how to use them.
- All policies have been developed to protect the health care worker and provide a safer hospital environment.

How Will Universal Precautions Interface with Our Infection Control Practices? (1, 2)

Specific Isolation Precautions
- Universal Precautions for blood and body fluids will be used in the care of all patients.

Figure 6-1. Part I Self-Test

Date ______________________________
Department ______________________________
Director/Supervisor ______________________________
Area/Unit ______________________________
Name/Position ______________________________
U.P. Implementation Date ______________________________

Circle the correct response.

True False 1. Health care workers and patients can be at risk for acquiring communicable bloodborne diseases in the hospital because isolation is not initiated until an infectious disease is suspected or proven.

True False 2. It is the responsibility of employers to provide safeguards and of health care workers to comply with hospital policy with regard to blood and body fluids/substances.

True False 3. The major communicable bloodborne disease in the health care industry today is HIV.

True False 4. Persons at high risk for exposure to hepatitis B infection at Children's Hospital include dentists, renal nurses, and respiratory therapists.

True False 5. Either the HB or the HBIG vaccine will be administered to an employee (not previously vaccinated) stuck by a contaminated needle.

True False 6. Prospective studies suggest the risk of HIV acquisition (by accidental needlesticks) with contaminated needles is 2 to 3 percent.

True False 7. HIV and HBV are usually transmitted through blood, amniotic fluid, and feces.

True False 8. Universal Precautions apply to all blood and any body fluid/substance.

True False 9. An exposure to blood and body fluids/substances may occur through the skin or mucous membranes.

True False 10. One reason routine testing for HIV is not recommended is because false-negative serology can occur with improperly performed tests.

True False 11. Health care workers may be tested for HIV to track an occupational exposure or at an employee's request.

True False 12. Patients should be tested at the time of admission to determine HIV status.

True False 13. If a health care worker is exposed to HIV, he or she must be tested at the time of exposure and at 6 weeks, 12 weeks, 6 months, and 1 year after exposure.

True False 14. Fundamental to the concept of Universal Precautions is wearing gloves for any patient contact.

True False 15. Health care workers with rashes, exudative lesions, or weeping dermatitis must be restricted from all work.

True False 16. Universal Precautions include separating general and potentially infectious waste.

True False 17. All direct care workers are assigned a pair of protective eyewear.

True False 18. The primary difference between high- and low-risk waste is the presence/absence of visible blood, body fluids containing blood, or body fluids to which Universal Precautions apply.

True False 19. All potentially infectious waste is disposed of in a clear plastic bag within a lidded waste receptacle.

True False 20. Dirty diapers are usually disposed of in a single brown plastic bag.

True False 21. I.V. tubing is treated as low-risk waste.

Answer Key

Answer	*Objective*	*Answer*	*Objective*	*Answer*	*Objective*
1. True	1	8. False	8	15. False	14
2. True	2	9. True	9	16. True	14
3. False	3	10. True	10	17. False	15
4. True	4	11. True	11	18. True	16
5. True	5	12. False	11	19. False	17
6. False	6	13. True	12	20. True	17
7. False	7	14. False	13	21. True	17

- Specific isolation precautions are required for the prevention of nonbloodborne pathogens. Modified category-specific isolation (based on disease) techniques will be used. (Implementation, December 1988.)

Critical Point

- Universal and Specific Isolation Precautions are intended to supplement rather than replace recommendations for routine infection control such as:
  - –Using gloves to prevent gross contamination
  - –Good hand washing

When Should Hands Be Washed? (3)

Critical Point

- Studies show that professionals wash hands about 30 percent of the time when it is called for.

Patient Circumstances

- The CDC recommends that we consider circumstances, that is, the intensity, duration, and sequence of activity with a patient, to determine the need for hand washing.
- Routine, brief patient care activities do not require hand washing, for example:
  - –Shaking hands
  - –Taking blood pressures

When to Wash

- Hands are to be washed:
  - –When coming on and going off duty
  - –When obviously soiled
  - –Before performing an invasive procedure
  - –Before/after contact with wounds
  - –Before contact with a susceptible patient
  - –After contact with a source likely to be contaminated with microorganisms
  - –Between contacts with patients
  - –Prior to leaving a patient's room
  - –After performing personal body functions
  - –Before and after meals or snacks
  - –After removal of barrier precautions, including gloves
  - –Before preparing and administering medications or food

Critical Point

- When in doubt, wash your hands.
- Hand washing continues to be the most effective procedure for preventing the spread of infection.
- Wearing gloves does not reduce the number of times hands should be washed.

How Should Hands Be Washed? (3)

Hand Washing Procedure

- The following steps outline the procedure for hand washing:
  - –Using continuously running warm water and one-half teaspoon of soap, make a good lather, and rub all hand surfaces together vigorously for 10 to 15 seconds. Friction counts.
  - –Check nailbeds, cuticles, and under the nails for the removal of debris.
  - –Hold hands down so that water drains from the fingertips into the sink rather than running back toward the elbows.

– Rinse well.
– Dry with a paper towel.

Critical Point
- Do not contaminate your hands after washing by turning off the faucet or raising the waste receptacle lid with hands (if necessary use a paper towel for this purpose).

Patient Education
- While we are working to reduce nosocomial infection, we also have the opportunity to educate children and families about the importance of good hand washing and personal hygiene.
- In addition to washing hands, the health care worker must also consider what protective barriers are appropriate.

How Does the Health Care Worker Determine What Protective Barriers Are Appropriate? (4)

- The following should be considered in order to determine what protective barriers are appropriate:

Procedure – The procedure being performed
Anticipated Exposure – The type of exposure anticipated
Types of Fluid – The type of potentially infectious body fluids/substances:
Blood
Body fluids containing blood tissues
Other body fluids to which Universal Precautions apply
Volume – The volume of blood and/or body fluids likely to be encountered
Route – The probable route of exposure:
Percutaneous
Mucous membrane
Probability – The probability of exposure

Critical Point
- In utilizing protective barriers, some judgment must be exercised based on patient and procedure variables suggesting the likelihood of blood and body fluid exposure.
- The likelihood of infection after skin exposure to HIV, HBV, or any bloodborne pathogens will depend on certain factors.

What Factors Influence the Likelihood of Infection with Bloodborne Pathogens? (5)

- The likelihood of infection after exposure to HIV or HBV depends on:

Viral Concentration – The concentration of the virus (viral concentration is higher for HBV than HIV)
Duration – The duration of the contact
Skin Lesions – The presence of skin lesions on the hands of health care workers
Immune Status – The immune status of the health care worker (for HBV)

Critical Point
- Therefore, immediately and thoroughly wash hands and skin surfaces that are contaminated with:
  – Blood
  – Body fluids/substances containing visible blood
  – Or other body fluids to which Universal Precautions apply

- Remember to wear protective barriers for any anticipated contact with:
  - Blood
  - Body fluids/substances containing visible blood
  - Or other body fluids to which Universal Precautions apply

Do You Wear Protective Barriers When Performing Activities of Daily Living, for Example, Bathing, Feeding, Diaper Changes? (6)

Critical Points

- Protective barriers are worn when performing activities of daily living when exposure to blood, body fluids containing visible blood, or other body fluids to which Universal Precautions apply is likely.

Bathing/Feeding

- Gloves are not routinely worn for bathing or feeding a child if the skin is intact.

Diaper Change

- Gloves are not required for the prevention of infection with bloodborne pathogens during diaper changes under normal circumstances.

Critical Points

- Gloves will not protect the health care worker from penetration (for example, bites).
- Gloves may be routinely worn during the manipulation of any indwelling tube.
- Gloves must be changed between patients (and hands washed) and between dirty and clean procedures on the same patient.

Where Are Protective Barriers Located on the Inpatient Care Unit? (7)

Nurse Servers

- Protective barriers, including masks, gowns, and gloves, will be stocked in the nurse servers by the Linen Department.
- In addition, linens, towels, washcloths, and chucks will be stocked by the Linen Department.
- Patient care supplies, including respiratory, may be stocked by the therapist or nurse.

Clean Utility Room

- Additional clothing (including aprons) and equipment (including protective eyewear) will be kept in unit-specific designated areas (that is, the clean utility rooms). It must be the responsibility of the charge nurse or designee to check these levels throughout the shift.

Dirty Utility Room

- A 1:10 bleach solution will be secured in the dirty utility rooms in all patient areas and prepared by Housekeeping daily.
  - Gallon jugs of bleach may be ordered by the unit secretary through Distribution.
  - Housekeeping will provide clear plastic spray bottles with a line delineating the amount of bleach to add (two squirts) so that the remainder can be filled with water if an additional supply is required.
  - The 1:10 bleach solution must be made every 24 hours.

Resuscitation Devices

- A Laerdal pocket mask will be available to all direct care givers as an additional means of protection to be used in any resuscitative efforts.

Child's Bedside

- Ambu® bags will continue to be available at the bedside of all children in the ICUs, where codes and emergency interventions are more frequent.
- Finally, sharps containers will be readily accessible in all clinical areas where needles/sharps are used, including patient rooms at each bedside.

How Do I Handle Needles and Sharp Objects? (8)

- Needles and sharp objects should be handled in such a manner as to prevent accidental cuts or punctures. Used needles should not be:
  - Bent
  - Broken
  - Reinserted into their own sheaths
  - Unnecessarily handled

Disposal Box

- They should be discarded intact immediately after use into a needle disposable box.

What Do I Do if a Personal Exposure (Such as a Needlestick, Mucosal Splash, or Contamination of an Open Wound) by Blood and/or Body Fluids/Substances Occurs? (9)

Needlestick Exposure

- For a needlestick exposure, milk the puncture to express blood and clean the wound vigorously with soap and water for 10 to 15 seconds, using friction.

Mucosal Splash

- For a mucosal splash to the eye, nose, or mouth, flush or rinse with saline or water.
- For a mucosal splash to the skin or contamination of an open wound, wash with soap and water (and change clothes if necessary).

Critical Point

- All needlesticks, mucosal splashes, and contamination of open wounds with blood and/or body fluids/ substances must be reported to Employee Health by completing a non-patient-related incident report and by notifying your supervisor (report to Employee Health for treatment/policy).

What Do I Do if a Spill Occurs or Equipment Is Contaminated?

Spills

- Spills of high-risk waste must be cleaned and disinfected.
  - Spills on nonporous surfaces (for example, countertops) should be absorbed and disinfected with a 1:10 solution of bleach and water.
  - Spills on porous surfaces (for example, carpets) should be absorbed and ESD personnel contacted to carry out (nonbleach) disinfection.

Personal Equipment

- In addition, protective eyewear, scissors, and clamps contaminated with blood and body substances should be washed with soap and water and wiped with a 1:10 bleach solution.

Nondisposable Supplies

- Nondisposable supplies and equipment used in procedures or codes (for example, cutdown trays and intubation trays) should be bagged and returned to SPD.

How Do I Protect Myself from Personal Exposure during an Emergency or Code? (10)

Gloves
- Gloves are located in every nurse server as well as treatment rooms and should be used to protect oneself from potentially infectious body fluids.

Ambu® Bags
- Ambu® bags are at the patient's bedside in all critical care areas and are located on the crash cart in all areas.

Laerdal Pocket Masks
- Laerdal pocket masks will be available to all direct care givers. Carry your mask with you at all times or know exactly where it is located.

Critical Points
- The mask is easy to clean. The one-way valve can be cleaned for repeated manikin training but should be discarded after one use on a patient.
- Remember that the risk of any single exposure remains extremely small. The emergency care of a child should never be delayed because protective barriers are not immediately available.

What Should I Tell Patients and Their Families about Universal Precautions? (11)

- You must assist children and families in understanding the benefits of applying Universal Precautions.

Good Work
- The routine use of appropriate work practices and protective barriers is a prudent step toward protecting the health of all.

Critical Point
- Remind children and families that potentially infectious agents are present in blood and body fluids/substances; while the health care workers practice Universal Precautions, children, families, and visitors should do their part to prevent contamination by:
  - Adhering to good hand washing and practicing personal hygiene
  - Wearing protective barriers when handling blood and body fluids/substances
  - Disposing of waste in the appropriate receptacle
  - Following directives on posted signs for specific isolation and Universal Precautions

Summary
- The risk of nosocomial transmission of HIV, HBV, and other bloodborne pathogens can be minimized if health care workers follow these general guidelines:
  - Take care to prevent injuries when using needles, scalpels, and other sharp instruments or devices.
  - Use protective barriers to prevent exposure to blood, body fluids/substances containing blood, and other fluids to which Universal Precautions apply. The type of protective barrier should be appropriate to the procedure and anticipated exposure.
  - Immediately and thoroughly wash hands and other skin surfaces that are contaminated with blood, body fluids containing visible blood, or other body fluids to which Universal Precautions apply.

Part II Self-Test

The self-test for part II is shown in figure 6-2. The learning module evaluation form is shown in figure 6-3.

Figure 6-2. Part II Self-Test

Date ______________________________
Department ______________________________
Director/Supervisor ______________________________
Area/Unit ______________________________
Name/Position ______________________________
U.P. Implementation Date ______________________________

Circle the correct response.

True False 1. Routine infection control includes using gloves to prevent gross contamination and using good hand-washing techniques.

True False 2. While Universal Precautions for blood and body fluids will be used in the care of all patients, specific isolation precautions are required for the prevention of nonbloodborne pathogens.

True False 3. Hands should be washed after any patient contact, including shaking hands.

True False 4. Wearing gloves reduces the number of times hand washing is required.

True False 5. Hands should be washed vigorously for 10 to 15 seconds.

True False 6. The health care worker must consider the procedure being performed and the type of exposure anticipated before deciding what protective barriers to wear.

True False 7. The likelihood of infection after exposure to HIV or HBV is based only on whether a needle penetrates the skin of both the patient and the health care worker.

True False 8. Gloves should be worn during the manipulation of any indwelling tube.

True False 9. Gloves should be worn when feeding toddlers who may bite.

True False 10. Protective barriers are located in all nurse servers.

True False 11. Needle boxes are located at the sinks in all patients' rooms.

True False 12. Baby and adult Ambu® bags are both located at each patient's bedside.

True False 13. Needles are separated from the syringe and discarded in a needle disposal box.

True False 14. For a mucosal splash to the skin or open wound, wash with soap and water.

True False 15. Spills of high-risk waste must be cleaned and disinfected with a 1:10 bleach solution on porous and nonporous surfaces.

True False 16. Gloves and resuscitative devices should be used to protect the health care worker during an emergency or code.

True False 17. Families need to be taught about good hand washing/personal hygiene, protective barriers, and directives for specific isolation to help minimize the spread of infection.

Answer Key

Answer	*Objective*
1. True	1
2. True	2
3. False	3
4. False	3
5. True	3
6. True	4
7. False	5
8. True	6
9. False	6
10. True	7
11. False	7
12. False	7
13. False	8
14. True	9
15. False	9
16. True	16
17. True	11

Figure 6-3. Universal Precautions Learning Module Evaluation

Please circle the appropriate response for each statement.

SD = Strongly disagree
D = Disagree
A = Agree
SA = Strongly agree
NA = Not applicable

Title of Module PART I ______________ PART II ______________

1. The directions in the module were clearly stated.	SD	D	A	SA	NA
2. The objectives for the module were clearly stated.	SD	D	A	SA	NA
3. The content presented in the module reinforced previous learning.	SD	D	A	SA	NA
4. The content was relevant to the objectives.	SD	D	A	SA	NA
5. The questions in the self-test were clearly related to the objectives.	SD	D	A	SA	NA
6. The exercises were appropriate and helpful.	SD	D	A	SA	NA
7. The content in the module was relevant to employee practice.	SD	D	A	SA	NA
8. The references were complete, covering major points.	SD	D	A	SA	NA
9. The self-test is coordinated with the objctives and content.	SD	D	A	SA	NA

10. What did you find most helpful? Please explain.
11. What did you find least helpful? Please explain.
12. Approximate time for completion? ______________
13. Overall rating of the module (please circle)

Poor				Outstanding
1	2	3	4	5

Thank you for your participation.

Tucson Medical Center
Tucson, Arizona

Body Substance Precaution System Educational Component

Purpose
To educate all hospital personnel to the Body Substance Precaution (BSP) system, HIV consents, and employee exposure protocols.

Timeline

- February 1–February 29, 1988, for all supervisory personnel
- March 1–March 31, 1988, for all other hospital personnel

Method

- Intensive inservice education of all supervisory personnel is to be carried out on the BSP system, HIV consents, and employee exposure protocol by the Infection Control Department.
- Supervisory personnel are to instruct personnel under their direct supervision during the regularly scheduled March staff meeting on the BSP system, HIV consents, and employee exposure protocols.
- All educational inservicing is mandatory.
- It will be the responsibility of the supervisors to enlist attendance of their personnel.

Expected Outcomes

- Allow more direct education in smaller groups.
- Supply a resource person on each shift.
- Allow supervisory personnel the tools necessary to adequately evaluate staff compliance, correction of noncompliance, and reeducation if needed.
- Reduce cost element directly related to the education of all hospital personnel to the BSP system.

Supervisor's Checklist
This checklist will help you set up and maintain the BSP system in your department.

Procedures
Review all your department's procedures to:

1. Determine risk classification (category I, II, or III)
2. List the body fluid to which workers most probably will be exposed and route of exposure
3. Revise any procedure for which the use of protective barriers is required (please send a copy of the rough draft of the revised procedure to the Infection Control Department by April 1, 1988, for review)

Job Description

1. Review all job descriptions by job title and assign to each a category of risk classification (I, II, or III).
2. Personnel Services will be notifying your department when this will be needed.

Training and Education

1. All staff members within your department must be inserviced during your regularly scheduled March staff meeting. A copy of the attendance sheet will need to be sent to the Infection Control Department.

2. Your department will need to include training and education for the BSP system in your decentralized orientation program. A checklist has been developed to assist you with this.

Monitoring

All departments will participate in observational audits quarterly. The PCR department audits will be coordinated by Nursing Quality Assurance. All other department audits will be coordinated by the Infection Control Department. The Training and Education Documentation Form is shown in figure 6-4.

Figure 6-4. Training and Education Documentation Form

Name: ______________________________

Unit: ______________________________

Tucson Medical Center
Decentralized Orientation Program

Each employee needs to document that the requirements of the BSP program have been met by dating and initialing the space adjacent to each item listed. This form will be used for documenting training and education for the BSP system. Following completion of BSP education, the form should be given to your immediate supervisor to be kept in your personnel file in the department.

Date and Initial

______________ Read in the Infection Control Manual: Section 5, Protective Care Guidelines, Section 4.14, Exposure to Blood and/or Body Fluids, and Section 2B 1-8, Policy and Procedure.

______________ Read HIV/HBV Fact Sheet located in Section 6.

______________ Take posttest. Correct answers and review the rationale provided.

______________ Locate the main table of contents at the front of the Infection Control Manual and review any other sections of interest to you.

Tucson Medical Center
Tucson, Arizona

Hepatitis B Virus and Human Immunodeficiency Virus Fact Sheet

Hepatitis B virus (HBV) is the major infectious occupational health hazard in the health care industry according to the Centers for Disease Control. Infection with the human immunodeficiency virus (HIV), the virus that causes AIDS, represents a small but real hazard to the health care worker.

According to the CDC, there are between 200,000 and 300,000 cases of HBV infection in the United States each year. The incidence of reported clinical HBV increases each year.

The most recent data available from the CDC report over 70,000 cases of AIDS diagnosed since 1981. They estimate that 1 to 1.5 million persons are infected with HIV in the United States currently. These are individuals who carry the virus but are either asymptomatic or have AIDS-related complex.

HBV is transmitted, according to the CDC's information, in the following ways:

1. By sexual contact involving the exchange of body fluids (blood, semen, or vaginal secretions)
2. Parenterally by contaminated needles or syringes or by contact with HBV-contaminated blood to mucous membrane or nonintact skin

HIV is transmitted, according to the CDC's information, in the following ways:

1. By sexual contact involving the exchange of body fluids (blood, semen, or vaginal secretions)
2. Parenterally by contaminated needles and syringes
3. Prenatally by transmission of HIV from the mother to the baby
4. Blood or blood product transfusions that have been contaminated by HIV or by contact with HIV-contaminated blood to mucous membrane of nonintact skin

HIV cannot be transmitted by casual contact (for example, sharing a telephone or shaking hands).

Tucson Medical Center
Tucson, Arizona

Body Substance Precaution System Educational Component Posttest

Answer the following questions. Review the answers and rationale that follow the test.

1. Which of the following do you believe is the most important procedure to interrupt transmission of infectious agents in the hospital?
   a. Double bagging
   b. Wearing gloves for contact with body fluids
   c. Terminal cleaning of rooms
2. A patient is incontinent of urine onto the bathroom floor. In wiping up the "spill," should you wear gloves?
   a. Yes
   b. No
3. HIV and HBV can be transmitted by:
   a. Contact with contaminated blood
   b. Sexual contact
   c. Parenteral contact (for example, contaminated needles)
   d. All of the above
4. The BSP system focuses on isolating:
   a. Diagnosed cases of infectious diseases
   b. All blood and body fluids from patients with AIDS or hepatitis B
   c. All blood and body fluids from all patients
5. How long should you wash your hands?
   a. 5 seconds
   b. 10 seconds
   c. 20 seconds
6. In deciding when gloves would be appropriate protective wear, these three factors must be considered:
   1. Contact with blood and body fluids is expected.
   2. Contact with blood and body fluids is possible–use judgment for each procedure.
   3. Contact with blood will not occur.

   Assign a 1, 2, or 3 to each task to describe your decision for or against glove protection.

_____ starting an I.V.	_____ taking a blood pressure
_____ bathing a patient	_____ emptying a Foley
_____ taking in a tray	_____ transfer to stretcher
_____ brushing patient's teeth	_____ assisting with a bronchoscopy or other invasive procedure.

7. The BSP system does not include precautions for which type(s) of disease transmission.
   a. Enteric
   b. Airborne
   c. Contact
   d. Airborne and contact
8. Wound dressings should be:
   a. Considered infectious waste and red bagged at all times
   b. Bagged as "closed and contained" with regular trash
   c. Discarded in regular trash

9. Fluid-filled containers should be:
   a. Considered infectious waste and red bagged
   b. Bagged as "closed and contained" with regular trash
   c. Discarded in regular trash
10. According to the BSP system, appropriate barrier precautions for contact via hands with mucous membranes or nonintact (for example, open cuts) skin would be:
    a. Gloves
    b. Gloves, gown
    c. Gloves, gown, mask
    d. Gloves, gown, mask, and eyewear
11. A nurse who has never had chickenpox has been assigned to care for a patient with disseminated herpes zoster infection. Which of the following is appropriate?
    a. Mask only
    b. Mask, gown and gloves
    c. Ask for a different assignment
    d. No barriers are needed
12. Any time a health care worker has open cuts on his/her hands and anticipates performing a procedure that possibly may put him/her at risk of exposure to blood/body fluids, he/she should wear gloves.
    a. Always
    b. Never
    c. Depending on his/her skill level

Answers and Rationale

1. b. Wearing gloves for contact with body fluids

   Many infectious agents are transferred by contact between personnel and patients. Hand washing and glove usage are the best ways to interrupt transmission.
2. a. Yes, you should wear gloves

   Always wear gloves when handling any body fluids.
3. d. Via contaminated blood, sexual contact, and parenterally

   HIV and HBV are transmitted via all of these routes.
4. c. All blood and body fluids from all patients

   All blood and body fluids from all patients are considered infectious.
5. b. 10 seconds

   Hands should be washed for at least 10 seconds with warm water, soap, and friction. Use lotion if hands are chapped.
6. Starting an I.V. (1)

   – It is a hospital policy that gloves are to be worn when performing any invasive procedure (for example, drawing blood or starting an I.V.).

   Bathing a patient (2)

   – Gloves may or may not be worn, depending on the condition of your hands, whether or not the patient is incontinent, has open sores, etc.

   Taking in a tray (3)

   – There is no anticipated contact with blood or body fluids.

   Brushing patient's teeth (1)

   – Gloves will be worn when coming in contact with blood or body fluids.

   Taking a blood pressure (2)

   – There is no anticipated contact with blood or body fluids; if the patient has open sores or is bleeding, etc., at this site, gloves would be appropriate, and the cuff would need cleaning following use.

Emptying a Foley (1)
– Any time you handle large amounts of body fluids, gloves should be worn.

Transfer to stretcher (2)
– For the most part, no barriers would be necessary; if the patient were bleeding, incontinent, etc., gloves would be necessary.

Assisting with a bronchoscopy (1)
– Gloves are necessary for anticipated contact with mucus and saliva.

7. b. Airborne

   The BSP system provides barriers for any contact with blood or body fluids. For diseases transmitted via the airborne route, special precautions are indicated, including the use of a private room.

8. b. Be bagged as "closed and contained" with regular trash

   Wound dressings are not considered infectious if they are "closed and contained" within another plastic bag or glove for disposal within the regular trash.

9. a. Considered infectious waste and red bagged

   Fluid-filled containers are considered infectious waste and need to be red bagged for proper disposal. Any large volume of blood or body fluid is considered infectious.

10. a. Gloves

    Gloves are to be used for contact with mucous membranes and nonintact skin.

11. c. Ask for a different assignment

    Anyone who has not had chickenpox should not enter the room of any patient with chickenpox or disseminated herpes zoster. A mask does not provide an adequate barrier for those individuals who are susceptible to chickenpox.

12. a. Always

    Gloves should always be worn when performing procedures that may put the health care worker at risk of exposure to blood or body fluids when hands are abraded, have dermatitis, or have any open cuts, sores, or lesions.

Return the finished posttest with the corrected answers to your immediate supervisor. Initial and date your orientation checklist for BSP.

Yale-New Haven Hospital
New Haven, Connecticut

Universal Blood and Body Fluids Precautions Departmental Trainers' Handbook and Reference Guide

Introduction

Since its founding, Yale-New Haven Hospital has traditionally and compassionately cared for the sick and injured. In the provision of such care, the safety of every member of the health care team remains a primary concern.

In anticipation of the need to care for patients infected with human immunodeficiency virus (HIV) (which causes AIDS), hepatitis B virus (HBV), and other bloodborne diseases, the Infection Control Committee adopted a "Universal Blood and Body Fluids Precautions" (Universal Precautions) policy in July 1987. The Universal Precautions policy, endorsed by the Centers for Disease Control (CDC), the American Hospital Association (AHA), and the Occupational Safety and Health Administration (OSHA), applies to all employees at all times, regardless of the patient's age, background, or diagnosis.

The policy focuses on isolating body substances (blood, feces, amniotic fluid, urine, wound drainage, oral secretions, etc.) from the hands and bodies of personnel, primarily by increased glove use, hand washing, and other barrier techniques (gowns, masks, goggles) at times when exposure to a patient's mucous membranes, nonintact skin, and moist body substances is anticipated. The emphasis is on the health care worker's *interaction* with the patient rather than on the *diagnosis* of the patient because the patient's medical history, examination, and laboratory testing cannot reliably identify all patients infected with HIV (AIDS virus), hepatitis B virus (HBV), and other bloodborne pathogens.

The consistent use of Universal Precautions is essential for the safety and well-being of YNHH employees. The provision of a safe work environment is a commitment the hospital takes very seriously. To that end, mandatory training of all employees on the Universal Precautions policy and vigilant compliance with the policy will determine the effectiveness of the Hospital's Universal Precautions program.

Goals of "Train-the-Trainer" Program

1. To assist trainers in gaining knowledge of the content, application, and rationale behind the Yale-New Haven Hospital Blood and Body Fluid Precautions (Universal Precautions) policy
2. To review the reasons why a diagnosis-driven isolation system fails to protect health care workers
3. To provide trainers with information concerning the anticipated changes in hospital infection control practices under an expanded Universal Precautions system
4. To inform trainers of the hospital's accident and incident reporting mechanisms and the medical monitoring services provided by the Personnel Health Service to employees with significant blood and body fluid exposure

Trainers' Curriculum Options

The training curriculum is designed so that trainers can customize their training curricula through the use of department-specific videos as well as answer questions that address the particular needs and concerns of individual departments, units, and services.

The Universal Precautions Trainers' Handbook and Reference Guide contains a suggested format for department-specific training sessions, reading materials, and references. Epidemiology and Infection Control staff are available to answer questions and consult on a department-specific basis.

Universal Precautions Phase I "Train-the-Trainer" Program Objectives

At the completion of the program, participants will be able to:

1. List the modes of transmission of HBV and HIV.
2. Discuss the YNHH Universal Precautions policy.
3. Relate the reasons why a diagnosis-driven isolation system fails to protect health care workers.
4. Identify what protective barriers are required to protect employees in specific patient–employee interactions as well as other situations that involve contact with blood and body fluids.
5. Describe at least three hospitalwide changes in infection control and isolation practices anticipated under an expanded Universal Precautions system.
6. Discuss the location of protective clothing and equipment in each department, unit, and service.
7. Discuss the appropriate actions to take and the persons to contact in the event of accident, needlestick, or significant blood and body fluid exposure.
8. Discuss medical monitoring procedures provided by the Personnel Health Service after an employee sustains a significant exposure to blood and body fluids.
9. Assess individual learning through completion of a learning assessment questionnaire.

Trainer's Checklist

Before beginning a training session, the trainer should consider the following points to help ensure the success of the presentation:

1. Notify participants of the date and time of the training well in advance. Post a notice in the department and remind employees of the date and time.
2. Make sure you have several copies of the attendance record and enough copies of the Universal Precautions assessment questionnaire to go around. Because training is mandatory, every employee must complete a learning assessment questionnaire.
3. Reserve a conference room that is large enough and has the necessary seating capacity for all the participants scheduled for training. If necessary, contact Training and Organization Development to reserve a room, or call the Department of Epidemiology.
4. Make arrangements for the department-specific video by calling the Department of Epidemiology.
5. Make arrangements for obtaining a video cassette player with a television monitor ahead of time.
6. Do not rely on the video alone to address employees' questions. Be sure to ascertain employees' concerns and departmental issues relating to Universal Precautions before showing the video. Write them down and be prepared to discuss the concerns/issues before, during, or after the video showing. Stop the video if necessary to discuss a point.
7. Right before the session is to begin, make sure the chairs are arranged so that everyone can see the television monitor. Make sure electrical cords are arranged so that they do not pose a safety hazard.
8. Plan ahead to have a stock of pencils available for participants attending the session without writing tools.
9. Make sure the lighting in the room is adjusted so that the video can be easily viewed and yet the room is bright enough that discussion can take place.
10. If refreshments are planned (that are optional), make sure they have been ordered well in advance and are delivered on time.
11. Collect the attendance sheet and the learning assessment questionnaires at the completion of the program.

12. File the attendance sheet, the assessment questionnaires, and the duplicate copy of the employee data sheets in the department.

Training Outline for Universal Precautions Trainers

1. Inform employees that they must sign the attendance sheet.
2. Introduce the Universal Precautions training module. During the introduction, discuss the content, application, and rationale for using Universal Precautions. Explain that Universal Precautions are not new and that the practice of wearing gloves, washing hands, and using other appropriate protective clothing (gowns, masks, goggles, etc.) to prevent skin and mucous membranes from coming in contact with blood and body fluids represents good infection control practice. This is something we should have been doing all along to prevent the transmission of microorganisms from patient to health care provider and health care provider to patient.
3. Show the department-specific video.
4. Summarize key points.
5. Administer the learning assessment questionnaire (figure 6-5).
6. After employees have completed their questionnaires, collect the questionnaires and review the correct answers with employees. This will generate further discussion.
7. Explain YNHH procedure for reporting an accident, needlestick, or other significant exposure to blood and body fluids.

Figure 6-5. Universal Precautions Learning Assessment Questionnaire

Yale-New Haven Hospital

Name ____________________ **Department** ____________________ **Date** __________

Universal Precautions Assessment
Phase III
Universal Precautions Respiratory Isolation System

Please check (✓) true or false.	True	False
1. The one-tier Universal Precautions/Respiratory Isolation system eliminates the use of all isolation signs except for Respiratory Isolation.	X	
2. Blood spills should be cleaned up immediately using ordinary soap and water.		X
3. Extraordinary room-cleaning procedures, beyond routine measures, are necessary when AIDS patients are discharged.		X
4. Gloves are necessary when performing routine procedures such as emptying urinals and bedpans and cleaning soiled patient equipment.	X	
5. Clinical specimens should be placed in a sealable plastic bag after collection and before transport to the lab.	X	
6. Waste generated by patients on Respiratory Isolation should be separated by regulated and nonregulated waste in the same manner as waste from other patients.	X	
7. Hand washing is necessary after gloves are removed.	X	
8. All soiled linen is handled in the same manner regardless of the patient's specific diagnosis.	X	
9. Masks should be worn entering a Respiratory Isolation room.	X	
10. Hepatitis B vaccine is recommended for all OSHA category I and II employees and is available through the YNHH Personnel Health Service.	X	

8. Show participants a copy of the Supervisor's Report of Employee Incident. Explain the procedure for completing the form and for reporting the incident to the Personnel Health Service.
9. Explain where protective clothing (gowns, gloves, masks, and goggles) is kept in each department.
10. Answer additional questions. Consult with hospital Epidemiology staff as necessary for assistance or further information regarding Universal Precautions. Be prepared to answer questions about employee compensation. Consult with Human Resources as necessary for additional information.
11. Collect the attendance sheet and the learning assessment questionnaires at the completion of the program.
12. File the attendance sheet, the assessment questionnaires, and the duplicate copy of the employee data sheets in the department.

Yale-New Haven Hospital
New Haven, Connecticut

List of Videotapes Available for Universal Precautions Training

Videotape/Source	Department
AIDS Prevention for Nursing Professionals/GA 6848	Nursing
Is It Worth the Risk?/AHA 067666	ER/Ambulatory Service/ Clinics/Nursing
Hospital Infection Control/Parker Productions	Support Services
AIDS Prevention for Laboratory Professionals/ GA 6847	Laboratory
AIDS/Hepatitis B Infection Control: Protecting the Medical Staff/Triad	Professional staff
AIDS, HIV and Seroconversion: What You Should Know/GA 6846	General

Note: Other videotapes are available from Epidemiology and Infection Control and from the AIDS Care Program.

Other Materials

- *Fight Fear with Fact*—Sabella/Burgess, April 1987. ½", 18 minutes, color. Overview of general AIDS information.
- *Sex, Drugs and AIDS*—ODN Productions, 1986. ½", 18 minute, color. Overview of AIDS. Specifically created for high school students. Excellent for everyone.
- *James E. Hurley—The Human Face of AIDS*—½", 18 minutes, color. Created for a conference on AIDS and Local Government Policy March 17, 1987. Rights reserved J. McBride, CCSU Philosophy Department.
- *AIDS: Everything You and Your Family Need to Know . . . but Were Afraid to Ask*—½", 39 minutes, color. Commonly asked AIDS questions answered by Surgeon General Koop. Well done.
- *An Epidemic of Fear: AIDS in the Workplace*—½", 23 minutes, color.
- *Overcoming Irrational Fear of AIDS—A Coping Strategy for Health Care Providers*—½", 22 minutes, color. Excellent teaching tool.
- *The ABCs of AIDS*—½", 35 minutes, color. Good overview, question/answer format.
- *The AIDS Antibody Test*—San Francisco AIDS Foundation. ½", 15 minutes, color. Good overview.
- *Connecticut Faces AIDS*—½", two separate programs on one 120-minute tape, color. Interviews by Connecticut Public Television with individuals fighting AIDS in Connecticut.
- *Chance of a Lifetime*—½", two separate programs on one 120-minute tape, color. Discussion of AIDS and prevention strategies.
- *Needle Talk—AIDS Prevention Information for IV Drug Users and Their Sexual Partners.* Featuring introduction by Dionne Warwick. ½", 27 minutes, color. New York City Department of Health, 1987.
- *AIDS and Health Care Workers*—Department of Health and Human Services, features Dr. Robert E. Wisdom, Assistant Secretary for Health. ½", 20 minutes, color. March 1988.

Yale-New Haven Hospital
New Haven, Connecticut

Revised Policy for HIV Precautions in Compliance with CDC/AHA Recommendations

The Infection Control Committee of Yale-New Haven Hospital (YNHH) has reviewed the recent Centers for Disease Control (CDC) update concerning HIV infection in three health care workers exposed to blood of infected patients and the subsequent recommendations from the CDC and the American Hospital Association (AHA) Advisory Committee on Infections in Hospitals. The Infection Control Committee endorses the CDC/AHA recommendation for the application of "Universal Body Substance Precautions" to all patients.

The CDC update noted that while "the precise risk of transmission during exposure of open wounds or mucous membranes to contaminated blood cannot be precisely defined, the studies indicate that it must be very low." There continues to be *no* evidence of HIV spread by casual contact or by the routine contacts of patient care.

Although nosocomial transmission is a rare event, the Infection Control Committee accepts the CDC/AHA recommendation for Universal Body Substance Precautions for *all* patients regardless of their individual diagnoses. These precautions include the following:

1. Hands should be washed before and after contact with *all* patients. If hands or other skin surfaces accidentally come in contact with blood or other body fluids, they should be immediately washed with soap and water.
2. Gloves should be worn when contact with blood or body fluids is anticipated, but gloves need not be worn by health care team members in ordinary patient contacts.
3. Gowns, masks, and goggles are *not* routinely required but are indicated where there is a risk of extensive exposure to blood or body fluids through close contact, splashing, or aerosol.

All other YNHH isolation policies and procedures, needlestick precautions, Personnel Health policies, decontamination procedures, and hazardous waste handling procedures will remain unchanged and in effect.

HIV infection is *not* easily transmitted. Documented transmission has been through (1) sexual contact, (2) sharing of contaminated needles and syringes, (3) transfusion of contaminated blood or blood products or contact with contaminated blood to mucous membranes or nonintact skin, and (4) transmission from infected mothers to their infants. All health care workers should be aware of these documented dangers, protect themselves accordingly, and assist in educating other members of our communities to the substantial dangers associated with these high-risk behaviors.

We are unable to predict the full scope of the AIDS epidemic but believe that it will increase, at least for the near future, and that every reasonable precaution for the protection of the hospital worker should be implemented while continuing our ethical responsibility for the optimum care of all our patients.

Implementing the Universal Body Substance Precautions system includes the following elements and should be followed by *all* personnel at *all* times regardless of the patient's diagnosis. Precautions apply to *all* patients (inpatients, outpatients, those seen in Emergency Services) and to contaminated medical equipment and materials. The precautions are based on degree and risk of exposure and the use of proven techniques.

Appropriate clinical judgment should be used when determining which protective barriers are needed. Each area must establish its own standards for consistent use of protective barriers. These unit standards should be based on the individual's skills and interaction with the patient's blood and/or body substances, nonintact skin, and mucous membranes. There is no evidence of HIV spread by casual contact (for example, taking a temperature or blood pressure, bathing or feeding a patient, or giving an oral medication).

1. Hands should be washed before and after contact with *all* patients, paying particular attention to around and under fingernails and between the fingers. If hands or other skin surfaces accidentally come in contact with blood or other body fluids, they should be washed immediately with soap and water.
2. Wear gloves when it is likely that hands will be in contact with blood or body substances (blood, urine, stool, oral secretions, wound, or other drainage). Discard gloves and wash hands after soiling or after contact with blood and body substances of patients prior to leaving the patient's room.
3. Wear protective clothing (gown or plastic apron) when soiling with blood or body substances is expected.
4. Wear masks and/or eye protection when it is likely that eyes and/or mucous membranes will be splashed with blood or body substances (for example, when suctioning a patient with copious secretions).
5. Discard uncapped needle/syringe units and sharps in puncture-resistant containers for this purpose. Containers are located in all patient rooms, treatment rooms, and intensive care units.
6. Discard trash in usual manner according to hospital policy.
7. Bag linen in usual manner according to hospital policy.
8. When accidental skin exposure occurs, remove blood or body substances by washing hands or other exposed areas with soap and water.
9. When significant exposure (needlestick, mucous membrane splash, or contact with nonintact skin) to blood occurs, report the incident to your supervisor, and report to Personnel Health Services for evaluation and follow-up.

Yale-New Haven Hospital
New Haven, Connecticut

Protective Barriers Needed for Specific Activities: Decision-Making Worksheet for Managers

Universal Body Substance Precautions apply to *all* personnel at *all* times, regardless of the patient's diagnosis. These precautions apply to *all* patients (inpatients, outpatients, and those seen in Emergency Services) and to contaminated medical equipment and materials. The precautions are based on the degree and the risk of exposure to blood and body fluids and on the use of proven techniques.

It is important for patient care providers and for those handling contaminated equipment and other materials to use common sense and judgment in determining when and what barriers are needed in particular situations. Departmental/unit standards of practice are to be based on the individual employee's skills and interactions with the patient's blood and body substances, nonintact skin, and mucous membranes. There is no evidence of HIV spread by casual contact (for example, taking a temperature or blood pressure, bathing a patient, feeding a patient, or giving an oral medication).

To begin this exercise, list 10 activities that you or members of your staff do routinely in your department. The activities listed should be those that are performed most frequently by the majority of the employees.

The 10 activities are as follows:

1. ______________________________
2. ______________________________
3. ______________________________
4. ______________________________
5. ______________________________
6. ______________________________
7. ______________________________
8. ______________________________
9. ______________________________
10. ______________________________

When it is being determined whether gloves, gowns, masks, goggles, etc., are required for direct patient care and for activities requiring the handling of blood/body substances or contaminated equipment and supplies, the following decision-making process should be systematically applied.

Activity Name Will this activity result in contamination of hands, arms, uniform, eyes, etc., with blood/body substances? Yes/No

If yes, then department/unit procedures are to be developed that address this activity. If no, the activity does not require the use of Universal Body Substance Precautions.

Activity Name Will this activity result in probable contamination of the hands and arms with blood/body substances? Yes/No

If yes, gloves are required for the activity. If no, the activity does not require gloves.

The following are examples of contacts likely to cause significant contamination of the hands, which require gloves:

- Objects in contact with patient secretions
- Patient contact in which secretions of mouth, nose, rectum, etc., are touched
- Materials contaminated by patient urine
- Materials contaminated by patient feces
- Direct contact with feces
- Materials contaminated with secretions or excretions from infected sites
- Direct contact with secretions or excretions from infected sites
- Direct contact with infected patient sites (wounds, tracheotomy, infected skin lesions, etc.)

The following are examples of contacts unlikely to cause significant contamination of the hands:

- Contact with sterile or autoclaved materials
- Contact with thoroughly cleaned or washed materials
- Contact with objects handled by patients either infrequently or not expected to be contaminated (for example, patient furniture)
- Contact with objects intimately associated with patients but not known to be contaminated (patient gowns, linens, dishes, bedside rails, etc.)
- Minimal or limited contact with patient (shaking hands, taking pulse, etc.)

In situations where unanticipated contact with blood and body fluids occurs, blood and body substances should be removed from exposed areas by careful washing of hands and areas exposed.

Activity Name Will this activity result in probable splashing of the face and eyes with blood and/or body substances? Yes/No

If yes, a face mask and goggles are required for this activity. If no, the activity does not require a mask and goggles.

When significant exposure (needlestick, mucous membrane splash, or contact with nonintact skin) to blood or other body fluids occurs, the employee should report the incident immediately to his/her immediate supervisor, have an incident report completed and signed by the supervisor, and be seen as soon as possible by Personnel Health Services following the incident for an evaluation and follow-up.

In the following examples, several situations are described to which Universal Body Substance Precautions would apply:

1. *Starting intravenous therapy and venipuncture:* A person starting intravenous therapy infusions and/or performing a venipuncture for drawing blood should generally wear gloves. This is especially important if the individual's practice usually results in blood getting on fingers and hands. The major risk in starting I.V.s and drawing blood is for needlestick injuries and/or blood coming in contact with nonintact skin, chapped hands, hangnails, fingers that have abrasions, etc. Careful needle handling is the most important safety measure in this interaction to prevent needlesticks. Under most circumstances, needles should not be recapped, bent, or broken. Used needles should be discarded directly into the designated needle disposal containers, which are strategically located in all patient rooms, treatment rooms, and other specified areas. Vacutainer® needles should be unscrewed using the slot on the Eagleguard® container, or in the case of phlebotomists, the needle disposal box on the venipuncture tray should be used.

2. *Manipulating stopcocks:* Persons who manipulate stopcocks as part of their regular duties often get blood on their fingers and hands during such manipulations. As a consequence, gloves should be worn during these manipulations. It is wise to develop a standard of practice of routinely wearing gloves to manipulate stopcocks to avoid contamination of the hands as well as inadvertent contamination of the line.
3. *Caring for incontinent patients:* Gloves should be worn routinely for activities that involve cleaning incontinent patients and helping patients with toilet hygiene. The major risk in such activities is getting stool underneath the fingernails. Gloves reduce this risk and make hand washing after completing the tasks easier and more efficient for the individual performing the task. The activity may sometimes require the use of a plastic apron or gown to protect the uniform as well as changing soiled pajamas and bed clothing soiled with urine and stool.
4. *Suctioning patients, giving mouth care, emptying suction bottles and other drainage bottles where splashing is anticipated:* All employees need to evaluate their particular situation and their patient's clinical condition, the degree or risk of exposure to a patient's oral secretions, and whether the patient is on a ventilator or not. All employees also need to evaluate their suctioning practices. Masks and eye protection should be used if splashing is likely to occur. Suctioning of a patient's airway should *always* be done with the care provider wearing gloves on both hands. The suction kit contains two gloves to make it convenient for staff to wear gloves on both hands. For mouth care, gloves should be worn if it is necessary to put fingers into a patient's mouth. For activities involving the emptying of suction bottles and other drainage bottles, gloves, gown or apron, masks, and goggles should be worn if splashing of the face and uniform is anticipated.
5. *Emptying urinary catheter bags, bedpans, emesis basins, urinals, etc.:* When patient care provider is emptying a urinary catheter bag, bedpan, urinal, emesis basin, etc., each activity should be viewed as a single interaction, and the tasks for one patient should be completed before going to the next patient. Wearing gloves for handling and cleaning any of these items is prudent because it is difficult to perform these activities without contaminating the hands. It is unacceptable to consider it a single task to empty the catheter bags of several patients in sequence without changing gloves and washing hands between patients. The reason is that studies have shown that health care workers sometimes carry organisms on their hands and spread them from one patient to another while performing sequential activities when they do not wash their hands appropriately between patients.
6. *When a patient has a rash or skin lesion:* Rashes are of multiple causes and may or may not be associated with breaks in the skin. For patients with open, draining lesions or rashes draining pustular or serious drainage, gloves should be worn for contact with the affected areas. New lesions and rashes should always be brought to the attention of the patient's physician to determine the cause and to initiate appropriate intervention.
7. *When should hands be washed and gloves be changed?* Hands should be washed before and after contact with all patients, with particular attention paid to around and under fingernails and between the fingers. If hands or other skin surfaces accidentally come in contact with blood or other body fluids, they should be washed immediately with soap and water. Gloves should be worn when it is likely that hands will be in contact with blood or body substances (blood, urine, stool, oral secretions, wound, or other drainage). Prior to leaving patients' rooms, health care workers should discard their gloves and wash their hands after soiling or after contact with the blood and body substances of patients.
8. *When should an apron or gown be worn?* Aprons and gowns should be worn if the activity performed is likely to result in splashing and soiling of the uniform.
9. *When should eye masks or eye protection be worn?* Protective eyewear and masks should be worn during activities that will result in splashing and aerosolization of secretions. Appropriate clinical judgment should be used in determining when and what barriers are needed.

Chapter 7

Employee Health

Introduction

The importance of employee health cannot be overlooked in an overall Universal Precautions program. This chapter discusses strategies for developing employee health programs that reduce the risk of occupationally acquired bloodborne infections among health care workers. Sample policies and procedures are also included for implementing specific components of a comprehensive program.

Effective employee health programs include strategies for screening and immunization, follow-up and management of exposures, and health counseling. The development and implementation of successful programs require cooperative effort among a number of key individuals, including representatives from the risk management department, the employee health and safety program, the legal department, and the infection control program. The hospital administration's commitment to an effective program and allocation of necessary resources is essential for the employee health program to succeed.

Standardized policies and procedures are needed to ensure the successful implementation of an effective employee health program to reduce the risk of occupationally acquired bloodborne infections. The first step is the identification of workers at risk of exposure to bloodborne pathogens so that educational programs can target methods of reducing the risk of infection, including the availability of vaccines, medical treatment and evaluation following exposures, and counseling.

The primary vaccine-preventable bloodborne infection is hepatitis B, for which a highly effective vaccine has been available since 1981. The most effective strategy in preventing hepatitis B is to immunize individuals prior to occupational exposure.

Preexposure vaccination programs should include the identification of all workers in need of vaccination, including medical house staff, attending physicians, paramedical staff, and students. The choice of specific health care workers to be included in preexposure vaccination programs depends on the philosophy of the institution and its available resources. Some facilities have made the vaccine widely available to employees. This approach is consistent with the health promotion and disease prevention philosophy of many health maintenance organizations that make hepatitis B vaccination widely available to employees regardless of their level of occupational risk. Specific protocols should also be developed for conducting preimmunization screening and obtaining consent, as well as specific recommendations for vaccine storage, dosage, route and method of administration, and contraindications. The Occupational Safety and Health Administration currently requires employers to provide hepatitis B vaccinations free to employees who are at substantial risk of exposure to blood or other potentially infectious materials.

However, the precise method for determining those employees at risk for occupational exposure is still being evaluated by OSHA.

Preexposure vaccination programs should also include strategies for ensuring that employees receive the entire three-dose vaccination series. This is often the most difficult aspect of operating the immunization program.

Postexposure protocols should include precise definitions of what an employee exposure entails, as well as standardized procedures for identifying and testing source patients for serologic evidence of hepatitis B (HBV) and human immunodeficiency virus (HIV) infection, testing exposed employees, and administering required prophylactic treatment for both known and unknown sources. Decisions also need to be made regarding a designated place for the treatment and follow-up of exposure cases. Care providers in these designated areas should be thoroughly familiar with the prescribed treatment protocols. Employees should also be released from their duties to report exposures and receive follow-up treatment. Written informed consent should be obtained, and the risks and benefits of follow-up testing and treatment should be clearly explained. When an employee refuses treatment, he or she should be asked to provide a written statement that he or she has refused treatment and was offered the opportunity for future follow-up. Confidentiality must be ensured throughout the treatment and follow-up process.

Because a bloodborne exposure is often a very stressful event, counseling should be provided for the exposed employee and his or her family members if they desire it. This counseling should be provided by a person specially trained to deal sensitively with the issues associated with exposures to AIDS, hepatitis, and other life-threatening diseases. Counseling should include a discussion of the health risks, recommended follow-up and treatment, life-style and sexual practices to be followed during the follow-up and monitoring period, and any worker's compensation issues.

Immunization recommendations have been published by the U.S. Public Health Service's Advisory Committee on Immunization Practices (ACIP). The ACIP's current recommendations, entitled "Protection against Viral Hepatitis. Recommendations of the Immunization Practices Advisory Committee (ACIP)" include recommendations for preexposure and postexposure screening and recommended preventive treatment, including hepatitis B immunization and the use of immune globulins.[1] [The recommendations are reproduced in chapter 10.]

Recommendations on the management of HIV-infected health care workers and additional information on employees exposed to HIV-infected source patients are contained in the CDC's "Recommendations for Prevention of HIV Transmission in Healthcare Settings."[2] [These recommendations are also reproduced in chapter 10.] Zidovudine (AZT, Retrovir®) is currently being offered as an option for postexposure prophylaxis by some physicians and institutions. However, because of the limitations in current knowledge regarding the efficacy and safety of zidovudine prophylaxis after occupational exposure to HIV, the Public Health Service cannot make a recommendation for or against its use in postexposure prophylaxis. Therefore, zidovudine prophylaxis cannot be considered a necessary component of postexposure prophylaxis management at this time. The Public Health Service does, however, recommend that workers at risk of occupational exposure to HIV should be informed of the considerations pertaining to the use of zidovudine for postexposure prophylaxis. These considerations for zidovudine use, as well as additional guidelines for postexposure management, are discussed in the CDC's "Public Health Service Statement on Management of Occupational Exposure to HIV, Including Zidovudine Use"[3] [reproduced in chapter 10 of this manual].

This chapter includes a sample hepatitis B immunization program from Lutheran General Hospital-Lincoln Park in Chicago. Postexposure protocols are included from a number of facilities.

The use of zidovudine is addressed in sample policies from three facilities representing the variety of approaches taken. The policy from the Veterans Administration Medical Center, Seattle, represents a facility that does not prescribe or administer zidovudine for postexposure prophylaxis but does provide information that can be shared with exposed employees' private physicians. The postexposure protocol from the University of Minnesota Hospital and Clinic includes a statement on providing zidovudine to employees with significant exposures to HIV. A protocol from San Francisco General Hospital is also included; it addresses the management of accidental exposures, including the administration of zidovudine and monitoring of its use. A policy from the Cleveland Clinic Foundation contains guidelines for HIV testing of patients and employees and management of HIV-infected employees, including benefits for employees with occupationally acquired HIV infection.

Because of specific concerns regarding exposures to patients with cytomegalovirus (CMV) and *Mycobacterium tuberculosis* (MTB) infections, sample policies have been included on these two infections. The policy discussing CMV infection is from San Francisco General Hospital, and the policy on the management of exposures to MTB patients is from Kaiser Permanente Medical Center, San Francisco.

☐ References

1. Centers for Disease Control. Protection against viral hepatitis: recommendations of the Immunization Practices Advisory Committee (ACIP). *Morbidity and Mortality Weekly Report* 39(Suppl. S-2):1–26, Feb. 9, 1990.
2. Centers for Disease Control. Recommendations for prevention of HIV transmission in health-care settings. *Morbidity and Mortality Weekly Report* 36(Suppl. 2S)3S–18S, Aug. 21, 1987.
3. Centers for Disease Control. Public Health Service statement on management of occupational exposure to human immunodeficiency virus, including considerations regarding zidovudine postexposure use. *Morbidity and Mortality Weekly Report* 39(Suppl. RR-1):1–14, Jan. 26, 1990.

Cleveland Clinic Foundation
Cleveland, Ohio

Policy Statement on Human Immunodeficiency Virus Infections for Patients and Health Care Workers

Introduction

Human immunodeficiency virus (HIV) infection has become a major epidemic, with serious medical, social, and economic consequences. Physicians must become familiar with the clinical manifestations of symptomatic HIV infection (AIDS and AIDS-related conditions) as well as the indications for, and limitations of, the various laboratory diagnostic tests that are currently available. It is the responsibility of any physician who wishes to perform these tests on his or her patients to inform them about the appropriate interpretation of the tests, the ethical and potential legal implications associated with performing these tests, the need for appropriate counseling before and after the test results are conveyed to the patient, and the need for medical follow-up if the test results are positive (see appendix I [p. 184]).

Definitions

For the purpose of this document, the following terms and definitions apply:

1. *HIV Testing:* This refers to all types of tests for HIV infection and is not specifically limited to testing for HIV antibodies.
2. *Medical Testing:* This refers to HIV testing that is physician initiated and used primarily for the clinical diagnosis and management of the patient.
3. *Educative Testing:* This refers to HIV testing that is patient initiated and used to meet special needs such as assessment of personal risk of infection, education, and personal reassurance. Employees who have sustained a needlestick, sharp injury, or mucous membrane splash of patient blood or other bodily fluids qualify for educative testing through the Primary Care Department.
4. *Preliminary Testing:* This refers to the first stage of an HIV testing algorithm designed for maximum sensitivity and specificity. The preliminary test is generally a test for antibodies to HIV as detected by enzyme-linked immunosorbent assay (ELISA).
5. *Confirmatory Testing:* This refers to the second stage of the HIV testing algorithm and is automatically performed on all initially positive preliminary tests. This is a more specific secondary test for HIV antibodies and generally employs Western blot methodology; however, other or additional secondary tests may be used in the diagnostic algorithm.

Medical Testing

1. Every Cleveland Clinic Foundation physician has the right to order HIV testing. Authority to write an order for HIV testing may be delegated to appropriately trained designees.
2. Patients will be tested for HIV infection only after giving informed consent. The person requesting the consent should be the physician desiring to order the test(s) or his or her appropriately trained designee.
3. In situations when consent may not be possible and when such information is deemed essential for the patient's medical management, consent can be presumed. In the case of minors, a parent or other legal guardian of that patient should provide consent.
4. Consent should be requested orally. A brief documentation of the consent should be made in the patient's chart, where appropriate.
5. Communication of a positive result to a patient should be made only after the results of the confirmatory test are available.

Educative Testing

1. Patients and employees who wish to determine their own status of HIV infection in an atmosphere of heightened confidentiality may participate in the currently available CCF HIV testing and education program.
2. After appropriate counseling, testing will be done in a confidential manner. A brief notation that the patient has been counseled and tested for HIV will be recorded in the chart.
3. If the test result is negative, the patient or employee will be informed and counseled, but neither the lab report nor the test result shall be entered in the patient's chart.
4. If the test result is positive, the result will not automatically be charted. The patient will be informed and counseled. A report will be submitted with the patient's knowledge to the designated primary physician. Subsequent physician charting may include the results of educative testing.

Postexposure HIV Testing of Health Care Workers

1. When an employee sustains a needlestick, sharp injury, or mucous membrane splash of patient blood or other body fluids, that employee should file an accident report with his/her supervisor (policy number 289).
2. The employee should be evaluated in the Primary Care Department as soon as practical after exposure has occurred, at which time the epidemiologic information surrounding the incident will be recorded.
3. After the employee has been counseled, he or she will be encouraged to undergo a baseline test for HIV within two weeks of exposure. Although participation is voluntary, any decision will be briefly documented in the employee's chart.
4. If the patient from such an exposure is identified, consent to permit HIV testing will be sought. In the absence of consent, the request to override a patient's refusal will be referred to the Infection Control Committee, which may authorize the testing of the patient's blood. Results of patient serologic testing will be conveyed to the employee.
5. Employees with exposure to patients whose HIV status is positive or cannot be determined will be encouraged to have follow-up testing at 3, 6, and 12 months after exposure.
6. Documentation and follow-up will be as described under educative testing.
7. Regular full-time employees who develop HIV infection as a result of job-related exposure will be eligible for special benefits (appendix II [pp. 184–85]). In the event of a known incident of exposure, eligibility for these benefits is contingent in part on the employee's immediate documentation of the incident and submission to postexposure HIV testing.

Charting of Test Results

1. Results of medical testing will be recorded in the chart.
2. Results of educative testing will not be recorded in the chart except as provided under #4, educative testing.
3. All CCF employees must preserve the confidential nature of patient testing and results. Employees are bound by Cleveland Clinic Foundation policy to maintain the confidentiality of a patient's record. Breach of confidentiality is grounds for dismissal (policy number 003).

Reporting of HIV Test Results to the Public Health Department

1. After a patient with suspected AIDS or AIDS-related complex (ARC) is found to be HIV infected, a case report will be submitted to the appropriate health department in a timely manner.
2. Reporting will be facilitated by the Infection Control Department.

Health Care Workers with HIV Infection

1. HIV-positive employees or applicants for employment will be treated under the existing policy provided for nondiscrimination against handicapped persons (policy number 18).
2. If any employee becomes physically unable to perform his or her job responsibilities, this situation will be handled under existing Medical Placement (policy number 293).
3. Employees with HIV infection will be evaluated on an individual basis. There is no need to routinely restrict them from working with patients. However, their physical ability to perform tasks must be reevaluated on a regular basis.
4. Infected employees will be excused from mouth-to-mouth resuscitation and other activities subject to medical determination. An integral part of this process includes assessing the type of patient contact required for the job, educating the employee about personal hygiene and infection control, and counseling.
5. Any employee who tests HIV positive at the CCF should be identified to the chairman of the Infection Control Committee. The nature of this information will be kept confidential.

Appendix I

Suggested Information to Be Provided to the Patient prior to Testing for Human Immunodeficiency Virus (HIV) Infection

1. The reason the patient is being asked to consent to and undergo the test
2. How the test is performed, that is, it is a blood test for antibodies to HIV
3. What HIV is
4. The significant implications of both positive and negative tests
5. The material advantages and benefits of having the test performed
6. The material disadvantages and risks of having the test performed
7. That the patient has the freedom to refuse the test and that the decision and/or test outcome will not affect his or her present or future health care
8. That the results of the test may become part of the patient's medical record and could be disclosed to third-party payers
9. That the results of the test (if a diagnosis of AIDS or ARC were to be made) would be reported to the appropriate health department

Appendix II

Benefit Provisions for Job-Related HIV-Infected Employees

Given the unique aspects of HIV infection and AIDS as life-threatening, regular full-time employees who develop HIV infection as a result of job-related exposure will be eligible for special benefits.

Eligibility for these benefits shall be determined by agreement of a Review Panel that the HIV infection is the result of Cleveland Clinic Foundation work-related activities. The panel shall consist of the chairman and vice-chairman of the Infection Control Committee and the director of the Section of Clinical Virology. In the event of a known incident of exposure, eligibility for these benefits is conditioned upon the employee's immediate documentation of the incident and submission to the procedures delineated in the Post-exposure HIV Testing of Health Care Workers section of the AIDS Policy. In the event of no known specific incident of exposure, the Review Panel may nonetheless conclude that an employee is eligible for these benefits if other evidence exists that supports this conclusion.

Benefit Coverage

During the initial six-month period when an employee is on medical leave of absence or restricted duty, the following benefits will continue according to normal plan provisions and as amended below:

- Health plan
  - Copays and deductibles for drugs required for the treatment of AIDS will be waived.
- Elected BeneFlex plans
- Core life insurance
- Pension service credit
- Salary continuation
  - Salary continuation will be extended to employees in their first year of employment for medical leaves associated with job-related HIV infection or AIDS. Pay will be continued given the schedule applicable to year one in the Salary Continuation Policy.

After six months of continuous disability, the employee will be placed on disabled status and the following will occur:

- Payments will be provided in an amount at least equivalent to the long-term disability benefit, even if this benefit has not been elected.
- Health plan coverage, including the drug waiver cited above, will continue with no premium charge for the plan in effect at the onset of disability.
- Core life insurance will continue with no premium charge.
- Optional life insurance may be converted if the employee chooses to remit the premium.
- Dental and DEH coverage under BeneFlex will stop unless the employee wants to continue at full plan cost.

Charlotte Hungerford Hospital
Torrington, Connecticut

Management of Employee Exposure to Blood/Body Fluids

Policy

1. It is the policy of The Charlotte Hungerford Hospital to investigate each incident of employee exposure to blood and body fluids and to provide appropriate care as specified in this procedure.
2. A quality assurance report must be filled out by the employee.

Definition: An *exposure* is defined as any percutaneous, mucous membrane, or nonintact skin contact with the blood or body fluids of a patient, either directly or indirectly. The exposure might be in the form of a puncture wound, bite, or splash or might involve nonintact skin (that is, dermatitis).

Procedure

1. The affected employee reports to the Emergency Department as soon after the incident as possible.
   (a) First aid is administered.
   (b) A brief account of the circumstances of the incident is elicited and recorded on the form ER Report of Employee Exposure to Blood/Body Fluids [see figure 7-1]. Forward the form, along with a copy of the Emergency Department record, to the Personnel Health Department.
2. Administer tetanus–diphtheria if necessary [see figure 7-2].
3. If there was no contact with a patient's blood/body fluids (that is, clean needle/sharp object-inflicted wound), nothing further needs to be done.
4. If there was contact with blood/body fluids or if the source was unknown, determine the hepatitis B vaccination status of the employee.
   (a) Follow the steps indicated [figure 7-3] for the hepatitis B vaccinated and nonvaccinated employee.
      (1) The HBsAb status of a vaccinated employee may be obtained from the Personnel Health Department if unknown by the employee.
      (2) For the unvaccinated employee, administer HBIG and initiate the vaccine series. An informed consent for HB vaccination must be signed by the employee [see figure 7-4]. Forward this form to Personnel Health.
5. Inform the employee that he/she may elect to have a baseline HIV antibody test done.
   (a) If the employee elects to have this test, an informed consent must be read and signed by the employee and by a physician [see figures 7-5 and 7-6].
   (b) If the employee elects not to have this test, a refusal form must be signed by the employee.
6. When ordering the necessary blood tests for the employee on the computer, confidentiality must be maintained.
7. Enter the Personnel Health code (613) for the doctor.
8. The Personnel Health Department will administer HBIG and HB vaccine to the employee only if these measures were indicated but not administered in the ER (that is, when prophylaxis is dependent on a blood test result).
9. When the source patient is known:
   (a) Order HBsAg on the patient. Indicate under "Comment" that the patient should not be charged, as it is an "employee exposure."

(b) Personnel Health will notify the patient's physician that the patient should be tested for HIV antibody. The physician is responsible for informing the patient, obtaining the consent, and informing the patient of the test results.

10. The Personnel Health nurse is responsible for obtaining patient test results, contacting and counseling the employee for blood test results, administering any additional blood tests if indicated, and maintaining records in the employee's health file.
11. The Laboratory is responsible for forwarding blood test results on the employee and the patient (if known) as soon as possible to the Personnel Health Department.

Figure 7-1. ER Report of Employee Exposure to Blood/Body Fluids

Complete the following: Date: ________________

Employee name: ____

Location in hospital where incident occurred: ____________________________

Nature of exposure: _____ Bite _____ Splash _____ Cut
_____ Needlestick _____ Nonintact skin

Other (specify): ____

____

Circumstances of injury:

_____ No human contact (object inflicting wound was never in contact with a patient or body fluid, i.e., piggyback needle, clean needle)

_____ Identifiable source (patient or body fluid) ____________________________
(Name and location of patient)

_____ Source unknown (i.e., needle in trash, etc.)

Explain ____

____

____

Checklist of ER

HBsAg ordered on source patient _____

Employee previously unvaccinated:

HBIG given _____

HB vaccine first dose given _____

—signed form attached _____

Employee previously vaccinated, Ab status unknown:

HBsAb done _____

HIV testing information given _____

Forward to Personnel Health with copy of emergency room record.

Figure 7-2. Management of Employee Wounds Acquired on the Job

	Clean, minor wounds		All other wounds[1]	
History of absorbed tetanus toxoid (doses)	**Td[2]**	**TIG**	**Td[2]**	**TIG**
Unknown or less than three	Yes	No	Yes	Yes
Greater than three[3]	No[4]	No	No[5]	No

[1] Such as, but not limited to, wounds contaminated with dirt, feces, soil, saliva, etc.; puncture wounds, avulsions; and wounds resulting from missles, crushing, burns and frostbite.

[2] For persons 7 years old and older, Td is preferred to tetanus toxoid alone.

[3] If only three doses of fluid toxoid have been received, a fourth dose of toxoid, preferably an absorbed toxoid, should be given.

[4] Yes, if more than 10 years since last dose.

[5] Yes, if more than 5 years since last dose. (More frequent boosters are not needed and can accentuate side effects.)

Notes

Tetanus toxoid (see notation 1 above)

Give tetanus toxoid if:

a. Fewer than three previous toxoid injections; or
b. Last injection more than 10 years prior; or
c. Wound is contaminated and last toxoid was given more than 5 years prior.

Tetanus immune globulin (human TIG)

1. For small, clean wounds, TIG is unnecessary.
2. For contaminated wounds, give TIG if:
   a. Fewer than two previous toxoid injections; or
   b. Wound is more than 24 hours old and fewer than three previous toxoid injections.

Reference: Centers for Disease Control, Recommendations of PHS Advisory Committee on Immunization Practices: diphtheria and tetanus toxoid and pertussis vaccine, *Morbidity and Mortality Weekly Report* 24:27, 1985.

Figure 7-3. Management of Employee Exposure to Blood/Body Fluids

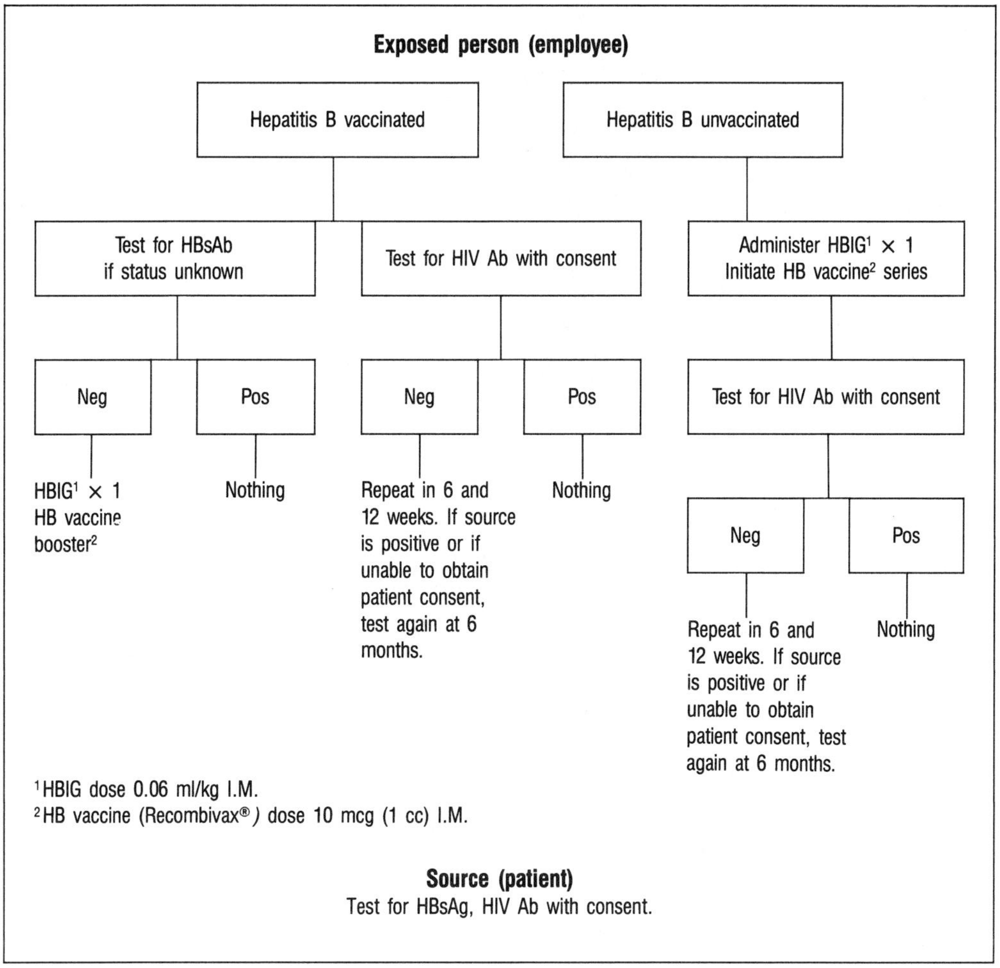

Figure 7-4. Hepatitis B Vaccine Information and Consent Form

The Disease
Hepatitis B is a viral infection caused by the hepatitis B virus (HBV), which causes death in 1 to 2 percent of patients. Most people with hepatitis B recover completely, but approximately 5 to 10 percent become chronic carriers of the virus. Most of these people have no symptoms but can continue to transmit the disease to others. Some may develop chronic active hepatitis and cirrhosis. HBV also appears to be a causative factor in the development of liver cancer. Thus, immunization against hepatitis B can prevent acute hepatitis and also reduce sickness and death from chronic active hepatitis, cirrhosis, and liver cancer.

The Vaccine
Recombivax-HB® is a noninfectious subunit viral vaccine derived from hepatitis B surface antigen (HBsAg) produced in yeast cells. A portion of the hepatitis B virus gene, coding for HBsAg, is cloned into yeast, and the vaccine for hepatitis B is produced from cultures of this recombinant yeast strain. The vaccine contains no detectable yeast DNA but may contain up to 4 percent yeast protein. It has been extensively tested for safety in chimpanzees and for safety and efficacy in large-scale clinical trials with human subjects. The vaccine against hepatitis B, prepared from recombinant yeast cultures, is free of association with human blood or blood products. A high percentage of healthy people who receive two doses of vaccine and a booster achieve high levels of surface antibody (anti-HBs) and protection against hepatitis B. Persons with immune-system abnormalities, such as dialysis patients, have less response to the vaccine, but over half of those receiving it do develop antibodies. Full immunization requires three doses of vaccine over a six-month period, although some persons may not develop immunity even after three doses. There is no evidence that the vaccine has ever caused hepatitis B, non-A/non-B hepatitis, or AIDS (acquired immunodeficiency syndrome). However, persons who have been infected with HBV prior to receiving the vaccine may go on to develop clinical hepatitis in spite of immunization. The duration of immunity is unknown at this time.

Possible Vaccine Side Effects
The incidence of side effects is very low. No serious side effects have been reported with the vaccine. A few persons experience tenderness, redness, and itching at the site of injection. Low-grade fever and/or headache may occur. Rash, nausea, joint pain, diarrhea, and mild fatigue have also been reported. The possibility exists that more serious side effects may be identified with more extensive use.

If you have any questions about hepatitis B or the hepatitis B vaccine, please ask.

Consent Form
I have read the above statements about hepatitis B and the hepatitis B vaccine. I have had an opportunity to ask questions and understand the benefits and risks of hepatitis B vaccination. I understand that I must have three doses of vaccine to confer immunity. However, as with all medical treatment, there is no guarantee that I will become immune or that I will not experience an adverse side effect from the vaccine. I request that it be given to me or to the person named below of whom I am the parent or guardian.

______________________________ Date Vaccinated Lot #

Name of Person to Receive Vaccine (Please Print)

(1) ______________ ______________

(2) ______________ ______________

(3) ______________ ______________

____

Signature of Person Receiving Vaccine or Parent or Guardian

____

Date Signed

Figure 7-5. Informed Consent for HIV Antibody Testing

I, the undersigned, hereby agree to have my blood tested for antibody to HIV, the agent of acquired immunodeficiency syndrome, with this understanding:

1. As with any test, false-positive and false-negative results may occur. I will be informed by a physician if my blood test is positive or negative.
2. The HIV antibody test is not a diagnostic test for AIDS.
3. Individuals with blood positive for HIV antibody should not donate blood, plasma, body organs, other tissue, or sperm.
4. I understand that I am free to decline to have my blood tested.
5. I understand that reasonable efforts will be made to keep my test results confidential to the extent possible. However, I understand that the hospital cannot guarantee confidentiality and that it must report diagnoses of AIDS to the State Department of Health Services and may become subject to other reporting requirements or the requirements of subpoena or court order with respect to test results. Furthermore, I understand that the hospital has no control over employers, insurance companies, and other third parties and is not responsible for their inquiries or policies with respect to AIDS and/or HIV antibody testing.
6. The physician witness below has discussed this informed consent with me and has explained it to my satisfaction, including the limitations upon the value of the test and the hazards attendant upon unwarranted disclosure of test results.

Date ____________________ Print Name ____________________

Signed ____________________
(and relationship if not self)

Physician Witness ____

Code number assigned to patient ______________

Figure 7-6. Reverse Side of Informed Consent for HIV Antibody Testing

Should I Be Tested for HIV Antibody?

You should consider the following factors and discuss your particular situation with your physician in attempting to answer this question:

A positive antibody test indicates infection with HIV—the virus that causes AIDS. However, only a portion of persons with HIV antibodies have AIDS.

An antibody test does not identify the HIV virus and cannot be used to diagnose AIDS. Nor can the test totally exclude infection with HIV, the virus that causes AIDS.

Antibody test results are difficult to interpret, especially when the positive test occurs in a healthy person whose life-style does not put him at risk of coming in contact with HIV.

A negative test result in an individual whose life-style does put him at risk of coming in contact with HIV does not guarantee that the person has never been infected with the virus or is not currently infected with the virus.

A positive antibody test result can have a significant psychological impact on both the person tested and those close to him or her. At the present time, the consequences for persons who are infected with HIV are unpredictable since no treatment is currently available for the infection.

Insurance companies or employers may seek information about positive test results as a condition of coverage or employment.

In some states, positive test results may have to be reported to the State Health Department. This is not a requirement in Connecticut at this time.

Although a diagnosis of AIDS must be reported to the Connecticut Department of Health Services, there is no requirement at this time for reporting of positive HIV antibody testing results.

University of Minnesota Hospital and Clinic
Minneapolis, Minnesota

Needlestick or Other Significant Exposure to Blood or Other Body Fluids

Policy

Needlestick or other significant exposure to blood or other body fluids has the potential of transmitting the hepatitis B virus (HBV), the viruses of non-A, non-B hepatitis, the human immunodeficiency virus (HIV, the virus of AIDS), and certain other pathogens. Exposures should be managed to minimize the chance of transmission and provide full documentation of their nature and consequences.

Procedure

1. **Report for Evaluation:** All persons who may have had a significant blood or body fluid exposure should notify their supervisor and report for evaluation immediately. Exposure evaluation and management should be carried out during regular hours as follows: hospital employees, residents, fellows, and volunteers in the UMHC Employee Health Service (EHS); students in Boynton Health Service (BHS); medical–dental staff, other specified hospital professional personnel (psychologists), nonhospital ancillary personnel, and other UM employees in the UMHC Emergency Department (ED). Persons in more than one of the aforementioned categories should be seen in the area relevant to the activity under way at the time of the exposure. During nonregular hours, all persons should be seen in the ED. UMHC will cover the cost of source evaluations of UMHC patients for all exposures and for serologies, IG, HBIG, HBV vaccine, and Zidovudine for hospital employees, residents, fellows, or volunteers. Exposure management may continue even after the exposed person has ended his or her affiliation with the University of Minnesota.
2. **Incident Report:** An incident report should be completed for all reported blood or body fluid exposures. The incident report should be initiated by the exposed person, completed by the evaluating site (EHS, ED, or BHS), and returned by the exposed person to his or her supervisor or department.
3. **First Report of Injury:** First Reports of Injury do not need to be completed if the exposure is judged nonsignificant. Required reports should be completed by the exposed person's supervisor or, if the exposed person prefers, the hospital epidemiologist.
   A. *Hospital employees, residents, fellows, volunteers:* The First Report of Injury should be completed within 72 hours after it is determined that the exposure was to a source positive for HBV, HIV, non-A, non-B hepatitis, or to other pathogens requiring Blood Precautions (see Policy 33.21).
   B. *Other personnel:* The First Report of Injury should be completed within 72 hours after the exposure is reported (regardless of the infectiousness of the source).
4. **Unaffiliated Persons:** If a person not affiliated with the University of Minnesota reports a significant blood or body fluid exposure during the course of health care delivery to, or law enforcement activities involving, an individual currently hospitalized at the UMHC, the UMHC will evaluate the exposure source. The exposed person should report to his or her occupational health physician or private physician. The physician should report the exposure to the UMHC hospital epidemiologist. The hospital epidemiologist or designee will deliver the form letter and requisitions as per paragraph 8. The hospital epidemiologist will communicate the results of the source studies to the physician.
5. **Exposed Patient:** For the management of potentially significant exposures of patients to blood or body fluids of personnel, see Policy 33.4, Management of Potentially Infectious Personnel.

6. **Significance:** An M.D. or R.N. will judge the significance of the exposure. Exposure is considered significant when there has been percutaneous inoculation, fresh (less than 24-hour) cut or mucous membrane contact (for example, splash to the eye or mouth or mouth-to-mouth resuscitation) by blood or body fluid or a contaminated instrument, sharp, or needle. A cutaneous exposure involving large amounts of blood or prolonged contact with blood, especially when the exposed skin is chapped, abraded, or afflicted with dermatitis, is also considered significant. If the exposure is judged nonsignificant, no further follow-up is required. Pregnant and immunosuppressed persons should be managed as are other persons except as indicated in 8A. Coagulation factor concentrate will be considered hazardous for HIV, HBV (see paragraphs 8A and 8B); the hazard from exposure to blood for autologous transfusion or pheresis products will be treated as would a known source exposure (see section 8); screened untreated blood components will be considered non-A, non-B hepatitis hazardous (see paragraph 8C) but not HIV or HBV hazardous.
7. **Immune Globulin:** All personnel who have had a significant blood or body fluid exposure will be offered a single dose of IG (0.06 ml/kg) unless they are judged to need HBIG [see algorithm in figure 7-7]. IG is not needed if the exposed person has received any immune globulin in the past month. IG is contraindicated in persons with agammaglobulinemia.
8. **Source Known:** If the exposure is significant and the source is known, the following laboratory information about the source person will be sought: an anti-HIV serology and a hepatitis B battery (HBsAg, anti-HBs, and anti-HBC). Either of these studies may be omitted if the source person has been tested within the three months prior to the exposure or if the source person is an established carrier. The laboratory studies will be sought by having the exposed person take a form letter and requisitions to the source's physician requesting that the physician order the appropriate studies. The letter will request that the physician discuss the implications of a positive anti-HIV serology with the patient before the test is ordered. The form letter and requisition may also be taken by the exposed person to the charge nurse or nurse manager, who should give the letter to the patient's physician. If the exposed person needs assistance, the EHS (or the ED or BHS) will assist in the delivery of the form letter and requisition. If a known source does not undergo HBV or HIV testing, the exposed person should be managed as if the source were unknown.
   A. *Hepatitis B exposure:* Significant hepatitis B exposure occurs (1) when the source is HBsAg positive, (2) when the source is anti-HBc positive, HBsAg negative, and anti-HBs negative, or (3) since hepatitis B immune globulin (HBIG) must be administered shortly after the exposure to be effective, when an untested source is likely to be hepatitis B infectious. When the HBV laboratory studies of the source are unknown or when negative studies were obtained more than three months previously, the physician will judge whether the source is likely to be a hepatitis B carrier so that HBIG administration, if appropriate, may be given at the time the exposed person is first seen. Persons likely to be HBsAg positive include needle-using addicts, patients who have had hemodialysis, recipients of multiple units of blood, male homosexuals, and Southeastern Asian immigrants.

      Significant HBV exposures will be managed using the algorithm [in figure 7-7]. In the algorithm, the "current HBV battery" refers to an HBsAg, anti-HBs, and anti-HBc drawn from the exposed person at the time of first evaluation. It should be obtained unless it had been performed within the previous three months. In the algorithm, "HBV marker positive" means anti-HBs positive (not "weak positive"), anti-HBc positive, or HBsAg positive. Immune globulin (IG) or HBIG, when indicated according to the algorithm, will be administered (0.06

ml/kg I.M.) immediately (not delayed until the results of the exposed person's current HB battery are available). IG or HBIG need not be given if administered in the prior month. HBV vaccine administration may be delayed until the results of the current HB battery on the exposed person and the HBV infectiousness of the source are known. If the exposed person is pregnant, she should have a HBsAg determination near term. If an exposed person becomes pregnant between the time of the exposure and the nine-month postexposure anti-HBc test and if the anti-HBc test is positive, she should also have an HBsAg determination near term.

B. *AIDS virus exposure:* Significant HIV exposure occurs when the source is anti-HIV seropositive (Western blot positive or indeterminant), HIV antigen positive,

Figure 7-7. Algorithm: Needlestick or Other Significant Exposure to Blood or Other Body Fluids

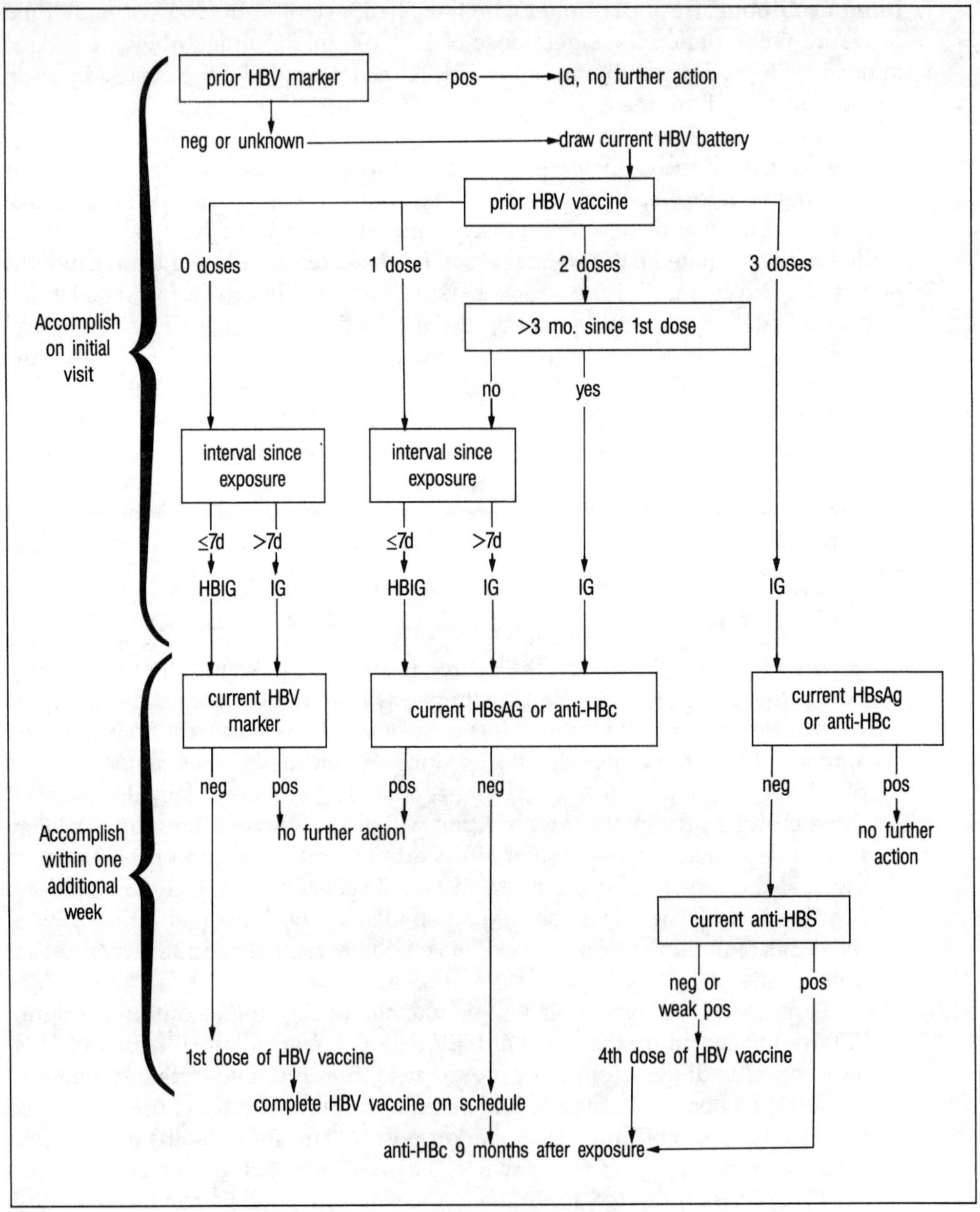

HIV culture positive; has AIDS; is untested and has clinical illness suggestive of HIV infection; or refuses a requested anti-HIV serology. The blood bank will perform source anti-HIV EIA tests within 24 hours of the arrival in the blood bank of source specimens. The results of the initial EIA, if reactive, will be immediately phoned to the director of the EHS, the ED physician on duty, the medical director of BHS, or the hospital epidemiologist. The physician phoned will judge whether the exposure is significant based on the strength of the reaction, other clinical and laboratory information about the source (for example, hepatitis B status, absolute lymphocyte count), and, possibly, a risk history interview of the source.

The exposed person will be offered an anti-HIV serology at the time of exposure unless he or she is known to have been HIV infected or had an anti-HIV serology obtained in the past month. The exposed person will be informed that establishing lack of infection at the time of exposure will strengthen worker's compensation claims. Follow-up anti-HIV serologies will be offered at 6 weeks, 12 weeks, 6 months, and 12 months after the exposure unless the exposed person has a prior positive test. The exposed, seronegative person should be advised of recommendations for preventing HIV transmission for at least 3 months after the exposure until the HIV serology status is known. The recommendations would include avoidance of (a) unprotected sexual activity, (b) donation of blood, body fluids, or organs, (c) pregnancy, and (d) needle sharing. In addition, the exposed person should be advised to report and seek medical evaluation for any acute febrile illness that occurs within 12 weeks of exposure.

Persons with significant blood or body fluid exposure to HIV-containing materials will be offered zidovudine 200 mg q 4 hours for 42 days. The prophylaxis should be discontinued if it was begun on the basis of an initial EIA that is subsequently determined to be a false positive. These exposures will be those occurring in the prior 96 hours. For persons electing to take zidovudine, monitoring of CBC and differential count will be performed every two weeks as long as the zidovudine is being taken.

If an exposed person is discovered to be HIV infected after exposure to a source found to be anti-HIV negative at the time of exposure, an effort will be made to retest the source patient.

C. *Non-A, non-B hepatitis:* Immediate administration of the single dose of IG should be strongly encouraged if the source is suspected of being a non-A, non-B hepatitis virus carrier.

D. *Other pathogens:* Other pathogens transmissible by blood exposure are listed in Policy 33.21. Management of exposure to these pathogens will be individualized in consultation with the hospital epidemiologist.

9. **Source Unknown:** A current HB battery should be obtained from the exposed person if the exposing body fluid contains blood unless he or she previously had hepatitis B or had an HBV battery obtained in the past three months. The exposed person will be offered an anti-HIV serology at the time of exposure unless he or she is known to have been AIDS virus infected or had an anti-HIV serology obtained in the past three months. The exposed person will be informed that establishing lack of infection at the time of exposure will strengthen worker's compensation claims. Unless a prior HB battery shows a positive HBV marker, an anti-HBc and anti-HBs will be obtained from the exposed person nine months after the exposure. Follow-up anti-HIV serology will be offered nine months after the exposure, unless a prior anti-HIV serology is positive.

San Francisco General Hospital, University of California at San Francisco, and the Consortium for Health Care Workers San Francisco, California

Protocol for Administering and Monitoring Zidovudine in Health Care Workers Exposed to HIV

I. Purpose

The purpose of this protocol is to outline a regimen for safely administering zidovudine to health care workers occupationally exposed to human immunodeficiency virus (HIV).

II. Background

A. *Risk of HIV Infection in Health Care Workers*

Human immunodeficiency virus, the cause of AIDS, can be transmitted to health care personnel exposed to blood and other materials containing the virus. The risk of infection following parenteral needlestick exposure to blood infected with HIV is approximately 0.4 percent (1 in 250) overall; the risk from mucous membrane exposure and inoculation of nonintact skin is not zero but is too low to be measured in the prospective studies of health care workers currently under way. No risk from contamination of normal skin or from other types of exposure has been documented. Other factors in addition to the route of exposure may influence transmission risk, e.g., titer of virus in the source material, volume of infected material involved, viability of the virus, etc.

Although few occupationally infected health care workers have so far developed AIDS, present evidence suggests that infection is likely to be eventually fatal in the majority. There is no known cure for AIDS; prevention of infection is therefore of paramount importance.

B. *Efficacy of Zidovudine*

Zidovudine is a drug that delays but does not prevent disease progression in patients with AIDS. Zidovudine inhibits reverse transcriptase, an essential virus enzyme required for replication and development of the latent state. The efficacy of zidovudine in preventing latent infection with HIV following occupational exposure is not known and will be difficult to ascertain because of the low risk of transmission.

Data derived from animal studies suggest that zidovudine may be at least partially effective in preventing viremia, disease, and perhaps latent infection in animals inoculated with nonhuman retroviruses. Benefit is most evident when the drug is administered before exposure (preexposure prophylaxis). Drug efficacy decreases when treatment is delayed. Efficacy of postexposure prophylaxis in animals inoculated with lower titers of retrovirus (more comparable to the amount of virus involved in a typical needlestick injury) has not been evaluated.

C. *Toxicity of Zidovudine*

Evaluation of toxicity from zidovudine in healthy health care workers treated for short intervals is incomplete. Persons with asymptomatic HIV infection rarely experience serious toxicity in the first four weeks of treatment. Headaches, nausea, diarrhea, fever, insomnia, parasthesia, neutropenia, macrocytic anemia, thrombocytopenia, hepatitis, myositis, and skin changes may be side effects of treatment. Irreversible toxicity is unusual even in patients treated for prolonged intervals. Delayed toxicity, teratogenicity, and mutagenicity have not been evaluated.

D. *Rationale for Administering Zidovudine*

The risk of HIV infection after exposure is not high, but the outcome, should infection occur, is likely to be fatal. Although the risks and benefits from postexposure treatment with zidovudine are unknown, some health care workers may choose to take zidovudine after occupational exposure. The risk/benefit ratio of postexposure prophylaxis is likely to be most apparent for exposures involving a higher risk of infection ("massive," "definite parenteral," and "possible parenteral" exposures, as defined in the appendix [pp. 201–11 of this manual]).

Toxicity is likely to be related to zidovudine dose and the duration of treatment. The optimal dosing regimen for zidovudine is unknown; however, current recommendations for treating patients with established infection are designed to provide drug levels in excess of the concentration required to inhibit HIV replication in tissue cultures (>1 micromole). The duration of treatment required to protect against infection after exposure is unknown and cannot be predicted from data currently available. Experience with nonretroviral viruses suggests that prophylactic treatment for more than a few days is not usually required, but the relevance of these data to HIV is unclear.

This protocol is designed to provide a consistent approach to treating health care workers occupationally exposed to HIV with zidovudine. The dose (200 mg five times a day for four weeks) was selected by a panel of experts experienced in assessing risks of occupational HIV exposure and viral therapies in California.

III. Eligible Health Care Workers

A. *Eligibility Criteria*

1. A health care worker with a discreet occupational exposure to HIV infective material four or fewer days before treatment is eligible for enrollment. Health care workers receiving zidovudine therapy in the past may be treated again if (a) more than three months has elapsed since the completion of the previous course and (b) no more than two prior courses of treatment have been given. Health care workers sustaining exposures more than four days before evaluation may be treated at the discretion of the supervising physician or his/her designee.
   a. Eligible exposures (defined in the appendix [pp. 201–11 of this manual]):
      - Massive parenteral exposure: Zidovudine definitely encouraged.
      - Definite parenteral exposure: Zidovudine should be offered.
      - Possible parenteral exposure: Zidovudine is not routinely recommended but may be indicated for select cases and should at least be discussed with the health care worker.
      - Doubtful parenteral exposure: Zidovudine is never recommended but can be prescribed in select cases; the health care worker should be advised of the extremely small risk of infection associated with this type of exposure.
      - Nonparenteral exposure: Zidovudine should not be prescribed.

   b. HIV-infected material:
      - (a) Body fluids/tissues (although infectivity is known to decrease with the age of the specimen, all can be considered potentially infectious, regardless of age): blood, blood products, bloody fluids; semen, cere-

brospinal fluid, amniotic fluid; menstrual discharge; pleural, peritoneal, or pericardial fluid; inflammatory exudates; any other body fluid or tissue contaminated with blood.

- And (b) HIV infection documented in source (one or more of the following criteria): clinically diagnosed AIDS/ARC or compatible symptoms/signs in patient at high risk; repeatedly reactive ELISA in source serum; confirmed by Western blot or IFA; p24 antigenemia in source serum; positive HIV culture from any site in source; positive polymerase chain reaction in source. Zidovudine treatment may be instituted pending the results of source patient testing at the discretion of the supervising physician.
- And (c) source fluid has not been physically or chemically inactivated.
- Or (d) fluids or tissues contaminated with HIV in research laboratories that have not been physically or chemically inactivated regardless of age of the specimen.

2. The health care worker must provide informed consent to receive an approved drug for a nonapproved indication.
3. This protocol must be approved by the responsible institution.

B. *Exclusion Criteria*

1. Health care workers sustaining nonparenteral exposures should be excluded.
2. Men or women of childbearing capacity who decline to perform acceptable contraception or abstinence during the period of chemoprophylaxis and for four weeks thereafter should be excluded.
3. Women who are pregnant or become pregnant and who elect to continue pregnancy should be excluded.
4. Women who elect to continue breast-feeding during the period of treatment should be excluded.
5. Health care workers with a prior diagnosis of HIV infection should be excluded. *Zidovudine should be discontinued if baseline HIV tests are found to be positive after treatment is begun.*
6. Health care workers with an underlying renal insufficiency (creatinine >3 × nl) should be excluded.
7. Health care workers with an underlying hepatic insufficiency (SGOT, Alk Phos, or total bilirubin >3 × N) should be excluded.
8. Health care workers with an endogenous or drug-induced immunosuppression should be excluded.
9. Health care workers with a bone marrow dysfunction (Hgb < 10 g/dl); granulocytes < 1500/mm^3, or platelets < 100,000/mm^3 should be excluded.
10. Health care workers who received a treatment with myelosuppressive/nephrotoxic/hepatotoxic drugs within two weeks prior to or concurrent with starting therapy should be excluded.
11. Health care workers with a probable noncompliance with treatment or follow-up should be excluded.

IV. Treatment Procedures

A. *Informed Consent*

Following a discussion of the study protocol with the supervising physician or his/her designee, employees choosing to receive zidovudine read and sign the consent form (Form 1 [figure 7-8 in this manual]). Individuals of childbearing potential must also sign the statement of intent to avoid pregnancy (Form 2 [figure 7-9]). To facilitate implementation of therapy as soon as possible after exposure,

Figure 7-8. Consent to Take an Approved Drug for a Nonapproved Indication

Zidovudine for Prevention of HIV Infection
after Occupational Exposure to HIV

I have been exposed to human immunodeficiency virus (HIV), the virus that causes AIDS, in my workplace. My clinician has offered me treatment with zidovudine, which might reduce my risk of infection. Although zidovudine is indicated for treatment of established HIV infection, it is not approved by the Food and Drug Administration (FDA) for preventing infection after exposure.

If I decide to be treated with zidovudine the following will occur:

1. Approximately four tablespoons of my blood will be drawn and tested for routine studies, including complete blood count, platelet count, liver function tests, kidney function tests, and CPK (muscle enzyme) as well as for human immunodeficiency virus (HIV) infection (separate consent).
2. A urine sample to evaluate my kidney function will be obtained.
3. A urine sample to determine whether I am pregnant will be obtained (women only).
4. I will be given a two-week supply of zidovudine and instructions for taking it. Dose will be two 100-mg tablets to be swallowed every four hours, five times a day. A second two-week supply of the drug will be provided at my next visit.
5. I will be required to return to my clinician every other week for six weeks and at three months, six months, and twelve months after my exposure. Blood and urine tests will be repeated at each visit.
6. If I experience adverse reactions or develop abnormal laboratory tests, zidovudine dose may be lowered or discontinued by my clinician.

Benefits of Treatment
The risk of infection from my exposure is not known with certainty. However, should HIV infection occur, the outcome eventually may be fatal. Zidovudine may prevent infection after exposure to HIV.

The benefit of zidovudine in preventing infection after exposure is unproven. Experiments in mice, cats, and monkeys suggest that zidovudine might prevent infection when treatment is started soon after exposure. If treatment is delayed for more than 24 hours, zidovudine is much less likely to prevent infection in these animals.

The duration of zidovudine treatment likely to prevent infection is not known but could be prolonged. For this reason, my clinicians recommend taking the drug for four weeks.

Risks
If I take zidovudine, I might develop symptoms, including headache, muscle pain, tiredness, loss of appetite, trouble sleeping, fever, nausea, vomiting, dizziness, and diarrhea. Although unlikely, I might also develop anemia, low white cell blood count, low platelet count, hepatitis (liver inflammation), nervous system inflammation (meningitis/encephalitis), muscle inflammation, or other serious adverse effects. These adverse effects are expected to disappear after zidovudine treatment is stopped but could be life-threatening or irreversible.

Although considered unlikely, delayed effects of zidovudine could include cancer (carcinogenesis) or mutations in my genetic material (mutagenesis).

Drawing blood may be painful and may cause a bruise or rarely an infection.

Treatment Options
Treatment with zidovudine is voluntary. If I decide to stop taking zidovudine, I should notify my clinician within 24 hours. If I elect to receive or discontinue zidovudine, neither my employment nor other treatment and follow-up for my exposure will be affected. Declining zidovudine treatment will not affect benefits to which I am otherwise entitled as a result of my exposure.

I have been given the opportunity to ask questions relevant to zidovudine treatment. If I have questions in the future, I may contact ______________________________ at ______________________ .
I have been given a copy of this consent.

My signature indicates my willingness to take zidovudine.

______________________________ ______________________
Participant Date

____
Name (print)

______________________________ ______________________
Supervising clinician Date

____
Name (print)

Figure 7-9. Voluntary Statement of Intent to Avoid Pregnancy—Women (top) and Men (bottom)

To the best of my knowledge, I am not currently pregnant. Furthermore, I agree to avoid pregnancy while I am taking zidovudine (AZT, Retrovir®) during the next four weeks and for four weeks thereafter. Should I have sexual relations during this period, I will practice a form of birth control (e.g., abstinence, oral contraceptives, intrauterine device, diaphragm plus condom) that is deemed reliable by my clinician. I will immediately contact my clinician if pregnancy is suspected. I may decline to sign this statement; my declining to sign will have no effect on future treatment by my clinician except that I will not be treated with zidovudine.

Participant's signature ____________________ Date __________

Name (print) ____________________ Date __________

Should I have sexual relations during the next four weeks and for four weeks following completion of zidovudine treatment, I will practice a form of birth control with my partner(s) (e.g., abstinence, oral contraception, condom plus diaphragm, intrauterine device) that is deemed reliable by my clinician. I may decline to sign this statement; my declining to sign will have no effect on future treatment by my physician except that I will not be treated with zidovudine.

Participant's signature ____________________ Date __________

Name (print) ____________________ Date __________

up to three doses of zidovudine may be provided after verbal (telephone) consent, provided that the health care worker can be seen by a clinician within 24 hours.

B. *Source Patient Evaluation*

When the source of the exposure is known, the source patient may be asked to consent to HIV testing if HIV infection has not been diagnosed. The procedure for obtaining consent must comply with existing institutional policies for source patient counseling and testing. The results of this evaluation will be disclosed to the exposed health care worker and the treating clinicians.

C. *Initial Laboratory Evaluation*

1. Routine lab studies: Complete blood count with differential and platelets; serum creatinine, urinalysis with micro; SGOT, AlkPhos, total bilirubin, CPK; urine pregnancy test (women only)
2. HIV studies and other virus studies: HIV antibody (ELISA); confirmatory test (WB or IFA); hepatitis B virus (HBsAg, HBsAb, HBcAb); HIV p24 antigen (optional); CD4 lymphocyte subset analysis (optional); peripheral blood lymphocytes (to be frozen for gene amplification or other virus studies if indicated in the future) (optional)
3. Source patient evaluation: HIV antibody (ELISA with WB or IFA confirmation); HIV p24 antigen titer (optional); peripheral blood lymphocytes (to be frozen for gene amplification or other virus studies if indicated in the future) (optional); HIV semiquantitative culture (optional); CD4 lymphocyte subset analysis (optional)

D. *Medication Instructions*

Health care workers should be given a two-week supply of zidovudine and instructed to take two tablets (200 mg) every four hours, five times a day. A convenient regimen may be two tablets at 7 a.m., 11 a.m., 3 p.m., 7 p.m., and 11 p.m. A second two-week supply will be provided at the time of the two-week follow-up visit, provided that no adverse effects requiring drug discontinuation or dosage adjustment are apparent.

Written instructions for taking zidovudine and a review of potential adverse effects warranting medical evaluation will be provided to each health care worker [figures 7-10 and 7-11 of this manual]. A clinician will be available 24 hours a day to answer questions and to arrange a medical consultation if indicated.

V. Follow-up

Each treated health care worker should be evaluated by a clinician at two weeks, four weeks, six weeks, three months, six months, and one year after therapy is started. Routine and HIV studies will be repeated at each visit. The health care worker's medical records [figures 7-12 through 7-16 of this manual] will be updated at each visit. Potential side effects will be evaluated and a physical exam performed as indicated by symptoms.

Zidovudine treatment will be reduced or discontinued in accordance with the guidelines included in the Symptom Adverse Side Effect Scale [figure 7-17 of this manual]. Life-threatening complications (or deaths) occurring in patients receiving zidovudine will be reported promptly to the Food and Drug Administration.

Appendix. Management of Accidental Exposures to Blood/Body Fluids

I. Definitions of HIV/HBV Exposure
   A. Massive Exposure
      1. Transfusion of blood
      2. Large-volume injections of blood (>1 ml)
      3. Parenteral exposure to laboratory materials containing high titer of virus
   B. Definite Parenteral Exposure
      1. Intramuscular (I.M./deep) injury with a blood/body fluid-contaminated needle
      2. Injection of blood/body fluid

Figure 7-10. Zidovudine Chemoprophylaxis for Health Care Providers Occupationally Exposed to HIV: Fact Sheet

Health care providers exposed to HIV (the AIDS virus) risk infection. The risk from a needlestick injury involving HIV-infected blood is approximately 0.4 percent (1 in 250) but may be higher or lower depending on the severity of injury. The risk from exposures involving mucous membranes or nonintact skin is believed to be lower than the risk from a needlestick but is not zero. HIV is likely to produce serious illness and death after several years of infection.

Zidovudine is a drug that prevents HIV reproduction and delays disease caused by HIV in persons already infected. Zidovudine might prevent infection if administered soon after occupational exposure to HIV, but this is unproven. AT THE PRESENT TIME, THERE IS INSUFFICIENT SCIENTIFIC DATA TO STRONGLY SUPPORT OR DISCOURAGE THE USE OF ZIDOVUDINE FOR PREVENTING INFECTION IN OCCUPATIONALLY EXPOSED HEALTH CARE WORKERS.

Zidovudine is approved by the Food and Drug Administration for treatment of some patients with HIV infection but is not approved for use as a postexposure prevention drug in health care workers. WRITTEN INFORMED CONSENT PRIOR TO ZIDOVUDINE TREATMENT THEREFORE IS REQUIRED. Life-threatening or serious irreversible toxicities from zidovudine, when taken for short intervals, are not expected but could occur. Serious reversible toxicities (detailed in the attached consent form) have been observed in a small percentage of persons in the first six weeks of treatment. The optimal dose and duration of zidovudine treatment is not known. Individual variations in drug tolerance are expected. CAREFUL MEDICAL MONITORING SUPERVISED BY A TRAINED CLINICIAN DURING ZIDOVUDINE TREATMENT IS THEREFORE MANDATORY.

The effect of zidovudine on unborn children is unknown. Because harmful effects to the fetus might occur, ZIDOVUDINE IS NOT RECOMMENDED FOR PREGNANT WOMEN (OR FOR MEN OR WOMEN ENGAGING IN SEXUAL PRACTICES THAT COULD LEAD TO PREGNANCY) DURING AND FOR AT LEAST FOUR WEEKS AFTER TREATMENT.

Figure 7-11. Zidovudine Chemoprophylaxis for Health Care Providers Occupationally Exposed to HIV: Treatment Instructions

- Store medication in the original container in a cool, dry location; do not refrigerate.
- Because zidovudine has a short half-life, it is essential that you take it every four hours as directed. A suggested schedule is 7 a.m., 11 a.m., 3 p.m., 7 p.m., and 11 p.m. (The 3 a.m. dose is not required.) The medication is best absorbed when taken on an empty stomach.
- If you miss a dose—If less than two hours late, take the medication and resume previous schedule; if more than two hours late, skip the dose and resume previous schedule. Notify your clinician of the date and time of the missed dose at the next visit.
- Other medications, including over-the-counter products, should not be taken without first consulting your clinician, with the following exceptions:
  (a) For headaches, muscle or joint aches and pains, low-grade fever: ibuprofen (Advil®, Nuprin®), 400 mg every six hours as needed for no more than two days. Call your physician if relief is not obtained within two days.
  (b) Nausea: phosphated carbohydrate solution (Emetrol®, Calm-X®, Nausetrol®, Eazol®, Especol®), one tablespoon, undiluted by other fluids, as needed to control nausea. Call if relief is not obtained in 36 hours.
- Discuss all medications taken, their dosage, and frequency with your clinician during your regular scheduled follow-up visits.
- You will be evaluated by your clinician every two weeks for six weeks and at three months and six months and twelve months from the date of your injury. A targeted physical exam may be performed as needed at any of these visits. Laboratory tests will be performed at each visit.
- You may call your clinician at __________________ to discuss problems or concerns requiring attention before your next appointment.

3. Laceration or similar wound produced by a visibly blood/body fluid-contaminated instrument that causes bleeding in health care worker
4. Laceration or similar fresh wound inoculated with blood/body fluid
5. Any parenteral inoculation of HIV/HBV virus samples (usually research settings) not included under massive exposure

C. Possible Parenteral Exposure
1. Subcutaneous (S.Q./superficial) injury with blood/body fluid-contaminated needle
2. A wound produced by blood/body fluid-contaminated instrument that does not cause visible bleeding
3. Prior wound or skin lesion contaminated with blood/body fluid
4. Mucous membrane inoculation with blood/body fluid

D. Doubtful Parenteral Exposure
1. Subcutaneous (S.Q./superficial) injury with a needle or device contaminated with noninfectious/nonbloody fluids
2. A wound produced by noninfectious/nonbloody body fluid-contaminated instrument
3. Prior wound or skin lesion contaminated with noninfectious/nonbloody body fluid
4. Mucous membrane inoculation with noninfectious/nonbloody body fluid

E. Nonparenteral Exposure
1. Intact skin visibly contaminated with blood/body fluid

Note: Body fluids deemed potentially infectious for HIV:
- Blood products, bloody fluids
- Semen, cerebrospinal fluid, amniotic fluid
- Menstrual discharge
- Pleural, peritoneal, or pericardial fluid inflammatory exudates

- Any other body fluid or tissue contaminated with blood

Body fluids not listed above are generally regarded as noninfectious.

II. Immediate Treatment
   A. Wound Care/First Aid
      1. Clean wound with soap and water.
      2. Flush mucous membranes with water/saline.
      3. Other wound care is dictated by injury or accident.
      4. Serious injuries requiring suturing or other physician intervention should be promptly evaluated in the ER; registration is required.
   B. Contact HIV Counseling and Testing Service Needlestick Hotline.

III. Early Treatment
   A. Tetanus prophylaxis if indicated (24 hours or less after serious "dirty" injury; requires ER visit); otherwise at Center for Municipal Occupational Safety and Health of San Francisco General Hospital (CMOSH) follow-up.
      1. Document refusal of treatment.
   B. HBV HBIg prophylaxis less than 24 hours after parenteral exposure (after drawing health care worker red top for HBsAb) if health care worker not completely vaccinated and:
      1. Source is known to be HBsAg positive.
      2. Source has clinical hepatitis and HBV has not been excluded.
      3. Document refusal of treatment.

Figure 7-12. Health Care Worker Medical Record: Baseline Visit for Zidovudine Chemoprophylaxis

Treatment Location: ____________________

Name of Treating Clinician: ____________________

Employee I.D. Number: ____________________

Date of Exposure: _____ / _____ / _____ Time of Exposure: __________

Date of Visit: _____ / _____ / _____

Date Zidovudine Started: _____ / _____ / _____ Time First Dose: __________

Severity of Exposure:
_____ Massive
_____ Definite Parenteral
_____ Possible Parenteral
_____ Doubtful Parenteral

EXPOSURE HISTORY

PHYSICAL EXAMINATION

Body weight __________ Height __________ Urine pregnancy test __________ (if indicated)

ASSESSMENT/PLAN

_____ Consent (Form 1) signed
_____ HIV testing consent signed
_____ Contraception/safer sex discussed
_____ Intent to avoid pregnancy (Form 2) signed
_____ Health care worker information packet provided
_____ Baseline laboratory tests/HIV test ordered
_____ Follow-up appointment given (____________________)

____

Provider's signature

Figure 7-13. Health Care Worker Medical Record: Follow-Up Visit for Zidovudine Chemoprophylaxis

(WEEK # _____ postexposure or MONTH # _____ postexposure)

Employee I.D. Number: ____________________

Date of Exposure: _____ / _____ / _____ Date of Visit: _____ / _____ / _____

Date Zidovudine Started: _____ / _____ / _____

INTERVAL HISTORY (include assessment of drug/safer sex compliance)

SYMPTOMS (complete chart)

PHYSICAL EXAMINATION

Body weight ________________

LAB VALUES (complete chart)

ABNORMAL VALUES/GRADE:

ASSESSMENT/PLAN

_____ Follow-up appointment given (________________________)

____

Provider's signature

C. Immune serum globulin prophylaxis as soon as possible less than 24 hours after parenteral exposure (after drawing health care worker red top for HBsAb):
   1. All other massive, definite, or possible parenteral exposures are included.
   2. Document refusal of treatment.

D. HBIg or ISG treatment when CMOSH follow-up within 24 hours not available:
   1. Counseling and Testing Service physician to call ER M.D./R.N.
   2. Treatment instructions provided to ER M.D./R.N.
   3. Health care worker to report to ER triage desk (no registration)
   4. Red top tube drawn, labeled with health care worker's name, and stored in ER
   5. ER R.N. to provide treatment and document visit in ER Employee Exposure Log
   6. Health care worker referred to CMOSH 8:00 a.m. next working day
   7. Health care worker given fact sheet regarding follow-up
   8. Counseling and Testing physician to call CMOSH N.P. and alert her/him that health care worker visited ER, to expect CMOSH follow-up visit, and to pick up red top tube in ER
   9. Detailed exposure documentation deferred to CMOSH

E. Heptavax® five days or less after parenteral exposure (at CMOSH follow-up) if:
   1. Health care worker is HBsAb negative.
   2. Document refusal of treatment.

F. Azidothymidine (ZIDOVUDINE, AZT, zidovudine) recommended as soon as possible (within hours) for:

Figure 7-14. Health Care Worker's Laboratory Record for Zidovudine Prophylaxis

Employee I.D. Number: ______________________

Date of Exposure: ___/___/___

Date AZT Commenced: ___/___/___

LABORATORY RECORD
(record **GRADE:**)

	Date of Visit / # Days of Therapy When Labs Performed						
	_/_/_ Day #_	_/_/_ Day #_	_/_/_ Day #_	_/_/_ Day #_	_/_/_ Day #_	_/_/_ Day #_	_/_/_ Day #_
White cells							
Differential (P/L/M/E)							
Hematocrit							
Hemoglobin							
Platelets							
SGOT							
Alkaline phosphatase							
Total bilirubin							
CPK							
Creatinine							
Urine specific gravity							
Urine heme							
Urine protein							
HIV antibody ELISA							
HIV antibody IFA							
Western blot bands							
p24 antigen titer							
PCR							
CD4 Count							
Other ________							

Figure 7-15. Health Care Worker's Symptoms Record for Zidovudine Prophylaxis

Employee I.D. Number: ______________________

Date of Exposure: ___/___/___

Date AZT Commenced: ___/___/___

SYMPTOMS RECORD
(record **GRADE:**)

	Date of Visit / # Days of Therapy When Symptoms Described						
	__/__/__ Day #__	__/__/__ Day #__	__/__/__ Day #__	__/__/__ Day #__	__/__/__ Day #__	__/__/__ Day #__	__/__/__ Day #__
Fever							
Diaphoresis							
Lymphadenopathy							
Rash							
Headache							
Change in taste							
Dizziness							
Insomnia							
Somnolence							
Anxiety							
Myalgia							
Arthralgia							
Paresthesia							
Weakness							
Malaise							
Dyspepsia							
Nausea/vomiting							
Loss of appetite							
Diarrhea							
Other ___________							

Figure 7-16. Health Care Worker Medical Record: Abnormal Lab Values/ Zidovudine Dosage Adjustment Schedule

Lab Value	Grade 1	Grade 2 (reduce dose)	Grade 3 (discontinue)
Hemoglobin (grams per deciliter)	(−) 1	(−) 2-3	(−) ≥4
Neutrophils (per cubic millimeter)	>2,500	1,000–2,499	<1,000
Platelets (per cubic millimeter)	>100,000	75,000–99,999	<75,000
Creatinine	<1.5 × B	1.5–2.5 × B	>2.5 × B
SGOT	<3 × B	3.0–5.0 × B	>5.0 × B
AlkPhos	<3 × B	3.0–5.0 × B	>5.0 × B
Bilirubin	<3 × B	3.0–5.0 × B	>5.0 × B
Proteinuria	0–trace	1-2 g/24 hours	>2 g/24 hours
Hematuria	0–micro	gross	clots

B = baseline laboratory values.

1. Massive exposure (transfusion of blood from source known to be HIV infected or source at high risk for HIV infection pending test)
2. High-titer exposure (parenteral exposure to concentrated virus, usually in research lab setting)
3. Treatment deferred if health care worker is pregnant
4. Rx: 200 mg P.0. every four hours pending subsequent evaluation by HIV Counseling and Testing or Employee Health Clinician within 24 hours
5. Zidovudine is not routinely encouraged for other exposures *but should be discussed.* It may be prescribed for definite and possible parenteral exposures to HIV and at the discretion of the supervising clinician for some doubtful parenteral exposures (see zidovudine protocol for details).
6. In all cases in which zidovudine is administered, every effort should be made to initiate treatment as soon as possible–within hour(s)–of exposure. This will be accomplished by maintaining a supply of zidovudine (three doses) in the pharmacy, which can be released 24 hours a day by phone order from a Counseling and Testing Service clinician. Health care worker identifiers should not be used when ordering zidovudine.
7. Counseling and Testing physician must arrange follow-up visit for treated health care worker within 24 hours of starting zidovudine; contact medical chief resident on call if needed.
8. Health care workers may request referral to non-UCSF/SFGH/VA clinicians for additional evaluation and nonprotocol treatment.

IV. Follow-up Evaluation and Treatment

A. Refer the health care worker to CMOSH (8:00 a.m. Monday through Friday except holidays) or instruct health care worker to call CMOSH (to arrange follow-up with N.P.). Call and leave message on CMOSH N.P. answering line to let N.P. know that health care worker is expected.

B. Source patient HIV testing will be coordinated by the Counseling and Testing Service when contacted by CMOSH N.P.

C. Assessing Risk of Infection in Source Patient

1. Source known and available for HBV evaluation; health care worker HBsAb negative or pending:
   a. Diagnosed HBV (HbsAg+ ± HBeAg+) test unnecessary.

Figure 7-17. Symptom Adverse Effect Scale
Retrovirus Exposure Surveillance Program Zidovudine Chemoprophylaxis

Symptoms	Grade 0	Grade 1	Grade 2	Grade 3 (reduce dose)	Grade 4 (discontinue treatment)
Headache	None	Occasional/no therapy required	Frequent/nonnarcotic analgesic required	Persistent/narcotic required	Intolerable, intractable headache despite therapy
Taste perception	None	Transient/selective changes	Persistent changes	Total loss of taste	
Dizziness	None	Intermittent episodes	Frequent episodes/therapy required	Frequent episodes, poorly responsive to therapy	Unable to perform daily functions
Somnolence	Alert	Drowsiness	Unnatural sleepiness	Unable to stay awake	Coma
Paresthesia/weakness	None	Mild paresthesia, decreased DTRs	Severe paresthesia, absent DTR, mild weakness	Intolerable paresthesia, marked weakness	Paralysis
Difficulty falling asleep	None	Subtle, minor changes	Nightly changes/medication required	Nightly changes, poorly responsive to medication	Persistent changes resulting in an inability to function
Sleep continuity disturbance	No change	Occasional disturbed sleep	Frequent waking/therapy required	Increased waking, poorly responsive to therapy	Inability to maintain sleep despite therapy
Increased anxiety	None	Transient anxiety	Persistent anxiety/medication required	Persistent anxiety, poorly responsive to medication	Unable to perform daily functions, inadequately responsive to medication
Malaise	None	Mild feeling of illness	Persistent feeling of illness that interrupts daily activities	Intolerable feeling of illness and fatigue with inability to function	
Fever/diaphoresis	None	37.8–38.4ºC	38.5–40.0ºC	>40.0ºC	Fever with hypotension
Lymphadenopathy	None	Lymphadenopathy not requiring symptomatic therapy	Lymphadenopathy requiring symptomatic therapy	Intolerable lymphadenopathy despite symptomatic therapy	
Loss of appetite	None	Transient loss of appetite	Persistent loss of appetite	Intolerable loss of appetite associated with weight loss of 10 lbs. or more or 10 percent body weight	
Dyspepsia	None	Transient indigestion/no therapy required	Persistent indigestion requiring therapy	Intolerable indigestion, no relief from therapy	

Figure 7-17. (Continued)

Symptoms	Grade 0	Grade 1	Grade 2	Grade 3 (reduce dose)	Grade 4 (discontinue treatment)
Nausea/vomiting	None	Transient nausea and/or vomiting not requiring symptomatic therapy	Persistent nausea and/or vomiting requiring therapy	Vomiting requiring I.V. therapy	Intractable vomiting
Diarrhea	None	Transient, less than two days/no therapy required	Present two or more days requiring therapy	Intolerable despite therapy	Hemorrhagic, dehydration
Myalgia	None	Mild myalgia/no therapy needed	Moderate myalgia requiring medication	Intolerable myalgia despite therapy	
Arthralgia	None	Minor arthralgia/no therapy needed	Moderate arthralgia/therapy required	Intolerable arthralgia despite therapy	
Rash	None	Erythremia	Mild desquamation, vesicles	Moderate desquamation, ulceration	Exfoliative dermatitis, necrosis requiring surgical intervention
Dyspnea	None	Mild symptoms	Exertional dyspnea	Dyspnea at rest	Complete bed rest required

b. High-risk HBV (drug user/gay man/Asian immigrant/dialysis patient, etc./clinical hepatitis)—test source.
c. HBV known seronegative (tested in last month)—test source (optional).
d. No apparent risk for HBV—test source (optional).
e. Rule of thumb: Test source unless source is known to be HBsAG positive.

2. Source known and available for HIV evaluation:
   a. Diagnosed HIV infection/AIDS/ARC—test unnecessary.
   b. High-risk HIV (multiple sexual partners/intravenous drug user/hemophiliac/etc.)—test source (with consent).
   c. HIV known seronegative (tested in last month)—test source with consent (optional).
   d. No apparent risk for HIV—test source with consent (optional).
   e. Rule of thumb: Test source (with consent) unless source is known to be HIV infected.
3. Source unknown/unavailable for evaluation:
   a. Individualize management depending on exposure severity.

D. Source Patient HIV Counseling and Testing
   1. Contact HIV Counseling and Testing Service.
   2. Counselor/Clinician assesses indications for testing.
   3. Request approval to seek testing from source patient's attending physician if appropriate.
   4. Patient counseled; informed consent required prior to testing.
   5. Source patient HIV test may be obtained on a STAT basis at the discretion of the counselor/clinician/N.P. Source patient HIV tests should be performed on a STAT basis when the exposed health care worker has elected to begin empiric zidovudine treatment.
   6. Test results are communicated to patient (with appropriate counseling and referral if indicated), CMOSH N.P./counselor, and exposed health care worker.
   7. Source patient test results are placed in the medical record envelope and filed in Counseling and Testing file.

E. Health Care Worker HIV Counseling and Testing
   1. HIV testing (baseline, six weeks, three months, six months) recommended if:
      a. Source is known to be HIV positive or have AIDS or ARC.
      b. Source tests HIV positive.
      c. Source is high risk for HIV.
      d. Source is unknown.
      e. Health care worker is anxious.
   2. HIV testing optional if:
      a. Source is low risk for HIV.
      b. Source is HIV test negative.
   3. Baseline serum specimen frozen: Document refusal of treatment.
   4. HIV testing available via:
      a. HIV Counseling and Testing Service confidential testing linked with counseling; in conjunction with CMOSH or Student Health Service; test results documentable for health care worker; turnaround time 10 days now at SFGH; will improve soon.
      b. Health Care Worker Study anonymous testing; ad hoc counseling only; test results documentable for health care worker; turnaround time 48 hours for postexposure follow-up testing.
      c. Outside referral/anonymous test sites.
   5. Health care worker counseling available via:
      a. HIV Counseling and Testing Service
      b. CMOSH M.D./R.N.
      c. CMOSH/Counseling and Testing counselor
      d. Outside referral

V. CMOSH Record Keeping, Documentation, and Required Reporting
   A. Regular CMOSH Medical Record
      1. Exposure occurred
      2. HBV treatment
   B. Coded Confidential CMOSH record
      1. Detailed exposure history form
      2. Employer's First Report (submit summary report to OSHA)
      3. Doctor's First Report of Illness (submit coded report to worker's compensation); health care worker must elect to uncode report when filing nonseroconversion claims; seroconversion claims remain coded except to specified worker's compensation personnel
      4. HIV test consents/results
      5. Declensions
      6. Zidovudine treatment record
      7. Counseling follow-up
      8. Other information relevant to exposure management

Veterans Administration Medical Center Seattle, Washington

AZT Prophylaxis after HIV Exposure

Procedure Following Health Care Worker's Exposure to HIV

1. All employees of Seattle VAMC, including volunteers, residents, and "without compensation" (WOC) workers, who sustain nonintact skin, mucous membrane, or percutaneous exposures to blood or body fluids will be initially evaluated and treated per the protocol outlined in Section E-3.0 of the Infection Control Manual, "Bloodborne Disease Exposure Follow-up Protocol."
2. Consent for HIV testing of both the employee and the source patient will conform to policy as defined in Memorandum 11-38. For exposures deemed by the Employee Health Practitioner or AOD to be in the "massive" or "definite" categories (as defined below), source blood samples will be processed on a STAT basis at the Blood Bank, with results available on the following administrative day.
3. Categories of exposures:
   a. Massive exposure: Includes large-volume (>1-ml) injections of blood and parenteral exposure to laboratory specimens containing high titer of virus.
   b. Definite parenteral exposure: Includes intramuscular (I.M./deep) injury with a blood/bloody body fluid-contaminated needle; injection of blood/bloody body fluid; laceration or similar wound, that causes bleeding in the health care worker produced by a visibly bloody body fluid-contaminated instrument; laceration or similar fresh wound inoculated with bloody body fluid; or any parenteral inoculation of HIV virus samples (usually research settings).
   c. Possible parenteral exposure: Includes subcutaneous (S.Q./superficial) injury with blood/bloody body fluid-contaminated needle; a wound produced by blood/bloody body fluid-contaminated instrument that does not cause visible bleeding; a prior wound or skin lesion contaminated with blood/bloody body fluid or mucous membrane inoculation with bloody body fluid.
   d. Doubtful parenteral exposure: Includes subcutaneous (S.Q./superficial) injury with nonbloody body fluid-contaminated needle; a wound produced by nonbloody body fluid-contaminated instrument that does not cause visible bleeding; a prior wound or skin lesion contaminated with nonbloody body fluid or mucous membrane inoculation with nonbloody body fluids.
   e. Nonparenteral exposure: Intact skin contamination with blood or body fluids is a nonexposure.
4. Employee pre- and posttest counseling will conform to Washington State law and will be documented in the Employee Health record.
5. Employees sustaining exposures from documented HIV-positive sources will be further counseled regarding the current medical data on postexposure prophylaxis with zidovudine (AZT). Seattle VA will not administer zidovudine for postexposure prophylaxis. A reference list identifying completed and ongoing research on zidovudine postexposure prophylaxis will be provided to the employee on request to share with his/her private physician.

Rationale for Not Prescribing AZT Prophylaxis

1. Zidovudine (AZT) and other inhibitors of viral reverse transcriptase are virustatic, not virucidal, agents. They are therefore more likely to merely suppress viral replication rather than eradicate infection. They do not kill cell-free virus and cannot eradicate virus from previously infected cells.
2. AZT and a related compound, dideoxycytidine (ddC), have been studied as prophylactic agents in three animal/retroviral models: mouse/murine leukemia virus, cat/feline

leukemia virus, and macaque/SRV-2. Both agents altered the natural history slightly by decreasing viremia and delaying development of an antibody response to the virus. Unfortunately, they were not effective in preventing establishment of chronic retroviral infections even when administered *prior* to the viral challenge. Although there is always uncertainty in extrapolating from animal models to humans, one can only conclude that there is little experimental evidence supporting the prophylactic use of AZT.

3. There are few data on the safety of short courses of AZT in otherwise healthy individuals. Much of the toxicity appears to be dose related, but even low doses have been associated with headache, fatigue, myalgia, insomnia, nausea, myositis, paresthesia, hepatitis, and anemia. Since AZT acts on DNA polymerase enzymes, there is the potential for mutagenesis and teratogenesis. AZT has been shown to produce neoplasms in mice, but the magnitude of this risk in humans is unknown. There are no data on the safety of AZT during pregnancy, but it is recommended that pregnant women *not* take AZT.
4. The one consistent effect of AZT observed in the animal studies cited above was to delay seroconversion. If it has the same effect in humans, it may give false assurance to exposed individuals who failed to seroconvert but who might nonetheless be infected and potentially infective.
5. The VA Chief Medical Director, in recognition of the data summarized above, has recommended that zidovudine prophylaxis be considered unproven and experimental and that it should only be administered as part of an approved research protocol.

San Francisco General Hospital
San Francisco, California

Occupational Risk of CMV Exposure to Health Care Workers [Excerpt from Body Substance Precautions Handbook for Clinical Staff]

Change in Infection Control policy for management of cytomegalovirus (CMV) exposures to hospital personnel:

1. Pregnant women will no longer be excluded from direct care of CMV excreters.
2. *All* employees caring for *all* patients, in order to protect themselves from the unknown carrier of CMV and other diseases, should use good personal hygiene during direct care. This includes hand washing before direct care, particularly in invasive procedures, and the use of gloves for contact with blood and other body fluids, particularly in the presence of fresh open areas on the skin.

Discussion

Background

Cytomegalovirus is a ubiquitous virus found in urine, saliva, breast milk, cervical secretions, and semen during primary or reactivated infection. It may also be in the bloodstream even though the infected person is asymptomatic; therefore, blood transfusion may be a source. CMV is the most common cause of posttransfusion mononucleosis. After infection with the virus, with or without symptoms, the virus may be excreted for as long as three to six years in infants and usually a shorter period in adults. Excretion may be reactivated with, but usually without, symptoms, during pregnancy (3 to 28 percent of pregnant women excrete virus[1]) or with immunodeficiency or immunosuppression.[2]

The most severe form of disease (involving the central nervous system, liver, sometimes the eyes, and the lungs) occurs during the perinatal period. The virus is so common that 0.5 to 2.2 percent of all newborns are congenitally infected, although the majority (999 out of 1,000) show no signs at birth.[3] However, 10 percent of these children with asymptomatic congenital infections will eventually develop some degree of neurosensory disability.[4]

Infection acquired in later life is usually inapparent but may cause symptoms like "mono." Posttransfusion infection is usually inapparent but may present like "mono." Widespread infection presenting as pneumonia and/or hepatitis is seen in persons who are immunodeficient or immunocompromised.

Since there can be more than one strain of virus, having a CMV antibody titer does not guarantee protection from other strains nor does it prevent reactivation of an already-acquired strain.[5]

Evidence of prior infection (CMV antibodies) has been shown in San Francisco to exist in 94 percent of homosexual men and 50 percent of heterosexual men.[6] It is estimated in California that 30 to 40 percent of women have had a primary infection before reaching childbearing age.[7]

Transmission

CMV is transmitted by intimate or very close contact between broken skin or mucous membranes and infected tissue. By far, the most efficient transmission occurs through oral or sexual contact. While asymptomatic excreters may be excreting less virus, it is enough to infect should the necessary intimate contact occur. Transmission has been effectively blocked by hand washing,[8] and the use of gloves for contact with body fluids may add a measure of assurance.[9-11]

Occupational Risk for Health Care Workers

A review of CMV excretion in hospitalized patients and studies of health care workers does not support frequent occurrence of CMV infection despite ample opportunity for exposure. The occurrence of CMV infection, with virus being excreted in our population, is about 3 percent of healthy adults,[12] 11 percent of renal transplant patients,[13] 1 to 2 percent of all newborns,[14] and up to 28 percent of pregnant women.[15] Most of these infections are asymptomatic and will not be known to the health care provider.

Despite health care workers caring for unknown CMV excreters, the seroconversion rates for nurses versus nonnurses of the same age was not significantly different when routine hygienic measures were taken.[16]

Some concern has been expressed about the ability of a patient with CMV pneumonia to transmit the virus by the airborne route. A review of the SFGH Health Care Workers Study shows many nurses have cared repeatedly for CMV pneumonia patients without protection of a mask. Their seroconversion rates are no different than those of other nurses or of the general public.[17]

Recommendations for CMV Infection Precautions for All Patients

1. Since CMV infection is so ubiquitous and usually inapparent, all patients of any age and any diagnosis should be cared for using good personal hygiene and standard good patient care practices. This includes hand washing after contact with body fluids, particularly urine and saliva, but including other body fluids as well. Gloves may be worn when large-volume exposure is expected or in the presence of fresh open wounds with ready access to the vascular system. Workers should be cautioned to use gloves only when actually needed because prolonged use promotes unhealthy skin problems.
2. Although women of childbearing age and immunosuppressed employees are at increased risk of experiencing disease as a result of CMV exposure, protection of these individuals is best accomplished by observing good personal hygiene as described above. Exclusion of pregnant women or immunosuppressed employees from the care of "known" CMV excreters does not accomplish the desired protection and may lead to a false sense of security. Therefore, health care workers (including pregnant women) who are otherwise able to care for patients will no longer be excluded from the care of "known" CMV excreters.
3. Screening of patients for CMV virus is not very useful because excretion may be intermittent and processing takes too long to be of practical value.
4. Screening employees for CMV antibody is not useful since this does not guarantee immunity to a different strain.

☐ References

1. Klanshaw, J. B. Cytomegalovirus. In: J. S. Remington and J. O. Klein, editors. *Infectious Diseases of the Fetus and the Newborns*, pp. 107–55. Philadelphia: W. B. Saunders, 1976.
2. Benenson, A. S., editor. *Control of Communicable Diseases in Man.* 14th ed. Washington, DC: American Public Health Association, 1985.
3. Pass, R. F., Stagno, S., Dworsky, M. E., et al. Excretion of cytomegalovirus in mothers: observations after delivery of congenitally infected and normal infants. *Journal of Infectious Diseases* 146:1–6, 1982.
4. Benenson.
5. Stagno, S., Pass, R. F., Dworsky, M. E., et al. Congenital cytomegalovirus infection: the relative importance of primary and recurrent matural infection. *New England Journal of Medicine* 306(16):945–49, 1982.
6. Drew, W. L., Mintz, L., Miner, R. C., et al. Prevalence of cytomegalovirus infections in homosexual men. *Journal of Infectious Diseases* 143:188–92, 1981.

7. *California Morbidity Supplement* 7, Feb. 25, 1983.
8. Brady, M. T. Cytomegalovirus infections: occupational risk for health professionals. *American Journal of Infection Control* 14:197–203, 1986.
9. Balfour, C. L., and Balfour, H. H. Cytomegalovirus is not an occupational disease for nurses in renal transplant and neonatal units. *Journal of the American Medical Association* 256(14):1909–14, 1986.
10. Ahlfors, K., Ivarsson, S. A., Johnson, T., and Renmarker, K. Risk of cytomegalovirus infection in nurses and congenital infection in their offspring. *Acta Paediatrica Scandinavica* 70:819–23, 1981.
11. Haneberg, B., Bertnes, E., and Haukenes, G. Antibodies to cytomegalovirus among personnel at Children's Hospital. *Acta Paediatrica Scandinavica* 69:407–9, 1980.
12. Benenson.
13. Balfour and Balfour.
14. Benenson.
15. *California Morbidity Supplement.*
16. *California Morbidity Supplement.*
17. Gerberding, J. L., Bryant LeBlanc, C. F., and Nelson, K. Risk of transmitting the human immunodeficiency virus, hepatitis B virus, and cytomegalovirus to health care workers exposed to patients with AIDS and AIDS-related conditions. *Journal of Infectious Diseases* 156:1–8, July 1987.

Kaiser Permanente Medical Center
San Francisco, California

Guidelines for Managing Exposure to Selected Communicable Diseases [Excerpt from Infection Control Manual]

An important exposure is one in which a person is subjected to an infectious agent in a way considered likely to lead to acquisition of disease. Whether an exposure to an infectious agent is important depends on various factors, including: (1) the mechanism of transmission of the agent involved and the person's infective potential (for example, a noncoughing patient with pulmonary tuberculosis poses little threat), (2) the type and duration of contact, (3) host susceptibility, and (4) whether suggested precautions are used. The hospital epidemiologist, with others who may be involved, will determine whether an important exposure has occurred and whether some intervention after the exposure is needed.

I. Exposure to a Patient with Tuberculosis (AFB Sputum Smear Positive)

A. Circumstances surrounding the incident usually include a sputum smear positive for AFB and a patient with a productive cough who has not been on Respiratory Precautions.

B. Department manager is notified and advised of the following procedure:

1. Health care workers who cared for such a patient while not on Respiratory Precautions should be questioned regarding recent or past tuberculin skin test results.
   a. Those health care workers who have had previously negative skin tests should be skin tested now for a baseline PPD result. (See number 2 for the procedure to follow when the exposure is from a patient with an AFB-positive smear diagnosed with AIDS or ARC.) If the baseline PPD is negative, then repeat the skin test two months after the exposure in question. Those persons who convert their PPD results from negative to positive at the baseline or two-month screening should be referred to their physician for a chest X-ray and evaluation for prophylaxis. Those persons with pulmonary symptoms suggestive of tuberculosis should also be referred to their physician for a chest X-ray.
   b. Those health care workers with a history of positive skin tests should be referred to their physician for a decision about the advisability of a chest X-ray.
2. When the exposure is from an AIDS or ARC patient, it is advisable to wait to place the PPD until the final AFB culture results are available. The majority of positive AFB smears in AIDS patients are due to nontuberculosis mycobacterial organisms. These organisms are called *Mycobacterium avium* complex (MAC). MAC are opportunistic organisms found in the environment that are nonpathogenic to a normal host. A much smaller percentage of AFB-positive smears in AIDS patients are due to *Mycobacterium tuberculosis* (TB). The final culture results will be known in about 10 to 30 days and will demonstrate whether the organism is TB or MAC.
   a. If the AFB organism is MAC, nothing further needs to be done.
   b. If the organism is TB, begin baseline skin testing in exposed health care workers and repeat the skin test two months after exposure.
3. Department managers will be given a table to facilitate tabulation of the above data.
4. Send a copy of the results to the Infection Control Department.
5. Notify the physician of any patient housed in the same room with a patient diagnosed with tuberculosis during the time s/he was not on Respiratory Precautions.

II. Exposure to Blood and Body Fluids/Substances

A. Introduction

Universal Precautions that include Guidelines for Preventing Transmission of Infections in Health Care Settings and Employee Health Issues are included in the Infection Control Manual, starting on p. 5. Compliance with these guidelines should minimize exposure of health care workers to blood and other body fluids/substances. However, inadvertent contact with blood or body fluids/substances may not be anticipated and exposure may occur.

B. Definition

Exposure to blood or body fluids/substances is defined as follows:

1. *Parenteral:* needlestick, cut, or other wound inflicted by a sharp object contaminated with the blood or body fluids/substances from any patient.
2. *Mucous membrane:* splash or aerosol to the eyes, nose, or mouth with blood or body fluids/substances of any patient.
3. *Cutaneous:* contact with blood or body fluids/substances when exposed skin (unprotected by gloves or other barriers) is abraded, severely chapped, or afflicted by dermatitis.

C. Procedure

Exposure to the blood or body fluids/substances of any patient may result in an infection. Health care workers should follow this procedure when an exposure has occurred:

1. Employee should immediately wash the contaminated area with soap and running water.
2. The employee should then notify his or her supervisor. The supervisor should report the employee's injury to:
   a. Personnel Department within 24 hours
   b. Infection Control Department
   c. Occupational Medicine Department
3. Employee should complete Employee's Report of Industrial Injury.
4. The employee should seek medical follow-up as soon as possible after the exposure.
   a. If known, the name and medical record number of the source of the exposure should be brought to the physician.
   b. Medical follow-up may be sought in the following locations at these times and on these days:
      (1) Monday through Friday, 8:30 a.m. to 5 p.m.—Employee Health Center (or if not open Medical Drop-In Clinic at 2200 O'Farrell, 4th floor).
      (2) Monday through Friday, 5 p.m. to 10 p.m., Saturday and Sunday, 8 a.m. to 10 p.m.—General Clinic, 2425 Geary.
      (3) All nights, 10 p.m. to 8 a.m.—Emergency Room.
   c. The physician may recommend or the employee may choose serial testing for human immunodeficiency virus antibody (anti-HIV).
      (1) Testing should be done at zero (baseline), at two months, and at six months postexposure.
      (2) The anti-HIV test may be obtained at Kaiser.
      (3) Pretest and posttest counseling should be done.
   d. For more information regarding hepatitis B, non-A, non-B hepatitis, and HIV transmission, see relevant sections of Infection Control Manual.
   e. The physician will initiate hepatitis B prophylaxis per hepatitis B exposure algorithms.
      (1) Algorithm I [figure 7-18] explains how to manage an exposure to blood and body fluids/substances in someone who has not received the hepatitis B vaccine.
      (2) Algorithm II [figure 7-19] explains how to manage an exposure to blood and body fluids/substances in someone who has completed the hepatitis B vaccine series.

Figure 7-18. Hepatitis B Postexposure Prophylaxis Protocol (for Persons Who Have Not Received Hepatitis B Vaccine)

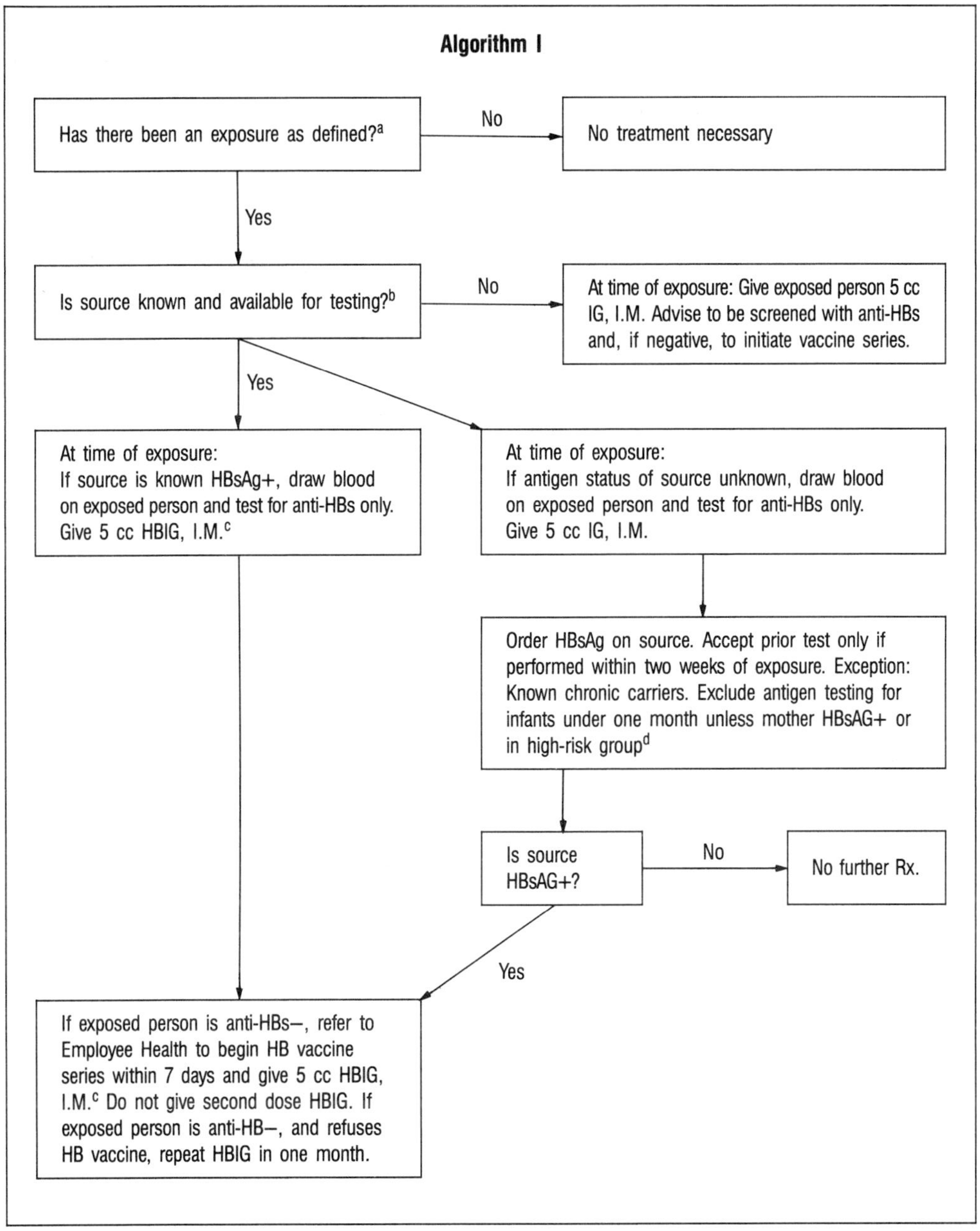

Footnotes

[a]Exposure is defined as (a) parenteral contact, that is, needlestick or laceration or open cut exposed to blood, laceration or open cut or conjunctivae exposed to known hepatitis B antigen-positive bodily materials, that is, such as urine, blood, saliva, pus, or stool; (b) known ingestion of bodily materials, that is, urine, blood, stool, saliva, pus; (c) known conjunctival splash with bodily materials, that is, urine, blood, stool, or pus.

[b]Testing includes only HBsAg on the source and anti-HBs on the exposed person. Routine testing for the antibody to hepatitis B core antigen (anti-HBc), e antigen (HBeAg), and DNA polymerase is not recommended.

[c]Employees who refuse HBIG but want to receive the vaccine series will be advised that it is a deviation from the recommendations for postexposure prophylaxis. Documentation is to be noted in the employee's medical record. HBIG should be given within 24 hours of exposure and not later than 7 days. Employees who for unavoidable circumstances are not able to meet the time constraints for HBIG as recommended in the protocol may receive HBIG after 7 days of exposure.

[d]High-risk group includes women of Asian, Pacific Island, or Alaskan Eskimo descent, whether immigrant or U.S. born, and women with histories of: (a) acute or chronic liver disease, (b) blood transfusions on repeated occasions, (c) household contact with an HBV carrier or hemodialysis patient, or (d) percutaneous use of illicit drugs.

Figure 7-19. Hepatitis B Vaccine Recipients Special Hepatitis B Postexposure Prophylaxis (for Persons Who Have Completed Hepatitis B Vaccine Series)

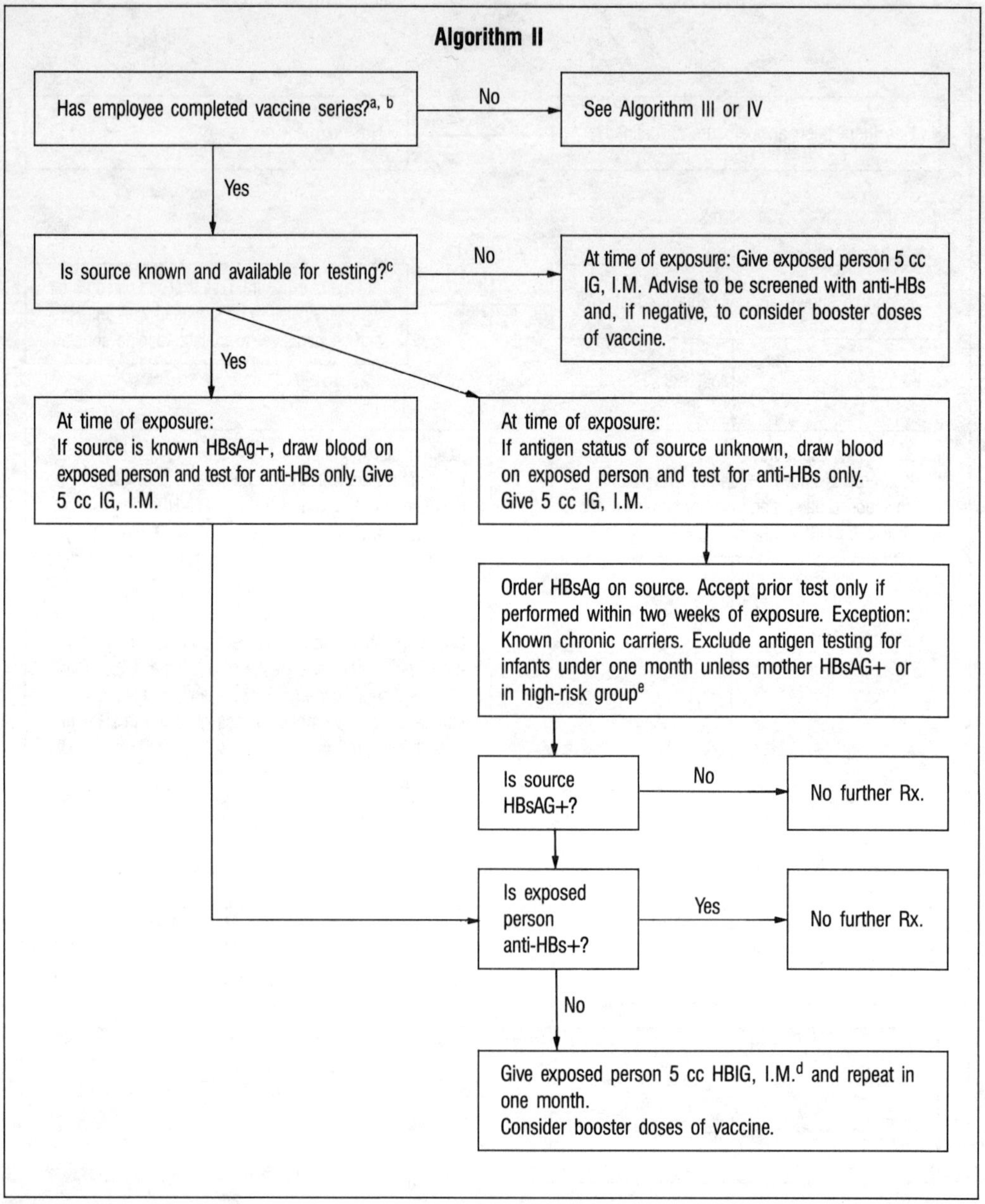

Footnotes

[a]If employee has been previously tested for anti-HBs and is positive, further testing is unnecessary. However, administer 5 cc IG, I.M. to employee.

[b]Exposure is defined as (a) parenteral contact, that is, needlestick or laceration or open cut exposed to blood, laceration or open cut or conjunctivae exposed to known hepatitis B antigen-positive bodily materials, that is, such as urine, blood, saliva, pus, or stool; (b) known ingestion of bodily materials, that is, urine, blood, stool, saliva, pus; (c) known conjunctival splash with bodily materials, that is, urine, blood, stool, or pus.

[c]Testing includes only HBsAg on the source and anti-HBs on the exposed person. Routine testing for the antibody to hepatitis B core antigen (anti-HBc), e antigen (HBeAg) and DNA polymerase is not recommended.

[d]Employees who refuse HBIG but want to receive the vaccine series will be advised that it is a deviation from the recommendations for postexposure prophylaxis. Documentation is to be noted in the employee's medical record. HBIG should be given within 24 hours of exposure and not later than 7 days. Employees who for unavoidable circumstances are not able to meet the time constraints for HBIG as recommended in the protocol may receive HBIG after 7 days of exposure.

[e]High-risk group includes women of Asian, Pacific Island, or Alaskan Eskimo descent, whether immigrant or U.S. born, and women with histories of: (a) acute or chronic liver disease, (b) blood transfusions on repeated occasions, (c) household contact with an HBV carrier or hemodialysis patient, or (d) percutaneous use of illicit drugs.

(3) Algorithm III [figure 7-20] explains how to manage an exposure to blood and body fluids/substances in someone who has received two doses of the hepatitis B vaccine.

(4) Algorithm IV [figure 7-21] explains how to manage an exposure to blood and body fluids/substances in someone who has received one dose of the hepatitis B vaccine.

f. Persons who receive the hepatitis B vaccine should have an anti-HBs test performed one month after the last dose of vaccine.

D. Abbreviations

HBsAg = Hepatitis B surface antigen
Anti-HBs = Antibody to the hepatitis B surface antigen
IG = Immune globulin (gamma globulin)
HBIG = Hepatitis B immune globulin

III. Exposure to Communicable Diseases by Prehospital Personnel

The following procedure should be followed by prehospital personnel (emergency medical technicians [EMTs], paramedics, police, etc.) following a possible exposure to a reportable disease:

A. Prehospital personnel who suspect that they have had an unprotected exposure to a communicable disease from a patient must register that information in a log provided for that purpose, located at reception desk in the Emergency Room.

B. A consultation sheet will be filled out by an Emergency Department physician and sent to the Infection Control Department.

C. The following information is needed in both the prehospital personnel exposure log book and the consultation sheet:

1. The type of exposure (the exposures that may pose a risk are mouth-to-mouth resuscitation, bites, needlesticks, mucous membrane splashes, nonintact skin contaminated by blood or body fluids/substances, airborne diseases, or any other type of exposure that the Emergency Room physician feels may pose a risk.
2. The exposed person's name, EMT number, address, and telephone number at work.
3. The patient's name, medical record number, location in medical center, presumptive diagnosis, address, and telephone number.

D. The Infection Control nurse will determine whether the patient has a reportable disease and notify the Department of Health Services as indicated.

Figure 7-20. Hepatitis B Vaccine Recipients Special Hepatitis B Postexposure Prophylaxis (for Persons Who Have Received Two Doses of Vaccine)

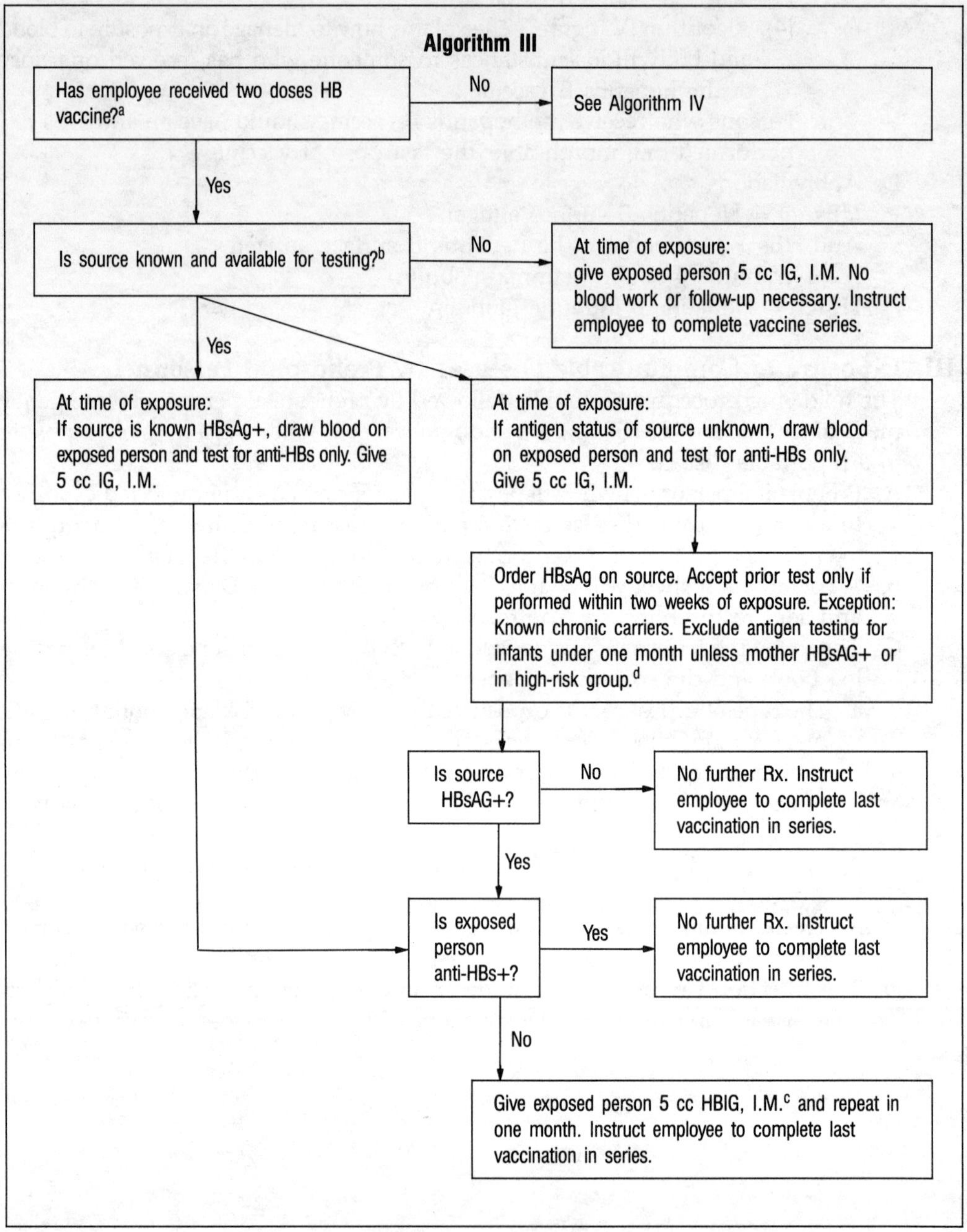

Footnotes

[a]Exposure is defined as (a) parenteral contact, that is, needlestick or laceration or open cut exposed to blood, laceration or open cut or conjunctivae exposed to known hepatitis B antigen-positive bodily materials, that is, such as urine, blood, saliva, pus, or stool; (b) known ingestion of bodily materials, that is, urine, blood, stool, saliva, pus; (c) known conjunctival splash with bodily materials, that is, urine, blood, stool, or pus.

[b]Testing includes only HBsAg on the source and anti-HBs on the exposed person. Routine testing for the antibody to hepatitis B core antigen (anti-HBc), e antigen (HBeAg), and DNA polymerase is not recommended.

[c]Employees who refuse HBIG but want to receive the vaccine series will be advised that it is a deviation from the recommendations for postexposure prophylaxis. Documentation is to be noted in the employee's medical record. HBIG should be given within 24 hours of exposure and not later than 7 days. Employees, who for unavoidable circumstances are not able to meet the time constraints for HBIG as recommended in the protocol, may receive HBIG after 7 days of exposure.

[d]High-risk group includes women of Asian, Pacific Island, or Alaskan Eskimo descent, whether immigrant or U.S. born, and women with histories of: (a) acute or chronic liver disease, (b) blood transfusions on repeated occasions, (c) household contact with an HBV carrier or hemodialysis patient, or (d) percutaneous use of illicit drugs.

Figure 7-21. Hepatitis B Vaccine Recipients Special Hepatitis B Postexposure Prophylaxis (for Persons Who Have Received One Dose of Vaccine)

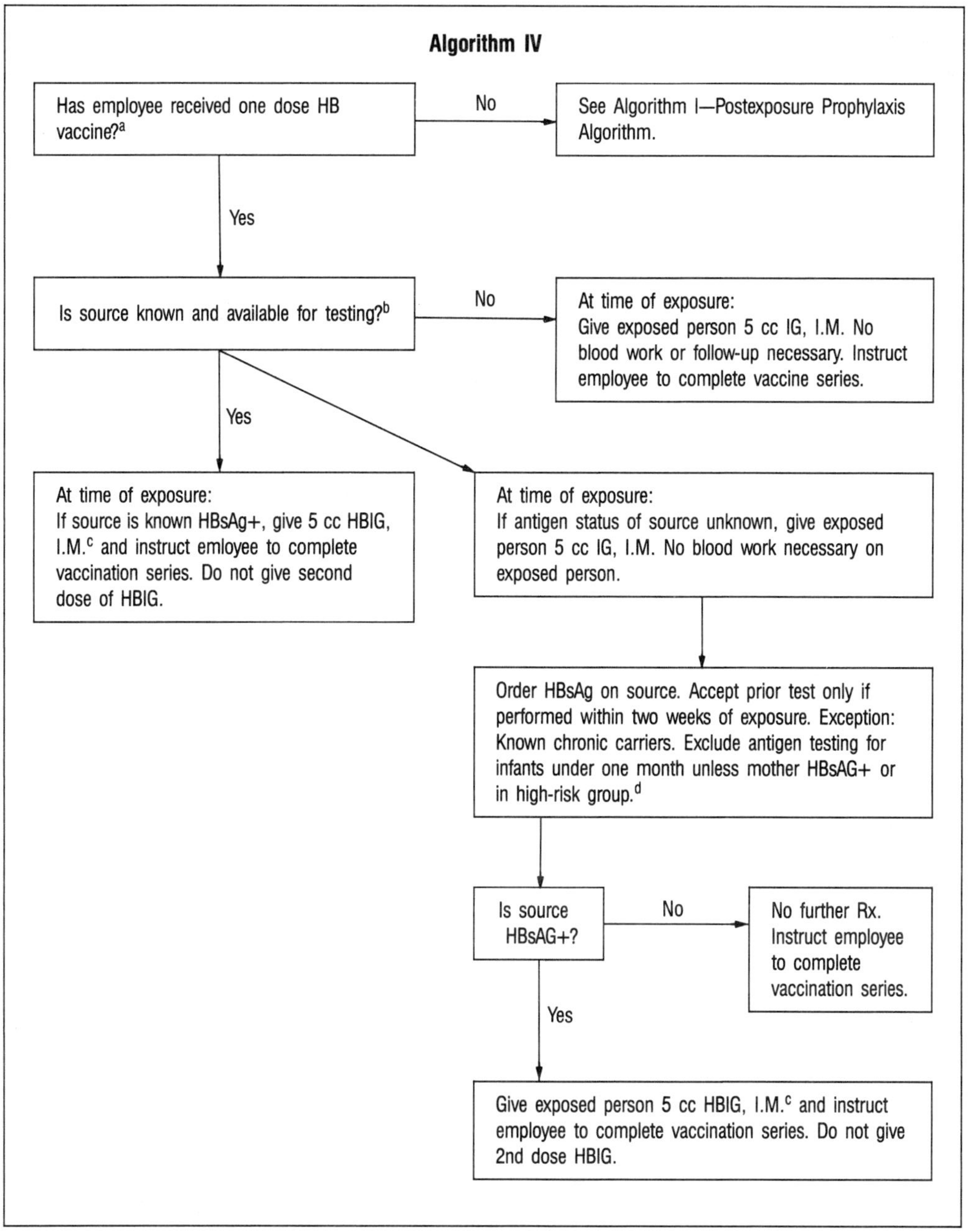

Footnotes

[a]Exposure is defined as (a) parenteral contact, that is, needlestick or laceration or open cut exposed to blood, laceration or open cut or conjunctivae exposed to known hepatitis B antigen-positive bodily materials, that is, such as urine, blood, saliva, pus, or stool; (b) known ingestion of bodily materials, that is, urine, blood, stool, saliva, pus; (c) known conjunctival splash with bodily materials, that is, urine, blood, stool, or pus.

[b]Testing includes only HBsAg on the source and anti-HBs on the exposed person. Routine testing for the antibody to hepatitis B core antigen (anti-HBc), e antigen (HBeAg), and DNA polymerase is not recommended.

[c]Employees who refuse HBIG but want to receive the vaccine series will be advised that it is a deviation from the recommendations for postexposure prophylaxis. Documentation is to be noted in the employee's medical record. HBIG should be given within 24 hours of exposure and not later than 7 days. Employees, who for unavoidable circumstances are not able to meet the time constraints for HBIG as recommended in the protocol, may receive HBIG after 7 days of exposure.

[d]High-risk group includes women of Asian, Pacific Island, or Alaskan Eskimo descent, whether immigrant or U.S. born, and women with histories of: (a) acute or chronic liver disease, (b) blood transfusions on repeated occasions, (c) household contact with an HBV carrier or hemodialysis patient, or (d) percutaneous use of illicit drugs.

Yale-New Haven Hospital
New Haven, Connecticut

Guidelines on Acquired Immune Deficiency Syndrome (AIDS) in the Workplace

I. Purpose

Acquired immune deficiency syndrome (AIDS) is an increasingly important issue for this hospital, its employees, its patients, and the general public. These AIDS in the workplace guidelines are intended as a broad, hospitalwide approach and represent the best judgment of the Yale-New Haven Hospital AIDS in the Workplace Task Force. These recommendations were based on the currently available scientific knowledge about the human immunodeficiency virus (HIV) and its manifestations. The purposes of this policy are (1) to clarify the work assignment guidelines of employees who have direct or indirect exposure to AIDS patients, (2) to outline the surveillance and monitoring procedures for employees who are infected with or exposed to HIV, and (3) to provide the means to disseminate information and educate hospital staff regarding exposure to this disease.

II. Establishment of Task Force on AIDS in the Workplace

Due to the medical complexity, the social and legal implications, and employee concerns about this disease, an AIDS in the Workplace Task Force will be established and designated as the appropriate group to review issues and establish workplace guidelines relative to AIDS. This Task Force will have representation from epidemiology, medical, clinical legal, nursing, and human resource functions. In addition, the Task Force may draw on other resources, internal and external, as it requires to evaluate medical developments and/or update these guidelines.

This task force will work closely with the AIDS Medical Task Force, the AIDS medical and nursing coordinators, the hospital epidemiology staff, the Infection Control Committee, Personnel Health Services (PHS), the Clinical Laboratories, and the Bioethics Committee where appropriate.

III. Employment

A. Applications

It is the responsibility of Personnel Health Services to assess, in a confidential setting, the applicant's medical history and physical condition in order to (1) determine the applicant's ability to perform the duties of the position applied for and (2) determine that the applicant can perform these duties in a manner that would not endanger the health or safety of the applicant or the health or safety of other employees or of patients. The communicable disease history would properly be directed to all serious or pertinent communicable diseases, including AIDS and AIDS-related syndromes. If the PHS nurse or physician elicited a history consistent with HIV infection, an HIV antibody test and counseling would be indicated.

B. Current Employees

The same evaluation procedures and medical inquiry guidelines used for applicants will be used for employees. Employees who have a history of a significant work-related exposure to HIV will be entered in the protocol established for monitoring these exposures. Employees who have exposures that are not work-related will be referred to their private physicians for monitoring and follow-up.

IV. Work Force Assignments

A. Care to Patients

The hospital has as its primary mission the provision of patient care, and all employees, directly or indirectly, must support this goal in caring for all patients.

There is no evidence that the risks in providing hands-on care to AIDS and other HIV-infected patients are any greater than the risks associated with caring for any patients with bloodborne or sexually transmitted infections. Employees are expected to perform their assigned duties and responsibilities in providing service and support to all patients, including AIDS or other HIV-infected patients. If an employee refuses to provide services to these patients, given the appropriate safety guidelines, then the employee's department head or immediate supervisor will immediately review the circumstances. If after education and counseling, the employee continues to refuse to provide care, appropriate administrative action will be pursued according to the hospital's personnel policies.

B. Working with Employees with AIDS/HIV Infection
Similarly, an employee's refusal to work with a fellow employee who has AIDS, HIV infection, or significant HIV exposure should be analyzed in the specific context in which it arises by the employee's department head and PHS. If after education and counseling, the employee continues to refuse to work with an infected or exposed employee, appropriate administrative action will be pursued according to the hospital's personnel policies.

C. Employees with AIDS or HIV Infection
Employees known to be infected with HIV (antibody-positive, AIDS, or ARC) will be considered individually as to their suitability for rendering patient care or being involved in invasive procedures. Supervision by the director, in conjunction with the employee's physician and the hospital epidemiologist, must determine on an individual and ongoing basis whether such an employee can adequately and safely perform patient care duties or invasive procedures. In addition, such employees must be provided with counseling and with instructions concerning infection control procedures.

D. Universal Precautions
Although nosocomial transmission is a rare event, the following Universal Blood and Body Substance Precautions (Universal Precautions) are recommended:

- Hands should be washed before and after contact with *all* patients. If hands or other skin surfaces accidentally come into contact with blood or other body fluids, they should be immediately washed with soap and water.
- Gloves should be worn when contact with blood or body fluids is anticipated, but gloves need not be worn by health care team members in ordinary patient contacts.
- Gowns, masks, and gloves are *not* routinely required but are indicated where there is a risk of exposure to blood or body fluids.
- Employees who have exudative lesions or weeping dermatitis must refrain from direct patient care and from handling patient care equipment until the condition resolves.

V. Testing and Monitoring

A. Monitoring Guidelines

1. Routine serologic testing of employees is not recommended. The risk of transmission of HIV to employees is extremely low and can be further minimized when routinely recommended infection control procedures are followed.

B. Management of Significant Exposures

1. *Definition:* Significant exposures include parenteral (needlestick, cut, bite), splashing to eyes, nose, or mouth, or contamination of open wound or skin lesion with blood or body fluids.
2. Source assessment will be done clinically and epidemiologically for likelihood of HIV (as well as hepatitis B) infection. If assessment suggests that an infection with HIV may exist, the patient's private physician will be informed by PHS

so that the patient may be counseled and requested to consent to serologic testing for HIV infection.

If the source patient declines testing or if the source cannot be precisely defined, that situation will be further evaluated epidemiologically by PHS and Hospital Epidemiology.

3. Monitoring of employees with significant exposure:
   a. This will be done in PHS for employees with work-related exposure that is significant by mode and source. This will include:
      (1) Documentation of the exposure
      (2) Medical history
      (3) Physical examination
      (4) Laboratory testing, including CBC with differential, HIV-antibody testing, and other tests as indicated
      (5) Hepatitis B exposure protocol (assessment of source, of health care worker's immune status, hepatitis screen, HBV prophylaxis as indicated, repeat hepatitis screen in one month)
   b. Above monitoring will be instituted as soon as possible after exposure and repeated at three and six months following exposure. This surveillance will be done only with the informed consent of the employee. All blood sampling and medical follow-up will be done in PHS.
4. Counseling of exposed employees will be done in PHS in collaboration with the AIDS nurse coordinator and will cover:
   a. The risk of infection
   b. Precautions to be observed during the monitoring period: refraining from donating blood, semen, or organs; avoiding exchange of blood, saliva, or other body fluids; use of condoms during sexual intercourse
   c. Being alert to the early clinical manifestations of HIV infection and the need for prompt reporting

   Concerned sexual partners will be included in counseling at the employee's request.
5. PHS will emphasize the need for completion of surveillance even if the employee should leave the hospital employ and will be responsible for maintaining contact with the employee, facilitating follow-up, and meeting its cost.

VI. Confidentiality of Employee Medical Records

In the event that it is necessary to screen or monitor an employee who has had exposure to HIV, specific procedures will be established within Personnel Health to maintain strict confidence.

Blood samples will be drawn in Personnel Health to avoid involvement of another department. All blood samples will be coded by date of birth. A log with code numbers and names will be kept separate from the confidential file. Any medical follow-up will also be done through Personnel Health.

VII. Employee Education, Orientation, and Counseling

A. The hospital recognizes its responsibility to identify and disclose to employees known health and safety issues and to provide a safe work environment. Therefore, it will make available to employees current information regarding AIDS and other serious communicable diseases in order to make health and safety guidelines meaningful in the context of particular work areas and improved patient care.

B. It is the responsibility of each department head to ensure that his/her employees receive adequate information, orientation, and if appropriate, individual counseling regarding AIDS and other communicable diseases.

C. This material will be disseminated to house staff, medical students, and attending physicians by those with appropriate responsibility.

Yale-New Haven Hospital
New Haven, Connecticut

Reporting and Accident Investigation of an Employee Incident

I. Purpose of Policy

The purpose of this policy is to outline procedures to be followed in reporting and investigating all accidents, injuries, and incidents where the potential for employee injury exists.

This policy only applies to employee accidents arising out of and during the course of employment by Yale-New Haven Hospital.

This policy does not apply to accidents involving only patients or visitors. For additional information concerning the reporting and investigation of an employee incident, contact the hospital safety coordinator.

II. Definition of "Reportable" Accident

For the purpose of this policy, an accident is "reportable" if an accident or other such occurrence has resulted in the injury, or the possibility of an injury, to an employee.

III. Procedure

If the employee is involved in an accident, with or without resulting injury, the following shall be done:

1. The employee shall report the accident and/or injury to his/her immediate supervisor regardless of how minor the resulting injury may be.
2. If the accident has resulted in an injury, the employee shall receive medical treatment for the injury at the Personnel Health Service Clinic during the regular business day or at the Emergency Service Department at any other time.
3. The employee's immediate supervisor will complete the Supervisor's Report of Employee Incident. The supervisor and the employee will sign the completed form.
4. If the accident has resulted in an injury, the Supervisor's Report of Employee Incident form must accompany, or follow shortly thereafter, the employee to Personnel Health Service Clinic or Emergency Department.
5. If the accident did not result in an injury, the Supervisor's Report of Employee Incident form must be forwarded to the hospital safety coordinator within one business day of the accident.
6. General guidelines for completion of the Supervisor's Report of Employee Incident include:
   - The report form is the only means of reporting on-the-job accidents and resulting injury.
   - Timeliness is essential to ensure prompt payment to employees losing time, prompt follow-up investigation of serious accidents, and the protection of the hospital against possible fraudulent cases.
   - The report should be completed when an injury occurs, no matter how slight, even if the injury does not require medical treatment. In addition, the form should be completed for accidents where the potential for injury existed, although no injury was actually incurred.
   - It is the supervisor's responsibility to complete this report. The injured employee or involved employee should not complete this report.
   - The report should be written legibly and contain factual details as opposed to editorial comment.

- The supervisor completing this report must conduct a preliminary investigation of the accident, noting what factors contributed to the accident and what actions have been taken or should be taken to prevent a recurrence of the accident.

IV. Investigation of Reportable Accidents

It shall be the responsibility of the immediate supervisor or the department head to conduct a preliminary investigation into the immediate and proximal causes of the accident.

It shall be the responsibility of the hospital safety coordinator to review the results of the preliminary investigation and, if deemed necessary, to extend the depth and scope of the investigation.

The immediate supervisor or the department head shall document any corrective or preventive action taken as indicated by the outcome of the preliminary investigation.

The immediate supervisor or the department head shall fully cooperate with the Safety Coordinator during any extension of the investigation deemed necessary.

Lutheran General Hospital-Lincoln Park
Chicago, Illinois

Hepatitis B Immunization: Preexposure

I. **Policy**
This policy is to establish the guidelines for providing hepatitis B immunization to Lutheran General Hospital-Lincoln Park employees who are known to be at occupational risk of exposure to hepatitis B infection.

II. **Definitions**
   A. This hepatitis B vaccination is a series of three I.M. injections of 1 cc Recombivax® or Heptavax B®. The first injection is given and then followed by reinforcing doses at one month and at six months.
   B. It will be the employee's responsibility to complete the scheduled three-dose series. Employees who do not return for their subsequent doses within the required time, but still wish to continue with the vaccine, will be required to purchase any doses in excess of the initial three necessary to complete the series.
   C. Employees who terminate their employment from LGH-Lincoln Park prior to the completion of the series may purchase the remaining doses from the Employee Health Service at cost plus handling.
   D. Employees not eligible for free vaccination may purchase it at cost plus handling through Employee Health.
   E. Risk category: Employees who have frequent, direct contact with blood or blood products during the course of their employment are thought to be at high or moderate risk. Based on the recommendations of the American Hospital Association Advisory Committee on Infections within Hospitals (ACIP), the CDC, and OSHA, employees of Lutheran General Hospital-Lincoln Park working in the following areas are assumed to be at risk:
      1. Anesthesiology—anesthesiologists and nurse anesthetists
      2. Cardiology—stress test personnel
      3. I.V. therapists
      4. Laboratory
      5. Operating room personnel who handle blood or tissue
      6. Pathologists
      7. Phlebotomists
      8. Radiologists and nonsurgical personnel who perform invasive procedures including angiograms and other special procedures requiring vascular access
      9. Housekeeping
      10. Central Service personnel
      11. Nurses, L.P.N.s, and nursing assistants from the following areas:
         a. Emergency Room
         b. ICU/CCU
         c. Obstetrics
         d. Recovery Room
         e. Surgery
         f. 3 East
         g. 3 West
         h. 5 East
         i. 6 East
         j. 8 East

      Consideration will also be given to shift assignment in each of the designated areas because the risk will vary.

F. Full-time employees are those employees working 60 hours or more in each pay period.
G. Part-time employees are those employees working 40 to 59.9 hours in each pay period.

III. Procedure

A. Employee Health will provide hepatitis B vaccine free to eligible full-time and part-time employees of LGH-Lincoln Park. Physicians and other employees may purchase the vaccine through Employee Health. This does not include contract or attending M.D.s. They will be charged the cost of the vaccine plus a handling fee. An employee's frequency of contact with blood and blood products is the primary factor in determining degree of risk.
B. Employees designated to be at risk of exposure who do not wish to receive the vaccine will sign a form acknowledging the vaccine's availability to them and their refusal to accept it.
C. Employee Health will advise new employees hired for high-risk areas of availability of the vaccine at the time of the employment physical. Eligible new employees will be eligible for vaccination upon successful completion of their three-month probationary period.
D. Employee transfers:
   1. Into risk area—will be offered the vaccine at no cost. It will be the supervisor's responsibility to ensure that the employee be immunized or sign a waiver.
   2. Out of risk area—those who have begun the immunization program may complete immunization at no cost.
E. Should an eligible employee in a risk area desire immunization at any time after the program has begun, he/she will be eligible for the vaccine at no cost.
F. The hepatitis B vaccine will be administered to employees by the employee health nurse. The nurse will discuss and perform the following steps with the employee:
   1. Obtain the following information to determine whether there are any contraindications to administering hepatitis B immunization:
      a. History of hepatitis B and/or documentation of positive hepatitis B antibodies. Employees who state a history of hepatitis B will be serologically tested to determine whether immunization is necessary.
      b. Current upper respiratory infection or other active infection.
      c. Allergies to thimerosal and/or formalin.
   2. Obtain a history of immunodeficiency or of immunosuppressive therapy. Recombivax® should not be used for immunocompromised patients. Heptavax® is available for such individuals.
   3. Ensure that the employee has received the information packet and responds to questions. Information packet and in-service program are developed and presented by infection control practitioner with the assistance of Employee Health. [The Hepatitis B Immunization Consent Form is reproduced in figure 7-22.]
   4. Obtain employee consent for administration. Recombinant vaccine, Recombivax®, will be given unless contraindicated. All three doses must be of the same vaccine. They cannot be interchanged.
   5. Shake the vial well before withdrawal and use. Administer Recombivax® or Heptavax B® 1 cc I.M. Immunocompromised persons receive 2 cc I.M. of Heptavax B®. Recombivax® is contraindicated for immunocompromised people. The vaccine is to be given in the deltoid muscle in adults.
   6. Observe employee for any systemic allergic reaction. In case of reaction, notify the Emergency Room physician immediately.

Figure 7-22. Hepatitis B Immunization Consent Form

A. Consent for Hepatitis B Immunization

I, ______________________, consent to be immunized against hepatitis B.

I acknowledge that:

1. I have been informed that I am at risk of acquiring hepatitis B because of the nature of my professional responsibilities.
2. I have attended the Hepatitis B® Inservice Program and have received and read the hepatitis B information pamphlet, which lists the indications, benefits, presently known side effects, and adverse reactions of Heptavax B®/Recombivax® vaccine. I have had an opportunity to ask questions and have had them answered to my satisfaction.
3. I must receive three (3) doses of vaccine over a six- (6-) month period of time to confer optimal immunity.
4. However, as with all medical treatment, there is no guarantee that I will become immune or that I will not experience an adverse side effect from the vaccine.
5. I understand I will be vaccinated using the synthetic vaccine, Recombivax®, unless medically contraindicated.

______________________ Witness

______________________ Employee's Signature

______________________ Section

______________________ Date

B. Employee's Responsibility

In the event that I should terminate employment at Lutheran General Hospital-Lincoln Park prior to receiving all three (3) doses of hepatitis B vaccine, I understand it will be my responsibility to complete the vaccination series on my own initiative and at my own expense.

______________________ Witness

______________________ Employee's Signature

__________ Date __________ Time

C. Refusal to Receive Immunization against Hepatitis B

I, ______________________, having been informed of the risks of acquiring hepatitis B because of the nature of my professional responsibilities and having been informed of the benefits of vaccination, at this time choose *not* to receive the hepatitis B immunization series.

______________________ Witness

______________________ Employee's Signature

__________ Date __________ Time

D. Administration Record

1. Allergies ______________________.
2. Are you allergic to mercury or formaldehyde?
   Yes ______ Specify ______________________ No ______
3. Do you presently have an upper respiratory infection or any other acute or chronic medical condition?
   Yes ______ No ______
4. Do you have a history of hepatitis B or documentation of hepatitis B antibodies?
   Yes ______ No ______
5. Do you have a history of being immunocompromised or receiving immunosuppressive therapy?
   Yes ______ No ______
6. Heptavax B®/Recombivax® Vaccine, 1.0 ml I.M., was administered to ______________________ Employee

	Date	Temp.	Site	Lot Number	Vaccinator
First Dose					
Second Dose					
Third Dose					

E. Nurses' Notes: ______________________

7. Instruct employee to apply cold compresses to any local reaction of erythema or induration and to notify Employee Health of additional symptoms so that they may be documented.
8. Inform employee of the importance of returning to Employee Health for remaining doses when scheduled.
9. Instruct employee to return to Employee Health for follow-up in event of needle puncture.
10. Document process in the employee's health record.
11. Upon return of the employee for the second dose, the nurse will:
    a. Question the employee regarding adverse effects from first dose.
    b. Verify that no fewer than three weeks and no more than five weeks have passed since initial dose.
    c. Administer second dose of Recombivax® 1 cc I.M. Immunocompromised patients receive 2 cc I.M. of Heptavax B® (Recombivax® contraindicated).
    d. Document process in the employee's health record.
    e. Observe the employee for reaction. See numbers 6 and 7.
12. Upon return of the employee for the third dose, the nurse will:
    a. Question the employee regarding adverse reactions from first two doses.
    b. Verify that no fewer than five months and no more than seven months have passed since the initial dose.
    c. Administer third dose of Recombivax® 1 cc I.M. Immunocompromised persons receive 2 cc I.M. of Heptavax B® (Recombivax® contraindicated).
    d. Document the process in the employee's health record.
    e. Observe the employee for reaction. See numbers 6 and 7.

G. If the three scheduled visits are not kept at the proper designated intervals, it may be necessary for the immunization process to be repeated from the beginning. The employee will be charged for doses in excess of the initial three required to complete the process.

H. Responsibility: The employee health nurse, employee, employee's unit supervisor, Emergency Room physician, and the Infection Control practitioner are responsible for ensuring that this policy is followed.

Lutheran General Hospital-Lincoln Park
Chicago, Illinois

Hepatitis Prophylaxis: Postexposure

I. Policy
This policy establishes the guidelines for employee prophylaxis against hepatitis B due to job-related incidents.

II. Definitions

A. The principal modes of transmission of hepatitis B are:
   1. Direct percutaneous inoculation of contaminated serum or plasma such as accidental needlestick
   2. Nonneedle percutaneous transfer of infected serum or plasma such as contamination of minute cutaneous scratches, abrasions, burns, or other lesions
   3. Contamination of mucosal surfaces by infected serum or plasma such as by mouth pipetting or accidental splashes in eye.

B. Some employees have received hepatitis B immunization. It is essential to identify the immune status of employees prior to prophylaxis. Employees will fall into one of the following categories:
   1. Susceptible. Not vaccinated. Not immune.
   2. Partially or fully vaccinated. Antibody level unknown.
   3. Immune. Antibody level known.

III. Procedure

A. Any employee who sustains an accidental needlestick, mucosal or cutaneous exposure, or oral ingestion involving serum or plasma shall receive an evaluation for prophylactic treatment for viral hepatitis.

B. The immunization status of the employee will be the basis on which the need for hepatitis B prophylaxis and blood screening is determined.
   1. A Report of Incident form shall be completed by the person involved and his or her immediate supervisor and must include:
      a. Source of needlestick, if known, patient's name, room number, physician, and diagnosis
      b. Circumstances of injury, such as during recapping of needle
   2. The employee must report to the Emergency Room for evaluation and prophylaxis.
      a. Employees who have completed the hepatitis B vaccine series and have adequate antibody levels on file within the past 12 months require no further follow-up.
      b. Employees who have completed the vaccination series against hepatitis B or who have received fewer than three injections and antibody levels are unknown will have an antibody test drawn to ensure immunity. If antibody levels are adequate, >10 RIA, no further follow-up is necessary.
      c. This result is received back from the laboratory in 48 hours. When the incident is reported, the patient's blood should be drawn and held in the laboratory. The specimen should be marked "DO NOT PROCESS–SAVE SERUM". Processing is only necessary when the employee is found not to be immune.
      d. Vaccinated employees found not to have adequate antibody levels for protection will be treated the same as unvaccinated employees. Vaccination if not complete should proceed on schedule. At this time, the patient's blood will be submitted for testing.

e. Serological testing shall be performed on the susceptible employee and the patient if the source is known.
   (1) Employee: HBsAg–Hepatitis B surface antigen
   Anti-HBs–Antibody to hepatitis B surface
   (2) Patient: HBsAg–Hepatitis B surface antigen
f. In all cases, the patient's physician must be notified by the floor nurse that serologic testing is being performed.
g. All laboratory requisitions must be labeled "Infection Control." This labeling is for accounting purposes and will ensure a "no charge" for the patient.
h. The Emergency Room physician will evaluate the serologic testing results and determine the need for further prophylactic immunization according to the following schedule:

Patient	Employee		
HBsAg	HBsAg	Anti-HBs	Prophylaxis Indications
Neg	Neg	Neg	Patient is not infective. No further follow up is necessary.
Pos	Pos	Neg	Patient infective. Employee already infective at time of needlestick. Refer employee to private physician for evaluation.
Pos	Neg	Pos	Patient infective. Employee already immune. No further action necessary.
Pos	Neg	Neg	Patient infective. Employee lacks immunity and is at risk. Administer HBIG × 1 plus hepatitis vaccine* 1 cc. Continue vaccine on schedule of one month and six months later.

*ACIP recommends the administration of HBIG plus hepatitis B vaccine for postexposure prophylaxis for hepatitis B. If employee refuses vaccine, a second dose of HBIG, 0.06 ml/kg I.M. is to be administered 30 days after the first injection.

C. Documentation and reporting:
   1. Copies of all serologic test results on employee and patient are to be kept in the employee's health file.
   2. The Hepatitis B Prophylaxis Flow Sheet [see figure 7-23] must be filled out by Emergency Room nurse and kept in employee's file when prophylaxis is completed.
   3. A copy of the incident report and ER record are to be sent to Employee Relations and the Infection Control practitioner.

Figure 7-23. Hepatitis B Postexposure Prophylaxis Flow Sheet

Occupational Exposure to Blood and Body Fluids

1. Report of Occurrence form completed by employee. ☐
2. Complete ER record: To include name of source patient, room number, physician, and diagnosis of source patient. If source unknown, document "source unknown." ☐

   Remember, all information supplied should be as specific as possible. This will help in evaluating the situation for follow-up.
3. Nature of injury:
   a. Mucous membrane exposure (splash). ☐
   b. Significant blood/bloody body fluid exposure to nonintact skin. ☐
   c. Percutaneous exposure (puncture wound). ☐
   d. Other. Please specify: ______________________________
4. All employees involved in exposures, as described above, will be baseline tested for HIV antibodies. If the employee refuses screening, a waiver must be signed.
   a. Employee has been counseled about HIV testing, and has signed the informed consent form. ☐
   b. Employee has refused HIV antibody testing and has signed the waiver. ☐
   c. Employee has refused to sign either form. Notify Employee Health or Infection Control immediately. ☐

☐ (a)	☐ (b)	☐ (c)
Employee consent signed	Employee signed waiver	Employee refused signature
↓	↓	↓
Draw HIV on employee		Contact Employee Health/Infection Control
↓		↓
Have HIV drawn on patient	Have HIV drawn on patient	Have HIV drawn on patient

5. All employees involved in exposures will be evaluated for hepatitis B susceptibility.
   a. Employee has completed hepatitis B vaccination or gives history of hepatitis B immunity, and hepatitis B antibodies, HbsAb, are *documented positive within the past 12 months.* Employee immune. No follow-up necessary.
   b. Employee has completed vaccine, gives history of immunity, and hepatitis B antibodies, HbsAb, are *not* documented within the past 12 months. Immune status unknown. Test employee for hepatitis B antibodies, HbsAb, *only.*
   c. Employee is partially vaccinated, never vaccinated, or known nonresponder to vaccine. Test employee for hepatitis B surface antigen (HbsAg) *only.*

☐ (a)	☐ (b)	☐ (c)
Employee HbsAb positive (documented within past 12 months)	Immune status unknown (employee)	Employee susceptible
↓	↓	↓
Employee immune	Draw HbsAb on employee	Draw HbsAg on employee
↓	↓	↓
No follow-up on patient necessary	Draw HbsAg on patient	Draw HbsAg on patient

6. Notify nursing unit:
   a. Of need for HIV testing on patient. ☐
   b. Of necessary hepatitis B tests on patient, as determined by #5 above. ☐
   c. To inform attending physician of tests requested. ☐
   d. To label requisitions "Infection Control" so the patient is not charged. ☐

Remember: All requisition forms must be marked Infection Control. If they are not, the employee will be billed for the tests performed!

7. Document results of patient's HbsAg in employee file. ☐
8. Document results of employee's HbsAg or HbsAb in employee file. ☐

(Figure continues.)

Figure 7-23. (Continued)

9. Evaluate patient and employee results and assess for necessary follow-up:

Patient	Employee			
HBsAg	HBsAg	Anti-HBs	Prophylaxis Indications	
Neg	Neg	Neg	Patient is not infective. No further treatment.	☐
Pos	Pos	Neg	Patient infective. Employee already infective at time of needlestick. Refer employee to private physician for evaluation.	☐
Pos	Neg	Pos	Patient infective. Employee already immune. No treatment.	☐
Pos	Neg	Neg	Patient infective. Employee lacks immunity and is *at risk.* Administer HBIG immediately and administer 1 cc Heptavax B® vaccine. See below.	☐

10. Call Pharmacy for HBIG (0.06 ml/kg I.M. of 5 ml for adults) and hepatitis B vaccine—either Heptavax® or Recombivax®. ☐
11. Administer HBIG and hepatitis B vaccine to employee. ACIP recommends the administration of HBIG *plus* vaccine for postexposure prophylaxis. If employee refuses vaccine, a second dose of HBIG (equal to the first) should be given 30 days after the first injection. ☐
12. Schedule employee for hepatitis B vaccine series one and six months from the initial injection date. If employee is already being immunized, follow original schedule. ☐
13. Send copy of incident report and ER record to Infection Control. ☐
14. File this flow sheet in the employee's file. ☐

Chapter 8

Occupational Safety and Health Administration

Introduction

The Occupational Safety and Health Administration (OSHA) has begun inspecting health care facilities to ensure that employers are providing appropriate safeguards for their employees against occupational exposure to bloodborne hazards. Because OSHA does not currently have a specific standard on bloodborne pathogens, it is relying on the CDC's guidelines for Universal Precautions as the accepted standard of practice to be followed by employers. To ensure that Universal Precautions programs are consistent with OSHA's requirements, health care facilities need to incorporate into their infection control programs both the current requirements related to enforcement of the CDC's guidelines and the components of OSHA's proposed standard on Occupational Exposure to Bloodborne Pathogens.

This chapter discusses the history of OSHA's recent activities in protecting employees against occupational exposures to bloodborne hazards and components of both current and proposed requirements. Sample materials for developing procedures on protective barriers for specific tasks are also included.

As a part of the Department of Labor, OSHA has the authority to conduct workplace inspections to determine whether employers are complying with standards issued by OSHA for safe and healthful workplaces. On May 30, 1989, OSHA published the proposed standard entitled Occupational Exposure to Bloodborne Pathogens in the *Federal Register* for public comment. This proposed rule represents the first time OSHA has been involved in regulating a biological hazard.

Although the release of a final standard is not expected until some time in 1991, OSHA's current authority to conduct inspections comes from the General Duty Clause of the Occupational Safety and Health Act (OSH Act) of 1970, which requires an employer to provide a safe work environment that is free from occupational hazards that are likely to cause death or serious harm. Until a final standard is published, OSHA is relying on the CDC's guidelines for Universal Precautions as the accepted standard of practice to be followed by employers in carrying out their responsibilities under the OSH Act.

The agency's involvement in regulating how health care institutions protect their employees from bloodborne pathogen hazards began in 1983, after it issued a set of voluntary guidelines designed to reduce the risk of occupational exposure to hepatitis B. In 1986, OSHA was petitioned by several unions representing health care employees to develop a *standard* for protecting workers from occupational exposures to bloodborne pathogens. The unions requested that this standard contain all of the provisions in the 1983 hepatitis B guidelines and special emphasis on providing hepatitis B vaccination free of charge to all high-risk employees. In response, the Department of Labor and the

Department of Health and Human Services published a Joint Advisory Notice entitled Protection against Occupational Exposures to Hepatitis B Virus and Human Immunodeficiency Virus Infection. This notice was published in the *Federal Register* on October 30, 1987, and advised employers of their legal responsibility to protect workers against bloodborne pathogen hazards and urged adherence to the CDC's guidelines for Universal Precautions. In addition, the notice announced OSHA's plans to begin a targeted inspection program to ensure that appropriate measures were being followed. The Joint Advisory Notice also recommended a classification of all job-related tasks, workers performing each task, and written procedures outlining the required protective barriers and workplace practices for each task.

On November 27, 1987, OSHA published an Advance Notice of Proposed Rulemaking to announce the initiation of the rule-making process. The comments received in response to this advance notice were used to develop OSHA's proposed standard entitled Occupational Exposure to Bloodborne Pathogens. Employers are not currently required to comply with the proposed standard. However, until a final standard is published, OSHA expects employers to comply with the CDC's guidelines on Universal Precautions.

To provide information for compliance safety and health officers handling the current inspection process, OSHA issued a compliance manual entitled *Enforcement Procedures for Occupational Exposures to Hepatitis B and Human Immunodeficiency Virus.* This directive provides information on the scope and method for conducting current inspections, guidelines for determining whether a hazard exists, and methods for assessing compliance and issuing citations and fines. The requirements outlined in this compliance manual are based on the CDC's guidelines as well as other existing OSHA general industry standards, including those on the use of personal protective equipment, housekeeping, waste disposal, and accident prevention signs and tags. (The compliance manual is reproduced in this chapter.) In the most recently revised directive (February 27, 1990), OSHA specified the employer's responsibility to offer hepatitis B vaccine free to employees at substantial risk of coming into contact with blood and body fluids.

The original task classification strategy outlined in the October 30, 1987, Joint Advisory Notice prompted many facilities to begin revisions in their infection control policies and procedures. However, OSHA's current requirements, as outlined in the compliance manual, do not dictate the use of a task classification strategy as outlined in the Joint Advisory Notice. As a result of numerous comments, OSHA is proposing a modification of the original task classification in the proposed standard that is now referred to as an "exposure determination." OSHA is proposing that this exposure determination include the identification of all tasks in which occupational exposure may take place and the employees performing these tasks. OSHA has explained that although a requirement for task-specific procedures outlining work practices and protective equipment is not going to be mandatory, it may be helpful as a training device for employees or for use as a reference guide for unusual or infrequently performed tasks. The proposed standard, as it is currently written, would require that employers complete an "exposure determination" within 90 days of the effective date of the final standard. OSHA has received a significant number of comments on this "exposure determination" requirement, but it is not known at this time what the final standard will require.

The proposed standard also contains requirements for an infection control plan that contains the exposure determination, the schedule and method of reducing risks of exposure, and the timetable for implementation of the plan. In addition, there are proposed requirements for housekeeping, handling and disposal of infectious waste and sharps, hepatitis B vaccination, postexposure evaluation, warning signs and labels to identify hazards, employee training, and record keeping. (Relevant portions of the proposed standard are reproduced in this chapter.)

Until a final standard is published, at a minimum employers must implement the CDC's recommendations for Universal Precautions. It will also be useful for employers to review OSHA's proposed standard on bloodborne pathogens to determine which elements may require a significant change in their current practices. It is anticipated that many of the elements in OSHA's proposed standard will not change significantly in the final standard, particularly those requirements that are based on the CDC's guidelines. (Elements of OSHA's proposed standard have been incorporated into many of the sample materials contained in this manual. Refer to the index to locate specific topics.)

Employers should be familiar with the OSHA inspection process and their rights and responsibilities. In general, workplace inspections are conducted by federal OSHA representatives except in states that have their own federally approved occupational safety and health programs, where inspections are conducted by the state OSHA program representatives. (The *OSHA Inspections Handbook* is reproduced in this chapter.) State OSHA plans may adopt more stringent requirements than federal OSHA; however, they must submit their plans to federal OSHA for approval. Employers should find out whether their states operate OSHA-approved state programs and, if so, become familiar with specific state requirements. OSHA's Office of Information (at 202/523-8148) may be contacted for the locations of federal OSHA regional offices and state plans.

Health care facilities should also become familiar with other applicable OSHA standards, because OSHA representatives have the authority to review compliance with any OSHA standard once they are on site in any facility. In fact, OSHA has announced its intention to assess compliance with the OSHA Hazard Communication Standard as part of its current inspections for occupational exposure to bloodborne pathogens. Because many of the OSHA standards cover groups of employees exposed to a variety of hazards, including biological, chemical, and physical hazards, required training, record keeping, medical evaluations, and compliance monitoring for the various hazards could be combined.

This chapter includes reproductions of documents from OSHA containing the current and proposed requirements for preventing and managing occupational exposures to bloodborne pathogens and for conducting inspection procedures. The sample policies included are based primarily on OSHA's original task classification strategy as published in the Joint Advisory Notice (October 1987). Although this task classification requirement will probably not appear in the final standard, the content of these policies may still be useful in developing department-specific guidelines and training programs for appropriate use of personal protective barriers.

Occupational Safety and Health Administration
Washington, D.C.

Enforcement Procedures for Occupational Exposure to Hepatitis B Virus (HBV) and Human Immunodeficiency Virus (HIV)

OSHA Instruction CPL 2-2.44B
February 27, 1990
Office of Health Compliance Assistance

A. *Purpose.* This instruction provides uniform inspection procedures and guidelines to be followed when conducting inspections and issuing citations under section 5 (a) (1) of the Act and pertinent standards for health care workers potentially exposed to HBV and HIV.

B. *Scope.* This instruction applies OSHA-wide.

C. *Cancellation.* This instruction cancels OSHA Instruction CPL 2-2.44A, August 15, 1988.

D. *References.*
   1. OSHA Instruction CPL 2.45B, June 15, 1989, the Field Operations Manual (FOM).
   2. OSHA Instruction ADM 1-1.12B, December 29, 1989, the Integrated Management Information System (IMIS) Forms Manual.
   3. OSHA Instruction CPL 2-2.36, November 30, 1983, Hepatitis B Risks in the Health Care System.
   4. Centers for Disease Control. Acquired Immunodeficiency Syndrome, AIDS—Recommendations and Guidelines November 1982-November 1986.
   5. Centers for Disease Control Morbidity and Mortality Weekly Report. Update on Hepatitis B Prevention. June 19, 1987; Vol. 36, No. 23.
   6. Centers for Disease Control Morbidity and Mortality Weekly Report. 1988 Agent Summary Statement for Human Immunodeficiency Virus and Report on Laboratory-Acquired Infection with Human Immunodeficiency Virus. April 1, 1988; Vol. 37, No. S-4.

E. *Action.* Regional Administrators and Area Directors shall ensure that the policies and procedures explained in this instruction are implemented in scheduling and conducting inspections. Regional Administrators shall further ensure that all relevant procedures established in this instruction are adhered to by State 7(c) (1) consultation projects.

F. *Federal Program Change.* This instruction describes a Federal Program change which affects State programs. Each Regional Administrator shall:
   1. Ensure that this change is promptly forwarded to each State designee.
   2. Explain the technical content of this change to the State designee as requested.
   3. Ensure that State designees are asked to acknowledge receipt of this Federal program change in writing, within 30 days of notification, to the Regional Administrator. Procedures and time frames for State notification, acknowledgment and plan supplement submission are set out in OSHA Instruction STP 2.22A, CH-2, Chapter II, Paragraph I.1.a.
      a. Paragraph I.1.a.(1) contains procedures Regional Administrations shall follow in notifying States of federal program changes via two-way memoranda.
      b. Paragraph I.1.a.(2) contains procedures for State response. (States should acknowledge receipt as soon as the State's intentions are known, but must do so no later than 70 calendar days after the date of issuance. The State's acknowledgment must indicate its intention to follow OSHA's policies and procedures, or describe its intended alternative policy and/or procedures, which must be "at least as effective" as OSHA's.
      c. State plan supplements must be submitted according to the schedule established in OSHA Instruction STP 2.22A, CH-2, Paragraph I.1.a.(3).

   d. Although States are not required to enforce General Duty Provisions, they are strongly urged to do so.
4. Advise State designees of the following:
   a. In order to ensure a sound and consistent national enforcement and litigation strategy in relation to the complex issues addressed by this instruction, State implementation of the procedures in this instruction, or comparable State procedures, must be carefully coordinated with OSHA.
   b. The State is also responsible for extending coverage under its procedures for addressing occupational exposure to HBV and HIV in the public sector, such as police, fire, ambulance and other emergency response workers.
   c. The Directorate of Technical Support is available to assist the States in locating expert witnesses. (See paragraph 0., Expert Witnesses.)
   d. In regard to paragraph I., Inspection Scheduling, Goal and Scope, the State's response to the Regional Administrator is to include a projection of the number of inspections the State expects to conduct in both the private and public sector.
5. After Regional review of the State plan supplement and resolution of any comments thereon, forward the State submission to the National Office in accordance with established procedures. The Regional Administrator shall provide a judgment on the relative effectiveness of each substantial difference in the State plan change and an overall assessment thereon with a recommendation for approval or disapproval by the Assistant Secretary.
6. Review policies, instructions and guidelines issued by the State to determine that this change has been communicated to State program personnel.

G. *Definitions.*
1. Health Care Facility. Those establishments listed under the Standard Industrial Classification (SIC) codes 80** and 7261; and clinics, health units, and nurses' stations at industrial work sites.
2. Health Care Worker. An employee of a health care facility including, but not limited to, nurses, physicians, dentists and other dental workers, optometrists, podiatrists, chiropractors, laboratory and blood bank technologists and technicians, research laboratory scientists, phlebotomists, dialysis personnel, paramedics, emergency medical technicians, medical examiners, morticians, housekeepers, laundry workers and others whose work may involve direct contact with body fluids, as defined below, from living individuals or corpses.
3. Universal Precautions. The term "universal precautions" refers to a system of infectious disease control which assumes that every direct contact with body fluids is infectious and requires every employee exposed to direct contact with body fluids to be protected as though such body fluids were HBV or HIV infected. Therefore, universal precautions are intended to prevent health care workers from parenteral, mucous membrane, and nonintact skin exposures to blood-borne pathogens.
4. Body Fluids. Fluids that have been recognized by CDC as directly linked to the transmission of HIV and/or HBV and/or to which universal precautions apply: blood, semen, blood products, vaginal secretions, cerebrospinal fluid, synovial fluid, pleural fluid, peritoneal fluid, pericardial fluid, amniotic fluid, and concentrated HIV or HBV viruses.
5. Phlebotomist. A phlebotomist is any health care worker who draws blood samples.
6. Infection Control (IC) Program. An IC program is the establishment's oral or written policy and implementation of procedures relating to the control of infectious disease hazards where employees may be exposed to direct contact with body fluids. An IC Program must address all of the areas outlined in this directive.
7. Joint Advisory Notice. Department of Labor/Department of Health and Human Services-Joint Advisory Notice (Federal Register, Vol. 52, No. 210; October 30, 1987)

is a list of recommendations developed to assist employers in implementing the Centers for Disease Control (CDC) guidelines.

H. *Background.* In September 1986, OSHA was petitioned by various unions representing health care employees to develop a standard to protect workers from occupational exposure to blood-borne diseases. Although the Agency has decided to pursue development of such a standard, as a result of recent rulemaking petitions and OSHA's evaluation of those petitions, the Agency has concluded that the risk of contracting hepatitis B and AIDS among members of various occupations within the health care system requires an immediate response through a variety of existing mechanisms.
   1. Occupational exposure may occur in many ways, including needlestick and cut injuries. Health care workers employed in certain occupations are assumed to be at high risk for blood-borne infections due to their routinely increased exposure to body fluids from potentially infected patients. These high risk occupations include but are not limited to physicians, pathologists, dentists and dental technicians, x-ray technicians, phlebotomists, emergency room, intensive care and operating room nurses and technicians, laboratory and blood bank technologists and technicians. Other health care workers who may be directly exposed to such body fluids depending on their exact work assignments include such occupations as housekeeping personnel, laundry workers, paramedics, medical examiners. Employees in any occupation where they are directly exposed to body fluids are considered to be at substantial risk of occupational exposure to HIV and/or HBV.
   2. Ward clerks and administrators have virtually no increased risk of contact with body fluids as a result of their employment; they are thus at no greater risk of contracting blood-borne diseases than other members of the general population.
   3. Neither HBV nor HIV is transmitted by casual contact in the workplace.
   4. The employer's obligations are those set forth in the Occupational Safety and Health Act (OSH Act) of 1970. However, the CDC has published guidelines to protect workers from HBV and HIV (See Appendices A & B). OSHA is relying on these guidelines as reflecting an appropriate and widely recognized and accepted standard of protection to be followed by health care employers in carrying out their responsibilities under the OSH Act.
   5. The same personal protective equipment and work practices used to prevent occupational transmission of HBV are effective in preventing occupational transmission of HIV. The CDC has called for use of "universal precautions" when working with blood and/or body fluids from any patients.
   6. One difference between the two viruses is that there is currently a vaccine to prevent HBV infection, which the CDC has recommended for persons at substantial risk of occupational exposure, but there is no vaccine for HIV.

I. *Inspection Scheduling, Goal, and Scope.*
   1. Inspection scheduling shall be conducted in accordance with the procedures outlined in the FOM, Chapter II, and for Federal agencies, Chapter XIII, except as modified in the following sections.
   2. The National Office shall develop and distribute a list of health care establishments by State to the appropriate Regional Administrators to identify the establishments to be programmed for inspection within the Region.
      a. This list shall be randomly selected from among all establishments identified as being within the health care industries, viz., those industries having primary Standard Industrial Classification (SIC) codes 80** (Health Sevices) and 7261 (Funeral Service and Crematories).
      b. A widely available commercial listing shall be the source of such establishments (Duns Marketing Service).
      c. All establishments listed as having less than 11 employees shall be excluded from the list.

   d. More establishments will be provided to the Regions than will actually be needed to allow for replacement of establishments.
3. The Regional Administrator shall use an additional random selection method to identify the establishments actually to be programmed for inspection within the Region.
   a. The number of health care establishments to be selected from the list provided by the National Office shall be at least equal to the inspection goal identified in the annual program plan developed for the Region.
   b. The names of the establishments selected by the Regional Administrator shall be distributed to the appropriate Area Office and shall constitute the Inspection Register for that office.
   c. An inspection of all establishments listed on the Inspection Register shall be conducted unless they are deleted for some legitimate reason.
4. Any establishment deleted shall be replaced by another establishment selected according to I.3.
   a. Area Directors shall inform the Regional Administrator of any deletions.
   b. The Regional Administrator shall select the next establishment by random number procedure from the list provided by the National Office.
   c. Because of the random number selection procedures, it may happen that the next establishment does not belong to the same Area Office jurisdiction and may have to be assigned to an Area Office other than the one deleting the first establishment.
5. When an inspection of an establishment listed on the Health Care Inspection Register is not conducted because the employer has refused entry, a warrant shall be sought in accordance with the current procedure for handling such refusals. Only if the court refuses to grant a warrant or if the Regional Solicitor declines to apply for a warrant, is such an establishment to be replaced according to I.3.
6. Each Region shall conduct the minimum number of health care facility inspections (e.g., hospital, clinical laboratories, blood donor center, etc.) annually identified in its program plan.
7. All inspections, programmed or unprogrammed, conducted at health care facilities or at other facilities (such as manufacturing plants) which support an onsite health care unit shall be directed to all areas involving the hazard of direct exposure to body fluids potentially contaminated with HBV or HIV.
   a. Primary areas of concern are emergency rooms, operating rooms, direct patient care areas, laboratories, and x-ray. Secondary areas of concern are laundry and housekeeping.
   b. Records review procedures for the purpose of conducting a records only inspection do not apply.
   c. Expansion to additional units may be appropriate when:
      (1) The IC program shows significant deficiencies in complying with OSHA requirements, as set forth in this instruction, that may indicate the existence of more widespread problems.
      (2) Relevant complaints are received from employees which are specifically related to direct exposures to body fluids.

J. *Inspection Procedures.* The procedures given in the FOM, Chapter III, shall be followed except as modified in the following sections.
1. When entering a hospital or health care facility, the CSHO shall locate the Hospital Administrator, the Medical Director or other person in charge and present credentials.
2. Health care facilities generally administer internal IC programs. This function may be performed by a committee or an individual. Upon entry the CSHO shall request the presence of the infection control nurses and/or other individuals who will be responsible for providing records pertinent to the inspection.

3. Careful examination of the facility's IC program is the core element of these inspections. Occupational injury and illness records shall be carefully scrutinized, and employees selected from all appropriate areas of the facility shall be interviewed to verify both the accuracy of the OSHA-200 records and the effectiveness of the IC program.
4. Needlesticks, like any other puncture wound, are considered injuries for recordkeeping purposes due to the instantaneous nature of the event. Only those work-related injuries that involve loss of consciousness, transfer to another job, restriction of work or motion, or medical treatment are required to be put on the OSHA 200 form. Use of prescription medication (beyond a single dose for minor injury or discomfort) is considered medical treatment. Therefore, any needlestick requiring medical treatment (e.g., gamma globulin, hepatitis B immune globulin, hepatitis B vaccine, etc.) shall be recorded. In addition, since this type of treatment is considered absolutely necessary, and must be administered by a physician or licensed medical personnel, such an injury cannot be considered minor.
5. In the event the facility being inspected does not have a formal IC program, employee interviews, combined with an inspection of appropriate areas of the facility shall be used to determine the effectiveness of the establishment's efforts to protect employees from exposure to potential infectious disease sources.
6. CSHOs shall use appropriate caution when entering patient care areas of the facility. When such visits are judged necessary for determining actual conditions in the facility, the privacy of patients shall be respected. Photographs of patients will not normally be necessary and in no event shall identifiable photographs be taken without their consent.
7. The walkaround portion of the inspection shall consist of a spot-check approach. The CSHO shall identify on the basis of professional judgment what areas should be physically checked out and to what extent. It is not expected that a comprehensive walkaround inspection of the workplace will be necessary. The CSHO is to be satisfied that an IC program is in place and judged to be effective.
8. If an inspection is conducted in an establishment outside of SIC codes 80** and 7261, and a health care unit is on site, the provisions of Sections J through T apply and shall be enforced.

K. *Federal Agency Facilities.* Health care facilities owned by agencies of the Federal Government are subject to inspection under this instruction.
1. Where an inspection other than one scheduled on the regular Federal establishment targeting list is to be made at a Federal health care facility in accordance with this instruction, notification of agency headquarters personnel, through the Office of Federal Agency Programs (OFAP), shall be accomplished prior to any facility visits.
2. Actual onsite visits shall be coordinated between Regional/Area Office and the establishment being inspected.

L. *Citation Policy.* The provisions of the FOM, Chapters IV and V, shall be followed when issuing citations for hazards related to blood-borne infectious diseases.
1. The following requirements apply when citing hazards found in health care facilities. Employers must comply with the provisions of these requirements whenever an employee may reasonably be expected to have direct contact with body fluids regardless of whether the patient is known to have been infected with HBV or HIV. This policy is based on the widespread nature of these viruses and the consequent risk to the health care workers described above. It is also based on the need to maintain patient confidentiality and HBV and HIV testing limitations.
   - 29 CFR 1910.132–Personal protective equipment.
   - 29 CFR 1910.22(a)(1) and (a)(2)–General requirements, Housekeeping.
   - 29 CFR 1910.141(a) (4) (i) and (ii)–Sanitation, Waste disposal.
   - 29 CFR 1910.145(f)–Specifications for accident prevention signs and tags.

- Section 5(a)(1)—General Duty Clause and Executive Order 13196, Section 1-201(a) for Federal facilities.

2. Whenever a hazardous condition exists that is not covered by one of the standards listed above, and the decision is made not to cite the condition under the general duty clause, the appropriate letter shall be sent advising the employer of the hazardous conditions and suggesting corrective action.
3. Such recommendations made to employers shall be noted in the case file for special attention in subsequent inspections.
4. Multi-Employer Work Site. The following citation guidelines apply in multi-employer work sites.
   a. Health care facilities shall be cited for standards and section 5(1) (1) violations to which their own employees are exposed.
   b. They shall also be cited for standards (but not 5(a) (1)) violations to which employees of other employers on their premises are exposed to the extent that they control the hazard. For example, they shall be cited for not providing personal protective equipment to unprotected employees of other employers on their premises.
   c. Physicians who are members of professional corporations are generally considered to be employees of that corporation. Therefore, the corporation may be cited for all violations affecting those physicians. Hospitals where they work may also be cited for standard violations (but not 5(a)(1) to which they are exposed.)
   d. No citation shall be issued where the only persons exposed are physicians who are sole practitioners or partners, and thus not employees under the Occupational Safety and Health Act.

M. *Violations.* The IC program shall be carefully evaluated to determine compliance with OSHA requirements, as clarified by those CDC guidelines relating to health care worker safety and health. The description of the OSHA requirements in this section is based upon those guidelines. Violations of OSHA requirements will normally be classified as serious.
   1. 29 CFR 1910.132(a) and (c). The standard provides in pertinent part: "(a) Application. Protective equipment, including personal protective equipment for eyes, face, head, and extremities, protective clothing, respiratory devices, and protective shields and barriers, shall be provided, used, and maintained in a sanitary and reliable condition wherever it is necessary by reason of hazards of processes or environment, . . . encountered in a manner capable of causing injury or impairment in the function of any part of the body through absorption, inhalation or physical contact. (c) Design. All personal protective equipment shall be of safe design and construction for work to be performed."

      The following personal protective measures shall have been addressed by the IC program and verified by interviews and walkaround.
      a. Gloves. The use of gloves will vary according to the procedure involved. The use of disposable gloves is indicated for procedures where body fluids are handled.
         (1) The use of gloves is particularly important in the following circumstances:
            (a) If the health care worker has cuts, abraded skin, chapped hands, dermatitis or the like.
            (b) During instrumental examination of otopharynx, gastrointestinal tract and genitourinary tract.
            (c) When examining abraded or non-intact skin or patients with active bleeding.
            (d) During invasive procedures.
            (e) During all cleaning of body fluids and decontaminating procedures.

(2) Gloves must be of appropriate material, usually intact latex or intact vinyl, of appropriate quality for the procedures performed, and of appropriate size for each health care worker. Where gloves do not meet these requirements 29 CFR 1910.132(c) shall be cited.
(3) Employers shall not wash or disinfect surgical or examination gloves for reuse.
(4) General purpose utility (rubber) gloves worn by maintenance, housekeeping, laundry or other non medical personnel may be decontaminated and reused.
(5) No gloves shall be used if they are peeling, cracked, or discolored, or if they have punctures, tears, or other evidence of deterioration. Failure to meet these requirements shall be cited under 29 CFR 1910.132(c).

b. Gowns. The use of gowns, aprons, or lab coats is required when splashes to skin or clothing with body fluids are likely to occur. Gowns, including surgical gowns, shall be made of or lined with fluid-proof or fluid-resistant material and shall protect all areas of exposed skin.
c. Masks and Eye Protectors. The use of masks and protective eyewear or face shields is required when contamination of mucosal membranes (eyes, mouth or nose) with body fluids such as splashes or aerosolization of such material (e.g., during surgical or dental procedures) is likely to occur. They are not required for routine care.
d. Resuscitation Equipment. Pocket masks, resuscitation bags, or other ventilation devices shall be provided in strategic locations as well as to key personnel (e.g. paramedics) where the need for resuscitation is likely. This will minimize the need for emergency mouth-to-mouth resuscitation.
e. Invasive Procedures. Personal protective equipment as described above shall be used when performing invasive procedures to avoid exposure. When a health care worker's skin or mucous membranes may come in contact with body fluids, gowns, masks, and eye protection shall be worn, as noted above.
f. Phlebotomy. Gloves shall generally be provided to and used by phlebotomists. Employers who do not make them available shall be cited for failure to provide under 29 CFR 1910.132(a). Employers who make gloves available, but discourage or prohibit their use shall be cited for failure to use under 29 CFR 1910.132(a), if in fact the gloves are not being used. However, no citation for failure to use shall be issued where the phlebotomist voluntarily and without the encouragement of the employer does not wear gloves, unless the following circumstances exist:
   (1) For performing phlebotomy when the health care worker has cuts, scratches or other breaks in his/her skin.
   (2) In situations where the CSHO and/or health care worker judges that hand contamination with blood may occur, for example, when performing phlebotomy on an uncooperative patient.
   (3) For performing finger and/or heel sticks in infants and children.
   (4) When persons are receiving training in phlebotomy.
g. Dentistry. Gloves are required for contact with oral mucous membranes. Surgical mask and protective eyewear or chin-length plastic face shields are required during dental procedures in which splashing, spattering or aerosolization of blood, saliva or gingival fluids is likely. (Saliva and gingival fluids are included because of the likelihood that they contain blood in their setting.)
h. Laboratories. The use of gloves are required for processing body fluid specimens. Masks and protective eyewear are required when the worker's mucosal membranes may come in contact with body fluids.
i. Postmortem Procedures. Persons performing or assisting in postmortem procedures are required to wear personal protective equipment as noted above to avoid exposure to body fluids.

2. 29 CFR 1910.22(a)(1) and (a)(2). The standard provides in pertinent part: "(a) Housekeeping. (1) All places of employment, passageways, storerooms, and service rooms shall be kept clean and orderly and in a sanitary condition. (2) The floor of every workroom shall be maintained in a clean and, so far as possible, a dry condition. . . ."

   The IC program shall have identified housekeeping operations involving substantial risk or direct exposure to body fluids and shall have addressed the proper precautions to be taken while cleaning rooms and blood spills. The application of these procedures shall be verified by employee interviews and the walkaround.
   a. Room Cleaning Where Body Fluids Are Present. Schedules shall be as frequent as necessary according to the area of the institution, types of surface to be cleaned, and the amount and type of soil present.
   b. Disinfectants. Following the initial cleanup, one of the following shall be used for cleaning blood and/or body fluids:
      (1) Chemical germicides that are approved for use as hospital disinfectants and are tuberculocidal when used at recommended dilutions.
      (2) Products registered by the Environmental Protection Agency as being effective against HIV with an accepted "HIV (AIDS virus)" label.
      (3) A solution of 5.25 percent sodium hypochlorite (household bleach) diluted between 1:10 and 1:100 with water.
3. 29 CFR 1910.141(a) (4) (i) and II). The standard provides in pertinent part: "(4) Waste disposal. (i) Any receptacle used for putrescible solid or liquid waste or refuse shall be so constructed that it does not leak and may be thoroughly cleaned and maintained in a sanitary condition. Such receptacle shall be equipped with a solid, tight-fitting cover, unless it can be maintained in a sanitary condition without a cover. This requirement does not prohibit the use of receptacles which are designed to permit the maintenance of a sanitary condition without regard to the aforementioned requirements. (ii) All sweeping, solid or liquid wastes, refuse, and garbage shall be removed in a manner as to avoid creating a menace to health and as often as necessary or appropriate to maintain the place of employment in a sanitary condition."

   The IC program shall have addressed the handling and disposal of the following potentially contaminated items. The effectiveness of the program in this regard shall be verified through employee interviews and the walkaround.
   a. Sharp instruments and disposable items. Needles shall not be recapped, purposely bent or broken by hand, removed from disposable syringes, or otherwise manipulated by hand. Resheathing instruments, self-sheathing needles, or forceps shall be used to prevent recapping needles by hand.
      (1) After they are used, disposable syringes and needles, scalpel blades, and other sharp items shall be placed in puncture-resistant containers for disposal.
      (2) Such containers shall be easily accessible to personnel needing them and located in all areas where needles are commonly used, including emergency rooms, intensive care units, and surgical suites and shall be so constructed that they will not spill their contents if knocked over and will not themselves allow injuries when handled.
      (3) These containers shall also be located on patient floors and any other setting where blood is drawn and needles are used.
   b. Lab Specimens. All specimen of body fluids shall be put in a well constructed container with a secure lid to prevent leaking during transport and shall be disposed of in an approved manner. Contaminated materials used in laboratory tests should be decontaminated before reprocessing or be placed in bags and disposed of in accordance with institutional policies for disposal of infectious waste.

4. 29 CFR 1910.145(f). The standard provides in pertinent part: "(f) (3) Use. Tags shall be used as means to prevent accidental injury or illness to employees who are exposed to hazardous or potentially hazardous conditions, equipment or operations which are out of the ordinary, unexpected or not readily apparent. Tags shall be used until such time as the identified hazard is eliminated or the hazardous operation is completed. Tags need not be used where signs, guarding or other positive means of protection are being used. (4) General Tag criteria. All required tags shall meet the following criteria: (i) Tags shall contain a signal word and a major message. (a) The signal word shall be . . . "BIOHAZARD," or the biological hazard symbol. (b) The major message shall indicate the specific hazardous condition or the instruction to be communicated to the employee. (ii) The signal word shall be readable at a minimum distance of five feet (1.52 m) or such greater distance as warranted by the hazard. (iii) The tag's major message shall be presented in either pictographs, written text or both. (iv) The signal word and the major message shall be understandable to all employees who may be exposed to the identified hazard. (v) All employees shall be informed as to the meaning of the various tags used throughout the workplace and what special precautions are necessary. (vi) Tags shall be affixed as close as safely possible to their respective hazards by a positive means such as string, wire, or adhesive that prevents their loss or unintentional removal. (f)(8) Biological hazard tags. (i) Biological hazard tags shall be used to identify the actual or potential presence of a biological hazard and to identify equipment, containers, rooms, experimental animals, or combinations thereof, that contain or are contaminated with hazardous biological agents."

   The IC program shall have addressed the labeling procedures to be followed in the facility. That these procedures are followed shall be confirmed by employee interviews and the walkaround.

   a. Bags or other receptacles containing articles contaminated with potentially infectious material, including contaminated disposable items, must be tagged or otherwise identified. The tag shall have the signal word "BIOHAZARD" or the biological hazard symbol. The tag shall indicate that the bag could contain infectious wastes and give any additional instructions; e.g., if the outside of the bag is contaminated with body fluids, a second outer bag should be used.
   b. If tags are not used, other equally effective means of identification shall be used (e.g., red bagging).
   c. Employees shall be informed of the meaning of tags. With respect to tagged material, they shall also be instructed to use double bagging where puncture or outside contamination is likely.

5. Section 5(a)(1). Section 5(a)(1) provides: "Each employer shall furnish to each of his employees employment and a place of employment which are free from recognized hazards that are causing or are likely to cause death or serious physical harm to his employees."
   a. Section 5(a)(1) citations must meet the requirements outlined in the FOM, Chapter IV, and can be issued only where there is a hazard which cannot be abated by implementing an abatement method required by the standards above. All applicable abatement methods identified as correcting the same hazard shall be issued under a single 5(a)(1) citation.
   b. If a citation under 5(a)(1) is justified, the citation, after setting forth the SAVE for section 5(a)(1), shall state: Health care workers (specify categories, such as doctors, nurses, etc.) (specify location) were exposed to the hazard of being infected by HBV and/or HIV through possible direct contact with blood or other body fluids. Feasible and useful abatement methods for reducing this hazard, among others, are: (List abatement methods not required by the standards which employer is not implementing.)

c. Recognition for purposes of citing section 5(a)(1) is recognition of the hazard of being infected with HBV and/or HIV through possible direct contact with body fluids. The health care industry generally accepts and, therefore, recognizes the determination of this hazard by the CDC, which is the acknowledged authority in this area. The employer's IC program can also constitute evidence of recognition.
d. The following are examples of feasible and useful abatement methods. The nonuse of any of these methods is likely to result in the continued existence of a serious hazard and, may, therefore, allow citation under 5(a)(1). Consequently, all of these methods shall have been implemented. To determine whether they are being implemented, the CSHO shall evaluate the IC program and verify with employee interviews and the walkaround.
    (1) Hepatitis B Vaccination. The facility's IC policy regarding hepatitis B vaccinations shall address all circumstances warranting such vaccinations and shall identify employees at substantial risk of directly contacting body fluids. All such employees shall be offered hepatitis B vaccinations free of charge in amounts and at times prescribed by standard medical practice.
    (2) Linen. The IC program shall have identified all laundry operations involving substantial risk of direct exposure to body fluids. Linen soiled with body fluids shall be handled as little as possible and with minimum agitation to prevent contamination of the person handling the linen. All soiled linen shall be bagged at the location where it was used; it shall not be sorted or rinsed in patient-care areas. Soiled linen shall be placed and transported in bags that prevent leakage.
    (3) Reusable Equipment. Standard sterilization and disinfection procedures currently recommended for hepatitis B in a variety of health care settings are adequate to sterilize or disinfect instruments, devices, or other items contaminated with body fluids. A recommended source of information is the CDC's Guidelines for Hospital Environmental Control: Cleaning, Disinfection and Sterilization of Hospital Equipment.
    (4) Bagging of Articles. Objects that are contaminated with potentially infectious materials shall be placed in an impervious bag. If outside contamination of the bag is likely, a second bag shall be added.
    (5) Handwashing. After removing gloves, hands or other skin surfaces shall be washed thoroughly and immediately after contact with body fluids.
    (6) Follow-up Procedures After Possible Exposure to HIV/HBV:
        (a) If a health care worker has a percutaneous (needlestick or cut) or mucous membrane (splash to eye, nasal mucosa, or mouth) exposure to body fluids or has a cutaneous exposure to blood when the worker's skin is chapped, abraded, or otherwise nonintact, the source patient shall be informed of the incident and tested for HIV and HBV infections, after consent is obtained.
        (b) If patient consent is refused or if the source patient tests positive, the health care worker shall be evaluated clinically and by HIV antibody testing as soon as possible and advised to report and seek medical evaluation of any acute febrile illness that occurs within 12 weeks after exposure. HIV seronegative workers shall be retested 6 weeks post-exposure and on a periodic basis thereafter (12 weeks and 6 months after exposure).
        (c) Follow up procedures shall be taken for health care workers exposed or potentially exposed to HBV. The types of procedures depends on the immunization status of the worker (i.e., whether HBV vaccination has been received and antibody response is adequate) and the HBV serologic status of the source patient. The CDC Immunization Practices

Advisory Committee has published its recommendations regarding HBV postexposure prophylaxis in table format in the June 7, 1985, Morbidity and Mortality Weekly Report.

(d) If an employee refuses to submit to the procedures in (b) or (c) above when such procedures are medically indicated, no adverse action can be taken on that ground alone since the procedures are designed for the benefit of the exposed employee.

(7) Training and Education of Health Care Workers. The employer's training program shall be evaluated in accordance with Appendix C.

(a) All high risk health care workers such as those listed in H.1. shall receive education on precautionary measures, epidemiology, modes of transmission and prevention of HIV/HBV. Health care workers shall be counseled regarding possible risks to the fetus from HIV/HBV and other associated infectious agents.

(b) In addition, such high risk workers must receive training regarding the location and proper use of personal protective equipment. They shall be trained concerning proper work practiced and, if the facility has implemented them, shall understand the concept of "universal precautions" as it applies to their work practices. They shall be trained about the meaning of color coding or other methods (except tags) used to designate contaminated articles or infectious waste. Where tags are used, training about tags and precautions to be used in handling contaminated articles or infectious waste is governed by 29 CFR 1910.145(f). (See section M.4.) Workers shall receive training about procedures to be used if they are exposed to needlestick or to body fluids.

N. *Other Standards.*

1. The hazard communication standard, 29 CFR 1910.1200 only applies to hazardous chemicals or physical hazards in the workplace and thus does not apply to biological hazards such as blood borne diseases.
2. A record concerning employee exposure to HIV and/or HBV is an employee exposure record within the meaning of 29 CFR 1910.20. A record about HIV and/or HBV status is also an employee medical record within the meaning of 29 CFR 1910.20 However, under 29 CFR 1913.10, the CSHO may obtain these records for purposes of determining compliance with 29 CFR 1910.20.
3. Generally, 29 CFR 1910.134 does not apply since there are no respirators approved for biohazards. However, placing respirators in areas where they could be contaminated by body fluids constitutes a violation of 29 CFR 1910.134(b)(6).

O. *Expert Witnesses.* The Directorate of Technical Support will assist the Regional Offices and the States in locating expert witnesses.

1. In the event that a 5(a)(1) citation is contested, proper expert witness support shall be immediately obtained. Issues which the expert must be prepared to address include:
   a. The risk to workers associated with the exposure circumstances.
   b. Existence, feasibility and utility of abatement measures.
   c. Recognition of the hazard in the industry, by the employer.
2. Expert witnesses may also be necessary in other cases, particularly those involving 29 CFR 1910.132(a).

P. *Recording in the IMIS.* Current instructions for completing the appropriate inspection classification boxes (Items 24 and 25) of the OSHA-1, Inspection Report, as found in the IMIS Manual shall be applied when recording inspections conducted at health care facilities or at facilities with health care units:

1. Inspections conducted in such facilities shall be coded as "Comprehensive" or "Partial" in Item 35 of the OSHA-1, as appropriate. Such inspections shall not be coded as records only inspections.

2. The OSHA-1 for health care facility or unit inspections scheduled as a result of a complaint shall be marked as "Safety" or "Health" as appropriate (Item 21.), "Complaint" (Item 24.), and "National Emphasis Program" (Item 25d.). Record "BLOOD" in the space in Item 25d.
3. The OSHA-1 for health care facility or unit inspections scheduled from the Safety or the health Establishment List or from the Health Care Establishment List shall be marked as "Safety" or "Health," as appropriate (Item 21.), "Planned" (Item 24h.), "Safety" or "Health Planning Guide" as appropriate (Item 25d.). Record "BLOOD" in the space in Item 25d.
4. The OSHA-1 for any unprogrammed safety or health inspection conducted in a health care facility or unit shall be marked "unprogrammed" (Item 24a. through g., as appropriate), "National Emphasis Program" (Item 25d) and "BLOOD" recorded in the space in Item 25d.

Q. *Referrals.*
1. When a complaint or inquiry is received from a source in a State plan State regarding occupational exposure to blood-borne disease, the Regional Administrator shall refer it to the State plan designee for action.
2. When a complaint or inquiry regarding occupational exposure to blood-borne disease in a State or local government health care facility is received in a State without an OSHA approved State plan, the Region Administrator shall refer it to the appropriate State public health agency or local health agency with jurisdiction over the health care facilities.

R. *Personal Protective Equipment for CSHOs.*
1. CSHOs shall not participate in activities that will require them to come into contact with body fluids, needles or other sharp instruments contaminated with blood. To evaluate such activities, CSHOs normally shall establish the existence of hazards and adequacy of work practices through employee interviews and shall observe them at a safe distance.
2. CSHOs shall take necessary precautions to avoid direct contact with body fluids. It will not normally be necessary for CSHOs actually to enter hazardous areas and, therefore, to use personal protective equipment. On the rare occasions when entry into potentially hazardous areas is judged necessary, the CSHO shall be properly equipped as required by the health care facility as well as by his/her own professional judgment, after consultation with the supervisor (FOM, Chapter III).

S. *Copies of Citations.* Copies of all citations issued pursuant to this program shall be sent expeditiously to the Office of Health Compliance Assistance through the Director of Fields Programs. Such information is necessary for program monitoring and evaluation.

T. *Informal Settlement Agreements and Notices of Contest.* Copies of all settlement agreements and notices of contest shall be sent expeditiously to the Office of Health Compliance Assistance through the Director of Fields Programs.

Occupational Safety and Health Administration Washington, D.C.

OSHA Inspections Handbook

Introduction

Under the Occupational Safety and Health Act of 1970 (the Act), the Occupational Safety and Health Administration (OSHA) is authorized to conduct workplace inspections determine whether employers are complying with standards issued by the Agency for safe and healthful workplaces. OSHA also enforces Section 5(a)(1) of the Act, known as the General Duty Clause, which requires that every working man and woman must be provided with a safe and healthful workplace. Workplace inspections are performed by OSHA compliance safety and health officers who are knowledgeable and experienced in the occupational safety and heath field and who are trained in the OSHA standards and in the recognition of safety and health hazards. Similarly, states with their own occupational safety and health programs conduct inspections using qualified State compliance safety and health officers.

Inspections are usually conducted without advance notice. In fact, alerting an employer without proper authorization in advance of an OSHA inspection can bring a fine of up to $1,000 and/or six-month jail term. This is true for OSHA compliance officers as well as state inspectors.

There are, however, special circumstances under which OSHA may give notice to the employer, but such a notice will normally be less than 24 hours. These circumstances include:

- Imminent danger situations which require correction as soon as possible;
- Inspections which must take place after regular business hours or which require special preparation;
- Cases where notice is required to assure that the employer and employee representative or other personnel will be present;
- Cases where an inspection must be delayed for more than 5 working days when there is good cause; and
- Situations in which the OSHA area director determines that advance notice would produce a more thorough or effective inspection.

Employers who receive advance notice of an inspection must inform their employees' representative or arrange for OSHA to do so.

If an employer refuses to admit an OSHA compliance officer or if an employer attempts to interfere with the inspection, the Act permits appropriate legal action.

Based on a 1978 Supreme Court ruling (Marshall v. Barlow's Inc.), OSHA usually may not conduct warrantless inspections without valid consent. The Agency may, however, inspect after acquiring a judicially authorized search warrant based upon administrative probable cause or upon evidence of a violation.

The remainder of this booklet is divided into five parts: inspection priorities; preparing for the inspection; the inspection process; inspection results; and appeals process.

Inspection Priorities

Obviously, not all 5 million workplaces covered by the Act can be inspected immediately. The worst situations need attention first. Therefore, OSHA has established a system of inspection priorities.

Imminent Danger

Imminent danger situations are given top priority. An imminent danger is any condition where there is reasonable certainty that a danger exists that can be expected to cause death or serious physical harm immediately or before the danger can be eliminated through normal enforcement procedures.

If an imminent danger situation is found, the compliance officer will ask the employer to voluntarily abate the hazard and to remove endangered employees from exposure. Should the employer fail to do this, OSHA, through the regional solicitor, may apply to the Federal District Court for an injunction prohibiting further work as long as unsafe conditions exist.

Catastrophes and Fatal Accidents

Second priority is given to investigation of fatalities and accidents resulting in hospitalization of five or more employees.

Such catastrophes must be reported to OSHA by the employer within 48 hours. OSHA investigates to determine the cause of such accidents, whether existing OSHA standards were violated, and whether additional standards are necessary to help avoid a recurrence of similar accidents.

Employee Complaints

Third priority is given to formal employee complaints of alleged violations of standards or of unsafe or unhealthful working conditions.

The Act gives each employee the right to request an OSHA inspection when the employee feels he or she is in imminent danger from a hazard or when he or she feels that there is a violation of an OSHA standard that threatens physical harm, OSHA will maintain confidentiality if requested, will inform the employee of any action it takes regarding the complaint and, if requested, will hold an informal review of any decision not to inspect.

Programmed Inspections

Next in priority are programmed inspections aimed at specific high hazard industries, occupations or health substances, or other industries identified in OSHA's current inspection procedures. Industries are selected for inspection on the basis of such factors as the injury incidence rates, previous citation history, employee exposure to toxic substances, or random selection. Special emphasis programs may also be developed and may be regional or national in scope, depending on the distribution of the workplaces involved. Comprehensive safety inspections in manufacturing will be conducted normally in those establishments with lost work-day injury rates at or above the BLS national rate for manufacturing currently in use by OSHA. States with their own occupational safety and health programs may use somewhat different systems to identify industries for inspection.

Follow-up Inspections

A follow-up inspection determines if previously cited violations have been corrected. If an employer has failed to abate a violation, the compliance officer informs the employer that he/she is subject to "Failure to Abate" alleged violations and proposed additional daily penalties while such failure to abate or violation continues.

Records Review

A records review is an examination of the employer's injury and illness records to determine whether there will be a comprehensive inspection of the workplace. The compliance officer reviews the OSHA Form 200 (log of occupational injuries and illnesses) and employment data of the establishment. Using these data, the compliance officer calculates the lost workday injury (LWDI) rate for the establishment. This figure is compared to the national average for manufacturing, published by the Bureau of Labor Statistics (BLS). If the calculated LWDI rate is below the BLS rate, the compliance officer will not normally conduct a comprehensive safety inspection. If the LWDI rate is above the national average, an inspection will be conducted.

Preparing for the Inspection

A compliance officer represents the Agency and is expected to demonstrate his/her knowledge and expertise in the safety and health field in a courteous and professional manner. Prior to the inspection, the compliance officer will become familiar with as many relevant facts as possible about the workplace, such as the inspection history of the establishment, the nature of the business, and the particular standards that might apply. This preparation provides the compliance officer with a knowledge of the potential hazards and industrial processes that may be encountered and aids in selecting appropriate personal protective equipment for protection against these hazards during the inspection.

Inspector's Credentials

When the OSHA compliance officer arrives at the establishment, he or she displays official credentials and asks to meet an appropriate employer representative. Employers should always ask to see the compliance officer's credentials.

An OSHA compliance officer carries U.S. Department of Labor credentials bearing his or her photograph and a serial number that can be verified by calling the nearest OSHA office. OSHA compliance officers may not collect a penalty at the time of inspection or promote the sale of a product or service at any time; anyone who attempts to do so is bogus and the FBI or local law enforcement officials should be contacted immediately.

Opening Conference

In the opening conference the compliance officer explains how the establishment was selected and determines whether it will be subject to a comprehensive safety inspection. The compliance officer also will ascertain whether an OSHA-funded consultation program is in progress or whether the facility is pursuing or has received an inspection exemption; if so, the inspection may be terminated.

The compliance officer explains the purpose of the visit, the scope of the inspection, and the standards that apply. The employer will be given copies of applicable safety and health standards as well as a copy of any employee complaint that may be involved (with the employee's name deleted, if the employee has requested anonymity).

The employer is asked to select an employer representative to accompany the compliance officer during the inspection.

An authorized employee representative also is given the opportunity to attend the opening conference and to accompany the compliance officer during the inspection. If the employees are represented by a recognized bargaining agent, the agent ordinarily will designate the employee representative to accompany the compliance officer. Similarly, if there is a plant safety committee, the employee members of that committee will designate the employee representative (in the absence of a recognized bargaining agent). Where neither employee group exists, the employee representative may be selected by the employees themselves, or the compliance officer may determine if any employee suitable represents the interest of other employees. Under no circumstances may the employer select the employee representative for the walk-around.

The Act does not require that there be an employee representative for each inspection. However, where there is no authorized employee representative, the compliance officer must consult with a reasonable number of employees concerning safety and health matters in the workplace.

The Inspection Process

After the opening conference, the compliance officer and accompanying representatives proceed through the establishment to inspect work areas for safety or health hazards.

The route and duration of the inspection are determined by the compliance officer. While talking with employees, the compliance officer makes every effort to minimize any work interruptions. The compliance officer observes safety and health conditions and practices, consults with employees, takes photos and instrument readings, examines records, collects air samples, measures noise levels, surveys existing engineering controls, and monitors employee exposure to toxic fumes, gases and dusts.

Trade secrets observed by the compliance officer will be kept confidential. An inspector who releases confidential information without authorization is subject to a $1,000 fine and/or one year in jail. The employer may require that the employee representative have confidential clearance for any are in question.

Employees are consulted during the inspection tour. The compliance officer may stop and question workers, in private, about safety and health conditions and practices in their workplaces. Each employee is protected, under the Act, from discrimination for exercising his or her safety and health rights.

OSHA places special importance on posting and recordkeeping. The compliance officer will inspect records of deaths, injuries and illnesses which the employer is required to keep. He or she will check to see that a copy of the totals from the last page of OSHA No. 200 has been posted and that the OSHA workplace poster (OSHA 2203) is prominently displayed. Where records of employee exposure to toxic substances and harmful physical agents have been required, they are also examined for compliance with the recordkeeping requirements.

The compliance officer also explains that while the following items are not required for all OSHA standards they should be recorded to accurately monitor and assess occupational hazards.

- Initial and periodic monitoring, including the date of measurement, for operations involving exposure; sampling and analytical methods used and evidence of their accuracy; number, duration, and results of samples taken; type of respiratory protective devices worn; and name, social security number, and the results of all employee exposure measurements. This records should be kept for 30 years.
- Employee physical/medical examinations, including the name and social security number of the employee; physicians' written opinions; any employee medical complaints related to exposure to toxic substances; and information provided to the examining physician. These records should me maintained for the duration of employment plus 30 years.
- Employee Training. These records should be kept for one year beyond the last date of employment of that employee.

The compliance officer also explains the requirements of the Hazard Communication Standard. Under that rule, manufacturing employers must establish a written, comprehensive hazard communication program which includes provisions for container labeling, material safety data sheets, and an employee training program. The program must contain a list of the hazardous chemicals in each work area and the means the employer will use to inform employees of the hazards of non-routine tasks.

During the course of the inspection, the compliance officer will point out to the employer any unsafe or unhealthful working conditions observed. At the same time, the compliance officer will discuss possible corrective action if the employer so desires.

Some apparent violations detected by the compliance officer can be corrected immediately. When they are corrected on the spot, the compliance officer records such corrections to help in judging the employer's good faith in compliance. Even though corrected, however, the apparent violations may still serve as the basis for a citation and, if appropriate, a notice of proposed penalty.

An inspection tour may cover part or all of an establishment, even if the inspection resulted from a specific complaint, fatality or catastrophe.

Closing Conference

After the inspection tour, a closing conference is held between the compliance officer, the employer, and the employer representative. It is a time for free discussion of problems and needs; a time for frank questions and answers.

The compliance officer will give the employer a copy of "Employer Rights and Responsibilities Following an OSHA Inspection," and then briefly discuss the information in the booklet and answer any questions.

The compliance officer discusses with the employer all unsafe or unhealthful conditions observed on the inspection and indicates all apparent violations for which a citation may be issued or recommended. The employer is also informed of appeal rights. The compliance officer will not indicate any specific proposed penalities. Only the OSHA area director has that authority.

During the closing conference, the employer may wish to produce records to show compliance efforts and to provide information which can help OSHA determine how much time may be needed to abate an alleged violation.

When appropriate, more than one closing conference may be held. This is usually necessary when health hazards are being evaluated or when laboratory reports are required.

If the employee representative did not participate in the opening conference held with the employer, a closing discussion is held with the employee representative, if requested to discuss matters of direct interest to employees.

The compliance officer explains that OSHA area offices are full-service resource centers that inform the public of OSHA activities and programs, such as new or revised standards, including the status or proposed standards, comment periods, or public hearings; provide technical experts and materials, including courses offered at the OSHA Training Institute; refer callers to other agencies and professional organizations as appropriate; and promote effective safety and health programs through voluntary protection programs and expanded employer abatement assistance efforts.

Inspection Results

After the compliance officer reports findings, the area director determines if citations will be issued and if penalities will be proposed.

Citations

Citations inform the employer and employees of the regulations and standards alleged to have been violated and of the length of time set for their abatement. The employer will receive citations and notices of proposed penalities by certified mail. The employer must post a copy of each citation at or near the place a violation occurred, for three days or until the violation is abated, whichever is longer.

Penalties

These are the types of violations which may be cited, and the penalities which may be proposed:

- Other Than Serious Violation — A violation that has a direct relationship to job safety and health, but probably would not cause death or serious physical harm. A proposed penalty of up to $1,000 for each violation is discretionary. A penalty for an other than serious violation may be adjusted downward by as much as 80 percent, depending on the employer's good faith (demonstrated efforts to comply with the Act), history of previous violations, and size of business. When the adjusted penalty amounts to less than $60, no penalty is proposed.
- Serious Violation — A violation where there is a substantial probability that death or serious physical harm could result. A mandatory penalty of up to $1,000 for each violation is proposed.a penalty for a serious violation may be adjusted downward based on the employer's good faith, history of previous violations, the gravity of the alleged violation, and size of business.
- Willful Violation — A violation that the employer intentionally and knowingly commits. The employer is aware that a hazardous condition exists, knows that the condition violates a standard or other obligation of the Act, and makes no reasonable effort to eliminate it. Penalities of up to $10,000 may be proposed for each willful violation. A proposed penalty for a willful violation may be adjusted downward, depending on the size of the business and its history of previous violations. Usually, no credit is given for good faith.

  An employer who is convicted of a willful violation of a standard that has resulted in the death of an employee may be fined up to $10,000 or imprisoned up to six months, or both. A second conviction doubles these maximum penalities.
- Repeated Violation — A violation of any standard, regulation, rule or order where, upon reinspection, a substantially similar violation is found and the original citation has become a final order. Repeated violations can bring a fine of up to $10,000 for each such violation.
- Failure to Correct Prior Violation — Failure to correct a prior violation may bring a civil penalty of up to $1,000 for each day the violation continues beyond the prescribed abatement date.

Additional violations for which citations and proposed penalties may be issued are as follows:

- Falsifying records, reports or applications can bring a fine of $10,000 or up to six months in jail, or both.
- Violations of posting requirements can bring a civil penalty of up to $1,000.
- Assaulting a compliance officer, or otherwise resisting, opposing, intimidating or interfering with a compliance officer in the performance of his or her duties is a criminal offense and is subject to a fine of not more than $5,000 and imprisonment for not more than three years.

Citation and penalty procedures may differ somewhat in states with their own occupational safety and health programs.

Appeals Process

Appeals by Employees

If an inspection was initiated due to an employee complaint, the employee or authorized employee representative may request an informal review of any decision not to issue a citation.

Employees may not contest citations, amendments to citations, penalities, or lack of penalities. They may, however, contest the time allowed for abatement of a hazardous condition. They may, however, contest the time allowed for abatement of a hazardous condition. They also may contest an employer's "Petition for Modification of Abatement" (PMA) which requests an extension of the abatement period. Employees must contest the PMA within 10 working days of its posting or within 10 working days after an authorized employee representative has received a copy.

Within 15 working days of the employer's receipt of a citation, the employee may submit a written objection to OSHA. The OSHA area director forwards the objection to the Occupational Safety and Health Review Commission, which operates independently of OSHA.

Employees may request an informal conference with OSHA to discuss any issues raised by an inspection, citation, notice of proposed penalty, or employer's notice of intention to contest.

Appeals by Employers

When issued a citation and notice of proposed penalty, an employer may request an informal meeting with OSHA's area director to discuss the case. The area director is authorized to enter into settlement agreements that revise citations and penalities to avoid prolonged legal disputes.

Petition for Modification of Abatement

Upon receiving a citation, the employer must correct the cited hazard by the abatement date unless he or she contests the citation or abatement date. However, factors beyond the employer's control may prevent the completion of corrections by that date. In such a situation, the employer who has made a good faith effort to comply may file for a "Petition for modification of Abatement" (PMA) date.

The written petition must specify the steps taken to achieve compliance, the additional time needed to comply, the reasons additional time is needed to comply, the reasons additional time is needed, and interim steps begin taken to safeguard employees against the cited hazard during the intervening period. The employer must certify that a copy of the PMA was posted in a conspicuous place at or near each place where a violation occurred and that the employee representative received a copy of the petition.

Notice of Contest

If the employer decides to contest either the citation, the abatement period or the proposed penalty, he or she has 15 working days from the time the citation and proposed penalty are received to notify the OSHA area director in writing. An orally expressed disagreement will not suffice. This written notification is called a "Notice of Contest."

There is no specific format for the Notice of Contest. However, it must clearly identify the employer's basis for filing — the citation, notice of proposed penalty, abatement period, or notification of failure to correct violations.

A copy of the Notice of Contest must be given to the employees' authorized representative. If any affected employees are not represented by a recognized bargaining agent, a copy of the notice must be posted in a prominent location in the workplace or given personally to each unrepresented employee.

Review Procedure

If the written Notice of Contest has been filed within the required 15 working days, the OSHA area director forwards the case to the Occupational Safety and Health Review Commission (OSHRC). The Commission is an independent agency not associated with OSHA or the Department of Labor. The Commission assigns the case to an administrative law judge.

The judge may investigate and disallow the contest if it is found to be legally invalid, or a hearing may be scheduled for a public place near the employer's workplace. The employer and the employees have the right to participate in the hearing; the OSHRC does not require that they be represented by attorneys.

Once the administrative law judge has ruled, any party to the case may request a further review by OSHRC. Any of the three OSHRC commissioners also may, at his or her own motion, bring a case before the Commission for review. Commission rulings may be appealed to the appropriate U.S. Court of Appeals.

Appeals in State Plan States

States with their own occupation safety and health programs have a state system for review and appeal of citations, penalties and abatement periods. The procedures are generally similar to federal OSHA's, but cases are heard by a state review board or equivalent authority.

Occupational Safety and Health Administration
Washington, D.C.

Occupational Exposure to Bloodborne Pathogens: Proposed Rule and Notice of Hearing [Excerpt from *Federal Register* 54(102):23134–23139, May 30, 1989]

PART 1910—[AMENDED]

Subpart Z—[Amended]

1. The general authority citation for Subpart Z of 29 CFR Part 1910 continues to read as follows and a new citation for § 1910.1030 is added:

Authority: Secs. 6 and 8, Occupational Safety and Health Act, 29 U.S.C. 655, 657, Secretary of Labor's Orders Nos. 12–71 (36 FR 8754), 8–76 (41 FR 25059), or 9–83 (48 FR 35736), as applicable; and 29 CFR Part 1911.

* * * * *

Section 1910.1030 also issued under 29 U.S.C. 653.

* * * * *

2. Section 1910.1030 is added to read as follows:

§ 1910.1030 Bloodborne pathogens.

(a) *Scope and application.* This section applies to all occupational exposure to blood or other potentially infectious materials as defined by paragraph (b) of this section.

(b) *Definitions.* For purposes of this section, the following shall apply:

"Assistant Secretary" means the Assistant Secretary of Labor for Occupational Safety and Health, or designated representative.

"Blood" means human blood, human blood components and products made from human blood.

"Bloodborne Pathogens" means pathogenic microorganisms that are present in human blood and can cause disease in humans. These pathogens include, but are not limited to, hepatitis B virus (HBV) and human immunodeficiency virus (HIV).

"Clinical Laboratory" means a workplace where diagnostic or other screening procedures are performed on blood or other potentially infectious materials.

"Director" means the Director of the National Institute for Occupational Safety and Health, U.S. Department of Health and Human Services, or designated representative.

"Disinfect" means to inactivate virtually all recognized pathogenic microorganisms but not necessarily all microbial forms (e.g. bacterial endospores) on inanimate objects.

"Engineering Controls" means controls that isolate or remove the hazard from the workplace.

"Exposure Incident" means a specific eye, mouth, other mucous membrane, non-intact skin, or parenteral contact with blood or other potentially infectious materials that results from the performance of an employee's duties.

"Infectious Waste" means blood and blood products, contaminated sharps, pathological wastes, and microbiological wastes.

"Occupational Exposure" means reasonably anticipated skin, eye, mucous membrane, or parenteral contact with blood or other potentially infectious materials that may result from the performance of an employee's duties. This definition excludes incidental exposures that may take place on the job, and that are neither reasonably nor routinely expected and that the worker is not required to incur in the normal course of employment.

"Other Potentially Infectious Materials" means

(1) The following body fluids: semen, vaginal secretions, cerebrospinal fluid, synovial fluid, pleural fluid, pericardial fluid, peritoneal fluid , amniotic fluid, saliva in dental procedures, and any body fluid that is visibly contaminated with blood.

(2) Any unfixed tissue or organ (other than intact skin) from a human (living or dead) and

(3) HIV- or HBV-containing cell or tissue cultures, organ cultures, and culture medium or other solutions; and blood, organs or other tissues from experimental animals infected with HIV or HBV.

"Parenteral" means exposure occurring as a result of piercing the skin barrier (e.g. subcutaneous, intramuscular, intravenous routes).

"Patient" means any individual, living or dead, whose blood, body fluids, tissues, or organs may be a source of exposure to the employee. Examples include, but are not limited to, hospital and clinic patients; clients in institutions for the mentally retarded; trauma victims; clients of drug and alcohol treatment facilities; residents of hospices and nursing homes; human remains prior to embalming; and individuals who donate or sell blood or blood components.

"Personal Protective Equipment" is specialized clothing or equipment worn by an employee to protect him/her from a hazard.

"Production Facility" means a facility engaged in industrial-scale, large-volume production of HIV or HBV or in high concentration production of HIV or HBV.

"Research Laboratory" means a laboratory producing research-laboratory-scale amounts of HIV or HBV.

"Sharps" means any object that can penetrate the skin including, but not limited to, needles, scalpels, and broken capillary tubes.

"Sterilize" means the use of a physical or chemical procedure to destroy all microbial life including highly resistant bacterial endospores.

"Universal precautions" is a method of infection control in which all human blood and certain human body fluids are treated as if known to be infectious for HIV, HBV and other bloodborne pathogens.

"Work Practice Controls" means controls that reduce the likelihood of exposure by altering the manner in which a task is performed.

(c) *Infection control*— (1) *Exposure Determination.* (i) Each employer who has employees with occupational exposure as defined by paragraph (b) of this section shall identify and document those tasks and procedures where occupational exposures may take place.

(ii) Each employer shall identify and document all positions with occupational exposure.

(iii) This exposure determination shall be made without regard to the use of personal protective equipment.

(2) *Infection Control Plan.* (i) Each employer having employees whose reasonably anticipated duties may result in occupational exposure shall establish a written infection control plan designed to minimize or eliminate employee exposure.

(ii) This infection control plan shall contain the following as a minimum:

(A) The exposure determination required by paragraph (c)(1) and

(B) The schedule and method of implementation for each of the applicable paragraphs of this standard.

(iii) This infection control plan shall be reviewed and updated as necessary to reflect significant changes in tasks or procedures.

(iv) The infection control plan shall be made available to the Assistant Secretary and the Director for examination and copying.

(d) *Methods of Compliance*— (1) *General.* Universal precautions shall be observed to prevent contact with blood and other potentially infectious materials, unless those precautions would interfere with the proper delivery of health care or public safety services in a particular circumstance, or would create a significant risk to the personal safety of the worker.

(2) *Engineering and work practice controls.* (i) Engineering controls shall be examined and maintained or replaced on a regular schedule to ensure their effectiveness.

(ii) Employees shall wash their hands immediately or as soon as possible after removal of gloves or other personal protective equipment and after hand contact with blood or other potentially infectious materials.

(iii) All personal protective equipment shall be removed immediately upon leaving the work area or as soon as possible if overtly contaminated and placed in an appropriately designated area or container for storage, washing, decontamination or disposal.

(iv) Used needles and other sharps shall not be sheared, bent, broken, recapped, or resheathed by hand. Used needles shall not be removed from disposable syringes.

(v) Eating, drinking, smoking, applying cosmetics or lip balm, and handling contact lenses are prohibited in work areas where there is a potential for occupational exposure.

(vi) Food and drink shall not be stored in refrigerators, freezers, or cabinets where blood or other potentially infectious materials are stored or in other areas of possible contamination.

(vii) All procedures involving blood or other potentially infectious materials shall be performed in such a manner as to minimize splashing, spraying, and aerosolization of these substances.

(viii) Mouth pipetting/suctioning is prohibited.

(3) *Personal protective equipment*— (i) *Provision and Use.* When there is a potential for occupational exposure, the employer shall provide and assure that the employee uses appropriate personal protective equipment such as, but not limited to, gloves; gowns, fluid-proof aprons, laboratory coats, and head and foot coverings; face shields or masks and eye protection; and mouthpieces, resuscitation bags, pocket masks, or other ventilation devices.

(ii) *Accessibility.* The employer shall assure that appropriate personal protective equipment in the appropriate sizes is readily accessible at the worksite or issued to employees. Hypoallergenic gloves shall be readily accessible to those employees who are allergic to the gloves normally provided.

(iii) *Cleaning.* The employer shall provide for the cleaning, laundering or disposal of personal protective equipment required by paragraphs (d) and (e) of this standard.

(iv) *Repair and replacement.* The employer shall repair or replace required personal protective equipment as needed to maintain its effectiveness.

(v) *Gloves.* Gloves shall be worn when the employee has the potential for the hands to have direct skin contact with blood, other potentially infectious materials, mucous membranes, non-intact skin, and when handling items or surfaces soiled with blood or other potentially infectious materials.

(A) Disposable (single use) gloves, such as surgical or examination gloves, shall be replaced as soon as possible when visibly soiled, torn, punctured, or when their ability to function as a barrier is compromised. They shall not be washed or disinfected for re-use.

(B) Utility gloves may be disinfected for re-use if the integrity of the glove is not compromised, however they must be discarded if they are cracked, peeling, discolored, torn, punctured, or exhibit other signs of deterioration.

(vi) *Masks, Eye Protection, and Face Shields.* Masks and eye protection or chin-length face shields shall be worn whenever splashes, spray, spatter, droplets, or aerosols of blood or other potentially infectious materials may be generated and there is a potential for eye, nose, or mouth contamination.

(vii) *Gowns, Aprons, and Other Protective Body Clothing.* Appropriate protective clothing shall be worn when the employee has a potential for occupational exposure. The type and characteristics will depend upon the task and degree of exposure anticipated; however, the clothing selected shall form an effective barrier.

(A) Gowns, lab coats, aprons, or similar clothing shall be worn if there is a potential for soiling of clothes with blood or other potentially infectious materials.

(B) Fluid-resistant clothing shall be worn if there is a potential for splashing or spraying of blood or other potentially infectious materials.

(C) Surgical caps or hoods shall be worn if there is a potential for splashing or splattering of blood or other potentially infectious materials on the head.

(D) Fluid-proof clothing shall be worn if there is a potential for clothing becoming soaked with blood or other potentially infectious materials.

(E) Fluid-proof shoe covers shall be worn if there is a potential for shoes to become contaminated and/or soaked with blood or other potentially infectious materials.

(4) *Housekeeping*—(i) *General.* Employers shall assure that the worksite is maintained in a clean and sanitary condition. The employer shall determine and implement the appropriate written schedule for cleaning and method of disinfection based upon the location within the facility, type of surface to be cleaned, type of soil present, and tasks or procedures being performed.

(ii) *Cleaning and Disinfection.* All equipment and environmental and working surfaces shall be properly cleaned and disinfected after contact with blood or other potentially infectious materials.

(A) Work surfaces shall be decontaminated with an appropriate disinfectant after completion of procedures; when surfaces are overtly contaminated; immediately after any spill of blood or other potentially infectious materials; and at the end of the work shift.

(B) Protective coverings such as plastic wrap, aluminum foil, or imperviously-backed absorbent paper may be used to cover equipment and environmental surfaces. These coverings shall be removed and replaced at the end of the work shift or when they become overtly contaminated.

(C) Equipment which may become contaminated with blood or other potentially infectious materials shall be checked routinely and prior to servicing or shipping and shall be decontaminated as necessary.

(D) All bins, pails, cans, and similar receptacles intended for reuse which have a potential for becoming contaminated with blood or other potentially infectious materials shall be inspected, cleaned, and disinfected on a regularly scheduled basis and cleaned and disinfected immediately or as soon as possible upon visible contamination.

(E) Broken glassware which may be contaminated shall not be picked up directly with the hands. It shall be cleaned up using mechanical means, such as a brush and dust pan, a vacuum cleaner, tongs, cotton swabs or forceps.

(F) Specimens of blood or other potentially infectious materials shall be placed in a closable, leakproof container labeled or color-coded according to paragraph (g)(1)(ii) prior to being stored or transported. If outside contamination of the primary container is likely, then a second leakproof container that is labeled or color-coded according to paragraph (g)(1)(ii) shall be placed over the outside of the first and closed to prevent leakage during handling, storage, or transport. If puncture of the primary container is likely, it shall be placed within a leakproof, puncture-resistant secondary container.

(G) Reusable items contaminated with blood or other potentially infectious materials shall be decontaminated prior to washing and/or reprocessing.

(iii) *Infectious Waste Disposal.* (A) All infectious waste destined for disposal shall be placed in closable, leakproof containers or bags that are color coded or labeled as required by paragraph (g)(1)(ii) of this standard.

(*1*) If outside contamination of the container or bag is likely to occur then a second leakproof container or bag which is closable and labeled or color-coded as described in paragraph (g)(1)(ii) shall be placed over the outside of the first and closed to prevent leakage during handling, storage, and transport.

(*2*) Disposal of all infectious waste shall be in accordance with applicable Federal, state, and local regulations.

(B) Immediately after use, sharps shall be disposed of in closable, puncture resistant, disposable containers which are leakproof on the sides and bottom and that are labeled or color-coded according to paragraph (g)(1)(ii).

(*1*) These containers shall be easily accessible to personnel and located in the immediate area of use.

(*2*) These containers shall be replaced routinely and not allowed to overfill.

(iv) *Laundry.* (A) Laundry from workplaces with employees covered under paragraph (a) of this section that is contaminated with blood or other potentially infectious materials or may contain contaminated sharps shall be treated as if it were contaminated and shall be handled as little as possible and with a minimum of agitation.

(*1*) Contaminated laundry shall be bagged at the location where it was used and shall not be sorted or rinsed in patient-care areas.

(*2*) Contaminated laundry shall be placed and transported in bags that are labeled or color-coded as described in paragraph (g)(1)(ii). Whenever this laundry is wet and presents the potential for soak-through of or leakage from the bag, it shall be placed and transported in leakproof bags.

(B) The employer shall ensure that laundry workers wear protective gloves and other appropriate personal protective equipment to prevent occupational exposure during handling or sorting.

(e) *HIV and HBV Research Laboratories and Production Facilities.* (1) This paragraph applies to research laboratories and production facilities engaged in the culture, production, concentration, and manipulation of HIV and HBV. It does not apply to clinical or diagnostic laboratories engaged solely in the analysis of blood, tissues, or organs. These requirements apply in addition to the other requirements of the standard.

(2) Research laboratories and production facilities shall meet the following criteria:

(i) *Standard microbiological practices.* All infectious liquid or solid waste shall be decontaminated before being disposed of.

(ii) *Special practices.* (A) Laboratory doors shall be kept closed when work involving HIV or HBV is in progress.

(B) Contaminated materials that are to be decontaminated at a site away from the work area shall be placed in a durable, leakproof container that is closed before being removed from the work area.

(C) Access to the work area shall be limited to authorized persons only. Policies and procedures shall be established whereby only persons who have been advised of the potential biohazard, who meet any specific entry requirements, and who comply with all entry and exit procedures shall be allowed to enter the work areas and animal rooms.

(D) When potentially infectious materials or infected animals are present in the work area or containment module, a hazard warning sign incorporating the universal biohazard symbol shall be posted on all access doors. The hazard warning sign shall comply with the provisions outlined in paragraph (g)(1)(i) of this standard.

(E) All activities involving potentially infectious materials shall be conducted in biological safety cabinets or other physical-containment devices within the containment module. No work shall be conducted in open vessels on the open bench.

(F) Laboratory coats, gowns, smocks, uniforms, or other appropriate protective clothing shall be used in the work area and animal rooms. Protective clothing shall not be worn outside of the work area and shall be decontaminated before being laundered.

(G) Special care shall be taken to avoid skin contamination with potentially infectious materials. Gloves shall be worn when handling infected animals and when making hand contact with potentially infectious materials is unavoidable.

(H) All waste from work areas including animal rooms shall be decontaminated before disposal.

(I) Vacuum lines shall be protected with high-efficiency particulate air (HEPA) filters and liquid disinfectant traps.

(J) Hypodermic needles and syringes shall be used only for parenteral injection and aspiration of fluids from laboratory animals and diaphragm bottles. Only needle-locking syringes or disposable syringe-needle units (i.e., the needle is integral to the syringe) shall be used for the injection or aspiration of potentially infectious fluids. Extreme caution shall be used when handling needles and syringes to avoid autoinoculation and the generation of aerosols during use and disposal. A needle shall not be bent, sheared, replaced in the sheath or guard, or removed from the syringe following use. The needle and syringe shall be promptly placed in a puncture-resistant container and decontaminated, preferably by autoclaving, before being discarded or reused.

(K) Spills and accidents that result in overt exposures of employees to potentially infectious materials shall be immediately reported to the laboratory director or other responsible person.

(L) A biosafety manual shall be prepared or adopted. Personnel shall be advised of potential hazards, shall be required to read instructions on practices and procedures, and shall be required to follow them.

(iii) *Containment equipment.* (A) Certified biological safety cabinets (Class I, II, or III) or other appropriate combinations of personal protection or physical containment devices, such as special protective clothing, respirators, centrifuge safety cups, sealed centrifuge rotors, and containment caging for animals, shall be used for all activities with potentially infectious materials that pose a threat of exposure to droplets, splashes, spills, or aerosols.

(B) Biological safety cabinets shall be certified when installed, whenever they are moved and at least annually.

(3) HIV and HBV research laboratories shall meet the following criteria:

(i) Each laboratory shall contain a sink for hand washing.

(ii) An autoclave for decontamination of infectious laboratory waste shall be available.

(4) HIV and HBV production facilities shall meet the following criteria:

(i) The work areas shall be separated from areas that are open to unrestricted traffic flow within the building. Passage through two sets of doors shall be the basic requirement for entry into the work area from access corridors or other contiguous areas. Physical separation of the high-containment work area from access corridors or other areas or activities may also be provided by a double-doored clothes-change room (showers may be included), airlock, or other access facility that requires passing through two sets of doors before entering the work area.

(ii) The interior surfaces of walls, floors and ceilings shall be water resistant so that they can be easily cleaned. Penetrations in these surfaces shall be sealed or capable of being sealed to facilitate decontamination of the work area.

(iii) Each work area shall contain a sink for washing hands. The sink shall be foot, elbow, or automatically operated and shall be located near the exit door of the work area.

(iv) Access doors to the work area or containment module shall be self-closing.

(v) An autoclave for decontamination of infectious waste shall be available within or as near as possible to the work area.

(vi) A ducted exhaust-air ventilation system shall be provided. This system shall create directional airflow that draws air into the work area through the entry area. The exhaust air shall not be recirculated to any other area of the building, shall be discharged to the outside, and shall be dispersed away from occupied areas and air intakes. The proper direction of the airflow shall be verified (i.e., into the work area).

(5) Training requirements. Additional training requirements for employees in HIV and HBV research laboratories and HIV and HBV production facilities are specified in paragraph (g)(2)(v).

(f) Hepatitis B Vaccination and Post Exposure Follow-up—(1) *General.* (i) The employer shall make available hepatitis B vaccination to all employees who have occupational exposure on average one or more times per month and post-exposure follow-up for all employees with an occupational exposure incident.

(ii) The employer shall assure that all medical evaluations and procedures are performed by or under the supervision of a licensed physician and that all laboratory tests are conducted by an accredited laboratory.

(iii) The employer shall assure that all evaluations, procedures, vaccinations, and post-exposure management are provided to the employee at a reasonable time and place, and according to standard recommendations for medical practice.

(2) *HBV Vaccination.* (i) HBV vaccination shall be offered to all employees occupationally exposed on an average of one or more times per month to blood or other potentially infectious materials, unless the employee has a previous HBV vaccination or unless antibody testing has revealed that the employee is immune. If the employee initially declines HBV vaccination but at a later date while still covered under the standard decides to accept the HBV vaccine, the employer shall provide the vaccine at that time. Should a booster dose(s) be recommended at a future date, such booster dose(s) shall be provided according to standard recommendations for medical practice.

(ii) HBV antibody testing shall be made available to an employee who desires such testing prior to deciding whether or not to receive HBV vaccination. If the employee is found to be immune to HBV by virtue of adequate antibody titer, then the employer is not required to offer the HBV vaccine to that employee.

(3) *Post exposure evaluation and follow-up.* Following a report of an exposure incident, the employer shall make available to each employee covered by paragraph (a) a confidential medical evaluation and follow-up, including at least the following elements:

(i) Documentation of the route(s) of exposure, HBV and HIV antibody status of the source patient(s) (if known), and the circumstances under which the exposure occurred.

(ii) If the source patient can be determined and permission is obtained, collection of and testing of the source patient's blood to determine the presence of HIV or HBV infection.

(iii) Collection of blood from the exposed employee as soon as possible after the exposure incident for the determination of HIV and/or HBV status. Actual antibody or antigen testing of the blood or serum sample may be done at that time or at a later date if the employee so requests.

(iv) Follow-up of the exposed employee including antibody or antige testing, counseling, illness reporting, and safe and effective post-exposure prophylaxis, according to standard recommendations for medical practice.

(4) *Information provided to the physician.* The employer shall provide the following information to the evaluating physician:

(i) A copy of this regulation and its appendices and

(ii) A description of the affected employee's duties as they relate to the employee's occupational exposure.

(5) *Physician's written opinion.* For each evaluation under this section, the employer shall obtain and provide the employee with a copy of the evaluating physician's written opinion within 15 working days of the completion of the evaluation. The written opinion shall be limited to the following information:

(i) The physician's recommended limitations upon the employee's ability to receive hepatitis B vaccination.

(ii) A statement that the employee has been informed of the results of the medical evaluation and that the employee has been told about any medical conditions resulting from exposure to blood or other potentially infectious materials which require further evaluation or treatment.

(iii) Specific findings or diagnoses, which are related to the employee's ability to receive HBV vaccination. Any other findings and diagnoses shall remain confidential.

(6) *Medical recordkeeping.* Medical records required by this standard shall be maintained in accordance with paragraph (h)(1) of this section.

(g) *Communication of Hazards to Employees*—(1) *Signs and Labels*—(i) *Signs.* The employer shall post signs at the entrance to work areas specified in paragraph (e) of this standard which shall bear the following legend:

BIOHAZARD

[Name of the Infectious Agent]

[Special requirements for entering the area]

[Name, telephone number of the laboratory director or other responsible person.]

(ii) *Labels.* (A) Warning labels shall be affixed to containers of infectious waste; refrigerators and freezers containing blood and other potentially infectious materials; and other containers used to store or transport blood or other potentially infectious materials except as provided in paragraph (g)(1)(ii) (E) and (F).

(B) Labels required by this section shall include the following legend:

BIOHAZARD

(C) These labels shall be fluorescent orange or orange-red or predominantly so, with lettering or symbols in a contrasting color.

(D) Labels required by paragraph (g)(1)(ii) shall either be an integral part of the container or shall be affixed as close as safely possible to the container by string, wire, adhesive, or other method that prevents their loss or unintentional removal.

(E) Red bags or red containers may be substituted for labels on containers of infectious waste.

(F) Containers of blood or blood components that are labeled as to their contents and have been released for distribution are exempted from the labeling requirements of paragraph (g).

(2) *Information and Training.* (i) Employers shall ensure that all employees with occupational exposure participate in a training program.

(ii) Training shall be provided at the time of initial employment or within 90 days after the effective date of this standard and at least annually thereafter.

(iii) Material appropriate in content and vocabulary to educational level, literacy, and language background of employees shall be used.

(iv) The training program shall contain the following elements:

(A) A copy of this standard and an explanation of its contents;

(B) A general explanation of the epidemiology and symptoms of bloodborne diseases;

(C) An explanation of the modes of transmission of bloodborne pathogens;

(D) An explanation of the employer's infection control program.

(E) An explanation of the appropriate methods for recognizing tasks and other activities that may involve exposure to blood and other potentially infectious materials;

(F) An explanation of the use and limitations of practices that will prevent or reduce exposure including appropriate engineering controls, work practices, and personal protective equipment;

(G) Information on the types, proper use, location, removal, handling, decontamination and/or disposal of personal protective equipment;

(H) An explanation of the basis for selection of personal protective equipment;

(I) Information on the hepatitis B vaccine, including information on its efficacy, safety, and the benefits of being vaccinated.

(J) Information on the appropriate actions to take and persons to contact in an emergency;

(K) An explanation of the procedure to follow if an exposure incident occurs, including the method of reporting the incident and the medical follow-up that will be made available. Also information on the medical counseling that the employer is providing for exposed individuals; and

(L) An explanation of the signs and labels and/or color coding required by paragraph (g)(1).

(v) Additional training. Employees in HIV or HBV research laboratories and HIV or HBV production facilities shall receive the following training in addition to the above training requirements:

(A) Employees shall be trained in and demonstrate proficiency in standard microbiological practices and techniques and in the practices and operations specific to the facility before being allowed to work with HIV or HBV.

(B) Employees shall be experienced in the handling of human pathogens or tissue cultures prior to working with HIV or HBV.

(C) A training program shall be provided to employees who have no prior experience in handling human pathogens. Initial work activities shall not include the handling of infectious agents. A progression of work activities shall be assigned as techniques are learned and proficiency is developed.

The employee shall participate in work activities involving infectious agents only after proficiency has been demonstrated.

(h) *Recordkeeping*—(1) *Medical records.* (i) The employer shall establish and maintain an accurate record for each employee subject to paragraph (f) of this section, in accordance with 29 CFR 1910.20.

(ii) This record shall include:

(A) The name and social security number of the employee;

(B) A copy of the employee's hepatitis B vaccination records and medical records relative to the employee's ability to receive vaccination or the circumstances of an exposure incident;

(C) A copy of all results of physical examinations, medical testing, and follow-up procedures as they relate to the employee's ability to receive vaccination or to post exposure evaluation following an exposure incident;

(D) The employer's copy of the physician's written opinion; and

(E) A copy of the information provided to the physician as required by paragraphs (f)(4).

(iii) Confidentiality. The employer shall assure that employee medical records required by paragraph (f) are:

(A) Kept confidential; and

(B) Are not disclosed or reported to any person within or outside the workplace except as required by this section or as may be required by law.

(iv) The employer shall maintain this record for at least the duration of employment plus 30 years in accordance with 29 CFR 1910.20.

(2) *Training Records.* (i) Training records shall include the following information:

(A) The dates of the training sessions;

(B) The contents or a summary of the training sessions;

(C) The names of persons conducting the training; and

(D) The names of all persons attending the training sessions.

(ii) These records shall be maintained for 5 years.

(3) *Availability.* (i) The employer shall assure that all records required to be maintained by this section shall be made available upon request to the Assistant Secretary and the Director for examination and copying.

(ii) Employee training records required by this paragraph shall be provided upon request for examination and copying to employees, employee representatives, and the Assistant Secretary in accordance with 29 CFR 1910.20.

(iii) Employee medical and training records required by this paragraph shall be provided upon request for examination and copying to the subject employee, to anyone having written consent of the subject employee, and to the Assistant Secretary in accordance with 29 CFR 1910.20.

(4) *Transfer of records.* (i) The employer shall comply with the requirements involving transfer of records set forth in 29 CFR 1910.20(h).

(ii) If the employer ceases to do business and there is no successor employer to receive and retain the records for the prescribed period, the employer shall notify the Director, at least three months prior to their disposal and transmit them to the Director if required by the Director to do so within that three month period.

(i) *Dates*—(1) Effective Date. The standard shall become effective on [Insert date 30 days after publication in the **Federal Register**].

(2) Exposure Determination. The exposure determination required by paragraph (c)(1) of this section shall be completed within 90 days of the effective date of this standard.

(3) Infection Control Plan. The Infection Control Plan required by paragraph (c)(2) of this section shall be completed within 120 days of the effective date of this standard.

(4) Paragraphs (d)(2) Engineering and Work Practice Controls, (d)(3) Personal Protective Equipment, (d)(4) Housekeeping, (e) HIV and HBV Research Laboratories and Production Facilities, (f) Hepatitis B Vaccination and Post-Exposure Follow-up, (g) Communication of Hazards to Employees, and (h) Recordkeeping shall take effect 150 days after the effective date of this standard. OSHA expects that the employer will have initiated, but perhaps not completed, the HBV vaccination series within this time period.

New Jersey Hospital Association
Princeton, New Jersey

Categories of Universal Precautions/Worker Protection/Barrier Protection

In order to protect health care workers from exposure to the unknown HIV-positive or Hepatitis-B patient as well as the diagnosed patient, a consistent approach is needed to manage blood, body fluids, or moist tissue from all patients. This approach, the primary component of universal precautions, should be utilized by all health care workers whether the patient is in the hospital setting or an emergency situation encountered by paramedics or the emergency department personnel.

Universal precautions require usage of barrier equipment to prevent contact with blood, body fluids, or moist tissue from any patient. The barrier equipment should be constructed in such a manner as to prevent moisture from penetrating the barrier and reaching the mucous membrane or skin of the health care worker. Barrier equipment includes:

- Gloves - vinyl, latex, heavy-duty rubberized, commercial household design
- Gowns - water-resistant paper or fabric
- Aprons - plastic, moisture-resistant paper, rubber (may be disposable)
- Masks - water and moisture resistant
- Goggles - shatterproof, fogless - able to go over prescription glasses' sides
- CPR (cardiopulmonary resuscitation) shields or masks

In their Joint Advisory Notice, the U.S. Departments of Labor, and Health and Human Services, emphasize universal precautions. Their approach supports categorizing the nature of all potential patient/health care worker contacts and protecting workers based upon the probability of direct contact with blood or body fluids. The key is categorization of contacts, not people. Thus, some people at different times during the workday may move among categories of tasks with varying exposures. They therefore will adjust their barrier protection in accordance with the duty being performed.

The tables which follow the text in this section are detailed listings of common hospital tasks, both those involving direct patient care and those which are more supportive or general in nature. Category I tasks are those which are likely to result in contact with blood or body fluids. Category II tasks are those which may produce such exposures unexpectedly. Category III tasks are highly unlikely to produce an exposure. The tables present information on barriers required, and they list examples of those personnel who are likely to be involved in each. In general, the quality of the barrier product is as important as the availability of that product. Having ample supplies of an item which does not protect employees adequately is pointless.

Guidelines for use of barrier equipment are summarized as follows:

- When there is contact with blood, body fluid, or moist tissue (for example, pus, feces, blood, urine, etc.) from any patient, gloves are worn.
- A gown is always required when suctioning; when there is any chance of a splash; and when inserting a central venous pressure line, or any catheterization procedure.

- When soilage of the uniform or clothing is likely or anticipated, a gown or apron is worn. As an example, an apron may be worn for routine wound dressing changes or incontinence bed changes.

- When aerosolization or splattering is likely, or anticipated, a mask covering the nose and mouth and goggles to protect the eyes are worn, in addition to gowning.

- If unanticipated contact of the health care worker's skin or mucous membrane occurs from blood, body fluids, or moist tissue of the patient, the exposed area should be washed as soon as possible. The health care worker should follow the protocol regarding exposure from his/her particular institution.

- Change standard design masks every 30 minutes to protect against barrier breakdown resulting from moisture of respiration.

Latex-type household gloves, such as "Playtex" brand, are suitable for protection in a variety of non-clinical tasks, including maintenance and housekeeping. Each employee should be issued his or her own pair since they are reuseable. In clinical areas, there should be a central, readily accessible stock of barrier equipment. In some areas, such as nursing units, multiple locations may be desirable. Hospitals may wish to consider using their infection control isolation carts for this purpose since universal precautions precludes the necessity for most types of isolation measures. Barrier equipment should be distributed through hospitals as widely as possible, particularly in non-clinical areas where Category I exposures may be unpredictable and not readily prepared for.

Particular attention should be paid to those persons engaged in Category II tasks. Protecting them against unexpected exposures may be difficult; and this requires some advance planning. As a minimum, all personnel who engage in Category II tasks should have gloves on their persons at all times. Gloves form the baseline as minimum protection for any task in Category I.

EXPOSURE CATEGORIES

Category I

TYPES OF BODY FLUIDS, BLOOD	BARRIER NEEDED	SAMPLES OF PROCEDURES	HEALTH CARE WORKERS
A. Oral/Pharyngeal Secretions Mouth Trachea Nares	1. Wash hands after contact 2. Gloves 3. Mask and goggles if aerosolization likely 4. Gowns if soilage of clothing is expected	Suctioning Oral/pharyngeal Endotracheal tubes Tracheostomies Intubation/Extubation Resuscitation Specimen obtaining and processing Oral examinations All dental procedures Tracheostomy care Handling linen or articles soiled with oral secretions	Physicians Nurses Nurses Aides/Orderlies Respiratory Therapists Laboratory Technicians Housekeepers Trash Handlers Linen Handlers Specimen Transporters Paramedics
B. Blood (from any site)	1. Wash hands after contact 2. Gloves 3. Mask and goggles if aerosolization or splattering likely 4. Gowns if soilage likely 5. Moisture-proof linen bags 6. Leak-proof trash bags	Venipunctures (any reason) Arterial punctures Processing specimens in Lab Hemodialysis (all patients) Transfusion therapy Central venous line access (including Swan-Ganz, etc.) Managing frank blood from wounds or drainage Serosanguineous wound drainage Irrigation of wounds Trauma wound care Delivery - Normal C-Section Handling of infant Blood, amniotic fluid Post-delivery care of umbilical cord	Physicians Nurses Nurses Aides/Orderlies Laboratory Technicians Respiratory Technicians Paramedics Radiology Technicians Housekeepers Linen Handlers Trash Handlers Departments: ER MICU Labor and Delivery Operating Room ICU/CCU Laboratory, etc Specimen Transporters

EXPOSURE CATEGORIES

Category I (continued)

TYPES OF BODY FLUIDS, BLOOD	BARRIER NEEDED	SAMPLES OF PROCEDURES	HEALTH CARE WORKERS
C. Urine Incontinency Fistula Catheters Specimen collection	1. Wash hands after contact 2. Gloves 3. Individual urine collection specimen containers 4. Closed urinary drainage system 5. Moisture resistant linen bags for soiled linen 6. Masks, goggles, gown, or aprons, if aerosolization splattering or soiling likely	Catheterization straight or foley Collecting/handling/ processing specimens Irrigation of catheters or ileoconduits Perineal care Toileting assistance Handling linen/articles soiled with urine	Nurses Nurses Aides/Orderlies Physicians Laboratory Technicians Housekeepers Linen Handlers Trash Handlers Specimen Transporters
D. Fecal Drainage Normal defecation Ostomy drainage Incontinency	1. Wash hands after contact 2. Gloves 3. Gown if soilage likely 4. Moisture-resistant linen bags	Administering enemas Incontinence care Ostomy care Diarrhea (all types) Gall bladder drainage (T. Tube) Rectal tubes - insertion and removal Toileting assistance Handling linen/articles contaminated with feces Rectal examination Performing barium enemas, VGI series X-rays	Physicians Nurses Nurses Aides/Orderlies Laboratory Technicians Housekeepers Linen Handlers Specimen Transporters X-Ray Technicians
E. Lesions or Wound Drainage ex. Traumatic Operative Necrotic Erosions	1. Wash hands after contact 2. Gloves 3. Mask, goggles, if aerosolization or splattering likely 4. Gown or apron if soilage likely 5. Moisture-resistant linen bags 6. Moisture-resistant bags for soiled dressings 7. Cover draining wound	Wound care Cleansing Irrigation (mask, gown and goggles at all times) Changing dressing (regardless of infective status) Handling linen/articles contaminated with drainage Bathing non-intact skin Wound examination	Physicians Nurses Nurses Aides/Orderlies Housekeepers Linen Handlers Trash Handlers

EXPOSURE CATEGORIES

Category I (continued)

TYPES OF BODY FLUIDS, BLOOD	BARRIER NEEDED	SAMPLES OF PROCEDURES	HEALTH CARE WORKERS
F. Other Body Fluids Moist tissue Cerebrospinal fluid Tears Peritoneal dialysis fluid Vaginal discharge Pleural fluid Abdominal fluid Vomitus/nasogastric tube drainage Tissues/organs Synovial (joint) fluid	1. Wash hands after contact 2. Gloves 3. Masks and goggles for aerosolization or splattering 4. Gowns/aprons if soilage likely 5. Secured specimens collection system	Peritoneal dialysis procedures Thoracentesis Paracentesis Vaginal exams Intracranial monitoring procedures Lumbar puncture Biopsies Bone marrow aspirations Organ procurement Arthroscopy Joint aspiration Handling specimens	Physicians Nurses Nurses Aides/Orderlies Laboratory Technicians Housekeepers Linen Handlers Trash Handlers Specimen Transporters
G. High Risk Procedures	Always Required: 1. Gloves 2. Masks 3. Goggles	Autopsies Surgery: Orthopedic procedures Heart surgery Vascular surgery Plumbing work on sewer systems (protective attire such as overalls) Handling/sorting soiled linen Management of trauma patients Bronchoscopy Endoscopy Contact with frank G.I. bleeding	All personnel in room Physicians Nurses Respiratory Therapists Technicians Perfusionists Nursing Attendants Plumbers/Assistants Housekeepers Linen Handlers

EXPOSURE CATEGORIES

Category II

TYPES OF BODY FLUIDS, BLOOD	BARRIER NEEDED	SAMPLES OF PROCEDURES	HEALTH CARE WORKERS
Tasks that involve no exposure to blood, body fluids, or tissues, but occupation may require performing unplanned Category I tasks.	Only if contact with blood or body fluids is required, use: 1. Gloves 2. Gowns/aprons, if soilage likely 3. Masks, if splashing, spraying, or aerosolization likely 4. Goggles, if splashing or spraying likely Otherwise, no barriers are needed.	Patient/family interviews, admission, counseling, etc.	Physicians Nurses Admitting Clerks Intake Clerks: E.R., Laboratory, Preadmission Testing, X-Ray, Chaplains, Social Workers, Dietitians, Therapists
		Patient transportation and transfers	Physicians Nurses Transporters Security Guards Volunteers
		Responding to emergencies involving combative persons	Physicians Nurses Security Guards Therapists Social Workers
		Delivering food trays/ collecting and handling food trays	Dietary Aides Dishwashers
		Handling soiled patient equipment	Central Service Personnel
		Performing routine physiotherapy	Physical Therapists
		Taking routine X-Rays and diagnostic tests	X-Ray Technicians Students EKG, Echo, Ultrasound, Noninvasive Testing

EXPOSURE CATEGORIES

Category II (continued)

TYPES OF BODY FLUIDS, BLOOD	BARRIER NEEDED	SAMPLES OF PROCEDURES	HEALTH CARE WORKERS
Tasks that involve no exposure to blood, body fluids, or tissues but occupation may require performing unplanned Category I tasks. (continued)	Only if contact with blood or body fluids is required, use: 1. Gloves 2. Gowns/aprons, if soilage likely 3. Masks, if splashing, spraying, or aerosolization likely 4. Goggles, if splashing or spraying likely Otherwise, no barriers are needed.	All nursing tasks not falling into Category I a. Bathing b. Dressing c. Feeding d. Ambulatory e. Routine assessments	Nurses
		Physical examinations excluding focused exams listed in Category I	Physicians Nurses
		Routine housekeeping in patient care areas	Housekeepers

EXPOSURE CATEGORIES

Category III

TYPES OF BODY FLUIDS, BLOOD	BARRIER NEEDED	HEALTH CARE WORKERS
Tasks that involve no exposure to blood or body fluids or tissues, and occupation does not require performing Category I tasks.	**No Barriers Needed**	1. Tasks routinely performed by: Cashiers Coffee Shop/Gift Shop Personnel Medical Records Clerks All Office Personnel e.g., Secretaries, Fiscal Staff, Personnel Staff Pharmacists Painters Electricians Information Desk Clerks Telephone Operators Library Personnel Purchasing Personnel Receiving Personnel Quality Assurance/Risk Management/Utilization Review Staff Volunteers 2. Routine maintenance: Maintenance Workers 3. Delivering clean laundry: Couriers 4. Delivering clean supplies: Couriers 5. Routine housekeeping, non-patient care areas: Housekeepers

Berks County Home/Berks Heim
Reading, Pennsylvania

Universal Precautions: Resident Care Index for Nursing and Therapies

Policy

This index identifies the minimum requirements for the implementation of Universal Precautions preventive measures (technique and equipment) for all routine nursing care of the resident. This list is not all-inclusive of resident care situations. Sterile technique is always used during sterile procedures. Other equipment may be required to protect the resident during certain procedures. Refer to the Berks Heim policy/procedure manual for any specific policy/procedure of nursing care.

When employees have open cuts or abrasions on their hands, they are responsible for protecting them through the use of gloves.

Purpose

- To prevent transmission of infectious agents from resident to health care worker to resident
- To prevent cross-contamination between residents
- To identify preventive measures and protective equipment of Universal Precautions in routine resident care.

Index

Legend: X = routinely; S = if soiling is likely; * = if splattering is likely.

	Hand Washing	Gloves	Plastic Aprons/ Gowns	Eye Protection	Mask
Transportation of residents	X				
Routine bath	X				
Cleanup of incontinent resident–urine	X				
Cleanup of incontinent resident–urine/feces	X				
Washing hair	X				
Shaving	X	S			
Hearing aid care	X				
Denture care	X				
Care of fingernails and toenails	X				
Changing of brief–urine	X				
Changing of brief–feces	X	X			
Sitz bath	X				
Enema	X	X	S		

(Table continues.)

	Hand Washing	Gloves	Plastic Aprons/ Gowns	Eye Protection	Mask
Emptying of Foley bag or urine receptacle, commode, bedpan, emesis basin	X				
Ketourine checks	X				
Ostomy care, teaching or irrigation	X	X	S		
Changing of visibly soiled beds–urine/feces	X	S	S		
Postmortem care	X	X	S		
Removal of fecal impaction	X	X	S		
Cleanup of blood spills or blood/body fluids	X	X			
Cleaning of surfaces soiled by blood/body fluids substances	X	S			
Emptying wastebaskets	X	S			
Vital signs–oral temperature, pulse, respiration, blood pressure	X				
Vital signs–rectal temperature	X	S			
Facial contact with residents with frequent and forceful coughing	X				*
Feeding resident	X				
Traction	X				
Collection of specimens–urine, stool, sputum, wound tissue, wound drainage	X	S	S		
Handling specimen containers	X				
Handling soiled equipment	X				
Starting an I.V. cannula	X	X			
Discontinuing an I.V. cannula	X	X			
I.V. tubing changes at the hub	X	X			

	Hand Washing	Gloves	Plastic Aprons/ Gowns	Eye Protection	Mask
Giving oral medications	X	X			
Giving intramuscular injections	X				
Application of eye ointments/meds	X	X (finger cots)			
Application of topical ointments to wounds	X	X			
I.V. piggyback medications	X				
I.V. direct or into the hub at catheter	X	X			
Inserting rectal suppository	X	X			
Inserting vaginal suppository	X	X			
Tube feeding to nasogastric tube or gastrostomy tube	X				
Applying pressure to control bleeding	X	X	S	*	
Oral exam	X	S			
Special mouth care	X	S			
Endotracheal suctioning	X	X	S	X	
Tracheostomy care	X	X	S	*	
Induced sputum specimen	X	S			
Oral suctioning–oral or nasal care	X	X	S	*	
Nasotracheal suctioning	X	X	S	X	
Placing oxygen mask or cannula	X				
Insertion of nasogastric tube	X	X	S		
Gastric lavage	X	X	S		
Vaginal irrigation	X	X	S		
Foley catheter insertion	X	X			
Foley catheter irrigation	X	S			
Foley catheter placement in rectum for fecal incontinence	X	X	S		

(Table continues.)

	Hand Washing	Gloves	Plastic Aprons/ Gowns	Eye Protection	Mask
Dressing changes and removal	X	X	S		
Wound care, routine	X	X	S		
Dressing changes/wounds with large amount of drainage	X	X	S		
Wound irrigation	X	X	S	*	
Wound packing or removal of packing	X	X	S		
Wound abscess irrigation and drainage	X	X	S	*	
Changing of Pleur-evac®	X	X	S		
Suture/staple removal	X	S	S		
Oxygen setup	X				
Spirometry	X				
Postural drainage	X	S	S		
Breathing treatment	X				
Ear oximetry	X				

North Carolina Memorial Hospital
Chapel Hill, North Carolina

Universal Blood and Body Fluid Precautions: Examples of Procedures and Required Protective Wear

Procedure	Gloves		Mask/ Eyewear	Apron/ Gown
	Nonsterile	Sterile		
Administration of medications (oral)				
Arterial blood gases (collection/processing)	X			
Arteriovenous access (initiating hemodialysis)*		X	If splashing is likely	If soiling is likely
Aspiration of urine from Foley				
Autolets® (fingerstick)	X			
Autopsy	X		X	X
Barium enema	X			If soiling is likely
Biopsy (percutaneous)*–bone, liver, skin, cervix		X		
Bleeding time	X			
Blood pressure				
Bladder irrigation (emptying solution)	X			
Bone marrow collection		X	If splashing is likely	
Bronchoscopy (performing)	X		X	X
Calibration of body-fluid-contaminated equipment (e.g., Medical Engineering)	X			
Central lines:* Broviac, umbilical artery, inserting Swanz-Ganz, Hickman, CVP, subclavian, triple lumen		X	X	X
Changing diapers	If soiling is likely			
Chemstrips®	X			
Clean catch urine	X			
Cleaning blood spills	X			If soiling is likely

(Table continues.)

Procedure	Gloves		Mask/ Eyewear	Apron/ Gown
	Nonsterile	Sterile		
Cleaning patient equipment	X		If splashing is likely	If soiling is likely
Condom catheters (placement)	X			
Colostomy care	X			If soiling is likely
Decubitus care	X			
Delivering patient food				
Diabetic urine	X			
Dialysis–peritoneal (discarding fluid)	X		If splashing is likely	If soiling is likely
Dressing–wet (not fresh wound), wet to dry*, changing of		X		
Endotracheal suctioning		X	If splashing is likely	If soiling is likely
Enemas	X			If soiling is likely
Environmental cleaning (mopping, vacuuming) (excludes exposure to toxic chemicals)				
Environmental cleaning in patient care areas (removal of trash liner from patient care area)	X			
Feeding infants (tube, bottle)				
Foley catheters (perineal care)	X			
Gastrostomy feeding				
Guaiac stool specimen	X			
Heparin lock (inserting, drawing blood, removing)	X			
Injections–intramuscular, subcutaneous				
Intraaortic balloon pump*		X	If splashing is likely	If soiling is likely
Intravenous therapy-insertion, site care	X			
I.V. piggyback medications				
Lumbar puncture*		X		
Minnesota four lumen				
Mouth care	X			

Procedure	Gloves Nonsterile	Gloves Sterile	Mask/ Eyewear	Apron/ Gown
Nasogastric tube–irrigation and removal	X		If splashing is likely	If soiling is likely
Pin care (orthopedic)	X			
Postmortem care	X		If splashing is likely	X
Postural drainage				
Rectal medications	X			
Removing linen contaminated with body fluid	X			If soiling is likely
Removing noncontaminated linen				
Repairing clogged sinks/toilets–maintenance	X		If splashing is likely	If soiling is likely
Sigmoidoscopy	X		X	X
Specific gravity of urine	X			
Specimen handling (contact with blood and body fluids)	X			
Tanking patients with open wounds	X		If splashing is likely	If soiling is likely
Temperatures–rectal	X			
Tracheal aspirate	X		If splashing is likely	If soiling is likely
Tracheostomy care (routine care)	X		If splashing is likely	If soiling is likely
Tube feeding				
Venipuncture	X			
Wound cleaning (fresh operative wound)*–irrigation, packing		X	If splashing is likely	If soiling is likely
Wound suction–emptying	X			

*These guidelines pertain to personnel protection only. Aseptic technique and isolation precautions (i.e., gown, glove, mask, draping) may need to be followed according to the procedure. Hand washing should always be done before and after direct patient contact.

Yale-New Haven Hospital
New Haven, Connecticut

Task Classification and Recommended Barriers for Rehabilitation Services

Classification of Departmental Tasks by Risk of Exposure to Blood and Body Fluids

Category I Position Titles

- Director
- Supervisor
- Senior physical therapist
- Senior occupational therapist
- Staff physical therapist
- Staff occupational therapist
- Rehabilitation aide

Category II Position Title

- Receptionist

Category III Position Title

- Secretary

Procedure

1. General
   a. Avoid accidental contact by anticipating the course of treatment.
   b. Clean blood spills promptly with a phenolic solution or a 10 percent bleach solution (for example, on equipment).
   c. Utilize the Eagleguard® system for all sharps. Do not attempt to recap needles or remove blades from scalpels.
   d. Hands shall be washed before and after contact with all patients. If hands or other skin surfaces come in contact with blood or other body fluids, they shall be washed immediately with soap and water.
   e. If the staff member has an exudative lesion or weeping dermatitis, they shall notify a supervisor.
2. Tasks with probable exposure to blood and body fluids: These tasks require the routine use of hand washing and barrier protection. See figure 8-1 for a complete list of activities and recommended levels of barrier protection.
3. Tasks with unlikely exposure to blood and body fluids: These tasks do not require the routine use of barrier protection. Hand washing is recommended for these tasks as part of good hygiene. See figure 8-2 for a complete list of activities.

Figure 8-1. Tasks That Routinely Involve Exposure to Blood, Body Fluids, and Tissues

The tasks listed below include the minimum requirements necessary to provide appropriate protection against skin, mucous membrane, or respiratory transmission of contagious microorganisms and to ensure the routine practice of good hygiene. Additional barrier protection may be required for less-controlled situations. Good judgment is required.

Legend: X = use routinely; * = use if soiling or splattering is likely.

Activity	Hand Washing	Gloves	Gown/ Plastic Apron	Mask	Eye Protection
Taking quantitative culture samples	X	X	*	*	*
Dressing removal/wound care	X	X	*	*	*
Transferring patients (e.g., bed to stretcher, etc.)	X	*	*		
Performing exercise programs with patients	X	*	*		
Gait training/ambulating patients using contact guarding techniques	X	*	*		
Cleanup of incontinent patients	X	X	*		
Cleanup of spills of blood, body fluids, or tissues	X	X			
Direct contact with patients with frequent, forceful coughing	X			X	*
Taking vital signs	X				
Changing soiled linens	X	X	*		
Cleaning surfaces contaminated by blood, body fluids, or tissues	X	X			
Cleaning equipment used in patient care (e.g., walkers)	X	X			
Setting up sterile fields and instruments	X				
Cleaning contaminated fields and instruments	X	X			
Cleaning whirlpools	X	X			
Emptying wastebaskets in patient areas	X	X			
Splinting	X	*			

Figure 8-2. Tasks That Do Not Routinely Involve Exposure to Blood, Body Fluids, and Tissues

The tasks listed below include the minimum requirements necessary to provide appropriate protection against skin, mucous membrane, or respiratory transmission of contagious microorganisms and to ensure the routine practice of good hygiene. Additional barrier protection may be required for less-controlled situations. Good judgment is required.

Legend: X = use routinely; * = use if soiling or splattering is likely.

Activity	Hand Washing	Gloves	Gown/ Plastic Apron	Mask	Eye Protection
Answering telephone	X				
Greeting/directing patients	X				
Emptying wastebaskets in office areas	X				
Clerical/secretarial activities	X				
Putting supplies in storeroom	X				

Chapter 9

Discussion of Viewpoints

Introduction

The sample policies and procedures in this manual represent diverse and sometimes conflicting viewpoints on particular issues. These differences are, in part, a result of the continuous evolution of the practice of infection prevention and control in health care facilities.

Ideally, infection prevention and control practices should be based on rigorously controlled scientific studies that demonstrate the practices' efficacy. However, not all practices are supported by definitive studies but instead may have been adopted because of a strong theoretical rationale or because they are considered effective by the majority of experts in the field. In addition, even scientifically valid practices may not be applicable or practical in all settings and may need to be adapted for various settings. Such adaptations often require that it be decided which practices best suit a particular facility's needs and resources or the methods of individual practitioners. For example, the application of Universal Precautions practices depends on the judgment of health care workers in specific situations.

This chapter provides brief commentary on a number of concepts, terms, and practices mentioned in the sample materials in this manual but for which there may be insufficient scientific background

Use of Personal Protective Apparel

In general, the purpose of using protective apparel such as masks, gowns, and gloves in health care settings has been to protect patients from nosocomial infection. Only recently has attention focused on protecting health care workers from bloodborne infections. Very little information exists to support the efficacy of the various items of protective apparel in actually preventing infections from specific bloodborne pathogens or biological agents in general. The complexity of the factors related to disease transmission and the wide range of performance capabilities among health care workers have made verifying such information difficult.

Much of the data that are currently available on performance and use criteria, as well as efficacy, apply to industrial workplace exposures to chemical and physical hazards but do not apply directly to exposures to biological agents in health care settings. Although the published performance standards, requirements, and specifications for protective apparel are not all directly applicable to health care settings, they do provide information on existing criteria that can be used as a basis for evaluating the efficacy of protective apparel used in health care settings. (A list of the organizations and agencies that have developed standards is included in the references at the end of this chapter.)

In general, the use of protective apparel should reduce the risk of exposure to bloodborne pathogens. The selection of appropriate apparel is determined by the health care worker's clinical situation. The selection usually depends on the following factors: (1) the probability of exposure to blood and body fluids, (2) the type of body fluid involved, (3) the amount of blood or body fluids likely to be encountered, and (4) the probable route of transmission.

Masks and Protective Eyewear

Surgical face masks have commonly been used to protect health care workers caring for patients infected with communicable diseases caused by airborne pathogens. However, surgical face masks were *not* designed to protect the wearer from external airborne hazards. Rather, they were designed to reduce the shedding of microorganisms from the surgical team into the operative field and so prevent wound contamination. There is little information on the ability of masks to prevent the passage of body fluids or biological agents from the patient through the mask to the wearer. It is believed that much of the migration of microorganisms from the surgical team to the patient occurs around the outside of the masks rather than through the masks. Surgical masks also have a varied range of filtration performance, from very high to very low, and there are no minimum performance requirements.

Masks are likely to reduce the risk of exposing the mucous membranes of the mouth and nose to splashed body fluids. However, masks probably offer little protection to susceptible workers caring for patients with viral infections transmitted via the respiratory route. For this reason, the Centers for Disease Control (CDC) recommends that for diseases for which immunity offers the only protection, such as varicella (chickenpox) and rubeola (measles), susceptible persons stay out of the rooms of infected patients. Masks need not be worn by health care workers and visitors who are immune to such diseases.

Protective eyewear includes face shields, goggles, and safety glasses with and without side shields. No information exists on performance criteria for the use of eye protection against infection by biological agents. The combination of masks and protective eyewear or the use of face shields is likely to reduce the risk of contaminating the mucous membranes of the eyes, nose, and mouth by splashing or spraying of blood and body fluids. Masks and protective eyewear should be selected on the basis of the clinical situation, including the potential for splashing or spraying of blood or body fluids, and the level of visibility required in specific clinical situations.

Gloves

In health care settings, gloves are worn by health care workers to protect patients from organisms on the hands of care givers as well as to protect the care giver's hands from exposure to blood and body fluids. The integrity of the skin appears to be an important factor in preventing transmission of bloodborne diseases. Gloves offer an extra layer of protection for the intact and nonintact skin of the wearer and the patient. In general, gloves should be changed between patient contacts to ensure that infectious agents are not carried from patient to patient on the hands of health care workers.

Because detergents and disinfecting agents may cause gloves to deteriorate, surgical or examination gloves should not be washed or disinfected for reuse.

Gloves cannot protect health care workers from injuries caused by needles and other sharp instruments. Some health care facilities do not require that gloves be worn for performing phlebotomy. Phlebotomists argue that exposure to blood is minimal during phlebotomy and that gloves reduce their manual dexterity and increase their risk for needlestick injuries. The CDC recognizes that the likelihood of hand contamination with blood depends on several factors, including the skill and technique of the phlebotomist and the type of procedure. As of 1988, the CDC recommends that gloves should be worn under the following conditions: (1) when health care workers are being trained in phlebotomy, (2) when health care workers have cuts, scratches, or other breaks in the skin, (3) when hand contamination is likely, for example, when health care workers perform phlebotomy on uncooperative patients, and (4) when health care workers perform fingersticks and/or heelsticks on infants and children.

The Occupational Safety and Health Administration (OSHA), however, is currently (1990) proposing that gloves be required for all procedures involving exposure to blood, including phlebotomy, and that the concern for "gloves increasing the risk of personal safety of the worker cannot be a basis for an exemption." It is not known whether OSHA will change this requirement in the final standard on exposure to bloodborne pathogens.

There are no reported differences in the barrier effectiveness between intact latex and intact vinyl gloves. Thus, the type of gloves selected should be appropriate for the task being performed. Sterile gloves are needed for procedures involving contact with areas of the body that are usually sterile. The use of nonsterile examination gloves is indicated for procedures involving contact with mucous membranes, nonintact skin, blood, body fluids, body substances, or items soiled with blood, body fluids, or body substances.

Gloves should be changed when torn or when a needlestick or other injury occurs as well as after each patient contact and before administering care to another patient. To protect patients, gloves may also need to be changed during the care of an individual patient to prevent nosocomial infections caused by the patient's own endogenous flora. That is, gloves should be changed after contact with a contaminated site (for example, an infected wound) and before contact with a clean site (for example, an intravascular insertion site) on the same patient. Health care workers should wash their hands immediately after they remove their gloves and before they put on clean gloves.

Gowns and Other Protective Clothing

Protective clothing includes gowns, aprons, lab coats, and other clothing. The use of surgical gowns and drapes that are designed to serve as a protective barrier has been advocated for more than three decades to prevent contamination of the operative field. However, no specific type of barrier material has yet been clearly shown to be more effective than others in reducing the risk of surgical wound infection.

Only recently has attention been paid to the use of clothing in protecting health care workers from disease. Few data exist on the efficacy of protective apparel in reducing the risk of exposure and infection from biological agents and, in particular, from bloodborne pathogens. Protective clothing is made of a wide variety of materials that provide a range of capabilities to resist the passage of microorganisms and fluids. These materials include both reusable "woven" fabrics and a variety of "nonwoven" disposable materials. Currently, no accepted performance standards are in place for testing the capability of specific materials to resist the penetration or permeation of body fluids or biological agents. The user must rely primarily on test data supplied by individual manufacturers for their products. Terms such as *barrier, impervious, fluid resistant,* and *fluid proof* are used to describe clothing designed to prevent exposure to body fluids. These terms, however, have never been precisely defined, and no minimum performance or use criteria are available.

In the absence of data to support the use or selection of a particular type of protective apparel, the wearer must choose the appropriate apparel on the basis of the area of the body to be protected, the amount and type of body fluids likely to be encountered, and the probability that exposed skin will be contaminated and clothing will be soiled. For example, an apron that covers the front of the uniform may be all that is needed for routine bedside patient care procedures. Lab coats and cover gowns are also commonly worn to prevent the soiling of the uniforms or street clothes underneath. For procedures that involve considerable splashing of blood or body fluids, such as surgical, trauma, or delivery procedures, clothing that provides an effective barrier is necessary, according to the CDC's recommendations (1987).

According to OSHA's proposed standard on bloodborne pathogens (1989), the type and characteristics of protective clothing "will depend on the tasks and degree of anticipated exposure." This statement appears to allow some decision making on the part of the facility and the individual health care worker. However, OSHA also specifies that "fluid-resistant gowns" are to be worn when there is a potential for splashing or spraying and that "fluid-proof gowns" are to be worn when there is a potential for clothing to become soaked. It is not known how health care facilities will be expected to comply with these standards in the absence of recognized criteria to determine the fluid-resistant and fluid-proof capabilities of protective apparel.

Use of the Term *Impervious*

The term *impervious* implies that an object or material has the ability to stop the passage or entrance of other materials. It is used in the sample policies in this manual to describe containers, bags, and protective clothing. The term is often used interchangeably with *leak proof, leak resistant, moisture proof,* and *nonpermeable.* However, these terms are sometimes used incorrectly to describe particular items, and the result may be that supplies are used inappropriately and in violation of a facility's stated policies and procedures. For example, most needle boxes are not impervious or puncture proof but instead should be called puncture resistant. Although it is not impervious, a densely woven cloth laundry bag does resist the passage of body fluids from soiled linen through other linens in the laundry. To state that an "impervious laundry bag" should be used implies that the laundry bag is to be made of plastic, although that may not have been what the policy was intended to require. In developing policies and procedures, it may be prudent to specify the precise container or barrier that should be used, such as a plastic trash bag, a cloth laundry bag, a hard plastic needle box, a reusable woven gown, a disposable gown, or a plastic apron.

Use of Biohazard Labeling

The adoption of Universal Precautions theoretically eliminates the need to identify patients known to be infected with bloodborne pathogens or their laboratory specimens. Some facilities, however, have chosen to continue identifying patients with diagnosed or suspected bloodborne infections by posting the Blood and Body Fluid Precaution signs on patients' doors without identifying the specific type of infection. Some facilities have continued to label the laboratory specimens of patients known to be infected with bloodborne pathogens in addition to practicing Universal Precautions techniques for all specimens. Those facilities that do not advocate the labeling of patients and their specimens believe that the identification of known or suspected patients or specimens will result in health care workers having a false sense of security and in their not following Universal Precautions as rigorously when they come into contact with patients or specimens that are not labeled.

The Occupational Safety and Health Administration has proposed requiring the use of specific biohazard tags to identify objects and equipment, including soiled laundry, that are contaminated with blood or body fluids. It is not known whether OSHA will recognize other identification methods, such as the use of color-coded bags. Whatever method is used to identify biological hazards, all personnel must be trained to recognize such hazards and follow appropriate procedures.

Use of Disinfection

Several policies in the manual state that "high-level disinfection" is to be used for furniture and environmental surfaces. High-level disinfection is usually necessary only for patient care equipment that touches mucous membranes. Routine cleaning of horizontal surfaces such as bedside tables and floors is usually done with a general disinfectant– detergent formulation registered with the Environmental Protection Agency (EPA). The actual physical removal of microorganisms by scrubbing is at least as important as, if not more important than, any antimicrobial effect of the cleaning agent. According to the CDC (1987), housekeeping procedures do not need to be changed because of concerns about contamination with human immunodeficiency virus or hepatitis B virus.

Therefore, if the facility is using an EPA-registered disinfectant–detergent for general housekeeping, its use can be continued. For cleaning and decontamination of large blood spills, the CDC (1987) recommends the use of one of the chemical germicides that are approved for use as a hospital disinfectant and are tuberculocidal when used as recommended. This is a special protocol applicable specifically to sites within the health care facility that have become significantly contaminated with blood. The CDC does not recommend specific commercial products but instead uses the EPA's system of classification for label claim registration, for example, a hospital disinfectant with a claim of tuberculocidal activity.

Use of Needle Recapping

Several of the policies in this manual state that used needles are never to be recapped. However, some procedures may require that needles be recapped, for example, vacuum collection systems for blood specimens, blood gas syringes, needles that must be carried through a crowded room, and a single syringe of medication administered in a series. Strictly speaking, the personnel performing such procedures would be in violation of their facility's policy. It is useful for policies and procedures to describe safe recapping techniques to be followed in those specific situations when recapping is necessary. In addition, there are a variety of new products on the market that reduce the need to recap used needles and that provide a safer design for recapping to eliminate the risk of injury.

Bagging of Specimens

Some facilities advocate bagging or double-bagging specimens for transport, some dictating the use of Ziploc® plastic bags. The important consideration is choosing a primary specimen container that is sturdy and leak proof, with a secure lid to prevent leaking during transport. Care should be taken when collecting and handling specimens to avoid contaminating the outside of the container and the laboratory requisition accompanying the specimen. When the primary container does leak, a secondary container or bag should be used, and the requisition should be placed on the outside of the secondary container. It should be noted that some specimen containers, such as urine cups, may be more likely to tip over and spill when they are in placed in plastic bags. In addition, the routine use of secondary bags is costly and may be unnecessary.

Use of Covered Linen Hampers and Trash Containers

Covers on linen hampers and trash containers are often mandated by state and local regulations. Historically, it was believed that trash and soiled linen could present an airborne infection hazard and that covers would reduce this perceived risk. However, there is no scientific evidence that open hampers and trash containers are a health hazard, and the practice of routinely using covers on bedside linen and trash containers does not reduce the risk of infection and only adds unnecessary expense. Facilities should consult their local and state regulations for specific requirements dictating the use of covered containers for medical waste during transport and disposal and additional fire hazard requirements.

☐ References

Publications

Centers for Disease Control. Recommendations for prevention of HIV transmission in health-care settings. *Morbidity and Mortality Weekly Report* Supplement 36(2S):3S–18S, Aug. 21, 1987.

Centers for Disease Control. Update: Universal Precautions for prevention of transmission of human immunodeficiency virus, hepatitis B virus, and other bloodborne pathogens in health-care settings. *Morbidity and Mortality Weekly Report* 37:377–88, June 24, 1988.

Department of Labor/Occupational Safety and Health Administration. Occupational exposure to bloodborne pathogens: proposed rule and notice of hearing. *Federal Register* 54(102):23042–139, May 30, 1989.

Garner, J. S., and Favero, M. S. *Guideline for Handwashing and Hospital Environmental Control.* Publication No. 99-1117. Atlanta: Centers for Disease Control, 1985.

Garner, J. S., and Simmons, B. P. Guidelines for isolation precautions in hospitals. *Infection Control* 4(Suppl.):245–326, 1983.

Northwest Center for Occupational Health and Safety, University of Washington. AIDS and personal protective equipment: report of a workshop. Seattle, May 17–18, 1989.

Organizations and Agencies with Consensus Standards and Regulations for Selection, Testing, and Use of Personal Protective Equipment

American Conference of Governmental Industrial Hygienists (ACGIH), 6500 Glenway Avenue, Building D-7, Cincinnati, OH 45211—Guidelines for the selection of chemical-protective clothing.

American National Standards Institute (ANSI), 1430 Broadway, New York, NY 10018—Standards on respiratory protection practices.

American Society for Testing and Materials (ASTM), 1916 Race Street, Philadelphia, PA 19103—Test methods and standards and specifications for protective barriers and equipment.

National Institute of Occupational Safety and Health (NIOSH), Centers for Disease Control, Atlanta, GA 30333—Standards and guidelines for industrial respiratory protection devices.

Occupational Safety and Health Administration. Code of Federal Regulations (CFR): 29 CFR 1910.132 July 1987—General industry standards: general requirements under OSHA regulations for personal protective equipment (PPE).

Chapter 10

Resources

Introduction

In many small health care facilities that do not have extensive medical libraries, it is often difficult to obtain reference materials. Therefore, for the reader's convenience, a number of key reference articles are reprinted in this chapter, including the Centers for Disease Control's (CDC's) guidelines on Universal Precautions, recommendations from the CDC's Immunization Practices Advisory Committee on protection against viral hepatitis, as well as articles on Body Substance Isolation and linen handling. Also included are an annotated list of audiovisual materials on Universal Precautions; sample posters, pocket cards, brochures, and wall signs developed for employees by hospitals and associations; and a list of selected references on infection control.

Centers for Disease Control
Atlanta, Georgia

Update: Universal Precautions for Prevention of Transmission of Human Immunodeficiency Virus, Hepatitis B Virus, and Other Bloodborne Pathogens in Health-Care Settings [Reprinted from *Morbidity and Mortality Weekly Report* 37(24):378–88, June 24, 1988]

Introduction

The purpose of this report is to clarify and supplement the CDC publication entitled "Recommendations for Prevention of HIV Transmission in Health-Care Settings" (*1*).*

In 1983, CDC published a document entitled "Guideline for Isolation Precautions in Hospitals" (*2*) that contained a section entitled "Blood and Body Fluid Precautions." The recommendations in this section called for blood and body fluid precautions when a patient was known or suspected to be infected with bloodborne pathogens. In August 1987, CDC published a document entitled "Recommendations for Prevention of HIV Transmission in Health-Care Settings" (*1*). In contrast to the 1983 document, the 1987 document recommended that blood and body fluid precautions be consistently used for all patients regardless of their bloodborne infection status. This extension of blood and body fluid precautions to **all** patients is referred to as "Universal Blood and Body Fluid Precautions" or "Universal Precautions." Under universal precautions, blood and certain body fluids of all patients are considered potentially infectious for human immunodeficiency virus (HIV), hepatitis B virus (HBV), and other bloodborne pathogens.

*The August 1987 publication should be consulted for general information and specific recommendations not addressed in this update.

Universal precautions are intended to prevent parenteral, mucous membrane, and nonintact skin exposures of health-care workers to bloodborne pathogens. In addition, immunization with HBV vaccine is recommended as an important adjunct to universal precautions for health-care workers who have exposures to blood (*3,4*).

Since the recommendations for universal precautions were published in August 1987, CDC and the Food and Drug Administration (FDA) have received requests for clarification of the following issues: 1) body fluids to which universal precautions apply, 2) use of protective barriers, 3) use of gloves for phlebotomy, 4) selection of gloves for use while observing universal precautions, and 5) need for making changes in waste management programs as a result of adopting universal precautions.

Body Fluids to Which Universal Precautions Apply

Universal precautions apply to blood and to other body fluids containing visible blood. Occupational transmission of HIV and HBV to health-care workers by blood is documented (*4,5*). **Blood is the single most important source of HIV, HBV, and other bloodborne pathogens in the occupational setting. Infection control efforts for HIV, HBV, and other bloodborne pathogens must focus on preventing exposures to blood as well as on delivery of HBV immunization.**

Universal precautions also apply to semen and vaginal secretions. Although both of these fluids have been implicated in the sexual transmission of HIV and HBV, they have not been implicated in occupational transmission from patient to health-care worker. This observation is not unexpected, since exposure to semen in the usual health-care setting is limited, and the routine practice of wearing gloves for performing vaginal examinations protects health-care workers from exposure to potentially infectious vaginal secretions.

Universal precautions also apply to tissues and to the following fluids: cerebrospinal fluid (CSF), synovial fluid, pleural fluid, peritoneal fluid, pericardial fluid, and amniotic fluid. The risk of transmission of HIV and HBV from these fluids is unknown; epidemiologic studies in the health-care and community setting are currently inadequate to assess the potential risk to health-care workers from occupational exposures to them. However, HIV has been isolated from CSF, synovial, and amniotic fluid (*6–8*), and HBsAg has been detected in synovial fluid, amniotic fluid, and peritoneal fluid (*9–11*). One case of HIV transmission was reported after a percutaneous exposure to bloody pleural fluid obtained by needle aspiration (*12*). Whereas aseptic procedures used to obtain these fluids for diagnostic or therapeutic purposes protect health-care workers from skin exposures, they cannot prevent penetrating injuries due to contaminated needles or other sharp instruments.

Body Fluids to Which Universal Precautions Do Not Apply

Universal precautions do not apply to feces, nasal secretions, sputum, sweat, tears, urine, and vomitus unless they contain visible blood. The risk of transmission of HIV and HBV from these fluids and materials is extremely low or nonexistent. HIV has been isolated and HBsAg has been demonstrated in some of these fluids; however, epidemiologic studies in the health-care and community setting have not implicated these fluids or materials in the transmission of HIV and HBV infections (*13,14*). Some of the above fluids and excretions represent a potential source for nosocomial and community-acquired infections with other pathogens, and recommendations for preventing the transmission of nonbloodborne pathogens have been published (*2*).

Precautions for Other Body Fluids in Special Settings

Human breast milk has been implicated in perinatal transmission of HIV, and HBsAg has been found in the milk of mothers infected with HBV (*10,13*). However, occupational exposure to human breast milk has not been implicated in the transmission of HIV nor HBV infection to health-care workers. Moreover, the health-care worker will not have the same type of intensive exposure to breast milk as the nursing neonate. Whereas universal precautions do not apply to human breast milk, gloves may be worn by health-care workers in situations where exposures to breast milk might be frequent, for example, in breast milk banking.

Saliva of some persons infected with HBV has been shown to contain HBV-DNA at concentrations 1/1,000 to 1/10,000 of that found in the infected person's serum (*15*). HBsAg-positive saliva has been shown to be infectious when injected into experimental animals and in human bite exposures (*16–18*). However, HBsAg-positive saliva has not been shown to be infectious when applied to oral mucous membranes in experimental primate studies (*18*) or through contamination of musical instruments or cardiopulmonary resuscitation dummies used by HBV carriers (*19,20*). Epidemiologic studies of nonsexual household contacts of HIV-infected patients, including several small series in which HIV transmission failed to occur after bites or after percutaneous inoculation or contamination of cuts and open wounds with saliva from HIV-infected patients, suggest that the potential for salivary transmission of HIV is remote (*5,13,14,21,22*). One case report from Germany has suggested the possibility of transmission of HIV in a household setting from an infected child to a sibling through a human bite (*23*). The bite did not break the skin or result in bleeding. Since the date of seroconversion to HIV was not known for either child in this case, evidence for the role of saliva in the transmission of virus is unclear (*23*). Another case report suggested the possibility of transmission of HIV from husband to wife by contact with saliva during kissing (*24*). However, follow-up studies did not confirm HIV infection in the wife (*21*).

Universal precautions do not apply to saliva. General infection control practices already in existence – including the use of gloves for digital examination of mucous membranes and endotracheal suctioning, and handwashing after exposure to saliva – should further minimize the minute risk, if any, for salivary transmission of HIV and HBV (*1,25*). Gloves need not be worn when feeding patients and when wiping saliva from skin.

Special precautions, however, are recommended for dentistry (*1*). Occupationally acquired infection with HBV in dental workers has been documented (*4*), and two possible cases of occupationally acquired HIV infection involving dentists have been reported (*5,26*). During dental procedures, contamination of saliva with blood is predictable, trauma to health-care workers' hands is common, and blood spattering may occur. Infection control precautions for dentistry minimize the potential for nonintact skin and mucous membrane contact of dental health-care workers to blood-contaminated saliva of patients. In addition, the use of gloves for oral examinations and treatment in the dental setting may also protect the patient's oral mucous membranes from exposures to blood, which may occur from breaks in the skin of dental workers' hands.

Use of Protective Barriers

Protective barriers reduce the risk of exposure of the health-care worker's skin or mucous membranes to potentially infective materials. For universal precautions, protective barriers reduce the risk of exposure to blood, body fluids containing visible blood, and other fluids to which universal precautions apply. Examples of protective barriers include gloves, gowns, masks, and protective eyewear. Gloves should reduce the incidence of contamination of hands, but they cannot prevent penetrating injuries due to needles or other sharp instruments. Masks and protective eyewear or face shields should reduce the incidence of contamination of mucous membranes of the mouth, nose, and eyes.

Universal precautions are intended to supplement rather than replace recommendations for routine infection control, such as handwashing and using gloves to prevent gross microbial contamination of hands (*27*). Because specifying the types of barriers needed for every possible clinical situation is impractical, some judgment must be exercised.

The risk of nosocomial transmission of HIV, HBV, and other bloodborne pathogens can be minimized if health-care workers use the following general guidelines:[†]

1. Take care to prevent injuries when using needles, scalpels, and other sharp instruments or devices; when handling sharp instruments after procedures; when cleaning used instruments; and when disposing of used needles. Do not recap used needles by hand; do not remove used needles from disposable syringes by hand; and do not bend, break, or otherwise manipulate used needles by hand. Place used disposable syringes and needles, scalpel blades, and other sharp items in puncture-resistant containers for disposal. Locate the puncture-resistant containers as close to the use area as is practical.
2. Use protective barriers to prevent exposure to blood, body fluids containing visible blood, and other fluids to which universal precautions apply. The type of protective barrier(s) should be appropriate for the procedure being performed and the type of exposure anticipated.
3. Immediately and thoroughly wash hands and other skin surfaces that are contaminated with blood, body fluids containing visible blood, or other body fluids to which universal precautions apply.

Glove Use for Phlebotomy

Gloves should reduce the incidence of blood contamination of hands during phlebotomy (drawing blood samples), but they cannot prevent penetrating injuries caused by needles or other sharp instruments. The likelihood of hand contamination with blood containing HIV, HBV, or other bloodborne pathogens during phlebotomy depends on several factors: 1) the skill and technique of the health-care worker, 2) the frequency with which the health-care worker performs the procedure (other factors being equal, the cumulative risk of blood exposure is higher for a health-care worker who performs more procedures), 3) whether the procedure occurs in a routine or emergency situation (where blood contact may be more likely), and 4) the prevalence of infection with bloodborne pathogens in the patient population. The likelihood of infection after skin exposure to blood containing HIV or HBV will depend on the concentration of virus (viral concentration is much higher for hepatitis B than for HIV), the duration of contact, the presence of skin lesions on the hands of the health-care worker, and – for HBV – the immune status of the health-care worker. Although not accurately quantified, the risk of HIV infection following intact skin contact with infective blood is certainly much less than the 0.5% risk following percutaneous

[†]The August 1987 publication should be consulted for general information and specific recommendations not addressed in this update.

needlestick exposures (*5*). In universal precautions, *all* blood is assumed to be potentially infective for bloodborne pathogens, but in certain settings (e.g., volunteer blood-donation centers) the prevalence of infection with some bloodborne pathogens (e.g., HIV, HBV) is known to be very low. Some institutions have relaxed recommendations for using gloves for phlebotomy procedures by skilled phlebotomists in settings where the prevalence of bloodborne pathogens is known to be very low.

Institutions that judge that routine gloving for *all* phlebotomies is not necessary should periodically reevaluate their policy. Gloves should always be available to health-care workers who wish to use them for phlebotomy. In addition, the following general guidelines apply:

1. Use gloves for performing phlebotomy when the health-care worker has cuts, scratches, or other breaks in his/her skin.
2. Use gloves in situations where the health-care worker judges that hand contamination with blood may occur, for example, when performing phlebotomy on an uncooperative patient.
3. Use gloves for performing finger and/or heel sticks on infants and children.
4. Use gloves when persons are receiving training in phlebotomy.

Selection of Gloves

The Center for Devices and Radiological Health, FDA, has responsibility for regulating the medical glove industry. Medical gloves include those marketed as sterile surgical or nonsterile examination gloves made of vinyl or latex. General purpose utility ("rubber") gloves are also used in the health-care setting, but they are not regulated by FDA since they are not promoted for medical use. There are no reported differences in barrier effectiveness between intact latex and intact vinyl used to manufacture gloves. Thus, the type of gloves selected should be appropriate for the task being performed.

The following general guidelines are recommended:

1. Use sterile gloves for procedures involving contact with normally sterile areas of the body.
2. Use examination gloves for procedures involving contact with mucous membranes, unless otherwise indicated, and for other patient care or diagnostic procedures that do not require the use of sterile gloves.
3. Change gloves between patient contacts.
4. Do not wash or disinfect surgical or examination gloves for reuse. Washing with surfactants may cause "wicking," i.e., the enhanced penetration of liquids through undetected holes in the glove. Disinfecting agents may cause deterioration.
5. Use general-purpose utility gloves (e.g., rubber household gloves) for housekeeping chores involving potential blood contact and for instrument cleaning and decontamination procedures. Utility gloves may be decontaminated and reused but should be discarded if they are peeling, cracked, or discolored, or if they have punctures, tears, or other evidence of deterioration.

Waste Management

Universal precautions are not intended to change waste management programs previously recommended by CDC for health-care settings (*1*). Policies for defining, collecting, storing, decontaminating, and disposing of infective waste are generally determined by institutions in accordance with state and local regulations. Information regarding waste management regulations in health-care settings may be obtained from state or local health departments or agencies responsible for waste management.

Reported by: Center for Devices and Radiological Health, Food and Drug Administration. Hospital Infections Program, AIDS Program, and Hepatitis Br, Div of Viral Diseases, Center for Infectious Diseases, National Institute for Occupational Safety and Health, CDC.

Editorial Note: Implementation of universal precautions does not eliminate the need for other category- or disease-specific isolation precautions, such as enteric precautions for infectious diarrhea or isolation for pulmonary tuberculosis (*1,2*). In addition to universal precautions, detailed precautions have been developed for the following procedures and/or settings in which prolonged or intensive exposures to blood occur: invasive procedures, dentistry, autopsies or morticians' services, dialysis, and the clinical laboratory. These detailed precautions are found in the August 21, 1987, "Recommendations for Prevention of HIV Transmission in Health-Care Settings" (*1*). In addition, specific precautions have been developed for research laboratories (*28*).

References

1. Centers for Disease Control. Recommendations for prevention of HIV transmission in health-care settings. MMWR 1987;36(suppl no. 2S).
2. Garner JS, Simmons BP. Guideline for isolation precautions in hospitals. Infect Control 1983:4;245–325.
3. Immunization Practices Advisory Committee. Recommendations for protection against viral hepatitis. MMWR 1985;34:313-24,329–35.
4. Department of Labor, Department of Health and Human Services. Joint advisory notice: protection against occupational exposure to hepatitis B virus (HBV) and human immunodeficiency virus (HIV). Washington, DC:US Department of Labor, US Department of Health and Human Services, 1987.
5. Centers for Disease Control. Update: Acquired immunodeficiency syndrome and human immunodeficiency virus infection among health-care workers. MMWR 1988;37:229–34,239.
6. Hollander H, Levy JA. Neurologic abnormalities and recovery of human immunodeficiency virus from cerebrospinal fluid. Ann Intern Med 1987;106:692–5.
7. Wirthrington RH, Cornes P, Harris JRW, et al. Isolation of human immunodeficiency virus from synovial fluid of a patient with reactive arthritis. Br Med J 1987;294:484.
8. Mundy DC, Schinazi RF, Gerber AR, Nahmias AJ, Randall HW. Human immunodeficiency virus isolated from amniotic fluid. Lancet 1987;2:459–60.
9. Onion DK, Crumpacker CS, Gilliland BC. Arthritis of hepatitis associated with Australia antigen. Ann Intern Med 1971;75:29–33.
10. Lee AKY, Ip HMH, Wong VCW. Mechanisms of maternal-fetal transmission of hepatitis B virus. J Infect Dis 1978;138:668–71.
11. Bond WW, Petersen NJ, Gravelle CR, Favero MS. Hepatitis B virus in peritoneal dialysis fluid: A potential hazard. Dialysis and Transplantation 1982;11:592–600.
12. Oskenhendler E, Harzic M, Le Roux J-M, Rabian C, Clauvel JP. HIV infection with seroconversion after a superficial needlestick injury to the finger [Letter]. N Engl J Med 1986;315:582.
13. Lifson AR. Do alternate modes for transmission of human immunodeficiency virus exist? A review. JAMA 1988;259:1353–6.
14. Friedland GH, Saltzman BR, Rogers MF, et al. Lack of transmission of HTLV-III/LAV infection to household contacts of patients with AIDS or AIDS-related complex with oral candidiasis. N Engl J Med 1986;314:344–9.
15. Jenison SA, Lemon SM, Baker LN, Newbold JE. Quantitative analysis of hepatitis B virus DNA in saliva and semen of chronically infected homosexual men. J Infect Dis 1987;156:299–306.
16. Cancio-Bello TP, de Medina M, Shorey J, Valledor MD, Schiff ER. An institutional outbreak of hepatitis B related to a human biting carrier. J Infect Dis 1982;146:652–6.

17. MacQuarrie MB, Forghani B, Wolochow DA. Hepatitis B transmitted by a human bite. JAMA 1974;230:723–4.
18. Scott RM, Snitbhan R, Bancroft WH, Alter HJ, Tingpalapong M. Experimental transmission of hepatitis B virus by semen and saliva. J Infect Dis 1980;142:67–71.
19. Glaser JB, Nadler JP. Hepatitis B virus in a cardiopulmonary resuscitation training course: Risk of transmission from a surface antigen-positive participant. Arch Intern Med 1985;145:1653–5.
20. Osterholm MT, Bravo ER, Crosson JT, et al. Lack of transmission of viral hepatitis type B after oral exposure to HBsAg-positive saliva. Br Med J 1979;2:1263–4.
21. Curran JW, Jaffe HW, Hardy AM, et al. Epidemiology of HIV infection and AIDS in the United States. Science 1988;239:610–6.
22. Jason JM, McDougal JS, Dixon G, et al. HTLV-III/LAV antibody and immune status of household contacts and sexual partners of persons with hemophilia. JAMA 1986;255:212–5.
23. Wahn V, Kramer HH, Voit T, Brüster HT, Scrampical B, Scheid A. Horizontal transmission of HIV infection between two siblings [Letter]. Lancet 1986;2:694.
24. Salahuddin SZ, Groopman JE, Markham PD, et al. HTLV-III in symptom-free seronegative persons. Lancet 1984;2:1418–20.
25. Simmons BP, Wong ES. Guideline for prevention of nosocomial pneumonia. Atlanta: US Department of Health and Human Services, Public Health Service, Centers for Disease Control, 1982.
26. Klein RS, Phelan JA, Freeman K, et al. Low occupational risk of human immunodeficiency virus infection among dental professionals. N Engl J Med 1988;318:86–90.
27. Garner JS, Favero MS. Guideline for handwashing and hospital environmental control, 1985. Atlanta: US Department of Health and Human Services, Public Health Service, Centers for Disease Control, 1985; HHS publication no. 99-1117.
28. Centers for Disease Control. 1988 Agent summary statement for human immunodeficiency virus and report on laboratory-acquired infection with human immunodeficiency virus. MMWR 1988;37(suppl no. S4:1S-22S).

Centers for Disease Control
Atlanta, Georgia

Recommendations for Prevention of HIV Transmission in Health-Care Settings [Reprinted from *Morbidity and Mortality Weekly Report* 36(Suppl. 2S):3S–18S, Aug. 21, 1987]

Introduction

Human immunodeficiency virus (HIV), the virus that causes acquired immunodeficiency syndrome (AIDS), is transmitted through sexual contact and exposure to infected blood or blood components and perinatally from mother to neonate. HIV has been isolated from blood, semen, vaginal secretions, saliva, tears, breast milk, cerebrospinal fluid, amniotic fluid, and urine and is likely to be isolated from other body fluids, secretions, and excretions. However, epidemiologic evidence has implicated only blood, semen, vaginal secretions, and possibly breast milk in transmission.

The increasing prevalence of HIV increases the risk that health-care workers will be exposed to blood from patients infected with HIV, especially when blood and body-fluid precautions are not followed for all patients. Thus, this document emphasizes the need for health-care workers to consider **all** patients as potentially infected with HIV and/or other blood-borne pathogens and to adhere rigorously to infection-control precautions for minimizing the risk of exposure to blood and body fluids of all patients.

The recommendations contained in this document consolidate and update CDC recommendations published earlier for preventing HIV transmission in health-care settings: precautions for clinical and laboratory staffs (*1*) and precautions for health-care workers and allied professionals (*2*); recommendations for preventing HIV transmission in the workplace (*3*) and during invasive procedures (*4*); recommendations for preventing possible transmission of HIV from tears (*5*); and recommendations for providing dialysis treatment for HIV-infected patients (*6*). These recommendations also update portions of the "Guideline for Isolation Precautions in Hospitals" (*7*) and reemphasize some of the recommendations contained in "Infection Control Practices for Dentistry" (*8*). The recommendations contained in this document have been developed for use in health-care settings and emphasize the need to treat blood and other body fluids from **all** patients as potentially infective. These same prudent precautions also should be taken in other settings in which persons may be exposed to blood or other body fluids.

Definition of Health-Care Workers

Health-care workers are defined as persons, including students and trainees, whose activities involve contact with patients or with blood or other body fluids from patients in a health-care setting.

Health-Care Workers with AIDS

As of July 10, 1987, a total of 1,875 (5.8%) of 32,395 adults with AIDS, who had been reported to the CDC national surveillance system and for whom occupational information was available, reported being employed in a health-care or clinical laboratory setting. In comparison, 6.8 million persons – representing 5.6% of the U.S. labor force – were employed in health services. Of the health-care workers with AIDS, 95% have been reported to exhibit high-risk behavior; for the remaining 5%, the means of HIV acquisition was undetermined. Health-care workers with AIDS were significantly more likely than other workers to have an undetermined risk (5% versus 3%, respectively). For both health-care workers and non-health-care workers with AIDS, the proportion with an undetermined risk has not increased since 1982.

AIDS patients initially reported as not belonging to recognized risk groups are investigated by state and local health departments to determine whether possible risk factors exist. Of all health-care workers with AIDS reported to CDC who were initially characterized as not having an identified risk and for whom follow-up information was available, 66% have been reclassified because risk factors were identified or because the patient was found not to meet the surveillance case definition for AIDS. Of the 87 health-care workers currently categorized as having no identifiable risk, information is incomplete on 16 (18%) because of death or refusal to be interviewed; 38 (44%) are still being investigated. The remaining 33 (38%) health-care workers were interviewed or had other follow-up information available. The occupations of these 33 were as follows: five physicians (15%), three of whom were surgeons; one dentist (3%); three nurses (9%); nine nursing assistants (27%); seven housekeeping or maintenance workers (21%); three clinical laboratory technicians (9%); one therapist (3%); and four others who did not have contact with patients (12%). Although 15 of these 33 health-care workers reported parenteral and/or other non-needlestick exposure to blood or body fluids from patients in the 10 years preceding their diagnosis of AIDS, none of these exposures involved a patient with AIDS or known HIV infection.

Risk to Health-Care Workers of Acquiring HIV in Health-Care Settings

Health-care workers with documented percutaneous or mucous-membrane exposures to blood or body fluids of HIV-infected patients have been prospectively evaluated to determine the risk of infection after such exposures. As of June 30, 1987, 883 health-care workers have been tested for antibody to HIV in an ongoing surveillance project conducted by CDC (*9*). Of these, 708 (80%) had percutaneous exposures to blood, and 175 (20%) had a mucous membrane or an open wound contaminated by blood or body fluid. Of 396 health-care workers, each of whom had only a convalescent-phase serum sample obtained and tested ≥90 days post-exposure, one – for whom heterosexual transmission could not be ruled out – was seropositive for HIV antibody. For 425 additional health-care workers, both acute- and convalescent-phase serum samples were obtained and tested; none of 74 health-care workers with nonpercutaneous exposures seroconverted, and three (0.9%) of 351 with percutaneous exposures seroconverted. None of these three health-care workers had other documented risk factors for infection.

Two other prospective studies to assess the risk of nosocomial acquisition of HIV infection for health-care workers are ongoing in the United States. As of April 30, 1987, 332 health-care workers with a total of 453 needlestick or mucous-membrane exposures to the blood or other body fluids of HIV-infected patients were tested for HIV antibody at the National Institutes of Health (*10*). These exposed workers included 103 with needlestick injuries and 229 with mucous-membrane exposures; none had seroconverted. A similar study at the University of California of 129 health-care workers with documented needlestick injuries or mucous-membrane exposures to blood or other body fluids from patients with HIV infection has not identified any seroconversions (*11*). Results of a prospective study in the United Kingdom identified no evidence of transmission among 150 health-care workers with parenteral or mucous-membrane exposures to blood or other body fluids, secretions, or excretions from patients with HIV infection (*12*).

In addition to health-care workers enrolled in prospective studies, eight persons who provided care to infected patients and denied other risk factors have been reported to have acquired HIV infection. Three of these health-care workers had needlestick exposures to blood from infected patients (*13-15*). Two were persons who provided nursing care to infected persons; although neither sustained a needlestick, both had extensive contact with blood or other body fluids, and neither observed recommended barrier precautions (*16,17*). The other three were health-care workers with non-needlestick exposures to blood from infected patients (*18*). Although the exact route of transmission for these last three infections is not known, all three persons had direct contact of their skin with blood from infected patients, all had skin lesions that may have been contaminated by blood, and one also had a mucous-membrane exposure.

A total of 1,231 dentists and hygienists, many of whom practiced in areas with many AIDS cases, participated in a study to determine the prevalence of antibody to HIV; one dentist (0.1%) had HIV antibody. Although no exposure to a known HIV-infected person could be documented, epidemiologic investigation did not identify any other risk factor for infection. The infected dentist, who also had a history of sustaining needlestick injuries and trauma to his hands, did not routinely wear gloves when providing dental care (*19*).

Precautions To Prevent Transmission of HIV

Universal Precautions

Since medical history and examination cannot reliably identify all patients infected with HIV or other blood-borne pathogens, blood and body-fluid precautions should be consistently used for **all** patients. This approach, previously recommended by CDC (*3,4*), and referred to as "universal blood and body-fluid precautions" or "universal precautions," should be used in the care of **all** patients, especially including those in emergency-care settings in which the risk of blood exposure is increased and the infection status of the patient is usually unknown (*20*).

1. All health-care workers should routinely use appropriate barrier precautions to prevent skin and mucous-membrane exposure when contact with blood or other body fluids of any patient is anticipated. Gloves should be worn for touching blood and body fluids, mucous membranes, or non-intact skin of all patients, for handling items or surfaces soiled with blood or body fluids, and for performing venipuncture and other vascular access procedures. Gloves should be changed after contact with each patient. Masks and protective eyewear or face shields should be worn during procedures that are likely to generate droplets of blood or other body fluids to prevent exposure of mucous membranes of the mouth, nose, and eyes. Gowns or aprons should be worn during procedures that are likely to generate splashes of blood or other body fluids.
2. Hands and other skin surfaces should be washed immediately and thoroughly if contaminated with blood or other body fluids. Hands should be washed immediately after gloves are removed.
3. All health-care workers should take precautions to prevent injuries caused by needles, scalpels, and other sharp instruments or devices during procedures; when cleaning used instruments; during disposal of used needles; and when handling sharp instruments after procedures. To prevent needlestick injuries, needles should not be recapped, purposely bent or broken by hand, removed from disposable syringes, or otherwise manipulated by hand. After they are used, disposable syringes and needles, scalpel blades, and other sharp items should be placed in puncture-resistant containers for disposal; the puncture-resistant containers should be located as close as practical to the use area. Large-bore reusable needles should be placed in a puncture-resistant container for transport to the reprocessing area.
4. Although saliva has not been implicated in HIV transmission, to minimize the need for emergency mouth-to-mouth resuscitation, mouthpieces, resuscitation bags, or other ventilation devices should be available for use in areas in which the need for resuscitation is predictable.
5. Health-care workers who have exudative lesions or weeping dermatitis should refrain from all direct patient care and from handling patient-care equipment until the condition resolves.
6. Pregnant health-care workers are not known to be at greater risk of contracting HIV infection than health-care workers who are not pregnant; however, if a health-care worker develops HIV infection during pregnancy, the infant is at risk of infection resulting from perinatal transmission. Because of this risk, pregnant health-care workers should be especially familiar with and strictly adhere to precautions to minimize the risk of HIV transmission.

Implementation of universal blood and body-fluid precautions for **all** patients eliminates the need for use of the isolation category of "Blood and Body Fluid Precautions" previously recommended by CDC (7) for patients known or suspected to be infected with blood-borne pathogens. Isolation precautions (e.g., enteric, "AFB" [7]) should be used as necessary if associated conditions, such as infectious diarrhea or tuberculosis, are diagnosed or suspected.

Precautions for Invasive Procedures

In this document, an invasive procedure is defined as surgical entry into tissues, cavities, or organs or repair of major traumatic injuries 1) in an operating or delivery room, emergency department, or outpatient setting, including both physicians' and dentists' offices; 2) cardiac catheterization and angiographic procedures; 3) a vaginal or cesarean delivery or other invasive obstetric procedure during which bleeding may occur; or 4) the manipulation, cutting, or removal of any oral or perioral tissues, including tooth structure, during which bleeding occurs or the potential for bleeding exists. The universal blood and body-fluid precautions listed above, combined with the precautions listed below, should be the minimum precautions for **all** such invasive procedures.

1. All health-care workers who participate in invasive procedures must routinely use appropriate barrier precautions to prevent skin and mucous-membrane contact with blood and other body fluids of all patients. Gloves and surgical masks must be worn for all invasive procedures. Protective eyewear or face shields should be worn for procedures that commonly result in the generation of droplets, splashing of blood or other body fluids, or the generation of bone chips. Gowns or aprons made of materials that provide an effective barrier should be worn during invasive procedures that are likely to result in the splashing of blood or other body fluids. All health-care workers who perform or assist in vaginal or cesarean deliveries should wear gloves and gowns when handling the placenta or the infant until blood and amniotic fluid have been removed from the infant's skin and should wear gloves during post-delivery care of the umbilical cord.
2. If a glove is torn or a needlestick or other injury occurs, the glove should be removed and a new glove used as promptly as patient safety permits; the needle or instrument involved in the incident should also be removed from the sterile field.

Precautions for Dentistry*

Blood, saliva, and gingival fluid from **all** dental patients should be considered infective. Special emphasis should be placed on the following precautions for preventing transmission of blood-borne pathogens in dental practice in both institutional and non-institutional settings.

1. In addition to wearing gloves for contact with oral mucous membranes of all patients, all dental workers should wear surgical masks and protective eyewear or chin-length plastic face shields during dental procedures in which splashing or spattering of blood, saliva, or gingival fluids is likely. Rubber dams, high-speed evacuation, and proper patient positioning, when appropriate, should be utilized to minimize generation of droplets and spatter.
2. Handpieces should be sterilized after use with each patient, since blood, saliva, or gingival fluid of patients may be aspirated into the handpiece or waterline. Handpieces that cannot be sterilized should at least be flushed, the outside surface cleaned and wiped with a suitable chemical germicide, and then rinsed. Handpieces should be flushed at the beginning of the day and after use with each patient. Manufacturers' recommendations should be followed for use and maintenance of waterlines and check valves and for flushing of handpieces. The same precautions should be used for ultrasonic scalers and air/water syringes.

*General infection-control precautions are more specifically addressed in previous recommendations for infection-control practices for dentistry (*8*).

3. Blood and saliva should be thoroughly and carefully cleaned from material that has been used in the mouth (e.g., impression materials, bite registration), especially before polishing and grinding intra-oral devices. Contaminated materials, impressions, and intra-oral devices should also be cleaned and disinfected before being handled in the dental laboratory and before they are placed in the patient's mouth. Because of the increasing variety of dental materials used intra-orally, dental workers should consult with manufacturers as to the stability of specific materials when using disinfection procedures.
4. Dental equipment and surfaces that are difficult to disinfect (e.g., light handles or X-ray-unit heads) and that may become contaminated should be wrapped with impervious-backed paper, aluminum foil, or clear plastic wrap. The coverings should be removed and discarded, and clean coverings should be put in place after use with each patient.

Precautions for Autopsies or Morticians' Services

In addition to the universal blood and body-fluid precautions listed above, the following precautions should be used by persons performing postmortem procedures:

1. All persons performing or assisting in postmortem procedures should wear gloves, masks, protective eyewear, gowns, and waterproof aprons.
2. Instruments and surfaces contaminated during postmortem procedures should be decontaminated with an appropriate chemical germicide.

Precautions for Dialysis

Patients with end-stage renal disease who are undergoing maintenance dialysis and who have HIV infection can be dialyzed in hospital-based or free-standing dialysis units using conventional infection-control precautions (*21*). Universal blood and body-fluid precautions should be used when dialyzing **all** patients.

Strategies for disinfecting the dialysis fluid pathways of the hemodialysis machine are targeted to control bacterial contamination and generally consist of using 500-750 parts per million (ppm) of sodium hypochlorite (household bleach) for 30-40 minutes or 1.5%-2.0% formaldehyde overnight. In addition, several chemical germicides formulated to disinfect dialysis machines are commercially available. None of these protocols or procedures need to be changed for dialyzing patients infected with HIV.

Patients infected with HIV can be dialyzed by either hemodialysis or peritoneal dialysis and do not need to be isolated from other patients. The type of dialysis treatment (i.e., hemodialysis or peritoneal dialysis) should be based on the needs of the patient. The dialyzer may be discarded after each use. Alternatively, centers that reuse dialyzers—i.e., a specific single-use dialyzer is issued to a specific patient, removed, cleaned, disinfected, and reused several times on the same patient only—may include HIV-infected patients in the dialyzer-reuse program. An individual dialyzer must never be used on more than one patient.

Precautions for Laboratories[†]

Blood and other body fluids from **all** patients should be considered infective. To supplement the universal blood and body-fluid precautions listed above, the following precautions are recommended for health-care workers in clinical laboratories.

[†]Additional precautions for research and industrial laboratories are addressed elsewhere (*22,23*).

1. All specimens of blood and body fluids should be put in a well-constructed container with a secure lid to prevent leaking during transport. Care should be taken when collecting each specimen to avoid contaminating the outside of the container and of the laboratory form accompanying the specimen.
2. All persons processing blood and body-fluid specimens (e.g., removing tops from vacuum tubes) should wear gloves. Masks and protective eyewear should be worn if mucous-membrane contact with blood or body fluids is anticipated. Gloves should be changed and hands washed after completion of specimen processing.
3. For routine procedures, such as histologic and pathologic studies or microbiologic culturing, a biological safety cabinet is not necessary. However, biological safety cabinets (Class I or II) should be used whenever procedures are conducted that have a high potential for generating droplets. These include activities such as blending, sonicating, and vigorous mixing.
4. Mechanical pipetting devices should be used for manipulating all liquids in the laboratory. Mouth pipetting must not be done.
5. Use of needles and syringes should be limited to situations in which there is no alternative, and the recommendations for preventing injuries with needles outlined under universal precautions should be followed.
6. Laboratory work surfaces should be decontaminated with an appropriate chemical germicide after a spill of blood or other body fluids and when work activities are completed.
7. Contaminated materials used in laboratory tests should be decontaminated before reprocessing or be placed in bags and disposed of in accordance with institutional policies for disposal of infective waste (*24*).
8. Scientific equipment that has been contaminated with blood or other body fluids should be decontaminated and cleaned before being repaired in the laboratory or transported to the manufacturer.
9. All persons should wash their hands after completing laboratory activities and should remove protective clothing before leaving the laboratory.

Implementation of universal blood and body-fluid precautions for **all** patients eliminates the need for warning labels on specimens since blood and other body fluids from all patients should be considered infective.

Environmental Considerations for HIV Transmission

No environmentally mediated mode of HIV transmission has been documented. Nevertheless, the precautions described below should be taken routinely in the care of **all** patients.

Sterilization and Disinfection

Standard sterilization and disinfection procedures for patient-care equipment currently recommended for use (*25,26*) in a variety of health-care settings—including hospitals, medical and dental clinics and offices, hemodialysis centers, emergency-care facilities, and long-term nursing-care facilities—are adequate to sterilize or disinfect instruments, devices, or other items contaminated with blood or other body fluids from persons infected with blood-borne pathogens including HIV (*21,23*).

Instruments or devices that enter sterile tissue or the vascular system of any patient or through which blood flows should be sterilized before reuse. Devices or items that contact intact mucous membranes should be sterilized or receive high-level disinfection, a procedure that kills vegetative organisms and viruses but not necessarily large numbers of bacterial spores. Chemical germicides that are registered with the U.S. Environmental Protection Agency (EPA) as "sterilants" may be used either for sterilization or for high-level disinfection depending on contact time.

Contact lenses used in trial fittings should be disinfected after each fitting by using a hydrogen peroxide contact lens disinfecting system or, if compatible, with heat (78 C-80 C [172.4 F-176.0 F]) for 10 minutes.

Medical devices or instruments that require sterilization or disinfection should be thoroughly cleaned before being exposed to the germicide, and the manufacturer's instructions for the use of the germicide should be followed. Further, it is important that the manufacturer's specifications for compatibility of the medical device with chemical germicides be closely followed. Information on specific label claims of commercial germicides can be obtained by writing to the Disinfectants Branch, Office of Pesticides, Environmental Protection Agency, 401 M Street, SW, Washington, D.C. 20460.

Studies have shown that HIV is inactivated rapidly after being exposed to commonly used chemical germicides at concentrations that are much lower than used in practice (*27-30*). Embalming fluids are similar to the types of chemical germicides that have been tested and found to completely inactivate HIV. In addition to commercially available chemical germicides, a solution of sodium hypochlorite (household bleach) prepared daily is an inexpensive and effective germicide. Concentrations ranging from approximately 500 ppm (1:100 dilution of household bleach) sodium hypochlorite to 5,000 ppm (1:10 dilution of household bleach) are effective depending on the amount of organic material (e.g., blood, mucus) present on the surface to be cleaned and disinfected. Commercially available chemical germicides may be more compatible with certain medical devices that might be corroded by repeated exposure to sodium hypochlorite, especially to the 1:10 dilution.

Survival of HIV in the Environment

The most extensive study on the survival of HIV after drying involved greatly concentrated HIV samples, i.e., 10 million tissue-culture infectious doses per milliliter (*31*). This concentration is at least 100,000 times greater than that typically found in the blood or serum of patients with HIV infection. HIV was detectable by tissue-culture techniques 1-3 days after drying, but the rate of inactivation was rapid. Studies performed at CDC have also shown that drying HIV causes a rapid (within several hours) 1-2 log (90%-99%) reduction in HIV concentration. In tissue-culture fluid, cell-free HIV could be detected up to 15 days at room temperature, up to 11 days at 37 C (98.6 F), and up to 1 day if the HIV was cell-associated.

When considered in the context of environmental conditions in health-care facilities, these results do not require any changes in currently recommended sterilization, disinfection, or housekeeping strategies. When medical devices are contaminated with blood or other body fluids, existing recommendations include the cleaning of these instruments, followed by disinfection or sterilization, depending on the type of medical device. These protocols assume "worst-case" conditions of extreme virologic and microbiologic contamination, and whether viruses have been inactivated after drying plays no role in formulating these strategies. Consequently, no changes in published procedures for cleaning, disinfecting, or sterilizing need to be made.

Housekeeping

Environmental surfaces such as walls, floors, and other surfaces are not associated with transmission of infections to patients or health-care workers. Therefore, extraordinary attempts to disinfect or sterilize these environmental surfaces are not necessary. However, cleaning and removal of soil should be done routinely.

Cleaning schedules and methods vary according to the area of the hospital or institution, type of surface to be cleaned, and the amount and type of soil present. Horizontal surfaces (e.g., bedside tables and hard-surfaced flooring) in patient-care areas are usually cleaned on a regular basis, when soiling or spills occur, and when a patient is discharged. Cleaning of walls, blinds, and curtains is recommended only if they are visibly soiled. Disinfectant fogging is an unsatisfactory method of decontaminating air and surfaces and is not recommended.

Disinfectant-detergent formulations registered by EPA can be used for cleaning environmental surfaces, but the actual physical removal of microorganisms by scrubbing is probably at least as important as any antimicrobial effect of the cleaning agent used. Therefore, cost, safety, and acceptability by housekeepers can be the main criteria for selecting any such registered agent. The manufacturers' instructions for appropriate use should be followed.

Cleaning and Decontaminating Spills of Blood or Other Body Fluids

Chemical germicides that are approved for use as "hospital disinfectants" and are tuberculocidal when used at recommended dilutions can be used to decontaminate spills of blood and other body fluids. Strategies for decontaminating spills of blood and other body fluids in a patient-care setting are different than for spills of cultures or other materials in clinical, public health, or research laboratories. In patient-care areas, visible material should first be removed and then the area should be decontaminated. With large spills of cultured or concentrated infectious agents in the laboratory, the contaminated area should be flooded with a liquid germicide before cleaning, then decontaminated with fresh germicidal chemical. In both settings, gloves should be worn during the cleaning and decontaminating procedures.

Laundry

Although soiled linen has been identified as a source of large numbers of certain pathogenic microorganisms, the risk of actual disease transmission is negligible. Rather than rigid procedures and specifications, hygienic and common-sense storage and processing of clean and soiled linen are recommended (*26*). Soiled linen should be handled as little as possible and with minimum agitation to prevent gross microbial contamination of the air and of persons handling the linen. All soiled linen should be bagged at the location where it was used; it should not be sorted or rinsed in patient-care areas. Linen soiled with blood or body fluids should be placed and transported in bags that prevent leakage. If hot water is used, linen should be washed with detergent in water at least 71 C (160 F) for 25 minutes. If low-temperature(≤70 C [158 F]) laundry cycles are used, chemicals suitable for low-temperature washing at proper use concentration should be used.

Infective Waste

There is no epidemiologic evidence to suggest that most hospital waste is any more infective than residential waste. Moreover, there is no epidemiologic evidence that hospital waste has caused disease in the community as a result of improper disposal. Therefore, identifying wastes for which special precautions are indicated is largely a matter of judgment about the relative risk of disease transmission. The most practical approach to the management of infective waste is to identify those wastes with the potential for causing infection during handling and disposal and for which some special precautions appear prudent. Hospital wastes for which special precautions appear prudent include microbiology laboratory waste, pathology waste, and blood specimens or blood products. While any item that has had contact with blood, exudates, or secretions may be potentially infective, it is not usually considered practical or necessary to treat all such waste as infective (*23,26*). Infective waste, in general, should either be incinerated or should be autoclaved before disposal in a sanitary landfill. Bulk blood, suctioned fluids, excretions, and secretions may be carefully poured down a drain connected to a sanitary sewer. Sanitary sewers may also be used to dispose of other infectious wastes capable of being ground and flushed into the sewer.

Implementation of Recommended Precautions

Employers of health-care workers should ensure that policies exist for:

1. Initial orientation and continuing education and training of all health-care workers—including students and trainees—on the epidemiology, modes of transmission, and prevention of HIV and other blood-borne infections and the need for routine use of universal blood and body-fluid precautions for **all** patients.
2. Provision of equipment and supplies necessary to minimize the risk of infection with HIV and other blood-borne pathogens.
3. Monitoring adherence to recommended protective measures. When monitoring reveals a failure to follow recommended precautions, counseling, education, and/or re-training should be provided, and, if necessary, appropriate disciplinary action should be considered.

Professional associations and labor organizations, through continuing education efforts, should emphasize the need for health-care workers to follow recommended precautions.

Serologic Testing for HIV Infection

Background

A person is identified as infected with HIV when a sequence of tests, starting with repeated enzyme immunoassays (EIA) and including a Western blot or similar, more specific assay, are repeatedly reactive. Persons infected with HIV usually develop antibody against the virus within 6-12 weeks after infection.

The sensitivity of the currently licensed EIA tests is at least 99% when they are performed under optimal laboratory conditions on serum specimens from persons infected for ≥12 weeks. Optimal laboratory conditions include the use of reliable reagents, provision of continuing education of personnel, quality control of procedures, and participation in performance-evaluation programs. Given this performance, the probability of a false-negative test is remote except during the first several weeks after infection, before detectable antibody is present. The proportion of infected persons with a false-negative test attributed to absence of antibody in the early stages of infection is dependent on both the incidence and prevalence of HIV infection in a population (Table 1).

The specificity of the currently licensed EIA tests is approximately 99% when repeatedly reactive tests are considered. Repeat testing of initially reactive specimens by EIA is required to reduce the likelihood of laboratory error. To increase further the specificity of serologic tests, laboratories must use a supplemental test, most often the Western blot, to validate repeatedly reactive EIA results. Under optimal laboratory conditions, the sensitivity of the Western blot test is comparable to or greater than that of a repeatedly reactive EIA, and the Western blot is highly specific when strict criteria are used to interpret the test results. The testing sequence of a repeatedly reactive EIA and a positive Western blot test is highly predictive of HIV infection, even in a population with a low prevalence of infection (Table 2). If the Western blot test result is indeterminant, the testing sequence is considered equivocal for HIV infection.

TABLE 1. Estimated annual number of patients infected with HIV not detected by HIV-antibody testing in a hypothetical hospital with 10,000 admissions/year*

Beginning prevalence of HIV infection	Annual incidence of HIV infection	Approximate number of HIV-infected patients	Approximate number of HIV-infected patients not detected
5.0%	1.0%	550	17-18
5.0%	0.5%	525	11-12
1.0%	0.2%	110	3-4
1.0%	0.1%	105	2-3
0.1%	0.02%	11	0-1
0.1%	0.01%	11	0-1

*The estimates are based on the following assumptions: 1) the sensitivity of the screening test is 99% (i.e., 99% of HIV-infected persons with antibody will be detected); 2) persons infected with HIV will not develop detectable antibody (seroconvert) until 6 weeks (1.5 months) after infection; 3) new infections occur at an equal rate throughout the year; 4) calculations of the number of HIV-infected persons in the patient population are based on the mid-year prevalence, which is the beginning prevalence plus half the annual incidence of infections.

When this occurs, the Western blot test should be repeated on the same serum sample, and, if still indeterminant, the testing sequence should be repeated on a sample collected 3-6 months later. Use of other supplemental tests may aid in interpreting of results on samples that are persistently indeterminant by Western blot.

Testing of Patients

Previous CDC recommendations have emphasized the value of HIV serologic testing of patients for: 1) management of parenteral or mucous-membrane exposures of health-care workers, 2) patient diagnosis and management, and 3) counseling and serologic testing to prevent and control HIV transmission in the community. In addition, more recent recommendations have stated that hospitals, in conjunction with state and local health departments, should periodically determine the prevalence of HIV infection among patients from age groups at highest risk of infection (*32*).

Adherence to universal blood and body-fluid precautions recommended for the care of all patients will minimize the risk of transmission of HIV and other blood-borne pathogens from patients to health-care workers. The utility of routine HIV serologic testing of patients as an adjunct to universal precautions is unknown. Results of such testing may not be available in emergency or outpatient settings. In addition, some recently infected patients will not have detectable antibody to HIV (Table 1).

Personnel in some hospitals have advocated serologic testing of patients in settings in which exposure of health-care workers to large amounts of patients' blood may be anticipated. Specific patients for whom serologic testing has been advocated include those undergoing major operative procedures and those undergoing treatment in critical-care units, especially if they have conditions involving uncontrolled bleeding. Decisions regarding the need to establish testing programs for patients should be made by physicians or individual institutions. In addition, when deemed appropriate, testing of individual patients may be performed on agreement between the patient and the physician providing care.

In addition to the universal precautions recommended for all patients, certain additional precautions for the care of HIV-infected patients undergoing major surgical operations have been proposed by personnel in some hospitals. For example, surgical procedures on an HIV-infected patient might be altered so that hand-to-hand passing of sharp instruments would be eliminated; stapling instruments rather than

TABLE 2. Predictive value of positive HIV-antibody tests in hypothetical populations with different prevalences of infection

	Prevalence of infection	Predictive value of positive test*
Repeatedly reactive enzyme immunoassay (EIA)†	0.2%	28.41%
	2.0%	80.16%
	20.0%	98.02%
Repeatedly reactive EIA followed by positive Western blot (WB)§	0.2%	99.75%
	2.0%	99.97%
	20.0%	99.99%

*Proportion of persons with positive test results who are actually infected with HIV.
†Assumes EIA sensitivity of 99.0% and specificity of 99.5%.
§Assumes WB sensitivity of 99.0% and specificity of 99.9%.

hand-suturing equipment might be used to perform tissue approximation; electrocautery devices rather than scalpels might be used as cutting instruments; and, even though uncomfortable, gowns that totally prevent seepage of blood onto the skin of members of the operative team might be worn. While such modifications might further minimize the risk of HIV infection for members of the operative team, some of these techniques could result in prolongation of operative time and could potentially have an adverse effect on the patient.

Testing programs, if developed, should include the following principles:

- Obtaining consent for testing.
- Informing patients of test results, and providing counseling for seropositive patients by properly trained persons.
- Assuring that confidentiality safeguards are in place to limit knowledge of test results to those directly involved in the care of infected patients or as required by law.
- Assuring that identification of infected patients will not result in denial of needed care or provision of suboptimal care.
- Evaluating prospectively 1) the efficacy of the program in reducing the incidence of parenteral, mucous-membrane, or significant cutaneous exposures of health-care workers to the blood or other body fluids of HIV-infected patients and 2) the effect of modified procedures on patients.

Testing of Health-Care Workers

Although transmission of HIV from infected health-care workers to patients has not been reported, transmission during invasive procedures remains a possibility. Transmission of hepatitis B virus (HBV)—a blood-borne agent with a considerably greater potential for nosocomial spread—from health-care workers to patients has been documented. Such transmission has occurred in situations (e.g., oral and gynecologic surgery) in which health-care workers, when tested, had very high concentrations of HBV in their blood (at least 100 million infectious virus particles per milliliter, a concentration much higher than occurs with HIV infection), and the health-care workers sustained a puncture wound while performing invasive procedures or had exudative or weeping lesions or microlacerations that allowed virus to contaminate instruments or open wounds of patients (*33,34*).

The hepatitis B experience indicates that only those health-care workers who perform certain types of invasive procedures have transmitted HBV to patients. Adherence to recommendations in this document will minimize the risk of transmission of HIV and other blood-borne pathogens from health-care workers to patients during invasive procedures. Since transmission of HIV from infected health-care workers performing invasive procedures to their patients has not been reported and would be expected to occur only very rarely, if at all, the utility of routine testing of such health-care workers to prevent transmission of HIV cannot be assessed. If consideration is given to developing a serologic testing program for health-care workers who perform invasive procedures, the frequency of testing, as well as the issues of consent, confidentiality, and consequences of test results—as previously outlined for testing programs for patients—must be addressed.

Management of Infected Health-Care Workers

Health-care workers with impaired immune systems resulting from HIV infection or other causes are at increased risk of acquiring or experiencing serious complications of infectious disease. Of particular concern is the risk of severe infection following exposure to patients with infectious diseases that are easily transmitted if appropriate precautions are not taken (e.g., measles, varicella). Any health-care worker with an impaired immune system should be counseled about the potential risk associated with taking care of patients with any transmissible infection and should continue to follow existing recommendations for infection control to minimize risk of exposure to other infectious agents (*7,35*). Recommendations of the Immunization Practices Advisory Committee (ACIP) and institutional policies concerning requirements for vaccinating health-care workers with live-virus vaccines (e.g., measles, rubella) should also be considered.

The question of whether workers infected with HIV—especially those who perform invasive procedures—can adequately and safely be allowed to perform patient-care duties or whether their work assignments should be changed must be determined on an individual basis. These decisions should be made by the health-care worker's personal physician(s) in conjunction with the medical directors and personnel health service staff of the employing institution or hospital.

Management of Exposures

If a health-care worker has a parenteral (e.g., needlestick or cut) or mucous-membrane (e.g., splash to the eye or mouth) exposure to blood or other body fluids or has a cutaneous exposure involving large amounts of blood or prolonged contact with blood—especially when the exposed skin is chapped, abraded, or afflicted with dermatitis—the source patient should be informed of the incident and tested for serologic evidence of HIV infection after consent is obtained. Policies should be developed for testing source patients in situations in which consent cannot be obtained (e.g., an unconscious patient).

If the source patient has AIDS, is positive for HIV antibody, or refuses the test, the health-care worker should be counseled regarding the risk of infection and evaluated clinically and serologically for evidence of HIV infection as soon as possible after the exposure. The health-care worker should be advised to report and seek medical evaluation for any acute febrile illness that occurs within 12 weeks after the exposure. Such an illness—particularly one characterized by fever, rash, or lymphadenopathy—may be indicative of recent HIV infection. Seronegative health-care workers should be retested 6 weeks post-exposure and on a periodic basis thereafter (e.g., 12 weeks and 6 months after exposure) to determine whether transmission has occurred. During this follow-up period—especially the first 6-12 weeks after exposure, when most infected persons are expected to seroconvert—exposed health-care workers should follow U.S. Public Health Service (PHS) recommendations for preventing transmission of HIV (*36,37*).

No further follow-up of a health-care worker exposed to infection as described above is necessary if the source patient is seronegative unless the source patient is at high risk of HIV infection. In the latter case, a subsequent specimen (e.g., 12 weeks following exposure) may be obtained from the health-care worker for antibody testing. If the source patient cannot be identified, decisions regarding appropriate follow-up should be individualized. Serologic testing should be available to all health-care workers who are concerned that they may have been infected with HIV.

If a patient has a parenteral or mucous-membrane exposure to blood or other body fluid of a health-care worker, the patient should be informed of the incident, and the same procedure outlined above for management of exposures should be followed for both the source health-care worker and the exposed patient.

References

1. CDC. Acquired immunodeficiency syndrome (AIDS): Precautions for clinical and laboratory staffs. MMWR 1982;31:577-80.
2. CDC. Acquired immunodeficiency syndrome (AIDS): Precautions for health-care workers and allied professionals. MMWR 1983;32:450-1.
3. CDC. Recommendations for preventing transmission of infection with human T-lymphotropic virus type III/lymphadenopathy-associated virus in the workplace. MMWR 1985;34:681-6, 691-5.
4. CDC. Recommendations for preventing transmission of infection with human T-lymphotropic virus type III/lymphadenopathy-associated virus during invasive procedures. MMWR 1986;35:221-3.
5. CDC. Recommendations for preventing possible transmission of human T-lymphotropic virus type III/lymphadenopathy-associated virus from tears. MMWR 1985;34:533-4.
6. CDC. Recommendations for providing dialysis treatment to patients infected with human T-lymphotropic virus type III/lymphadenopathy-associated virus infection. MMWR 1986;35:376-8, 383.
7. Garner JS, Simmons BP. Guideline for isolation precautions in hospitals. Infect Control 1983;4 (suppl) :245-325.
8. CDC. Recommended infection control practices for dentistry. MMWR 1986;35:237-42.
9. McCray E, The Cooperative Needlestick Surveillance Group. Occupational risk of the acquired immunodeficiency syndrome among health care workers. N Engl J Med 1986;314:1127-32.
10. Henderson DK, Saah AJ, Zak BJ, et al. Risk of nosocomial infection with human T-cell lymphotropic virus type III/lymphadenopathy-associated virus in a large cohort of intensively exposed health care workers. Ann Intern Med 1986;104:644-7.
11. Gerberding JL, Bryant-LeBlanc CE, Nelson K, et al. Risk of transmitting the human immunodeficiency virus, cytomegalovirus, and hepatitis B virus to health care workers exposed to patients with AIDS and AIDS-related conditions. J Infect Dis 1987;156:1-8.
12. McEvoy M, Porter K, Mortimer P, Simmons N, Shanson D. Prospective study of clinical, laboratory, and ancillary staff with accidental exposures to blood or other body fluids from patients infected with HIV. Br Med J 1987;294:1595-7.
13. Anonymous. Needlestick transmission of HTLV-III from a patient infected in Africa. Lancet 1984;2:1376-7.
14. Oksenhendler E, Harzic M, Le Roux JM, Rabian C, Clauvel JP. HIV infection with seroconversion after a superficial needlestick injury to the finger. N Engl J Med 1986;315:582.
15. Neisson-Vernant C, Arfi S, Mathez D, Leibowitch J, Monplaisir N. Needlestick HIV seroconversion in a nurse. Lancet 1986;2:814.
16. Grint P, McEvoy M. Two associated cases of the acquired immune deficiency syndrome (AIDS). PHLS Commun Dis Rep 1985;42:4.
17. CDC. Apparent transmission of human T-lymphotropic virus type III/lymphadenopathy-associated virus from a child to a mother providing health care. MMWR 1986;35:76-9.
18. CDC. Update: Human immunodeficiency virus infections in health care workers exposed to blood of infected patients. MMWR 1987;36:285-9.
19. Kline RS, Phelan J, Friedland GH, et al. Low occupational risk for HIV infection for dental professionals [Abstract]. In: Abstracts from the III International Conference on AIDS, 1-5 June 1985. Washington, DC: 155.
20. Baker JL, Kelen GD, Sivertson KT, Quinn TC. Unsuspected human immunodeficiency virus in critically ill emergency patients. JAMA 1987;257:2609-11.
21. Favero MS. Dialysis-associated diseases and their control. In: Bennett JV, Brachman PS, eds. Hospital infections. Boston: Little, Brown and Company, 1985:267-84.

22. Richardson JH, Barkley WE, eds. Biosafety in microbiological and biomedical laboratories, 1984. Washington, DC : US Department of Health and Human Services, Public Health Service. HHS publication no. (CDC) 84-8395.
23. CDC. Human T-lymphotropic viruś type III/lymphadenopathy-associated virus: Agent summary statement. MMWR 1986;35:540-2, 547-9.
24. Environmental Protection Agency. EPA guide for infectious waste management. Washington, DC :U.S. Environmental Protection Agency, May 1986 (Publication no. EPA/530-SW-86-014).
25. Favero MS. Sterilization, disinfection, and antisepsis in the hospital. In: Manual of clinical microbiology. 4th ed. Washington, DC: American Society for Microbiology, 1985;129-37.
26. Garner JS, Favero MS. Guideline for handwashing and hospital environmental control, 1985. Atlanta: Public Health Service, Centers for Disease Control, 1985. HHS publication no. 99-1117.
27. Spire B, Montagnier L, Barré-Sinoussi F, Chermann JC. Inactivation of lymphadenopathy associated virus by chemical disinfectants. Lancet 1984;2:899-901.
28. Martin LS, McDougal JS, Loskoski SL. Disinfection and inactivation of the human T lymphotropic virus type III/lymphadenopathy-associated virus. J Infect Dis 1985; 152:400-3.
29. McDougal JS, Martin LS, Cort SP, et al. Thermal inactivation of the acquired immunodeficiency syndrome virus-III/lymphadenopathy-associated virus, with special reference to antihemophilic factor. J Clin Invest 1985;76:875-7.
30. Spire B, Barré-Sinoussi F, Dormont D, Montagnier L, Chermann JC. Inactivation of lymphadenopathy-associated virus by heat, gamma rays, and ultraviolet light. Lancet 1985;1:188-9.
31. Resnik L, Veren K, Salahuddin SZ, Tondreau S, Markham PD. Stability and inactivation of HTLV-III/LAV under clinical and laboratory environments. JAMA 1986;255:1887-91.
32. CDC. Public Health Service (PHS) guidelines for counseling and antibody testing to prevent HIV infection and AIDS. MMWR 1987;3:509-15..
33. Kane MA, Lettau LA. Transmission of HBV from dental personnel to patients. J Am Dent Assoc 1985;110:634-6.
34. Lettau LA, Smith JD, Williams D, et. al. Transmission of hepatitis B with resultant restriction of surgical practice. JAMA 1986;255:934-7.
35. Williams WW. Guideline for infection control in hospital personnel. Infect Control 1983;4 (suppl) :326-49.
36. CDC. Prevention of acquired immune deficiency syndrome (AIDS): Report of inter-agency recommendations. MMWR 1983;32:101-3.
37. CDC. Provisional Public Health Service inter-agency recommendations for screening donated blood and plasma for antibody to the virus causing acquired immunodeficiency syndrome. MMWR 1985;34:1-5.

Centers for Disease Control
Atlanta, Georgia

Public Health Service Statement on Management of Occupational Exposure to Human Immunodeficiency Virus, Including Considerations Regarding Zidovudine Postexposure Use [Reprinted from *Morbidity and Mortality Weekly Report* 39(Suppl. RR-1):1–14, Jan. 26, 1990]

INTRODUCTION

CDC has issued guidelines to reduce the risk of human immunodeficiency virus (HIV) infection among health-care workers, emergency-response and public-safety workers, and others who might be exposed to HIV while performing job duties (*1-4*). The safety practices outlined in these guidelines remain the primary means of preventing occupational acquisition of HIV infection (*5*). Additionally, some physicians and some institutions have offered the option of using zidovudine (azidothymidine, AZT, ZDV, Retrovir) after occupational exposure to HIV (*6*). Data collected in an ongoing CDC surveillance project of health-care workers who have been occupationally exposed to blood from HIV-infected patients (*7*) indicate that during the period April-December 1989, 13 (8.6%) of 151 newly enrolled participants began a postexposure regimen of zidovudine.

This report reviews Public Health Service (PHS) recommendations for postexposure management of workers who have occupational exposures that may place them at risk of acquiring HIV infection, provides background information on zidovudine and experience with zidovudine postexposure prophylaxis, and presents considerations relevant to a decision to offer postexposure prophylaxis.

Definition of Occupational Exposure

For purposes of this document, an occupational exposure (i.e., exposure that occurs during the performance of job duties) that may place a worker at risk of HIV infection is defined as a percutaneous injury (e.g., a needlestick or cut with a sharp object), contact of mucous membranes, or contact of skin (especially when the exposed skin is chapped, abraded, or afflicted with dermatitis or the contact is prolonged or involving an extensive area) with blood, tissues, or other body fluids to which universal precautions apply, including: a) semen, vaginal secretions, or other body fluids contaminated with visible blood, because these substances have been implicated in the transmission of HIV infection (*2*); b) cerebrospinal fluid, synovial fluid, pleural fluid, peritoneal fluid, pericardial fluid, and amniotic fluid, because the risk of transmission of HIV from these fluids has not yet been determined (*2*); and c) laboratory specimens that contain HIV (e.g., suspensions of concentrated virus).

PHS RECOMMENDATIONS FOR MANAGEMENT OF PERSONS AFTER OCCUPATIONAL EXPOSURES THAT MAY PLACE THEM AT RISK OF ACQUIRING HIV INFECTION

Employers should make available to workers a system for promptly initiating evaluation, counseling, and follow-up after a reported occupational exposure that may place the worker at risk of acquiring HIV infection. Workers should be educated to report exposures immediately after they occur, because certain interventions that may be appropriate, e.g., prophylaxis against hepatitis B, must be initiated promptly to be effective (*3,8,9*). Workers who might reasonably be considered at risk of occupational exposure to HIV should be familiarized with the principles of postexposure management as part of job orientation and ongoing job training.

If an exposure occurs, the circumstances should be recorded in the worker's confidential medical record. Relevant information includes the following:

- date and time of exposure
- job duty being performed by worker at time of exposure
- details of exposure, including amount of fluid or material, type of fluid or material, and severity of exposure (e.g., for a percutaneous exposure, depth of injury and whether fluid was injected; for a skin or mucous-membrane exposure, the extent and duration of contact and the condition of the skin, e.g., chapped, abraded, intact)
- description of source of exposure—including, if known, whether the source material contained HIV or HBV
- details about counseling, postexposure management, and follow-up

After an occupational exposure, both the exposed worker and the source individual should be evaluated to determine the possible need for the exposed worker to receive prophylaxis against hepatitis B according to previously published CDC recommendations (*3,8,9*). Because of the potentially severe consequences of hepatitis B virus infection, hepatitis B vaccine, which is both safe and highly effective (*10*), should be offered to any susceptible health-care worker who has an occupational exposure and has not previously been vaccinated with hepatitis B vaccine. Hepatitis B immune globulin may also be indicated, particularily if the source patient or material is found to be positive for hepatitis B surface antigen (HBsAg) (*3,8,9*).

In addition, the source individual should be informed of the incident and, if consent is obtained, tested for serologic evidence of HIV infection. If consent cannot be obtained (e.g., patient is unconscious), policies should be developed for testing source individuals in compliance with applicable state and local laws. **Confidentiality of the source individual should be maintained at all times.**

If the source individual has AIDS, is known to be HIV-seropositive, or refuses testing, the worker should be evaluated clinically and serologically for evidence of HIV infection as soon as possible after the exposure (baseline) and if seronegative, should be retested periodically for a minimum of 6 months after exposure (e.g., 6 weeks, 12 weeks, and 6 months after exposure) to determine whether HIV infection has occurred. The worker should be advised to report and seek medical evaluation for any acute illness that occurs during the follow-up period. Such illness, particularly if characterized by fever, rash, myalgia, fatigue, malaise, or lymphadenopathy, may be indicative of acute HIV infection, drug reaction, or another medical condition. During the follow-up period, especially the first 6-12 weeks after the exposure when most infected persons are expected to seroconvert, exposed workers should follow PHS recommendations for preventing transmission of HIV. These recommendations include refraining from blood, semen, or organ donation and abstaining from or using measures to prevent HIV transmission during sexual intercourse (*11-14*). In addition, in countries such as the United States where safe and effective alternatives to breast-feeding are available, exposed women should not breast-feed infants during the follow-up period in order to prevent the infant's possible exposure to HIV in breast milk. **During all phases of follow-up, confidentiality of the worker should be protected.**

If the source individual is HIV-seronegative and has no clinical manifestations of AIDS or HIV infection, no further HIV follow-up of the exposed worker is necessary unless epidemiologic evidence suggests that the source individual may have recently been exposed to HIV or if testing is desired by the worker or recommended by the health-care provider. In these instances, the guidelines may be followed as described above.

If the source individual cannot be identified, decisions regarding appropriate follow-up should be individualized, based on factors such as whether potential sources are likely to include a person at increased risk of HIV infection.

The employer should make serologic testing available to all workers who are concerned about possible infection with HIV through an occupational exposure. Appropriate psychological counseling may be indicated as well.

ZIDOVUDINE

Background

Zidovudine is a thymidine analogue that has been shown in vitro to inhibit replication of some retroviruses, including HIV, by interfering with the action of viral ribonucleic acid (RNA)-dependent deoxyribonucleic acid (DNA) polymerase (reverse transcriptase) and possibly also by other mechanisms (*15*).

In a double-blind, placebo-controlled trial, zidovudine was shown to increase the length and quality of life of patients with advanced HIV infection and AIDS (*16*). Largely on the basis of the results of this trial, zidovudine was approved for marketing by the Food and Drug Administration (FDA) and is indicated for treatment of adults with symptomatic HIV infection, including AIDS, who have a history of cytologically confirmed *Pneumocystis carinii* pneumonia or an absolute CD_4 lymphocyte count of $<200/mm^3$. The dose of zidovudine originally approved for oral use by patients who have AIDS and advanced symptomatic HIV infection was 200 mg every 4 hours. On January 16, 1990, FDA approved a change in the labeling that now recommends administering the drug at 600 mg/day (100 mg every 4 hours) after a patient has received 1 month of zidovudine therapy at a dose of 1,200 mg/day (200 mg every 4 hours).

Later studies (National Institute of Allergy and Infectious Diseases [NIAID] AIDS Clinical Trial Group Protocols #016 and #019) have indicated that zidovudine can delay disease progression in patients with less advanced HIV infection (patients with an absolute CD_4 count of $<500/mm^3$, whether symptomatic or asymptomatic) (NIAID Administrative Report: "AIDS Clinical Trials Alert," August 29, 1989).

Toxicity

Among patients who have AIDS or symptomatic HIV infection and who are treated with zidovudine, the most frequently reported adverse events are granulocytopenia and anemia. Other adverse events that affect ≥5% of zidovudine recipients include one or more of the following: headache, nausea, insomnia, myalgia, diaphoresis, fever, malaise, anorexia, diarrhea, dyspepsia, vomiting, dyspnea, rash, and taste abnormalities (*17*). Occurrences less commonly reported in the published literature include polymyositis, peripheral neuropathy, and seizures.

Among 3,200 patients with asymptomatic HIV infection treated in NIAID protocol #019 with placebo or with zidovudine doses of either 1,500 mg or 500 mg daily (either 300 mg or 100 mg given every 4 hours, five times daily), investigators have reported the following toxicity after a median of 44 weeks of therapy: in the 1,500-mg/day group, approximately 12% of the subjects developed moderate to severe hematologic toxicity, defined as hemoglobin of <8 g/dl, granulocytes of <750/mm^3, or platelets of <50,000/mm^3. In the 500-mg/day group, this toxicity occurred at a rate of about 3%, compared with approximately 2% in the placebo group. Nausea was rarely reported in the placebo group; however, 3%-5% of zidovudine recipients, irrespective of dose group, experienced moderate to severe nausea. No statistically significant difference was observed between zidovudine dose and placebo for any other moderate to severe clinical adverse experiences (NIAID Administrative Report: "AIDS Clinical Trials Alert," August 29, 1989).

Preliminary data from a study sponsored by the Burroughs-Wellcome Company of health-care workers who received 200 mg of zidovudine or placebo every 4 hours for 6 weeks after occupational exposure to HIV indicate that adverse effects most frequently consisted of nausea and vomiting. In no instance did the prescribing physician discontinue a participant's study drug or placebo because of hematologic or other serious toxicity; however, during the therapy period, 14 (28.6%) of 49 participants who received zidovudine had a hemoglobin concentration between 9.5 and 12 g/dl, compared with one (2.9%) of 35 participants in the placebo group. Seven (14.3%) of the 49 participants who received zidovudine, compared with one (2.9%) of the 35 placebo recipients, elected to discontinue therapy because of subjective, reversible symptoms, including nausea, vomiting, fatigue, headache, myalgia, or cough.

Several anecdotal reports of short-term toxicity among health-care workers receiving zidovudine have been received by PHS. Symptoms include fever, myalgia, fatigue, nausea, and vomiting. Single reports have been received of severe anemia, reversible peripheral neuropathy, and transient clinical hepatitis.

Although the risk of acute zidovudine toxicity for exposed health-care workers cannot be determined from this limited information, data from the NIAID protocol #019 trial and from the Burroughs-Wellcome study of exposed health-care workers suggest that the risk of acute toxicity associated with short-term use of the drug is lower than the risk observed during long-term therapy of symptomatic HIV-infected individuals.

For healthy persons not infected with HIV, the risk of long-term toxicity, including teratogenic and carcinogenic effects, related to a course of zidovudine is not known. It is not known whether zidovudine can cause fetal harm when administered to a pregnant woman or whether it can affect reproductive capacity (*17*). To assess the safety of zidovudine use during pregnancy, the Burroughs-Wellcome Company has developed a registry to evaluate pregnancy outcomes of women who took zidovudine during pregnancy. Physicians are encouraged to register such persons by telephoning the pregnancy registry, (919) 248-8465 (collect) or 1-800-722-9292. It is also not known whether zidovudine is excreted in human milk. However, because of the potential for adverse side effects among breast-fed infants, as well as the potential for transmission of HIV if the mother is infected, mothers should be instructed to discontinue breast-feeding whether or not they are receiving zidovudine (*17*).

In other studies conducted by the Burroughs-Wellcome Company (Appendix I), vaginal tumors, including carcinomas, were observed in mice and rats receiving zidovudine at doses that the FDA has determined resulted in plasma levels in mice approximately equal to human plasma levels at the dose originally approved for treatment of persons with symptomatic HIV infection (200 mg every 4 hours). In rats, the plasma levels were determined by the FDA to be about 10 times higher than human plasma levels achieved with the originally approved dose. The results of these rodent carcinogenicity studies are of uncertain predictive value for humans.

Studies of Zidovudine Postexposure Prophylaxis Involving Animals

Data involving studies of laboratory animals (Appendix II) are limited and must be interpreted with caution, as they have most often been derived by using nonhuman retroviruses having pathogenic mechanisms different from the pathogenesis of HIV infection in humans. In one study using HIV in a mouse model, zidovudine prophylaxis was begun 24 hours before intrathymic injection of a large inoculum of HIV and continued for 2 weeks thereafter. HIV infection was not prevented in any of the animals studied, although the course of infection was modified. It is not known whether prophylaxis would be effective in conditions that more closely resemble occupational exposures, i.e., zidovudine begun after exposure, with the exposure consisting of a percutaneous injection of a lower inoculum of HIV. **Data from animal studies are inadequate to support or reject the hypothesis that zidovudine may be effective prophylaxis for persons who have been occupationally exposed to HIV.**

Studies of Zidovudine Postexposure Prophylaxis Involving Humans

The efficacy of zidovudine prophylaxis for humans after exposure to HIV cannot be assessed because of insufficient data. The Burroughs-Wellcome Company recently sponsored a double-blind, placebo-controlled study to evaluate 6 weeks of zidovudine prophylaxis (200 mg orally every 4 hours) involving health-care workers who had experienced occupational percutaneous, mucous-membrane, or nonintact-skin exposures to HIV-infected blood. Of 84 workers who initially enrolled in the study (49 of whom were given zidovudine), none developed HIV infection after at least 6 months of follow-up. The risk of transmission of HIV per episode of percutaneous exposure to HIV-infected blood is, on the average, approximately 0.4% (*7*). Thus, the absence of seroconversions in this small group of participants is not unexpected, regardless of whether they took zidovudine. Enrollment in this study was terminated in June 1989.

NIAID has enrolled three persons in an ongoing open trial of zidovudine prophylaxis after a "massive exposure" to HIV. The first person received a blood transfusion from an HIV-infected donor, was started on zidovudine 7 days after exposure, and was culture-positive for HIV 4 months after completing 6 weeks of chemotherapy. The second person was exposed to a high concentration of HIV on abraded skin in a research laboratory, was started on zidovudine within 24 hours postexposure, and remains HIV-seronegative after 11 months. The risk of seroconversion after this type of laboratory exposure is unknown. The third person was exposed to a high concentration of HIV on broken skin in a research laboratory, was started on zidovudine within 24 hours after the exposure, and is HIV-seronegative 3 months after the exposure. The risk of seroconversion after this type of laboratory exposure also is unknown. All individuals were able to complete a 6-week course of therapy (200 mg orally every 4 hours) without clinically significant adverse effects. Information regarding enrollment in this study can be obtained by calling the NIAID study coordinator at (800) 537-9978.

Prophylaxis Schedules Currently Used After Occupational Exposure

Various regimens have been prescribed for zidovudine prophylaxis after occupational exposure. No data are available to enable investigators to determine the efficacy or compare the toxicity of these or other regimens. At the National Institutes of Health Clinical Center, workers who elect to receive zidovudine are treated with 200 mg every 4 hours (six times daily) for 6 weeks (*6*). At San Francisco General Hospital, workers who elect to receive zidovudine are treated with 200 mg every 4 hours (five times daily; no dose is given at 4:00 a.m.) for 4 weeks (*6*). Some clinicians have used an initial dose of 400 mg, and others have prescribed treatment courses ranging from 4 days to 4 months. At several institutions, attempts are made to begin prophylaxis within 1 hour after exposure for workers who elect to receive the drug.

DISCUSSION

Data from animal and human studies are inadequate to establish the efficacy or safety of zidovudine for prophylaxis after occupational exposure to HIV. However, some physicians believe that zidovudine should be offered as prophylaxis to persons after certain occupational exposures for the following reasons: the severity of the illness that may result from HIV infection, the documented antiviral effect of zidovudine in the treatment of persons with established HIV infection, the apparent reversibility of acute toxicity in persons taking zidovudine for a brief period, and the suggestion that in some animal studies, zidovudine postexposure may modify the course of some retroviral infections. Other physicians believe that zidovudine should not be recommended for uninfected persons after occupational exposures because of the lack of data demonstrating efficacy in postexposure prophylaxis, the limited data on toxicity in uninfected individuals, and the fact that zidovudine has been shown to be carcinogenic in rats and mice.

At this time, prophylaxis with zidovudine cannot be considered a necessary component of postexposure management. However, workers who might be at risk of occupational exposure to HIV should be informed, as part of job orientation and ongoing job training, of the considerations pertaining to the use of zidovudine for postexposure prophylaxis. The PHS recommends that if a physician decides to offer zidovudine to a worker after an exposure incident, that decision by the physician and the decision by the worker to take zidovudine should take into account the following considerations.

Considerations Regarding Use of Zidovudine After an Occupational Exposure

Risk of HIV infection after exposure

Evaluation of the risk of HIV infection after exposure should take into account existing knowledge from prospective studies of exposed workers, which demonstrate that on the average the risk of transmission of HIV per episode of percutaneous exposure (e.g., a needlestick or cut with a sharp object) to HIV-infected blood is approximately 0.4%. These studies also suggest that the risk of HIV transmission per episode of mucous-membrane or skin exposure to HIV-infected blood is less than that after a percutaneous exposure (*7,18-21*). The risk of HIV transmission after occupational exposure to body fluids other than blood, for which universal precautions are recommended, is unknown. The risk of HIV infection for persons who take zidovudine postexposure prophylaxis cannot be determined at present because of the small number of persons studied.

Risk evaluation should also include an assessment of factors that may increase or decrease the probability of HIV transmission after an individual occupational exposure. These factors are not well understood, but include the likelihood that the source fluid contained HIV and probably also the concentration of HIV in the source fluid, the route of exposure, and the volume of fluid involved. For example, a percutaneous exposure to concentrated HIV in a research laboratory is probably more likely to result in transmission of infection than a similar exposure to HIV-infected blood in a clinical setting. A percutaneous exposure to HIV-infected blood is probably more likely to result in transmission than a mucous-membrane exposure to the same blood. Finally, an exposure to a larger quantity of HIV-infected blood, such as injection of several milliliters, is probably more likely to result in HIV transmission than an exposure to a smaller quantity of the same blood, such as in a needlestick exposure.

Interval between exposure and initiation of prophylaxis, if given

Data from animal studies suggest that prophylaxis against certain retroviral infections other than HIV may be more effective when started within hours after exposure (*22,23*). Because in vitro studies indicate that human HIV infection may be established in human lymphocytes within hours after exposure (*24*), and epidemiologic studies of exposed health-care workers indicate that acute retroviral illness may occur as early as 2 weeks after exposure (*7*), it appears that if the decision is made to use postexposure prophylaxis, prophylaxis should be initiated promptly.

Counseling and informed consent

If zidovudine prophylaxis is being considered, the worker should be counseled regarding a) the theoretical rationale for postexposure prophylaxis, b) the risk of occupationally acquired HIV infection due to the exposure, c) the limitations of current knowledge of the efficacy of zidovudine when used as postexposure prophylaxis, d) current knowledge of the toxicity of zidovudine (including the data from animal and human studies) and the limitations of this knowledge in predicting toxicity in uninfected individuals who take the drug after occupational exposures, and e) the need for postexposure follow-up (including HIV serologic testing), regardless of whether zidovudine is taken. **The worker should also be informed that there are diverse opinions among physicians regarding the use of zidovudine for postexposure**

prophylaxis, and the PHS cannot make a recommendation for or against the use of zidovudine for this purpose because of the limitations of current knowledge.

The duration of follow-up needed to detect evidence of HIV transmission or delayed toxicity among workers who take zidovudine is presently unknown. Workers taking zidovudine postexposure may require follow-up to detect HIV seroconversion for a longer period than that recommended for workers who do not take zidovudine. Regardless of the length of follow-up, mechanisms should be developed to permit workers taking zidovudine to be contacted if future information indicates the need for additional evaluation.

If a physician offers zidovudine as prophylaxis after an occupational exposure and the exposed worker elects to take the drug, the physician or other appropriate health-care provider should obtain written informed consent from the worker for this use of this drug. The consent document should reflect the information presented in the counseling session, as outlined above, emphasizing the need for follow-up medical evaluations and for precautions to prevent the transmission of HIV infection during the follow-up period, including refraining from blood, semen, or organ donation, refraining from breast-feeding, and either abstaining from sexual intercourse or using latex condoms during sexual intercourse, as discussed below.

Considerations regarding sexual intercourse for exposed workers taking zidovudine include 1) the possible risk of teratogenesis associated with zidovudine use, and 2) the risk of transmission of HIV to a sexual partner. The risk of teratogenesis among offspring of either men or women taking zidovudine is unknown. Therefore, men and women of reproductive age who are receiving zidovudine should abstain from, or use effective contraception during, sexual intercourse throughout the time zidovudine is being taken. In addition, to prevent HIV transmission to sexual partners, all exposed workers, including pregnant women, should abstain from, or use latex condoms during, sexual intercourse throughout the follow-up period.

Research Needs

Further data are needed to determine risk factors for occupational exposure to HIV, to evaluate measures for preventing these exposures, and to identify risk factors for HIV transmission after occupational exposure. Appropriate animal models of HIV infection are needed, and animal studies should be conducted under experimental conditions that mimic the circumstances of occupational exposure affecting humans. Studies involving humans should be conducted to determine whether postexposure prophylaxis with zidovudine or other agents is effective, and, if effective, should define the optimal time that postexposure prophylaxis should be initiated and the optimal duration of prophylaxis. Studies should also assess the toxicity of candidate prophylactic agents, establish the optimal dosage for healthy individuals and for persons with preexisting hepatic or renal dysfunction, and define the duration of follow-up needed to detect evidence of HIV infection in persons receiving prophylaxis. Strains of HIV isolated from treated workers should be monitored to detect development of drug resistance.

Expanded Surveillance of Workers with Occupational Exposures to HIV

CDC has expanded its ongoing surveillance of workers with occupational exposures to HIV (7) to collect additional information on postexposure chemoprophylaxis. No names or other personal identifiers of workers are collected.

Information is collected on the following:

- circumstances associated with exposures
- extent to which zidovudine and other antiretroviral agents are prescribed for postexposure chemoprophylaxis, including dosage and timing
- incidence of associated toxicity
- rate of HIV seroconversion among workers who do and do not receive postexposure chemoprophylaxis

All physicians who provide care to a worker within 1 month after an occupational exposure to HIV, regardless of whether an antiretroviral agent is prescribed, are encouraged to enroll the worker in the CDC surveillance system. Enrollment and follow-up requirements have been simplified; in particular, it is no longer necessary to send blood specimens to CDC for HIV serologic testing unless the enzyme immunoassay (EIA) performed by a licensed local laboratory is reactive or equivocal. CDC will continue, however, to offer EIA testing at no charge on specimens from surveillance participants on request. Additional information and enrollment materials can be obtained from the Hospital Infections Program, Center for Infectious Diseases, Centers for Disease Control, Mail Stop C-10, Atlanta, GA 30333; telephone (404) 639-1644.

CONTACTS FOR PHYSICIANS AND FOR INFECTION CONTROL AND OCCUPATIONAL HEALTH PROFESSIONALS

- To enroll persons who have had a "massive exposure" to HIV in NIAID study of zidovudine prophylaxis, telephone (800) 537-9978.
- To report adverse effects associated with zidovudine to FDA, use "Adverse Reaction Report" forms (FDA #1639), obtainable from:
  Food and Drug Administration
Office of Epidemiology and Biostatistics
HFD-730
Rockville, MD 20857
(301) 443-4580.
- To enroll an exposed worker in the CDC prospective surveillance system, telephone (404) 639-1644.
- To enroll pregnant women who receive zidovudine during pregnancy, contact:
  Zidovudine in Pregnancy Registry
Epidemiology, Information, and Surveillance Division
Burroughs-Wellcome Company
3030 Cornwallis Road
Research Triangle Park, NC 27709
(919) 248-8465 (collect) or (800) 722-9292.

References

1. CDC. Recommendations for prevention of HIV transmission in health-care settings. MMWR 1987;36(no. 2S).
2. CDC. Update: universal precautions for prevention of transmission of human immunodeficiency virus, hepatitis B virus, and other bloodborne pathogens in health-care settings. MMWR 1988;37:377-88.
3. CDC. Guidelines for prevention of transmission of human immunodeficiency virus and hepatitis B virus to health-care and public-safety workers. MMWR 1989;38(no. S-6).
4. CDC. 1988 Agent summary statement for human immunodeficiency virus and report on laboratory-acquired infection with human immunodeficiency virus. MMWR 1988;37 (no. S-4).
5. US Department of Labor, US Department of Health and Human Services. Joint advisory notice: protection against occupational exposure to hepatitis B virus (HBV) and human immunodeficiency virus (HIV). Washington, DC: US Department of Labor, US Department of Health and Human Services, 1987.
6. Henderson DK, Gerberding JL. Prophylactic zidovudine after occupational exposure to the human immunodeficiency virus: an interim analysis. J Infect Dis 1989;160:321-7.
7. Marcus R, CDC Cooperative Needlestick Study Group. Surveillance of health-care workers exposed to blood from patients infected with the human immunodeficiency virus. N Engl J Med 1988;319:1118-23.
8. CDC. Recommendations for protection against viral hepatitis: recommendations of the Immunization Practices Advisory Committee (ACIP). MMWR 1985;34:313-35.
9. CDC. Protection against viral hepatitis: recommendations of the Immunization Practices Advisory Committee (ACIP). MMWR 1990 (in press).
10. CDC. Update on hepatitis B prevention. MMWR 1987;36:353-66.
11. CDC. Public Health Service guidelines for counseling and antibody testing to prevent HIV infection and AIDS. MMWR 1987;36:509-15.
12. CDC. Additional recommendations to reduce sexual and drug abuse-related transmission of human T-lymphotropic virus type III/lymphadenopathy-associated virus. MMWR 1986; 35:152-5.
13. CDC. Prevention of acquired immune deficiency syndrome (AIDS): report of inter-agency recommendations. MMWR 1983;32:101-3.
14. CDC. Provisional Public Health Service inter-agency recommendations for screening donated blood and plasma for antibody to the virus causing acquired immunodeficiency syndrome. MMWR 1985;34:1-5.
15. Yarchoan R, Mitsuya H, Myers C, Broder S. Clinical pharmacology of 3′-azido-2′, 3′-dideoxythymidine (zidovudine) and related dideoxynucleosides. N Engl J Med 1989; 321:726-38.
16. Fischl MA, Richman DD, Grieco MH, et al. The efficacy of azidothymidine (AZT) in the treatment of patients with AIDS and AIDS-related complex. N Engl J Med 1987;317:185-91.
17. Huff BB, ed. 1989 Physicians' desk reference. 43rd ed. Oradell, New Jersey: Edward R. Barnhart, 1989:793-5.
18. Henderson DK, Fahey BJ, Saah AJ, Schmitt JM, Lane HC. Longitudinal assessment of risk for occupational/nosocomial transmission of human immunodeficiency virus, type 1 in health care workers [Abstract]. In: Program and abstracts of the twenty-eighth Interscience Conference on Antimicrobial Agents and Chemotherapy (Los Angeles). Washington, DC: American Society for Microbiology, 1988:221.
19. Gerberding JL, Littell CG, Chambers HF, et al. Risk of occupational HIV transmission in intensively exposed health-care workers: follow-up [Abstract]. In: Program and abstracts of the twenty-eighth Interscience Conference on Antimicrobial Agents and Chemotherapy (Los Angeles). Washington, DC: American Society for Microbiology, 1988:169.
20. Elmslie K, Mulligan L, O'Shaughnessy M. National surveillance program: occupational exposure to human immunodeficiency virus (HIV-1) infection in Canada. V International Conference on AIDS. Montreal, June 4-9, 1989:148.
21. McEvoy M, Porter K, Mortimer P, Simmons N, Shanson D. Prospective study of clinical, laboratory, and ancillary staff with accidental exposures to blood or body fluids from patients infected with HIV. Br Med J 1987;294:1595-7.
22. Ruprecht RM, O'Brien LG, Rossoni LD, Nusinoff-Lehrman S. Suppression of mouse viraemia and retroviral disease by 3′-azido-3′-deoxythymidine. Nature 1986;323:467-9.
23. Tavares L, Roneker C, Johnston K, Nusinoff-Lehrman S, de Noronha F. 3′-Azido-3′-deoxythymidine in feline leukemia virus-infected cats: a model for therapy and prophylaxis of AIDS. Cancer Res 1987;47:3190-4.
24. Sunyoung K, Byrn R, Groopman J, Baltimore D. Kinetics of HIV gene expression during the one-step multiplication of HIV [Abstract]. IV International Conference on AIDS. Book 1. Stockholm, June 12-16, 1988:119.

APPENDIX I

Results of Studies Conducted by the Burroughs-Wellcome Company of Zidovudine Carcinogenicity Involving Animals

In lifetime carcinogenicity bioassays, mice and rats were given various doses of zidovudine, up to the maximum tolerated doses, for most of their lifespans. Dose reductions were necessary for both species during the study because of the onset and persistence of drug-related anemia. Mice were treated initially with 30, 60, or 120 mg/kg/day; after 90 days, these doses were reduced to 20, 30, or 40 mg/kg/day, respectively. Rats were treated initially with 80, 220, or 600 mg/kg/day; after 90 days, the 600-mg/kg/day group was reduced to 450 mg/kg/day; and after 280 days, this group was further reduced to 300 mg/kg/day. Although anemia persisted at the reduced doses, drug treatment did not adversely affect survival in either species.

Among mice dosed for approximately 22 months, seven vaginal neoplasms occurred in 60 female animals at the highest dose. The earliest a tumor was discovered was after 19 months of continuous dosing; most tumors were discovered after 21 months of treatment. The tumors consisted of five nonmetastasizing squamous cell carcinomas and two benign tumors (one squamous cell papilloma and one squamous cell polyp). One benign vaginal tumor (squamous cell papilloma) was discovered in the middle-dose group after 22 months of treatment. In all instances, these lesions were discovered during histologic examination of tissues from animals that either died or were sacrificed, late in life from nontreatment-related causes, or sacrificed upon completion of lifetime dosing.

Among rats dosed for approximately 22 months, two nonmetastasizing vaginal squamous cell carcinomas were diagnosed on the basis of histologic examination of tissues from animals receiving the highest dose. These carcinomas were discovered after 20-22 months of dosing. No vaginal tumors occurred among rats given the middle or low dose.

No other drug-related tumors were observed among animals of either sex or of either species (Burroughs-Wellcome Company [letter to physicians], Dec. 5, 1989).

APPENDIX II

Studies of Zidovudine Prophylaxis Involving Animals

Studies of retrovirus infections other than HIV in mice and cats suggest that zidovudine may alter the course of some retroviral infections when given before or shortly after exposure to the virus. In one study, mice were injected with a large challenge inoculum (1 X 10^4 plaque-forming units) of Rauscher murine leukemia virus (RMLV) and were given a 20-day course of zidovudine, at various doses, beginning 4 hours after inoculation. By day 69, all untreated mice had died of RMLV infection, whereas those treated with high doses of zidovudine had no clinical signs of infection and were not viremic. Both the protective effect of zidovudine and the incidence of zidovudine-induced bone marrow depression were greater with increasing doses (*1*).

In another study, cats were injected with a large challenge dose (2 X 10^3 focus-inducing units) of Rickard feline leukemia virus (RFLV) and were given zidovudine at various doses and various intervals after inoculation. Of eight cats injected with RFLV and treated with a 6-week course of zidovudine beginning 1 hour after inoculation, none developed clinical evidence of RFLV disease, none had virus isolated from serum, and one had evidence of infection manifested by the development of neutralizing antibody within 3 months after treatment with zidovudine was stopped. In contrast, 11 of 12 untreated cats either became viremic or died of infection in the same period. When zidovudine prophylaxis was initiated 3 or 7 days after inoculation, a substantial proportion of animals in different dosage groups became viremic, developed neutralizing antibody, or both. All animals treated beginning 28 days after inoculation were viremic when zidovudine treatment was initiated (*2*).

Limited studies involving primates have not shown success in postexposure prophylaxis against simian immunodeficiency virus (SIV). In one study, macaque monkeys were inoculated with a small dose (10 $TCID_{50}$) of a rapidly lethal variant of SIV (SMM/PBj-14) and later treated with zidovudine for 14 days. Of three animals whose treatment was begun 1 hour after inoculation, two developed infection, and one died. Of three animals treated within 24 hours, all developed infection, and two died. Of three animals treated within 72 hours, all developed infection, and two died. Of three control animals that were inoculated with the virus but not given zidovudine treatment, all developed infection, and two died (*3*). In another study of macaque monkeys, a 1-week course of zidovudine begun 8 hours before the animals were inoculated with SIV did not prevent viremia, but delayed its onset until 1-2 days after the zidovudine treatment was completed (*4*).

Finally, studies have been conducted by using the SCID-hu mouse model, an immunodeficient mouse with an immune system that has been reconstituted with transplanted human hematolymphoid organs susceptible to infection with HIV (*5*). Seventeen mice were treated with zidovudine for 24 hours before and for 2 weeks after intrathymic injection of a standard challenge dose of HIV (400-4,000 IU), the smallest dose causing infection in all animals. At 2 weeks after injection, none of the mice tested positive for HIV DNA by the polymerase chain reaction (PCR), although the presence of HIV RNA in some cells was detected by in situ hybridization. Four weeks after zidovudine was stopped, HIV DNA was detected by PCR in all 17 mice. In comparison, all of 40 mice not receiving zidovudine tested positive for HIV DNA by PCR 2 weeks after injection (*6*).

References

1. Ruprecht RM, O'Brien LG, Rossoni LD, Nusinoff-Lehrman S. Suppression of mouse viraemia and retroviral disease by 3'-azido-3'-deoxythymidine. Nature 1986;323:467-9.
2. Tavares L, Roneker C, Johnston K, Nusinoff-Lehrman S, de Noronha F. 3'-Azido-3'-deoxythymidine in feline leukemia virus-infected cats: a model for therapy and prophylaxis of AIDS. Cancer Res 1987;47:3190-4.
3. McClure HM, Anderson DC, Fultz P, Ansari A, Brodie A, Lehrman A. Prophylactic effects of AZT following exposure of macaques to an acutely lethal variant of SIV (SIV/SMM/PBj-14) [Abstract]. V International Conference on AIDS. Montreal June 4-9, 1989;522.
4. Lundgren B, Hedström KG, Norrby E, Oberg B, Wahren B. Inhibition of early occurrence of antigen in SIV-infected macaques as a measurement of antiviral efficacy [Abstract]. Symposium on Nonhuman Primate Models for AIDS. November 1988.
5. Namikawa R, Kaneshima H, Lieberman M, Weissman IL, McCune JM. Infection of the SCID-hu mouse by HIV-1. Science 1988;242:1684-6.
6. McCune JM, Namikawa R, Shih CC, Rabin L, Kaneshima H. 3'-Azido-3' deoxythymidine suppresses HIV infection in SCID-hu mouse. Science 1990 (in press).

Centers for Disease Control
Atlanta, Georgia

Protection against Viral Hepatitis: Recommendations of the Immunization Practices Advisory Committee (ACIP) [Reprinted from *Morbidity and Mortality Weekly Report* 39(Suppl. S-2):1–26, Feb. 9, 1990]

*The following statement updates all previous recommendations on protection against viral hepatitis, including use of hepatitis B vaccine and hepatitis B immune globulin for prophylaxis of hepatitis B (*MMWR *1985;34:313-24,329-35 and* MMWR *1987,36:353-66), universal screening of pregnant women to prevent perinatal hepatitis B transmission (*MMWR *1988;37:341-46,51), and use of immune globulin to prevent other types of viral hepatitis* (MMWR *1985;34:313-24,329-35).*

INTRODUCTION

The term "viral hepatitis" is commonly used for several clinically similar diseases that are etiologically and epidemiologically distinct (*1*). Two of these, hepatitis A (formerly called infectious hepatitis) and hepatitis B (formerly called serum hepatitis), have been recognized as separate entities since the early 1940s and can be diagnosed with specific serologic tests. A third category, currently known as non-A, non-B hepatitis, includes two epidemiologically distinct types of hepatitis: parenterally transmitted and enterically transmitted non-A, non-B hepatitis. Parenterally transmitted non-A, non-B hepatitis is associated with both posttransfusion and sporadic cases of acute hepatitis and may be caused by at least two different agents. Part of the genome for one of these agents has recently been cloned, and a candidate serologic assay for antibody to this virus (proposed as hepatitis C virus) has been developed (*2,3*). Enterically transmitted non-A, non-B hepatitis, which is spread by the fecal-oral route and is different from the types seen in the United States, has been reported in parts of Asia, Africa, and Mexico (*4*). Another distinct type of hepatitis, delta hepatitis, is an infection dependent on the hepatitis B virus. It may occur as a coinfection with acute hepatitis B infection or as superinfection of a hepatitis B carrier (*5*).

HEPATITIS SURVEILLANCE

Approximately 28,500 cases of hepatitis A, 23,200 cases of hepatitis B, 2,620 cases of non-A, non-B hepatitis, and 2,470 cases of hepatitis type unspecified were reported in 1988 in the United States. Most cases of each type occur among young adults. Since reporting from many localities is incomplete, the actual number of hepatitis cases occurring annually is thought to be several times the reported number.

IMMUNE GLOBULINS

Immune globulins are important tools for preventing infection and disease before or after exposure to hepatitis viruses. Immune globulins used in medical practice are sterile solutions of antibodies (immunoglobulins) from human plasma. They are prepared by cold ethanol fractionation of large plasma pools and contain 10%-18% protein. In the United States, plasma is primarily obtained from paid donors. Only plasma shown to be free of hepatitis B surface antigen (HBsAg) and antibody to human immunodeficiency virus (HIV) is used to prepare immune globulins.

Immune globulin (IG) (formerly called immune serum globulin, ISG, or gamma globulin) produced in the United States contains antibodies against the hepatitis A virus (anti-HAV) and the HBsAg (anti-HBs). Hepatitis B immune globulin (HBIG) is an IG prepared from plasma containing high titers of anti-HBs.

There is no evidence that hepatitis B virus (HBV), HIV (the causative agent of acquired immunodeficiency syndrome [AIDS]), or other viruses have ever been transmitted by IG or HBIG commercially available in the United States (*6*). Since late April 1985, all plasma units for preparation of IGs have been screened for antibody to HIV, and reactive units are discarded. No instances of HIV infection or clinical illness have occurred that can be attributed to receiving IG or HBIG, including lots prepared before April 1985. Laboratory studies have shown that the margin of safety based on the removal of HIV infectivity by the fractionation process is extremely high (*7*). Some HBIG lots prepared before April 1985 have detectable HIV antibody. Shortly after being given HBIG, recipients have occasionally been noted to have low levels of passively acquired HIV antibody, but this reactivity does not persist (*8*).

Serious adverse effects from IGs administered as recommended have been rare. IGs prepared for intramuscular administration should be used for hepatitis prophylaxis. IGs prepared for intravenous administration to immunodeficient and other selected patients are not intended for hepatitis prophylaxis. IG and HBIG are not contraindicated for pregnant or lactating women.

HEPATITIS A

Hepatitis A is caused by the hepatitis A virus (HAV), a 27-nm ribonucleic acid (RNA) agent that is classified as a picornavirus. Patients with illness caused by HAV characteristically have abrupt onsets of symptoms including fever, malaise, anorexia, nausea, abdominal discomfort, dark urine, and jaundice. Severity is related to age. Among children, most infections are asymptomatic, and illness is usually not accompanied by jaundice. Most infected adults become symptomatically ill with jaundice. The case-fatality rate among reported cases is about 0.6%.

Hepatitis A is primarily transmitted by person-to-person contact, generally through fecal contamination and oral ingestion. Transmission is facilitated by poor personal hygiene, poor sanitation, and intimate (intrahousehold or sexual) contact. In recent years, cases of hepatitis A among intravenous drug users, most likely due to person-to-person contact, have been reported with increasing frequency (*9*). Common-source epidemics from contaminated food and water also occur. Sharing utensils or cigarettes or kissing is not believed to transmit the hepatitis A virus.

The incubation period of hepatitis A is 15-50 days (average 28). High concentrations of HAV (10^8 particles/g) are found in stool specimens from infected persons.

Virus in the feces reaches its highest concentration late in the incubation period and early in the prodromal phase of illness, and it diminishes rapidly once jaundice appears. Greatest infectivity is during the 2-week period immediately before the onset of jaundice. Viremia probably occurs during the period that the virus is shed in feces. Virus has not been found in urine. A chronic carrier state with HAV in blood or feces has not been demonstrated. Transmission of HAV by blood transfusion has been reported but is uncommon (*10*).

The diagnosis of acute hepatitis A is confirmed by finding IgM anti-HAV in serum collected during the acute or early convalescent phase of the disease. IgG anti-HAV, which appears in the convalescent phase of the disease and remains detectable in serum thereafter, confers enduring protection against the disease. Commercial tests are available to detect IgM anti-HAV and total anti-HAV in serum.

Although the incidence of hepatitis A in the United States in the 1980s was lower than that in the 1970s, a 26% increase in incidence was observed between 1983 and 1988. It is still a common infection among older children and young adults. In 1988, 50% of reported cases of hepatitis in this country were attributable to hepatitis A.

Recommendations for IG Prophylaxis for Hepatitis A

Numerous field studies conducted in the past 4 decades confirm that IG given before exposure or during the incubation period of hepatitis A is protective against clinical illness (*11-13*). Its prophylactic value is greatest (80%-90%) when given early in the incubation period and declines thereafter (*13*). Recent tests have shown slightly decreased titers of anti-HAV in current IG lots compared with lots tested 8 years previously; however, no differences in IG efficacy have been noted.

Preexposure Prophylaxis

The major group for whom preexposure prophylaxis is recommended is international travelers. The risk of hepatitis A for U.S. citizens traveling abroad varies with living conditions, length of stay, and the incidence of hepatitis A infection in areas visited (*14-16*). In general, travelers to developed areas of North America, western Europe, Japan, Australia, and New Zealand are at no greater risk of infection than they would be in the United States. For travelers to developing countries, risk of infection increases with duration of travel and is highest for those who live in or visit rural areas, trek in back country, or frequently eat or drink in settings of poor sanitation. Nevertheless, recent studies have shown that many cases of travel-related hepatitis A occur in travelers with "standard" tourist itineraries, accommodations, and food and beverage consumption behaviors (*16* and CDC unpublished data). In developing countries, travelers should minimize their exposure to hepatitis A and other enteric diseases by avoiding potentially contaminated water or food. Travelers should avoid drinking water (or beverages with ice) of unknown purity and eating uncooked shellfish or uncooked fruits or vegetables that they did not prepare.

IG is recommended for all susceptible travelers to developing countries (*17*). IG is especially important for persons who will be living in or visiting rural areas, eating or drinking in settings of poor or uncertain sanitation, or who will have close contact with local persons (especially young children) in settings with poor sanitary conditions. Persons who plan to reside in developing areas for long periods should receive IG regularly.

For travelers, a single dose of IG of 0.02 ml/kg of body weight is recommended if travel is for <3 months. For prolonged travel or residence in developing countries, 0.06 ml/kg should be given every 5 months. For persons who require repeated IG prophylaxis, screening for total anti-HAV before travel is useful to define susceptibility and eliminate unnecessary doses of IG for those who are immune. IG produced in developing countries may not meet the standards for purity required in most developed countries. Persons needing repeat doses overseas should use products that meet U.S. license requirements.

Postexposure Prophylaxis

Hepatitis A cannot be reliably diagnosed on clinical presentation alone, and serologic confirmation of index patients is recommended before contacts are treated. Serologic screening of contacts for anti-HAV before they are given IG is not recommended because screening is more costly than IG and would delay its administration.

For postexposure IG prophylaxis, a single intramuscular dose of 0.02 ml/kg is recommended. IG should be given as soon as possible after last exposure; giving IG more than 2 weeks after exposure is not indicated.

Specific recommendations for IG prophylaxis for hepatitis A depend on the nature of the HAV exposure.

1. Close personal contact. IG is recommended for all household and sexual contacts of persons with hepatitis A.
2. Day-care centers. Day-care facilities attended by children in diapers can be important settings for HAV transmission (*18-20*). IG should be administered to all staff and attendees of day-care centers or homes if a) one or more children or employees are diagnosed as having hepatitis A, or b) cases are recognized in two or more households of center attendees. When an outbreak (hepatitis cases in three or more families) occurs, IG should also be considered for members of households that have children (center attendees) in diapers. In centers not enrolling children in diapers, IG need only be given to classroom contacts of an index patient.
3. Schools. Contact at elementary and secondary schools is usually not an important means of transmitting hepatitis A. Routine administration of IG is not indicated for pupils and teachers in contact with a patient. However, when an epidemiologic investigation clearly shows the existence of a school- or classroom-centered outbreak, IG may be given to persons who have close contact with patients.
4. Institutions for custodial care. Living conditions in some institutions, such as prisons and facilities for the developmentally disabled, favor transmission of hepatitis A. When outbreaks occur, giving IG to residents and staff who have close contact with patients with hepatitis A may reduce the spread of disease. Depending on the epidemiologic circumstances, prophylaxis can be limited or can involve the entire institution.
5. Hospitals. Routine IG prophylaxis for hospital personnel is not indicated. Rather, sound hygienic practices should be emphasized. Staff education should point

out the risk of exposure to hepatitis A and should emphasize precautions regarding direct contact with potentially infective materials (*21*).

Outbreaks of hepatitis A occur occasionally among hospital staff, usually in association with an unsuspected index patient who is fecally incontinent. Large outbreaks have occurred from contact with infected infants in neonatal intensive care units (*10*). In outbreaks, prophylaxis of persons exposed to feces of infected patients may be indicated.

6. Offices and factories. Routine IG administration is not indicated under the usual office or factory conditions for persons exposed to a fellow worker with hepatitis A. Experience shows that casual contact in the work setting does not result in virus transmission.
7. Common-source exposure. IG use might be effective in preventing foodborne or waterborne hepatitis A if exposure is recognized in time. However, IG is not recommended for persons exposed to a common source of hepatitis infection after cases have begun to occur, since the 2-week period during which IG is effective will have been exceeded.

   If a food handler is diagnosed as having hepatitis A, common-source transmission is possible but uncommon. IG should be administered to other food handlers but is usually not recommended for patrons (*22*). However, IG administration to patrons may be considered if all of the following conditions exist: a) the infected person is directly involved in handling, without gloves, foods that will not be cooked before they are eaten, and b) the hygienic practices of the food handler are deficient or the food handler has had diarrhea, and c) patrons can be identified and treated within 2 weeks of exposure. Situations in which repeated exposures may have occurred, such as in institutional cafeterias, may warrant stronger consideration of IG use.

HEPATITIS B

Hepatitis B infection is caused by the hepatitis B virus (HBV), a 42-nm, double-shelled deoxyribonucleic acid (DNA) virus of the class hepadnaviridae. Several well-defined antigen-antibody systems are associated with HBV infection (Table 1). HBsAg is found on the surface of the virus and is also produced in excess amounts, circulating in blood as 22-nm spherical and tubular particles. HBsAg can be identified in serum 30-60 days after exposure to HBV and persists for variable periods. Anti-HBs develops after a resolved infection and is responsible for long-term immunity. Antibody to the core antigen (anti-HBc) develops in all HBV infections and persists indefinitely. IgM anti-HBc appears early in infection and persists for ≥6 months. It is a reliable marker of acute or recent HBV infection. A third antigen, hepatitis B e antigen (HBeAg), may be detected in samples from persons with acute or chronic HBV infection. The presence of HBeAg correlates with viral replication and high infectivity. Antibody to HBeAg (anti-HBe) develops in most HBV infections and correlates with the loss of replicating virus and with lower infectivity.

TABLE 1. Hepatitis nomenclature

	Abbreviation	Term	Definition/Comments
A. Hepatitis A	HAV	Hepatitis A virus	Etiologic agent of "infectious" hepatitis; a picornavirus; single serotype.
	Anti-HAV	Antibody to HAV	Detectable at onset of symptoms; lifetime persistence.
	IgM anti-HAV	IgM class antibody to HAV	Indicates recent infection with hepatitis A; detectable for 4-6 months after infection.
B. Hepatitis B	HBV	Hepatitis B virus	Etiologic agent of "serum" hepatitis; also known as Dane particle.
	HBsAg	Hepatitis B surface antigen	Surface antigen(s) of HBV detectable in large quantity in serum; several subtypes identified.
	HBeAg	Hepatitis B e antigen	Soluble antigen; correlates with HBV replication, high titer HBV in serum, and infectivity of serum.
	HBcAg	Hepatitis B core antigen	No commercial test available.
	Anti-HBs	Antibody to HBsAg	Indicates past infection with and immunity to HBV, passive antibody from HBIG, or immune response from HB vaccine.
	Anti-HBe	Antibody to HBeAg	Presence in serum of HBsAg carrier indicates lower titer of HBV.
	Anti-HBc	Antibody to HBcAg	Indicates prior infection with HBV at some undefined time.
	IgM anti-HBc	IgM class antibody to HBcAg	Indicates recent infection with HBV; detectable for 4-6 months after infection.
C. Delta hepatitis	HDV	Hepatitis D virus	Etiologic agent of delta hepatitis; can cause infection only in presence of HBV.
	HDAg	Delta antigen	Detectable in early acute delta infection.
	Anti-HDV	Antibody to delta antigen	Indicates present or past infection with delta virus.
D. Non-A, non-B hepatitis	PT-NANB	Parenterally transmitted	Diagnosis by exclusion. At least two candidate viruses, one of which has been proposed as hepatitis C virus; shares epidemiologic features with hepatitis B.
	ET-NANB	Enterically transmitted	Diagnosis by exclusion. Causes large epidemics in Asia, Africa, and Mexico; fecal-oral or waterborne.

TABLE 1. Hepatitis nomenclature – Continued

	Abbreviation	Term	Definition/Comments
E. Immune globulins	IG	Immune globulin (previously ISG, immune serum globulin, or gamma globulin)	Contains antibodies to HAV, low-titer antibodies to HBV.
	HBIG	Hepatitis B immune globulin	Contains high-titer antibodies to HBV.

The incubation period of hepatitis B is long (45-160 days; average = 120), and the onset of acute disease is generally insidious. Clinical symptoms and signs include anorexia, malaise, nausea, vomiting, abdominal pain, and jaundice. Extrahepatic manifestations of disease—such as skin rashes, arthralgias, and arthritis—can also occur. The case-fatality rate for reported cases is approximately 1.4%.

A variable proportion of individuals infected with HBV will become chronically infected with the virus. The HBV carrier is central to the epidemiology of HBV transmission. A carrier is defined as a person who is either HBsAg-positive on at least two occasions (at least 6 months apart) or who is HBsAg-positive and IgM anti-HBc negative when a single serum specimen is tested. Although the degree of infectivity is best correlated with HBeAg-positivity, any person positive for HBsAg is potentially infectious. The likelihood of becoming chronically infected with HBV varies inversely with the age at which infection occurs. HBV transmitted from HBsAg-positive mothers to their newborns results in HBV carriage for up to 90% of infants. Between 25% and 50% of children infected before 5 years of age become carriers, whereas only 6%-10% of acutely infected adults become carriers.

Carriers and persons with acute infection have the highest concentrations of HBV in blood and serous fluids. A lower concentration is present in other body fluids, such as saliva and semen. Transmission occurs via percutaneous or permucosal routes, and infective blood or body fluids can be introduced at birth, through sexual contact, or by contaminated needles. Infection can also occur in settings of continuous close personal contact (such as in households or among children in institutions for the developmentally disabled), presumably via inapparent or unnoticed contact of infective secretions with skin lesions or mucosal surfaces. Transmission of infection by transfusion of blood or blood products is rare because of routine screening of blood for HBsAg and because of current donor selection procedures. Transmission of HBV from infected health-care workers to patients is uncommon but has been documented during types of invasive procedures (e.g., oral and gynecologic surgery) (*23,24*). HBsAg-positive health-care workers need not be restricted from patient contact unless they have been epidemiologically associated with HBV transmission. Rather, they should be educated about the potential mechanisms of HBV transmission. Adherence to aseptic techniques minimizes the risk of transmission. HBV is not transmitted via the fecal-oral route.

Worldwide, HBV infection is a major cause of acute and chronic hepatitis, cirrhosis, and primary hepatocellular carcinoma. The frequency of HBV infection and patterns of transmission vary markedly in different parts of the world. In the United States,

Western Europe, and Australia, it is a disease of low endemicity, with infection occurring primarily during adulthood and with only 0.2%-0.9% of the population being chronically infected. In contrast, HBV infection is highly endemic in China and Southeast Asia, most of Africa, most Pacific Islands, parts of the Middle East, and in the Amazon Basin. In these areas, most persons acquire infection at birth or during childhood, and 8%-15% of the population are chronically infected with HBV. In other parts of the world, HBV infection is moderately endemic, with 2%-7% of the population being HBV carriers. Prevention strategies for populations in which HBV infection is highly endemic are directed at vaccinating infants with hepatitis B vaccine, usually beginning at birth, to prevent both perinatal and childhood transmission of infection (*25*). Recommendations for hepatitis B prophylaxis in other areas should be designed to maximize the interruption of HBV transmission in accordance with local patterns of transmission. The recommendations that follow are intended for use in the United States.

Hepatitis B Virus Infection in the United States

Each year, an estimated 300,000 persons, primarily young adults, are infected with HBV. One-quarter become ill with jaundice, more than 10,000 patients require hospitalization, and an average of 250 die of fulminant disease. The United States currently contains an estimated pool of 750,000-1,000,000 infectious carriers. Approximately 25% of carriers develop chronic active hepatitis, which often progresses to cirrhosis. Furthermore, HBV carriers have a risk of developing primary liver cancer that is 12-300 times higher than that of other persons. An estimated 4,000 persons die each year from hepatitis B-related cirrhosis, and more than 800 die from hepatitis B-related liver cancer.

Serologic surveys demonstrate that, although HBV infection is uncommon among adults in the general population, it is highly prevalent in certain groups. Those at risk, based on the prevalence of serologic markers of infection, are described in Table 2. Persons born in areas of high HBV endemicity and their descendents remain at high risk of infection, as do certain populations in which HBV is highly endemic (Alaskan Natives and Pacific Islanders). Certain lifestyles (e.g., homosexual activity, intravenous drug abuse) result in early acquisition of HBV infection and high rates of infection. Persons who have heterosexual activity with multiple partners are at significant risk of infection. Inmates of prisons have a high prevalence of HBV markers, usually because of parenteral drug abuse before or during imprisonment. Patients in custodial institutions for the developmentally disabled are also at increased risk of having HBV infection. Household contacts and sexual partners of HBV carriers are at increased risk, as are hemodialysis patients and recipients of certain plasma-derived products that have not been inactivated (e.g., anti-hemophilic factor).

Those at occupational risk of HBV infection include medical and dental workers, related laboratory and support personnel, and public service employees who have contact with blood, as well as staff in institutions or classrooms for the mentally retarded.

Hepatitis B Prevention Strategies in the United States

The incidence of reported acute hepatitis B cases increased steadily over the past decade and reached a peak in 1985 (11.50 cases/10^5/year), despite the introduction of hepatitis B vaccine 3 years previously. Incidence decreased modestly (18%) by 1988, but still remains higher than a decade ago. This minimal impact of hepatitis B vaccine on disease incidence is attributable to several factors. The sources of infection for most cases include intravenous drug abuse (28%), heterosexual contact with infected persons or multiple partners (22%), and homosexual activity (9%). In addition, 30% of patients with Hepatitis B deny any of the recognized risk factors for infection.

The present strategy for hepatitis B prevention is to vaccinate those individuals at high risk of infection. Most persons receiving vaccine as a result of this strategy have been persons at risk of acquiring HBV infection through occupational exposure, a group that accounts for approximately 4% of cases. The major deterrents to vaccinating the other high-risk groups include their lack of knowledge about the risk of disease and its consequences, the lack of public-sector programs, the cost of vaccine, and the inability to access most of the high-risk populations.

For vaccine to have an impact on the incidence of hepatitis B, a comprehensive strategy must be developed that will provide hepatitis B vaccination to persons before they engage in behaviors or occupations that place them at risk of infection. Universal HBsAg screening of pregnant women was recently recommended to prevent perinatal HBV transmission. The previous recommendations for selective screening failed to identify most HBsAg-positive pregnant women (*27*). As an alternative to high-risk-group vaccination, universal vaccination of infants and adolescents needs to be examined as a possible strategy to control the transmission of disease.

TABLE 2. Prevalence of hepatitis B serologic markers in various population groups

	Prevalence of serologic markers of HBV infection	
Population group	**HBsAg (%)**	**Any marker (%)**
Immigrants/refugees from areas of high HBV endemicity	13	70-85
Alaskan Natives/Pacific Islanders	5-15	40-70
Clients in institutions for the developmentally disabled	10-20	35-80
Users of illicit parenteral drugs	7	60-80
Sexually active homosexual men	6	35-80
Household contacts of HBV carriers	3-6	30-60
Patients of hemodialysis units	3-10	20-80
Health-care workers— frequent blood contact	1-2	15-30
Prisoners (male)	1-8	10-80
Staff of institutions for the developmentally disabled	1	10-25
Heterosexuals with multiple partners	0.5	5-20
Health-care workers— no or infrequent blood contact	0.3	3-10
General population (NHANES II)*		
Blacks	0.9	14
Whites	0.2	3

*Second National Health and Nutrition Examination Survey (*26*).

Hepatitis B Prophylaxis

Two types of products are available for prophylaxis against hepatitis B. Hepatitis B vaccines, first licensed in 1981, provide active immunization against HBV infection, and their use is recommended for both preexposure and postexposure prophylaxis. HBIG provides temporary, passive protection and is indicated only in certain postexposure settings.

HBIG

HBIG is prepared from plasma preselected to contain a high titer of anti-HBs. In the United States, HBIG has an anti-HBs titer of >100,000 by radioimmunoassay (RIA). Human plasma from which HBIG is prepared is screened for antibodies to HIV; in addition, the Cohn fractionation process used to prepare this product inactivates and eliminates HIV from the final product.There is no evidence that the causative agent of AIDS (HIV) has been transmitted by HBIG (*6*).

Hepatitis B Vaccine

Two types of hepatitis B vaccines are currently licensed in the United States. Plasma-derived vaccine consists of a suspension of inactivated, alum-adsorbed, 22-nm, HBsAg particles that have been purified from human plasma by a combination of biophysical (ultracentrifugation) and biochemical procedures. Inactivation is a threefold process using 8M urea, pepsin at pH 2, and 1:4,000 formalin. These treatment steps have been shown to inactivate representatives of all classes of viruses found in human blood, including HIV (*28*). Plasma-derived vaccine is no longer being produced in the United States, and use is now limited to hemodialysis patients, other immunocompromised hosts, and persons with known allergy to yeast.

Currently licensed recombinant hepatitis B vaccines are produced by *Saccharomyces cerevisiae* (common baker's yeast), into which a plasmid containing the gene for the HBsAg has been inserted. Purified HBsAg is obtained by lysing the yeast cells and separating HBsAg from yeast components by biochemical and biophysical techniques. These vaccines contain more than 95% HBsAg protein. Yeast-derived protein constitutes no more than 5% of the final product.

Hepatitis B vaccines are packaged to contain 10-40 μg HBsAg protein/ml and are adsorbed with aluminum hydroxide (0.5 mg/ml). Thimerosal (1:20,000 concentration) is added as a preservative.

The recommended series of three intramuscular doses of hepatitis B vaccine induces an adequate antibody response* in >90% of healthy adults and in >95%of infants, children, and adolescents from birth through 19 years of age (*29-31*). The deltoid (arm) is the recommended site for hepatitis B vaccination of adults and children; immunogenicity of vaccine for adults is substantially lower when injections are given in the buttock (*32*). Larger vaccine doses (two to four times normal adult dose) or an increased number of doses (four doses) are required to induce protective antibody in a high proportion of hemodialysis patients and may also be necessary for other immunocompromised persons (such as those on immunosuppressive drugs or with HIV infection) (*33,34*).

*An adequate antibody response is ≥10 milliInternational Units (mIU)/ml, approximately equivalent to 10 sample ratio units (SRU) by RIA or positive by enzyme immunoassay (EIA), measured 1-6 months after completion of the vaccine series.

Field trials of the vaccines licensed in the United States have shown 80%-95% efficacy in preventing infection or clinical hepatitis among susceptible persons (*31,35*). Protection against illness is virtually complete for persons who develop an adequate antibody response after vaccination. The duration of protection and need for booster doses are not yet fully defined. Between 30% and 50% of persons who develop adequate antibody after three doses of vaccine will lose detectable antibody within 7 years, but protection against viremic infection and clinical disease appears to persist (*36-38*). Immunogenicity and efficacy of the licensed vaccines for hemodialysis patients are much lower than in normal adults. Protection in this group may last only as long as adequate antibody levels persist (*33*).

Vaccine Usage

Primary vaccination comprises three intramuscular doses of vaccine, with the second and third doses given 1 and 6 months, respectively, after the first. Adults and older children should be given a full 1.0 ml/dose, while children <11 years of age should usually receive half (0.5 ml) this dose. See Table 3 for complete information on age-specific dosages of currently available vaccines. An alternative schedule of four doses of vaccine given at 0, 1, 2, and 12 months has been approved for one vaccine for postexposure prophylaxis or for more rapid induction of immunity. However, there is no clear evidence that this regimen provides greater protection than the standard three-dose series. Hepatitis B vaccine should be given only in the deltoid muscle for adults and children or in the anterolateral thigh muscle for infants and neonates.

For patients undergoing hemodialysis and for other immunosuppressed patients, higher vaccine doses or increased numbers of doses are required. A special formu-

TABLE 3. Recommended doses and schedules of currently licensed HB vaccines

	Vaccine					
	Heptavax-B*,†		Recombivax HB*		Engerix-B*§	
Group	Dose (μg)	(ml)	Dose (μg)	(ml)	Dose (μg)	(ml)
Infants of HBV-carrier mothers	10	(0.5)	5	(0.5)	10	(0.5)
Other infants and children <11 years	10	(0.5)	2.5	(0.25)	10	(0.5)
Children and adolescents 11-19 years	20	(1.0)	5	(0.5)	20	(1.0)
Adults >19 years	20	(1.0)	10	(1.0)	20	(1.0)
Dialysis patients and other immunocompromised persons	40	(2.0)¶	40	(1.0)**	40	(2.0)¶,††

*Usual schedule: three doses at 0, 1, 6 months.
†Available only for hemodialysis and other immunocompromised patients and for persons with known allergy to yeast.
§Alternative schedule: four doses at 0, 1, 2, 12 months.
¶Two 1.0-ml doses given at different sites.
**Special formulation for dialysis patients.
††Four-dose schedule recommended at 0, 1, 2, 6 months.

lation of one vaccine is now available for such persons (Table 3). Persons with HIV infection have an impaired response to hepatitis B vaccine. The immunogenicity of higher doses of vaccine is unknown for this group, and firm recommendations on dosage cannot be made at this time (*34*).

Vaccine doses administered at longer intervals provide equally satisfactory protection, but optimal protection is not conferred until after the third dose. If the vaccine series is interrupted after the first dose, the second and third doses should be given separated by an interval of 3-5 months. Persons who are late for the third dose should be given this dose when convenient. Postvaccination testing is not considered necessary in either situation.

In one study, the response to vaccination by the standard schedule using one or two doses of one vaccine, followed by the remaining doses of a different vaccine, was comparable to the response to vaccination with a single vaccine. Moreover, because the immunogenicities of the available vaccines are similar, it is likely that responses in such situations will be comparable to those induced by any of the vaccines alone.

The immunogenicity of a series of three low doses (0.1 standard dose) of plasma-derived hepatitis B vaccine administered by the intradermal route has been assessed in several studies. The largest studies of adults show lower rates of developing adequate antibody (80%-90%) and twofold to fourfold lower antibody titers than with intramuscular vaccination with recommended doses (*39* and CDC unpublished data). Data on immunogenicity of low doses of recombinant vaccines given intradermally are limited. At this time, intradermal vaccination of adults using low doses of vaccine should be done only under research protocol, with appropriate informed consent and with postvaccination testing to identify persons with inadequate response who would be eligible for revaccination. Intradermal vaccination is not recommended for infants or children.

All hepatitis B vaccines are inactivated (noninfective) products, and there is no evidence of interference with other simultaneously administered vaccines.

Data are not available on the safety of hepatitis B vaccines for the developing fetus. Because the vaccines contain only noninfectious HBsAg particles, there should be no risk to the fetus. In contrast, HBV infection of a pregnant woman may result in severe disease for the mother and chronic infection of the newborn. Therefore, pregnancy or lactation should not be considered a contraindication to the use of this vaccine for persons who are otherwise eligible.

Vaccine storage and shipment

Vaccine should be shipped and stored at 2 C-8 C but not frozen. *Freezing destroys the potency of the vaccine.*

Side effects and adverse reactions

The most common side effect observed following vaccination with each of the available vaccines has been soreness at the injection site. Postvaccination surveillance for 3 years after licensure of the plasma-derived vaccine showed an association of borderline significance between Guillain-Barré syndrome and receipt of the first vaccine dose (*40*). The rate of this occurrence was very low (0.5/100,000 vaccinees) and was more than compensated by disease prevented by the vaccine even if Guillain-Barré syndrome is a true side effect. Such postvaccination surveillance information is not available for the recombinant hepatitis B vaccines. Early concerns about safety of plasma-derived vaccine have proven to be unfounded, particularly the concern that infectious agents such as HIV present in the donor plasma pools might contaminate the final product.

Effect of vaccination on carriers and immune persons

Hepatitis B vaccine produces neither therapeutic nor adverse effects for HBV carriers (*41*). Vaccination of individuals who possess antibodies against HBV from a previous infection is not necessary but will not cause adverse effects. Such individuals will have a postvaccination increase in their anti-HBs levels. Passively acquired antibody, whether acquired from HBIG or IG administration or from the transplacental route, will not interfere with active immunization (*42*).

Prevaccination serologic testing for susceptibility

The decision to test potential vaccine recipients for prior infection is primarily a cost-effectiveness issue and should be based on whether the costs of testing balance the costs of vaccine saved by not vaccinating individuals who have already been infected. Estimation of cost-effectiveness of testing depends on three variables: the cost of vaccination, the cost of testing for susceptibility, and the expected prevalence of immune individuals in the group.

Testing in groups with the highest risk of HBV infection (HBV marker prevalence >20%, Table 2) is usually cost-effective unless testing costs are extremely high. Cost-effectiveness of screening may be marginal for groups at intermediate risk. For groups with a low expected prevalence of HBV serologic markers, such as health professionals in their training years, prevaccination testing is not cost-effective.

For routine testing, only one antibody test is necessary (either anti-HBc or anti-HBs). Anti-HBc identifies all previously infected persons, both carriers and those who are not carriers, but does not differentiate members of the two groups. Anti-HBs identifies persons previously infected, except for carriers. Neither test has a particular advantage for groups expected to have carrier rates of <2%, such as health-care workers. Anti-HBc may be preferred to avoid unnecessary vaccination of carriers for groups with higher carrier rates. If RIA is used to test for anti-HBs, a minimum of 10 sample ratio units should be used to designate immunity (2.1 is the usual designation of a positive test). If EIA is used, the positive level recommended by manufacturers is appropriate.

Postvaccination testing for serologic response and revaccination of nonresponders

Hepatitis B vaccine, when given in the deltoid, produces protective antibody (anti-HBs) in >90% of healthy persons. Testing for immunity after vaccination is not recommended routinely but is advised for persons whose subsequent management depends on knowing their immune status (such as dialysis patients and staff). Testing for immunity is also advised for persons for whom a suboptimal response may be anticipated, such as those who have received vaccine in the buttock, persons ≥50 years of age, and persons known to have HIV infection. Postvaccination testing should also be considered for persons at occupational risk who may have needle-stick exposures necessitating postexposure prophylaxis. When necessary, postvaccination testing should be done between 1 and 6 months after completion of the vaccine series to provide definitive information on response to the vaccine.

Revaccination of persons who do not respond to the primary series (nonresponders) produces adequate antibody in 15%-25% after one additional dose and in

30%-50% after three additional doses when the primary vaccination has been given in the deltoid (*36*). For persons who did not respond to a primary vaccine series given in the buttock, data suggest that revaccination in the arm induces adequate antibody in >75%. Revaccination with one or more additional doses should be considered for persons who fail to respond to vaccination in the deltoid and is recommended for those who have failed to respond to vaccination in the buttock.

Need for vaccine booster doses

Available data show that vaccine-induced antibody levels decline steadily with time and that up to 50% of adult vaccinees who respond adequately to vaccine may have low or undetectable antibody levels by 7 years after vaccination. Nevertheless, both adults and children with declining antibody levels are still protected against hepatitis B disease. Current data also suggest excellent protection against disease for 5 years after vaccination among infants born to hepatitis B-carrier mothers. For adults and children with normal immune status, booster doses are not routinely recommended within 7 years after vaccination, nor is routine serologic testing to assess antibody levels necessary for vaccine recipients during this period. For infants born to hepatitis B-carrier mothers, booster doses are not necessary within 5 years after vaccination. The possible need for booster doses after longer intervals will be assessed as additional information becomes available.

For hemodialysis patients, for whom vaccine-induced protection is less complete and may persist only as long as antibody levels remain above 10 mIU/ml, the need for booster doses should be assessed by annual antibody testing, and booster doses should be given when antibody levels decline to <10 mIU/ml.

Groups recommended for preexposure vaccination

Persons at substantial risk of HBV infection who are demonstrated or judged likely to be susceptible should be vaccinated. They include the following:

1. Persons with occupational risk. HBV infection is a major infectious occupational hazard for health-care and public-safety workers. The risk of acquiring HBV infection from occupational exposures is dependent on the frequency of percutaneous and permucosal exposures to blood or blood products. Any health-care or public-safety worker may be at risk for HBV exposure depending on the tasks that he or she performs. If those tasks involve contact with blood or blood-contaminated body fluids, such workers should be vaccinated. Vaccination should be considered for other workers depending on the nature of the task (*43*).

   Risks among health-care professionals vary during the training and working career of each individual but are often highest during the professional training period. For this reason, when possible, vaccination should be completed during training in schools of medicine, dentistry, nursing, laboratory technology, and other allied health professions before workers have their first contact with blood.
2. Clients and staff of institutions for the developmentally disabled. Susceptible clients in institutions for the developmentally disabled should be vaccinated. Staff who work closely with clients should also be vaccinated. The risk in institutional environments is associated not only with blood exposure but may also be consequent to bites and contact with skin lesions and other infective secretions. Susceptible clients and staff who live or work in smaller (group)

residential settings with known HBV carriers should also receive hepatitis B vaccine. Clients discharged from residential institutions into community settings should be screened for HBsAg so that the community programs may take appropriate measures to prevent HBV transmission. These measures should include both environmental controls and appropriate use of vaccine.

Staff of nonresidential day-care programs (e.g., schools, sheltered workshops for the developmentally disabled) attended by known HBV carriers have a risk of HBV infection comparable to that among health-care workers and therefore should be vaccinated (*44*). The risk of HBV infection for clients appears to be lower than the risk for staff. Vaccination of clients in day-care programs may be considered. Vaccination of classroom contacts is strongly encouraged if a classmate who is an HBV carrier behaves aggressively or has special medical problems that increase the risk of exposure to his/her blood or serous secretions.

3. Hemodialysis patients. Hepatitis B vaccination is recommended for susceptible hemodialysis patients. Although seroconversion rates and anti-HBs titers are lower than those for healthy persons, for those patients who do respond, hepatitis B vaccine will protect them from HBV infection and reduce the necessity for frequent serologic screening (*45*). Some studies have shown higher seroconversion rates and antibody titers for patients with uremia who were vaccinated before they required dialysis (*46*). Identification of patients for vaccination early in the course of their renal disease is encouraged.
4. Sexually active homosexual men. Susceptible sexually active homosexual men should be vaccinated regardless of their age or the duration of their homosexual practices. Persons should be vaccinated as soon as possible after their homosexual activity begins. Homosexual and bisexual men known to have HIV infection should be tested for anti-HBs response after completion of the vaccine series and should be counseled accordingly.
5. Users of illicit injectable drugs. All users of illicit injectable drugs who are susceptible to HBV should be vaccinated as early as possible after their drug abuse begins.
6. Recipients of certain blood products. Patients with clotting disorders who receive clotting-factor concentrates have an increased risk of HBV infection. Vaccination is recommended for these persons, and it should be initiated at the time their specific clotting disorder is identified. Prevaccination testing is recommended for patients who have already received multiple infusions of these products.
7. Household and sexual contacts of HBV carriers. Household contacts of HBV carriers are at high risk of HBV infection. Sexual contacts appear to be at greatest risk. When HBV carriers are identified through routine screening of donated blood, diagnostic testing in hospitals, prenatal screening, screening of refugees from certain areas, or other screening programs, they should be notified of their status. All household and sexual contacts should be tested and susceptible contacts vaccinated.
8. Adoptees from countries of high HBV endemicity. Families accepting orphans or unaccompanied minors from countries of high or intermediate HBV endemicity should have the children screened for HBsAg. If the children are HBsAg-positive, family members should be vaccinated (*47*).

9. Other contacts of HBV carriers. Persons in casual contact with carriers in settings such as schools and offices are at minimal risk of HBV infection, and vaccine is not routinely recommended for them. At child-care centers, HBV transmission between children or between children and staff has rarely been documented. Unless special circumstances exist, such as behavior problems (biting or scratching) or medical conditions (severe skin disease) that might facilitate transmission, vaccination of contacts of carriers in child care is not indicated.
10. Populations with high endemicity of HBV infection. In certain U.S. populations, including Alaskan Natives, Pacific Islanders, and refugees from HBV-endemic areas, HBV infection is highly endemic, and transmission occurs primarily during childhood. In such groups, universal hepatitis B vaccination of infants is recommended to prevent disease transmission during childhood. In addition, more extensive programs of "catch-up" childhood vaccination should be considered if resources are available.

    Immigrants and refugees from areas with highly endemic HBV disease (particularly Africa and eastern Asia) should be screened for HBV markers upon resettlement in the United States. If an HBV carrier is identified, all susceptible household contacts should be vaccinated. Even if no HBV carriers are found within a family, vaccination should be considered for susceptible children <7 years of age because of the high rate of interfamilial HBV infection that occurs among these children (*48*). Vaccination is recommended for all infants of women who were born in areas in which infection is highly endemic.
11. Inmates of long-term correctional facilities. The prison environment may provide a favorable setting for the transmission of HBV because of the use of illicit injectable drugs and because of male homosexual practices. Moreover, it provides an access point for vaccination of percutaneous drug abusers. Prison officials should consider undertaking screening and vaccination programs directed at inmates with histories of high-risk behaviors.
12. Sexually active heterosexual persons. Sexually active heterosexual persons with multiple sexual partners are at increased risk of HBV infection. Risk increases with increasing numbers of sexual partners. Vaccination is recommended for persons who are diagnosed as having recently acquired other sexually transmitted diseases, for prostitutes, and for persons who have a history of sexual activity with multiple partners in the previous 6 months.
13. International travelers. Vaccination should be considered for persons who plan to reside for more than 6 months in areas with high levels of endemic HBV and who will have close contact with the local population. Vaccination should also be considered for short-term travelers who are likely to have contact with blood from or sexual contact with residents of areas with high levels of endemic disease. Ideally, hepatitis B vaccination of travelers should begin at least 6 months before travel to allow for completion of the full vaccine series. Nevertheless, a partial series will offer some protection from HBV infection. The alternative four-dose schedule may provide better protection during travel if the first three doses can be delivered before travel (second and third doses given 1 and 2 months, respectively, after first).

Postexposure Prophylaxis for Hepatitis B

Prophylactic treatment to prevent hepatitis B infection after exposure to HBV should be considered in the following situations: perinatal exposure of an infant born to an HBsAg-positive mother, accidental percutaneous or permucosal exposure to HBsAg-positive blood, sexual exposure to an HBsAg-positive person, and household exposure of an infant <12 months of age to a primary care giver who has acute hepatitis B.

Various studies have established the relative efficacies of HBIG and/or hepatitis B vaccine in different exposure situations. For an infant with perinatal exposure to an HBsAg-positive and HBeAg-positive mother, a regimen combining one dose of HBIG at birth with the hepatitis B vaccine series started soon after birth is 85%-95% effective in preventing development of the HBV carrier state (*35, 49-51*). Regimens involving either multiple doses of HBIG alone, or the vaccine series alone, have 70%-85% efficacy (*52,53*).

For accidental percutaneous exposure, only regimens including HBIG and/or IG have been studied. A regimen of two doses of HBIG, one given after exposure and one a month later, is about 75% effective in preventing hepatitis B in this setting (*54,55*). For sexual exposure, a single dose of HBIG is 75% effective if given within 2 weeks of last sexual exposure (*56*). The efficacy of IG for postexposure prophylaxis is uncertain. IG no longer has a role in postexposure prophylaxis of hepatitis B because of the availability of HBIG and the wider use of hepatitis B vaccine.

Recommendations on postexposure prophylaxis are based on available efficacy data and on the likelihood of future HBV exposure of the person requiring treatment. In all exposures, a regimen combining HBIG with hepatitis B vaccine will provide both short- and long-term protection, will be less costly than the two-dose HBIG treatment alone, and is the treatment of choice.

Perinatal Exposure and Recommendations

Transmission of HBV from mother to infant during the perinatal period represents one of the most efficient modes of HBV infection and often leads to severe long-term sequelae. Infants born to HBsAg-positive and HBeAg-positive mothers have a 70%-90% chance of acquiring perinatal HBV infection, and 85%-90% of infected infants will become chronic HBV carriers. Estimates are that >25% of these carriers will die from primary hepatocellular carcinoma (PHC) or cirrhosis of the liver (*57*). Infants born to HBsAg-positive and HBeAg-negative mothers have a lower risk of acquiring perinatal infection; however, such infants have had acute disease, and fatal fulminant hepatitis has been reported (*58,59*). Based on 1987 data in the United States, an estimated 18,000 births occur to HBsAg-positive women each year, resulting in approximately 4,000 infants who become chronic HBV carriers. Prenatal screening of all pregnant women identifies those who are HBsAg-positive and allows treatment of their newborns with HBIG and hepatitis B vaccine, a regimen that is 85%-95% effective in preventing the development of the HBV chronic carrier state. The following are perinatal recommendations:

1. All pregnant women should be routinely tested for HBsAg during an early prenatal visit in each pregnancy. This testing should be done at the same time that other routine prenatal screening tests are ordered. In special situations

(e.g., when acute hepatitis is suspected, when a history of exposure to hepatitis has been reported, or when the mother has a particularly high-risk behavior, such as intravenous drug abuse), an additional HBsAg test can be ordered later in the pregnancy. No other HBV marker tests are necessary for the purpose of maternal screening, although HBsAg-positive mothers identified during screening may have HBV-related acute or chronic liver disease and should be evaluated by their physicians.

2. If a woman has not been screened prenatally or if test results are not available at the time of admission for delivery, HBsAg testing should be done at the time of admission, or as soon as possible thereafter. If the mother is identified as HBsAg-positive >1 month after giving birth, the infant should be tested for HBsAg. If the results are negative, the infant should be given HBIG and hepatitis B vaccine.
3. Following all initial positive tests for HBsAg, a repeat test for HBsAg should be performed on the same specimen, followed by a confirmatory test using a neutralization assay. For women in labor who did not have HBsAg testing during pregnancy and who are found to be HBsAg-positive on first testing, initiation of treatment of their infants should not be delayed by more than 24 hours for repeat or confirmatory testing.
4. Infants born to HBsAg-positive mothers should receive HBIG (0.5 ml) intramuscularly once they are physiologically stable, preferably within 12 hours of birth (Table 4). Hepatitis B vaccine should be administered intramuscularly at the appropriate infant dose. The first dose should be given concurrently with HBIG but at a different site. If vaccine is not immediately available, the first dose should be given as soon as possible. Subsequent doses should be given as recommended for the specific vaccine. Testing infants for HBsAg and anti-HBs is recommended when they are 12-15 months of age to monitor the success or failure of therapy. If HBsAg is not detectable and anti-HBs is present, children can be considered protected. Testing for anti-HBc is not useful, since maternal anti-HBc can persist for >1 year. HBIG and hepatitis B vaccination do not interfere with routine childhood vaccinations. Breast-feeding poses no risk of HBV infection for infants who have begun prophylaxis
5. Household members and sexual partners of HBV carriers identified through prenatal screening should be tested to determine susceptibility to HBV infection, and, if susceptible, should receive hepatitis B vaccine.

TABLE 4. Hepatitis B virus postexposure recommendations

	HBIG		Vaccine	
Exposure	Dose	Recommended timing	Dose	Recommended timing
Perinatal	0.5 ml IM	Within 12 hours of birth	0.5 ml IM*	Within 12 hours of birth†
Sexual	0.06 ml/kg IM	Single dose within 14 days of last sexual contact	1.0 ml IM*	First dose at time of HBIG treatment†

*For appropriate age-specific doses of each vaccine, see Table 3.
†The first dose can be given the same time as the HBIG dose but in a different site; subsequent doses should be given as recommended for specific vaccine.

6. **Obstetric and pediatric staff should be notified directly about HBsAg-positive mothers so that neonates can receive therapy without delay after birth and follow-up doses of vaccine can be given. Programs to coordinate the activities of persons providing prenatal care, hospital-based obstetrical services, and pediatric well-baby care must be established to assure proper follow-up and treatment both of infants born to HBsAg-positive mothers and of other susceptible household and sexual contacts.**
7. In those populations under U.S. jurisdiction in which hepatitis B infection is highly endemic (including certain Alaskan Natives, Pacific Island groups, and refugees from highly endemic areas accepted for resettlement in the United States), universal vaccination of newborns with hepatitis B vaccine is the recommended strategy for hepatitis B control. HBsAg screening of mothers and use of HBIG for infants born to HBV-carrier mothers may be added to routine hepatitis B vaccination when practical, but screening and HBIG alone will not adequately protect children from HBV infection in endemic areas. In such areas, hepatitis B vaccine doses should be integrated into the childhood vaccination schedule. More extensive programs of childhood hepatitis B vaccination should be considered if resources are available.

Acute Exposure to Blood That Contains (or Might Contain) HBsAg

For accidental percutaneous (needle stick, laceration, or bite) or permucosal (ocular or mucous-membrane) exposure to blood, the decision to provide prophylaxis must include consideration of several factors: a) whether the source of the blood is available, b) the HBsAg status of the source, and c) the hepatitis B vaccination and vaccine-response status of the exposed person. Such exposures usually affect persons for whom hepatitis B vaccine is recommended. For any exposure of a person not previously vaccinated, hepatitis B vaccination is recommended.

Following any such exposure, a blood sample should be obtained from the person who was the source of the exposure and should be tested for HBsAg. The hepatitis B vaccination status and anti-HBs response status (if known) of the exposed person should be reviewed. The outline below and Table 5 summarize prophylaxis for percutaneous or permucosal exposure to blood according to the HBsAg status of the source of exposure and the vaccination status and vaccine response of the exposed person.

For greatest effectiveness, passive prophylaxis with HBIG, when indicated, should be given as soon as possible after exposure (its value beyond 7 days after exposure is unclear).

1. Source of exposure HBsAg-positive
   a. Exposed person has not been vaccinated or has not completed vaccination. Hepatitis B vaccination should be initiated. A single dose of HBIG (0.06 ml/kg) should be given as soon as possible after exposure and within 24 hours, if possible. The first dose of hepatitis B vaccine (Table 3) should be given intramuscularly at a separate site (deltoid for adults) and can be given simultaneously with HBIG or within 7 days of exposure. Subsequent doses should be given as recommended for the specific vaccine. If the exposed person has begun but not completed vaccination, one dose of HBIG should be given immediately, and vaccination should be completed as scheduled.

b. Exposed person has already been vaccinated against hepatitis B, and anti-HBs response status is known.
   (1) If the exposed person is known to have had adequate response in the past, the anti-HBs level should be tested unless an adequate level has been demonstrated within the last 24 months. Although current data show that vaccine-induced protection does not decrease as antibody level wanes, most experts consider the following approach to be prudent.
      a) If anti-HBs level is adequate, no treatment is necessary.
      b) If anti-HBs level is inadequate,* a booster dose of hepatitis B vaccine should be given.
   (2) If the exposed person is known not to have responded to the primary vaccine series, the exposed person should be given either a single dose of HBIG and a dose of hepatitis B vaccine as soon as possible after exposure, or two doses of HBIG (0.06 ml/kg), one given as soon as possible after exposure and the second 1 month later. The latter treatment is preferred for those who have failed to respond to at least four doses of vaccine.

*An adequate antibody level is ≥10 milliInternational Units (mIU)/ml, approximately equivalent to 10 sample ratio units (SRU) by RIA or positive by EIA.

TABLE 5. Recommendations for hepatitis B prophylaxis following percutaneous or permucosal exposure

	Treatment when source is found to be:		
Exposed person	**HBsAg-positive**	**HBsAg-negative**	**Source not tested or unknown**
Unvaccinated	HBIG x 1* and initiate HB vaccine[†]	Initiate HB vaccine[†]	Initiate HB vaccine[†]
Previously vaccinated Known responder	Test exposed for anti-HBs 1. If adequate,[§] no treatment 2. If inadequate, HB vaccine booster dose	No treatment	No treatment
Known nonresponder	HBIG x 2 or HBIG x 1 plus 1 dose HB vaccine	No treatment	If known high-risk source, *may treat as if source were HBsAg-positive*
Response unknown	Test exposed for anti-HBs 1. if inadequate,[§] HBIG x 1 plus HB vaccine booster dose 2. If adequate, no treatment	No treatment	Test exposed for anti-HBs 1. If inadequate[§], HB vaccine booster dose 2. If adequate, no treatment

*HBIG dose 0.06 ml/kg IM.
[†]HB vaccine dose - see Table 3.
[§]Adequate anti-HBs is ≥10 SRU by RIA or positive by EIA.

c. Exposed person has already been vaccinated against hepatitis B, and the anti-HBs response is unknown. The exposed person should be tested for anti-HBs.
   (1) If the exposed person has adequate antibody, no additional treatment is necessary.
   (2) If the exposed person has inadequate antibody on testing, one dose of HBIG (0.06 ml/kg) should be given immediately and a standard booster dose of vaccine (Table 3) given at a different site.

2. Source of exposure known and HBsAg-negative
   a. Exposed person has not been vaccinated or has not completed vaccination. If unvaccinated, the exposed person should be given the first dose of hepatitis B vaccine within 7 days of exposure, and vaccination should be completed as recommended. If the exposed person has not completed vaccination, vaccination should be completed as scheduled.
   b. Exposed person has already been vaccinated against hepatitis B. No treatment is necessary.
3. Source of exposure unknown or not available for testing
   a. Exposed person has not been vaccinated or has not completed vaccination. If unvaccinated, the exposed person should be given the first dose of hepatitis B vaccine within 7 days of exposure and vaccination completed as recommended. If the exposed person has not completed vaccination, vaccination should be completed as scheduled.
   b. Exposed person has already been vaccinated against hepatitis B, and anti-HBs response status is known.
      (1) If the exposed person is known to have had adequate response in the past, no treatment is necessary.
      (2) If the exposed person is known not to have responded to the vaccine, prophylaxis as described earlier in section I.b.(2) under "Source of exposure HBsAg-positive" may be considered if the source of the exposure is known to be at high risk of HBV infection.
   c. Exposed person has already been vaccinated against hepatitis B, and the anti-HBs response is unknown. The exposed person should be tested for anti-HBs.
      (1) If the exposed person has adequate anti-HBs, no treatment is necessary.
      (2) If the exposed person has inadequate anti-HBs, a standard booster dose of vaccine should be given.

Sexual Partners of Persons with Acute HBV Infection

Sexual partners of HBsAg-positive persons are at increased risk of acquiring HBV infection, and HBIG has been shown to be 75% effective in preventing such infections (*56*). Because data are limited, the period after sexual exposure during which HBIG is effective is unknown, but extrapolation from other settings makes it unlikely that this period would exceed 14 days. Before treatment, testing of sexual partners for susceptibility is recommended if it does not delay treatment beyond 14 days after last exposure. Testing for anti-HBc is the most efficient prescreening test to use in this population.

All susceptible persons whose sexual partners have acute hepatitis B infection or whose sexual partners are discovered to be hepatitis B carriers should receive a single dose of HBIG (0.06 ml/kg) and should begin the hepatitis B vaccine series if prophylaxis can be started within 14 days of the last sexual contact, or if ongoing sexual contact with the infected person will occur. Giving the vaccine with HBIG may improve the efficacy of postexposure treatment. The vaccine has the added advantage of conferring long-lasting protection.

An alternative treatment for persons who are not from a high-risk group for whom vaccine is routinely recommended and whose regular sexual partners have acute HBV infection is to give one dose of HBIG (without vaccine) and retest the sexual partner for HBsAg 3 months later. No further treatment is necessary if the sexual partner becomes HBsAg-negative. If the sexual partner remains HBsAg-positive, a second dose of HBIG should be given and the hepatitis B vaccine series started.

Household Contacts of Persons with Acute HBV Infection

Since infants have close contact with primary care givers and they have a higher risk of becoming HBV carriers after acute HBV infection, prophylaxis of an infant <12 months of age with HBIG (0.5 ml) and hepatitis B vaccine is indicated if the mother or primary care giver has acute HBV infection. Prophylaxis for other household contacts of persons with acute HBV infection is not indicated unless they have had identifiable blood exposure to the index patient, such as by sharing toothbrushes or razors. Such exposures should be treated similarly to sexual exposures. If the index patient becomes an HBV carrier, all household contacts should be given hepatitis B vaccine.

DELTA HEPATITIS

The delta virus (also known as hepatitis D virus [HDV]) is a defective virus that may cause infection only in the presence of active HBV infection. The HDV is a 35- to 37-nm viral particle, consisting of single-stranded RNA (mw 500,000) and an internal protein antigen (delta antigen [HDAg]), coated with HBsAg as the surface protein (*5*). Infection may occur as either coinfection with HBV or superinfection of an HBV carrier, each of which usually causes an episode of clinical acute hepatitis. Coinfection usually resolves, whereas superinfection frequently causes chronic HDV infection and chronic active hepatitis. Both types of infection may cause fulminant hepatitis.

HDV infection may be diagnosed by detecting HDAg in serum during early infection and by the appearance of total or IgM-specific delta antibody (anti-HDV) during or after infection. A test for detection of total anti-HDV is commercially available. Other tests (HDAg, IgM anti-HDV) are available only in research laboratories.

Routes of transmission of HDV are similar to those of HBV. In the United States, HDV infection most commonly affects persons at high risk of HBV infection, particularly parenteral drug abusers and persons with hemophilia.

Since HDV is dependent on HBV for replication, prevention of hepatitis B infection, either preexposure or postexposure, will suffice to prevent HDV infection for a person susceptible to hepatitis B. Known episodes of perinatal, sexual, or percutaneous exposure to serum or exposure to persons known to be positive for both HBV and HDV should be treated exactly as such exposures to HBV alone.

Persons who are HBsAg carriers are at risk of HDV infection, especially if they participate in activities that put them at high risk of repeated exposure to HBV (parenteral drug abuse, male homosexual activity). However, at present no products are available that might prevent HDV infection in HBsAg carriers either before or after exposure.

NON-A, NON-B HEPATITIS

Parenterally Transmitted (PT) Non-A, Non-B Hepatitis

Parenterally transmitted non-A, non-B hepatitis accounts for 20%-40% of acute viral hepatitis in the United States and has epidemiologic characteristics similar to those of hepatitis B (*60*). Recently, a portion of the genome of a virus thought to be responsible for PT non-A, non-B hepatitis was cloned (*2*). A candidate serologic assay for antibody to this virus (proposed as hepatitis C virus) has been developed. This assay appears to detect a substantial number of persons with chronic infection and is being evaluated for screening potential blood donors (*3*). Although PT non-A, non-B hepatitis has traditionally been considered a transfusion-associated disease, most reported cases have not been associated with blood transfusion (*61-64*). Groups at high risk of acquiring this disease include transfusion recipients, parenteral drug users, and dialysis patients (*62,63*). Health-care work that entails frequent contact with blood, personal contact with others who have had hepatitis in the past, and contact with infected persons within households have also been documented in some studies as risk factors for acquiring PT non-A, non-B hepatitis (*63-65*). However, the role of person-to-person contact in disease transmission has not been well defined, and the importance of sexual activity in the transmission of this type of hepatitis is unclear.

Multiple episodes of non-A, non-B hepatitis have been observed among the same individuals and may be due to different bloodborne agents. An average of 50% of patients who have acute PT non-A, non-B hepatitis infection later develop chronic hepatitis (*66*). Experimental studies of chimpanzees have confirmed the existence of a carrier state, which may be present in 1%-3% of the population (*67,68*).

The risk and consequences of perinatal transmission of PT non-A, non-B hepatitis are not well defined. Only one small study has been published in which infants born of 12 women who had acute PT non-A, non-B hepatitis during pregnancy were followed. Six infants developed transient alanine aminotransferase (ALT) elevations at 4-8 weeks of age (*69*).

The results have been equivocal in several studies attempting to assess the value of prophylaxis with IGs against PT non-A, non-B hepatitis (*70-72*). For persons with percutaneous exposure to blood from a patient with PT non-A, non-B hepatitis, it may be reasonable to administer IG (0.06 ml/kg) as soon as possible after exposure. In other circumstances, no specific recommendations can be made.

Enterically Transmitted (ET) Non-A, Non-B Hepatitis

A distinct type of non-A, non-B hepatitis acquired by the fecal-oral route was first identified through investigations of large waterborne epidemics in developing countries. This ET non-A, non-B hepatitis, which has occurred in epidemics or sporadically in parts of Asia, North and West Africa, and Mexico, is serologically distinct from other known hepatitis viruses (*4,73*). Young to middle-aged adults are most often affected, with an unusually high mortality among pregnant women. The disease has been transmitted to experimental animals, and candidate viruses have been identified; however, no serologic tests have yet been developed (*74*).

ET non-A, non-B hepatitis has not been recognized as an endemic disease in the United States or Western Europe, and it is unknown whether the causative agent is present in these areas. Cases have been documented, however, among persons returning from travel to countries in which this disease occurs (*75*).

Travelers to areas having ET non-A, non-B hepatitis may be at some risk of acquiring this disease by close contact with infected persons or by consuming contaminated food or water. There is no evidence that U.S.-manufactured IG will prevent this infection. As with hepatitis A and other enteric infections, the best means of preventing ET non-A, non-B hepatitis is avoiding potentially contaminated food or water.

References

1. Francis DP, Maynard JE. The transmission and outcome of hepatitis A, B, and non-A, non-B: a review. Epidemiol Rev 1979;1:17-31.
2. Choo Q-L, Kuo G, Weiner AJ, et al. Isolation of a cDNA clone derived from a blood-borne non-A, non-B hepatitis genome. Science 1989;244:359-62.
3. Kuo G, Choo Q-L, Alter HJ, et al. An assay for circulating antibodies to a major etiologic virus of human non-A, non-B hepatitis. Science 1989;244:362-4.
4. Ramalingaswami V, Purcell RH. Waterborne non-A, non-B hepatitis. Lancet 1988;1:571-3.
5. Rizzetto M. The delta agent. Hepatology 1983;3:729-37.
6. CDC. Safety of therapeutic immune globulin preparations with respect to transmission of human T-lymphotropic virus type III/lymphadenopathy-associated virus infection. MMWR 1986;35:231-3.
7. Wells MA, Wittek AE, Epstein JS, et al. Inactivation and partition of human T-cell lymphotropic virus, type III, during ethanol fractionation of plasma. Transfusion 1986;26:210-3.
8. Tedder RS, Uttley A, Cheingsong-Popov R. Safety of immunoglobulin preparation containing anti-HTLV-III [Letter]. Lancet 1985;1:815.
9. CDC. Hepatitis A among drug abusers. MMWR 1988;37:297-300,305.
10. Noble RC, Kane MA, Reeves SA, et al. Posttransfusion hepatitis A in a neonatal intensive care unit. JAMA 1984;252:2711-5.
11. Kluge I. Gamma-globulin in the prevention of viral hepatitis: a study of the effect of medium-size doses. Acta Med Scand 1963;174:469-77.
12. Stokes J Jr, Neefe JR. Prevention and attenuation of infectious hepatitis by gamma globulin; preliminary note. JAMA 1945;127:144-5.
13. Mosley JW, Reisler DM, Brachott D, Roth D, Weiser J. Comparison of two lots of immune serum globulin for prophylaxis of infectious hepatitis. Am J Epidemiol 1968;87:539-50.
14. Woodson RD, Cahill KM. Viral hepatitis abroad. Incidence in Catholic missionaries. JAMA 1971;219:1191-3.
15. Woodson RD, Clinton JJ. Hepatitis prophylaxis abroad. Effectiveness of immune serum globulin in protecting Peace Corps volunteers. JAMA 1969;209:1053-8.
16. Steffen R, Rickenbach M, Wilhelm U, Helminger A, Schar M. Health problems after travel to developing countries. J Infect Dis 1987;156:84-91.
17. CDC. Health information for international travel 1989. Atlanta: CDC, 1989; HHS publication no. (CDC) 89-8280.
18. Storch G, McFarland LM, Kelso K, Heilman CJ, Caraway CT. Viral hepatitis associated with day-care centers. JAMA 1979;242:1514-8.
19. Hadler SC, Webster HM, Erben JJ, Swanson JE, Maynard JE. Hepatitis A in day-care centers. A community-wide assessment. N Engl J Med 1980;302:1222-7.
20. Hadler SC, Erben JJ, Matthews D, Starko K, Francis DP, Maynard JE. Effect of immunoglobulin on hepatitis A in day care centers. JAMA 1983;249:48-53.
21. Favero MS, Maynard JE, Leger RT, Graham DR, Dixon RE. Guidelines for the care of patients hospitalized with viral hepatitis. Ann Intern Med 1979;91:872-6.

22. Carl M, Francis DP, Maynard JE. Food-borne hepatitis A: recommendations for control. J Infect Dis 1983;148:1133-5.
23. Lettau LA, Smith JD, Williams D, et al. Transmission of hepatitis B with resultant restriction of surgical practice. JAMA 1986;255:934-7.
24. Kane MA, Lettau L. Transmission of HBV from dental personnel to patients. JADA 1985;110:634-6.
25. Maynard JE, Kane MA, Hadler SC. Global control of hepatitis B through vaccination: role of hepatitis B vaccine in the expanded programme on immunization. Rev Infect Dis 1989;11(S3):S574-8.
26. McQuillan GM, Townsend TR, Fields HA, et al. Seroepidemiology of hepatitis B virus infection in the United States: 1976 to 1980. Am J Med 1989;87(3A):5S-10S.
27. CDC. Prevention of perinatal transmission of hepatitis B virus: prenatal screening of all pregnant women for hepatitis B surface antigen. MMWR 1988;37:341-6,351.
28. Francis DP, Feorino PM, McDougal S, et al. The safety of hepatitis B vaccine: inactivation of the AIDS virus during routine vaccine manufacture. JAMA 1986;256:869-72.
29. Zajac BA, West DJ, McAleer WJ, Scolnick EM. Overview of clinical studies with hepatitis B vaccine made by recombinant DNA. J Infect 1986;13(suppl A):39-45.
30. Andre FE, Safary A. Clinical experience with a yeast-derived hepatitis B vaccine. In: Zuckerman AJ, ed. Viral hepatitis and liver disease. New York, Alan R. Liss, 1988:1023-30.
31. Szmuness W, Stevens CE, Harley EJ, et al. Hepatitis B vaccine: demonstration of efficacy in a controlled clinical trial in a high-risk population in the United States. N Engl J Med 1980;303:833-41.
32. CDC. Suboptimal response to hepatitis B vaccine given by injection into the buttock. MMWR 1985;34:105-13.
33. Stevens CE, Alter HJ, Taylor PE, et al. Hepatitis B vaccine in patients receiving hemodialysis. Immunogenicity and efficacy. N Engl J Med 1984;311:496-501.
34. Collier AC, Corey L, Murphy VL, Handsfield HH. Antibody to human immunodeficiency virus and suboptimal response to hepatitis B vaccination. Ann Intern Med 1988;109:101-5.
35. Stevens CE, Taylor PE, Tong MJ, et al. Yeast-recombinant hepatitis Bvaccine: efficacy with hepatitis B immune globulin in prevention ofperinatal hepatitis B virus transmission. JAMA 1987;257:2612-6.
36. Hadler SC, Francis DP, Maynard JE, et al. Long term immunogenicity and efficacy of hepatitis B vaccine in homosexual men. N Engl J Med 1986:315:209-14.
37. Wainwright RB, McMahon BJ, Bulkow LR, et al. Duration of immunogenicity and efficacy of hepatitis B vaccine in a Yupik Eskimo population. JAMA 1989;261:2362-6.
38. Hadler SC. Are booster doses of hepatitis B vaccine necessary? Ann Intern Med 1988;109:457-8.
39. Redfield RR, Innis BL, Scott RM, Cannon HG, Bancroft WH. Clinical evaluation of low-dose intradermally administered hepatitis B vaccine, a cost reduction strategy. JAMA 1985;254:3203-6.
40. Shaw FE, Graham DJ, Guess HA, et al. Postmarketing surveillance for neurologic adverse events reported after hepatitis B vaccination. Experience of the first three years. Am J Epidemiol 1988;127:337-52.
41. Dienstag JL, Stevens CE, Bhan AK, et al. Hepatitis B vaccine administered to chronic carriers of hepatitis B surface antigen. Ann Intern Med 1982;96:575-9.
42. Szmuness W, Stevens CE, Oleszko WR, et al. Passive-active immunization against hepatitis B: immunogenicity studies in adult Americans. Lancet 1981;1:575-7.
43. CDC. Guidelines for prevention of transmission of human immunodeficiency virus and hepatitis B virus to health-care and public-safety workers. MMWR 1989;38(no.S-6).
44. Breuer B, Friedman SM, Millner ES, et al. Transmission of hepatitis B in school contacts of retarded HBsAg carriers. JAMA 1985;254:3190-5.
45. CDC. Routine screening for viral hepatitis in chronic hemodialysis centers. Hepatitis Surveillance Report No. 49. Atlanta: CDC, 1985:5-6.
46. Seaworth B, Drucker J, Starling J, Drucker R, Stevens C, Hamilton J. Hepatitis B vaccine in patients with chronic renal failure before dialysis. J Infect Dis 1988;157:332-7.
47. Hershow RC, Hadler SC, Kane MA,: Adoption of children from countries with endemic hepatitis B: transmission risks and medical issues. Pediatr Infect Dis J 1987;6:431-7.
48. Franks AL, Berg CJ, Kane MA, et al. Hepatitis B virus infection among children born in the United States to Southeast Asian refugees. N Engl J Med 1989;321:1301-5.

49. Beasley RP, Hwang L-Y, Lee GC, et al. Prevention of perinatally transmitted hepatitis B virus infections with hepatitis B immune globulin and hepatitis B vaccine. Lancet 1983;2:1099-102.
50. Wong VCW, Ip HMH, Reesink HW, et al. Prevention of the HBsAg carrier state in newborn infants of mothers who are chronic carriers of HBsAg and HBeAg by administration of hepatitis-B vaccine and hepatitis-B immunoglobulin: double-blind randomised placebo-controlled study. Lancet 1984;1:921-6.
51. Stevens CE, Toy PT, Tong MJ, et al. Perinatal hepatitis B virus transmission in the United States: prevention by passive-active immunization. JAMA 1985;253:1740-5.
52. Beasley RP, Hwang LY, Stevens CE, et al. Efficacy of hepatitis B immune globulin for prevention of perinatal transmission of the hepatitis B virus carrier state: final report of a randomized double-blind, placebo-controlled trial. Hepatology 1983:3:135-41.
53. Xu ZY, Liu CB, Francis DP, et al. Prevention of perinatal acquisition of hepatitis B virus carriage using vaccine: preliminary report of a randomized, double-blind placebo-controlled and comparative trial. Pediatrics 1985;76:713-8.
54. Seeff LB, Wright EC, Zimmerman HJ, et al. Type B hepatitis after needlestick exposure: prevention with hepatitis B immune globulin. Final report of the Veterans Administration Cooperative Study. Ann Intern Med 1978;88:285-93.
55. Grady GF, Lee VA, Prince AM, et al. Hepatitis B immune globulin for accidental exposures among medical personnel: final report of a multicenter controlled trial. J Infect Dis 1978;138:625-38.
56. Redeker AG, Mosley JW, Gocke DJ, McKee AP, Pollack W. Hepatitis B immune globulin as a prophylactic measure for spouses exposed to acute type B hepatitis. N Engl J Med 1975;293:1055-9.
57. Beasley RP, Hwang L-Y. Epidemiology of hepatocellular carcinoma. In: Vyas GN, Dienstag JL, Hoofnagle JH, eds. Viral hepatitis and liver disease. New York: Grune & Stratton, 1984:209-24.
58. Sinatra FR, Shah P, Weissman JY, Thomas DW, Merritt RJ, Tong MJ. Perinatal transmitted acute icteric hepatitis B in infants born to hepatitis B surface antigen-positive and anti-hepatitis Be-positive carrier mothers. Pediatrics 1982;70:557-9.
59. Delaplane D, Yogev R, Crussi F, Schulman ST. Fatal hepatitis B in early infancy: the importance of identifying HBsAg-positive pregnant women and providing immunoprophylaxis to their newborns. Pediatrics 1983;72:176-80.
60. Alter MJ, Hadler SC, Francis DP, Maynard JE. The epidemiology of non-A, non-B hepatitis in the United States. In: Dodd RY, Barker LF, eds. Infection, immunity, and blood transfusion. New York: Alan R. Liss, Inc, 1985:71-9.
61. Alter HJ, Purcell RH, Holland PV, et al. Clinical and serological analysis of transfusion-associated hepatitis. Lancet 1975;2:838-41.
62. Dienstag JL. Non-A, non-B hepatitis. I. Recognition, epidemiology, and clinical features. Gastroenterology 1983;85:439-62.
63. Alter MJ, Gerety RJ, Smallwood LA, et al. Sporadic non-A, non-B hepatitis: frequency and epidemiology in an urban U.S. population. J Infect Dis 1982;145:886-93.
64. Alter MJ, Coleman PJ, Alexander WJ, et al., Importance of heterosexual activity in the transmission of hepatitis B and non-A, non-B hepatitis. JAMA 1989;262:1201-5.
65. Guyer B, Bradley DW, Bryan JA, Maynard JE. Non-A, non-B hepatitis among participants in a plasmapheresis stimulation program. J Infect Dis 1979; 139:634-40.
66. Dienstag JL, Alter HJ. Non-A, non-B hepatitis: evolving epidemiologic and clinical perspectives. Semin Liver Dis 1986;6:67-81.
67. Tabor E, Seeff LB, Gerety RJ. Chronic non-A, non-B hepatitis carrier state: transmissible agent documented in one patient over a six-year period. N Engl J Med 1980;303:140-3.
68. Aach RD, Szmuness W, Mosley JW, et al. Serum alanine aminotransferase of donors in relation to the risk of non-A, non-B hepatitis in recipients: the Transfusion-Transmitted Viruses Study. N Engl J Med 1981;304:989-94.
69. Tong MJ, Thursby M, Rakela J, et al. Studies on the maternal-infant transmission of the viruses which cause acute hepatitis. Gastroenterology 1981;80:999-1003.

References 70 through 75 may be obtained by writing to the Hepatitis Branch, Division of Viral and Rickettsial Diseases, Center for Infectious Diseases, Mailstop A33, Centers for Disease Control, Atlanta, Ga. 30333.

American Journal of Infection Control

Implementing and Evaluating a System of Generic Infection Precautions: Body Substance Isolation [Reprinted from an article by P. Lynch, M. J. Cummings, P. L. Roberts, M. J. Herriott, B. Yates, and W. E. Stamm, *American Journal of Infection Control* 18:1–12, 1990]

In early 1984 the Infection Control Committee at Harborview Medical Center (HMC), a 330-bed municipal teaching hospital affiliated with the University of Washington, decided to implement a system of generic infection precautions. For years the hospital had used the category system of isolation practices developed by the Centers for Disease Control (CDC) for patients with recognized infections.[1] Our rationale for changing the isolation system at HMC has been described in detail previously[2] but in brief included the following: (1) Application of these barrier precautions both in our hospital and in other institutions was inconsistent and frequently incorrect.[3-5] (2) Microorganisms continued to be transmitted to patients or to hospital personnel from index patients who were not in isolation, because they lacked signs or symptoms of clinical disease. For example, we observed frequent transmission of marker organisms such as *Serratia marcescens*, *Pseudomonas aeruginosa*, and amikacin-resistant gram-negative rods from one patient to another in our hospital because the patients who were reservoirs for such agents often did not have clinically evident disease, were not being treated under "isolation precautions," and were thus not considered infectious by hospital personnel. (3) Rates of seropositivity for hepatitis B virus among health care workers who came into frequent contact with serum or blood were higher, suggesting a need for more widely applied precautions that reduce employee exposure to blood and secretions.[6, 7] (4) Employees were becoming increasingly concerned about protecting themselves against human immunodeficiency virus (HIV) infection. (5) Some employees believed that some isolation precautions, for example, the use of paper plates and double bagging of linen and wastes, were rooted in tradition and lacked a sound theoretic rationale.[8, 9]

Because HMC personnel were using category isolation precautions, our initial approach was to maintain the major elements of this system and to encourage the staff to use barrier precautions consistently when they were likely to have contact with blood or body fluids from any patient. Throughout 1984 this strategy was presented in new employee orientations and in many education programs for all clinical staff. By the end of 1984 it was apparent that the additional precautions were being used with increased frequency but usually only for patients who were already in category isolation. Observation of patient care activities in the critical care units indicated that two standards of precautions persisted: one for patients who were designated as being "on isolation" and another for patients who were not.

It became apparent to us that a major change in the nature of our isolation system would be necessary to accomplish the changes in practice that we believed were necessary. The major changes needed were to (1) stop, to the greatest extent possible, designating certain patients as "isolation patients"; (2) emphasize the potential infectiousness of all moist body substances; (3) specify exactly what precautions were to be used for all patients; and (4) convey the rationale for such a system to our staff to maximize compliance.

By implementing a generic precautions system the committee hoped to (1) decrease nosocomial transmission of infectious agents among patients; (2) reduce the risk among health care workers for infections transmitted by blood and other body substances such as lesion drainage, airway secretions, or feces; (3) simplify the indications for isolation precautions so that health care workers could understand them and perform them correctly; and (4) reduce the costs expended by our hospital for prevention of nosocomial infections in patients and personnel.

KEY ELEMENTS OF THE BODY SUBSTANCE ISOLATION SYSTEM

The term "body substance isolation" (BSI) was coined to describe the new approach. The word *isolation* was used to reinforce the idea that these precautions were adequate for all patients except for those with the few diseases transmitted via the airborne route. In addition, because a major focus of the system was to isolate body substances, mucous membranes, and nonintact skin from the hands of health care workers by using gloves, the use of the word *isolation* was appropriate. The words *body substance* rather than *body fluids* were selected to emphasize that the precautions were to be used for solids such as tissue and feces as well as for fluids. As previously described,[2] the elements of the BSI system are as follows:

- Clean gloves are put on just before contact with mucous membranes or with nonintact

Table 1. Estimate of necessary time and sequence for planning and implementing the BSI system

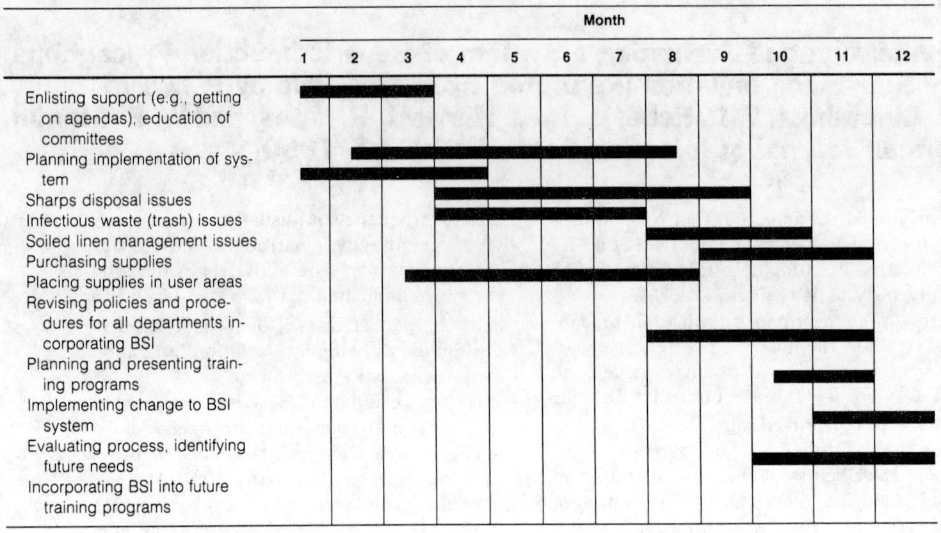

skin for all patients. To accomplish this, gloves are changed between patients and sometimes between activities with the same patient. This practice serves the dual purpose of protecting patients from cross-infection via hand carriage of microorganisms and personnel from acquisition of agents in the patient's blood or moist body substances.

- Handwashing is indicated whenever the hands are soiled and before each new patient contact
- Additional barriers such as gowns or plastic aprons, masks, goggles or glasses, hair covers, and shoe covers are used as necessary to keep moist body substances off the clothing, skin, or mucous membranes of the wearer. Hair covers are most commonly used in the burn/critical care unit, and shoe covers are used for trauma surgery.
- Sharps and needles are placed in puncture-resistant plastic containers. When needles are resheathed, recapping devices are used when possible.
- Laboratory specimens from all patients are handled as if they were infectious. Biohazard labels are not used.
- Handling and reprocessing practices are uniform for all articles and equipment used on all patients (e.g., soiled reusable articles are transported in plastic bags or rigid containers)
- Soiled linen is bagged securely before transport, and laundry workers wear gloves and gowns to sort all soiled linen. At the laundry visibly soiled linen is run through a cold water rinse before washing, to prevent staining.
- Trash is placed in plastic bags and transported to a landfill. Trash from the laboratories and from the pathology department, as well as all sharps and fluid-filled containers, are autoclaved before being transported to the landfill.
- Private rooms are used for patients with communicable diseases transmitted via the air. A large red sign reading "STOP," placed at the door of such patients, instructs all persons, "Check with the nurse before entering." For certain diseases (e.g., meningococcal meningitis and tuberculosis) masks are worn when personnel enter the patient's room. For childhood diseases in which immunity offers the best protection against employee acquisition of disease (e.g., measles, mumps, rubella, and varicella), susceptible personnel do not care

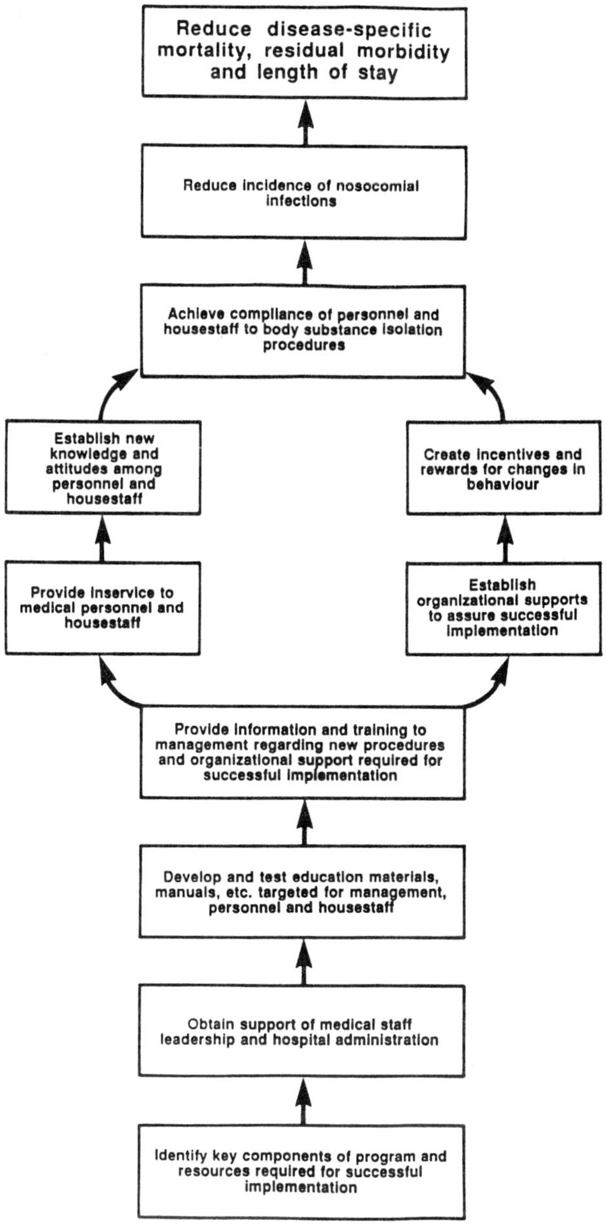

Fig. 1. BSI implementation model.

for the patient. Roommates who are immune to the patient's disease or who are currently infected with the same disease may share rooms. Private rooms are also used for patients who soil the room with body substances to such an extent that a roommate would be likely to have inadvertent contact.

- Reminder signs describing BSI precautions are placed in patient care areas such as the patient bedside, utility rooms, clinics, laboratories, and other locations

IMPLEMENTATION OF THE BSI SYSTEM

Implementing a program that required personnel to accept a philosophic change and also to change some of their basic practices and habits was complex and took more than a year (Table 1). The steps used in implementation of the model are summarized in Fig. 1. Each step in the implementation model was addressed sequentially and depended on the completion of the step preceding it. Before implementation, infection control personnel met twice with committees from all clinical and nonclinical departments to familiarize them with the BSI concept and to hear concerns or difficulties anticipated in each department. Members of the committees also identified needed supplies and structural changes (such as glove box holders) and estimated the time necessary to complete the implementation process in their areas.

As in most health care facilities, written departmental infection prevention practices at HMC were included in all department procedure manuals. Additionally, many departments had extensive unwritten customs related to management of patients with known infections. These written and unwritten practices were identified and changed in each department to conform with the new system. Written policies and procedures were revised accordingly.

In some departments compliance with BSI recommendations was made a part of employee performance review at the beginning of the implementation process. Although the effect of this approach was not formally evaluated, it demonstrated to the staff that infection prevention practices are important to the department head and that compliance would be included as a requirement for satisfactory job performance. Subsequently, more departments have adopted this approach at HMC and believe that it improves personnel compliance.

EVALUATION OF THE BSI SYSTEM

During the planning process, several aspects of the implementation of the system were selected for formal evaluation. These included (1) ascertaining attendance at 50 initial training programs that were offered to hospital personnel, including medical staff; (2) measuring by written examination the infection control knowledge as well as attitudes and self-reported practices of our hospital personnel; (3) measuring by direct observation the compliance of personnel with recommendations for glove use; and (4) monitoring colonization and infection of hospitalized patients with marker organisms previously associated with cross-infection in our hospital. For clarity, methods and results are presented together for each of the four aspects selected for study.

Attendance at training sessions

Methods. Fifty training sessions, each including a 45-minute slide presentation and discussion format, were offered on all shifts during October and November 1985. Staff rosters from every department were used to ascertain attendance. Departments with attendance of fewer than 50% of staff were contacted, and special presentations were made for their benefit and convenience and to increase attendance.

Results. By the end of the initial training sessions, 422 (70%) of 603 inpatient nurses, 37 (26%) of 141 physicians, 67 (39%) of 172 laboratory employees, and 438 (51%) of 859 employees in all other categories had attended one of the sessions. At the end of the entire training period (December 1985), including the special presentations, approximately 75% of all clinical personnel (including physicians) had attended a training session. This was the minimum attendance level that we believed was acceptable.

Questionnaire assessment of changes in attitudes, knowledge, and reported practices

Methods. Of the employees (including 717 clinical staff) who attended the scheduled train-

Table 2. Survey on BSI proportion of correct responses to test items before and immediately after training clinical staff

	% correct (*n* = 717)	
	Before	**After**
A nurse is caring for a patient who is bleeding from a disconnected IV. She has gotten blood on her hands and the linen is bloody.		
Q1. The nurse should wear gloves to keep from soiling her hands with blood.		
A1. Strongly agree/agree	92	99*
Q2. How often in the past year would you have worn gloves for a similar situation?		
A2. Always/usually	56	NA
Q4. The proportion of all cases of hepatitis B that are clinically unrecognized is approximately		
A4. ⅔	25	89*
Q5. Do you know where in your department you would find clean gloves to wear in a situation such as this?		
A5. Yes	96	NA
Q6. Are there enough gloves conveniently located in your department for these kinds of situations?		
A6. Yes	90	NA
A young girl with chickenpox is in the burn unit. A resident is pretty sure he has never had chickenpox and wears a mask while he is in the room for her dressing change.		
Q7. The resident should not have gone in the room if he believed he was susceptible to chickenpox, even with a mask.		
A7. Strongly agree/agree	58	93*
A patient with AIDS is hospitalized in a two-bed room for treatment of pneumonia. He has good personal hygiene and never soils the environment with body substances. The patient in the next bed is recovering from a stroke and has no incisions or indwelling lines; he also has good personal hygiene.		
Q8. These two patients are an acceptable roommate combination in terms of risk of transmission of infectious agents.		
A8. Strongly agree/agree	68	91*
Q9. The AIDS patient needs to go to radiology for a chest x-ray. The transport orderly wants to wear a gown, mask, and gloves himself, and drape and mask the patient for the trip to x-ray. He is told that the patient presents no special infection risk since he is not soiling the environment with body substances and the additional precautions are inappropriate.		
A9. Strongly agree/agree	78	88
The patient has had a urinary catheter in place for several weeks. Usually when the staff empties the bag, they get urine on their hands because the spout always drips a little.		
Q10. The staff should wear clean gloves to empty the urine bag.		
A10. Strongly agree/agree	95	99*
Q11. Approximately what proportion of people with indwelling catheters for several weeks have urine colonized with potentially pathogenic microorganisms?		
A11. 100%	28	69*
Q12. How often in the past year have you worn clean gloves to empty urine containers?		
A12. Always/usually	55	NA
A patient on a ventilator needs frequent suctioning. The therapist wears gloves on only one hand for the suctioning and for oral care.		
Q13. The personnel suctioning the patient should wear gloves on both hands when in contact with mucous membranes or airway secretions.		
A13. Strongly agree/agree	91	99*
Q14. How often in the past year would you have worn gloves on both hands for situations like this?		
A14. Always/usually	73	NA
Q15. What proportion of people have airway secretions colonized with potentially pathogenic microorganisms?		
A15. 100%	20	59*

NA, Not applicable.
*Significant by McNemars test ($p < 0.01$).

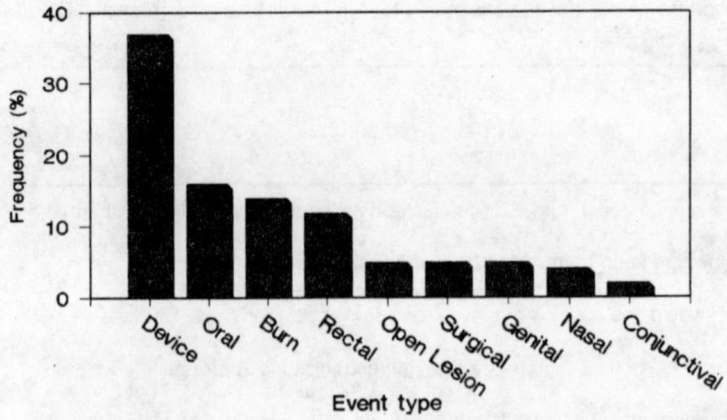

Fig. 2. Types of patient contact observed: August 1985 to April 1987.

ing sessions, 818 completed written pretests and posttests given before and after the training session. The same test was administered at each session, and the test format was multiple choice with a forced response style. A situation or vignette describing a health care worker–patient interaction was presented and was then followed by questions on knowledge, attitude, and self-reported practices.

Results. As shown in Table 2, statistically significant increases in infection control knowledge and understanding of the BSI system occurred immediately after the formal training sessions. The responses indicated that some personnel were already aware of glove use recommendations for body substance contacts before the training sessions (questions 1, 10, 13), but their own self-reported glove use practices for these same contacts did not reflect compliance with these recommendations (questions 2, 12, 14).

Observation of glove use before and after implementation of BSI

Methods. Appropriate glove use by hospital personnel was measured in critical care units and on general wards in an observational study conducted between August 1985 and April 1987. The general purpose of the study, "to evaluate infection prevention practices," was announced to the hospital staff, but staff were not told that glove use was being specifically monitored. Results of the first observation periods were not reported to staff until the data collection and analysis were complete.

Seven 40-hour observation periods were conducted. Patient care units were selected for observation randomly. The time of day that a unit was observed and the observers' locations within a unit were also randomized.

Observers were hired and trained to achieve more than 80% interrater reliability in recognizing and defining recordable events. Events were recorded each time a caregiver had contact with a patient's nonintact skin, with an indwelling device insertion site, or with mucous membranes (defined as oral, nasal, conjunctival, rectal, or genital sites). Nonintact skin included burns, surgical incisions, and open skin lesions. The discipline of the caregivers was recorded but not their names or other identifying information.

Appropriate glove use was defined as the application of clean gloves just before contact with mucous membranes, nonintact skin, or indwelling device insertion sites. When the observer noted such glove use, it was recorded as compliance. Failure to use gloves in these situations was counted as noncompliance. Gloves worn from one "event" to another on the same or a different patient was also recorded as noncompliance. Using gloves for non-patient-related contact with moist body substances (e.g., cleaning an incontinent patient's bed or cleaning a blood spill from the floor) was not recorded.

Table 3. Appropriate glove use during two observation periods before and after implementing BSI at HMC

	Observation period			
	1 and 2 (Aug.-Sept. 1985)		7 and 8 (June-April 1987)	
	*n**	Compliance (%)	*n**	Compliance (%)
Personnel				
Medical	3/10	30	16/19	84
Nursing	57/91	63	89/110	81
Type of contact				
Indwelling device	16/33	48	51/65	78
Oral/nasal/conjunctival	20/37	54	20/27	74
Nonintact skin†	26/33	79	29/35	83
Rectal/genital	16/24	67	22/24	92
TOTAL	183/228	61	227/280	81

*Number of events with compliance divided by total number of observed events.
†Includes burns, incisions, and open lesions.

Results. In 250 hours of observation, 697 events that met the previously described definitions were recorded, an average of less than 3 per hour. Four hundred ninety-four (71%) of the events occurred in critical care units, and nursing personnel performed 488 (70%) of all the recorded events. Physicians and respiratory therapists each performed 97 (14%) of the events, and the small number of events remaining were performed by physical therapists and other personnel. The most numerous events were contacts with indwelling medical device insertion sites, including contact with oral and nasal endotracheal tubes, chest tubes, surgical drains, and central lines. Oral contacts were the next most frequent event and usually involved mouth care or inspecting the oral cavity (Fig. 2).

Before implementation of BSI and before the first training sessions offered in October and November 1985, glove use was judged appropriate in 61% of the observed interactions. By the end of the observation period (April to June 1987), overall appropriate glove use had increased to 81% ($p < 0.001$). Significant increases in appropriate glove use were observed in both physicians and nurses. Although the number of physicians observed was small, physicians achieved the greatest improvement in gloving practices (Table 3). Appropriate glove use by nursing department personnel improved from 63% to 81%. Consistency was usually observed within each nursing unit, but considerable variation was seen among the units. Overall compliance at the completion of the study ranged from 59% to 90% in various units.

By type of interaction, the biggest improvements in gloving practices were seen with gloving for manipulating indwelling devices and for rectal/genital mucosal contacts (Table 3). Although there was an immediate initial improvement in compliance after the training programs, we continued the structured observational study for 18 months. This continuation permitted us to observe fluctuations over time and to determine whether the initially observed improvement would be sustained.

Prevalence of *Serratia* organisms and amikacin-resistant gram-negative rods in clinical specimens before and after BSI

Methods. Because *S. marcescens* and aerobic gram-negative bacilli that are resistant to many antimicrobials are nearly always acquired during hospitalization, Marrie et al.[10] have used these strains as "marker organisms" to assess the occurrence of nosocomial transmission in a given hospital. At HMC, nosocomial colonization and infection with *S. marcescens* and amikacin-resistant strains of gram-negative bacilli have been monitored since 1984. Microbiology laboratory reports were re-

Table 4. Patients colonized or infected with *Serratia* organisms or amikacin-resistant gram-negative rods: July 1, 1984-June 30, 1988

	1984-85	1985-86	1986-87	1987-88
All inpatient units				
Patient days*	82,721	83,723	79,833	80,433
Serratia				
No. of patients	166	93	67	36
Rate†	2.0	1.1	0.8	0.4
Amikacin-resistant GNR‡				
No. of patients	48	35	27	23
Rate†	0.58	0.42	0.34	0.29
Critical care units				
Patient days*	10,997	10,320	10,311	11,350
Serratia				
No. of patients	116	43	30	19
Rate†	10.5	4.2	2.9	1.7
Amikacin-resistant GNR‡				
No. of patients	28	18	15	13
Rate†	2.5	1.7	1.5	1.1

GNR, Gram-negative rods.
*Excluding psychiatric patients.
†Rate given in cases per 1000 patient days.
‡Includes *Acinetobacter*, *Serratia*, *P. aeruginosa*, *Enterobacter*, and *Klebsiella*.

viewed weekly to identify these marker organisms in routine clinical specimens. Medical record review was then performed to determine whether the specimen was obtained more than 3 days after admission and to verify the site of colonization or infection. If more than one site was colonized, the site from which the organism was first cultured was recorded. Each patient, regardless of the number of sites from which a particular marker organism was isolated, was counted only once.

Results. Overall, the incidence of *Serratia* colonization and infection declined from 166 cases in fiscal year 1984 to 1985 to 36 cases in 1987 to 1988 (Table 4). A consistent decline was seen for each year, but the most dramatic fall was between 1984 to 1985 and 1985 to 1986. Nosocomial colonization and infection with these marker organisms occurred most frequently in the critical care units, where most of the decline in incidence was observed. In the critical care units the decrease was apparent at several specific sites of infections, including sputum, burn wounds, and vascular line sites. Similarly, a marked decrease in the prevalence of amikacin-resistant gram-negative bacilli occurred during this period.

During this same time period, no significant changes in the numbers of admission, length of stay, total patient days, or numbers of cultures taken at the hospital were found. Aminoglycoside use increased slightly during this period, whereas the use of both imipenem and third-generation cephalosporins increased dramatically in 1987 (Table 5).

DISCUSSION

In 1983 the CDC published a newly revised "Guideline for Isolation Precautions in Hospitals."[11] The Guideline suggested that hospitals use either the traditional category-specific isolation or an alternative disease-specific isolation or that they design their own system as we have done. Since the original Guideline was published in 1983, the CDC have subsequently recommended that all hospitals use universal precautions to reduce the risk that health care workers will acquire hepatitis B virus, HIV, and other blood-borne infectious agents.[12] These CDC recommendations focus on those body substances (especially blood) known to transmit hepatitis B virus, HIV, and other blood-borne infectious agents. Unless visible blood is also present, feces, nasal secretions, airway

Table 5. Factors that may have influenced the decline in *Serratia* organisms and in amikacin-resistant gram-negative rods

	1984-85	1985-86	1986-87	1987-88
Census				
No. of admissions	8,888	9,422	9,243	9,267
Patient days	82,721	83,723	79,833	80,433
Length of stay (days)	9.3	8.9	8.6	8.7
No. of inpatient cultures	28,867	28,059	25,820	28,064
Antimicrobial therapy (gm)				
Gentamicin/tobramycin	1,456	1,483	1,753	1,905
Ceftriaxone ceftazidime, cefoperzone, or cefotetan	178	3,648	3,928	10,208
Imipenem	0	0	885	2,505

secretions, sputum, urine, and vomitus are specifically excluded from the universal precautions recommendations.[13] The CDC suggest that universal precautions be combined with traditional category or disease-specific isolation precautions that focus on reducing the risk of transmission of infectious agents from diagnosed infected patients. The efficacy of category- and disease-specific isolation in reducing the frequency of nosocomial infections has never been formally evaluated.

Compared with these recommendations, BSI is a single system of infection precautions intended to reduce the risk of nosocomial infection in both patients and personnel. It thus encompasses all body sites and substances for which precautions are appropriate. The system is based on the rationale that infectious agents are frequently present at all moist body sites in hospitalized patients regardless of whether active infection exists and that transmission of infectious agents to and from these sites occurs whether or not the patient is infected.[14] As previously described, the BSI system provides a consistent rationale for when to use precautions, simplifies the choice of which precautions to use, and, we hope, would be associated with a reduction in nosocomial infections and their costs.

BSI and universal precautions involve the use of the same barrier precautions, but universal precautions are not intended to reduce cross-transmission of organisms among patients. Specifically, glove use recommendations differ. To comply with BSI, personnel must put on clean gloves just before contact with mucous membranes, nonintact skin, and indwelling device insertion sites. For universal precautions gloves are recommended only for anticipated contact with blood or with bloody secretions. Health care workers who believe that the purpose of wearing gloves is to protect themselves from blood-borne illnesses often wear gloves excessively and fail to put on clean gloves just before contact with mucous membranes and nonintact skin. We believe that excessive glove use may reduce the risk of transmission of blood-borne illnesses to personnel but is likely to increase cross-transmission of organisms among patients.

Because HMC was the first hospital in the United States to implement fully an interaction-driven system of infection precautions, we were interested in evaluating the effectiveness of our teaching methods, the degree of compliance with the system, and its effect on infections in our institution. As anticipated, we found that implementation of a program that was based on a different rationale than the traditional diagnosis-driven system required extensive training and frequent reinforcement to ensure compliance. At HMC we were unsuccessful in combining a generic precautions system with a diagnosis-driven system, category isolation, because personnel continued to link the need for precautions only with diagnosed infected cases. Personnel also questioned the inconsistency inherent in recommending a standardized approach as effective and safe and then adding additional special precautions based on the patient's diagnosis. Our personnel responded by failing to carry out the recommended precautions routinely, and they often added additional and unnecessary rituals such as using gloves for delivering trays to rooms of all patients in isolation. We thus decided to implement fully the generic isolation system, BSI, without continued use of category-specific isolation.

Involving key personnel early in the decision-making and training processes was critical in gaining acceptance of the BSI concept and in implementing it. At HMC the influence of head nurses was an important factor that affected whether BSI principles were fully implemented on each nursing unit. In units with higher levels of compliance, the head nurse involved influential unit and ancillary personnel in planning for the change, sought feedback on staff performance, and regularly reinforced performance with both personnel and house staff. The levels of appropriate glove use on such units generally exceeded 90%.

Our data regarding appropriate glove use after implementation of BSI are highly encouraging. Overall, we significantly increased appropriate glove use from 60% to more than 80% after BSI was fully implemented. On some units appropriate glove use was observed in more than 90% of expected circumstances after the BSI system had been in use for 12 months. These results are particularly encouraging because we suspect that in our institution appropriate glove use was already being performed at a reasonably high level at the time of our first observation period because of the emphasis on glove use in the 12 months when generic precautions were encouraged but when BSI was not yet implemented. In contrast to these results, appropriate handwashing has usually been observed after only 30% to 45% of patient contacts at our hospital and elsewhere.[3, 5]

Assessing the effectiveness of BSI in terms of reducing rates of nosocomial colonization and infection was obviously of interest to us. As a measure of the effect of BSI on hospital-acquired infections at HMC, we selected two groups of marker organisms that could be easily followed longitudinally, were prevalent in our institution, and were essentially always nosocomially acquired. We observed significant declines in the occurrence of both marker strains after BSI was implemented. However, a number of potential weaknesses in this type of evaluation of colonization and infection rates before and after BSI should be noted. First, we did not measure overall nosocomial infection rates in patients nor did we measure infections in hospital employees before and after implementation of BSI. Second, our evaluation with marker organisms was longitudinal in nature and could have been influenced by factors other than BSI. However, we found no significant differences in rates of admission, length of stay, or culture practices during the time period studied. Antibiotic use clearly changed during the study period as several newer β-lactam antibiotics were added to the formulary. How this might have influenced the organisms we studied is not clear. Use of alternate study designs, such as randomization of individual units to BSI or category-specific isolation, was not feasible in our hospital because of the different patient populations on each unit and the relatively small size of the hospital. Studies of this type would be of interest in hospitals where such a design is feasible.

Previous studies also suggest that universal glove use (and gown use where appropriate) reduces the nosocomial transmission of certain kinds of microorganisms. Leclair et al.[15] demonstrated that increased compliance with gloving and gowning markedly reduced nosocomial transmission of respiratory syncytial virus among pediatric patients. Similarly, Klein et al.[16] observed a significant decline in all nosocomial infections when glove use was encouraged routinely for care of infants in a neonatal intensive care unit. However, it should be pointed out that glove use was only one aspect of the programs implemented in these two studies; other factors may have been of importance also. Finally, Gerding et al.[17] demonstrated a significant reduction in nosocomial incidence of *Clostridium difficile*–associated diarrhea after implementation of policies similar to BSI. These studies all support the concept that implementation of appropriate glove use as a routine infection control procedure reduces nosocomial infections. However, we encourage more comprehensive studies of the effects of BSI on overall nosocomial infection rates with the use careful experimental designs. In these studies assessing both the effectiveness and cost effectiveness of BSI would also be of interest.

We acknowledge with deep appreciation the contribution of Marguerite Jackson, who reviewed the early drafts of the manuscript; Leslie Taylor, who assisted with several iterations; Christine Coffin and the nurse coordinators at our hospital; and the staff and personnel whose cooperation made possible the implementation and evaluation of BSI.

References

1. Centers for Disease Control. Isolation techniques for use in hospitals. 2nd ed. Atlanta: Centers for Disease Control, 1975.
2. Lynch P, Jackson MM, Cummings MJ, Stamm WE. Rethinking the role of isolation practices in the prevention of nosocomial infections. Ann Intern Med 1987;107:243-6.
3. Larson E. Compliance with isolation technique. AM J INFECT CONTROL 1983;11:221-5.
4. Larson E, Killien M. Factors influencing handwashing behavior of patient care personnel. AM J INFECT CONTROL 1982;10:93-9.
5. Albert RK, Condie F. Handwashing patterns in medical intensive care units. N Engl J Med 1981;304:1465-6.
6. Dienstag JL, Ryan DM. Occupational exposure to hepatitis B virus in hospital personnel: infection or immunization? Am J Epidemiol 1982;115:26-39.
7. Denes AE, Smith JL, Maynard JE, Doto IL, Berquist KR, Finkel AJ. Hepatitis B infection in physicians: results of a seroepidemiologic study. JAMA 1978;239:210-2.
8. Jackson MM. From ritual to reason—with a rational approach for the future: an epidemiologic perspective. AM J INFECT CONTROL 1984;12:213-20.
9. Maki DG, Alvarado C, Hassemer C. Double-bagging of items from isolation rooms is unnecessary as an infection control measure: a comparative study of surface contamination with single- and double-bagging. Infect Control 1986;7:535-7.
10. Marrie TJ, Noble MA, Haldane EV, et al. *Serratia marcescens:* a marker for an infection control program. Infect Control 1982;3:134-42.
11. Centers for Disease Control. Guideline for isolation precautions in hospitals. Infect Control 1983;4:245-325.
12. Centers for Disease Control. Recommendations for prevention of HIV transmission in health-care settings. MMWR 1987;36 (suppl 2S):3S-5S.
13. Centers for Disease Control. Update: universal precautions for prevention of transmission of human immunodeficiency virus, hepatitis B virus, and other bloodborne pathogens in health-care settings. MMWR 1988;37:377-88.
14. Olson B, Weinstein RA, Nathan C, Chamberlin W, Kabins SA. Epidemiology of endemic *Pseudomonas aeruginosa:* why infection control efforts have failed. J Infect Dis 1984;150:808-16.
15. Leclair JM, Freeman J, Sullivan BF, Crowley CM, Goldmann DA. Prevention of nosocomial respiratory syncytial virus infections through compliance with glove and gown isolation precautions. N Engl J Med 1987;6:317-34.
16. Klein BS, Perloff WH, Maki DG. Protective isolation reduces nosocomial infection in a pediatric intensive care unit. Twenty-seventh Interscience Conference on Antimicrobial Agents and Chemotherapy. New York: American Society for Microbiology, Oct 4-7, 1987: Abstract 1297.
17. Gerding DN., Johnson S, Olson M, Wuler M, Hughes R, Clabots C. Prospective controlled study of vinyl glove use to interrupt *Clostridium difficile* nasocomial transmission. In: Abstracts of the Eighty-eighth Annual Meeting of American Society for Microbiology, May 8-13, 1988, Miami Beach, Fla. Washington, DC: American Society for Microbiology, 1988:416. Abstract No. L-32.

Health Facilities Management

Isolating and Double-Bagging Laundry: Is It Really Necessary? [Reprinted from an article by G. Pugliese, *Health Facilities Management* 2(2):16–21, Feb. 1989]

The AIDS epidemic has prompted many health institutions to adopt guidelines — many of which are not based on scientific evidence — for handling and processing soiled linen in hopes of reducing the risk of transmission of this greatly feared disease.

One ritual has been to handle the soiled linen from patients in isolation differently from that of other patients' linen. This is based on the belief that "isolation linen" poses a greater risk of disease transmission. For example, isolation linen has been double-bagged and not sorted in the laundry before being washed. Often the inner bag is made of a water soluble material that the linen can be placed directly into the washer with minimum handling. Once washed, the lined is then sorted and rewashed. These procedures were recommended in 1981 by the Centers for Disease Control (CDC), Atlanta[1].

In 1985, the CDC recognized that the risk of disease transmission associated with soiled linen was negligible. The CDC revised its guidelines to recommend hygienic and commonsense storage and processing of soiled linen rather than dictating rigid rules and regulations[2]. These recommendations are based on the knowledge that environmental surfaces, including walls, floors, carpets, curtains, and soiled linen, rarely, if ever, contribute to the transmission of infections, including bloodborne infections such as AIDS and hepatitis B. In updating the guidelines, the CDC attempted to reduce or eliminate expensive practices that are not likely to prevent infections and advocate only those practices that are either scientifically valid or based on reasonable rationale. The CDC has also charged the users of the guidelines with keeping abreast of new studies in the filed.

Two recent studies have looked at double-bagged isolation linen. In 1986, Dennis Maki, M.D., and his colleagues at the University of Wisconsin Medical Center in Madison compared the bacterial contamination of the outside of the bags of single-and double-bagged isolation linen[3]. The study showed the level of contamination to be similar. Since there was no infection control advantage to double-bagging, the medical center converted to a single-bag system for both soiled linen and contaminated waste for a savings of more than $9,000 in one year.

Another study was performed in 1987 by Steven Weinstein and his associates at the University of Massachusetts Medical Center, Worcester, in collaboration with colleagues from St. Vincent Hospital, also in Worcester[4]. That comparison between single-versus double-bagged isolation linen also showed no difference in the level of contamination. The investigators noted, however, that the nonisolation linen was often more grossly soiled with feces, urine, and blood than the isolation line. They concluded that the degree of soiling was often more closely related to whether the patient was incontinent and to the type of procedures being performed on the patient, rather than to the patient's isolation status. Based on the study findings, the two facilities eliminated the use of water-soluble laundry bags, the labeling of linen as biohazardous, and the use of double bags for isolation linen. Discontinuing the use of water-soluble bags alone resulted in a savings of more than $21,000 in one year.

Interpretation of universal precautions. Many health care facilities that use special procedures for handling and processing isolation linen, including the use of double bags, water-soluble bags, and special tagging, have expanded these procedures to include the linen from all patients. This was not the intent of the CDC in its recommendations for universal precautions. In 1987, the CDC again summarized its position on handling soiled linen[5]: "Rather than rigid procedures and specifications, hygienic and commonsense storage and processing of clean and soiled linen are recommended." The CDC further stated that "all soiled linen should be bagged at the location where it was used; should not be sorted or rinsed in patient care areas; and if soiled with blood or body fluids, should be placed in bags that prevent leakage." The CDC also outlines proper procedures for laundry cycles using high-or-low-temperature water.

OSHA participates. The recent activities of the Occupational Safety and Health Administration (OSHA), Washington, DC, in the inspection of health care facilities has added another perspective to laundry operations. Under the General Duty Clause of the Occupational Safety and Health Act of 1970, OSHA has general enforcement authority to protect health care workers from the risks of bloodborne diseases such as AIDS and hepatitis B. Although OSHA does not currently follow a specific standard design to reduce occupational exposure to bloodborne infections, it uses existing recommendations such as the CDC's universal precautions to assist in assessing the risk of these occupational exposures.

OSHA field staff members use a compliance manual that was most recently revised on August 15, 1988[6]. The section entitle "Linen" clearly restates the CDC recommendations cited above. Some of the recent laundry literature suggests that OSHA does not allow sorting of soiled linen and that OSHA requires not only double bagging of soiled linen, but also the use of impervious bags, such as plastic bags. This is not correct. In a separate section of the manual entitled "Bagging of

Articles." OSHA did suggest the use of impervious bags for the bagging of contaminated articles and the use of a second bag if contamination of the first bags is likely. However, OSHA did not intend this to apply to the bagging of linen but rather to the packaging of single-use contaminated items and specimens for disposal.

It should also be noted that the compliance manual used by the OSHA field staff is only a guideline for conducting inspections. In the absence of specific enforcement standards for handling soiled linen, OSHA is relying on the CDC guidelines for universal precautions as reflecting an appropriate and widely accepted practice to be followed[5,7].

The focus of concern recently has been to prevent occupational exposure to blood and certain body fluids to reduce the risk of infection from bloodborne pathogens. Nevertheless, all linen used in patient care settings should be considered soiled, whether it be with blood, urine, feces, or other body fluids; and it should be handled and processed in the same manner regardless of patient source. The goal should be to use hygienic and practical measures to contain the linen and minimize employee exposure until the soil can be removed by washing.

Collection and bagging. All soiled linen should be bagged at the location where it is generated. The linen should also undergo a minimum of agitation to prevent contamination of the air and the people handling the linen.

The people who collect and bag the linen should be sure that all nonlaundry items such as instruments, needles, or plastic under pads are removed. The greatest risk to health care workers for acquiring bloodborne infections is from accidental needle punctures or injuries with sharp items that are contaminated with the blood of infected patients. All personnel should be trained to put needles and other sharp items immediately into puncture-resistant containers for proper disposal. Sharp items not only place laundry personnel at risk but also damage laundry equipment and linen.

The bag used to contain and transport the linen should prevent leakage. If the linen is entirely soaked with blood or body fluids, such as the linen from some surgical or trauma procedures, a plastic bag may be needed.

Nevertheless, a cloth bag is adequate for the majority of soiled linen. The linen can be collected in such a manner as to keep the visibly or heavily soiled portion contained in the center of the bundle. This can be achieved by either folding or rolling the soiled spot into the center. This technique will reduce the risk of contamination of the worker bagging the linen and prevent the laundry bag from soaking through.

Gloves and a gown or apron may be needed for bagging heavily soiled linen. Although it may be more efficient to have the laundry bag immediately accessible, the rolled package of linen can be safely carried a short distance for placement in the laundry bag.

In some settings, both cloth and plastic laundry bags are available. The type of bag used would then depend on the amount and type of that cloth bags can be used for the majority of patient care linen that is lightly soiled and plastic bags for linen that is wet or heavily soiled.

The use of cloth bags, which can be washed and reused, will reduce the cost associated with single-use plastic bags. Also, using plastic bags to collect all soiled linen may place an additional burden on the laundry service. For example, in some states, the disposable laundry bag may be classified as infectious waste and as such would require special disposal practices that may be costly and/or not readily available.

There is no need to double-bag laundry unless the primary bag leaks. The use of water-soluble bags generally is not necessary for a variety of reasons. First, it further adds to the cost of bagging and processing. Second, linen in water-soluble bags must be washed in hot water, which make the removal of stains difficult and often requires replacement of the stained linen. Third, the linen must be rewashed after the initial washing, further adding to the cost of processing as well as reducing the use-life of the linen. And fourth, linen in water soluble bags is not sorted before washing; as a result, instruments and other items inadvertently left in the linen can damage both the washing machines and the linen.

Identifying soiled laundry. Linen should be identified as soiled for the protection of those involved in collecting, transporting, and processing it. All personnel should be aware of the type of bags used for soiled linen and be trained in the proper procedures for processing it. If the CDC recommendations are followed, there is no need to identify certain linen as infectious or biohazardous.

The precise length of time that soiled linen can remain bagged and stored prior to washing is based on emotional and aesthetic concerns rather than a risk of disease transmission. If soiled linen is bagged to prevent leakage, it can be held for varying lengths of time while it is being collected, transported, and stored for washing. Nevertheless, schedules should be developed to accomplish these activities within a reasonable time frame.

Training personnel. All personnel who handled soiled linen, including those involved in collecting, sorting, and washing, should be trained to reduce their risk of exposure. Appropriate procedures should include the use of protective apparel, such as gloves and gowns or aprons, to reduce the risk of contamination of exposed areas of skin and soiling of clothing. Protective eyewear is not necessary because splashing of blood or body fluids, is unlikely in the laundry setting. If latex or vinyl gloves are worn, they should be discarded after use and reused. If general-purpose gloves, such as rubber household gloves are worn, they may be washed after use and reused. They should be discarded if they are peeling, cracked, punctured, torn, or show other evidence of deterioration. Reusable protective apparel, such as gowns, may be washed and reused.

Facility managers must work together, in addition to working with local, state, and federal regulatory agencies, to eliminate unnecessary laundry practices.

References

1. Centers for Disease Control Guidelines. Atlanta: CDC, 1981.
2. Centers for Disease Control. Guidelines for handwashing and environmental control — Laundry. In: Guidelines for the Prevention and Control of Nosocomial Infections, Atlanta: CDC. 1985.
3. Maki D.G., Alvarado C., and Hassemer C. Double-bagging items from isolation rooms is unnecessary as an infection control measure: A comparative study of surface contamination with single- and double-bagging. Infection Control 7:535, 1986.
4. Weinstein, S., Gantz, N., Pelletier, O., and Hibert D. Bacterial surface contamination of linen from patients on isolation precautions versus standard care. American Journal of Infection Control, 15; 2, 1987.
5. Centers for Disease Control. Recommendations for the prevention of HIV transmission in health-care settings, Morbidity and Mortality Weekly Report, 36:2S, 1987 Supplement.
6. United States Department of Labor, Occupational Safety and Health Administration: Office of Health Compliance Assistance Enforcement Procedures for Occupational Exposure to Hepatitis B Virus and Human Immunodeficiency Virus, OSHA Instruction CPL 2-2, 44A., August 15, 1988.
7. Centers for Disease Control. Update: Universal precautions for prevention of transmission of human immunodeficiency virus, hepatitis B virus, and other bloodborne pathogens in the health-care setting; Morbidity and Mortality Weekly Report 37:377, 1988.

Association for Practitioners in Infection Control, Dallas-Fort Worth Regional Chapter Dallas, Texas

Audiovisual Materials on Universal Precautions

The following list of audiovisual materials was compiled by the APIC Dallas-Fort Worth Regional Chapter as a guide for its members. The inclusion of any particular product in this list does not constitute an endorsement by the APIC Dallas-Fort Worth Regional Chapter. This summary does not contain all of the audiovisual materials that are currently available. Practitioners are urged to obtain and review additional materials.

Universal Precautions: The Transmission and Prevention of AIDS and Hepatitis

Company: Cinecraft Productions Inc.
2515 Franklin Blvd
Cleveland, OH 44113
216/781-2300

Product Description: 15 minutes; color videotape; English

Audience: For professional staff including nurses, physicians, and other health care professionals

Price: $250.00; 2-week rental $125.00; preview for one week $60.00

Content/Comments: Explains Universal Precautions and potentially infectious blood and body fluids as defined by the CDC but comments on other infections transmitted from other substances. Explains options for glove use during phlebotomy as recommended by the CDC. Cites examples of procedures requiring protective apparel and techniques to reduce exposures, including scenes from in-room patient care, handling and disposal of needles, suctioning, linen handling, reprocessing of instruments, use of disinfectants. Comments on lack of need for double bagging and reserve/protective isolation. Some recommendations may need to be adapted to particular facility, for example, use of "moisture-repellant/barrier-proof apparel," "impermeable laundry bags," use of "impermeable bags" to transport specimens.

Overall Impression: Fair to good

Universal Precautions: AIDS and Hepatitis B—Prevention for the Health Care Worker

Company: Medcom Inc. (MEDCOM/TRAINEX)
12601 Industry Street
Garden Grove, CA 92641
714/891-1443 or 800/877-1443

Product Description: Program includes separate video segments for workers and management staff; workbook lesson guide or a self-study guide for professional staff; materials for evaluation and documentation and record keeping

Audience: All levels of professional and nonprofessional staff

Price: $1200 per employee (minimum order of $2000 per facility; includes 165 workbooks for allied and professional staff; one instructor's guide for every 100 employees; one five-part video for staff per 100 employees; one videotape and compliance manual for management staff/per facility

Content/Comments: Program/video segments and training materials for staff include risk of transmission of HIV and HBV; Universal Precautions procedures, including safe work practices, barriers, and other controls. Information presented in learning modules that can be used for self-study or class settings as a comprehensive program or to supplement existing program. Separate program (video and manual) for management includes employer responsibilities, including record-keeping methods, workplace monitoring, and OSHA requirements. Optional update service available as new information from OSHA available. Company guarantees worker compliance with Universal Precautions or agreement to pay OSHA penalties.

Overall Impression: Excellent

Protecting Asepsis—A Contemporary Approach to Infection Control
Company: Surgikos, Inc.
Education Department
P.O. Box 130
Arlington, TX 76011
817/493-5857 or 800/433-5170

Product Description: 15 minutes; color videotape; English; 1988

Audience: General hospitalwide audience

Price: Free

Content/Comments: Discusses infection control practices and concepts, including chain of infection, hand washing, glove usage, protective apparel, sharps disposal, and linen handling. Reinforces single level of care concept, whereby all patients and procedures are considered potentially contaminated.

Overall Impression: Very good to excellent

Any Questions?
Company: Quality Line Enterprises
309 Santa Monica, Room 202
Santa Monica, CA 90401
800/356-0986 or 213/451-5994

Product Description: 15 minutes; color videotape; English

Audience: General hospitalwide

Price: $295; previews and rentals available

Content/Comments: Discusses Universal Precautions and includes concept of Body Substance Isolation; provides good examples of patient care and support service examples of appropriate protective measures.

Overall Impression: Excellent

If We Take Care
Company: Quality Line Enterprises
309 Santa Monica, Room 202
Santa Monica, CA 90401
800/356-0986 or 213/451-5994

Product Description: 12 minutes; color videotape; English; 1988

Audience: General hospitalwide

Price: $199.00; previews available

Content/Comments: Universal Precautions including potentially infectious fluids as defined by the CDC; short and concise with good overview of Universal Precautions.

Overall Impression: Good

For Your Sake—For Everybody's Sake—Universal Precautions

Company: Woodbridge Video
672 Woodbridge Drive
Detroit, MI 48226
313/259-8505

Produced By: Detroit Medical Center

Product Description: 20 minutes; color videotape; English

Audience: Professionals, surgeons in OR, trauma, patient care, OB, and support services including dietary, housekeeping, and chaplains

Price: $295

Content/Comments: Discusses both Body Substance Isolation and Universal Precautions as recommended by the CDC; interactive and didactic format.

Overall Impression: Good to excellent

Techniques for Preventing HIV and HBV in Healthcare Workers

Company: Glaxo Pharmaceuticals
Video Library
Regent Place 1000 Parliament Court
Research Triangle Park, NC 27560
800/824-2896 or 919/941-3340

Product Description: 12 minutes; color videotape; English; 1989

Audience: Professional staff

Price: Free; contact facilities Glaxo Pharmaceuticals sales representative

Content/Comments: Overview of Universal Precautions; discusses myths of casual contact transmission; includes differentiation of risk of HIV versus HBV; focuses on blood exposures and needlesticks as greatest risk of transmission; discusses proper sharps handling procedures; gives good examples of appropriate protective barriers in clinical situations, for example, placement and manipulation of arterial lines, dentistry, suctioning, intubation, and emergency procedures.

Overall Impression: Excellent

Biological Hazards in Critical Care

Company: Glaxo Pharmaceuticals
Video Library
Regent Place 1000 Parliament Court
Research Triangle Park, NC 27560
800/824-2896 or 919/941-3340

Product Description: 12 minutes; color videotape; English; 1989

Audience: Professional staff

Price: Free; contact facilities Glaxo Pharmaceuticals sales representative

Content/Comments: Reviews Universal Precautions as recommended by the CDC; body fluids not specifically defined so could be used for a variety of institutionally defined potentially infectious fluids; emphasizes staff with weeping dermatitis refraining from patient care, HBV immunization, postexposure reporting and follow-up; provides examples of modes of transmission of a variety of infections including CMV, VZV, herpes simplex, Salmonella; discusses the need for administrative support for provision of protective barriers and staff education. Script; monograph; posttest; and CEU application included.

Overall Impression: Excellent

Universal Precautions for Infection Control
Company: Healthcare Video
444 Main Street
LaCrosse, WI 54601

Product Description: 14 minutes; color videotape; English

Audience: General hospitalwide

Price: $275; preview available

Content/Comments: General overview of Universal Precautions

Overall Impression: Good

Universal Precautions—HBV and HIV in the Hospital Setting, Universal Precautions—HBV and HIV in Prehospital Setting, Universal Precautions—HBV and HIV in Long Term Care Setting, Universal Precautions—Clinics, and Body Substance Isolation
Company: Lincoln Medical Education Foundation
Lincoln Area Health Education Center
4600 Lincoln Road NE
Lincoln, NE 68510
402/483-4581

Product Description: Approximately 20–30 minutes; color videotapes; English (Body Substance Video available also in Spanish)

Audience: General audience for each specific setting

Price: $75–250; previews available

Content/Comments: Each includes summary of transmission of bloodborne infections; recommendations for application of Universal Precautions in specific settings includes HBV vaccination; appropriate protective apparel, hand washing, disposal of sharps, CPR, cleaning and disinfecting procedures, follow-up for accidental exposures, and information for pregnant health care workers.

Overall Impression: Good to excellent

AIDS and Hepatitis B—Protecting Hospital Support Staff
Company: Triad Communications, Inc.
2233 North Hamline Avenue
St. Paul, MN 55113
800/727-9700

Product Description: 15 minutes; color videotape; 1988; English

Audience: Direct patient care and support staff

Price: $600.00; preview available (regular updates of program available)

Content/Comments: Program includes administrative packet, instructor's guide, student workbook, pretests and posttests, and record keeping. Includes discussion of Universal

Precautions as recommended by the CDC, as well as recommended protective measures, environmental considerations, laboratory precautions, accidental exposures.

Overall Impression: Good to excellent

AIDS Prevention for Laboratory Professionals, AIDS Prevention for Support Service Employees, AIDS Prevention for Nursing Professionals, and AIDS, HIV and Seroconversion: What You Should Know

Available From: Guidance Associates
Communications Park, Box 3000
Mt. Kisco, NY 10549
800/431-1242

Developed By: College of American Pathologists and American Society of Clinical Pathologists

Product Description: 30 minutes; videotapes; 1988; support staff video also available in Spanish

Audience: Targeted for intended audiences

Price: $199 each; complete series $499 (AIDS, HIV Seroconversion video free with any purchase)

Content/Comments: Includes discussion of routes of transmission of HIV and HBV, Universal Precautions, department-specific precautions to reduce risk of transmission. The laboratory video includes precautions for autopsy.

Overall Impression: Good

Hospital Infection Control

Company: Parker Productions, Inc.
P.O. Box 1476
San Mateo, CA 94401
800/227-2463 or 415/573-8122

Product Description: 17 minutes; color videotape; English

Audience: General health care workers

Price: $420; rentals and previews available

Content/Comments: Includes general infection control concepts such as chain of infection, also discusses modes of transmission of HIV and HBV, Universal Precautions as recommended by the CDC; protective clothing and equipment to reduce risk; postexposure follow-up procedures.

Overall Impression: Good to excellent

A Matter of Protection: Barrier Techniques for Healthcare Workers

Company: MEDCO Media, Inc.
Laurel Avenue at State Hwy. 35
Sea Girt, NJ 08705
201/974-0230

Product Description: 26 minutes; color videotape; English

Audience: Professional and support staff

Price: $249

Content/Comments: Emphasizes use of barrier techniques for contact with all body fluids, mentions Body Substance Isolation and the CDC's Universal Precautions as methods of barrier protection; traditional and unique examples of situations for barrier protection including plumber cleaning out a pipe, dietary handling of dishes and trays; includes some procedures where barrier protection is not needed; refers you to your institution's procedure manual for specific information.

Overall Impression: Excellent

Is It Worth the Risk? Safe Handling of Blood and Body Fluids
Company: American Hospital Association
Order Processing
840 North Lake Shore Drive
Chicago, IL 60611
800/242-2626 or 312/280-6020

Product Description: 22 minutes; color videotape; English; 1987

Audience: General hospitalwide audience

Price: $25.00 (AHA member price)

Content/Comments: Discusses the need to use appropriate protective barriers when there is risk of exposure to any blood or body fluids; an infection control practitioner takes an emergency room nurse on a tour of the hospital to show how Universal Precautions can be successfully implemented in each department.

Overall Impression: Good to excellent

Body Substance Precautions for Healthcare Professionals, Body Substance Precautions for Support Staff, and Body Substance Precautions for Laboratory
Company: Syntex Laboratories
Palo Alto, CA 94304
415/855-5371

Product Description: 18 minutes each; color videotapes; English; 1988

Audience: Professional/direct patient care staff, support staff, laboratory staff

Price: Free; available from Syntex Laboratories sales representatives

Content/Comments: Professional staff video provides detailed discussion of pathophysiology; diagnosis, epidemiology, and transmission of HIV; discusses concept of Body Substance Isolation; includes recommended barrier precautions for specific patient care procedures as well as common mistakes in techniques. Support staff and laboratory videos provide similar content geared to these audiences.

Overall Impression: Excellent

Overcoming the Irrational Fear of AIDS
Company: Carle Medical Communications
110 West Main
Urbana, IL 61801-2700
217/384-4838

Product Description: 22 minutes; color videotape; English; 1987

Audience: Patient care personnel

Price: $385; rental and preview available

Content/Comments: Discusses feelings and fears about AIDS patients with a group of health care providers and offers a training model to assist workers in overcoming negative thinking; gives examples of issues and conflicts of people who treat AIDS patients. Includes a discussion leader's guide and selected bibliography.

Overall Impression: Very good

Of Critical Importance—AIDS Precautions in Radiology
Company: Carle Medical Communications
110 West Main
Urbana, IL 61801-2700
217/384-4838

Product Description: 13 minutes; color videotape; English

Audience: Radiology staff

Price: $325.00

Content/Comments: Discusses the CDC's Universal Precautions and the use of protective barriers during specific radiology procedures; includes safe needle handling and cleaning and disinfection procedures.

Overall Impression: Very good

Body Substance Precautions
Company: University of Michigan Hospitals
Attention: Candace Friedman
300 North Ingalls N12B01
Ann Arbor, MI 48109-0458

Product Description: 13 minutes; color videotape; 1988

Audience: Direct patient care and support staff

Price: $150.00

Content/Comments: Discusses the rationale for replacing traditional category-specific isolation with body substance precautions; includes chain of infection, summary on general hospital-acquired infection risks, good hand-washing demonstration; provides examples of appropriate measures to reduce risk of transmission when in contact with all moist body substances.

Overall Impression: Very good

Body Substance Isolation Slide Module—Acute Care and Body Substance Isolation Slide Module—Long-Term Care
Company: Marvik Educational Services, Inc
3937 Southview Drive
San Diego, CA 92117

Product Description: Approximately 45 slides in each series and script

Audience: Professional and support staff

Price: $95.00 for each slide set ($39.00 for supplemental workbook containing key elements of BSI model, timelines and worksheets for implementation, and bibliography)

Content/Comments: Produced by the infection control practitioners Marguerite Jackson and Patricia Lynch, who developed Body Substance Isolation (BSI). Contains a discussion of the purpose of infection precautions, rates of nosocomial infections, prevalence of HBV in specific job categories, complete discussion of the rationale for BSI, measures to reduce risk of infections, and measures that have been proven ineffective. The long-term care slide series also contains information on rates of nosocomial infections in nursing homes and symptoms of serious diseases and emphasizes early recognition of symptoms.

Overall Impression: Very good to excellent

AIDS, Herpes, and Hepatitis: Preventative Measures for Infection Control
Company: Videolink
846 Jefferson Avenue
Scranton, PA 18510
717/963-1366 or 800/648-3858

Product Description: 22 minutes; color videotape

Audience: Professional and direct patient care staff

Price: $99.00

Content/Comments: Good dramatization about risk of certain types of infections to health care workers; interesting combination of HIV, HBV, HAV, and herpes simplex; includes discussion on signs, symptoms, and risks of transmission of each type of infection and methods to reduce risks; emphasizes Universal Precautions as recommended by the CDC. Refers to measures to reduce risk to staff from contact with both patients and residents and provides examples of interactions with residents—thus applicable for training of long-term care staff. Handout materials provided for viewer with pretest and posttest included.

Overall Impression: Good

On Guard: Infection Control for Safety and Healthcare Professionals
Company: Pyramid Film and Video
2801 Colorado Avenue
Santa Monica, CA 90404
213/828-7577

Product Description: 30 minutes; color videotape; English

Audience: Fire departments, ambulance services, police departments, hospital emergency departments, and industrial health care centers

Price: $295; previews available

Content/Comments: Contains reenactments of actual situations discussing the risk of transmission of bloodborne pathogens and precautions to reduce risk including barrier precautions, general infection control measures, mouth-to-mouth resuscitation, and needlestick prevention.

Overall Impression: Excellent

Infection Control in Child Care Settings
Company: Pyramid Film and Video
2801 Colorado Avenue
Santa Monica, CA 90404
213/828-7577

Product Description: 30 minutes; videotape; English

Audience: Child care providers in day-care and home settings

Price: $165

Content/Comments: Using an engaging clown mime who interacts with children throughout this videotape, basic terms explain how infections are spread and discusses policies that protect both children and workers; includes a summary of the common childhood infections and method of spread; and contains specific information about AIDS and hepatitis B. Designed for child care providers in daycare and home settings but can also be used to teach basic principles to parents.

Overall Impression: Excellent

Tennessee Hospital Association
Nashville, Tennessee

Universal Precautions [Poster]

UNIVERSAL PRECAUTIONS

Blood and Body Fluids
Infection Control Procedures

Universal blood and body fluid precautions should be used routinely for ALL patients whenever there is a potential for exposure to blood or other body fluids, secretions, excretions and tissues. Be familiar with the infection control procedures within your department. Practice universal blood & body fluid precautions on all patients for your own protection.

NEEDLES & SHARP INSTRUMENTS—The greatest risk of exposure to HBV and HIV is through needlesticks and cuts with sharp instruments. Never break, bend or re-cap a used needle or other instrument. Dispose of needles and sharp instruments in puncture-resistant containers designed for their disposal. Handle all sharp instruments and broken glass with extreme caution. Immediately report any cut or needlestick to your immediate supervisor.

WASH HANDS—Routine handwashing is a basic infection control procedure. Hands always should be washed before and after contact with each patient. Wash hands with soap under a steady stream of water for at least 10 seconds.

WEAR GLOVES—Latex gloves always should be worn whenever patients are examined and you may be exposed to their blood, body fluids, secretions, excretions, tissues or mucous membranes. Wash hands before putting on gloves and after gloves have been removed. Gloves should be used when cleaning soiled instruments, surfaces, and when handling linens soiled with blood or body fluids, or when cleaning up spills of blood or body fluids. Housekeeping personnel may use standard rubber gloves.

WEAR GOWNS—Protective gowns or aprons should be worn when there is a potential for blood or body fluid splatters or spraying. Examples: arterial punctures, endoscopies, inserting arterial lines, hemapherasis, hemodialysis, intubation, surgery.

WEAR GOGGLES—Protective eyewear, such as goggles, should be worn when there is a potential for blood or body fluid splatters or spraying. Examples: arterial punctures, dental and orthopedic drilling, intubation, inserting arterial lines, endoscopies, etc.

WEAR MASKS—Generally, masks are unnecessary when in casual contact with patients, but should be used when there is a potential for blood or body fluid splatters or spraying. HIV and HBV are blood-borne and are not spread through the air. Masks also should be worn if the patient is on respiratory isolation for his or her protection. See examples under gowns.

CLEAN UP SPILLS—Spilled or splattered blood and body fluids should be cleaned up immediately. Use of a daily fresh solution of household bleach and water (1:10 dilution) is adequate and gloves should be worn. Some instruments require special disinfectants. Check departmental policy.

LAUNDRY—Standard hospital laundry detergents and wash cycles are sufficient for linens contaminated with blood and body fluids. Handle linens and patient clothing with gloved hands when they are soiled with blood or other body fluids, secretions and excretions. Check departmental policy regarding bagging and labeling of patient laundry.

DISHES & UTENSILS—Standard hospital dishwashing is sufficient and special handling is not indicated. Gloves should be worn only if dishes and utensils are visibly soiled with blood or body fluids. Gloves are not indicated when serving patient food.

HOUSEKEEPING—Standard hospital housekeeping procedures are adequate for routine, daily cleaning of patient rooms. Routine cleanup of patient rooms following discharge or transfer is adequate unless there is visible contamination with blood or body fluids.

CASUAL CONTACT—Casual contact with patients does not pose a risk of infection with HIV or HBV. Handshaking, touching, talking, visiting and other casual contact with patients does not require any special infection control procedures since HIV and HBV are not spread through casual contact.

Always report to your immediate supervisor whenever you believe you may have been exposed to HIV or HBV through contact with a patient's blood or body fluids. Your department has adopted infection control measures with which you should be familiar and should use routinely as indicated for all patients.

PROTECT YOURSELF
ALWAYS OBSERVE UNIVERSAL PRECAUTIONS

Yale-New Haven Hospital
New Haven, Connecticut

Universal Precautions [Pocket Card]

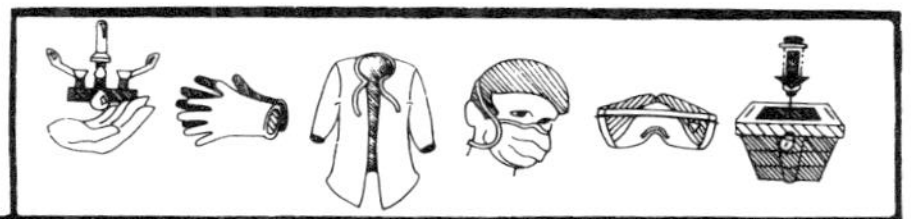

Talking to Patient						
Adjusting IV rate or non-invasive equipment; food tray delivery						
Sharps disposal	X	X				X
Examining patient without touching blood, body fluids, mucous membranes, or non-intact skin	X					
Examining patient, including contact with blood, body fluids, mucous membranes, or non-intact skin	X	X				
Intravenous catheter insertion, drawing blood	X	X				
Suctioning	X	X	Use gown, mask, eyewear if bloody fluid splattering likely			
Handling materials soiled with blood or body fluids; plumbing repairs	X	X	Use gown, mask, eyewear only if waste or linen are extensively contaminated and splattering likely			
Intubation and CPR	X	X	X	X	X	
Inserting arterial access; endoscopy; operative and other procedures which produce extensive splattering of blood and body fluids	X	X	X	X	X	

UNIVERSAL PRECAUTIONS apply to all health care personnel at **ALL** times regardless of the patient's age, background, or diagnosis. The consistent use of Universal Precautions is essential for your safety. The patient's medical history, examination, and laboratory testing **CANNOT RELIABLY IDENTIFY** all patients **INFECTED** with **HIV (AIDS** virus) or other blood-borne, pathogens (e.g., Hepatitis B).

The Universal Precautions chart on the reverse side of this card is a guide for infection control practice. Use common sense and judgment when determining appropriate barrier precautions.

Use **GLOVES** for touching blood and body fluids, mucous membranes, or non-intact skin for **ALL PATIENTS** and for handling items or touching surfaces soiled with blood or body fluids. **GLOVES** should be **CHANGED** when soiled or torn. Use **CLEAN** gloves with each patient and **WASH HANDS** after removing gloves.

Wear **GOWNS, MASKS**, and protective **EYEWEAR** in addition to gloves during procedures where splattering of blood and body fluids may occur.

Always **DISPOSE** of **SHARPS** in the collection container located in each patient room. **DO NOT RECAP, CLIP**, or **BEND** needles or **THROW** them in the **TRASH.**

DO NOT wear gloves or protective clothing when contact with the patient or objects used by the patient is **UNLIKELY** to result in exposure to blood or potentially infectious body fluids. **EXAMPLES:** shaking hands, delivering supplies and medications, delivering food trays, touching cleaned or washed objects, and so forth.

Yale New Haven Hospital
1826

Kaiser Permanente Medical Care Program, Northern California Region San Francisco, California

Infection Control Precautions [Pocket Card]

KAISER PERMANENTE
Medical Care Program
Northern California Region

The Kaiser Permanente Medical Care Program Supports the Following:

GUIDELINES FOR PREVENTING TRANSMISSION OF INFECTIONS IN HEALTH CARE SETTINGS

INFECTION CONTROL PRECAUTIONS

1. **Handle the blood and body fluid/substances of ALL patients as potentially infectious.**
2. Wash hands before and after all patient or specimen contact.
3. Wear gloves when contact with blood or body fluid/substances is anticipated; remove gloves after each individual task.
4. Wear a gown or disposable plastic apron when splashing with blood or body fluid/substances is anticipated.
5. Wear a mask for protection against airborne transmitted diseases. (HIV is not airborne.)
6. Wear protective eyewear and mask if facial splatter with blood or body fluid/substances is anticipated.
7. Place used syringes immediately in a nearby puncture-resistant container; generally, needles should not be recapped or manipulated in any way.
8. Process **ALL** laboratory specimens as potentially infectious.
9. Place equipment needed for emergency resuscitation, e.g. Ambubags and/or mouth pieces, in areas in which the need for resuscitation is predictable.

EMPLOYEE HEALTH ISSUES

1. Wash your hands, arms, face, etc., immediately and thoroughly if you have had unprotected contact with body substances.
2. Protect your non-intact skin (e.g. chapped, abraded or afflicted with dermatitis) from contact with body substances.
3. Contact your supervisor when you have had an exposure to blood or body fluid/substances such as a needle stick or a splash of blood onto non-intact skin or mucous membranes.

Johns Hopkins Health System
Baltimore, Maryland

Universal Precautions for Care of All Patients [Wall Sign]

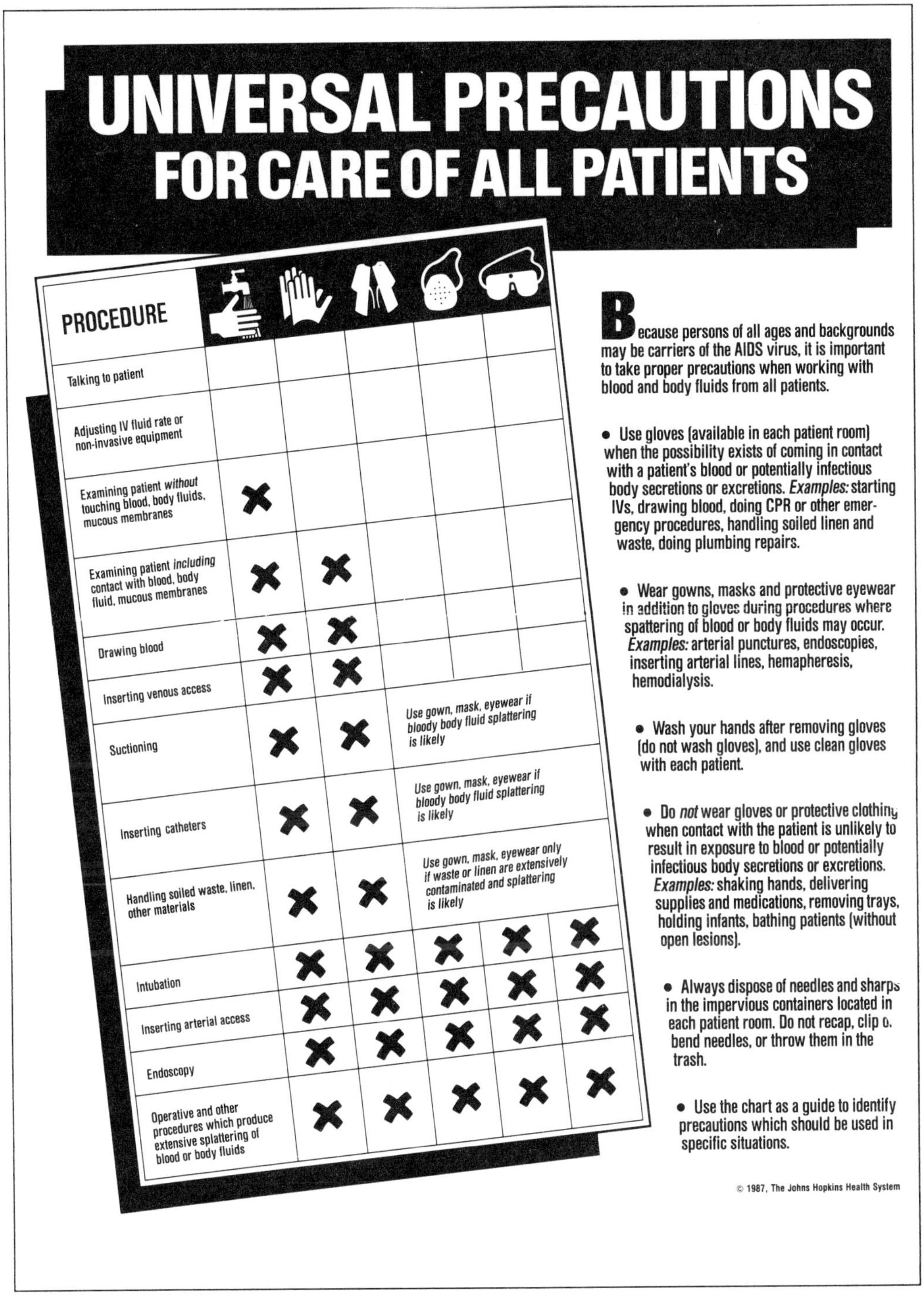

UNIVERSAL PRECAUTIONS
FOR CARE OF ALL PATIENTS

PROCEDURE					
Talking to patient					
Adjusting IV fluid rate or non-invasive equipment					
Examining patient *without* touching blood, body fluids, mucous membranes	X				
Examining patient *including* contact with blood, body fluid, mucous membranes	X	X			
Drawing blood	X	X			
Inserting venous access	X	X			
Suctioning	X	X	*Use gown, mask, eyewear if bloody body fluid splattering is likely*		
Inserting catheters	X	X	*Use gown, mask, eyewear if bloody body fluid splattering is likely*		
Handling soiled waste, linen, other materials	X	X	*Use gown, mask, eyewear only if waste or linen are extensively contaminated and splattering is likely*		
Intubation	X	X	X	X	X
Inserting arterial access	X	X	X	X	X
Endoscopy	X	X	X	X	X
Operative and other procedures which produce extensive splattering of blood or body fluids	X	X	X	X	X

Because persons of all ages and backgrounds may be carriers of the AIDS virus, it is important to take proper precautions when working with blood and body fluids from all patients.

- Use gloves (available in each patient room) when the possibility exists of coming in contact with a patient's blood or potentially infectious body secretions or excretions. *Examples:* starting IVs, drawing blood, doing CPR or other emergency procedures, handling soiled linen and waste, doing plumbing repairs.
- Wear gowns, masks and protective eyewear in addition to gloves during procedures where spattering of blood or body fluids may occur. *Examples:* arterial punctures, endoscopies, inserting arterial lines, hemapheresis, hemodialysis.
- Wash your hands after removing gloves (do not wash gloves), and use clean gloves with each patient.
- Do *not* wear gloves or protective clothing when contact with the patient is unlikely to result in exposure to blood or potentially infectious body secretions or excretions. *Examples:* shaking hands, delivering supplies and medications, removing trays, holding infants, bathing patients (without open lesions).
- Always dispose of needles and sharps in the impervious containers located in each patient room. Do not recap, clip or bend needles, or throw them in the trash.
- Use the chart as a guide to identify precautions which should be used in specific situations.

Johns Hopkins Health System
Baltimore, Maryland

Universal Precautions for Laboratory Workers [Wall Sign]

UNIVERSAL PRECAUTIONS FOR LABORATORY WORKERS

Because patients of all ages and backgrounds may be carriers of the AIDS virus or other blood-borne diseases, it is important that laboratory workers take the following precautions when working with the blood or body fluids of any and all patients.

- Handle sharp items with safety awareness. Maintain eye contact with the item.
- Discard sharp objects in puncture-resistant containers. Place filled container in autoclave bucket for decontamination. Put autoclaved container in red bag for incineration.
- Use mask, safety glasses, goggles or face shield to protect eyes, nose and mouth during procedures when specimen splashing, spattering, or aerosolization is expected.
- Remove protective equipment and lab coat prior to leaving the lab.
- Wash hands when procedures are completed, before leaving the lab, and whenever there is a tear in a glove.
- Wear gloves when processing human specimens. Change gloves and wash hands when processing is finished.
- Decontaminate reusable instruments and devices before reprocessing.
- Place contaminated disposable items in appropriate bag (red or autoclavable).
- Clean up spills of blood or body fluids promptly and disinfect the spill site. Decontaminate work bench and laboratory equipment after liquid spills.
- When collecting specimens, do not force liquid into a vacutainer tube.
- Choose a suitable specimen container, avoid contaminating the outside of the container or the requisition, and be sure the lid is on tight. Decontaminate the outside of the container before transporting.
- Wrap a cotton or gauze pad moistened with disinfectant around rubber stoppers or lyophilized containers while opening them.
- Use capped tubes when vortexing or centrifuging specimens.
- Shield machines which emit splash or splatter.
- Use biological safety cabinets for procedures which are likely to create aerosols, such as blending.
- Use a pipetting aid. Never pipette by mouth.

PROCEDURE					biosafety
Writing or handling paper work	Always				
Collecting blood with needle and syringe or vacutainer tube	Always	Always	Always		
Transporting specimens	Always	Optional	Optional		
Removing rubber stoppers	Always	Always	Always	Optional	
Vortexing or centrifuging specimens	Always	Always	Always	Optional	Optional
Filtering specimens under pressure	Always	Always	Always	Optional	Optional
Opening containers of lyophilized infectious agents	Always	Always	Always	Optional	Optional
Transferring, splitting, or culturing specimens	Always	Always	Always	Optional	Optional

Always Optional

Association for Practitioners in Infection Control and Society for Hospital Epidemiologists of America
Mundelein, Illinois

AIDS Information for Health Care Workers [Brochure]

AIDS
INFORMATION
FOR
HEALTH CARE
WORKERS

PRESENTED BY THE

ASSOCIATION FOR
PRACTITIONERS
IN INFECTION CONTROL

AND

SOCIETY FOR
HOSPITAL
EPIDEMIOLOGISTS
OF AMERICA

FEBRUARY 1988

SHEA

HOW IS HUMAN IMMUNODEFICIENCY VIRUS TRANSMITTED?

1. *Sexual contact involving the exchange of body fluids (blood, semen, or vaginal secretions);*
2. *As a result of sharing contaminated needles and syringes;*
3. *Transfusion of blood or blood products contaminated by HIV or contact with HIV contaminated blood to mucous membranes or non-intact skin;*
4. *Transmission from infected mothers to their infants.*

CAN AIDS BE ACQUIRED BY CASUAL CONTACT?

AIDS is not an easily transmissible disease. There is NO EVIDENCE that AIDS is spread by:

— toilet seats, bathtubs, showers, swimming pools, hot tubs
— handshakes, hugging, or other non-sexual physical contact
— drinking fountains, dishes, utensils or food handled by a person with AIDS
— doorknobs, telephones, linen, clothing, money, or other articles touched by a person with AIDS
— sneezing, coughing or spitting
— being around a person with AIDS even if contact is daily
— insects

HOW MANY CASES OF AIDS HAVE BEEN REPORTED AND WHAT ARE THE TRANSMISSION CATEGORIES?

Over 50,000 cases of AIDS have been reported in the U.S. In addition, nearly two million people in the U.S. may be carrying the HIV virus. It is important to remember that "risk behaviors" are much more relevant than "risk groups". It isn't who you are, its what you do, that matters. AIDS cases nationally have occurred among the following groups of people:

66% - Homosexual/Bisexual Male
16% - I.V. Drug Users

8% - Homosexual Male & I.V. Drug User
4% - Heterosexual Cases
2% - Transfusion, Blood/Components
1% - Hemophilia
1% - Children who apparently acquired AIDS from infected mothers
3% - Unknown

WHAT IS THE FUTURE COURSE OF THE EPIDEMIC?

Estimates of the future course of the epidemic are important to the planning of health care, public health measures, and research. The Public Health Service has issued the following projections of the course of the epidemic through 1991:

- By the end of 1991, there will have been a cumulative total of more than 270,000 cases of AIDS in the United States, with more than 74,000 of those occurring in 1991 alone.
- By the end of 1991, there will have been a cumulative total of more than 179,000 deaths from AIDS in the United States, with 54,000 of those occurring in 1991 alone.
- Because of the typical time between infection with HIV and the development of clinical AIDS is four or more years, most of the persons who will develop AIDS between now and 1991 are already infected.
- The vast majority of AIDS cases will continue to come from the currently recognized high-risk groups.
- New AIDS cases in men and women acquired through heterosexual contact will increase from 1,100 in 1986 to almost 7,000 in 1991.
- Pediatric AIDS cases will increase almost 10-fold in the next five years, to more than 3,000 cumulative cases by the end of 1991.

RECOMMENDATIONS FOR PREVENTION OF HIV TRANSMISSION IN HEALTH CARE SETTINGS

The Centers for Disease Control has received several reports of Human Immunodeficiency Virus (HIV) infection in health care workers (HCW's) apparently following needlesticks, splashes to the face or blood contamination of an open wound. The occupational risk of acquiring HIV for Health Care Workers is very low and is estimated to be less than 1% in those who have parenteral contact with blood of infected patients.

UNIVERSAL PRECAUTIONS

Since medical history, examination, or laboratory testing cannot reliably identify all patients infected with HIV or other blood-borne pathogens (e.g. Hepatitis B), **blood and body-fluid precautions** should be consistently used for **all** patients. This approach of "universal blood and body-fluid precautions" or "universal precautions" should be used in the care of **all** patients, especially including those in emergency-care settings in which the risk of blood exposure is increased and the infection status of the patient is usually unknown. Universal precautions include, but are not limited to the following procedures:

1. **Gloves** should be worn for touching blood and body fluids, mucous membranes, or non-intact skin of all patients, for handling items or surfaces soiled with blood or body fluids, and for performing venipuncture and other vascular access procedures. Gloves should be changed when torn and after contact with each patient.
2. **Hands** and other skin surfaces should be washed immediately and thoroughly if contaminated with blood or other body fluids. Hands should also be washed immediately after gloves are removed.
3. **Gowns** or plastic aprons are indicated if blood splattering is likely.
4. **Mask** and **Protective Goggles** should be worn if aerosolization or splattering are likely to occur such as in certain dental and surgical procedures, wound

irrigations, post-mortem exam, bronchoscopy and suctioning procedures.

5. To minimize the need for emergency mouth-to-mouth resuscitation, mouthpieces, resuscitation bags, or other ventilation devices should be strategically located and available for use in areas where the need for resuscitation is predictable.
6. Sharp objects should be handled in such a manner to prevent accidental cuts or punctures. Used needles should not be bent, broken, reinserted into their original sheath or unnecessarily handled. They should be discarded intact immediately after use into an impervious needle disposal box which should be readily accessible (placed in all clinical areas, including patient rooms). All needlestick accidents, mucosal splashes or contamination of open wounds with blood or body fluids should be reported immediately.
7. Blood spills should be cleaned up promptly with a disinfectant solution such as a 1:10 dilution of bleach. Gloves should be worn.
8. All patient's blood specimens should be considered biohazardous.
9. Health Care Workers who have exudative lesions or weeping dermatitis should refrain from all direct patient care and from handling patient care equipment until the condition resolves.
10. Pregnant health care workers are not known to be at greater risk of contracting HIV infection than health care workers who are not pregnant; however, if a HCW develops HIV infection during pregnancy, the infant is at risk of infection resulting from perinatal transmission. Because of this risk, pregnant health care workers should be especially familiar with and strictly adhere to precautions to minimize the risk of HIV transmission.

ENVIRONMENTAL CONSIDERATIONS FOR HIV TRANSMISSION

Outside the human body, HIV is a fragile virus that is easy to kill. However, some people have expressed concern because laboratory experiments in which large amounts of HIV were placed on environmental surfaces have shown that small amounts of the virus could be isolated from the surface several days later. It is important to note that the amount of virus used in these experiments was much higher than would be present in even a large spill of blood from an infected person.

Environmental contamination of surfaces or equipment in health care facilities has not been a means of transmitting HIV to people. Nevertheless, the precautions described below should be taken routinely in the care of all patients.

1. *Standard sterilization and disinfection procedures for patient care equipment are adequate. Chemical germicides that are approved for use as "hospital disinfectants" and are tuburculocidal when used at recommended dilutions can be used to decontaminate spills of blood and other body fluids.*
2. *Gloves should be worn during all cleaning and decontaminating procedures.*
3. *Strategies for decontaminating spills of blood and other body fluids in a patient care setting are different than for spills of cultures or other materials in clinical, public health, or research laboratories. In patient care areas, visible material should first be removed and then the area should be decontaminated. With large spills of cultured or concentrated infectious agents in the laboratory, the contaminated area should be flooded with a liquid germicide before cleaning, then decontaminated with fresh germicidal chemical.*

Page 5

MANAGEMENT OF EXPOSURES

A blood or body fluid exposure in a health care worker is defined as follows:

1. contaminated needlestick accident,
2. mucous membrane exposure (e.g. splash to the eye or mouth).
3. cutaneous exposure (i.e. contact with large amounts of blood or body fluids on ungloved hands or other skin surfaces that may be cut, chapped, abraised, or afflicted with dermatitis).

The health care facility's Employee Health and Infection Control Departments should develop specific policies regarding potential HIV testing of both the source patient and the employee. Detailed recommendations from the Centers for Disease Control are available (MMWR Supplement: Recommendations for Prevention of HIV Transmission in Health Care Settings, Vol. 36, No. 2S, August 21, 1987).

ADDITIONAL RESOURCES

Public Health Service AIDS HOTLINE:
1-800-342-AIDS

National Sexually Transmitted Disease HOTLINE:
1-800-227-8922

National Gay Task Force AIDS Information HOTLINE:
1-800-221-7044

REFERENCES

Material for this brochure was adapted from recommendations and educational materials from the U.S. Department of Health and Human Services - Centers for Disease Control.

Page 6

Massachusetts General Hospital
Boston, Massachusetts

Universal Precautions [Employee Brochure]

MASSACHUSETTS GENERAL HOSPITAL

UNIVERSAL PRECAUTIONS

All health care workers must routinely use "Universal Precautions" to protect themselves from the blood or body fluids from all patients, regardless of their diagnosis. Appropriate clinical judgement must be used in determining additional protective equipment necessary in addition to the required protection, as outlined in your department's classifications of job related tasks. The Centers for Disease Control and the Occupational Safety and Health Administration have published recommendations promoting the use of Universal Precautions for your protection.

The "MGH Manual of Precaution Techniques" contains specific considerations and information on Universal Precautions and infection control prevention measures. Diseases and conditions requiring Respiratory Precautions, such as tuberculosis and chickenpox, and Immunocompromised Host Precautions are detailed in the manual. These are currently the only TWO category-specific precautions, requiring labeling with isolation cards, in addition to Universal Precautions. Reportable diseases are identified, as well as their modes of transmission

MASSACHUSETTS GENERAL HOSPITAL
UNIVERSAL PRECAUTIONS

Gloves

1. Universal Precautions applies to <u>all</u> patients (inpatients, outpatients, Emergency Room, etc.) regardless of their diagnosis and applies to all contaminated medical equipment and materials.

Gowns

2. Use appropriate clinical judgement in determining when protective barriers are necessary. Protective barriers should be used when having direct contact with blood, body substances, mucous membranes, or non-intact skin.

Masks

3. Wear gloves when hands are likely to be in contact with blood or body substances (urine, oral secretions, wound or other drainage). Immediately wash hands if they become contaminated with blood or body substances. Routinely wash hands before and after all patient contacts. Carry a set of gloves with you at all times if your job-related tasks may expose you to blood or body substances.

Goggles

4. Wear an impervious gown when soiling of clothing is likely to occur.

5. Wear a mask <u>and</u> safety glasses (goggles) when it is likely that eyes or mucous membranes will be splashed with blood or body substances.

Needleboxes

6. Use extreme caution when handling contaminated sharps: needles, scalpels, blades, pipettes, glass slides, etc. Discard them immediately into strategically located puncture-resistant needle-box containers. Needles should not be recapped before discarding.

Infectious Wastes

7. Discard trash in the usual manner <u>unless</u> the item or material is saturated or heavily contaminated with blood or blood contaminated body substances. Then the item should be disposed of according to the MGH procedure for disposing of infectious waste, as outlined in the <u>Manual of Precaution Techniques</u>

Linen

8. Bag all hospital linen in the usual manner. No special bagging or labelling will be necessary. However, if linen is heavily soiled with body substances, double wrap it with linen before placing it into the laundry bag. If the outside of the linen bag becomes wet, place it into another linen bag.

Reprocessed Items

9. Pre-clean or soak instruments, or other reusable equipment being returned to Central Supply (CSR) for reprocessing, to remove blood, tissue or body substances. Forward all items back to CSR in designated, puncture-resistant boxes. No special bagging or labelling will be required, just extreme care in handling and transporting the items.

Approved Disinfectants

10. Use only approved hospital germicides, disinfectants or sterilants.

Clean blood spills with the use of gloves and paper towels before applying the disinfectant.

Specimens in Plastic Bags

11. Handle all laboratory specimens and blood tubes with gloves. Place each patient's specimen (container or tubes) into a plastic bag. The lab requisition <u>must</u> be affixed to the outside of the plastic bag by a rubber band (no staples or tape please). No special labeling or identification of specimens is required.

Resuscitation Bags

12. Avoid mouth-to-mouth resuscitation by placing resuscitation devices with patients who are likely to require resuscitation.

Employee Health Service

13. Be familiar with the "MGH Employee Health Service Policies", as detailed in the Manual of Precaution Techniques. In particular, report all needlestick and mucous membrane exposures for adequate HIV/HBV follow-up and management.

EMPLOYEE HEALTH - PROTECTING YOURSELF Rx

1. Report all needlestick and mucous membrane exposures to the Employee Health Service (ext.2217, Bulf.1, Mon-Fri, 8:00am-4:00pm) or the Emergency Ward (Any day, 4:00pm-8:00am) for appropriate HIV/HBV followup and management. An incident report MUST be filed documenting the exposure for your Employee Health record.
2. If an eyesplash with blood or body fluids occurs, rinse your eye, then go directly to the MEEI Emergency Room for immediate irrigation.
3. Carry an extra set of gloves with you at all times for unanticipated exposures to blood or body fluids.
4. Protect your co-workers: immediately dispose of used, UNCAPPED, needles into needleboxes; assist in confining or containing hazardous (e.g. bloody) situations to protect one another from exposures; and wear protective materials and assure that others do the same.
5. To avoid needlstick injuries DO NOT RECAP contaminated needles. Discard immediately into strategically located needleboxes. DO NOT CUT OR BREAK contaminated needles to avoid aerosolization of blood.
6. If you are susceptible to Hepatitis B or are unsure of your antibody status, go to Employee Health for anti-HBs testing and receive free "Recombivax" Hepatitis B vaccine if necessary.
7. Carry your safety glasses, distributed through your service chief or director, with you at all times.

American Hospital Association
Chicago, Illinois

Resource List for AIDS and Universal Precautions

Written Materials

AIDS and Alzheimer's Disease: A Training Manual for Health-Care Teams about Coping with Chronic and Terminal Illness (manual; 87 pages; 1988)

This educational program from the Greater New York Hospital Foundation, Inc., contains three curricula, Chronic and Terminal Illness, AIDS, and Alzheimer's Disease, each designed to enhance the functioning of the total health care team. Each curriculum includes comprehensive lecture notes, handout materials, and references; two detailed care studies present opportunities for team problem solving.

Member price: $49.95 Nonmember price: $49.95

AIDS/HIV Infection: Recommendations for Health-Care Practices and Public Policy (booklet; 54 pages; 1988)

This report provides guidance for ensuring a safe environment in the hospital, appropriate health care delivery practices for caring for AIDS patients, financing of treatment and care for AIDS patients, and public health issues. It also looks at clinical infection control issues, the need for AIDS education, social attitudes, and policy issues.

Member price: $8.00 Nonmember price: $15.00

Management of HIV Infection in the Hospital, 3rd ed. (booklet; 50 pages; 1988)

This booklet describes the natural history of HIV infection, risk factors associated with transmission in the occupational setting, and methods of reducing risk of HIV, HBV, and other bloodborne pathogens. Guidelines are included for interpretation of HIV serologic tests, management of personnel, and development of Universal Precautions policies and procedures.

Member price: $8.00 Nonmember price: $15.00

Planning for AIDS Care (booklet; 46 pages; 1989)

This book examines the experiences of eight case-study hospitals as they define and direct their AIDS care policies and practices.

Member price: $25.00 Nonmember price: $50.00

Audiovisual Materials

Working Together: Needlestick Prevention (packaged program: two 18-minute videotapes and 125-page training manual; 1990)

This comprehensive audiovisual training program emphasizes teamwork in identifying prevention strategies and training in proper handling and disposal of needles. Two videotapes are included for both support and clinical staff. The training manual contains materials for conducting discussion and training sessions, sample agenda, evaluation forms, and guidelines for developing policies and procedures. This program also contains needlestick posters and stickers.

Member price: $225.00 Nonmember price: $300.00

Is It Worth The Risk? Safe Handling of Blood and Body Fluids (20-minute videotape, 1987)

This video addresses the need for health care employers to wear protective barriers to reduce the risk of occupational exposure to blood or other body fluids. It demonstrates how Universal Precautions can be successfully implemented in each department.

Member price: $25.00 Nonmember price: $300.00

Universal Precautions (Slide presentation)

This 75-slide set series describes the routes of transmission, risks, and methods to reduce risk of occupational exposure to hepatitis B, HIV, and other bloodborne pathogens, including recommended workplaces and protective barriers for both patient care and non-patient care personnel; stresses the importance of reporting occupational exposures and the need for hepatitis B immunization. Narrative script is included.

Member price: Not available Nonmember price: Not available

OSHA's Bloodborne Pathogens Standard: Preparing for the New Rule (90-minute videotaped teleconference, November 1989)

This teleconference provides an update on proposed OSHA standards, scope of current inspection process, and methods for implementing Universal Precautions. It includes special interviews with representatives of the CDC discussing risks of occupational transmission of HIV and HBV and OSHA discussing the scope and key provisions of the proposed rule. A 50-page workbook is included.

Member price: $350.00 Nonmember price: Not available

AIDS Policies: Hospital/Medical Staff Dialogue (90-minute videotaped teleconference, March 1988)

This teleconference addresses the major AIDS policy issues facing hospitals, including testing for HIV, patient confidentiality, and duty to treat. It explores ways that hospital medical staff and key individuals can work together to resolve conflicts and develop policies on these issues.

Member price: $300.00 Nonmember price: Not available

Buckle Down Your Medical Waste Program (Video packaged program: 25-minute videotape and resource book; 1989)

Package discusses methods for objectively assessing your medical waste program and tips for handling, storing, and disposing of medical waste. Resource book contains a leader's guide, sample policies and strategies for cost containment and minimizing liabilities.

Member price: $175.00 Nonmember price: $250.00

Selected References on Infection Precautions*

Albert, R. K., and Condie, F. Hand-washing patterns in medical intensive-care units. *New England Journal of Medicine* 304:1465–66, 1981.

American Hospital Association. AIDS: protecting the hospital worker. Panel discussion by Patricia Lynch, Marguerite Jackson, Steven Trosty, and Carson Dye, Aug. 12, 1987. Chicago: AHA. [Videotape copies provided all AHA member hospitals, Sept. 1987.]

Bennett, J. V., and Brachman, P. S., editors. *Hospital Infections*, 2nd ed. Boston: Little, Brown & Co., 1986.

Burke, J. F., Quinby, W. C., Bondoc, C. C., et al. The contribution of a bacterially isolated environment in the prevention of infection in seriously burned patients. *Annals of Surgery* 186:377–85, 1977.

Centers for Disease Control. *Isolation Techniques for Use in Hospitals*, rev. ed. Atlanta: CDC, 1975.

Centers for Disease Control. *Guideline for Isolation Precautions in Hospitals.* Atlanta: CDC, 1983.

Centers for Disease Control. Update: human immunodeficiency virus infections in health-care workers exposed to blood of infected persons. *Morbidity and Mortality Weekly Report* 36(19):285–89, May 22, 1987.

Centers for Disease Control: Recommendations for prevention of HIV transmission in health-care settings. *Morbidity and Mortality Weekly Report* 36(Suppl. 2S):3S–18S, Aug. 21, 1987.

Centers for Disease Control. Update: AIDS and HIV infection among health-care workers. *Morbidity and Mortality Weekly Report* 37(15):229–39, Apr. 22, 1988.

Centers for Disease Control. Update: Universal Precautions for prevention of transmission of HIV, HBV, and other bloodborne pathogens in health-care settings. *Morbidity and Mortality Weekly Report* 37(24):377–88, June 24, 1988.

Centers for Disease Control. AIDS and HIV infection in the United States: 1988 update. *Morbidity and Mortality Weekly Report* 38(Suppl. S-4):1–38, May 12, 1989.

Centers for Disease Control. *Guidelines for the Prevention and Control of Nosocomial Infections.* Atlanta: CDC, 1981–1985, revised periodically.

Department of Labor/Department of Health and Human Services. Joint advisory notice: HBV/HIV. *Federal Register* 52(219):41818–24, Oct. 30, 1987.

Department of Labor/Occupational Safety and Health Administration. Advance notice of proposed rulemaking. *Federal Register* 52(228):45438–41, Nov. 27, 1987.

Department of Labor/Occupational Safety and Health Administration. Enforcement Procedures for Occupational Exposure to HBV and HIV (OSHA Instruction CPL 2-2.44A), Aug. 15, 1988.

Department of Labor/Occupational Safety and Health Administration. Occupational exposure to bloodborne pathogens; proposed rule. *Federal Register* 54(102):23042–39, May 30, 1989.

Dienstag, J. L., and Ryan, D. M. Occupational exposure to hepatitis B virus in hospital personnel: infection or immunization? *American Journal of Epidemiology* 115:26–39, 1982.

Donowitz, L. G., Wenzel, R. P., and Hoyt, J. W. High risk of hospital-acquired infection in the ICU patient. *Critical Care Medicine* 10:355–57, 1982.

Friedland, G. H., and Klein, R. S. Transmission of the HIV. *New England Journal of Medicine* 317:1125–35, 1987.

*Prepared by Marguerite M. Jackson, San Diego, CA.

Friedland, G. H., Saltzman, B. R., Rogers, M. F., et al. Lack of transmission of HTLV-III/LAV infection to household contacts of patients with AIDS or AIDS-related complex with oral candidiasis. *New England Journal of Medicine* 314:344–49, 1986.

Garner, J. S., and Hughes, J. M. Editorial: options for isolation precautions. *Annals of Internal Medicine* 107:248–50, 1987.

Gerberding, J. L., Bryant-LeBlanc, C. E., Nelson, K., et al. Risk of transmitting the human immunodeficiency virus, cytomegalovirus, and hepatitis B virus to health care workers exposed to patients with AIDS and AIDS-related conditions. *Journal of Infectious Diseases* 156:1–8, 1987.

Gerberding, J. L. Occupational HIV transmission: risk reduction. *Occupational Medicine: State of the Art Reviews* 4(special issue):21–24, 1989.

Gestal, J. J. Occupational hazards in hospitals: risk of infection. *British Journal of Industrial Medicine* 44:435–42, 1987.

Grady, G. F., Lee, V. A., Prince, A. M., et al. Hepatitis B immune globulin for accidental exposures among medical personnel: final report of a multicenter controlled trial. *Journal of Infectious Diseases* 138625–38, 1978.

Handsfield, H. H., Cummings, J., and Swenson, P. D. Prevalence of antibody to human immunodeficiency virus and hepatitis B surface antigen in blood samples submitted to a hospital laboratory: implications for handling specimens. *Journal of the American Medical Association* 258:3395–97, 1987.

Jackson, M. M. From ritual to reason—with a rational approach for the future: an epidemiologic perspective. *American Journal of Infection Control* 12:213–20, 1984.

Jackson, M. M. Rituals without reason: updating the curriculum in infection control. In: *Patterns in Specialization: Challenge to the Curriculum*, pp. 171–88. New York City: National League for Nursing, 1986.

Jackson, M. M. Implementing Universal Body Substance Precautions. *Occupational Medicine: State of the Art Reviews* 4(special issue):39–44, 1989.

Jackson, M. M., guest editor. Special issue: AIDS. In: *Today's OR Nurse.* Thorofare, NJ: Charles B. Slack Co., 1989.

Jackson, M., Dechairo, D. C., and Gardner, D. F. Perceptions and beliefs of nursing and medical personnel about needle-handling practices and needlestick injuries. *American Journal of Infection Control* 14:1–10, 1986.

Jackson, M. M., Healy, S. A., Straube, R. C., McPherson, D. C., and Greenawalt, N. C. The AIDS epidemic: dilemmas facing nursing managers. *Nursing Economics* 4(3):109–16, 1986.

Jackson, M. M., and Lynch, P. Infection control: too much or too little? *American Journal of Nursing* 84:208–10, 1984.

Jackson, M. M., and Lynch, P. Isolation practices: a historical perspective. *American Journal of Infection Control* 13:21–31, 1985.

Jackson, M. M., Lynch, P., McPherson, D. C., Cummings, M. J., and Greenawalt, N. G. Clinical savvy: why not treat all body substances as infectious? *American Journal of Nursing* 87:1137–39, 1987.

Jackson, M. M., Lynch, P., and Adams, S. *Nosocomial Infection and Medical Devices: Reducing the Risk.* Videotape CNE 9924 (28.5 minutes) produced by Hospital Satellite Network, Los Angeles, June 1986. Distributed by American Journal of Nursing Company, New York City.

Jagger, J., Hunt, E. H., Brand-Elnagger, J., and Pearson, R. D. Rates of needle-stick injury caused by various devices in a university hospital. *New England Journal of Medicine* 318: 284–88, 1988.

Klein, B. S., Perloff, W. H., and Maki, D. G. Reduction of nosocomial infection during pediatric intensive care by protective isolation. *New England Journal of Medicine* 320:1714–21, 1989.

Kuhls, T. C., and Cherry, J. D. The management of health care workers' accidental parenteral exposures to biological specimens of HIV seropositive individuals. *Infection Control* 8:211–13, 1987.

Larson, E. Compliance with isolation technique. *American Journal of Infection Control* 11:221–25, 1983.

Larson, E. Handwashing: it's essential, even when you use gloves. *American Journal of Nursing* 89:934–39, 1989.

Lynch, P., and Jackson, M. M. Isolation practices: how much is too much or not enough? *Asepsis, the Infection Control Forum* 8(4):2–5, 1986.

Lynch, P., Jackson, M. M., and Adams, S. *Nosocomial Infection Control: Body Substance Isolation.* Videotape CNE 9923 (28.5 minutes) produced by Hospital Satellite Network, Los Angeles, June 1986. Distributed by American Journal of Nursing Company, New York City.

Lynch, P., Jackson, M. M., Cummings, M. J., and Stamm, W. E. Rethinking the role of isolation practices in the prevention of nosocomial infections. *Annals of Internal Medicine* 107:243–46, 1987.

Maki, D. G. Risk factors for nosocomial infection in intensive care. *Archives of Internal Medicine* 149:30–35, 1989.

Maki, D. G., Alvarado, C., and Hassemer, C. Double-bagging of items from isolation rooms is unnecessary as an infection control measure: a comparative study of surface contamination with single- and double-bagging. *Infection Control* 7:535–37, 1986.

Maki, D. G., Alvarado, B. S., Hassemer, C. A., and Zilz, M. A. Relation of the inanimate hospital environment to endemic nosocomial infection. *New England Journal of Medicine* 307:1562–66, 1982.

Marcus, R. A. Surveillance of health care workers exposed to blood from patients infected with the HIV. *New England Journal of Medicine* 319:1118–23, 1988.

McCray, E. The cooperative needlestick surveillance group: occupational risk of the acquired immunodeficiency syndrome among health care workers. *New England Journal of Medicine* 314:1127–32, 1986.

McPherson, D. C., and Jackson, M. M. Isolation precautions for a changing environment: a new approach. *Journal of Healthcare Materiel Management* 5(6):28–32, 1987.

McPherson, D. C., Jackson, M. M., and Rogers, J. C. Evaluating the cost of the Body Substance Isolation System. *Journal of Healthcare Materiel Management* 6(6):20–28, 1988.

Meintz, S. L., and Jackson, M. M., issue editors. AIDS: community perspective. *Family and Community Health* 12(2; special issue), Aug. 1989.

Nauseef, W. M., and Maki, D. G. A study of the value of simple protective isolation in patients with granulocytopenia. *New England Journal of Medicine* 304:448–53, 1981.

Quraishi, Z. A., McGuckin, M., and Blais, F. X. Duration of handwashing in intensive care units: a descriptive study. *American Journal of Infection Control* 12:83–87, 1984.

Ribner, B. S., Landry, M. N., and Gholson, G. L. Strict versus modified isolation for prevention of nosocomial transmission of methicillin-resistant *Staphylococcus aureus. Infection Control* 7:317–20, 1986.

Seef, L. B., Wright, E. C., Zimmerman, H. J., et al. Type B hepatitis after needlestick exposure: prevention with hepatitis B immune globulin. *Annals of Internal Medicine* 88:285–93, 1987.

Stamm, W. E. Infections related to medical devices. *Annals of Internal Medicine* 89(part 2):764–69, 1978.

Vlahov, D., and Polk, B. F. Transmission of human immunodeficiency virus within the health care setting. *Occupational Medicine: State of the Art Reviews* 2:429–50, 1987.

Weinstein, R. A. Multiply resistant strains: epidemiology and control. In: *Hospital Infections,* 2nd ed., J. V. Bennett and P. S. Brachman, editors, pp. 151–69. Boston: Little, Brown & Co., 1986.

Index